Readings in Animal Cognition

Readings in Animal Cognition

Edited by
Marc Bekoff
Dale Jamieson

A Bradford Book
The MIT Press
Cambridge, Massachusetts
London, England

This book was set in Palatino by Asco Trade Typesetting Ltd., Hong Kong and was printed and bound in the United States of America.

Unless otherwise indicated, the chapters in this volume are reprinted from *Interpretation and Explanation in the Study of Animal Behavior*, edited by Marc Bekoff and Dale Jamieson (Boulder, Colorado: Westview Press, 1990). Reprinted by permission of Westview Press, Boulder, Colorado.

Library of Congress Cataloging-in-Publication Data

Readings in animal cognition / edited by Marc Bekoff, Dale Jamieson.
    p. cm.
    A Bradford book."
    Selected excerpts from *Interpretation and explanation in the study of animal behavior* originally published in 1990.
    Includes bibliographical references and index.
    ISBN 0-262-52208-X (pbk. : alk. paper)
    1. Cognition in animals. I. Bekoff, Marc. II. Jamieson, Dale.
III. Interpretation and explanation in the study of animal behavior.
QL785.R27   1996
591.51—dc20   95-386
                                                          CIP

This book is dedi
From whom we h

Contents

Preface

The main purpose of this book is to introduce readers to the rapidly growing inter-disciplinary field of animal cognition. While there is a number of excellent books in this area (e.g., Cheney and Seyfarth 1990; Ristau 1991; Griffin 1992; Dawkins 1993), there is no comprehensive collection of essays that includes most of the important topics and leading figures. This reader presents a coherent selection of essays that will fill this gap for people in various disciplines, including biology, philosophy, psy-chology, anthropology, and cognitive science.

The book begins with some general perspectives on nonhuman animal (hereafter animal) cognition. John Andrew Fisher discusses the supposed sin of anthropo-morphism. He identifies two broad categories: *interpretive* anthropomorphism ("to refer to all of the usual cases of ascribing M[entalistic]-predicates to animals on the basis of their behavior") and *imaginative* anthropomorphism ("the productive activity of representing imaginary or fictional animals as similar to us"). Fisher claims that there are no sound reasons for always regarding anthropomorphism as an embarrass-ment to be avoided and leaves open the door for what may be called "inflationary" interpretations and understandings. He concludes: "Without a plausible argument that ascribing mental states to non-human animals is a categorical fallacy the most basic assumption of critics of anthropomorphic thinking is seen to be untenable." In her essay, Lori Gruen discusses how gender influences the construction of categories and thus our interpretations and understandings of animal behavior. She presents three different views about the relationship between gender and knowledge and takes studies of sexual selection as an example of an area in which gender bias has affected our view of what animals are doing. Gruen also shows how language is involved in masking our biases and structuring our views. Hugh Wilder, in the following chapter, claims that interpretation is unavoidable in cognitive ethology because problems of interpreting data are inseparable from problems of theory construction. He discusses the "Clever Hans" phenomenon (the unintentional cueing of an experimental subject) in some detail, arguing that it may never be eliminable from many studies of animal cognition. However, he does not think that this threatens the scientific status of cog-nitive ethology. Wilder also discusses the proper interpretation of Morgan's Canon (the law of parsimony) and assesses its importance to the understanding of animal behavior. He argues that "The Canon may rule when available evidence under-determines the choice between competing explanations of animal behavior, but it is misused when it inhibits the gathering of new data or the generation of new ex-planatory hypotheses." Finally, Colin Allen and Marc Hauser deal with how concepts can be ascribed to animals. They write that "Concepts are capable of explaining complex abilities to generalize over variable stimuli, to rapidly produce appropriate responses to the common features underlying those stimuli, and to modify behavior when it is discovered that perceptual stimuli are unreliable guides to underlying features." Allen and Hauser go on to describe a series of thought experiments involving the behavior of animals towards dead conspecifics that may help to determine whether a particular behavior is concept-mediated.

The second section addresses cognitive and evolutionary explanations in detail. Dale Jamieson and Marc Bekoff relate cognitive ethology to classical ethology, especially to the pioneering work of Nobel laureate Niko Tinbergen. They argue that cognitive concepts usefully can be employed in both the description and explanation of behavior. Carolyn Ristau shows how the cognitive approach can be used to motivate and structure field studies of animal cognition. She discusses injury-feigning behavior by piping plovers and argues that the best explanation supposes that piping plovers are intentional creatures: They "monitor the approaches of intruders and modify their behavior accordingly." Bennett Galef considers what has been called "tradition" in animals. He points out that the term "traditional" has often been confused with "locale-specific," and that this conflation suggests that we have explanations when we do not. Galef argues for deflationary accounts of such phenomena as sweet potato washing in Japanese macaques; on his view the case for social learning has not been made. The chapters by Randy Thornhill and Sandra Mitchell are an exchange about how to study adaptation. Although Thornhill identifies some fallacies in adaptationist thinking, he is more sympathetic to this form of reasoning than is Mitchell. Mitchell is especially skeptical about adaptationist thinking when it is applied to animals who have the capacity for cultural learning. She discusses rape, pointing out that in order to explain human rape on the basis of the behavior of other animals (such as Thornhill's explanations that rely on scorpionfly behavior), we must be certain that the same behavior has been identified across species. However, since human rape is "essentially intentional," there is no reason to believe that the same behavior is being compared in these cases. In the final essay in this section, Walter Koenig and Ronald Mumme concentrate on helping behavior in birds and consider how methodological and analytical procedures can influence the acquisition of knowledge. They address the challenge put forth by Ian Jamieson and his colleagues concerning functional explanations of helping, namely that helping "originated and is currently maintained nonadaptively as a result of its tight linkage with the clearly adaptive behaviors associated with normal parental care." On this view, helping is an unselected consequence of what has been selected for. Koenig and Mumme argue that there are ample data to support the notion that helping has current adaptive value.

The third section is devoted to recognition, choice, vigilance, and play. Andrew Blaustein and Richard Porter discuss recognition in general but focus especially on kin recognition. If individuals favor relatives in the way predicted by kin selection theory and "selfish gene" views, then they must be able to recognize them and even be able to assess different degrees of relatedness. Blaustein and Porter consider various ideas of how recognition abilities may have evolved and may be acquired. They suggest that in some instances animals behave in such a way as to suggest that recognition abilities may involve intentionality. However, they conclude that little actually is known about the functions of kin recognition for most species in the habitats in which they live. In his chapter, Michael Rosenzweig considers habitat choice and points out that differential use of available space does not always indicate real choice. Furthermore, he notes that flexibility of response is not a guarantee of choice. In the absence of knowing how animals sense their worlds, it is difficult if not impossible to tease apart situations in which animals are constrained to use a particular area from instances in which they actively choose when and where to go. However, Rosen-zweig does think that in at least some instances the case for choice is quite strong. Steven Lima's paper on the relationship between cognition and scanning behavior focuses on recent research on vigilance in birds. He is skeptical about the "many eyes" hypothesis—that since most birds can either feed or scan for predators but not do both simultaneously, individuals benefit from living in large groups in which one can scan for many. Lima opens up many research questions: For example, does an individual monitor her or his behavior based on an awareness of what others have done, are doing, or are likely to do? Available information suggests that this is the case in many instances (Bekoff 1995). Finally, the topic of play is discussed in the essay by Alexander Rosenberg and the response by Colin Allen and Marc Bekoff. Rosenberg focuses on problems with defining play. Because play is a category that must be intentionally and functionally characterized, and because there can be no evolutionary biology of intentionality, Rosenberg argues that there can be no evolu-tionary biology of play and thus it is not a proper object of biological investigation. Allen and Bekoff counter that play is a behavioral phenotype that is suitable for evo-lutionary explanation, and that Rosenberg's arguments, if sound, would threaten many projects in cognitive ethology, and not just play research.

The fourth section considers communication and language. W. John Smith argues that "social communication is context-dependent, and so requires complex cognitive work that evaluates and integrates information from many sources." Smith defines communication broadly as "a process in which an individual shares some of the in-formation that it has with other individuals." Michael Philips and Steven Austad take issue with broad-based definitions of communication, including Smith's, and propose a narrower definition. In their view, communication occurs when "(a) an animal trans-fers information to an appropriate audience by use of signals; or (b) an animal gains information that another animal intends to convey by means of signs." While recog-nizing Smith's important contributions to the field of animal communication, they are concerned that "he does not provide an account of sharing that helps distinguish be-tween communicative behavior and behavior that successfully coordinates activity by other means." Interest in communication and language also finds a home in research on linguistic abilities in apes and dolphins. Sue Savage-Rumbaugh and Karen Brakke admit that ape language experiments have often been disappointing, but attribute this to the failure to provide the apes with a proper communicative environment. When allowed to communicate in more natural ways about what interests them, many apes show remarkable linguistic skills. Reporting on their work with Kanzi, a bonobo, they suggest that the linguistic gap between humans and other apes may be one of degree rather than kind. Louis Herman and Palmer Morrel-Samuels, reporting on their studies of dolphins, suggest that some animals may have more highly developed abilities for comprehending language than for producing it. This is an important in-sight, since most studies of animal language have been concerned with production rather than comprehension. On the basis of their studies, these authors conclude that dolphins "utilize a rich network of mental representations when responding to language-mediated tasks."

The final section of this collection is concerned with the broad question of animal minds. It is haunted by the apparent unanswerability of Thomas Nagel's (1974) famous question, "What is it like to be a bat?" Roger Crisp argues for the common-sense view that many animals have conscious experiences and mental lives. He employs four lines of argument to support the view that psychological states cannot be unique to a single species: arguments from other minds, arguments from behavior, arguments from neurology, and arguments from evolution. According to Crisp, just because we do not know what it is like to be a bat or a hamster is no reason to deny that there is something that it is like to be these animals. John Dupré rejects Nagel's question and also the burden of proving that animals have minds. In his view if such proof were required it could not be given for either humans or animals. We know that many animals have minds, and confusion about this reflects a lack of clarity about our concepts rather than any confusion about animals and what they are like. What is primarily needed to answer questions about animal minds, according to Dupré, is conceptual appreciation and analysis, not fieldwork or data. Nevertheless, many scientists do engage in field studies that bear on questions of animal minds, and some of the most important research has been done by Robert Seyfarth and Dorothy Cheney. Their controversial claim in this chapter is that the vervet monkeys whom they studied for many years do not have a theory of mind that "allows them to recognise their own knowledge and attribute mental states to others." Seyfarth and Cheney conclude that "while vervet monkeys are acutely sensitive to other animals' behavior, they know little about what causes them to do what they do." The concluding essay by Kathleen Akins returns us to Nagel's question. The force of this question rests on the intuition that there is a profound chasm between representational properties of the sorts that humans and bats may share with computers, and qualitative properties that are only instantiated in some biological creatures. It is the qualitative properties, some have argued, that science can never fully capture. By using the example of a film of a bat's phenomenology that is produced at the end of neuroscience, Akins tries to erode this distinction between representational and qualitative properties. She concludes that we can only know what science can tell us after it has done so. Perhaps the scientific investigation of mental representation will tell us what it is like to be a bat after all. Finally, in the last chapter Dale Jamieson and Marc Bekoff discuss relationships between ethics and the study of animal cognition.

Seventeen essays in this reader are drawn from a two-volume collection (now out of print) entitled *Interpretation and Explanation in the Study of Animal Behavior* (Bekoff and Jamieson 1990). One paper (Akins) originally appeared in this collection but was subsequently revised, five were published elsewhere, and this preface and the last chapter are new. The papers reprinted from the two-volume collection have been heavily cited, and we have been urged to make them available again. The five additional papers are recent examples of much-needed critical thinking in cognitive ethology. All previously published papers have been updated and corrected. These essays taken together provide the nucleus for an excellent course in animal cognition (cognitive ethology and comparative psychology), philosophy of biology, or philosophy of mind. We have added the final chapter because we believe that any discussion of what animals are like without a treatment of how we should relate to them is seriously incomplete. We hope that this essay will help to facilitate classroom discussion of our moral relations with animals.

We thank Claudia Mills for comments on this preface, and Paul Moriarity for compiling the index.

References

Bekoff, M., and Jamieson, D., eds. 1990. *Interpretation and Explanation in the Study of Animal Behavior. Volume I: Interpretation, Intentionality, and Communication; Volume II: Explanation, Evolution, and Adaptation.* Boulder, Colorado: Westview Press.

Bekoff, M. 1995. Vigilance, flock size, and flock geometry: Information gathering by Western Evening Grosbeaks (Aves, Fringillidae). *Ethology* 99: 150–161.

Cheney, D. L., and Seyfarth, R. M. 1990. *How Monkeys See the World: Inside the Mind of Another Species.* Chicago: University of Chicago Press.

Dawkins, M. S. 1993. *Through Our Eyes Only? The Search for Animal Consciousness.* San Francisco: W. H. Freeman.

Griffin, D. R. 1992. *Animal Minds.* Chicago: University of Chicago Press.

Nagel, T. 1974. What is it like to be a bat? *Phil. Rev.* 83: 435–450.

Ristau, C., ed. 1991. *Cognitive Ethology: The Minds of Other Animals. Essays in Honor of Donald R. Griffin.* Hillsdale, N.J., Lawrence Erlbaum Associates.

Perspectives on Animal Cognition

Chapter 1

The Myth of Anthropomorphism

John Andrew Fisher

Anthropomorphism is usually regarded as an embarrassment to be avoided. Philosophers and scientists often approach anthropomorphism as an obstacle to be overcome by those who wish to attribute cognitive or emotional states to non-human animals. Thus Donald Davidson (1975: 7) suggests that "Attributions of intentions and beliefs to animals smack of anthropomorphism." Even those who favor animal rights try to avoid being accused of it. Annette Baier (1985: 150), for example, feels obliged to say, "I see nothing at all anthropomorphic or in *any other way absurd* in saying that one may "break faith with" an animal, exploit its trust, disappoint expectations one has encouraged it to have" (my emphasis). And Mary Midgley (1978: 106) asserts, "There is nothing anthropomorphic in speaking of the motivation of animals." Contrary to this loose consensus, I will argue that there is a considerable amount of confusion about anthropomorphism. I will argue that the mistake or fallacy of anthropomorphism is neither well-defined nor clearly fallacious. There are many different conceptions of anthropomorphism and the common ones do not support their common rhetorical use. The charge of anthropomorphism oversimplifies a complex issue—animal consciousness—and it tries to inhibit consideration of positions that ought to be evaluated in a more open-minded and empirical manner.

Matching Rhetoric and Logic

It is useful to begin by recalling the historical roots of the concept of anthropomorphism. "Anthropomorphism" was originally a term used in theological contexts for views that characterize God in literal human terms. In particular, to view God as a person of sorts, with indefinitely amplified human powers and characteristics (loving, just, knowing) can be labeled anthropomorphic. Since Christian doctrine was to be distanced from such primitive forms of understanding, whether exemplified by uneducated belief or by pagan religions, anthropomorphism was viewed as a vulgar mistake. (I suggest it is no accident that, as P. J. Asquith [1986] tells us, Japanese primatologists are singularly unconcerned about issues of anthropomorphism in their studies of primates. Cultural history cannot be ignored in explaining this fact.)

Other strands wind through the history of science. With the emergence of modern science, a more primitive form of thinking was to be replaced by a more sophisticated and educated style of thought. For many historians of science, for example Cassirer (1950), "anthropomorphism" names those outmoded forms of explanation (e.g. Aristotelian causal explanations) that were eliminated in favor of mechanistic ones. Cassirer associates "anthropomorphism" with the trends of thought that the rise of modern science had to overcome. To go back to anthropomorphic ways of under-standing the physical world would be like going back on the Copernican revolution, going back to the dark ages.

Given its history it is easy to understand many of the rhetorical features of "anthropomorphism": It is a term of negative criticism that associates a type of understanding with an invalid or fallacious mode of thought long since hounded from respectable intellectual company.

Looking at this history helps to characterize the rhetorical meaning of the charge of anthropomorphism: in ordinary use anthropomorphism is treated partly like a fal-lacy, partly like a heresy. However, nothing said so far provides a sound argument that "anthropomorphism" is merely a vacuous rhetorical weapon; the rhetorical effect could well be based on a logical reality. It will be urged, indeed, that the explanation for the way "anthropomorphism" functions is to be found, simply enough, in the fact that it refers to a blatant logical mistake, namely, a category mistake. Category mistakes are made when one treats an entity of one type as if it were an entity of a different type, as in Gilbert Ryle's (1949) famous example of seeing the buildings of the University and yet asking where the University is located. Many assume that anthropomorphism is the category mistake of ascribing human attributes to some-thing not human.

If anthropomorphism is a blatant category mistake, then it is natural that it would be a criticism made casually and with the negative meanings we have explored. However, a criterion of an adequate analysis of anthropomorphism is that it appro-priately characterizes those cases where the charge of anthropomorphism is made, that is, cases of ascribing mental states to animals. This the category-mistake analysis fails to do.

If it's correct to say that species have natures (and I'll grant it for the sake of argu-ment), then human beings have a unique nature, perhaps equatable with the human genetic material each of us carries. Suppose further that humans turn out to be the only creatures we know with various capacities, such as full-blown language and a certain sort of self-consciousness. Does this then settle the question? Is it then a fallacy to view animals as having human characteristics? This obviously depends on what we mean by "human characteristics." If we mean those characteristics that de-fine the unique human nature, then the answer is, yes. But which are those character-istics? If they are on the molecular level, then they have little to do with the question of animal mentality and the sorts of comparisons in question between animals and humans. A biological answer to the question of how to define human nature, there-fore, can hardly settle that issue.

Even if humans are in a different category than other animals, it doesn't follow that to compare them with other animals is a category mistake. Quite the contrary. We share many features, physical, biological and social, with other animals, and it remains an empirical question which, if any, mental characteristics humans have uniquely. Even if scientists conclude that there are some such characteristics, that other animals only have (say) signalling systems, while human languages are much richer (e.g. in syntax), they had to look and see; it is not an a priori conclusion they can make in any other way.

Many philosophers (e.g. Descartes 1637/1969; Bennett 1988) have written as if the main issue concerning animal mentality is whether humans are unique in the animal world. And it seems a short step from arguing that humans have some unique property (or properties) to the conclusion that to think of animals as similar to humans is anthropomorphism. To put the position most tendentiously: if there is a difference in kind between persons (i.e., humans) and animals, isn't it anthropomorphism to treat animals as if they are similar to persons?

That way of putting it brings out the intuition that the charge of anthropomorphism rises or falls on there being a distinction between humans and animals. We can formulate it this way:

(*)   There is a difference in kind between humans and other animals *if and only if* anthropomorphism (i.e. thinking of animals as similar to humans) is a mistake.

But, as we have just seen, anthropomorphism and a difference in kind between humans and other animals are logically separate concepts. What causes confusion is the Cartesian heritage concerning (*). Descartes thought he had established a special distinction that attributed to humans (i.e., mental substance) all real mentality and to animals (i.e., machines) none. So, if we understand "anthropomorphism" to be the attribution to animals of mental terms (thoughts, feelings, intentions), then if the distinction mentioned in (*) is the *Cartesian* distinction, (*) would be true.

To a Cartesian, the comparison between animals and humans might seem like comparing humans and a leaf, and thus to be a category mistake, at least with respect to comparisons concerning an inner mental life. But this Cartesian dogma has long been repudiated by scientists in favor of an evolutionary story of biological continuity, in which humans are nothing but animals of a certain kind. In the contemporary context, therefore, it would seem that it is at least a genuine question as to what attributes, say, primates possess. And if so, it cannot be a mere category mistake to ascribe the attributes of human mentality to them. For it is not obvious that the attributes cannot literally apply to animals.

A Framework for Analysis

There are three questions we need to answer to give a logical characterization of anthropomorphism:

What is it? I.e., what sort of mistake is it?
When does it occur? Under what conditions do we make this mistake?
Why is it a mistake?

Different answers to these questions yield different conceptions of anthropomorphism. I believe that theorists often have different conceptions of anthropomorphism without being aware of it.

With respect to what anthropomorphism is, I propose that there are two broad categories: *Interpretive Anthropomorphism* and *Imaginative Anthropomorphism*. Before explaining these it is necessary to define the class of extended mentalistic predicates: predicates referring to mental states and processes, cognitive and emotional, as well as verbs of action (e.g. "hunt," "play") and predicates of moral character and personality (e.g. "loyal," "brave," "sneaky"). Call these M-predicates.

I intend "interpretive anthropomorphism" to refer to all of the usual cases of ascribing M-predicates to animals on the basis of their behavior. Interpretive anthropomorphism, then, refers to cases of inference, from animal behavior to M-predicates, where these include descriptions of the animal's physical behavior in terms of intentional actions (the deer are playing, the chimp is trying to solve the puzzle). So in these cases anthropomorphism is an *inference* from the animal's behavior described in terms of bodily movement; it also could be considered an *interpretation* of the animal's behavior or an *explanation* of the animal's behavior based on positing the truth of the ascribed M-predicates. The variations don't matter since the inference (or interpretation) is meant to be a sort of explanation. Since the charge of anthropomorphism presupposes that a mistake has been made, we can say that anthropomorphism on this conception is a fallacious inference. Interpretive anthropomorphism is surely the intended target of criticism by philosophers and scientists when they claim that anthropomorphism is a mistake to be avoided in explanations of animal behavior. Like any other fallacy, we need an account of the conditions under which it is committed and an account of why it is a fallacy.

By "imaginative anthropomorphism" I mean the productive activity of representing imaginary or fictional animals as similar to us. Examples of such representations are the animal characters in animations, books, drawings, movies and oral tales that are treated as similar to us, not only in having M-predicates, but in behaving in a similar way, for example, speaking, etc. This form of thought is obviously intertwined with interpretive anthropomorphism, and while not targeted by philosophers and scientists concerned about scientific explanations of animals, it can just as properly be called anthropomorphic. It too sometimes elicits complaints from critics. In a review of John Crompton's novels about social insects, Kendrick (1988: 59) notes Crompton's tendency to make insects talk: "Superficially, this smacks of anthropomorphism, anathema to today's nature writers."

With a view toward clarifying the way philosophers have talked about anthropomorphism, I propose making a further distinction, subdividing interpretive anthropomorphism into Categorical and Situational Anthropomorphism. *Categorical Anthropomorphism* involves ascribing M-predicates to creatures to which the predicates don't ever in fact apply. Categorical anthropomorphism is almost like making a category mistake; relative to the type of creature, it is always a mistake to ascribe a particular M-predicate, a mistake of interpretation. By contrast, *Situational Anthropomorphism* occurs when we misinterpret an animal's behavior in ways that could possibly apply to that animal in other circumstances, but which do not in the situation in question. An observer might, e.g. interpret a chimp's show of teeth as a sign of anger when it is (let's imagine) a sign of affection; the M-predicate chosen, while mistaken, is not categorically inapplicable to the animal in question.

We can further subdivide categorical anthropomorphism in terms of the conditions under which it is committed. *Species Type*: application of mentalistic predicates could be counted as anthropomorphism depending on the species of animal. What wouldn't be anthropomorphism concerning a chimp might be concerning a worm. *Predicate Type*: application of mentalistic predicates could be counted as anthropomorphic depending on the predicate. I have in mind applying the wrong types of predicates, e.g. predicates of moral character, to a given creature. While perhaps it can be said that a horse is trying hard to win the race, perhaps it cannot be said that he is courageous. So, to answer whether any use of mentalistic predicates is anthropomorphic we need to consider both the creature and the predicate applied. A clear example of a claim involving both predicate and species comes from Peter Carruthers (1989: 261) who claims, "only the most anthropomorphic of us would be prepared to ascribe second-order beliefs to toads and mice; and many of us would have serious doubts about ascribing such states even to higher mammals such as chimpanzees."

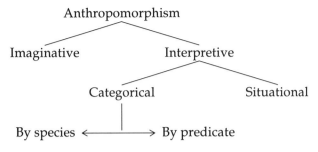

Figure 1.1

The typology of anthropomorphism is summarized in Fig. 1.1.

Clearly there is a range of potential targets for the charge of categorical anthropomorphism, and correlatively, a range of positions for critics of anthropomorphism to occupy. The most extreme critical position seems also to be the common one: I will call (on analogy with hard determinism) *Hard Anthropocentrist* ("Hard Centrists" for short) those critics of anthropomorphism who regard the application of *any* M-predicate (perhaps with the exception of pain and other sensations) to *any* non-human animal as categorical anthropomorphism. In other words, hard anthropocentrists are those who charge that inferences from behavior to M-predicates are categorically anthropomorphic. Hard Centrists see categorical anthropomorphism as a universal problem. Hard Centrists are committed to a sharp division between humans and other animals, such that, excepting pain and other sensations, it is always a mistake of categorical anthropomorphism to attribute M-predicates to animals, and never a categorical mistake to ascribe them to humans. Hard anthropocentrism seems to be the standard position among tough-minded philosophers and scientists, certainly among those who freely make the charge of anthropomorphism.

It is important to keep in mind that anthropocentrism is defined relative to the charge of anthropomorphism. Anthropocentrists are not just those who believe as a matter of empirical fact that certain M-predicates do not truly apply to certain animals. In addition they must hold that to ascribe the relevant M-predicates, on the basis of the animal's typical behavior, is to commit a mistake of categorical anthropomorphism. Donald Davidson, for example, is anthropocentric in my sense *only* when he suggests that those who are inclined to ascribe thoughts to animals on the basis of their purposive behavior are anthropomorphic. To claim that it is anthropomorphic to ascribe self-consciousness to a chimp, for instance, is to say more than merely that the ascription is false. For otherwise, the disagreement might just be an empirical one, about which conscientious investigators could disagree, and about which they could change their minds. Anthropomorphism, with its rhetorical implications, need not enter in. Consider, for example, those who believed on the basis of his performances, and before the mechanism of cue transmission was discovered, that Clever Hans could add numbers. Such observers were mistaken about Hans' mathematical comprehension, but there wasn't anything necessarily anthropomorphic about their reasoning.

Many of us, while less extreme than hard anthropocentrists, would hesitate to apply mentalist terms in some cases, e.g. to individual insects. So most of us think it *can* be categorical anthropomorphism to apply most M-predicates to some species, e.g. worker ants. Also there are some M-predicates that most of us would hesitate to apply to any non-human animals (e.g. Wittgenstein's famous example of a dog expecting his master day after tomorrow.) Thus there is a whole range of positions possible for the anthropocentrist concerning where to draw the line, relative to species and predicate, in making the charge of anthropomorphism.

Elsewhere I have explored the varieties of anthropomorphism in great detail (Fisher 1991). I will limit myself here to an examination of categorical anthropomorphism.

Categorical Anthropomorphism and the Philosophers

Categorical anthropomorphism occurs when, for a certain predicate and species, the anthropomorphic inference is mistaken in principle. Consider this example: when prairie dogs meet they greet each other with an apparent kiss. The anthropocentrist will argue: surely it is a mistake in principle to think that prairie dogs really kiss, that they kiss as we kiss, with similar intentions, thoughts, emotions and so forth—that what they do can literally be said to be a *kiss*. And this is not just a question of situational anthropomorphism, that is, of prairie dogs having other intentions (like an unfamiliar tribe), or of having strange or alien intentions (like Martians), but that there are simpler explanations (e.g. it is merely a sign of recognition) that do not attribute any of the rich complex of intentions, cognitions, feelings or social relations associated with kissing. It is only anthropomorphism to think that superficial behavioral similarities are to be understood as caused by underlying mentality of a familiar sort.

Generalize the reasoning just formulated, and you have the usual theme of philosophers who have worried about animal mentality. Most philosophers have tended to think there is a sharp division between humans and other animals—either humans have minds and animals do not, or humans are rational and animals are not, or humans use language and animals do not—such that it is a mistake in principle to apply various M-predicates to animals. And always this division is a hierarchy, with humans at the top and animals underneath separated by a gulf. Thus philosophers have not been concerned with getting the animal's mentality right, that is, to avoid the anthropological error of mistaking the expression of one mental state for that of another; nor have they been concerned to ban anthropomorphic interpretations to make room for another sort of mentality, alien to our understanding. Rather they have aimed to ban anthropomorphic interpretations in order to deny to animals any sort of mentality. Of course each philosopher draws his line at a slightly different point; Davidson worries about anthropomorphism in connection with ascription of any thought to animals, others might draw the line more or less extremely. It would be fair to sum up this tradition however as one that supposes the dangers of anthropomorphism are quite general; that is, the charge of categorical anthropomorphism is made in the case of most M-predicates and most species. In short, when philosophers have been concerned about anthropomorphism they have tended to adopt ways of speaking that make them sound like Hard Anthropocentrists.

Having already described the sort of mistake categorical anthropomorphism is supposed to be, I will focus here on the reasons why attribution of M-predicates to animals (i.e., the anthropomorphic inference) is thought to be the mistake of categorical anthropomorphism. I will examine not only the few discussions of anthropomorphism by philosophers but in addition other potential objections that I believe implicitly lie behind the categorical rejection of anthropomorphic inferences.

Anthropomorphic Inference Is Connected with Falsehood

It's safe to say that most references to anthropomorphism in the scientific and philosophical literature occur in discussions of whether animals think or have other M-states. I have maintained in preceding sections, however, that the question whether animals think and the issue of anthropomorphism, though related, are logically distinguishable. Those who fail to see this tend to assert that it is anthropomorphism to ascribe M-states to animals. On the contrary, an ascription of M-states to animals is not necessarily anthropomorphism even if it is false.

The idea that anthropomorphism is simply false belief or assertion can be located at two points in the anthropomorphic inference. Some may claim that ascription of M-predicates is anthropomorphism because it is based on false premises or assumptions. Others have the idea that it is anthropomorphism because it draws a false conclusion. I shall argue that neither of these is anthropomorphism in the proper sense.

Consider, first, the idea that the anthropomorphic inference is based on a false assumption, an assumption of similarity between the animals in question and humans. The question is: why is this a false similarity? Human physiology and human behavior have both evolved from that of other animals, so it is not obvious that the analogies that ground the anthropomorphic inference are not a valid basis for it. Indeed, it appears that, in attacking the assumptions underlying the inference, the Centrist who charges anthropomorphism gives a circular argument. In *Rationality*, Jonathan Bennett (1964: 11) suggests as much:

> [I]t begs the question to say that it is merely "sentimental" or "anthropomorphic" to credit bees with rationality. If "It is anthropomorphic to credit bees with rationality" means "To credit bees with rationality is to liken them to humans," then this is true but unhelpful; on the other hand, if it means "To credit bees with rationality is wrongly to liken them to humans," then it begs the question.

The very point at issue is whether it is mistaken to draw the anthropomorphic inference, so an argument needs to be given by the Centrist as to why the general analogy is mistaken, and mistaken, not just in this case, but in principle. It is difficult to see how such an argument would go. Whether or not the analogy is a good one seems to be an empirical question and, as such, the claim that it is not a good analogy, even if sustainable, would not ground a charge of anthropomorphism but merely one that the inference is mistaken.

Consider some particular assumptions that underlie anthropomorphic inferences. For example, we assume that elephants who appear to greet each other know each other and have appropriate social relations. For, such social relations would seem to be required for the application of our concept of a greeting. Whether such assumptions are true is an empirical question, however, and hence the assertion that they are not true does not justify the charge of categorical anthropomorphism, which holds that the anthropomorphic inference is wrong in principle.

Sometimes thinkers reason that if the conclusion of the anthropomorphic inference is false, even empirically false, then the inference is guilty of categorical anthropomorphism. This way of thinking equally misuses the charge of anthropomorphism to rule out what might be a reasonable empirical dispute. Consider the Clever Hans example. It is conceivable that there was another and smarter horse called Clever Shmans; a horse that, as far as anyone could tell from his behavior, could add numbers and did not use cues from spectators. How could it be asserted that to accept the claim of Shmans' ability is anthropomorphic? It is possible that we might argue on empirical grounds that Shmans cannot add. For example, it might be claimed that there is something missing in a horse's brain that is required in the human brain to understand numbers. If such evidence were found, however, it would not support a charge of anthropomorphism against those who accepted the ascription of numerical ability on the basis of Shmans' behavior.

Anthropomorphic Inference Has Suspect Origins
One of the most interesting reasons for being a Hard Centrist can be located in the general role that anthropomorphic inferences play in human cognitive development. The connection of anthropomorphism in literal thinking about animals to imaginative anthropomorphism and of imaginative anthropomorphism to imagination and childhood provides a motive to question anthropomorphic inference and to see it as categorical anthropomorphism.

Children invest dolls and other objects with personalities as part of normal cognitive development. They see personalities everywhere. Even when we grow up we still easily see human forms in clouds, cracks, cars, etc.; indeed, much visual art is based on our ability to see human forms in vague lines and shapes. Clearly humans have a capacity to perceive objects as having personalities. It is not just a capacity to imagine; it is a sort of imaginative representation of a perceived object. As children we often accept these representations as real.

One is inclined to say that to *accept* these characters is not, and does not require, anthropomorphism, because to accept them requires no beliefs at all. Instead it may be like treating them as, or seeing them as people. I need to be facilitated in that perception; they have to look and act like people. But I don't have to believe that frogs are persons in order to understand the character of Kermit the frog any more than I have to *believe* that trains are persons in order to understand the Little Engine that could. We can say that fictions are anthropomorphic when they represent animals as more like humans than in fact they are. But spectators are often not taken in by such representations, nor are they influenced by them. Even children know that raisins aren't really like the California Raisins, and that trains are not alive. Spectators are guilty of anthropomorphism only when they accept that the false nearness to humans is possible. When dogs talk in *The Plague Dogs* this is anthropomorphic, but viewers are not taken in. In *Bambi* most of the other details of forest life, in contrast to *The Plague Dogs*, are entirely misrepresented. If viewers are taken in, and accept the fiction as realistic, they are guilty of anthropomorphism.

Our general capacity to understand such anthropomorphic representations makes suspect the way we understand real animal behavior. What is at stake here is the validity of commonsense explanations of animals and their behavior. The Hard Centrist may wish to suggest that commonsense explanations, in terms of M-predicates, are too closely allied to childish anthropomorphism, indeed dependent upon those imaginative capacities, that we all grew up with and which we regularly apply in imaginary fictions. Just as we can easily imagine a Bambi on screen as a preadolescent human child, so when we see a real deer there probably is a certain amount of imagination going on in how we relate to and understand the deer. It seems likely that imaginative representations play an important role in how we understand animals commonsensically. Surely these imaginative capacities are often misused; and just as surely they do not provide the sort of foundation we hope to have for scientific explanation.

That we are able and inclined to see personality in some animals can be given an evolutionary explanation. William Calvin (1983: 16) suggests that human affection for cats has an evolutionary explanation in protective mimicry:

> One has only to observe a human holding a cat to realize what is going on: the pet is invoking the same reactions that a cuddly baby sets off. Their contented responses when cradled set off the same flood of emotions in us. Babies babble and nuzzle, cats purr and rub.

The idea is that there "is a symbiotic relation between parent and offspring: the infant needs much assistance to survive, and the parent "needs" to propagate genes.... A gene leading to cooing can interact with a gene leading to cradling to the benefit of both." Thus, if "the cat's purr can substitute for the coo, the cat has lucked into a good deal" (Calvin 1983: 17). So the cat may have evolved into a niche created by human need to nurture human infants.

I don't mean to suggest that such an evolutionary explanation can be extended to our responses to all other animals. Obviously, many animals would be either potential predators or potential prey for humans. Failure to be able to distinguish them from human infants would confer a selective disadvantage. Still, what I think is most salient about Calvin's hypothesis is that it gives us a plausible example of a form of perception and emotional response that may be genetically programmed and is relatively crude and inaccessible to modification through learning or experience. Perhaps our general response to animals is also based on an innate but crude cognitive-emotional framework within which there is no clear differentiation between ourselves and other animals and in which we view animals as similar to ourselves (as having reasons, motives, thoughts, emotions). Hard Centrists suspect as much, and would view the process of educational maturation to be a process of learning to disengage as much as possible from this framework, which is so uncalibrated in the very young.

Although I find it plausible to speculate that our commonsense explanations of animal behavior are based on an innate framework of concepts for understanding others, both human and animal, I don't think this possibility provides a substantial case against anthropomorphic inferences.

First, our perceptual apparatus in general is innate (hardwired) and yet not for that reason to be discarded; we do not reject the validity of the reports of vision, for example, on these grounds. In addition, it is plausible to hold that our way of understanding each other is a system that is largely innate, rather than an inductive generalization built up from experience (see Fodor & Chihara (1965) on the sort of theory we might have of other minds, and for the argument that the theory can be partly innate like a grammar and is not based on criteria or symptoms defining M-predicates in terms of behavior). So, unless we also wish to reject our ways of understanding each other, there is a problem in rejecting the system for understanding animals. The capacity itself is not necessarily defective or invalid in its operation. Second, as we grow up we do learn to make distinctions between things that are really alive and things that are not, and between living things that really have mentality and those that do not. We don't for a moment think that dolls, raisins or engines really have feelings. But commonsense persistently refuses to draw a sharp line between humans and other animals, and persists in retaining sympathetic feelings for animals and in understanding them along human lines in terms of M-predicates.

To demand that we draw a further line between humans and other animals such that we only apply our innate capacity to understand another mentality to fellow humans is to beg the question at issue. It cannot be that this capacity always produces invalid results, but rather that it is invalidly being "extended" to other creatures which it misconstrues. But to make that claim, a separate argument is required. It is not enough to speak of the evolutionary origins, the cognitive impenetrability of this capacity or the misconceptions it leads us to in childhood. To return to the cat, is it not *really* cuddly? Is it a mistake to find it cuddly, even if it is true that we have such a response because of the similarity of cats to infants? Obviously, to avoid begging the question the Hard Centrist must come up with a further argument to support his rejection of the application of this capacity to animals.

Anthropomorphic Inference Involves Invalid Methods

In addition to the Hard Centrist's worry about the cognitive schemes with which we perceive and understand animals, philosophers have raised a related objection. Some of them have characterized the anthropomorphic inference in such a way as to make it dubious or even absurd. They have suggested that at bottom the inference requires a process of "projection." Jonathan Bennett (1988: 200) associates this view with Quine:

> [Some philosophers] hold that we have no good *standards* governing our moves to conclusions about thoughts from premises about nonlinguistic behavior.... Quine, for instance, says that when we attribute beliefs to other animals we are speaking in a "dramatic idiom," imagining ourselves in the animal's shoes, so to speak, and saying on its behalf what we imagine *we* would think or be prone to say if *we* were barking at a cat up a tree or lunging at a toreador with our horns.

Bennett does not himself accept this view: "Despite recent skeptical literature tending the other way, I unashamedly conjecture that many animals have beliefs and wants, and that this is not anthropomorphism—not a "dramatic" way of pretending to be a mouse or a gorilla" (Bennett: 201). But as other influential philosophers obviously accept the idea that in ascribing thoughts to animals each of us is projecting ourselves onto the animal, we need to examine the tenability of this idea.

Although Bennett associates the idea of projection with anthropomorphism, Quine (1960: 219) does not use the term. He does, however, suggest that all ascriptions of propositional attitudes to fellow humans as well as to non-human animals involve projection, and he insinuates that projection is not in general an adequate method, and in the case of animals, absurd:

> Casting our real selves thus in unreal roles, we do not generally know how much reality to hold constant. Quandaries arise. But despite them we find ourselves attributing beliefs, wishes, and strivings even to creatures lacking the power of speech, such is our dramatic virtuosity. We project ourselves even into what from his behavior we imagine a mouse's state of mind to have been, and dramatize it as a belief, wish, or striving, verbalized as seems relevant to us in the state thus feigned.

A Quinian Hard Centrist would no doubt base her case on the quandaries emphasized by Quine.

Like most of the ideas associated with the charge of anthropomorphism, projection has not been analyzed by those who casually invoke it to explain our thinking about animals. It therefore requires careful scrutiny. There are three points in particular that need investigation: (1) How is projection connected to anthropomorphism? (2) What is wrong with projection? Why does it lead to falsehood? (3) Does the anthropomorphic inference *depend upon* projection? Is it plausible to hold that projection is the mechanism that underlies anthropomorphic inferences? I will argue for two points. First, it is not clear that, if it is construed in a non-question begging way, projection necessarily delivers falsehoods. Second and more important, it is not at all obvious that anthropomorphic inferences depend upon projection. Projection is a red herring.

Imagining what I would do or think in the animal's situation, may be an unreliable method—but how unreliable, and why? It's clear that if this is how I reason about what you will do or are thinking, I will get it wrong *some* of the time. But translated to the animal case, that would only yield situational anthropomorphism. Presumably what Quine and others have in mind is that it is always wrong or even entirely absurd. The Hard Centrist's claim is that projection yields categorical anthropomorphism.

There is another ambiguity. In Quine's (1960) view, projection underlies attribution of all propositional attitudes. For instance, "in indirect quotation we project ourselves into what, from his remarks and other indications we imagine the speaker's state of mind to have been, and then we say what, in our language, is natural and relevant for us in the state of mind thus feigned" (Quine 1960: 218). But is projection supposed to underlie how I know in general that other people have M-states? Or is it only supposed to underlie how I arrive at beliefs about particular M-states, *given that I can correctly assume they have M-states*? If the latter, then translated into the animal case, this would again yield only situational anthropomorphism. To make a Hard Centrist case out of projection we must suppose that it is the former, that is, it is how we know at all that animals have M-states. To take this as an extension of the human case we have to accept the once common assumption in the philosophy of mind that on the basis of what I think and feel in particular circumstances, I ascribe to other humans thoughts and feelings in similar circumstances. I argue from my own case. If this is the role of projection, and projection is essentially defective when applied to animals, then any anthropomorphic inference that projection underlies becomes categorical anthropomorphism.

If projection works at all in the case of fellow humans, why can't it work for animals? If there really is such a mechanism of the imagination that enables each of us to overcome the required counterfactual ("if I were her"), why cannot the same mechanism overcome the counterfactuals involved in thinking about animals ("if I were Lassie")? By hypothesis, I can abstract from sex, age, cultural and physical differences in ascribing M-states to persons; why can't I go farther and abstract from greater physical differences? To deny that we can successfully project ourselves onto animals assumes that animals are too different from us for me to reason validly in this way. That assumption begs the very question at issue. Part of the absurdity of projection comes from the difficult counterfactual on which projection is supposed to be based. But if it is not absurd to reason this way in some cases, why does it become categorically impossible as soon as we reason about other animals?

The Quinian position has a further problem. In so far as we are to take seriously the idea that we only know from our own case, one can ask how Quine knows that projection, this mechanism of the imagination he claims structures our thinking about animals, is actually how we arrive at our ascription of M-predicates. Perhaps this is how Quine thinks about other people and perforce, other animals; but how does he know that anyone else does it this way? How could he have evidence for the truth of his own claim? Is this in fact an example of an invalid projection?

If in fact anthropomorphic inference does not depend on projection, then this whole case collapses. And indeed, I do not see any clear reason to suppose that this mechanism must underlie all anthropomorphic inferences and plenty of reason to deny it. For instance, much that is counted as paradigmatic of anthropomorphism cannot be plausibly understood as projection. If I find a baby elephant cute, how am I projecting myself?

No doubt we sometimes reason this way, at least about fellow humans, but when we do there is an important requirement. Consider a chess example: I may ask, what would I do in the situation of my opponent? Equally, I may reason: I would do X, but Karpov is the type who will do Y. Even to think, "suppose I were Karpov," don't I have to know what Karpov is like, how he differs from me? In short don't I need a theory of Karpov, a model representing him? And in the case of animals ("Suppose I were that elephant") don't I need some theory of the animal, a modeling of what its like to be the animal? But if so, projection looses its alleged function, for it only works if I already have some basis for understanding. Take the simplest example: next door a deer is munching on my neighbor's grass. I immediately think: that deer must be hungry. I haven't arrived at this thought by thinking: if I were to eat my neighbor's grass I would be hungry. If I went next door and started to munch on the lawn, I would perhaps have had a nervous breakdown or be under the influence of a drug. My reasoning was, rather, based on how I represent deer, as creatures who make grass a regular part of their diet.

There is an obvious contrast between making ascriptions to the other based on understanding how the other responds mentally to a given situation, with making them based on how I would respond in the other's situation. What appears absurd in the projection argument is the idea that I can only reason from my own case, that I know about myself and only about myself from the inside and must somehow project myself onto the outside world to form any further inferences about people or animals. Such a picture has been convincingly shown to be a failure, however compelling it may seem if we accept the idea that each of us is an isolated Cartesian ego. On the one hand, the philosophical literature on the Other Minds problem demonstrates the thorough inability of the argument from analogy (the philosopher's version of projection) to avoid total skepticism about other humans' mental states. On the other hand, the private language argument, stemming from Wittgenstein (1953), has shown that we could not learn about our mental states from our own case. In particular we could not, I think, learn what our states are if we did not already know that other people have such states. It's not that one could never justifiably reason from analogy or by projection, but that this cannot be offered as the basis for how one knows that other humans have minds. Just as we don't make up our own language first and translate it into the public language, so we don't identify our own mental states first and then translate them into public discourse about mind. Rather, it is from learning the public language that we learn about M-states and that we have the M-states that others have. But if the projection mechanism is not the foundation for our *general* understanding of other humans, why insist that it is for our *general* understanding of animals? (And to say less is to reduce the projection objection to saying that projection can lead to situational anthropomorphism.) Why suppose that projection must be the mechanism except for a commitment to the discredited view that "I know from my own case"?

A general dilemma reinforces this rejection of the claim that projection underlies the anthropomorphic inference. In so far as projection is understood as requiring an impossible thought ("if I were that deer"), and for that reason provides an invalid basis for anthropomorphic inferences, why suppose that those who ascribe M-predicates to animals are engaged in entertaining it? This convicts the person who ascribes thoughts to animals not just of irrationality, but of impossible thoughts. Moreover, it is not as if anyone has any direct evidence that other people who ascribe thought to animals are reasoning this way. If there is nonsense in the thought that constitutes projection, the nonsense is Quine's not that of those who do attribute M-predicates animals. They may be wrong, but they cannot be doing the impossible when they infer the animal's M-state from its behavior.

The projection model of how we reason about others gains credibility only if there are no other conceivable possibilities. Yet other possibilities are conceivable. Rather than reasoning from our own cases, we could be born with an innate tendency to develop a theory of mentality that develops in parallel with our development of linguistic competence. We develop the theory primarily in application to people, but in addition we learn to apply it to higher animals on the basis of some of the same behavioral criteria that we apply in the human case. We learn such things as, when we cry we are sad, when we strike out we are angry, when we romp around with each other we are playing, when we ignore food we are not hungry, etc. This theory may be mistaken if extended to non-humans—and certainly it would be if we ignored the differences between us and them—but the question here is only whether we can think about animals without using the dubious mechanism of Quinian projection, and surely we can. If we "project" anything in thinking about animals it is human characteristics that we project upon them (rather than our own individual qualities). This is projection in an entirely different and unproblematic sense. It may be incorrect, but it is far from impossible or even absurd. We have only to assume that animals are members of the class of creatures that have roughly similar responses to our own.

Conclusion

I conclude that the idea that "anthropomorphism" names a widespread fallacy in commonsense thinking about animals is largely a myth. We have found that people commit no simple category mistake when they reason according to what I have termed the anthropomorphic inference. With the more complicated account of anthropomorphism suggested above, we can agree that anthropomorphism exists, namely situational and imaginative anthropomorphism. But we have found no adequate defense of the idea that common sense thinking about animals instances the more fundamental mistake anthropocentrists commonly suppose it does: categorical anthropomorphism. Without a plausible argument that ascribing mental states to non-human animals is a categorical fallacy the most basic assumption of critics of anthropomorphic thinking is seen to be untenable.

Acknowledgements

The author wishes to thank Marc Bekoff and Dale Jamieson for encouraging the larger research project that this paper summarizes (see Fisher 1991), as well as for editorial suggestions concerning earlier versions of this paper.

Literature Cited

Asquith, P. J. 1986. Anthropomorphism and the Japanese and western traditions in primatology. In: *Primate Ontogeny, Cognition and Social Behaviour* (ed. by J. Else & P. Lee), pp. 61–71. Cambridge: Cambridge University Press.

Baier, A. 1985. Knowing our place in the animal world. In: *Postures of the Mind*, pp. 139–156. Minneapolis, Minnesota: University of Minnesota Press.

Bennett, J. 1964. *Rationality*. London: Routledge & Kegan Paul.

———. 1988. Thoughtful brutes. Presidential Address. *Proceedings and Addresses of the American Philosophical Association* 62, 197–210.

Calvin, W. 1983. The lovable cat: mimicry strikes again. In: *The Throwing Madonna: Essays on the Brain*, pp. 14–21. New York: McGraw-Hill.

Cassirer, E. 1950. *The Problem of Knowledge*. New Haven: Yale University Press.

Carruthers, P. 1989. Brute experience. *Journal of philosophy* 86, 258–69.

Davidson, D. 1975. Thought and talk. In: *Mind and Language* (ed. by S. Guttenplan). pp. 7–23. Oxford: Oxford University Press.

Descartes, René. 1637/1969. *Discourse on the Method of Rightly Conducting the Reason*. In: *The Philosophical Works of Descartes, Volume I* (transl. by E. Haldane & G. Ross), pp. 79–130. Cambridge: Cambridge University Press.

Fisher, J. A. 1991. Disambiguating anthropomorphism: An interdisciplinary review. *Perspectives in Ethology*, 9, 49–85.

Fodor, J., & Chihara. C. 1965. Operationalism and ordinary language: a critique of Wittgenstein. *American Philosophical Quarterly* 2, 281–95.

Kendrick, W. 1988. Creepshow; John Crompton's Wild Kingdom. *Village Voice*, June 28, 1988, 59.

Midgley, M. 1978. *Beast and Man*. Ithaca, New York: Cornell University Press.

Quine, W. V. O. 1960. *Word and Object*. Cambridge Massachusetts: MIT Press.

Ryle, G. 1949. *The Concept of Mind*. New York: Barnes & Noble.

Wittgenstein, L. 1953. *Philosophical Investigations*. Oxford: Basil Blackwell.

Chapter 2

Gendered Knowledge? Examining Influences on Scientific and Ethological Inquiries

Lori Gruen

Introduction

Ethologists may study animals "because they provide specific instances of more general theories" (Bekoff & Jamieson 1991: 31), because they live and move, or simply in order to understand more fully animal and human behavior. Whatever the reason, the study is never direct. Knowledge about animals is mediated by a complex network of metaphors and various processes of categorization. To understand these behavioral metaphors and categories we must examine the unstated background assumptions on which they are formed. One way to do this is by analyzing the non-static interaction between knowledge seekers, the social context in which they seek knowledge, and the objects of knowledge themselves. To put it differently, in order to understand how categories can affect inquiry, those engaged in scientific discourse, either as participants or commentators, must first evaluate the consequences of the recognition that facts are theory-laden, theories are value-laden, and values are molded by historical and philosophical ideologies, social norms, and individual processes of categorization.

Scientists, ethologists, and philosophers, like everyone else, acquire particular views in particular places at particular moments in time. The culture, history, and society in which they emerge as thinking, feeling subjects necessarily shapes their beliefs, opinions, hopes, and desires. The questions that they find most pressing, the methods they choose to use in answering those questions, and the way the answers are interpreted has everything to do with their perspectives, beliefs, values, opinions, and so on (Bleier 1984; Birke 1986; Haraway 1986, 1989; Hubbard 1990 and many others). The way we categorize and interpret the world around us has much to do with our context—the external events that we notice and those we do not notice.

> There is always much more going on around us than enters our awareness, not only because some of it occurs outside our sensory range or behind our backs, but also because in giving coherence to our experience we necessarily select certain facts and ignore others. The choice of facts to be explained by scientific means is a function of the reality constructed by this process of selection. What counts as fact—as reality—will thus vary according to culture, institutional perspective, and so on.... (Longino & Doell 1987: 167)

Observing that the scientific enterprise is susceptible to a range of influences at virtually every level—from developing hypotheses to interpreting data—has forced many to reexamine our very conception of reality. As Bernstein (1990: 54) suggests

"We make categories to catalog the world and our experiences. These categories are often extremely useful to us, but that does not mean that they are real," nor does it necessarily mean that they are unreal. By understanding what categories we construct and the motivations and influences that affect their construction, we may be able to understand more clearly what it is that we mean by "reality."

Throughout this chapter I will be assuming that science is a social process (see Rouse 1987; Hull 1988; Longino 1990). All social processes have political dimensions. Just as social influences affect scientific projects, so too scientific projects affect society. While it is important to examine the far-reaching and often subtle effect that science has on humans (see for example Habermas 1970, 1974; Rose & Rose 1976; Farganis 1989) and nonhumans alike (see for example Kheel 1989; Bekoff & Jamieson 1991; Singer 1990), for present purposes I will be focusing on the epistemological and methodological issues that are raised by recognizing the role society plays in shaping scientific knowledge. Specifically, I will examine the role gender plays in influencing how we interpret and understand the world, focusing on a number of ethological examples (see also Wasser 1983).

How Gender Affects Category Construction

Feminists have argued that one of the major influences involved in the process of category construction is gender, a pervasive but subtle influence that has systematically failed to enter the awareness of many scientists. Sandra Harding (1986) has urged that we view gender as one of the fundamental analytic categories through which various activities and beliefs gain meaning and value. Theories about how gender affects our understanding of the world, and particularly our attitudes about science, vary in the feminist literature. This multiplicity has generated a host of complex and useful insights, many of which challenge the predominant conceptions of science in profound ways. Indeed, one might suggest that these critiques serve as systematic paradigms for many legitimate critiques of science, ranging from those examining epistemic inadequacies to those focusing on social injustices (see Dupré 1989). Ultimately, one would hope, these challenges will lead to a reevaluation that results in the development of a science that provides a richer understanding of the world.

In what follows I will present three different feminist critiques. While the critiques are heterogeneous in many respects, all point to "androcentric bias," that is male-centered bias, in science. The way in which bias affects how we ordinarily go about knowledge acquisition varies for each critique, however the meaning of the term "bias" is consistent throughout. "Bias" in this literature is short-hand for beliefs, opinions, attitudes, hopes and the range of subjective states, conscious or not, that influence the way individuals perceive the world. The first feminist critique that I shall discuss focuses on bias located in the fundamental assumptions on which the pursuit of knowledge rests. This criticism cuts at the very notions of objectivity and rationality. The second critique observes bias in the social institutions and practices that influence the choice of questions asked and the methods chosen to answer those questions. I will call this "investigative bias." The third locates androcentric bias in a scientist's process of categorizing information. This critique focuses on what I will call "interpretive bias," which influences how the data generated through scientific inquiry are interpreted and understood.

Because dismissive responses to such criticisms have often been the result of serious misunderstandings of the issues, and because these criticisms have much to offer by way of enriching our understanding of ourselves, other animals, and the rest of nature, it is important to recognize the differences between the three critiques. While the first is radical and indeed controversial in that it seems not to provide much room for grounding knowledge, it nonetheless highlights deeply rooted and largely unexamined assumptions and is therefore important to consider. The criticism that focuses on investigative bias raises relevant concerns for all areas of scientific inquiry by pointing to the inherently political nature of the enterprise. This criticism differs from the related criticism of interpretive bias in that it applies to both "hard" and "soft" sciences. The critique of interpretive bias in most applicable to behavioral research, and for this reason I will focus mainly on it.

Objectivity as Male Bias

Feminists who criticize objectivity and rationality maintain that these concepts are the product of a socialization process which exalts "masculine" charateristics. They deny that a sharp distinction between "subjective" and "objective," between fact and value, can be made. They argue that the notion that facts can be discovered about objects which are not only distinct (causally and physically) from the observer, but which are accessible to that observer through unbiased reason, requires a detachment or separation and an elevation of reason over emotion that parallels the ideological division between the sexes (for a more developed discussion see Fee 1983; Bleier 1986; Harding 1986; Berman 1989; Jaggar & Bordo 1989). Feminist critics of objectivity see "context stripping" scientists as asserting an authority by positioning themselves as active pursuers of truth in a world full of passive objects (for a historical examination of the development of the passive/active dichotomy see Merchant 1980). Some even argue, following the "strong programme" of social constructionism (see for example Latour & Woolgar, 1988), that the assertion of knowledge claims is, in essence, an assertion of power which serves to promote the hegemonic ideology of a particular institution at a given point in history.

There are a variety of problems with this critique, many of which have been pointed out by feminist scientists. Evelyn Fox Keller, for example, argues that this wholesale rejection of objectivity "dooms women to residing outside of realpolitik modern culture; it exacerbates the very problem it wishes to solve" (Fox Keller 1987: 233). Indeed, this retreat from rationality may easily lead to a radical relativism in which all knowledge claims, those of logical positivists, phrenologists, sociobiologists, and so forth are on par. The task for feminist critics is to move beyond the hostility of the objectivity/subjectivity split, to establish a "middle ground" as it were, and to reveal bias in scientific inquiry while taking care not to throw out the baby with the bath water.

Investigative Bias

This is the approach that the more productive criticisms take. The first of these criticisms asserts that science is fundamentally a political or social activity insofar as the criteria used to determine what research should be conducted are based on the interests of dominant groups from which support for particular projects is acquired. A research project is deemed important or relevant based on the way in which it does or potentially will contribute to a base of knowledge that serves particular interests.

The influence the military and industry has in the process of determining what questions scientists ask is the most obvious case of how societal values influence the scientific enterprise in this way. Feminist critics suggest that much of the work designed to investigate physiological and behavioral differences between men and women, such as research in intelligence (e.g. Shields 1987; Genova 1988), the influence of hormones on behavior (e.g. Bleier 1978; Longino & Doell 1987), studies on aggression, competition, and dominance (e.g. Haraway 1978a; Sayer 1982; Gross & Averill 1983), and projects designed to study evolutionary strategies (e.g. Slocum 1975; Fisher 1979; Zihlman 1981) serves to further predominantly male interests.

This bias also manifests itself in the establishment and perpetuation of certain ideologies within particular disciplines (for a discussion of scientific "bandwagoning" see Hull 1979). Often the popularity of a theory influences decisions about whether or not to conduct research in a particular area. The kinds of questions that are asked in ethology, for example, are strongly influenced by current trends popular among ethologists at a particular point in time. How an ethologist chooses the questions to ask will be determined by what he "hopes, believes, wants or needs to be true" within a particular social context (Bleier 1984: 4).

The way in which social values become embedded in science can often be observed in how experiments are designed (Fausto-Sterling 1985). Gender influence (perhaps together with maintenance requirements—e.g. learning studies in rats done primarily with males because females have a four-day reproductive cycle that complicates experiments; Fox Keller 1987: 235) can lead researchers to design experiments using males only and then to generalize the findings to an entire species. This bias also can occur in research in which the more observable and attention-getting animals (often males) are used as behavioral samples for the rest of a population. As these cases show, investigative bias may not only affect the selection of problems to be studied, but also experimental design.

In response to suggestions made by feminists that scientific investigation is susceptible to investigative bias, some scientists may respond: "Sure, science is influenced by societal concerns, and this is desirable because the direction of scientific research should be set by the concerns of the society in which they are conducted." In many ways, this is a welcome response, an advance from the misguided but well-entrenched view of science as value-free. However, it is important to recognize that powerful interests are those most clearly represented, while other concerns are largely ignored. Indeed, these powerful interests, heavily supported by male dominated institutions, can and do use scientific evidence to promote themselves and their conceptions of reality.

Interpretive Bias

This third critique of androcentric bias focuses primarily on how individual cognitive processes or psychological dispositions which have been influenced by social values in turn shape the interpretation and understanding of data. If there is gender bias present in the interpretation of data, we can generally discover a similar bias in the formulations of the questions the data are meant to answer (although this may not always be the case). However, it is important to distinguish between investigative and interpretive bias in that each has a unique force when applied to different scientific endeavors. Often, particularly in studies of chemical, electrical or other strictly physical interactions, there may not be much room for gender-based interpretive bias.

When a spark is observed in a spark chamber, for example, the assumption of the presence of certain subatomic particles would not seem to be affected by gender bias. However even in these cases it is appropriate to look for investigative bias (see Pickering 1984). It is in the area of biological and behavioral research, where the bulk of work is interpretive in nature, that the examination and analysis of bias is undeniably important.

Androcentric bias enters interpretations of data in a variety of ways. As Longino (1990: 86) points out " . . . values can affect the description of data, that is, value-laden terms may be employed in the description of experimental or observational data and values may influence the selection of data. . . ." Furthermore, interpretive bias can and does shape how categories are selected for sorting and understanding information. In animal behavior studies, for example, the belief that heterosexual behavior is "natural" often leads researchers to overlook or ignore the potential social importance and causes of homosexual activity. The focus on competition and aggression among males may lead researchers to overlook cooperation among males and both types of behaviors among females. In addition, gender stereotyping, extracted from human social interaction, can often be observed in both the language and the interpretation of animal behavior.

For example in studies of animal social organization, the belief that many ethologists have about the dominance of the human male has sometimes influenced the ways in which they have observed and interpreted the behavior of males of other species. In the early days of primatology investigators, influenced by the myth of male dominance, used the notion of a "harem" to describe colorfully what they perceived to be male dominance hierarchies in primate social groups. (This way of describing social arrangements has also been used in studies of elephant seals, Cox & LeBoeuf 1977; black antelopes, Dubost & Feer 1981; and many other mammals and birds, see Dagg 1983). Later work in primatology (see Goodall 1971; Rowell 1972; Lancaster 1975; and Haraway 1978a, 1978b, 1989) reveals a rich, often complex variety of social behaviors that were presumably always there. In many primate species males live on the periphery of the troops which are held together by females and their young. As Dutch ethologist Frans de Waal (1982: 32) wrote "we only see what we recognize." In the earlier studies, researchers saw male animals interacting with large numbers of female animals; what they "recognized" and then reported was male animals controlling a harem. Androcentric interpretation can also be clearly seen in the sociobiological literature on "prostitution" and "rape" among animals (see for example Bleier 1984, chapter 2; Hubbard 1990, chapter 8; S. Mitchell, chapter 9 of this reader).

Androcentric Bias in Practice

> Traditions of male-focused behavioral research have not merely meant a detour in our efforts to understand female behaviors, but also a temporary block for understanding the full complexity of animal mating systems. They have also led to a misuse of the biological evidence to bolster sexist preconceptions. (Hrdy & Williams 1983: 14)

Studies of Sexual Selection

Androcentric bias is readily observed in studies of sexual behavior in animals. While not widely commented on, the potential for this type of bias can be observed in

Darwin's theory of sexual selection. In *The Descent of Man and Selection in Relation to Sex* one can see the beginnings of a theory which posits males as active and aggressive. Darwin (1871: 567, 580) wrote:

> the male possesses certain organs of sense or locomotion, of which the female is quite destitute, or has them more highly developed, in order that he may readily find or reach her; or again the male has special organs of prehension for holding her securely ... in order that the males should seek efficiently, it would be necessary that they should be endowed with strong passions.

While Darwin believed that the males were the pursuers of sexual behavior, he also believed females, in their own way, did participate in the act—"the female, though comparatively passive, generally exerts some choice and accepts one male in preference to others" (Darwin 1871: 579).

Whether Darwin was actually the first to formulate the theory suggesting male promiscuity and female coyness and submission is open to debate. Some would deny that Darwin was operating under an androcentric bias, pointing to his allowance for female choice. They would say that this bias enters only in the misappropriation of certain of Darwin's views by later biologists. However Ruth Hubbard (1990: 93) has written that "it is important to expose Darwin's androcentrism, and not only for historical reasons, but because it remains an integral and unquestioned part of contemporary biological theories." Sara Blaffer Hrdy (1986) suggests that while the seeds may have been sown in Darwin, the most insidious version of the myth did not emerge until around 1948 with the work of A. J. Bateman. Bettyann Kevles (1986) has suggested that the myth was clearly articulated by Patrick Geddes and J. Arthur Thompson (1889) in their influential publication *The Evolution of Sex*. The origins of androcentric bias in sexual selection theory is not what is important. What is important is that male bias has a long history in biological theory. Male bias is apparent in Darwin's primary focus on male activity, and glaringly obvious in the work of many post-Darwinian biologists.

This bias has led to the formulation of a theory in which males and females are quite distinct, males are ardent and sexually undiscriminating while females are sexually restrained and passive. Bateman's work with *Drosophila* and resulting extrapolation to the rest of nature suggested a significant dichotomy between males and females: "... there is nearly always a combination of an undiscriminating eagerness in the males and a discriminating passivity in the females" (Bateman 1948: 365). This bias and its effect on interpretation can also be found in more recent ethological writings.

> Even among very simple organisms such as algae, which have threadlike rows of cells one behind the other, one can observe that during copulation the cells of one thread act as males with regard to the cells of a second thread, but as females with regard to the cells of a third thread. The mark of male behavior is that the cell actively crawls or swims over to the other; the female cell remains passive. (Wickler 1973: 23)

Starting with Darwin's observations of great sexual activity on the part of males, coupled with Bateman's pronouncement of the lack of sexually motivated activity on the part of females, Wickler suggests that, in principle, active behavior is "male" and passive behavior "female."

While the strict dichotomy between male and female was uncritically incorporated into theories of sexual selection, a new picture began to emerge in the 1970s. A growing number of field studies and some laboratory work revealed that female mammals and birds were indeed active in directing their own reproductive lives. Some females actively sought mates, engaged in sexual activity with multiple partners, left their own social units to seek sexual activity, caused males to engage in competitive activity, and some females just refused to have anything to do with males. Studies of chimpanzees (Goodall 1971, 1986; de Waal 1982), langurs (Jay 1963; Hrdy 1977), baboons (Rowell 1972; Altmann 1980; Smuts 1985; Moos-Heilen & Sossinka 1990), elephant seals (Cox & LeBœuf 1977), widowbirds (Andersson 1982), spotted sandpipers (Oring et. al 1989), and many other species (for numerous examples see Bateson 1983; Wasser 1983; Bradbury & Andersson 1987; Krebs & Davies 1987 chapter 8; Alcock 1989 chapter 13) revealed what had been overlooked or ignored in previous studies—females are not necessarily coy, chaste, passive, monandrous creatures. While Darwin primarily focused his attention on male behavior, Bateman carelessly generalized from fruitflies to all animals, Wickler displayed bias in his analogies, and some other biologists have selectively chosen to interpret data to maintain the male/female distinctness in sexual behavior, it has become apparent that gender values have strongly influenced our understanding of sexual selection. Current research on behavior patterns that "were always there" shows that predispositions to see things in a particular light result in myopic, value-laden interpretations of results.

Some Implications

One possible response to these feminist critiques is to concede that certain research, particularly in the area of behavior, has been affected by androcentric bias and at the same time maintain that this research was not paradigmatic of the enterprise as a whole. Particular research projects in which bias is revealed is just "bad science." Some scientists would maintain that the method and integrity of science ("science as usual") precludes such bias. This is a response some feminists, referred to by Harding and others as "feminist empiricists" take. Feminist empiricists argue that male bias is correctable by stricter adherence to the principles and methodology of scientific inquiry.

Some have suggested that the problem of "bad science" can be remedied by shifting to a more feminist science. Proponents of this solution argue that an androcentric bias can be cancelled out by a "gynocentric" one (see for example Ginzberg 1987). Recognizing same sex identification in primate observers, Thelma Rowell (1984: 16) argues along these lines: "... it is easier for females to empathize with females [and males with males] ... resulting [in a] stereoscopic picture of social behavior of primates more sophisticated than that current for other groups." However this is not an adequate solution. The answer is not to replace one bias with another and compound the problem from the other direction, nor to combine the biases in a hope that they will blend into a complete picture of reality. What is needed is an analysis of the assumptions that underlie various ways of seeing and knowing in order to determine which might lead to more informative methods. Incorporating the observations and interpretations of both men and women, with their respective biases, will not necessarily lead to more accurate or "truer" studies.

One does not have to cling to the integrity of the scientific method in order to escape the relativism discussed earlier. The choice isn't between "radical constructivism versus feminist critical empiricism" (Haraway 1988: 580). Scientists are not required to embrace absolute relativism or spend their lives undoing androcentric bias by either adding gynocentric bias or constantly struggling to remove bias altogether. Both courses of action are problematic. To reject objectivity and rationality is to accept the possibility that knowledge lacks foundation; to correct "bad science" is to admit that science without bias is possible, that is, to deny that science is susceptible to the influence of societal values. This apparent dilemma can be escaped by developing an account of the value-ladenness of knowledge claims while at the same time recognizing a commitment to accounts of what is "real."

Haraway proposes "feminist objectivity" as one way around the impasse. Feminist objectivity exists in partial perspectives which do not purport to "totalize" knowledge and leave us blind in the way that absolutist knowledge claims and their opposite, relativistic assertions of the impossibility of knowledge, do.

> Feminist objectivity is about limited location and situated knowledge, not about transcendence and splitting subject and object. It allows us to become answerable for what we learn how to see.... Situated knowledges require that the object of knowledge be pictured as an actor and agent, not as a screen or a ground or a resource, never finally as slave to the master that closes off the dialectic in his unique agency and his authorship of "objective" knowledge. (Haraway 1988: 583, 592)

While this seems a step in the right direction, more needs to be said about the mechanisms that stabilize partial perspectives. The relationship between the object and subject of knowledge can potentially become quite intimate and further distort the process of knowledge acquisition. A clear understanding of the interconnections of such a relationship must be explored in order to determine where knowledge is located. If science via feminist objectivity is to be useful, some way to determine which stories are better than others must be posited.

Helen Longino attempts to transcend the dilemma by focusing on "evidential reasoning" and arrives at a "contextualized" empiricist solution. Her way of stabilizing the partiality that Haraway suggests is to locate knowledge claims in a wide social context.

> If scientific inquiry is to provide knowledge, rather than a random collection of opinions, there must be some way of minimizing the influence of subjective preferences and controlling the role of background assumptions. The social account of objectivity solves this problem.... Social interactions determine what values remain encoded in the theories and propositions taken as expressing scientific knowledge at any given time. Values are not incompatible with objectivity, but objectivity is analyzed as a function of community practices.... (Longino 1990: 216)

Both Longino and Haraway have suggested a way of resolving the dilemma with which we are left after examining how bias exists at different levels of inquiry. Their approaches provide opportunities for moving beyond the conception of science as either arbitrary or flawed, yet more work needs to be done.

Conclusion

A careful look at the history of science reveals that the choice of questions asked, the methods of answering the questions and the interpretation of the answers are based on a multitude of influences or biases. By pointing out and examining androcentric bias, feminists have provided a systematic impetus for a reexamination of the scientific enterprise in order to more fully appreciate what it is that we know. This process requires that the individual seeking knowledge be aware of him or herself as both the subject and the object of knowledge generation. By accepting limitations on objectivity, however, one need not necessarily fall into radical relativism. As Fox Keller (1987: 238) suggests, we need to

> reconceptualize objectivity as a dialectical process so as to allow for the possibility of distinguishing the objective effort from the objectivist illusion.... Rather than abandon the quintessentially human effort to understand the world in rational terms, we need to refine that effort. To do this, we need to add to the familiar methods of rational and empirical inquiry the additional process of critical self-reflection.

This process of self-reflection requires an analysis of the historical and philosophical ideologies, the social norms, and the psychological dispositions of those conducting scientific inquiries. This analysis will not only illuminate how particular scientific projects can generate knowledge, but will presumably allow self-reflective knowledge seekers to understand the influence they have on their work and the influence their work has on the world. Feminist critiques of science remind us that, at a time in which scientific inquiry has the potential to affect the lives and well-being of billions of humans and nonhumans, it is imperative that the meaning of the work and its implications be as fully comprehended as humanly possible.

Acknowledgements

I would like to thank the following people for helpful comments and discussion of earlier drafts of this paper: Dale Jamieson, Ken Knowles, Mike Peirce, Regina Pistilli, and Peter Singer. My special thanks to Marc Bekoff for his enthusiasm and encouragement for this work.

Literature Cited

Alcock, J. 1989. *Animal Behavior: An Evolutionary Approach*, 4th Edition. Sunderland, Massachusetts: Sinauer Associates.

Altmann, J. 1980. *Baboon Mothers and Infants*. Cambridge, Massachusetts: Harvard University Press.

Andersson, M. 1982. Female choice selects for extreme tail length in a widowbird. *Nature* 299, 818–820.

Bateman, A. J. 1948. Intra-sexual selection in *Drosophila. Heredity* 2, 349–368.

Bateson, P. (ed.) 1983. *Mate Choice*. New York: Cambridge University Press.

Bekoff, M. & Jamieson, D. 1991. Reflective ethology, applied philosophy, and the moral status of animals. *Perspectives in Ethology*, 9, 1–47.

Berman, R. 1989. From Aristotle's dualism to materialist dialectics: Feminist transformations of science and society. In: *Gender/Body/Knowledge: Feminist Reconstructions of Being and Knowing* (ed. by A. Jaggar & S. Bordo), pp. 224–255. New Brunswick, New Jersey: Rutgers University Press.

Bernstein, I. S. 1990. An idiosyncratic approach to the study of relationships. In: *Interpretation and Explanation in the Study of Animal Behavior, Vol. 1* (ed. by M. Bekoff and D. Jamieson), pp. 35–55. Boulder, Colorado: Westview Press.

Birke, L. 1986. *Women, Feminism, and Biology*. New York: Methuen.

Bleier, R. 1978. Bias in biological and human sciences: Some comments. *Signs* 4, 159–162.

———. 1984. *Science and Gender: A Critique of Biology and Its Theories on Women*. New York: Pergamon Press.

———. (ed.) 1986. *Feminist Approaches to Science*. New York: Pergamon Press.

Bradbury, J. W. & Andersson, M. B. (eds.) 1987. *Sexual Selection: Testing the Alternatives*. New York: John Wiley & Sons.

Cox, C & LeBoeuf, B. 1977. Female incitation of male competition: A mechanism in sexual selection. *The American Naturalist* 111, 317–335.

Dagg, A. 1983. *Harems and Other Horrors: Sexual Bias in Behavioral Biology*. Waterloo, Ontario: Otter Press.

Darwin, C. 1871. *The Origin of Species and The Descent of Man*. New York: Modern Library.

de Waal, F. 1982. *Chimpanzee Politics: Power and Sex Among Apes*. New York: Harper and Row.

Dubost, G. & Feer, F. 1981. The behavior of the male *Antilope cervicapra* L., its development according to age and social rank. *Behaviour* 76, 62–127.

Dupré, J. 1989. Contemporary feminist perspectives on biological science. *Biology and Philosophy* 4, 107–119.

Farganis, S. 1989. Feminism and the reconstruction of social science. In: *Gender/Body/Knowledge: Feminist Reconstructions of Being and Knowing* (ed. by A. Jaggar & S. Bordo). pp. 207–223. New Brunswick, New Jersey: Rutgers University Press.

Fausto-Sterling, A. 1985. *Myths of Gender*. New York: Basic Books.

Fee, E. 1983. Women's nature and scientific objectivity. In: *Woman's Nature: Rationalizations of Inequality* (ed. by M. Lowe & R. Hubbard), pp. 9–27. New York: Pergamon Press.

Fox Keller, E. 1987. Feminism and science. In: *Sex and Scientific Inquiry* (ed. by S. Harding & J. O'Barr), pp. 233–246. Chicago, Illinois: University of Chicago Press.

Fisher, E. 1979. *Woman's Creation: Sexual Evolution and the Shaping of Society*. New York: McGraw Hill.

Geddes, P. & Thompson, J. A. 1889. *The Evolution of Sex*. New York: Scott.

Genova, J. 1988. Women and the mismeasure of thought. *Hypatia* 3, 101–118.

Ginzberg, Ruth. 1987. Uncovering gynocentric science. *Hypatia* 2, 89–106.

Goodall, J. 1971. *In the Shadow of Man*. Boston, Massachusetts: Houghton Mifflin.

———. 1986. *The Chimpanzees of Gombe*. Cambridge, Massachusetts: Harvard University Press.

Gross, M. & Averill, M. B. 1983. Evolution and patriarchal myths of scarcity and competition. In *Discovering Reality: Feminist Perspectives of Epistemology, Metaphysics, Methodology and Philosophy* (ed. by S. Harding & M. Hintikka), pp. 71–96. Boston, Massachusetts: D. Reidel Publishing Company.

Habermas, J. 1970. *Toward a Rational Society: Student Protest, Science and Politics*. Boston, Massachusetts: Beacon Press

———. 1974. *Theory and Practice*. Boston, Massachusetts: Beacon Press.

Haraway, D. 1978a. Animal sociology and a natural economy of the body politic, part I. A political physiology of dominance. *Signs* 4, 21–36.

———. 1978b. Animal sociology and a natural economy of the body politic, part II. The past is the contested zone: Human nature and theories of production and reproduction in primate behavior studies. *Signs* 4, 37–60.

———. 1986. Primatology is politics by other means. In: *Feminist Approaches to Science* (ed. by R. Bleier), pp. 77–118. New York: Pergamon Press.

———. 1988. Situated knowledges: The science question in feminism and the privilege of partial perspective. *Feminist Studies* 14, 575–600.

———. 1989. *Primate Visions: Gender, Race, and Nature in the World of Modern Science*. New York: Routledge.

Harding, S. 1986. *The Science Question in Feminism*. Ithaca, New York: Cornell University Press.

Harding, S. & Hintikka, M. (eds.) 1983. *Discovering Reality: Feminist Perspectives of Epistemology, Metaphysics, Methodology and Philosophy*. Boston, Massachusetts: D. Reidel Publishing Company.

Harding, S. & O'Barr, J. (eds.) 1987. *Sex and Scientific Inquiry*. Chicago, Illinois: University of Chicago Press.

Hrdy, S. B. 1977. *The Langurs of Abu: Female and Male Strategies of Reproduction*. Cambridge, Massachusetts: Harvard University Press.

———. 1986. Empathy, polyandry, and the myth of the coy female. In: *Feminist Approaches to Science* (ed. by R. Bleier), pp. 119–146. New York: Pergamon Press.

Hrdy, S. B., & Williams, G. C. 1983. Behavioral biology and the double standard. In: *Social Behavior of Female Vertebrates* (ed. by S. Wasser), pp. 3–17. New York: Academic Press.

Hubbard, R. 1990. *The Politics of Women's Biology*. New Brunswick, New Jersey: Rutgers University Press.

Hull, D. L. 1979. Sociobiology: Scientific bandwagon or traveling medicine show. In: *Sociobiology and Human Nature* (ed. by M. S. Gregory, A. Silvers, & D. Sutch) pp. 136–163. San Francisco, California: Jossey-Bass.

————. 1988. *Science as a Process: An Evolutionary Account of the Social and Conceptual Development of Science*. Chicago, Illinois: University of Chicago Press.

Jaggar, A & Bordo, S. (eds.) 1989. *Gender/Body/Knowledge: Feminist Reconstructions of Being and Knowing*. New Brunswick, New Jersey: Rutgers University Press.

Jay, P. 1963. The female primate. In: *The Potential of Women* (ed. by S. Farber & R. Wilson), pp; 3–12. New York: McGraw Hill.

Kevles, B. 1986. *Females of the Species: Sex and Survival in the Animal Kingdom*. Cambridge, Massachusetts: Harvard University Press.

Kheel, M. 1989. From healing herbs to deadly drugs: Western medicine's war against the natural world. In: *Healing the Wounds: The Promise of Ecofeminism* (ed. by J. Plant), pp. 96–111. Philadelphia, Pennsylvania: New Society Publishers.

Krebs, J. R. & Davies, N. B. 1987. *An Introduction to Behavioural Ecology*, 2nd Edition. Sunderland, Massachusetts: Sinauer Associates.

Lancaster, J. 1975. *Primate Behavior and the Emergence of Human Culture*. New York: Holt, Rinehart and Winston.

Latour, B. & Woolgar, S. 1988. *Laboratory Life: The Construction of Scientific Facts*, 2nd Edition. Princeton, New Jersey: Princeton University Press.

Longino, H. & Doell, R. 1987. Body, bias, and behavior: A comparative analysis of reasoning in two areas of biological science. In: *Sex and Scientific Inquiry* (ed. by S. Harding J. & O'Barr), pp. 165–186. Chicago, Illinois: University of Chicago Press.

Longino, H. 1990. *Science as Social Knowledge: Values and Objectivity in Scientific Inquiry*. Princeton, New Jersey: Princeton University Press.

Merchant, C. 1980. *The Death of Nature: Women, Ecology and the Scientific Revolution*. San Francisco, California: Harper & Row.

Moos-Heilen, R. & Sossinka, R. 1990. The influence of oestrus on the vocalization of female gelada baboons *(Theropithecus gelada) Ethology* 84, 35–46.

O'Donald, P. 1983. Sexual selection by female choice. In: *Mate Choice* (ed. by P. Bateson), pp. 53–66. New York: Cambridge University Press.

Oring, L. W., Fivizzani, A. J., & El Halawani, M. E. 1989. Testosterone-induced inhibition in the spotted sandpiper. *Hormones and Behavior* 23, 412–423.

Pickering, A. 1984. *Constructing Quarks: A Sociological History of Particle Physics*. Chicago, Illinois: University of Chicago Press.

Rose, H. & Rose, S. (eds.) 1980. *Ideology of/in the Natural Sciences*. New York: Schenkman.

Rouse, J. 1987. *Knowledge and Power: Toward a Political Philosophy of Science*. Ithaca, New York: Cornell University Press.

Rowell, T. 1972. *The Social Behaviour of Monkeys*. Middlesex, England: Penguin Books.

————. 1984 Introduction: Mothers, infants and adolescents. In: *Female Primates: Studies by Women Primatologists* (ed. by M. F. Small), pp. 13–16. New York: Allan Liss.

Sayer, J. 1982. *Biological Politics: Feminist and Anti-Feminist Perspectives*. New York: Tavistock Publications.

Shields, T. 1987. The variability hypothesis: The history of a biological model of sex differences in intelligence. In: *Sex and Scientific Inquiry* (ed. by S. Harding & J. O'Barr), pp. 187–216. Chicago, Illinois: University of Chicago Press.

Singer, P. 1990. *Animal Liberation*, 2nd Edition. New York: New York Review of Books.

Slocum, S. 1975. Woman the gatherer: Male bias in anthropology. In: *Toward an Anthropology of Women* (ed. by R. Reiter), pp. 36–50. New York: Monthly Review Press.

Smuts, B. 1985. *Sex and Friendship in Baboons*. Chicago, Illinois: Aldine Publishing Company.

Wasser, S. K. (ed.). 1983. *Social Behavior of Female Vertebrates*. New York: Academic Press.

Wickler, W. 1973. *The Sexual Code: The Social Behavior of Animals and Man*. Garden City, New York: Doubleday.

Zihlman, A. 1981. Women as shapers of the human adaptation. In: *Woman the Gatherer* (ed. by F. Dahlberg), pp. 75–120. New Haven, Connecticut: Yale University Press.

Chapter 3

Interpretive Cognitive Ethology

Hugh Wilder

I am interested in the large question of the possibility of cognitive ethology, the study of the cognitive abilities of animals and the psychophysiological and evolutionary processes underlying these abilities. The field has its detractors; some, for example, thinking that only humans (or only language users, the two sets often being coextensive for these critics) have any cognitive abilities to speak of, argue that cognitive ethology reduces immediately to cognitive anthropology. I am among the believers in the field, and will defend it here (see also Dennett 1987, especially Chapter 7; Griffin 1984; and Premack & Woodruff 1978). I will not, however, mount an abstract defense of the discipline by establishing its philosophical "credentials," nor will I meet head-on the arguments of any detractors (for such defenses, see, for example, Routley 1981). Rather, I will argue here that the discipline is possible because it is actual. In a series of case studies, I illustrate the practice of cognitive ethology. These cases show that while I am skeptical about the cognitive abilities of some animals, I am skeptical in these cases precisely because it *is* possible to study the cognitive abilities of whatever animals in which they occur.

I will look at the classic case of Clever Hans, the performing horse, and several of the relatively recent primate language studies. These cases dramatically demonstrate problems in the (human) interpretation of (nonhuman) animal behavior, but they also demonstrate how reliance on certain interpretive principles can solve these problems and contribute to the practice of good ethology. The problem I focus on is the Clever Hans Phenomenon, and the interpretive principle I discuss is Lloyd-Morgan's Canon. (For more on the Clever Hans Phenomenon see Sebeok & Rosenthal 1981; on "Morgan's Canon" [to which it is commonly referred] see Rollin 1990.) Ethologists certainly face other problems and rely on other methodological and heuristic principles in conducting their inquiries, but focus on these two will be sufficient for the sort of defense I offer of cognitive ethology.

Because of the importance of such interpretive principles as Morgan's Canon, cognitive ethology is best understood as an interpretive discipline, i.e., one in which common hermeneutic problems—problems in the interpretation of data—are inseparable from problems of theory construction and confirmation on the basis of the data. Morgan's Canon helps guide us in our attributions of rationality and other cognitive capacities to our animal subjects, but these attributions are more interpretations than discoveries of their rationality. And application of Morgan's Canon is not easy. My discussion of the case studies will emphasize the difficulty of the problems posed by the Clever Hans Phenomenon, as well as difficulties in using Morgan's Canon to help solve these problems. The picture of cognitive ethology which will emerge may, in its stress on the interpretive nature of the enterprise, be quite different from the more common behavioristic and positivistic pictures which remain from the discipline's earlier days. But I think my picture is defensible, and that it also makes for the best defense of cognitive ethology, for our abilities to understand the abilities of others.

Clever Hans: The Horse

Hans was exhibited in Berlin at the turn of this century by his owner and trainer, von Osten. (The classic presentation of the case of Clever Hans is Rosenthal 1965, on which the following review is based. See also de Luce & Wilder 1983.) The horse was trained to answer questions by tapping his hoof and shaking his head. von Osten had translated a wide variety of concepts into numbers, so that Hans appeared able to communicate on many different topics by tapping his hoof and shaking his head a certain number of times. Reports claimed that Hans was able, using this code, to count and solve arithmetic problems. He could work in whole numbers, fractions and decimals, and could convert one to the other. He could identify and reidentify objects of all sorts. He could match people with their photographs. Besides understanding the spoken German in which the questions were put to him, he could read and spell many German words. He knew the value of German coins, and could accurately make change. He could tell time and recognize musical tones and intervals. He could correlate the day and date in a given calendar year. When he perceived his questioner's ignorance, Hans would himself refuse to answer. But Hans answered as accurately for any intelligent and confident questioner as he did for his trainer, von Osten.

Although his performances were immensely popular, Hans' training and exhibitions were conducted in a sober scientific fashion. von Osten sincerely believed he had a gifted horse; he and others also believed that Hans had demonstrated that, with proper training, animal intelligence can be developed which is of the same kind and even (in certain domains) the same magnitude as human intelligence. Other observers were of course skeptical; many suspected fraud, and searched for some sort of communication between Hans and von Osten. However, no one could ever discover any deliberate communication or means of control von Osten or anyone else had over Hans.

However, in 1904 Pfungst and Stumpf began to look for unconscious and nondeliberate communication between Hans and his questioners. Pfungst noticed that Hans could answer questions in the absence of von Osten, which rendered improbable any explanation in terms of communication or control by von Osten. Pfungst also noticed that Hans' abilities diminished when he could not see his questioner, and when the questioner himself did not know the answers. These observations led Pfungst to hypothesize that Hans' abilities depended not on his own apparently human—indeed, peculiarly Germanic—intelligence, but on visual cues passed to Hans by his intelligent questioners.

Pfungst finally discovered such cues in the unintentional subtle motions of the questioner in asking his question and watching Hans answer. Pfungst's analysis of these cues remains a classic piece of scientific investigation, with implications for experimental design and observation in every branch of the behavioral sciences. Cues discovered by Pfungst included changes in the posture and inclination of the head of the questioner, raising of eyebrows, and dilation of nostrils. Certain subtle motions were made indicating expectancy when the questioner asked his question, these motions functioning as "go" signs, prompting Hans to begin tapping or shaking his head. Other motions were made indicating relief or satisfaction when the questioner thought Hans had tapped enough times to answer his question; these motions functioned as "stop" signs. What Hans had learned to do was to "read" these nearly subliminal cues in his questioners' behavior; he had not learned German, or arithmetic, or how to tell time, or how to correlate faces with photographs, days with dates, etc. He had learned to recognize and act on some stop and go signs. When the observers thought they perceived humanlike intelligence in Hans' behavior, what they were actually seeing was their own human intelligence projected onto the animal.

Clever Hans: The Phenomenon

Rosenthal (1966) revived interest in Clever Hans and suggested some important implications of the case for the practice of the behavioral sciences. He also dubbed the key discovered by Pfungst which finally unlocked the mystery of Hans' clever performances the "Clever Hans Phenomenon." In summary terms, as we have just seen, this Phenomenon is the subtle and unintentional cuing or prompting of an experimental subject. Some comments on the Phenomenon itself are in order before we discuss its implications.

First, as already noted in my presentation of the case, the cuing of the experimental subject need not be done by the experimenter; as in the eponymous case, cues may be passed by other participants in the experiments, and even by disinterested observers. (This basic point has often been missed. Broadhurst [1963: 26], for example, says that Hans responded correctly only in the presence of his trainer, and that Pfungst showed that it was von Osten alone who cued Hans. As we have seen, both claims are false. Rosenthal [1965: xxii] himself incorrectly summarizes the Clever Hans Phenomenon as "the subtle and unintentional cuing of the subject *by the experimenter*" [emphasis added].) It follows that the Clever Hans Phenomenon cannot be precluded simply by preventing direct experimenter-subject contact, as well constructed double-blind experiments are designed to do; more sophisticated techniques are required in order to eliminate Clever Hans type cuing.

Second, these cues need not be iconic; although they may, they need not resemble the behavior prompted in the animal by the cue. The cues are signs in the semiotic sense, and—as most signs in natural as well as artificial semiotic systems—need bear no physical resemblance or similarity to the information conveyed or the behavior resulting from reception of the sign. (A classic and still useful discussion of semiotic systems in general and iconic signs in particular is Morris 1938.) The signs passed to Hans signalled him to start and stop tapping his hoof and shaking his head, and the signs in no way resembled hoof tapping or head shaking. Nor were the signs "natural" start and stop signs, whatever those might be. It follows that animal responses to Clever Hans type cues need not *imitate* those cues. Animal behavior *may* imitate experimenter prompting (as it often does in the training phase of animal experimentation: I get Polly to say "Polly want a cracker" by saying "Polly want a cracker" myself), but Clever Hans cuing can occur without imitation (I say "Talk!" and Polly says "Polly want a cracker"). This is an important point, since some of the best understood and most widely recognized instances of the Clever Hans Phenomenon in the ape language studies are cases of animal imitation of trainer cues (see Terrace et al. 1979). Perhaps because Terrace's discovery of the imitative nature of his subject's behavior was so decisive and well publicized, other investigators have been especially concerned to design out the possibility of subject imitation of trainer cues from their investigations. The point here is that success in these attempts does not ensure success in the general problem of designing out *all* Clever Hans type experimental cuing.

Third, as with other behavioral stimuli, Clever Hans cues can be generalized and/or mediated by other variables. Hans' cues were direct and immediate: his questioner produced "start" signs (forward inclination of the head, raising the eyebrows, etc.) which Hans saw, and then Hans immediately began to tap. But in other experimental and performance situations signs may be passed indirectly to the subject (via intermediaries, for example), and the occurrence of the behavior elicited by the sign may be delayed (but maintained, for example, by the schedule of reinforcement in use). Nonhuman variables may cue the subject; for example, simple placement of the subject in a particular environment may, after suitable training, prompt the animal to begin behaving in particular ways. These points are of course familiar to behavioral scientists, but surprisingly easy to ignore in experimental design and interpretation of results.

Fourth, Clever Hans cues may be passed in any sensory modality available to the experimental subject. Hans' cues were visual, but it is easy to imagine how he might have been prompted in other modalities (auditory cues were first suspected, in fact). Note that the modality of the cues need not be consciously or even subliminally accessible to the sender of the cue (think ol animals more sensitive than humans to certain olfactory stimuli; these animals might respond to cues, unwittingly sent by their human observers, which could not be detected by the observers themselves). This is one reason Clever Hans cues are so hard to detect and control.

Fifth, while Clever Hans cues prompt, in the first instance, behavior in the animal subject, they may "rebound" and elicit particular behavior in the human observer. The role of expectancy and even wish-fulfillment in the (everyday *and* scientific) observation and recording of data is well established, and the point here is that the Clever Hans Phenomenon can strengthen an experimenter's tendency to observe and record what she or he expects or wants to see rather than what actually occurs. Cues passed to Clever Hans elicited behavior which *mimicked* real understanding of German and the principles of arithmetic, and his observers faithfully reported his comprehension of German and solution of arithmetic problems. Hans' reputation preceded his public performances, and his behavior reinforced his reputation; his behavior prompted his observers to perceive his success and to overlook the cues which they themselves were sending him. The Clever Hans Phenomenon confounds experimental results by prompting behavior in *both* subject and experimenter. For this as well as the reasons already cited, Clever Hans cues may take an indefinitely large number of forms and have a wide range of effects; it will be better, then, to think of Clever Hans *Phenomena* rather than a monolithic phenomenon.

Two kinds of implications of the Clever Hans case are especially important for our purposes: methodological and hermeneutic. The methodological implication, obvious in principle but surprisingly difficult to put into practice, is that behavioral scientists need to be on the lookout in their observational techniques and experimental design for the presence of Clever Hans Phenomena. Because of the diversity and subtlety of Clever Hans cues, they are difficult to detect. And because they are typically produced unintentionally, the perfectly good will and eternal vigilance of the experimenter is insufficient in precluding occurrence of Clever Hans Phenomena. As noted above, even well-designed double-blind studies which succeed in blocking direct experimenter-subject communication may fail to block other kinds of Clever Hans cuing (Umiker-Sebeok & Sebeok 1980).

The hermeneutic implication is related: if any Clever Hans Phenomena are present, then interpretations of observations and experimental results may be incorrect; the subject animal may not be doing what the observer thinks it is doing, even though each competing interpretation of the animal's behavior is compatible with all available observations (e.g., Hans was responding to simple stop and go signals, not doing addition; Polly is responding to my entry into the room, not saying she wants a cracker). Even when Phenomena *might* be present (i.e., when they have not been definitively designed out of the procedure), the subject *might* not be doing what the observer takes it to be doing. Since experimental results and interpretive hypotheses may be undermined by the mere possibility of presence of these Phenomena, behavioral scientists must (I repeat) proceed with great care in their observational and experimental work and with great modesty in advancing interpretive hypotheses. (Rosenthal 1965 and others [Umiker-Sebeok & Sebeok 1980; Gardner 1980; Sebeok & Rosenthal 1981] have taken evident pleasure in showing how Clever Hans Phenomena infect serious science in exactly the same way in which they occur in much pseudo-science [e.g. E.S.P.] and conjury.)

Clever Hans Meets Morgan

Rosenthal (1965: xiii) claims that "Pfungst's findings solved not only the riddle of Clever Hans but in principle the problem of other 'clever' animals." By "solved" here, Rosenthal means that a "reasonable explanation" is finally provided for the apparently extraordinary feats of the allegedly clever animals (it is "reasonable" to believe that Hans was responding to simple stop and go signals, and by implication unreasonable—or at least less reasonable—to believe either that Hans was understanding German and doing arithmetic or that von Osten was intentionally defrauding his public). By "reasonable," Rosenthal means *deflationary*: the animals are less clever than they seemed to be, because their behavior can be explained in terms of simpler cognitive (or perhaps even noncognitive, mechanistic or reflex) capacities than was originally thought.

Rosenthal is relying here on a particular interpretive principle which guides both his own (i.e., the scientist's) sense of rationality (determining what does and what does not count as a "reasonable" explanation) and his attributions of rationality (and any cognitive capacities generally) to animal subjects. The principle is known as Morgan's Canon, and it counsels parsimony in attributions of reason to animals: "In no case may we interpret an action as the outcome of the exercise of a higher psychical faculty, if it can be interpreted as the outcome of the exercise of one which stands lower in the psychical scale" (Lloyd-Morgan 1894: 53). There are problems here, to which we will return soon. But the basic idea is clear enough. Modern ethologists accept the Canon (perhaps in part contrary to Morgan's original intentions; see Rollin 1990) as counseling parsimony in attributing cognitive capacities to animals when explaining their behavior. When they are truly explanatory, explanations in terms of noncognitive factors (e.g., genetic determination, evolutionary value, exter-

nal cuing and prompting, internal reflexive responses, etc.) are preferable over explanations in terms of cognitive capacities (e.g., learned responses, goal-directed behavior,
reasoned actions); and explanations in terms of lower-order cognitive capacities (e.g.,
imitation), again, when truly explanatory, are preferable over explanations in terms
of higher-order abilities (e.g., conscious, rational deliberation).

Pfungst himself need not have relied on Morgan's Canon in defense of his explanation (since he witnessed Hans' intelligence diminish when the horse could not
see his intelligent human questioner [Rosenthal 1965]). But Pfungst's explanation is
consistent with Morgan's Canon, eschewing as it does the attribution of reason to
Hans; and Morgan's Canon is commonly used to justify such deflationary accounts of
the behavior of "clever" animals, when the choice between deflationary and inflationary accounts is underdetermined by the available evidence. (See Broadhurst 1963,
in which the Clever Hans case is cited as an instance in which application of Morgan's
Canon contributed to ethological progress.)

Thus Rosenthal claims, as we saw, that the Clever Hans Phenomenon solves *"in
principle"* the problem of other "clever" animals. Besides tacitly assuming the validity
and universal applicability of Morgan's Canon, this sweeping claim begs central
questions in cognitive ethology: Which animals are merely "clever" (scare-quotes)
and which are really clever (no quotes)? Which animals are clever in which ways?
Which are the animals for whom detection of Clever Hans Phenomena will deflate
our estimation of their cleverness? Rosenthal offers no clues, but he seems to be suggesting that the possibility of the presence of Clever Hans Phenomena is enough to
assure us in advance of any other empirical study of a "clever" animal's behavior that
that animal is less clever than claimed.

There are two related problems with this. First, Clever Hans Phenomena pervade
human social behavior (e.g., verbal and nonverbal communication) as well as non-
human/human interaction. And second, Morgan's Canon applies across the ethological board, to the study of human as well as nonhuman animal behavior. While it
is no doubt often reasonable to be as cautious and parsimonious in our attributions of
rationality to our conspecifics as we should be toward aliens, I think it reasonable to
believe that some of us sometimes behave really cleverly, and so might those aliens.
Fascination with the Clever Hans Phenomenon and uncritical adherence to Morgan's
Canon might blind ethologists to the occurrence of genuine cleverness in ourselves
and others. As Broadhurst (1963) points out, Morgan's Canon in particular is a powerful
tool for weeding out anthropomorphism in our interpretations of animal behavior;
the problem here is that some of us animals *are* sometimes anthropomorphic, and
it's not easy to decide which are when. If we knew, then we could use the Canon to
deflate claims on behalf of the others; but since we don't, we wield Morgan's sword
(fire the cannon?) at our own peril.

Beyond this, Morgan's Canon faces other problems as well. First, as we saw,
Morgan's Canon was originally formulated in terms of higher and lower psychical
faculties. More recent formulations mention cognitive capacities rather than psychical faculties (e.g., Broadhurst 1963). The problem here is how (and even whether)
Morgan's Canon survives the rejection of faculty psychology, what the conceptual
descendents of psychical faculties—those "cognitive capacities"—look like in
modern cognitive science. I think that some version of Morgan's Canon does survive and is defensible in modern terms, but the details need to be worked out. The

Canon must be revised in order to bring it into accord with the current state of cognitive science.

Second, how are we (now) to interpret Morgan's "higher" and "lower" designations? As Rollin (1990) shows, Lloyd-Morgan recognized three psychical faculties: from lower to higher, they were instinct, intelligence and reason. Lloyd-Morgan hypothesized that humans were the exclusive possessors of reason. But, in the first place, are there really just three (*these* three) "psychical faculties," however this concept is modernized? Without pursuing here this problem as far as it deserves, I simply note grounds for skepticism. Animal intelligence and cognitive capacities may not sort themselves neatly into (*any*) three kinds; rather, "the evolutionary message about intelligence, like the message about so many other dimensions in biology, is a message about pluralism and diversity, about the variety of intelligence in the biological world" (Jerison 1988: 10, as quoted in Bekoff 1989). And, in the second place, by what standard could something like Lloyd-Morgan's "reason" be the highest "psychical faculty"? While I am not entirely skeptical about the prospects of developing *some* perhaps rough measure of degrees of complexity and sophistication in animal intelligence, success here will require revision of the Canon's simplistic notions of "higher" and "lower." Such a measure must recognize the apparent diversity of intelligence in the biological world.

Such a measure must also avoid blatant *or* latent anthropocentrism—the third problem with Morgan's Canon I want to mention. As already noted, the Canon may serve as a welcome prophylactic against sentimental and unwarranted attributions of finer sensibilities to our favorite animals. But there may be a pernicious hidden agenda here: if all finer sensibilities and higher psychical faculties turn out to be exclusively *ours*, and especially if this turns out as a matter of definitional fiat rather than as a tentative matter of empirical fact, then Morgan's Canon may provide the "phylocentric chauvinist" an all-too convenient rationalization for his or her speciesism (see Pylyshyn 1978). Humans are of course different from other species in many ways, and not every mention of such differences amounts to speciesism (as not every mention of intraspecific human differences amounts to sexism or racism). Not all uses of Morgan's Canon are speciesist assertions of human dominion over the other animals. But *a priori* relegation of all nonhumans to second-class rational and cognitive status *can* be done from malevolent motives and have pernicious effects; and Morgan's Canon can aid and abet this anthropocentric project.

While ethologists of course need to respect differences between species, they also need to acknowledge inter-species structural (especially neurophysiological) similarities and evolutionary continuities (see Darwin 1872). In cases where such similarities and continuities are pronounced, it may make sense for the ethologist to advance attributions of cognitive capacities to nonhumans at which "phylocentric chauvinists" balk. In these sorts of cases, precisely the *opposite* of Morgan's Canon may be in order: "Assume until proven otherwise that others are just as intelligent, complicated, and so on, in their own way as you are in yours. And be very skeptical of your own motives and intellect if you think you have proved otherwise" (Menzel & Johnson 1978: 587, referring specifically to *nonhuman* animals).

The moral here is that care must be taken in the interpretation and application of Morgan's Canon. In particular, application of the Canon cannot substitute for or inhibit empirical investigation of animals' different cognitive abilities. The Canon may rule when available evidence underdetermines the choice between competing explanations of animal behavior, but it is misused when it inhibits the gathering of new data or the generation of new explanatory hypotheses.

The fourth and last problem I will mention with the Canon is its assumption of a single standard of optimality in the interpretation of animal behavior: accounts in terms of "lower" psychical faculties or cognitive capacities are preferable, when available, over accounts in terms of "higher" ones. However "lower" and "higher" get defined, they provide the univocal standard for assessing ethological interpretations. But ethological explanation, as all scientific explanation, is a pragmatic endeavor. Always, particular scientists engaged at a particular point in a particular research program are trying to understand for particular purposes a particular kind of behavior of a particular kind of animal. The "particular purposes" of the scientists are especially salient to the pragmatic nature of ethological explanations. Different ethologists will have different interests and purposes—specifically, different explanatory interests and purposes—and different kinds of explanations will be optimal for these different purposes. For example, investigators with an interest in training animal subjects (as in many of the ape language studies) may find behavioral interpretations rejecting mentalistic concepts altogether sufficient for their purposes, while observers of many animals in the field may find it more helpful to attribute (rudimentary, perhaps, but still recognizable) beliefs, desires and other intentional slates to the animals they are trying to understand. *Not* all optimal ethological explanations will be as parsimonious in doling out rationality as counseled by Morgan's Canon. While the Canon assumes a single standard of optimality requiring relative parsimony of all optimal explanations, ethological practice suggests a pluralistic conception of optimal explanation types, some of which will be less parsimonious than others in attributions of cognitive capacities.

To adapt a framework developed by Dennett (1978 and 1987) to our ethological concerns, we may divide the explanatory interests and purposes of ethologists among three broad (and fuzzy) categories. First, there are those ethologists whose interests are mainly physiological; these scientists are concerned to explain animals' cognitive capacities in terms of the physiological structures underlying these capacities. The leading question for these physiological ethologists is "*How* is that particular type of behavior possible?" and the typical answer is "Because of the types of physiological structures possessed by the animal in question." Modern ethology is thoroughly materialistic (though not necessarily reductionistic), assuming that all animal behavior and cognitive capacities are made possible by and explainable in terms of physical properties of the animals. And when the focus of inquiry is the physiological "platform" underlying an animal's behavior and cognitive capacities, then the ethologist will adopt the "physical stance" toward that animal. From this stance, explanations of the animal's behavior and capacities will be given in terms of the animal's physical states and physiological structures. While no doubt extraordinarily complex, ethology's commitment to materialism assumes that such explanations delivered from this physical stance can succeed in showing how types of behavior and capacities—including cognitive ones—are possible.

But this concern for the physiological structures underlying behavior and cognitive capacities is not the only concern ethologists may have. A second general interest of ethologists—emphatically *not* incompatible with the first just described—is in the evolutionary dynamics underlying animal behavior. Here the leading question is

"*Why* is that animal doing what it is doing?" and the typical answer is "Because of the evolutionary history of that animal and the evolutionary pressures sustaining that type of behavior." These evolutionary answers to ethological questions will be teleological, citing the "design" of an animal and explaining behavior in terms of such functional concepts as need and satisfaction, adaptation and reproductive success. Ethologists who have this kind of explanatory concern adopt what we may call the "evolutionary stance" toward their subjects (switching terminology from Dennett's original "design stance" to highlight the biological roots of ethology). Evolutionary stance answers to questions about why an animal does what it does and has the capacities it has supplement (rather than contradict) physical stance questions about how it is possible for the animal to be able to do those things and to have those capacities. And neither evolutionary stance nor physical stance explanations will answer questions about an animal's behavior and capacities in terms of that animal's intentional states, its beliefs and desires.

Ethologists may also be interested in what we shall call "hermeneutical problems" concerning animal behavior: here the leading questions are "*What* is that animal doing when engaging in that type of behavior? What is the *meaning* of that behavior in the life of that animal? How can we *make sense* of that behavior?" And answers to these hermeneutical questions may well be given in intentional terms: "That behavior is an expression of (manifestation of, etc.) particular intentional states of the animal, particular sorts of beliefs, desires, intentions and the like." Ethologists with these hermeneutical interests adopt the "intentional stance" toward their subjects, and may attribute a kind of (again, perhaps rudimentary) rationality to them, assuming that the animal has (perhaps nonconscious) beliefs, desires, intentions, and other intentional states. There may be both evolutionary and neurophysiological thresholds beyond which ethologists will be unwilling to adopt the intentional stance toward their animal subjects (paramecia might be excluded while chimpanzees are included, for example). And this intentional stance is no more incompatible with the physical and evolutionary stances than the latter are to each other; intentional stance explanations of animal behavior supplement rather than replace or supercede physical and evolutionary stance explanations of the same behavior.

Now, in counseling parsimony in doling out cognitive capacities to animal species, Morgan's Canon might be interpreted as saying that, where available, physical stance and evolutionary stance explanations are to be preferred over intentional stance explanations—since the last is certainly less parsimonious than the others in attributions of cognitive capacities. And, the Canon might be interpreted as always preferring, within the intentional stance, more over less parsimonious attributions, explanations in terms of simpler, more rudimentary cognitive capacities over more complex ones. Both interpretations are mistaken, I think, and their adoption would impoverish ethology.

Within the intentional stance, at certain (usually early) stages in the development of a research program, frankly inflationary accounts of animal behavior may be warranted. The animal may be (intentionally) more complex and sophisticated than its neurophysiology and evolutionary history would suggest, and research strategies should not blind us to that result. Inflationary accounts—flying in the face of Lloyd-Morgan's conservative counsel—might be fecund, yielding insights into patterns of animal behavior otherwise invisible. And again, at certain (especially early) stages in the development of a research program, considerations of fecundity may outweigh considerations of prudence in generating testable hypotheses. For traditional Popperian reasons, inflationary accounts may at certain historical moments be strategically helpful precisely because they turn out to be false; the falsification of accounts is one of the driving forces of the history of science.

Further, there is no need ever (let alone always) to prefer physical and evolutionary stance explanations in ethology over intentional stance explanations. The explanatory concerns of the three stances are different, and—as already noted—the three kinds of explanation, even explanations of the same type of behavior, are *not* incompatible with each other. Perhaps latent dualistic tendencies lead one to suspect that intentional stance explanations are incompatible with the materialistic, biological framework of physical and evolutionary stance explanations. But this is simply not so. While I cannot demonstrate it here, modern cognitive science—to which cognitive ethology is making crucial contributions—is making progress in showing how the most complex cognitive capacities can have a material basis. The questions of *which* animal species have *which* cognitive capacities is one of the central issues of ethology, and the best way to answer these questions may be to adopt the intentional stance toward animal subjects and try out intentional explanations of the animals' behavior. If a particular intentional explanation succeeds where others have failed in answering the ethologist's hermeneutical questions about the meaning of the animal's behavior, then the ethologist's tentative attribution of some kind of rationality to the animal has been to that extent justified. Of course the questions of whether, when and how intentional explanations of animal behavior can succeed are much debated. My point here is that Morgan's Canon can be and has been (mis)used to beg these questions rather than to help answer them. When the Canon is used to inhibit rich intentional explanations of animal behavior, it may blind ethologists to the possibly rich intentional lives of their animal subjects.

Despite all these problems, some version of Morgan's Canon may be essential to the science of ethology, as it helps to separate the science from its merely anecdotal and anthropomorphizing ancestors and neighbors. My review of some problems it faces shows that the Canon requires revision and reinterpretation and judicious application, but I leave to others and to other occasions all this important revisionist work. My point has been that while its good use can illuminate the lives of animals, the Canon can also obscure. That its good use is such a fine art shows again how cognitive ethology is an interpretive discipline.

Some Apes

I return now to the Clever Hans Phenomenon, and examine its possible occurrence in several of the more recent ape language experiments. Connections with Morgan's Canon will soon become apparent. The pervasiveness of the Clever Hans Phenomenon in the conduct of the behavioral sciences cannot now be doubted. Hediger (1974: 29) has offered an *a priori* argument suggesting its ineradicability "... every experimental method is necessarily a human method and must thus *per se* constitute a human influence on the animal.... The concept of an experiment with animals—be it psychological, physiological or pharmacological—without some direct or indirect contact between human being and animals is basically untenable." And where such contact cannot be eliminated, the possibility of inadvertent direct or indirect experimenter or observer cuing and prompting cannot be eliminated either.

Beginning with Rosenthal (1965), other investigators have offered empirical evidence suggesting the presence of Clever Hans Phenomena in particular experiments and research programs. Ensuing debates have been especially interesting concerning evidence found for the presence of Clever Hans Phenomena in many of the primate language studies of the 1960s, '70s and '80s. Terrace (1979) and Terrace et al. (1979) report finding experimenter prompting in his own work with Neam Chimpsky (Nim). Umiker-Sebeok & Sebeok (1980) describe ways in which a wider range of Clever Hans Phenomena may have occurred in several other ape language projects. (Ristau & Robbins 1982 is a reliable review of these projects. Of course Umiker-Sebeok & Sebeok's claims about Clever Hans "infection" are disputed by some of the principle investigators [but accepted by others; see Terrace et al. 1979 and Miles 1983].) If such Phenomena are present in a particular experiment, or even if their presence cannot be definitively ruled out, then—in accord with a revised Morgan's Canon—that experiment offers limited support for the hypothesis that the ape subjects can use and comprehend the language in which they were trained. The apes might be responding to Clever Hans-ish cues of their trainers, handlers or observers, rather than communicating in the language. Further research is required, and—at a minimum—careful double-blind experimental procedures must be followed. Such procedures may be difficult to implement, given the informal and social relations between investigators and subjects otherwise deemed appropriate in the ape language studies (on the importance of these informal and highly social investigator-subject relations, see Gardner & Gardner 1989 and O'Sullivan & Yeager 1989). And even when implemented, standard double-blind procedures may not eliminate cuing (see above and Umiker-Sebeok & Sebeok 1980). But unless the presence of Clever Hans Phenomena can be ruled out, this kind of deflationary interpretation of the apes' behavior will always be available and may be, in accord with Morgan's Canon, rationally preferable to less parsimonious interpretations.

I will illustrate this point by discussing three ape language projects, selected because they have as yet been insufficiently investigated for presence of Clever Hans Phenomena and because they are relatively "crucial cases" for their respective research programs. They are crucial because each involves minimal human intervention, thus minimizing the possibility of human prompting; also, they have been conducted and reported on after and partly in response to the accusations of Clever Hans Phenomena infection of other projects.

I will first describe two of Fouts' projects and argue that Clever Hans Phenomena may occur in each in the same ways. The first is Fouts' series of studies of chimpanzee-to-chimpanzee (*Pan troglodytes*) communication using acquired ASL (American Sign Language) signs; the second is his later set of studies of the transmission of acquired ASL signs from one chimpanzee to another. In the first (Fouts 1975a; Fouts 1975b; Fouts 1983; Fouts et al. 1973; Fouts et al. 1984), the chimpanzees are reared as much as possible as human children, with ASL the primary means of communication between chimpanzees and humans (see Gardner & Gardner 1969). Chimpanzees are taught ASL signs in formal training sessions, using modeling and reinforcement to train the animals to form signs and to build and maintain their ASL vocabularies (Fouts 1972). Fouts reports that chimpanzees raised and trained in this way eventually spontaneously communicate with each other using the signs of ASL (of course not exclusively; the animals continue communicating in their usual nonverbal ways as well). His primarily observational studies of this apparent intraspecific communication in ASL minimizes human intervention, suggesting a lower possibility for Clever Hans type prompting.

The second project began with Fouts' studies of a mother chimpanzee's (Washoe's, in fact) transmission of already acquired signs of ASL to her infant, and continued to study the general possibility of chimpanzee-to-chimpanzee transmission of ASL (Fouts et al. 1982; Fouts 1983; Fouts & Fouts 1989; Fouts et al. 1989). Fouts (1983: 71) stresses that this is an observational study, contrasting it with "the highly structured human-imposed training sessions" found in earlier experiments. The study began with the 1979 placement of Loulis, a ten month old chimpanzee, under Washoe's maternal care. Washoe, of course, was already trained in ASL; Loulis was never subjected to ASL training by his human handlers. (They did use seven ASL signs in his presence, but the rest of their communication with the chimpanzees and with each other was in spoken English.) Within several months, Fouts reports, Loulis had acquired 17 ASL signs; he could form the signs and use them on appropriate occasions in communication with Washoe and in manipulating objects. Fouts hypothesizes that Loulis acquired his signs through imitation of the other signing animals around him as well as through a surprising amount of apparently deliberate "tutorial" work done by Washoe. Since human intervention was again minimal, it might seem unlikely that Loulis' use of the ASL signs can be attributed to Clever Hans type prompting.

Direct trainer prompting in these two projects may be, as Fouts suggests, minimal. However, the Clever Hans case itself shows how much further Clever Hans Phenomena extend beyond direct trainer prompting. And in both of the projects just described, there is ample opportunity for cuing of animal subjects in such a way as to render suspect hypotheses that the animals—in either study—are "using the signs of ASL" in the sense of communicating with each other in ASL. If such cuing is in fact present, the animals may be responding to the cues in the same way in which Clever Hans responded to his.

I do not question the chimpanzees' acquired abilities to form ASL signs (forming the signs is different from using them in communication), nor do I suggest deliberate cuing by the animals' handlers. The real problem is that Fouts' procedures for observing his signing chimpanzees included no barriers to observer-to-chimpanzee communication and (hence) cuing. In fact, Fouts' observers included the animals' trainers, and were actually "participant observers" in the chimpanzees' conversations (particularly in the first study of chimpanzee-to-chimpanzee conversation). The observers' recordings of animal signing were checked for accuracy, but too late; the possibility for cuing had already been introduced with the entry of the observers.

Further, because the observers and data recorders in these studies were participant observers, the likelihood of observer-expectancy bias is enhanced. Clever Hans cuing can reinforce this tendency. Animal responses to Clever Hans cues look like the genuine article (e.g., communication in ASL); and if observers expect the genuine article, they may tend to overlook counterfeits. Note that observation by disinterested nonparticipants will help here no more than it did with Clever Hans; Clever Hans type cues are *not* (typically) produced deliberately, and may even be passed undetected by anyone (except the animal cued!). Nor does observation of videotapes of apparently spontaneous and private chimpanzee-to-chimpanzee communication eliminate the possibility of prompting. As we saw, prompting can have delayed results and can be mediated by a variety of factors including other people and particular environments.

Fouts' chimpanzee-to-chimpanzee ASL conversations introduce another source of cues: the animals themselves. No one doubts that the chimpanzees have been trained (by their human trainers or by each other) to form ASL signs; the issue is whether any chimpanzee has ever used these signs *as* linguistic signs, i.e., to perform speech acts. (The issue of what exactly it is to use signs "as linguistic signs" or in speech acts is of course contested. I here rely on the intuitive distinction between speaking and mimicking speech [and its equivalent for ASL].) The literature is enormous; for starters, see Chomsky 1965; Searle 1969; Terrace et al. 1979; and Savage-Rumbaugh et al. 1980.) And once one chimpanzee (e.g., Washoe) has been trained to make signs in ASL, another (e.g., Loulis) may imitate her signs. Subsequent "dialogue" in ASL between them may in fact be each responding to the immediate promptings of the other. Parrots can appear to converse with each other in English without the direct intervention of humans; but here, as in Fouts' studies of chimpanzee to chimpanzee communication in and transmission of ASL, appearances can be deceiving.

The last project I will describe is Savage-Rumbaugh's work with pygmy chimpanzees (*Pan paniscus*) (Savage-Rumbaugh 1984; Savage-Rumbaugh 1986; Savage-Rumbaugh and Brakke this volume). This project is noteworthy for many reasons, among them its demonstration of how in the same set of studies informal practices create opportunities for the occurrence of Clever Hans Phenomena, while formal testing procedures can (apparently) succeed in designing out at least its most blatant forms.

Savage-Rumbaugh's project again studies an animal's ability to acquire language skills without explicit human training. The pygmy chimpanzee subject, Kanzi, was reared in a rich social environment including other apes and humans. At least one member of a small and very stable group of human companions is always with Kanzi. Humans communicate with Kanzi in English and gestures, as well as the Yerkes lexigram symbol system. Kanzi receives no explicit training in any communication system. Savage-Rumbaugh (1986: 386) reports that after a period of time Kanzi began spontaneously to use gestures to communicate basic desires; later he began to "display elementary comprehension of vocal speech"; and later still "spontaneously started using lexigram symbols in a communicative manner."

In informal settings, Kanzi's lexigram utterances are directly observed and recorded by one of his human companions (some of which are checked by another person against a videotape recording).

> Each utterance is classified, when it occurs, as correct or incorrect and as spontaneous, structured, or prompted/imitated. Spontaneous utterances are those initiated by Kanzi with no prior prompting, querying, or other behavior on the part of human companions designed to elicit an utterance. Structured utterances are those initiated by questions, requests, or object-showing behavior on the part of the companion. Prompted utterances are those including any part of the companion's prior utterance. Although Terrace (Terrace *et al.* 1979) found it necessary to perform an analysis of video material in order to decide when Nim was imitating his teachers, we have found it reasonable to determine this at the time of the utterance. Since the symbols are displayed visually, the teachers

know which ones they have just used, and if Kanzi uses similar symbols, his utterance is scored as a prompted utterance. (Savage-Rumbaugh 1986: 387–388)

I have quoted Savage-Rumbaugh's description of her informal observational and recording procedures at length in order to show how ample are the opportunities in this setting for Clever Hans type cuing. Opportunities arise from several different factors. First, Kanzi's lexigram utterances are recorded by participants in conversations with him or by observers who know the language and can follow the conversations. This informal procedure precludes blind recording of data. Kanzi can see (and touch, smell, hear …) the participant/observer/recorder, whose behavior can cue him. And *Kanzi's* behavior can cue his observers, prompting them to see and record unreliable data; as we saw, Clever Hans cuing can reinforce experimenter-expectancy factors. This tendency is enhanced when observers and recorders are also (interested) participants.

Second, the human cues of Kanzi's behavior need not resemble in any way his responses (as we saw with Clever Hans). Therefore, many of Kanzi's utterances will be scored as spontaneous when they may in fact have been prompted by noniconic signs passed by an observer or participant.

Third, Clever Hans type cues are normally passed *unwittingly* by the observer or participant to the animal; so again many of Kanzi's utterances will be scored as spontaneous when they may in fact have been passed unintentionally by the person, perhaps even without her or his own knowledge (again, exactly as in Clever Hans' case). Since Savage-Rumbaugh's procedures score utterances as spontaneous when they have not been preceded by behavior *designed* to elicit the utterance, unintentional cues will pass through her procedural filter.

Fourth and last, while Kanzi's teachers may know which lexigram symbols they have just visually displayed, it does not follow that they know or are even aware of all the Clever Hans type signs they and others may have passed to Kanzi. These signs need not resemble the signs Kanzi produces, nor need they be visual signs. Since Kanzi is interacting with her conversants in a normal, unrestricted way, cues could be passed in a variety of forms and sensory modalities. Nor would examination of a video record of the session guarantee detection of any cues. Terrace and his co-workers succeeded in discovering their cues by studying videotapes, but they found only iconic ones (i.e., cases of Nim imitating his teachers); subtle noniconic and non-visual cues may have escaped Terrace's notice, and may escape Savage-Rumbaugh's as well.

Savage-Rumbaugh (1986: 392) claims that "since no symbol training tasks are employed at any time with Kanzi," the possibility of inadvertent cuing "is much reduced, if not eliminated entirely." As has just been shown, since Clever Hans cuing extends so far beyond explicit training sessions, its possibility has *not* in fact been eliminated from the informal procedures of the pygmy chimpanzee project. However, Savage-Rumbaugh has subjected Kanzi to formal tests which *do* seem to control for the forms of cuing just described which might occur in informal settings. These tests include just the sorts of double-blind procedures required in any serious attempt to eliminate Clever Hans Phenomena. (Pfungst's own tests of Hans' abilities still provide a model for such double-blind procedures [Rosenthal 1965; see also Umiker-Sebeok & Sebeok 1980, especially pp. 36–44].) Kanzi performed extremely well on the tests, successfully selecting appropriate lexigrams in response to spoken English words, selecting photographs in response to spoken English words, and selecting photographs when shown lexigrams (Savage-Rumbaugh 1986: 392–96). Savage-Rumbaugh interprets these results as suggesting that Kanzi has some understanding of spoken English and has mastered some basic elements of the linguistic practices of naming and reference. If Clever Hans Phenomena are, in fact, absent from the formal tests to which Kanzi has been subjected, and if, in accord with Morgan's Canon, no more parsimonious interpretation of his behavior is available, then perhaps Kanzi has indeed mastered these elements of language.

Of course, problems remain—problems with Savage-Rumbaugh's studies of Kanzi, but which are easily generalizable across the whole domain of cognitive ethology. First, how could we ever establish that Clever Hans Phenomena are absent from particular experimental conditions? The skeptic can always say that some may have still escaped our attention, and as long as their possible occurrence has not been precluded, the experimental results are unreliable. Second, how could we ever know that Morgan's Canon is satisfied, that no more parsimonious interpretation is available? Again the skeptic can always say that perhaps we haven't looked hard enough for a more parsimonious interpretation, or that perhaps one will be found next week.

The appropriate response to these skeptical arguments is agreement without concession. Certainty about our interpretations of Kanzi's cognitive abilities is beyond the reach of our own cognitive abilities, as is elimination of all general grounds for skepticism about any hypothesis in cognitive ethology. Certainty in any science is unattainable and inappropriate anyway, especially those in which interpretive problems loom as large as they do in cognitive ethology.

And, uncertainty comes in degrees. As we saw, Savage-Rumbaugh's formal double-blind testing procedures relieve some of our skeptical worries about her informal procedures. That grounds for skepticism remain means that she (and we!) are still doing science, not that we should now reject her hypotheses. Her double-blind procedures specifically help to rule out possible contamination of her results by infection with Clever Hans type cuing. And, reduction of the possibility of cuing reduces in turn the plausibility of *one* deflationary account of her subject's behavior, namely that he was merely responding to cues. Another deflationary account may be found next week, and Morgan's Canon requires us to keep looking. But it does not require us to reject Savage-Rumbaugh's hypotheses *this* week.

My overall aim in this paper has been to show that cognitive science is a possible science because it is an actual one. My case studies have been designed to illustrate the practice of ethology, both good and bad. The results of the practice of very good ethology—Pfungst's and Savage-Rumbaugh's, for example—may leave us in a state of some uncertainty about the real abilities of their animal subjects. But uncertainty is not peculiar to cognitive ethology; it is the hallmark of all good science.

Literature Cited

Bekoff, M. 1989. Tools, terms, and telencephalons: Neural correlates of "complex" and "intelligent" behavior. *The Behavioral and Brain Sciences* 12, 591–593.

Broadhurst, P. L. 1963. *The Science of Animal Behavior*. Harmondsworth: Penguin.

Chomsky, N. 1965. *Aspects of the Theory of Syntax*. Cambridge, Massachusetts: MIT Press.

Darwin, C. 1872. *The Expression of Emotion in Man and Animals*. New York: Greenwood Press.

de Luce, J. & Wilder, H. 1983. Introduction. In: *Language in Primates: Perspectives and Implications* (ed. by J. de Luce & H. Wilder), pp. 1–17. New York: Springer-Verlag.

Dennett, D. 1978. *Brainstorms: Philosophical Essays on Mind and Psychology*. Montgomery, Vermont: Bradford Books.

————. 1987. *The Intentional Stance*. Cambridge, Massachusetts: MIT Press.

Fouts, R. S. 1972. The use of guidance in teaching sign language to a chimpanzee. *Journal of Comparative and Physiological Psychology* 80, 515–522.

————. 1975a. Capacities for language in great apes. In: *Socioecology and the Psychology of Primates* (ed. by R. H. Tuttle), pp. 371–389. The Hague: Mouton.

————. 1975b. Communication with chimpanzees. In: *Hominisation und Verhalten* (ed. by G. Kurth & I. Eibl-Eibesfeldt), pp. 137–158. Stuttgart, West Germany: Gustav Fischer.

————. 1983. Chimpanzee language and elephant tails: A theoretical synthesis. In: *Language in Primates: Perspectives and Implications* (ed. by J. de Luce & H. Wilder), pp. 63–75. New York: Springer-Verlag.

Fouts, R. S. & Fouts, D. H. 1989. Loulis in conversation with the cross-fostered chimpanzees. In: *Teaching Sign Language to Chimpanzees* (ed. by R. A. Gardner, B. T. Gardner & T. E. Van Cantford), pp. 293–307. Albany, New York: SUNY Press.

Fouts, R. S., Fouts, D. H. & Schoenfeld, D. 1984. Sign language conversational interaction between chimpanzees. *Sign Language Studies* 42, 1–12.

Fouts, R. S., Fouts, D. H. & Van Cantfort, T. E. 1989. The infant Loulis learns signs from cross-fostered chimpanzees. In: *Teaching Sign Language to Chimpanzees* (ed. by R. A. Gardner, B. T. Gardner & T. E. Van Cantfort), pp. 280–292. Albany, New York: SUNY Press.

Fouts, R. S., Hirsch, A. & Fouts, D. 1982. Cultural transmission of a human language in a chimpanzee mother/infant relationship. In: *Psychobiological Perspectives: Child Nurturance Series*, Volume III (ed. by H. E. Fitzgerald, J. A. Mullins & P. Page), pp. 159–193. New York: Plenum Press.

Fouts, R. S., Mellgren, R. & Lemmon, W. 1973. American sign language in the chimpanzee: Chimpanzee to chimpanzee communication. Presented at: Midwestern Psychological Association Meeting, Chicago.

Gardner, M. 1980. Monkey business. *New York Review of Books* 27, 3–6.

Gardner, R. A. & Gardner, B. T. 1969. Teaching sign language to a chimpanzee. *Science* 165, 644–672.

————. 1989. A cross-fostering laboratory. In: *Teaching Sign Language to Chimpanzees* (ed. by R. A. Gardner, B. T. Gardner & T. E. Van Cantfort), pp. 1–28. Albany, New York: SUNY Press.

Griffin, D. R. 1984. *Animal Thinking*. Cambridge, Massachusetts: Harvard University Press.

Hediger, H. 1974. Communication between man and animal. *Image Roche* 62, 27–40.

Jerison, H. J. 1988. Evolutionary biology of intelligence: The nature of the problem. In: *Intelligence and Evolutionary Biology* (ed. by H. J. Jerison and I. Jerison), pp. 1–71. New York: Springer-Verlag.

Lloyd-Morgan, C. 1894. *An Introduction to Comparative Psychology*. London: Walter Scott.

Menzel, E. W. & Johnson, M. K. 1978. Should mentalistic concepts be defended or assumed? *The Behavioral and Brain Sciences* 4, 586–587.

Miles, H. L. 1983. Apes and language: The search for communicative Competence. In: *Language in Primates: Perspectives and Implications* (ed. by J. de Luce and H. Wilder), pp. 43–61. New York: Springer-Verlag.

Morris, C. 1938. *Foundations of the Theory of Signs*. Chicago, Illinois: University of Chicago Press.

O'Sullivan, C. & Yeager, C. P. 1989. Communicative context and linguistic competence: The effects of social setting on a chimpanzee's conversational skill. In: *Teaching Sign Language to Chimpanzees* (ed. by R. A. Gardner, B. T. Gardner & T. E. Van Cantfort), pp. 269–279. Albany, New York: SUNY Press.

Premack, D. & Woodruff, G. 1978. Does the chimpanzee have a theory of mind? *The Behavioral and Brain Sciences* 4, 515–526.

Pylyshyn, Z. 1978. When is attribution of beliefs justified? *The Behavioral and Brain Sciences* 4, 592–93.

Ristau, C. A. & Robbins, D. 1982. Language in the great apes: A critical review. *Advances in the Study of Behavior* 12, 141–255.

Rollin, B. E. 1990. How the animals lost their minds: Animal mentation and scientific ideology. In: *Interpretation and Explanation in the Study of Animal Behavior, vol. 1* (Ed. by M. Bekoff & D. Jamieson), pp. 375–393. Boulder, Colorado: Westview Press.

Rosenthal, R. 1965. *Clever Hans (The Horse of Mr. von Osten), by Oskar Pfungst*. New York: Holt, Rinehart & Winston.

Routley R. 1981. Alleged problems in attributing beliefs, and intentionality, to animals. *Inquiry* 24, 385–417.

Savage-Rumbaugh, E. S. 1984. *Pan paniscus* and *Pan troglodytes*. Contrasts in preverbal communicative competence. In: *The Pygmy Chimpanzee: Evolutionary Biology and Behavior* (ed. by R. L. Susman), pp. 395–414. New York: Plenum Press.

————. 1986. *Ape Language: From Conditioned Response to Symbol.* New York: Columbia University Press.

Savage-Rumbaugh, E. S., Rumbaugh, D. M. & Boysen, S. 1980. Do apes use language? *American Scientist* 68, 49–61.

Searle, J. R. 1969. *Speech Acts: An Essay in the Philosophy of Language.* Cambridge: Cambridge University Press.

Sebeok, T. A. & Rosenthal, R. (eds.) 1981. *The Clever Hans Phenomenon: Communication with Horses, Whales, Apes and People. Annals of the New York Academy of Science,* Volume 364.

Terrace, H. S. 1979. *Nim.* New York: Knopf.

Terrace, H. S., Petitto, L. A., Sanders, R. J. & Bever, T. G. 1979. Can an ape create a sentence? *Science* 206, 891–902.

Umiker-Sebeok, J. & Sebeok, T. A. 1980. Introduction: Questioning apes. In: *Speaking of Apes: A Critical Anthology of Two-Way Communication with Man* (ed. by J. Umiker-Sebeok & T. A. Sebeok), pp. 1–59. New York: Plenum Press.

Chapter 4

Concept Attribution in Nonhuman Animals: Theoretical and Methodological Problems in Ascribing Complex Mental Processes

Colin Allen and Marc D. Hauser

1 Introduction

Recent willingness to use mentalistic vocabulary to describe animal behavior has resulted from a decline in the popularity of the behaviorist approach to psychology introduced by Watson and championed by Skinner. It has not gone unnoticed that the current problems associated with the use of mentalistic vocabulary to describe animal behavior are similar to those that were faced by comparative psychologists of the nineteenth and early twentieth centuries (see Burghardt 1985 for a comparison of the problems). Then, as now, critics of mentalistic vocabulary in science have suggested that it is overly anthropomorphic and cannot be applied in a testable manner. Behaviorism was a reaction to the often unbridled anthropomorphism of the comparative psychologists. As Burghardt points out, if modern cognitive ethology is to successfully incorporate mentalistic descriptions, it is in need of a methodology that can avoid the charge of excessive anthropomorphism.

In this paper we explore the use of mentalistic terms by cognitive ethologists to describe animal behavior. As an example of a mentalistic term, we consider the notion of concept. We consider different aspects of behavior that are associated with human concepts, and address the question of whether it might be appropriate to say that nonhuman animals have concepts. Although, in recent times, philosophers have discussed concepts rather less than they have discussed other cognitive entities such as beliefs, we have chosen to look at concepts because of the somewhat more frequent use of this term by cognitive scientists. This paper is not intended as a review of the literature on categorization by animals (see Harnad 1987 for a series of papers that describe recent research). Neither is it intended as a review of philosophical literature on concepts. Instead, we intend to raise some methodological issues that attend attempts to attribute concepts to animals. In the latter part of the paper, we specifically focus on animal behavior with respect to death and describe a series of experiments that would allow comparison between animal responses to death and concept-mediated human behavior in response to death. These experiments will be posed as thought experiments, enabling us to focus on the particular methodological problems that are associated with such tests. Our analysis of concepts in nonhuman animals is intended to provide ethologists with a level of description of animal cognition that is useful to them in the design of experiments. Philosophers should be interested in the mental abilities of animals since the issues that arise provide a testing ground for philosophical theories of mind.[1]

From *Philosophy of Science*, 1991, 58: 221–240. Reprinted by permission.

Griffin (1981) has been foremost in challenging cognitive ethologists to pay more attention to the mental states of animals, especially animal awareness. We have chosen to phrase our discussion in terms of mental states rather than the less innocuous "cognitive processes" since the former are often taken to imply the attribution of properties to animals that are closer to those Griffin challenges ethologists to investigate.

Although biologists have become increasingly more willing to use terms that suggest complex mental states, the use of such terms is sometimes not intended to be taken literally. Terms such as "strategy," "deceit," "cheating," and "rape" have been deliberately introduced into behavioral ecology (Krebs and Davies 1984) with explicit disavowals of the necessity to invoke any mental states underlying the behaviors described by these terms. As an example of this, Munn (1986) describes a case of "deceitful" alarm calls in mixed species flocks of birds where "deceit" is given a nonmentalistic interpretation. For most philosophers, the question naturally arises whether it is appropriate to call this behavior "deceit" at all since many philosophical analyses of deceit (e.g., ones based on a Gricean account of communication) would require the attribution of complex intentions that the birds almost certainly do not have. Nonetheless, this metaphorical use of terms such as "deceit" is an accepted part of behavioral ecology which must be understood on its own terms.

Other researchers in both behavioral ecology and experimental psychology have intended their use of mentalistic vocabulary much less metaphorically. This is particularly true of those whose research has focused on cognition in nonhuman primates. The apparent sophistication of primates in comparison to most other animals makes them prime candidates for investigation of mental properties. Hinde (1982) remarks that the dangers of anthropomorphism have been much overemphasized and that analysis of primate behavior seems to require use of some mentalistic terms. Behavioral ecologists interested in the link between evolutionary theory and complex mental processes (e.g., Bachmann and Kummer 1980, Kummer 1982, Cheney and Seyfarth 1985) have shown themselves willing to use terms such as "knowledge" and "meaning" to describe the primates they study. It is our view, to be explained below, that mentalistic terminology gives ethologists a mode of description of animals that enables them to explain behavior within an evolutionary framework.

Experimental psychologists cum comparative psychologists have also helped themselves to the use of mentalistic terms. Premack's (1986) elegant experiments on causal inference in chimpanzees illustrate this approach. Although mentalistic terms have most commonly been used for nonhuman primates, behavioral descriptions of other organisms have also drawn upon mentalistic vocabulary (e.g., Gould and Gould 1982). On the basis of Skinnerian experiments, Herrnstein et al. (1976) have implied that pigeons have concepts. Herrnstein's experiments will be discussed in some detail below.

Despite this use of mentalistic terms, most behavioral ecologists, cognitive ethologists and comparative psychologists have not explicitly discussed the theoretical role played by such terms (for exceptions see contributions in Griffin 1982, and Harré and Reynolds 1984). Some philosophers have suggested that mentalistic vocabulary or moderate anthropomorphism might play a heuristic role in hypothesis generation (Dennett 1983, and Asquith 1984) and this view has been endorsed by some researchers of animal behavior (e.g., Burghardt 1985). However, one implication behind some of these suggestions appears to be that mentalistic vocabulary does not directly correspond to any underlying reality. Dennett, for instance, claims that mentalistic terms ultimately will not play any role in scientific description of organisms, eventually being eliminated by descriptions at some other level such as neurophysiology (Dennett 1969, 1983). In contrast, Griffin's proposal for the scientific exploration of animal awareness apparently presupposes that the mental states of animals are real phenomena in need of scientific explanation. This seems to us to be a more reasonable attitude towards mental states in animals than the eliminationist position implied by the view that talk of mental states is merely heuristic. Although it is our view that mental attributions are necessary for the adequate explanation of the behavior of some animals, our aim in this paper is not to provide arguments for this claim. Rather, we are concerned with discussing the kinds of experiments that might make mental attributions plausible.

In order to explicate the proper use of mentalistic terms in ethological explanations of nonhuman animal behavior, it is necessary to have at least an approximate understanding of the theoretical role these terms are expected to play and how they might systematically be applied. Ethology is the study of animal behavior within the context of evolutionary theory. In particular, an animal's behavior is examined in light of its function and its evolution (see Hinde 1982 for a full explanation of the nature of ethology). Questions about the function of a particular behavior are commonly answered by explaining how the behavior in question contributes to the fitness of the organism. Mentalistic terms provide a level of description that is appropriate to the functional level of description that is the concern of evolutionary hypotheses. Mental states relate organisms to their environments through the notion of content. A mental state will be adaptive insofar as its content provides for appropriate links between environment and behavior. Mentalistic terms thus provide a natural vocabulary for cognitive ethologists to frame their hypotheses.

In the next section, we consider the concept of concept and its role in ethological explanations of nonhuman animal behavior. Moreover, we discuss whether the concept of concept can be used to describe some of the mental representations that explain animal behavior. Our intent is not to provide an extensive philosophical treatment of the concept of concept. In particular, we cannot hope to consider all the constraints on concept ascription that have been discussed in the recent philosophical literature. Among such topics are the alleged holism of belief and concept attribution (Quine 1960), the role of the environment in fixing belief (Putnam 1975, and Burge 1979) and the role of discrimination under ideal conditions in concept individuation (see Rey 1983 for discussion of this last issue and the various theoretical roles played by the concept of concept). Rather, we are concerned with elucidating a minimal constraint on cognitive representations for them to count as concepts. This analysis will enable us to suggest how one might search for empirical data to support the attribution of concepts to nonhuman animals.

2 Concepts of Concept

The "concept of 'concept'" has the ring of a philosophical topic, rather like the "meaning of 'meaning.'" This latter topic has been extensively discussed by philosophers (e.g., Grice 1957, and Putnam 1975) and has led to specific methlological suggestions for cognitive ethologists. For instance, Dennett has made use of Grice's notion of levels of intentionality to suggest research strategies for cognitive ethologists (Dennett 1983). A recently published volume of papers arising from an interdisciplinary conference has also explored the possibilities of a fruitful interaction between philosophers and biologists on the topic of the meaning of primate signals (Harré and Reynolds 1984). In contrast, philosophical work on the concept of concept has been of little use to ethologists.

Many researchers in cognitive science regard the notion of internal representation to be a unifying theme in the different disciplines that make up cognitive science. Cooper, a psychologist, describes the task of the cognitive sciences as determining "the content, structure, and organization of knowledge" (1982, 145) which she equates with "the internal representations of the external world" (ibid.). The notion of an internal representation seems closely related to the notion of abstract idea found in Locke and Hume. Abstract ideas were the means by which human beings were supposed to be able to think about the individuals of some class without having to think about a particular individual. Thus the abstract idea of a horse included just those properties common to horses. Berkeley was famous for his attack on Locke's theory of abstract ideas, claiming that it was not possible to think of a horse without it having some particular color, height, and so on. One interpretation of Berkeley's objection suggests that it is based on the mistaken idea that the only way in which horses might be represented internally is in the form of a picture. The description of other possible forms of representation will go some way towards meeting Berkeley's objection, as well as going towards providing cognitive ethologists with a workable notion of concept. In addition, unlike a picture, an adequate representation for an abstract concept has a logical structure, or syntax, that connects its components (Fodor 1975). The search for representations with suitable structures is a primary goal for researchers in acquisition of concepts by computers (Schank et al. 1986).

The notion of concept is not identical with the notion of an internal representation since attributing internal representations in cases where one would not want to attribute a concept is possible. To develop this point, we will examine the research by Herrnstein et al. (1976) on pigeons. In their influential and widely cited paper, Herrnstein et al. have been taken to show that pigeons have concepts corresponding to certain natural categories (see, for example, Griffin 1981, and Dasser 1985). The three experiments conducted by Herrnstein et al. consisted of showing pigeons respectively pictures of trees, water, and a person. Included in these pictures were examples of each category that were considered "hard" by the experimenters. For instance, some pictures contained only parts of trees, or showed trees in the distance. In each case, the pictures falling into these categories were randomly mixed with pictures that showed non-examples of the categories, including pictures that were considered near misses. Examples of near misses for trees include a picture of celery and a picture of a vine climbing a wall. The pigeons were capable of differentially pecking at a feeder key according to whether the pictures fell into the category or not. These results have been widely cited as demonstrating that pigeons have concepts.

The title of the paper by Herrnstein et al. is simply "Natural Concepts in Pigeons," but it is notable that the only other place in their paper where the word "concept" appears is in reference to human concept formation. "Concept" is never once defined, and it is replaced throughout by the potentially less innocuous, and philosophically less interesting, "category." The term "category" is less interesting since it is more easily interpreted to pertain to the human classificatory scheme rather than that of the pigeons. To say that the pigeons sort pictures into categories of tree or person is thus a considerably less specific claim about the internal representations involved than the claim that pigeons have concepts of those things.[2]

Herrnstein and his colleagues correctly make the point that no simple classification of the pictures in terms of common visual elements can be specified that will uniquely characterize those pictures that contain trees. Rather, they believe that the notion of "family resemblance" from Wittgenstein is more likely to describe what enables the classification of trees together. They suggest that pigeons have an innate disposition to infer a tree category from seeing instances of trees.

What seems to follow from these experiments is that pigeons are able to recognize specific properties in particular examples, and use these properties to recognize a general class or category. We are supposing that an explanation of this ability will attribute some kind of internal representation to guide the classification. But is this enough to allow us to say that the pigeons possess the corresponding concepts?[3] It is possible to teach a human being to sort distributors from other parts of car engines based on a family resemblance between shapes of distributors. But this ability would not be enough for us to want to say that the person has the concept of a distributor. In a suitably constrained environment, such a person need not have a representation of any information other than the shape to accomplish the sorting.[4]

It is beyond the scope of this paper to provide a theory of concept individuation. Our aim instead is to provide means of assessing the similarity between human mental processes and those of animals. Humans may represent environmental features in different ways and the question arises whether animals do likewise. In order to explain the different forms of representation, it will be useful to introduce a distinction between different ways of using the notion of recognition. The distinction to be made is between recognizing an X, and recognizing something *as* an X or recognizing it to be an X.[5] The first of these can be thought of as an extensional characterization of a discriminatory ability. The organism said to have the ability has some way of sorting things into the classes specified (X and not-X), but this may be achieved by way of properties that are accidentally coextensive (see discussion below). The second says something about the organism's system of internal representation. To have a concept of X where the specification of X is not exhausted by a perceptual characterization, it is not enough just to have the ability to discriminate X's from non-X's. One must have a representation of X that abstracts away from the perceptual features that enable one to identify X's. In the case of distributors, for example, once a person knows what distributors do, they have a representation that takes them away from mere shape recognition. We are not trying here to give an account of either necessary or sufficient conditions for the attribution of the concept of a distributor to someone. Rather, we are pointing out that some forms of representation of distributors allow for more sophisticated behavior with respect to distributors. For instance, having knowledge of the function of distributors will help subjects to categorize anything that plays that role even if its shape radically diverges from the pattern they originally based their discriminations upon. It might also allow them to reject some distributor-shaped non-distributors.

We are not denying the possibility that pigeons have concepts. However, the experiments conducted by Herrnstein et al. do not warrant the conclusion that pigeons have abstract concepts such as those of tree or person. The limitations of the Herrnstein approach have recently been discussed by D'Amato and van Sant (1988). They used slide presentations to cebus monkeys to determine whether monkeys have the concept of a person. The monkeys were trained in a manner similar to the pigeons in Herrnstein's experiments. While D'Amato and van Sant claim to have evidence for the representation of the person concept in cebus monkeys, they express reservations. In particular, they admit that their experiments do not successfully distinguish between stimulus generalization and concept-mediated behavior. They also state that "continued efforts along similar lines are not likely to prove fruitful" (1988, 54), citing uncertainty about the concept of concept as one of the reasons. In the next section, we hope to defuse this kind of pessimism.

In this paper, we will not concern ourselves with the attribution of concepts such as those of red or square. Such concepts, while they may involve abstraction from stimuli, are likely to be more perceptually direct than concepts like tree, person or distributor. We will deal with the structure of these higher level concepts. As an example of how theoretical considerations about concepts apply to empirical research, we turn our attention to behavior towards the concept of death. The next section discusses why death is a suitable topic and provides empirical observations that have been made of animal responses to death.

3 Behaviors in Response to Death

Animal response to death is a subject which has been of considerable interest to researchers in animal cognition (Griffin 1981). For some species, death of a group member represents a substantial loss. In the case of death of a mature animal, this constitutes a loss of group resources (e.g., defense against predators or competitors). When an infant dies, any further "caring" behavior shown by the parents represents a potential waste of that organism's resources. In many species, the presence of dead organisms poses a hazard thus making behavior which removes the dead individual adaptive. The ubiquity of death in animal experience, and the clear advantage for some individuals of some species of being able to recognize death and modify behavior accordingly, makes it of considerable interest to ethologists. In addition to the theoretical interest in death is a considerable body of empirical work describing the response of individuals to dead animals across a variety of taxa. This body of data makes death a suitable topic for cross-species comparisons.

While scientific literature presents a fair amount of discussion of animal reactions to death, much of what is written is anecdotal in nature. Although we must be careful about the conclusions we draw from published reports, it is possible to distinguish some trends in the varying abilities of different species to recognize and react to death. In no species are reactions to death catalogued as thoroughly as they are in humans. However, in the examples discussed below, analogues to several of the human responses to death can be seen. We will describe some of the responses to death that have been reported in the animal literature before attempting to interpret the responses.

Some of the most thoroughly understood behavior in reaction to dead conspecifics occurs in ants, particularly *Pogonomyrmex barbatus*. Their behavior is described by E. O. Wilson (1971) as follows:

> The transport of dead nestmates from the nest is nevertheless one of the most conspicuous and stereotyped patterns of behavior exhibited by ants.... When a

corpse of a *Pogonomyrmex barbatus* worker is allowed to decompose in the open air for a day or more and is then placed in the nest or outside near the nest entrance, the first sister worker to encounter it ordinarily investigates it briefly by repeated antennal contact, then picks it up and carries it directly away towards the refuse piles.... It was soon established that bits of paper treated with acetone extracts of *Pogonomyrmex* corpses were treated just like intact corpses ... the worker ants appear to recognize corpses on the basis of a limited array of chemical breakdown products. They are, moreover, very narrow-minded on the subject. Almost any object possessing an otherwise inoffensive odor is treated as a corpse when daubed with oleic acid. This classification extends to living nestmates. (Pp. 278–279)

Cowgill (1972) has described the reaction of potto monkeys kept in captivity to the death of a cagemate. Two mated pairs of pottos had been kept in a single cage. The death of the dominant male's mate was followed by a period where his rate of feeding and overall activity level decreased. After a few days, the dominant male also died. Following this second death, the remaining pair were watched for a few months. The remaining pair spent a considerable part of their time apparently "searching" for their cagemate. Additionally, the two remaining animals would leave a portion of their food untouched, even when the food supply was reduced.

Among primates in the wild, a number of researchers have recorded observations of mothers carrying their dead infants for considerable periods of time. Jeanne Altmann's (1980) description of yellow baboon mothers in Kenya provides a perfect description of the general phenomenon:

Mothers persist in the apparently automatic embracing of their infants even after death. They continue to carry the decomposing and increasingly dehydrated corpse, despite the fact that this usually means that they walk three-legged, setting the corpse down whenever they stop to feed and then retrieving it again.... After about three days ... mothers leave the corpse on the ground for gradually increasing periods of time while they forage at greater distances away, eventually either lose it or leave it, looking back at the corpse with repeated signs of conflict and ambivalence and sometimes giving alarm barks. (Pp. 129–130)

Among human cultures, reactions to death vary considerably. Differing cultural, religious and scientific beliefs affect the treatment of dead bodies and the concept of death held by individuals in the different cultures. Although these differences exist, there is much that is common. For instance, all human cultures have some method for disposal or treatment of dead bodies. While the methods vary, they all have the effect of isolating living individuals from contact with a decomposing corpse. Other human reactions to death include various types of formal and informal mourning. Again, while these are different between cultures, it seems that there is a universal need for some sort of mourning behavior in response to death of close associates. The strength of the mourning response may be great enough to interfere with other behaviors related to death. For instance, some parents may be unable or unwilling to make the arrangements for the burial of a dead child. Examples such as this raise questions about the relationship between concepts and beliefs. However, since we are interested only in establishing that a certain level of mental representation is involved, we can avoid questions about the precise specification of the content of the representations.

4 Interpretation of Animal Response to Death

In ethology, what counts as a useful interspecific comparison between two behaviors is determined by the role those behaviors play in the survival and evolution of the respective species. In the behaviors described in the previous section, there are a number of analogies to human responses to death. The ambivalent baboons are like the distraught parents who will not accept the fact of their child's death. Even the ants' behavior is comparable to the human insistence on removing a corpse from the normal living and working areas. Some such parallels have been drawn in the popular science media, but there may be a useful scientific reason for such comparisons.

From an ethological perspective, the ants' behavior may have the same explanation at one level as human burial practices. That is, removal of dead conspecifics from the living quarters is adaptive (e.g., for reasons of disease control). The general statement of the hypothesis might be that the ability to recognize dead conspecifics will evolve in any species where removal of the dead confers a selective advantage. However, the mechanisms underlying this recognition ability will vary between different species. The stereotypicality of the ants' behavior is not enough to make us say that the ants do not recognize dead nestmates. However, it seems unreasonable to say that the ants recognize that their nestmates are *dead*. The ants are using chemical cues that within the normal limits of their environment serve to correctly pick out dead nestmates. Extensionally, within this environment, the class of dead ants and the class of objects with oleic acid are the same. Thus it is reasonable to say that they are able to recognize dead ants. But, their behavior is mediated by nothing more than the perceptual stimulus provided by oleic acid. Therefore, it is not reasonable to assert that they recognize nestmates as dead, or that they have a concept of death.

Humans, and indeed other animals, may not just respond to stimuli features of their environment that happen to latch onto the right extensional class. In the case of ants, no indication of death is independent of the presence of oleic acid. In humans, however, a variety of perceptual inputs count as evidence for death. Even more important than this variety is the fact that humans are able to modify what kinds of evidence will prompt them towards the normal behaviors (e.g., disposal and mourning) directed towards dead bodies. Thus, for instance, the advent of cardiopulmonary resuscitation means that lack of a pulse is no longer to be taken to mean that the victim is dead, although, of course, it still counts as evidence. Also, like ants, humans may be duped into believing that someone is dead when they are not (e.g., by the effects of some drugs). But unlike ants, humans who have been duped in this way normally will modify what they take in the future to be evidence of death so as to be careful not to be fooled by appearances. Humans are capable of recognizing something *as* dead because they have an internal representation of death that is distinct from the perceptual information that is used as evidence for death. It is this separate representation that is capable of explaining the human ability to reason about rather than merely respond to death in the environment.[6]

We would attribute an abstract concept to an organism if there is evidence supporting the presence of a mental representation that is independent of solely perceptual information. In the following sections, we discuss two experiments that might provide such evidence.

5 Experiments

We have thus far developed an analysis of the notion of a nonperceptual concept that involves representation of some feature independently of its perceptual components. This analysis has not been developed with full philosophical sophistication. It is, however, sufficient for us to suggest the kinds of experiments that enable one to determine to what extent the mental processing of nonhuman organisms reacting to death is similar to human mental processing.[7] In our view, the experiments we present below do not enable us to make claims about the precise specification of the content of animal concepts. Instead, what we try to do is make plausible the claim that animals can be shown to be operating with internal representations that function rather like human concepts.

With this objective in mind, we can suggest two testable features of behavior. First, an organism whose internal representations are concept-like should be able to generalize information obtained from a variety of perceptual inputs and use that information in a range of behavioral situations. For example, suppose animal A recognizes animal B as dead. Subsequently, A is presented with a stimulus that would ordinarily have evoked a response towards B were it alive. If A is operating with a concept of death, it should be able to use the perceptual input that informed it of B's death to modify its response with respect to the subsequent stimulus.[8] Observation of this kind of behavioral modification would make talk of concepts plausible. Our first experiment investigates the possibility of attaining the appropriate behavioral evidence. Secondly, organisms that can be said to possess a concept should be able to alter what they take as evidence for an instance of that concept. For example, when first presented with evidence that something is dead but then presented with conflicting evidence that it is alive, an animal should alter its responses to the first kind of evidence. Our second experiment is designed to address this feature.

Ethologists have traditionally preferred experiments that are "natural" over laboratory situations. The reasons for this are varied, but most can be related to the ethologists' attempt to provide evolutionary explanations of behavior. It is argued that these explanations are most valid when observations of animals are gathered in their natural habitats (i.e., those habitats in which natural selection has shaped their behavior, physiology, morphology, and so on). Thus, the experiments we describe are designed for a natural setting, although it would be possible to perform similar experiments in captivity.

The subjects for the first of our hypothetical experiments are East African vervet monkeys. Vervets are appropriate subjects for such an experiment because a great deal of work has been done to address the possibility that their behavior is guided by complex mental abilities (Cheney and Seyfarth 1985, Hauser 1988). The experiment involves an analysis of how female vervet monkeys respond to the death of their own infants. It is well established that female vervets are capable of recognizing the individual distress calls of their infants and that other females in a group will look towards the mother of an infant that has just uttered such a call. These responses indicate knowledge of mother-infant pairings (Cheney and Seyfarth 1980). Adult males also appear to recognize the calls of their potential offspring (Hauser 1986). In cases where infants have recently died, these facts can be exploited by playing one of their previously recorded distress calls from a concealed speaker (see Cheney and Seyfarth 1980 for description of concealed playback experimental method; in such experiments, the response of vervets to the recorded calls is no different from their response to naturally occurring calls).

Vervet mothers might respond in three ways when presented with distress call from their dead offspring:

1. They might respond as they do while the infant is alive (i.e., look towards speaker).
2. They might respond in a more agitated fashion (e.g., initiation of searching behavior).
3. They might not respond at all, continuing the activity in which they were engaged prior to the playback.

For (1), it seems correct to say that this would not provide any evidence of a concept associated with death unless gradations in response are too subtle to be distinguished by visual observation. (This, of course, is not the same as saying that it provides evidence that they do not have a concept.) However, (2) and (3) present more interesting possibilities. For (2), two possible explanations suggest themselves. Either the mothers have taken the distress call as evidence that the infant is nearby, or the call has elicited some kind of "surprise" reaction. Whether or not the mother had seen the infant die is relevant here. If the mother saw her infant carried away by a predator, or saw it die due to disease, then the first explanation would seem likely only if the infant was not recognized *as* dead.[9] The second explanation would be more likely for animals that had recognized the infants as dead. Control experiments that could distinguish between the two explanations would help in the determination of whether the animals are operating with a concept. Reactions to distress calls by females other than the mother could help provide such a control. Vervets are vulnerable to predation by leopards (Struhsaker 1967, and Seyfarth et al. 1980), so it would be reasonable for a mother who saw her infant carried away in the jaws of a leopard to infer that it was dead even if this could not be precisely determined. One could compare the response of a mother who saw the infant carried away by a leopard to the response of a second female who did not. The only evidence available to the second female is that the infant is no longer present with the group. The cause of this is unknown to her. In such a situation one might expect the mother to be startled upon hearing the infant's call. On the other hand, one would not necessarily expect the second female to show the same response.

It is important to realize that, so far, the experimental outcomes described would not enable the experimenters to distinguish between animals that have a concept related to our concept of death versus some other concept such as that of being missing. Possibility (3), however, is more decisive in this regard. The ability to "turn off" a response seems to indicate that the animal has recognized the finality of the disappearance of the infant.[10] If the infant were just believed to be missing, then the most adaptive response would be to begin searching when the distress call was heard. For vervet monkeys, since young infants are rarely separated from other group members for more than one to two hours, it seems unlikely that a failure to respond after a period of several days indicates a belief that the infant is missing. This "turning off" response could provide the basis for an adaptive explanation of conceptual representation of dealth. The ability to use an independent representation of death (a concept of death) to guide behavior would be advantageous if it allowed rapid modification of behavior in a wide variety of situations. For instance, if energy would be wasted by fruitless searching, then recognition of death will be advantageous if it deters such searching behavior. In the case of the ants described above, the direct link between perceptual input and behavior, without the intermediate step of conceptualization, leads to the "inappropriate" removal of live ants treated with oleic acid. In the ants' normal environment, dissociation of oleic acid from death is not needed. It might be wondered where the adaptive benefit from having a concept lies. Any mechanism that turned off the vervets' response would do. The answer to this question is not simple, but we would argue that adaptiveness of the general ability to form concepts arises from a history of variability in the vervets' environment that is not matched in the ants' (Allen 1989).

While thinking of a number of important controls that one would like to conduct for this experiment is possible, the majority turn out to be unacceptable, primarily for ethical reasons. One obvious control would involve removing infants from the group by direct intervention and then observing the mother's response to distress calls over a variety of conditions and period of time. However, the practical and ethical difficulties associated with such a procedure are often enormous, particularly with wild primate populations.[11] Some of these difficulties might be alleviated in captive populations. The responses of captive animals are, however, often difficult to interpret and may be unreliable as guides to the responses of animals in their natural environment. Captive animals are often removed from their living groups for short periods of time (e.g., for medical testing); thus, most captive populations are accustomed to frequent removal and return of individuals from the group. In contrast, free-ranging vervets are rarely out of visual or auditory contact for extended periods of time. This means that disappearance can either be interpreted as death or as migration into another group. Although males leave their natal groups upon reaching reproductive maturity and transfer into neighboring groups, infants never do so (Cheney and Seyfarth 1983).

It is worth noting that the most interesting response (3) was, in fact, a lack of response to the call on the part of the vervets. The interpretation of a lack of behavior is tricky since there are a number of alternative explanations. For instance, the animal might not have heard the playback or it might have been so engrossed in what it was doing that it failed to notice the distress call. While it is possible to reasonably discount some of these possibilities, the experimenter is always faced with the possibility of some unconsidered factor interfering between the playing of the call and the production of a response on the part of the targeted individual. In addition to the problem of interference, a lack of response presents a further problem of interpretation. A definite behavioral response (e.g., searching) leads reasonably directly to an interpretation (e.g., that the infant is believed to be nearby). The interpretation is aided by the apparent purposiveness of the behavior. In contrast, no response could be interpreted in a number of ways; for example: the mother hears the call but does not believe it is her infant's, the mother hears the call but infers that she must have heard another infant since her own is dead, she thinks she hears the call but infers that she must not have heard anything since the infant is dead. Undoubtedly, some of these interpretations are overly anthropomorphic. However, the general point is that the scant behavioral evidence itself does not distinguish between them.

Another disadvantage of the current experiment is its lack of general applicability to other animal species. Since the experiment relies on the ability of females to recognize the calls of their young, duplicating the experiment on other species would not always be possible.[12] The second experiment we consider is constructed with this problem in mind, and has the benefit of being applicable to a wide range of species, including humans.

The second experiment attempts to investigate whether animals have the ability to alter what they take as evidence for death. To do this, we take an individual of any species and administer a drug that causes unconsciousness and depression of vital signs. As we remarked above, a human is unlikely to be fooled twice into thinking that someone administered this drug was in fact dead. In the first trial of our experiment, animals are placed in a situation where they are expected to react as if the drugged animal were dead. As the effects of the drug wear off, the animal revives and we record the behavior of the other individuals. For the second trial, the experiment is repeated some time later with the original animal being drugged and the other animals watched to see whether they react in the same way. The final trial of our experiment involves the same drug procedure, but a different individual as the target for the drug. The question here is whether a change or modification in response is generalized to any individual.

As with the first experiment, there are a number of possible responses and alternative interpretations of those responses. If the animals fail to modify their behavior between trials, this would tend to indicate that they make no distinction between death and its perceptual signs. On this basis, describing the behavior as concept-mediated would be unreasonable. If the animals modify their response both when the original animal is drugged again, and when the drug is administered to a new individual, this would seem to provide the strongest evidence that the animals are operating with a concept. A suitable control for this would be to see whether the animals continued to produce their normal responses to death in cases where they had additional evidence that the animal was dead (e.g., they saw the animal get killed). A third possibility is that the animals modify their response only in the case where the original animal was redrugged, but did not transfer this to cases where other animals were drugged. Although this case is perhaps less likely, it would present some interesting difficulties for interpretation. One possible interpretation is that the animals have a concept of death, but that they believe that the first animal is faking being dead. Alternatively, one might interpret the results as showing that the animals do not have a concept of death since they do not generalize its conditions to all conspecifics.

This possibility raises a potential worry about concepts of death. Humans are capable of applying their concept to a wide variety of species, both plant and animal. But what if we discover that some animals only react to death in a more limited range of species (e.g., vervet monkeys recognize death in other monkeys and apes, but not in birds)? One might argue that this shows that individuals of this species do not have the concept of death. After all, it might be claimed, if a monkey cannot recognize that a tree is dead, then it does not know what *dead* means. Alternatively, one might argue that the animals do have the concept of death, but do not recognize that or do not care whether certain objects are capable of falling into its extension.

One view of concepts that is popular among philosophers (Quine 1960) and computer scientists (Quillian 1968) is that concepts are part of a network and that individual concepts can only be understood in the context of the network in which they are embedded. If such a view is correct, the animals' concepts will match the human concepts to the extent to which they are embedded in similar conceptual schemes.[13] However, whether or not one thinks that a particular species of animal has some human concept of *death*, experiments such as those we have suggested, which would show whether animals have representations of information that are sufficiently dissociated from perceptual stimuli to count as concepts, may still lead one to claim that the species have some other, perhaps related, concepts.

Our second experiment is applicable to a broad range of species because it does not rely on communicative abilities or other organism-specific qualities. Nonetheless, in common with the preceding experiment, it is not without its own practical and ethical difficulties. This is made vivid by the suggestion of conducting the experiment on young human children, which would obviously be unacceptable. Nonetheless, it provides a uniform base for comparison across those species where such experiments are considered acceptable.

6 Summary

In this paper, we have attempted to describe a particular class of internal representations that we believe can be investigated in animals and humans alike, without danger of overanthropomorphizing. In many respects, the problems facing the animal researcher are similar to those facing psychologists studying prelinguistic children. It is possible to see how the experiments we have suggested could have analogues for investigation of human children. The problems are also relevant to philosophers interested in the interpretation of terms like "Gavagai" by radical translators (Quine 1960).

The notion of concept we have suggested is of particular use to ethologists. It fits well into functional explanations of flexibility in animal behavior. Concepts are capable of explaining complex abilities to generalize over variable stimuli, to rapidly produce appropriate responses to the common features underlying those stimuli, and to modify behavior when it is discovered that perceptual stimuli are unreliable guides to underlying features. Furthermore, this notion of a concept can be tested by suitably ingenious experimental design. We have attempted to describe two possible experiments. Our discussion of these experiments illustrates the difficulties associated with conducting this kind of research. However, many of the difficulties are practical or ethical rather than theoretical.

Notes

We wish to thank Tyler Burge, Philip Clark, Lisa Hauser, Alan Nelson, anonymous reviewers for this journal, and, especially, Georges Rey and Keith Donnellan for criticism of earlier drafts of this paper.

1. In this paper, we cannot hope to take on Wittgensteinean worries about internal representations. One path for cognitive science is to proceed on the assumption that representations guide behavior, and to set itself the task of finding the grammar of those representations (e.g., *à la* Fodor 1981). It is the task of applying this strategy to animals with which we are concerned in this paper.

2. One might criticize the paper by Herrnstein et al. as providing nothing more than an argument by suggestion for the claim that pigeons have concepts. Since, however, they never say that pigeons do have concepts, it might be argued that they were never claiming that they do. Instead, it could be claimed that they were investigating the ability of pigeons to recognize and discriminate objects that are distinguished in human conceptual schemes. Unfortunately, their research its widely cited for having shown concepts in pigeons, so even if that was not their intention, it has, nonetheless, been the

consequence. Subsequent publications by Herrnstein reinforce the view that he meant concepts in pigeons to be equated with human concepts (e.g., Herrnstein 1984).

3. This question has also occurred to some psychologists. See, for example, Lea (1984).

4. In case one thinks that the real reason for saying human subjects do not have the concept of distributor is that they would incorrectly sort a distributor-shaped non-distributor, consider that the pigeons were not tested on pictures of accurate models of trees either. Allen (1989) argues elsewhere that the possibility of classification errors of objects outside the normal range of experience does not impugn attributions of intentional states to humans or animals.

5. This distinction is often ignored in the practice of ordinary speech. We are not making any claim that ordinary speech is incorrect, or that its practice should be changed.

6. Thanks to L. Hauser for clarification on this point.

7. These experiments, though focusing on the concept of death, should be useful for thinking about concepts in general.

8. Here, the relation between concepts and beliefs might appear to raise its ugly head. Behavioral evidence notoriously appears to be unable to provide grounds for distinguishing between on the one hand believing X falls under concept C, and behavior B is appropriate to C's, and on the other hand believing X is D, but B is appropriate to D's. But while this might present a problem for determining whether the subject has concept C or D, it need not present a problem for deciding whether or not the subject has any concepts at all.

9. Again, one might worry about being unable to rule out other interpretations. Perhaps the mother does recognize the infant as dead, but has other beliefs that interact so as to produce the observed behavior. In humans, certain beliefs in the existence of spirits might account for such behavior. But such an interpretation would require supporting evidence for those beliefs that is unlikely to be forthcoming in the case of the vervets.

10. We are assuming that the response to the distress call has been modified too quickly to make a behavioristic explanation, in terms of deconditioning, plausible. We have some indication (Hauser, unpublished data) that such quick changes in responsiveness do indeed occur in vervets.

11. Such removal experiments are more common is studies of small mammals (e.g., rodents), birds and insects.

12. Note, however, that in several species, females recognize the calls of their young.

13. Contrary to Quine, we believe that the discovery of these conceptual schemes is a matter for empirical research.

References

Allen, C. (1989), "Attributing Intentional States to Animals: Philosophical Issues Arising in Cognitive Ethology." Ph.D. Dissertation, University of California, Los Angeles.

Altmann, J. (1980), *Baboon Mothers and Infants*. Cambridge, MA: Harvard University Press.

Asquith, P. J. (1984), "The Inevitability and Utility of Anthropomorphism in Description of Primate Behaviour," in R. Harré and V. Reynolds (eds.), *The Meaning of Primate Signals*. Cambridge: Cambridge University Press; Paris: Editions de la Maison des Sciences de l'Homme, pp. 138–174.

Bachmann, C. and Kummer, H. (1980), "Male Assessment of Female Choice in Hamadryas Baboons," *Behavioral Ecology and Sociobiology* 6:315–321.

Burge, T. (1979), "Individualism and the Mental," in P. French, T. Uehling and H. Wettstein (eds.), *Midwest Studies in Philosophy*, Vol. 4, *Studies in Metaphysics*. Minneapolis: University of Minnesota Press, pp. 73–121.

Burghardt, G. (1985), "Animal Awareness: Current Perceptions and Historical Perspective," *American Psychologist* 40:905–919.

Cheney, D. L. and Seyfarth, R. M. (1980), "Vocal Recognition in Free-ranging Vervet Monkeys," *Animal Behaviour* 28:362–367.

———. (1983), "Nonrandom Dispersal in Free-ranging Vervet Monkeys: Social and Genetic Consequences," *American Naturalist* 122:392–412.

———. (1985), "Social and Non-social Knowledge in Vervet Monkeys," *Philosophical Transactions of the Royal Society of London B* 308:187–201.

Cooper, L. A. (1982), "Internal Representation," in D. R. Griffin (ed.), *Animal Mind, Human Mind: Report of the Dahlem Workshop on Animal Mind-Human Mind*. Berlin: Springer-Verlag, pp. 145–158.

Cowgill, U. M. (1972), "Death in *Perodicticus*," *Primates* 13:251–256.

D'Amato, M. R. and van Sant, P. (1988), "The Person Concept in Monkeys (*Cebus apella*)," *Journal of Experimental Psychology: Animal Behavior Processes* 14:43–55.

Dasser, V. (1985), "Cognitive Complexity in Primate Social Relationship," in R. A. Hinde, A. Perret-Clermont and J. Stevenson-Hinde (eds.), *Social Relationships and Cognitive Development*. Oxford: Clarendon Press, pp. 9–22.

Dennett, D. C. (1969), *Content and Consciousness*. London: Routledge & Kegan Paul.

———. (1983), "Intentional Systems in Cognitive Ethology: The 'Panglossian Paradigm' Defended," *The Behavioral and Brain Sciences* 6:343–390.

Fodor, J. A. (1975), *The Language of Thought*. New York: Crowell.

———. (1981), *Representations: Philosophical Essays on the Foundations of Cognitive Science*. Cambridge, MA: MIT Press.

Gould, J. L. and Gould, C. G. (1982), "The Insect Mind: Physics or Metaphysics?," in D. R. Griffin (ed.), *Animal Mind, Human Mind: Report of the Dahlem Workshop on Animal Mind-Human Mind*. Berlin: Springer-Verlag, pp. 269–298.

Grice, H. P. (1957), "Meaning," *Philosophical Review* 66:377–388.

Griffin, D. R. (1981), *The Question of Animal Awareness: Evolutionary Continuity of Mental Experience*. Revised and Enlarged Edition. New York: Rockefeller University Press.

———. (ed.) (1982), *Animal Mind, Human Mind: Report of the Dahlem Workshop on Animal Mind-Human Mind*. Berlin: Springer-Verlag.

Harnad, S. (ed.) (1987), *Categorical Perception: The Groundwork of Cognition*. Cambridge: Cambridge University Press.

Harré, R. and Reynolds, V. (eds.) (1984), *The Meaning of Primate Signals*. Cambridge: Cambridge University Press; Paris: Editions de la Maison des Sciences de l'Homme.

Hauser, M. D. (1986), "Male Responsiveness to Infant Distress Calls in Free-ranging Vervet Monkeys," *Behavioral Ecology and Sociobiology* 19:65–71.

———. (1988), "Invention and Social Transmission: New Data From Wild Vervet Monkeys," in R. Byrne and A. Whiten (eds.), *Machiavellian Intelligence: Social Expertise and the Evolution of Intellect in Monkeys, Apes, and Humans*. Oxford: Clarendon Press, pp. 327–343.

Herrnstein, R. J. (1984), "Objects, Categories, and Discriminative Stimuli," in H. L. Roitblat, T. G. Bever and H. S. Terrace (eds.), *Animal Cognition: Proceedings of the Harry Frank Guggenheim Conference, June 2–4, 1982*. Hillsdale, NJ: Lawrence Erlbaum Associates, pp. 233–261.

Herrnstein, R. J.; Loveland, D. H.; and Cable, C. (1976), "Natural Concepts in Pigeons," *Journal of Experimental Psychology, Animal Behavior Processes* 2:285–302.

Hinde, R. A. (1982), *Ethology: Its Nature and Relations with Other Sciences*. New York: Oxford University Press.

Krebs, J. R. and Davies, N. B. (1984), *Behavioral Ecology: An Evolutionary Approach*. 2d ed. Sunderland: Sinauer Press.

Kummer, H. (1982), "Social Knowledge in Free-ranging Primates," in D. R. Griffin (ed.), *Animal Mind, Human Mind: Report of the Dahlem Workshop on Animal Mind-Human Mind*. Berlin: Springer-Verlag, pp. 113–130.

Lea, S. E. G. (1984), "In What Sense Do Pigeons Learn Concepts?," in H. L. Roitblat, T. G. Bever and H. S. Terrace (eds.), *Animal Cognition: Proceedings of the Harry Frank Guggenheim Conference, June 2–4, 1982*. Hillsdale, NJ: Lawrence Erlbaum Associates, pp. 263–276.

Munn, C. A. (1986), "The Deceptive Use of Alarm Calls by Sentinel Species in Mixed-Species Flocks of Neotropical Birds," in R. W. Mitchell and N. S. Thompson (eds.), *Deception: Perspectives on Human and Nonhuman Deceit*. Albany: State University of New York Press, pp. 169–175.

Premack, D. (1986), *Gavagai! or The Future History of the Animal Language Controversy*. Cambridge, MA: MIT Press.

Putnam, H. (1975), "The Meaning of 'Meaning,'" in K. Gunderson (ed.), *Minnesota Studies in the Philosophy of Science*. Vol. 7, *Language, Mind, and Knowledge*. Minneapolis: University of Minnesota Press, pp. 131–193.

Quillian, M. R. (1968), "Semantic Memory," in M. Minsky (ed.), *Semantic Information Processing*. Cambridge, MA: MIT Press, pp. 227–270.

Quine, W. V. (1960), *Word and Object*. Cambridge: Technology Press of MIT.

Rey, G. (1983), "Concepts and Stereotypes," *Cognition* 15:237–262.

Schank, R. C.; Collins, G. C.; and Hunter, L. E. (1986), "Transcending Inductive Category Formation in Learning," *Behavioral and Brain Sciences* 9:639–686.

Seyfarth, R. M.; Cheney, D. L.; and Marler, P. (1980), "Monkey Responses to Three Different Alarm Calls: Evidence of Predator Classification and Semantic Communication," *Science* 210:801–803.

Struhsaker, T. T. (1967), "Auditory Communication Among Vervet Monkeys (*Cercopithecus aethiops*)," in S. A. Altmann (ed.), *Social Communication Among Primates*. Chicago: University of Chicago Press, pp. 281–324.

Wilson, E. O. (1971), *The Insect Societies*. Cambridge, MA: Belknap Press of Harvard University Press.

Cognitive and Evolutionary Explanations

Chapter 5

On Aims and Methods of Cognitive Ethology[1]

Dale Jamieson and Marc Bekoff

1 Introduction

In 1963 Niko Tinbergen published a paper, "On Aims and Methods of Ethology," dedicated to his friend Konrad Lorenz. This essay is a landmark in the development of ethology. Here Tinbergen defines ethology as "the biological study of behavior" and seeks to demonstrate the "close affinity between Ethology and the rest of Biology" (p. 411). Building on Huxley (1942), Tinbergen identifies four major problems of ethology: causation, survival value, evolution, and ontogeny. Concern with these problems, under different names (mechanism, adaptation, phylogeny, and development), has dominated the study of animal behavior during the last half century (Dawkins, et al. 1991; Dewsbury 1992).

With his emphasis on the importance of innate structures internal to animals, Tinbergen was resolutely antibehaviorist. Yet he remained hostile to the idea that ethology should employ any form of teleological reasoning or make reference to "subjective phenomena" such as "hunger" or the emotions. He wrote that teleological reasoning was "seriously hampering the progress of ethology" and that "[b]ecause subjective phenomena cannot be observed objectively in animals, it is idle to either claim or to deny their existence" (1951, p. 4).[2]

Since the 1976 publication of Donald Griffin's landmark book, *The Question of Animal Awareness*, a growing band of researchers has been attempting to study the cognitive states of nonhuman animals (for samples of this work see Bekoff & Jamieson 1990, and Ristau 1991). Although vigorous debate surrounds this research, cognitive ethology as a field has not yet been clearly delineated, adequately characterized, or sufficiently explained.

Our goal in this paper is to attempt for cognitive ethology what Tinbergen succeeded in doing for ethology: to clarify its aims and methods, to distinguish some of its varieties, and to defend the fruitfulness of the research strategies that it has spawned.

This paper is divided into five main parts. In the first part we briefly sketch the history of ethology and explain the motivation behind the cognitive turn. Next we discuss the groundbreaking work of Donald Griffin and the rise of cognitive ethology. In the third section we distinguish two varieties of cognitive ethology ("weak" and "strong") and provide some reasons for preferring the latter to the former. The

From *Philosophy of Science Association 1992*, 2: 110–124. © 1993 by the Philosophy of Science Association.

fourth part of the paper is a discussion of one area of research in cognitive ethology: social play. Finally we make some concluding remarks.

2 The Story of Animal Behavior

During the third quarter of the nineteenth century, Charles Darwin was the most important contributor to the foundations of animal behavior (Boakes 1984, Richards 1987). Darwin argued for mental continuity between humans and other animals, and claimed that "the lower animals, like man, manifestly feel pleasure and pain, happiness, and misery" (Darwin 1871, p. 448).[3] According to Darwin monkeys are capable of elaborate deceit (1896), insects can solve problems, and many animals can deliberate about what to do (1871, 1896).

Darwin's approach can be characterized as "anecdotal cognitivism." He attributed cognitive states to many animals on the basis of observation of particular cases rather than controlled experiments or manipulations. Darwin's follower, George Romanes, followed in this tradition although he was more critical than Darwin of various cognitive attributions to nonhuman animals. Even Lloyd Morgan, mainly remembered for his canon—"in no case may we interpret an action as the outcome of the exercise of a higher psychical faculty, if it can be interpreted as the outcome of the exercise of one which stands lower in the psychological scale" (Morgan 1894, p. 53)—accepted the Darwin-Romanes view of the continuity of mental states. Indeed, as Rollin (1989) points out, Morgan's canon is not only consistent with the view that animals have mental states, it actually presupposes it.

Behaviorism arose in part as an attempt to overcome the anecdotal approach and to bring rigor to the study of behavior. Controlled experiments rather than field observations provided the primary data, and basic concepts were supposed to be grounded in direct observation. Against this background, animal consciousness came to be seen as "... mystical, unscientific, unnecessary, obscure, and not amenable to study" (Rollin 1989, p. 68).

Jacques Loeb, who was active from about 1890–1915, was an influential forerunner of behaviorism in biology. Although he believed that consciousness was an emergent property of higher organisms, he argued that all animal behavior could be explained nonteleologically in terms of tropisms (Pauly 1987). Throughout the 1920s, with the work of Watson and others, behaviorism became increasingly influential. By 1930 the behaviorist revolution was complete and anecdotal cognitivism had virtually vanished from mainstream science.

Classical ethology developed in Europe with the work of Lorenz and Tinbergen, and arrived in America in the post–World War II period (although as Dewsbury 1992 points out, there were contacts before the war). The roots of classical ethology were in the investigations of Darwin, Charles Otis Whitman, and Oskar Heinroth. Classical ethology signified a return to some of the ideas of Darwin and the early anecdotal cognitivists, especially in its appeals to evolutionary theory, the close association with natural history, and the reliance on anecdote and anthropomorphism in motivating more rigorous study.

Lorenz, who was trained as a physician, comparative anatomist, psychologist and philosopher, did little fieldwork but his knowledge of animal behavior was enormous. His method was to watch various animals, both domestic and wild, who lived near his homes in Austria and Germany. He freely used anecdotes and did very little experimentation. Lorenz thought that empathy, intuition and emotion were important in understanding animals and that science should not be pursued "in the belief that it is possible to be objective by ignoring one's feelings" (Lorenz 1988/1991, p. 7). He attributed to animals such states as love, jealousy, envy, and anger.

Tinbergen complemented Lorenz's naturalistic and anecdotal approaches by doing elegant, simple and usually relatively noninvasive field experiments. Tinbergen also worked with Lorenz on several classical problems, including egg-rolling in geese.

Theoretically what was most important about Lorenz and Tinbergen was the emphasis they placed on internal states such as "instincts," "drives," "motivational impulses" and "outward flowing nervous energy." On their view behavior is typically caused by internal states; external stimuli mainly release or block behavior. This emphasis on internal states was in sharp contrast with the behaviorist tradition.

However by 1973 when Lorenz and Tinbergen were awarded the Nobel Prize (shared with Karl von Frisch), many thought that their grand theory was already in tatters (Kennedy 1992). As early as 1968 Patrick Bateson wrote that "[w]orship of the old gods and the intellectual baggage that went with it still survives quaintly in odd corners. But for the most part proponents of a Grand Theory have either been forced to close their eyes to awkward evidence or modify their ideas to the point of unfalsifiability" (p. 33). Marian Dawkins has written that "[m]ost contemporary textbooks on animal behavior tend to dismiss 'instinct' altogether and attempt to consign it to honorable retirement" (Dawkins 1986, p. 67).

In recent years no grand theory has arisen to replace the Lorenz-Tinbergen theory of instinct. However the question of adaptation (survival value) has become increasingly central in animal behavior studies. Indeed, many researchers write as if a behavior is completely explained if it can be shown that it might contribute to inclusive fitness. This is surprising since adaptationist explanations are often radically underdetermined by empirical evidence; and when they are not, the availability of a good adaptationist story does not drive out other forms of explanation.

The Lorenz-Tinbergen theory of instinct was meant to be an account of the mechanisms of behavior. With the decline of the "grand theory" some researchers have turned to neuroethology as the replacement for the study of instinct. However, despite great advances in neuroethology, much of what we want to know about animals cannot be explained in these terms alone. If we want to know why Grete (the dog) barked at the postman, an explanation in terms of neural pathways may not be very helpful (Dennett 1987).

Like many of the animals it studies, animal behavior needs all four legs (mechanism, adaptation, phylogeny, and development). And perhaps as never before animal behavior needs to countenance a variety of forms of explanation. Cognitive ethology has the potential to make important contributions to our understanding in a number of areas, for the cognitive vocabulary can help to deliver important insights about animals that may otherwise not be available.

3 Griffin and the Rise of Cognitive Ethology

Many of the same forces that led to the development of cognitive psychology in the 1960s began to gather in animal behavior in the 1970s. Lorenz and Tinbergen had already made appeals to "unobservable" internal states respectable, and philosophers such as Hilary Putnam (1960/1975) and Jerry Fodor (1968) had shown that materialism and mentalism could be made compatible. In addition, Jane Goodall and Dian Fossey were popularizing the idea that the other African apes, including chimpanzees and mountain gorillas (see Cavalieri & Singer 1993), have rich cognitive and emotional lives (Montgomery 1991).

The rise of cognitive ethology can conveniently be dated from the publication of Donald Griffin's *The Question of Animal Awareness* (1976). In view of its historical significance it is surprising that the expression "cognitive ethology" occurs only twice in the first edition of this landmark book, and then only in the last four pages. By 1978, however, this term figured in the title of Griffin's *Behavioral and Brain Sciences* target article. In each succeeding book (Griffin 1984, 1992) this expression has become more frequent (on Griffin's development see Bekoff 1993, Hailman 1978).

One explanation for Griffin's apparent reluctance to use the term "cognitive ethology" is his hostility to cognitive psychology. This hostility may be surprising since, as we have suggested, the cognitive turn in ethology can be related to similar developments in psychology. However Griffin appears to think of cognitive psychology as a variety of behaviorism. Indeed, he claims that "conspicuously absent from most of contemporary cognitive psychology is any serious attention to conscious thoughts or subjective feelings" (Griffin 1984, p. 11). Yet it is "conscious thoughts" and "subjective feelings" that Griffin is most interested in exploring. Griffin writes that the challenge of cognitive ethology "is to venture across the species boundary and try to gather satisfactory information about what other species may think or feel" (Griffin 1984, p. 12).

Griffin's picture is of a world of creatures with different subjectivities leading their own individual lives. Trying to learn about the minds of other animals involves trying to get "a window" on their minds (Griffin 1984, Chapter 8). Griffin seems to think that communication offers such a window, and in his writings he focuses on the communication systems of various animals.

Griffin's cognitive ethology has been attacked from several directions. Scientists, especially those of a behaviorist persuasion, often argue that cognitive or mental concepts cannot be operationally defined, thus there are no researchable questions in cognitive ethology. On this view cognitive ethology should be banished from the citadel of science and consigned to the scrapheap of idle speculation (for discussion see Bekoff & Allen 1996).

Griffin seems to be of two minds about this objection. In much of his work he has been concerned to satisfy his critics by framing definitions. Yet he seems impatient with the demand for definition and sometimes dismissive of it. In his early work (1976, 1981) Griffin is concerned to define such terms as "conscious awareness" and "mental experience." In Griffin (1982, 1984) he tries to define "mind," "aware," "intend," "conscious," "feeling," and "think"; but he is most concerned to define "consciousness." Although Griffin seems to think that it is important to define these key terms, he never seems completely happy with the definitions that he gives. In 1981 he writes that "almost any concept can be quibbled to death by excessive insistence on exact operational definitions" (p. 12). By 1991 he is claiming that "it is therefore neither necessary nor advisable to become so bogged down in quibbles about definitions that the investigation of animal cognition and consciousness is neglected altogether" (pp. 4–5). But despite his interest in getting on with it, even if the central terms cannot precisely be defined, Griffin returns again and again to the problem of definition.

In our view classical definitions cannot be given for key terms in cognitive ethology but it is not necessary to give them in order to have a viable field of research. Classical definitions preserve meaning and provide necessary and sufficient conditions for the application of a term. An area in which there is controversy is likely to be one in which the definitions of key expressions are contested. It is not only the application of cognitive terms that is contested, there are also competing definitions of such terms as "fitness," "recognition," "communication," "play," "choice," "dominance," "altruism," and "optimality." With respect to mental concepts, a huge literature has developed over the years about whether or not it is part of the meaning of mental terms that what they refer to is private, introspectable, incorrigible, and so on. One result of scientific inquiry is to help fix and refine definitions. As science advances, definitions change and become more precise and entrenched. In order to get an area of inquiry going, what is needed is some common understanding of the domain to be investigated, not agreement about the meaning of key terms. Key terms in cognitive ethology are well enough understood to begin inquiry, even if classical definitions are difficult to come by.

Griffin's cognitive ethology is not sunk by the failure of definition. Yet it should be clear from this discussion that Griffin is tempted by some key assumptions of his critics. It is another assumption, one that Griffin shares with some of his critics, that is especially problematical for his version of cognitive ethology.

Griffin appears to accept a fundamentally Cartesian notion of the mind, at least with respect to its epistemological status. Although he formulates his central question in different ways, what Griffin really wants to know is whether animals are conscious. He assimilates the question of consciousness to the question of whether animals have subjective states. When the question is posed in this way, the link between mind and behavior seems highly contingent: two creatures may be in the same subjective (i.e. mental) state, but in only one does this have any objective (i.e. behavioral) consequence; two creatures may be in the same objective (i.e. behavioral) state, but in only one is the behavior caused by a subjective (i.e. mental) state. Knowledge of the minds of others is, on this view, inferential and probabilistic (Griffin 1992, p. 260). From our observations of objective states we make inferences to unobservable, subjective states. But since the connections between observable, objective states and unobservable, subjective states are weak and contingent, these inferences can be incorrect. On this view the passage from behavioral observations to the attribution of mentality is always uncertain and possibly treacherous. Nevertheless Griffin believes that many animals are conscious and he appeals to three sorts of evidence in support of his view.

The first sort of evidence can be viewed as a generalization of an argument given by Mill (1884) for the existence of other human minds. It involves noting that in my own case various forms of consciousness are associated with various behaviors, physical states and structures; and inferring that these behaviors, states, and structures are probably associated with various forms of consciousness in other creatures as well. It has often been pointed out that this argument fails in its goal of establishing the existence of other human minds; for generalizing to countless cases from my own involves a very large generalization from a very small sample (Rosenthal 1991, Part II.A.). When the analogies are weaker, as they are when drawn between humans and nonhumans, the induction is even more suspect.

Other arguments that Griffin gives involve appeals to novel or flexible behaviors. These appeals often have the rhetorical power of "gee whiz" stories. When people hear about the neat things that animals do they are often inclined to infer consciousness. But such inferences are open to the following objection. If flexible and novel behaviors can fully be explained by reference to noncognitive states or processes whose existence is relatively uncontroversial, then it is reasonable to explain them in these noncognitive terms. In many cases such behavior can be explained in such non-cognitive terms (e.g. see Galef 1990, chapter 7 of this reader). In other cases it cannot, but Griffin's critics say that cognitive explanations are just temporary placeholders for the "real" explanations of which we are currently ignorant. Put in these terms, the dispute appears to be a standoff.

In the light of these difficulties with other forms of argument, it is not surprising that the evidence that Griffin most relies on involves communication. Just as Descartes placed a great deal of weight on the importance of language, so Griffin views communication as providing a window on other minds.

Commmunication can provide important evidence for various views about the nature of animal minds (see Cheney & Seyfarth 1990; Smith 1990, chapter 16 of this reader; 1991). But this concept as it is used in the ethological literature has its problems (Philips & Austad 1990, chapter 17 of this reader). Communication is not a transparent window that permits us to see into another "subjectivity." Thus facts about animal communication do not always provide support for views about the kinds of minds that Griffin believes that animals have.

So the objectors are right (in a way) but for the wrong reasons. They point out that the existence of Griffin-style minds in nonhuman animals is highly speculative and cannot convincingly be demonstrated by inferences from behavioral data. From this they conclude that animals do not have minds, or that if they do, they cannot systematically be studied. Instead the correct conclusion is that animals do not have Griffin-style minds, but for that matter neither do we. Our minds are closely tied to behavior and so are the minds of other animals. However our knowledge of other minds is not generally a matter of inference from behavior.

We agree with Griffin that many animals have mental states and that this belief is supported by close observations of their behavior. As we shall suggest in section four, minds that are closely tied to behavior can systematically be studied. In our view cognitive ethology is not only possible, but it is an active field of ongoing research.

In summary, Griffin's great contributions are to insist that questions about animal minds be addressed, to argue that what we say about animal minds must be continuous with our views about human minds, to bring a fully comparative perspective to bear on these questions, and to have motivated empirical research in a neglected area. However, despite his contributions and his immensely important historical role, cognitive ethology must develop more sophisticated conceptions of the mind and its relation to behavior, and develop research programs that are capable of answering some very specific questions. In the next two sections we will take some initial steps towards discharging these obligations.[4]

4 Two Concepts of Cognitive Ethology[5]

Cognitive ethology is an area that is undergoing growth and expansion. Among the different sorts of practices, two kinds of cognitive ethology can be distinguished. We will refer to them as "weak cognitive ethology" and "strong cognitive ethology," and discuss them in turn.

Weak Cognitive Ethology (WCE)

WCE is the most common form of cognitive ethology. WCE countenances the use of a cognitive vocabulary for the explanation of behavior, but not its description. The following passage is a characteristic expression of WCE (although in this passage it is offered as a "definition" of cognitive psychology).

> [I]t is the study of the mental processes that result in behavior. These internal processes act on sensory input: transforming, reducing, elaborating, storing, retrieving, and combining. Because these processes are usually not directly observable, their characteristics and the information upon which they act are inferred from behavior. Hypotheses about internal events (i.e. cognitive theories) generate predictions of how environmental inputs will be transformed in the production of behavior (Yoerg 1991, p. 288).

WCE is an advance over behaviorism because it takes information processing seriously. Behaviorists typically treated organisms as "black boxes" whose internal states were irrelevent to the real job of science which involves mapping environmental inputs on to behavioral outputs. WCE pries the lid off the black box and treats its contents as important.

However the description of the contents of the black box often relies on fashionable computer metaphors. Indeed, one might say that WCE simply replaces the mechanical metaphors of the behaviorist tradition with the computer mataphors of cognitive science. It may be, as many think, that the computer metaphor marks a real advance over mechanical ones. Digital computers have impressive formal powers that old-fashioned machines that rely on gears and pulleys do not. But Griffin and others (e.g. Searle 1992) remain unimpressed. They say that something is left out even in these very sophisticated models (e.g. "consciousness," "intrinsic intentionality").

Whether or not something has been left out, there appears to be a double-standard between humans and nonhumans that is implicit in much work that is done in WCE. Nonhumans are often assimilated to computers in a way in which humans are not. But the significant border, if there is one, is not between animals and computers on the one hand and humans on the other, but between biological creatures and nonbiological entities. Both may process information but they seem importantly different. The capacity for having affective states is a feature of many biological creatures, but one that computers do not seem to share. Many biological creatures suffer pain, distress, fear, and can be happy or contented. WCE leaves out the affective states of biological organisms. Cognition may play a role in emotion, but emotional and affective states cannot simply be reduced to cognitive states.

Another weakness of WCE is that it attempts to protect the description of behavior from the cognitive vocabulary. Researchers in the tradition of WCE seem to share the bahaviorist presumption that the behavior that is to be explained can and should be described in a cognitive-free language that makes reference only to bodily movements. Appeals to cognitive states enter only with attempts at explanation. We believe that a great deal of animal behavior cannot meaningfully be described without using cognitive and affective vocabularies. What distinguishes strong cognitive ethology from WCE (in part) is the willingness to deploy these vocabularies in the interpretation of behavior as well as in its explanation.

Strong Cognitive Ethology (SCE)

SCE underwrites a range of research programs in which both cognitive and affective vocabularies are willingly employed for purposes of interpretation and explanation. We will explain these concepts of interpretation and explanation in turn.

One important function of ethological investigation is to describe the behavior of animals. This role is not as highly prized as it was in the early days of ethology and is often dismissed as a hangover from natural history and sometimes likened to stamp-collecting. Yet any science must provide a description of its domain and it is important to know what animals do if we are to explain why they do it.

In recent animal behavior studies there has been a search for canonical descriptions that reflect the basic categories of behavior (e.g. Golani 1992; see also Purton 1978). The idea is that for any behavior it is possible to produce a description in a common vocabulary that is solely based on what is observable. Other descriptions of behavior, though they may be useful, involve "reading into the behavior" and are ultimately eliminable. This view is untenable for a number of reasons.

First, although we cannot argue the point in detail here, we believe that the search for basic nonhuman behaviors is doomed for the same reasons that the search for basic human actions is doomed. At time T1 Kelly presses the button, rings the door-bell, and displaces some molecules. Did Kelly do one thing or many things? If one thing, which thing? If many things, which thing is basic? Grete (the dog) may simultaneously engage in a play behavior, bow, bend her front legs, kick up some dust, and displace some molecules. The same questions arise about how many things Grete did and which they are. We believe that no plausible answers to these questions can be given that are independent of pragmatic factors. What an animal does and how this is conceptualized is a contextual matter.

A second reason why this approach is untenable is related to this point. In our view descriptions of behavior are intrinsically plural and multidimensional. What counts as "the best" description is relative to the questions being asked and the interests of the interrogator. It would be unfruitful and perhaps impossible to constrain all descriptions of animal behavior by a set of basic categories (Mason 1986). This point is perhaps most obvious with respect to primates. Primatologists virtually always describe the behavior of their subjects in highly abstract and functional terms. Later, often for purposes of publication, they may try to translate these descriptions into the vocabulary of bodily movements. But if primatologists were forbidden to use abstract, functional vocabularies, one wonders if they could describe the behavior of their subjects at all (Bekoff 1995). Indeed, what would be the title, or the subject for that matter, of a classic book like De Waal's *Peacemaking Among Primates*.

A third problem with this approach is that in many cases descriptions of an animal's behavior in the canonical language would deprive us of insights into the meaning of the behavior. Predator-avoidance may take many forms, and since nonhuman animals are no more infallible than human animals, such behavior may fail, or occur when no predator is within striking distance. In many cases we might be disposed to say that the animal is trying to avoid a predator, yet a description of the animal's behavior just in terms of her observable bodily movements would not allow this insight.

Finally, an animal's behavioral repertoire is organized functionally as well as in other ways. The same bodily movements may have different meanings; and the same behavior, defined in functional terms, may involve different bodily movements. For example, the same bodily movements involved in canid play are also involved in aggression and reproduction (see section 5). And the same behavior from a functional point of view, for example predator avoidance, may involve tree climbing in one case and running in another.

For these reasons we believe that the search for canonical descriptions of animal behavior fails. This approach is rooted in the positivist dream of a value-free observation language that can be used to characterize the phenomena that covering laws are supposed to explain. Whatever the plausibility of this model for the physical sciences, it is highly implausible for ethology.

Because the attempt to describe behavior in a canonical vocabulary that reflects basic categories is unsuccessful, we favor the use of the term "interpretation" where others use the term "description." This acknowledges the fact that describing what animals do involves interpreting their behavior.

A central role of explanation is to specify why something happened. Although we cannot tell the story here, we would defend a view of explanation that is similar to our account of interpretation: explanations can be plural, noncompetitive, and occur at different levels of abstraction. In our view appeal to generalizations that involve cognitive and affective states can genuinely be explanatory.

However a word of caution is in order. We have tried to defeat a picture of ethology that leaves no room for cognitive and affective interpretations and explanations. But even if what we have said is correct, no one is compelled to employ such vocabularies. It is still open to someone to object that such vocabularies are illegitimate—neither suitable for interpretation nor explanation. The rejection of the "canonical description view" does not imply the legitimacy—much less the fruitfulness—of the SCE alternative. A second objection is weaker. It may be admitted that although cognitive and affective vocabularies can be employed legitimately in interpretation and explanation, we are not compelled to use them and indeed would do better if we did not.

With respect to the second objection, we concede that no one is driven to apply cognitive and affective vocabularies to animals on pain of logical contradiction. Quine and Skinner could write their autobiographies as narratives of their bodily movements without falling into logical inconsistency. No doubt the same would be true of Digit and Koko. But Quine's autobiography is boring: it lacks insight and inspiration. One has the feeling that much of what is important has been left out. In our view the same is true with respect to interpreting and explaining the behavior of many nonhuman animals: one can avoid cognitive and affective vocabularies, but as we will try to show in the next section, in many cases one does this on pain of giving up interesting and insightful perspectives.

With respect to the first objection, this charge most plausibly comes either from those who espouse a double standard with respect to humans and nonhumans (or languageless creatures and those with language [e.g. Carruthers 1989]), or eliminativists with respect to cognitive and affective vocabularies. We have argued elsewhere, as have many others, that a principled double standard cannot be maintained, so we will not repeat those arguments here (Bekoff & Jamieson 1991; Jamieson & Bekoff 1992). With respect to eliminativism, if it is true that cognitive and affective vocabularies will one day bite the dust, then SCE would cease to exist. But SCE is not singularly vulnerable. The elimination of cognitive and affective vocabularies would fell other scientific enterprises as well and be part of a radical revision of the way that we think about the world. It is enough here to defend SCE against those who are more modest in their claims.[6]

In this section we have distinguished two concepts of cognitive ethology, spoken in favor of one, and defended it against two objections. The heart of the case for SCE, however, rests with its fruitfulness as a conceptual guide to empirical research. In the next section we will discuss one area of research in cognitive ethology.

5 Social Play

Space does not allow us to cover the many areas of research (e.g. mate choice, habitat selection, individual recognition and discrimination, injury-feigning, assessments of dominance, foraging for food, caching food, various types of social communication, observational learning, tool use, imitation, teaching) in which cognitive ethological approaches have been useful in gaining an understanding of the behavior of animals (for examples see Griffin 1984, 1992; Mitchell & Thompson 1986; Byrne & Whiten 1988; Cheney & Seyfarth 1990; Bekoff & Jamieson 1990, 1991; Ristau 1990; Bekoff 1995). Here we will discuss only one area: social play.

Social play is a behavior that lends itself to cognitive studies, and poses a great challenge to researchers (Mitchell 1990; Bekoff & Allen 1992). In particular, the question of how mammals communicate their intention to engage in social play presupposes cognitive states, without which it would be difficult or impossible to describe the social encounter (Bekoff 1995).

The canid "play bow" is a highly stereotyped movement that seems to function to stimulate recipients to engage (or continue to engage) in social play (Bekoff 1977). When an animal performs a play bow she crouches on her forelimbs, leaves her hind legs fairly straight, and may wag her tail and bark. Such play-soliciting signals appear to transmit the message that "what follows is play." Play-soliciting signals are used to communicate to others that actions such as biting, biting and shaking of the head from side-to-side, and mounting are to be taken as play and not as aggressive, predatory, or reproductive behavior.

Play-soliciting signals appear to foster cooperation between players so that each responds to the other in a way consistent with play and different from the responses that the same actions would elicit in other contexts (Bekoff 1975). This cooperation may occur because each of the participants has a belief about the intentions of the other animals who are involved in the social encounter. For example, in coyotes the response to a threat gesture is very different if it is immediately preceeded by a play signal or if a play signal is performed at the beginning of the interaction (Bekoff 1975). The play signal can be viewed as altering the meaning of a threat signal by establishing (or maintaining) a "play mood." When a play signaler bites or mounts the recipient of a play signal, the recipient is not disposed to injure or to mate with the signaler.

It is difficult to describe canid play behavior without using a cognitive vocabulary. One and the same bodily movement can be aggression or play. The difference between a movement that is aggressive and one that is playful is naturally described in terms of one animal's intention and another animal's appreciation of the intention.

Similarly the cognitive vocabulary appears to provide the resources for explaining some play behavior. For example, suppose that we want to know why Grete permitted Jethro to nip at her ears. One explanation may be that Grete believes that Jethro is playing. This gives rise to further questions, such as whether Jethro believes that Grete believes that Jethro is playing. One of the challenges of research in cognitive ethology is to investigate the extent to which such questions are well-formed and what the possible answers to them might be.

In this section we have been able to provide only a brief summary of some questions about social play. Because of the brevity of this account, we have not been able to discuss behaviors in which the affective vocabulary gains a foothold. Nor did we discuss what might be reasonable empirical constraints on cognitive interpretations and explanations.

It is important to remember that we are pluralists with respect to both explanation and interpretation. Cognitive explanations do not exclude other causal ones, nor do they rule out explanations that are adaptationist, phylogenetic, or developmental. In our view we need to employ a large range of conceptual resources in order to understand behavior.

6 Concluding Remarks

We have argued that cognitive ethology can be defended against its critics. In addition, we have discussed some of its varieties and forms and briefly sketched one area of research in cognitive ethology. Before closing, it is worth mentioning what cognitive ethology can contribute to cognitive studies generally.

Cognitive ethology can help to broaden the perspective of cognitive studies in two ways. First, cognitive ethology can help to situate the study of cognition in an evolutionary framework. It should be a necessary condition for postulating a cognitive state in a human that the existence of this state is at least consistent with evolutionary history. Although lip service is sometimes given to this constraint, talk of evolution in cognitive science is too often metaphorical. Cognitive ethology has the potential to make cognitive science take evolution seriously. Second, the fact that cognitive ethology is fully comparative can help to make cognitive science less parochial. Although there has been a great deal of concern about parochialism with respect to nonbiological systems, this concern has often coexisted with a surprising degree of "chimpocentrism" (Beck 1982). Many people are more willing to countenance cognition in computers or space aliens than in rodents, amphibians, or insects. Even in cognitive studies there is a tendency to view cognition as "essential" to humans and instantiated in various (lesser) degrees only in those who are phylogenetically close to humans. With its view of cognition as a strategic evolutionary response to problems that might have been faced by a variety of diverse organisms, cognitive ethology can help to overcome this form of parochialism.

There is no question but that the issue of animal minds is difficult and complex. Like questions about the human mind, it is tangled in issues of definition, conception, relation to behavior and so on. Yet in our view cognitive ethology is here to stay. For the adoption of cognitive and affective vocabularies by ethologists opens up a range of explanations, predictions, and generalizations that would not otherwise be available. As long as there are animals to behave and humans to wonder why, cognitive interpretations and explanations will be offered. In our view this is not only permissible, it is often enlightening. Sometimes it is even science.

Notes

1. We are grateful to all those who participated in discussions of this material at the University of Wyoming and the 1992 Philosophy of Science Association meetings. We especially thank Colin Allen, Marc Hauser, David Resnik and Carolyn Ristau.
2. However Tinbergen seems to suggest only a page later that "the study of subjective phenomena" is "consistent in the application of its own methods" but that this study should be kept distinct from the study of causation (1951, p. 5).
3. However there is a passage in Darwin (1871, Chapter 2) where he seems to suggest discontinuity between humans and other animals. Humans are dominant, according to Darwin, because of language, and language in part depends on human intellectual faculties. This suggests that discontinuities in power between humans and other animals may reflect discontinuities in intellect.
4. There is an important strand in Griffin's work that we have not addressed: He wants to understand creatures from "the inside out," he wants to know what it is like to be a bat (for example), and he assumes (following Nagel 1974) that such knowledge does not consist in knowing some set of "objective" facts about bats (for a contrary view see Akins 1990, and this reader). If Griffin is right in supposing that such radical subjectivity exists, cognitive ethology as we understand it will not deliver a deep appreciation of it. Griffin's concerns about radical subjectivity may be of profound importance, but they go beyond the boundaries of science as it is currently understood.
5. In what follows we make several simplifying assumptions including these: first, that cognitive ethology is directed towards explaining behavior rather than cognitive competencies; second, that for many organisms in many cases intentional interpretations and explanations count as cognitive ones; and third, that information processing in many organisms counts as cognitive activity. All of these assumptions warrant further discussion.
6. As suggested in the text, the existence of a cognitive vocabulary is a necessary condition for the persistence of cognitive ethology. However cognitive ethology is not committed to "folk psychology." Cognitive ethology is committed to the view that the behavior of nonhuman animals can usefully be interpreted or explained in ways consistent with our best understanding of cognitive states, whether these involve folk psychological concepts or not. If our best understanding of cognitive states involves some alternative to folk psychology, then cognitive ethology should embrace the alternative.

References

Akins, K. (1990), "Science and Our Inner Lives: Birds of Prey, Bats, and the Common Featherless Bi-ped," in Bekoff & Jamieson (1990), volume 1, pp. 414–27.

Bateson, P. (1968), "Ethological Methods of Observing Behavior," in *Analysis of Behavioral Change*, L. Weiskrantz (ed.). New York: Harper and Row, pp. 389–99.

Beck, B. (1982), "Chimpocentrism: Bias in Cognitive Ethology," *Journal of Human Evolution* 11:3–17.

Bekoff, M. (1975), "The Communication of Play Intention: Are Play Signals Functional?," *Semiotica* 15:231–39.

———. (1977), "Social Communication in Canids: Evidence for the Evolution of a Stereotyped Mammalian Display," *Science* 197:1097–99.

———. (1993), Review of Griffin (1992). *Ethology*. 95:166–170.

———. (1995), "Cognitive Ethology and the Explanation of Nonhuman Animal Behavior," in *Comparative Approaches to Cognitive Science*, H. Roitblat & J.-A. Meyer (eds.). Cambridge MA: MIT Press, pp. 119–149.

Bekoff, M. & Allen, C. (1992), "Intentional Icons: Towards an Evolutionary Cognitive Ethology," *Ethology* 91:1–16.

Bekoff, M. & Allen, C. (1996), "Cognitive Ethology: Slayers, Skeptics, and Proponents," in *Anthropomorphism, Anecdotes, and Animals: The Emperor's New Clothes?*, in R. Mitchell, N. Thompson, & L. Miles (eds.). Albany: SUNY Press.

Bekoff, M. & Jamieson, D. (eds.) (1990), *Interpretation and Explanation in the Study of Animal Behavior*, two volumes. Boulder, CO: Westview Press.

Bekoff, M. & Jamieson, D. (1991), "Reflective Ethology, Applied Philosophy, and the Moral Status of Animals," in *Perspectives in Ethology 9: Human Understanding and Animal Awareness*, P. Bateson & P. Klopfer (eds.). New York: Plenum Press, pp. 1–47.

Boakes, R. (1984), *From Darwin to Behaviorism: Psychology and the Minds of Animals*. New York: Cambridge University Press.

Byrne, R. & Whiten, A. (eds.) (1988), *Machiavellian Intelligence: Social Expertise and the Evolution of Intellect in Monkeys, Apes, and Humans*. Oxford: Oxford University Press.

Carruthers, P. (1989), "Brute Experience," *Journal of Philosophy* 86:258–69.

Cavalieri, P. & Singer, P. (eds.) (1993), *The Great Ape Project*. London: Fourth Estate.

Cheney, D. & Seyfarth R. (1990), *How Monkeys See the World: Inside the Mind of Another Species*. Chicago: The University of Chicago Press.

Darwin, C. (1871), *The Descent of Man, and Selection in Relation to Sex*, two volumes. London: Murray.

————. (1896), *The Variation of Animals and Plants Under Domestication*, two volumes. New York: Appleton.

Dawkins, M. (1986), *Unraveling Animal Behavior*. Essex, England: Longman Group.

Dawkins, M., Halliday, T., and Dawkins, R. (eds.) (1991), *The Tinbergen Legacy*. London: Chapman & Hall.

Dennett, D. (1987), *The Intentional Stance*. Cambridge, MA: The MIT Press.

Dewsbury, D. (1992), "On the Problems Studied in Ethology, Comparative Psychology, and Animal Behavior," *Ethology* 92:89–107.

Fodor, J. (1968), *Psychological Explanation*. New York: Random House.

Galef, B. (1990), "Tradition in Animals: Field Observations and Laboratory Analyses," in Bekoff & Jamieson (1990), volume 1, pp. 74–95.

Golani, I. (1992), "A Mobility Gradient in the Organization of Vertebrate Movement." *The Behavioral and Brain Sciences* 15:249–308.

Griffin, D. (1976), *The Question of Animal Awareness*. New York: The Rockefeller University Press.

————. (1978), "Prospects for a Cognitive Ethology." *The Behavioral and Brain Sciences.*" 4:527–38.

————. (1981), *The Question of Animal Awareness: Evolutionary Continuity of Mental Experience*, revised and enlarged edition. New York: The Rockefeller University Press.

————. (ed.) (1982), *Animal Mind—Human Mind*. New York: Springer-Verlag.

————. (1984), *Animal Thinking*. Cambridge, MA: Harvard University Press.

————. (1991), "Progress Towards Cognitive Ethology," in Ristau (1991), pp. 3–17.

————. (1992), *Animal Minds*. Chicago: The University of Chicago Press.

Hailman, J. (1978), Review of Griffin (1976). *Auk* 95: 614–15.

Huxley, J. (1942), *Evolution: The Modern Synthesis*. New York: Harper.

Jamieson, D. & Bekoff, M. (1992), "Carruthers on Nonconscious Experience," *Analysis* 52:23–8.

Kennedy, J. (1992), *The New Anthropomorphism*. Cambridge: Cambridge University Press.

Lorenz, K. (1988/1991), *Here Am I—Where Are You? The Behavior of the Greylag Goose*. New York: Harcourt, Brace, Jovanovich, Publishers.

Mason, W. (1986), "Behavior Implies Cognition," in *Science and Philosophy: Integrating Scientific Disciplines*, W. Bechtel (ed.). Boston: Kluwer, pp. 297–307.

Mill, J. (1884), *An Examination of Sir William Hamilton's Philosophy*. New York: Henry Holt.

Mitchell, R. (1990), "A Theory of Play," in Bekoff & Jamieson (1990), volume 1, pp. 197–227.

Mitchell, R. & Thompson, N. (eds.) (1986), *Deception: Perspectives on Human and Nonhuman Deceit*. Albany: State University of New York Press.

Morgan, L. (1894), *Introduction to Comparative Psychology*. London: Scott.

Montgomery, S. (1991), *Walking With the Great Apes*. Boston: Houghton Mifflin Company.

Nagel, T. (1974), "What Is It Like to Be a Bat?," *Philosophical Reivew* 83:435–50.

Pauly, P. (1987), *Controlling Life: Jacques Loeb and the Engineering Ideal in Biology*. Berkeley: University of California Press.

Philips, M. & Austad, S. (1990), "Animal Communication and Social Evolution," in Bekoff & Jamieson (1990), volume 1, pp. 254–68.

Purton, A. (1978), "Ethological Categories of Behavior and Some Consequences of Their Conflation," *Animal Behaviour* 26:653–70.

Putnam, H. (1960/1975), "Minds and Machines," in *Mind, Language and Reality, Philosophical Papers*, Volume 2. New York: Cambridge University Press, pp. 362–85.

Richards, R. (1987), *Darwin and the Emergence of Evolutionary Theories of Mind and Behavior*. Chicago: The University of Chicago Press.

Ristau, C. (ed.) (1991), *Cognitive Ethology: The Minds of Other Animals*. Hillsdale, NJ: Erlbaum.

Rollin, B. (1989), *The Unheeded Cry: Animal Consciousness, Animal Pain and Science*. New York: Oxford University Press.

Rosenthal, D. (ed.) (1991), *The Nature of Mind*. New York: Oxford University Press.

Searle, J. (1992), *The Rediscovery of the Mind*. Cambridge, MA: MIT Press.

Smith, W. (1990), "Communication and Expectations: A Social Process and the Cognitive Operations It Depends Upon and Influences," in Bekoff & Jamieson (1990), volume 1, pp. 234–53.

———. (1991), "Animal Communication and the Study of Cognition," in Ristau (1991), pp. 209–30.

Tinbergen, N. (1963), "On Aims and Methods of Ethology," *Zeitschrift für Tierpsychologie* 20:410–29.

———. (1991), *The Study of Instinct*. Oxford: Oxford University Press.

Yoerg, S. I. 1991. "Ecological Frames of Mind: The Role of Cognition in Behavioral Ecology." *Quarterly Review of Biology* 66: 287–301.

Chapter 6

Aspects of the Cognitive Ethology of an Injury-Feigning Bird, the Piping Plover

Carolyn A. Ristau

The Injury Feigning Plovers

The Plovers' Behaviors Toward Intruders

I shall concentrate on the piping plover *Charadrius melodus* and also include data from Wilson's plover *C. Wilsonia*, two shorebirds which typically nest on beaches or sand dunes of the eastern United States. Both parents incubate the eggs for about 4 weeks. At this point precocial young hatch; they can run freely and feed themselves on their first day. The young are able to fly in another 3 weeks.

The nest, eggs, young, and adult are all extremely well-camouflaged on the sand. The nest, like that of many birds that perform distraction displays, is simply a scrape on the ground sometimes lined with commonly found sand-colored shells. In some regions the nest may be further hidden because it is located among light grasses. Because the nest is easily accessible to predators, protection of the eggs depends on camouflage, preventing potential predators' knowledge of the nest's location, and keeping them out of the nest's vicinity.

In order for a plover to be conspicuous special behaviors or vocalizations are required. During incubation and before the young can fly, both parents of both species perform distraction displays to intruders which move along the ground. (See review of various species' behavior in Gochfeld, 1984.)

There are several different kinds of distraction behaviors. The bird, especially piping plovers, may peep loudly while walking and keeping apace or ahead of the intruder. The plover may also fly conspicuously and slowly exposing its underside and bright wing stripes as it circles within about 30 meters and returns again to the vicinity of the predator. As it flies or walks at a distance from its young, it can be heard to vocalize a "peep" or "peep-lo." This is, in fact, often what first attracts the human's attention to the cryptically colored bird against the sandy beach. Sometimes the plover may engage in false brooding that is, sit down with feathers slightly fluffed, wriggling as it does so giving the appearance of sitting on a nest when, in fact, there are no eggs in that particular location. Or it may merely pace back and forth in the general vicinity of a human, seeming to eye the presumed predator as it does so.

On some approaches of an intruder, the bird may do a gradation of broken-wing displays (BWD), which may perhaps begin with a fanning tail and gradually increase the awkwardness of walk until it has one and then both wings widely arched, fluttering, and dragging. It may then vocalize loud raucous squawks as well. The broken-wing display is usually made while the bird is moving forward along the ground, although stationary displays are also made. The full display, as made by piping plovers, consists of outstretched widely arched wings that flutter and drag along the ground. The bird presents a convincing case for being injured, and the observer often trudges hundreds of meters after the bird only to see it suddenly fly away with agility. At that point one is far from the nest or young.

Note that the plover does not always make a broken-wing display (BWD) when its offspring are approached by a ground-moving object. In the course of my experiments conducted on Long Island, New York in 1983, parents gave broken-wing displays during approximately 40% of the close approaches to the nest. In other cases the plover left the nest cryptically with a silent low run. It may also silently hide in hollows with its tail towards the intruder making it very difficult to be seen.

Furthermore, a related species, the killdeer *C. vociferous*, only rarely performs broken-wing displays at the approach of grazing animals such as cattle, which do not eat eggs but may accidentally trample the nest. Instead, when cattle come quite close to the nest, the killdeer may lunge in a cow's face thereby startling it and causing it to veer away (Armstrong, 1947; Graul, 1975; Walker, 1955). A somewhat similar set of reactions to mammals occurs among southern lapwings in Africa (Walters, 1980). Cattle and horses were typically ignored until the animal approached within about 5 meters of the nest or young. At such times, the parent bird either lunged with a characteristic defensive posture, wings spread wide and held low, or else did a brief mild distraction display. In short, at least some species which perform broken wing displays exhibit flexibility in their use of the behavior.

But precisely what is it that the bird is doing? Is this a stereotyped reflex, a fixed action pattern (FAP), or possibly a disorganized "hysterical" behavior as some have termed it? (Skutch, 1976, p. 403).

Does the bird have to do it? Can it control initiation or stopping of the BWD? Can the behavior be construed as intentional? What is evidence for the existence of an intention? Finally, can we answer any of these questions in a satisfying way?

It will be important to distinguish between "intentional" meaning "on purpose" and the philosophical use of the term to mean "aboutness"—a mark of the mental. I shall discuss both meanings.

What Are Some Possible Hypotheses About the Plover's Behavior?
Note that the following hypotheses are not mutually exclusive; it is quite possible that some combination may finally prove to be the most satisfactory.

Reflexive or Fixed Action Pattern Response   The bird's behavior is a reflex or an FAP which occurs when the parent bird is in a certain hormonal condition and is in the presence of an intruder and the plover's nest or young. A reflex is a simple stimulus-response connection in which a specific input is inevitably followed with little or no intervening processing by a unitary output. For example, the human knee-jerk response or the eye-blink response to a puff of air are reflexes. Complex behaviors are considered to be constructed by a chain of reflexes. In contrast, a fixed action pattern, a concept developed by the ethologists Lorenz and Tinbergen, is described in a recent textbook as follows:

The distinguishing characteristics of the behavior are the innate and stereo-typed coordination and patterning of several muscle movements which, when released, proceed to completion without requiring further sensory input. In terms of its almost total independence of feedback, the fixed-action pattern represents an extreme class of prewired behavioral performances which have come to be known as "motor programs." (Gould, 1982, p. 37)

For either a reflex or an FAP, there are several possibilities about the direction in which the plover makes a broken-wing display. In all cases, given the complexity of the motor acts involved, an FAP seems a more reasonable construct than does a reflexive interpretation. The possible directions are the following:

1. The BWD is made in random directions. This hypothesis predicts that the displaying bird should be just as likely to display toward as away from the nest or young.
2. The displaying bird merely goes away from the nest or young.
3. The displaying bird merely goes away from the intruder.
4. The displaying bird moves away from both the nest or young and the intruder. This hypothesis requires that the plover must know the location and movements or trajectories of the young and the intruders in order to respond appropriately. That is no small feat. (And it is difficult to conceive of as reflexive or an FAP.)

Conflict Behavior   Earlier investigators often interpreted the broken-wing display to be the result of conflicting motivations. The displaying bird's behavior was thought to be "convulsive," "deliriously excited," and "its behavior patterns were more or less disorganized" (Skutch, 1976, p. 403). If the bird's behavior were indeed so disorganized, one would predict random directions of display or at least inconsistent leading away from the nest or young.

Approach/Withdrawal Tendencies   This point of view, espoused by students of Schneirla (1972), is similar to the conflict hypothesis but emphasizes more orderly behaviors by the bird than those predicted by a simple conflict hypothesis. It is hypothesized that the bird would make a broken-wing display at the point of conflict. Not one of the many possible predicted behaviors suffices to account for the complexity of the observed behaviors.

Pre-programmed Sequence of Behavior   According to this hypothesis, the bird behaves according to a programmed sequence of behavior in which stimuli such as direction of movement of the intruder, size of intruder, nearness to nest, and so forth determine the response of the parent bird. At least for the piping and Wilson's plovers, the variability observed in their behavior does not lend itself to an interpretation of a rigidly programmed sequence of behavior. If we allow for great flexibility in that programming, we are including the possibility of learning (see Learning), and if we allow reprogramming, we might well be talking about purposeful behaviors. Recognize, however, no program yet exists that adequately accounts for the behavior of a whole animal in the real world, so the kind of "super" program that could include descriptions of intentional behavior is not plausibly included as part of the hypothesis of pre-programmed behavior.

Learning   Plovers might be able to learn about various aspects of a situation. This might include the ability to distinguish potential predators from those that are not. We have investigated that possibility in work discussed in Ristau (1986). Except for a simple reflexive interpretation of the plover's behavior and the conflict hypothesis, none of the other hypotheses necessarily preclude the possibility of learning.

An explanation of all the complexities of the parent bird's behavior in terms of operant conditioning is not viable if only because the infrequent interactions with predators are not likely to provide the extensive learning history required. A plover may, however, over one or more breeding seasons learn to improve its strategy for effective use of a BWD.

Intentional or Purposeful Behavior   The plover wants to lead the intruder away from the nest or young. It behaves so as to achieve this objective, which might include using the broken-wing display. I do not mean to imply that every plover has independently thought of or learned to make a BWD. The BWD is exhibited throughout the species and is undoubtedly an evolved genetically transmitted behavior. (There is no direct evidence for this assertion for no studies have been made of the ontogeny of the BWD.) However, strategies for its effective use may well be learned both directly and by observation. The fact that a behavior or some aspect of it is learned or genetically prewired does not preclude the possibility of conscious thinking associated with it (see Griffin, 1984, 1985). The hypothesis of purposeful behavior requires that the plover must know the location and movements of young and intruders. In the next section, this hypothesis is discussed more fully.

Evidence Needed to Evaluate the Hypothesis: The Plover Wants to Lead the Intruder Away from Nest/Young
Based on the previous discussion concerning descriptive characteristics of intentional behavior, I propose the following observable behaviors as suggestive evidence in support of the following hypothesis: The plover wants to lead the intruder away from nest/young. I can make no claim that these are necessary and sufficient conditions for intentional behavior. I have not succeeded where centuries of philosophical thought have failed, that is, in proposing unassailable connections between observable behaviors and accompanying mental states. In evaluating the hypothesis, I will concentrate on broken-wing displays because they are very conspicuous and easily observed; other behaviors may also distract a predator.

1. The direction in which a bird moves during BWDs made in different encounters between intruders, nest or young, and parents should usually be appropriate or adequate to accomplish the objective of leading the intruder away. However, one should not expect that the parent bird will always move in a correct direction; in fact completely accurate performance might well be suspect. Neither is it required that the displaying bird move in an optimal direction.
2. The displaying birds should monitor the intruder to determine the intruder's attention, location, and behavior, particularly whether it is following the displaying bird.
3. Once the intruder's behavior is monitored, the displaying bird, if necessary, should modify its own behavior in a variety of ways in response to the intruder's behavior so as to achieve the goal of leading an intruder away. For

instance, if the intruder is not paying attention to the displaying bird, as indicated either by eye gaze or failure to follow, the plover should try to gain the intruder's attention by loud vocalizing or by flying or walking into the visual field of the intruder. As one example, the displaying bird could reapproach the intruder to try again from a closer distance to attract the intruder's attention. If the intruder stops following, the bird could increase the intensity of its display or stop displaying and change its behavior.

4. The bird should exhibit appropriate flexibility of behaviors in other circumstances. For example, it should not make BWDs before eggs are laid or after young can fly safely away. If we encounter a parent away from nest or young (e.g., feeding on its favorite mud flat), it should not make BWDs. If predators destroy the eggs or the eggs hatch and the young leave the nest, parents should no longer make BWDs leading away from the nest site. Flexibility could extend to other aspects of the bird's behavior, for example, the ability to learn which intruders are potentially dangerous and which are not.

Methods

The data being reported were gathered in the breeding season of 1982 on piping plovers and Wilson's plovers on a barrier island off the coast of Virginia. In that work, human intruders approached the nest or young, walked in the area of offspring, stopping at the nest and at other locations, and either followed or did not follow the displaying adult. Directions of the intruder's initial approach and changes in movements were varied so as to make the intruder's behavior unpredictable to the birds. Observations of the birds' behavior and of the location and direction of movement of the birds, chicks, and intruder were recorded by means of audio dictations and often videotape as well. Directions were given in compass points such as northeast or north northeast, which was the most precise specification of direction used. One observer was frequently located in a portable blind, while the other also functioned as an intruder. Sometimes both observers were the intruders.

Results

The reported data are drawn only from interactions in which the locations and directions of intruder, displaying birds, and nest or all chicks could be determined. The data derive from 19 different experimental sessions and from 10 birds which were members of 4 different pairs of piping plovers and 2 different pairs of Wilson's plovers. Data are combined for sessions with one and two intruders and for the stages of incubation and unfledged young. In 45 instances of broken-wing displays, the data were sufficiently detailed for analysis.

Evidence that the Plovers Make Broken-Wing Displays in a Direction "Appropriate" to Lead Intruders Away from the Nest or Young

Definitions of "Appropriate Direction"   The first question I asked was whether the bird was displaying in a direction so as to cause an intruder to move toward or away from the offspring. In 44 out of 45 cases (98%), the bird's direction of display would have caused an intruder who followed it (i.e., went to the locations of the displaying bird) to get further from the young at the end of the period of injury-simulating display than at the beginning. One can also use a more stringent definition of the intruder moving away from eggs or young. Would the intruder ever, in the course of following the displaying bird, pass closer to the offspring? By those requirements, in 39 of the 45 cases (87%), the most direct path by which an intruder could have followed the displaying bird would never bring it closer to the nest or young. These data indicate that the birds' direction of display is adequate to get an intruder further from offspring.

Where in the Intruder's Visual Field does the Bird Make Broken-Wing Displays?   If the bird is displaying in order to attract the intruder's attention, one would expect the bird to be selective about where it displays; it should display where the intruder will see it. With respect to location, 44 of the 45 BWDs were made in front of the intruder rather than behind, that is, within a 180 degree arc of the intruder's visual field. The one possible exception occurred when an intruder was searching for young (very near them) and moving in a somewhat unpredictable fashion. The parent made a BWD to the side of the intruder, directed away from the young, and headed opposite to the general trend of the intruder's movement toward the chicks. In this situation, because the intruder was moving in a zigzag fashion, she was likely to turn so that sometimes the BWD would be within her visual field, and sometimes it would not.

These data do not determine which intruder characteristics the bird was responding to because, in most cases, the intruder was moving so that direction of movement, eye gaze, and facial and body orientation could be cues for the bird. When the intruder was stationary, it is conceivable the bird opted to display with respect to remembered direction of intruder movement rather than simply direction of eye gaze.

Positioning by the Bird Before Making a BWD   Another question examined in detail was the location of the bird when it began its broken-wing displays. If this behavior is a reflex that is elicited whenever an intruder approaches closely enough, one might expect the display to occur wherever the bird is located. However, the bird always moves before displaying. Sometimes the bird moves by flying, which is an easily and accurately observable form of locomotion. One can argue that by flying to a location rather than walking, a slower form of locomotion, it is probably important to the plover to get to that location rapidly. In all 13 cases of flying, the bird's new position was closer to the intruder than was its position before flight. One would not expect such positioning if, as some have suggested, the bird were attempting to get away from the intruder.

Furthermore, in 11 of those 13 cases, not only was the bird closer to the intruder, but it was closer to the front of the intruder than it had been, that is, more directly in the center of the intruder's visual field and/or the path of the moving intruder.

Evidence that Birds Making a BWD Monitor the Intruder's Behavior   To engage in these various behaviors strongly suggests the birds are monitoring the intruders. Are they? How can one determine what a plover is monitoring? Plovers have eyes that are placed laterally with both frontal and side (temporal) foveas so they can see can see over a wide field. It would be difficult to specify exactly what they are attending to within that field. They cannot, however, see behind them. Observations, photographs, and videotapes show that as a plover is making a broken-wing display while moving away from an intruder, it often turns its head sharply back over its shoulder its eye toward the intruder. The change in head/eye orientation strongly suggests monitoring of the intruder.

Modification of Displays in Response to Changing Intruder Behavior   Further indications of intentionality are provided by the behaviors of plovers when intruders do not follow the displaying bird. Detailed information is available in 36 of the 45 total cases of broken-wing displays. In five instances the intruder followed the displaying bird and in all five cases the bird continued its display and did not stop to move closer to the intruder. Because five is a small number of cases, I looked through the data in 1983, 1984, and 1985 and found 12 additional cases (with adequate data) when the intruder followed the displaying bird; the bird did not reapproach the intruder in any of these cases.

In 31 cases of the original data set, the intruder did not follow the displaying bird or ceased to follow it. It seems sensible to expect that a bird that was not sensitive to the intruder's response to its display would simply continue what it was doing, that is, making a BWD. However, the bird did not typically do this. In 17 of these 31 instances (55%) when the intruder did not follow the display, the bird stopped its display and reapproached the intruder by either flying or walking closer. In nine instances (29%), the bird either continued to make a BWD or increased the intensity of the display, for example, by flapping its wings more vigorously or vocalizing raucously while displaying. Of the remaining five cases, after displaying, (a) the bird flew to the location of the young (three instances), (b) flew away (one instance), or (c) in one other case did not reapproach or fly.

Summary

In summary, the use of intense distraction displays, at least by the plovers in this study, indicates that they usually perform the displays in a direction that would cause an intruder following them to get further away from the threatened nest or young. Furthermore, the birds monitor the intruder's approach and modify their behavior in response to changes in intruder locomotion. I interpreted the data as providing at least suggestive evidence for the purposive nature (or first order intentional analysis) of the birds' behavior. I don't mean to claim that it is the very flexible, fully cognitive, fully conscious, purposeful behavior we humans sometimes have. (Of course, conscious intention is almost impossible to demonstrate in a totally unequivocal fashion even in other human beings, but these data are the beginnings.)

To those who are discomforted by attempts to study "consciousness" in animals, recognize that even taking the stance of purposeful or intentional behavior without ever implying consciousness is a fruitful enterprise. The stance led me to design experiments that I had not otherwise thought to do, that no one else had done, and that revealed complexities in the behavior of the piping plover's distraction behavior not heretofore appreciated. I invite readers to adopt the stance of intentional behavior and to help delineate the levels and kinds of knowledge and purposiveness an organism might have.

Discussion

The Benefits of Limited Anthropomorphism and of using an Intentional Stance

One may question why we should describe the way animals behave in terms of an intentional stance, that is, with respect to goals or beliefs and desires as philosophers use the terms. J. Bennett (in Ristau 1991) has discussed this issue by focusing on the explanatory value of beliefs and desires and other mental states in understanding behavior. He, in fact, extends the ideas developed by Grice (1967), Dennett (1978, 1983, 1987) and Bennett (1976) to emphasize the importance of grounding the beliefs, desires, and behavior in the environment. When a simple, "triggered" stimulus-motor response description of behavior does not suffice, Bennett argues that an explanation may be needed in terms of a class of situations which are characterized by the organism's having certain beliefs and desires which make possible a variety of behaviors to achieve the goal.

Some, such as Burghardt (in Ristau 1991), consider an intentional stance a possibly useful heuristic device in suggesting experiments to be done and emphasizes that it should be considered just one of many possible approaches; he underscores the need for empirical data. I couldn't possibly disagree. Of course other approaches should be followed and, of course, every scientist needs empirical data. Yoerg and Kamil (in Ristau 1991) go a step further and state that anything that helps provoke a scientist to design experiments is OK—in that limited way. Thus, any sort of event might be the seed for a reasonable experiment, but the method of conjuring up an experiment should not be confused with the appropriate interpretation of the experiment or with a useful theoretical approach. For example, they suggest one may wish to imagine how an organism might feel or think when one makes field observations or designs an experiment, but that is not evidence that the organism actually feels that way. Their statements are also very sensible, but there are several other issues to be considered in conjunction with them.

Among these issues we should examine why it should be fruitful to be anthropomorphic in at least a limited way or to use an intentional stance when designing experiments or interpreting observational data. Why do these approaches work? Griffin and others propose that the approach of anthropomorphism works because animals may indeed have mental states including mental experiences. He uses several arguments to support his claim; most relevant here is the continuity of nature and of evolution. It is highly unlikely given all the continuities between humans and other organisms that humans alone should be aware or conscious, and have thoughts, purposes, beliefs, and desires. It is more likely that creatures other than humans should have a mind. The anthropomorphism, of course, should be limited. Another organism is not a human; it lives in different circumstances and sometimes has quite different sensory apparati. (See also Burghardt's ideas about critical anthropomorphism in Ristau 1991.)

Why should an intentional stance be particularly useful? Recall that, in Dennett's view, an intentional stance need not imply consciousness. The stance can be applied to a thermostat, a chess-playing computer program, a plover, or a human (a snake too?—see Burghardt in Ristau 1991) Other philosophers, for example, Searle (1980), distinguish between the derived intentionality of a thermostat or a computer program (intentionality derived from its designer) and the intrinsic intentionality of a human and perhaps a plover. A human actually does want a vacation or a dinner, whereas it is simply a useful strategy to deal with a chess-playing computer program to say it wants to bring its queen out early.

An intentional stance, at least the first level, can include a purposive interpretation of behavior (e.g., my studies in which I suggested that the plover wants to lead the intruder away from its nest). Because I took that stance, predictions about the plover's behaviors were made and experiments were designed to test the predictions.

Many ethologists who may not wish to deal with questions of animal mentality might opt to describe the plovers' injury feigning in terms of its function; the behavior functions to lead an intruder away from the nest. It has evolved to have that function. As proposed by the ethologist Tinbergen (1969), the function of a behavior is one of the four kinds of explanations of behavior scientists seek to answer. (The other three "whys" of behavior are evolution, ontogeny, and proximate mechanism —the last typically phrased in terms of physiological information; note the absence of any mentalistic explanation.) The concept of "proper function" (Millikan, 1984, 1986) of a behavior or a morphological structure, as developed by Millikan is related to this ethological formulation. (Millikan's ideas are described in Beer in Ristau 1991.)

It appears to me that a purposive or functional interpretation of behavior is useful because we may have struck upon an organizational principle of organisms. This is a most important point that I wish to emphasize. At an extreme level, the blowfly, upon encountering a sucrose solution with the chemoreceptors on its feet, extends it proboscis and imbibes the solution. We may say of the blowfly that its goal or the function of its behavior was to drink the sugar. At other extremes, there are the cases of the plover leading an intruder away from its nest or the human wanting dinner. For the blowfly, or some other organism, if you prefer, the proboscis extension and drinking behavior is probably under little if any voluntary control whereas there is extensive voluntary control, at least at the human end, for how to go about getting dinner. The degree of flexibility is a most important characteristic of the behaviors that are described as purposeful, and they may vary in interesting ways ontogenetically and across species. The description of the blowfly's behavior may be made in terms of the stimulus-response triggers as discussed by Bennett (in Ristau 1991) whereas that of the plover and the human appear to be better described by goals (desires) to be accomplished by a variety of behaviors.

Methodology
How then should one undertake studies using a limited or critical anthropomorphic approach or an intentional stance?

1. Empirical data are essential. Discussions of the possible mind states of animals without reference to their sensory and cognitive capabilities will be limited. It would be most useful to gather data so as to be descriptive of the organisms' behavior even to scientists uninterested in a mentalistic approach.
2. A hypothesis or stance and alternative interpretations must be specified as clearly as possible. Hypotheses must be falsifiable. Evidence must include not only data in support of a (mentalistic) hypothesis, but data which disconfirm simpler alternative interpretations. Precisely how the empirical data disconfirm alternative explanations must be carefully delineated.
3. In applying an intentional stance one should look for gaps in intentionality; that is, deviations from the expected behavior of a fully rational creature which, indeed, even we humans are not. One should look for errors and limitations of abilities in order to specify them more precisely.
4. Comparative studies are most useful. In this way, one can accumulate evidence about the different kinds of abilities. In particular, the degree of flexibility exhibited by different species may reveal differences along the continuum from rigidly programmed control of behavior to more voluntary control (Ristau,

1988). If we consider a potentially purposive behavior, the flexibility could be observed in terms of the breadth of stimuli to which the organism is responsive in achieving its goal; the situations or contexts in which the behavior can occur; and the ability to overcome obstacles in achieving the goal, particularly with respect to the variety and novelty of responses utilized.

Are Piping Plovers Intentionalist Creatures?

This is a tough question to answer. Remember that the philosophical meaning of intentional does not mean on purpose, although purposeful behavior and "wants it to be the case that" are among various intentional idioms. For a plover to be intentional it must be shown to have mind states. An intentional creature will have beliefs and knowledge, and it will act in accordance with them. Its behavior, such as a broken-wing display, will not simply appear, like a reflex or fixed action pattern, only in the presence of certain very specific stimulu. An intentionalist plover would be aware of its goal, and alters its behavior in ways appropriate to achieve its goal. There may be other and better ways of stating all this. I am simply exploring the possible application of an intentional stance to an animal's behavior—in this case, the piping plover.

It is for the previously mentioned reasons that I examined the ability of the piping plovers to attempt to continue to attract an intruder's attention and to cause the intruder to follow it away from nest/young as part of a body of evidence needed to indicate that the plover had a goal achievable by a variety of means. (Other behavioral flexibilites are discussed in Ristau, 1986). The plover is sensitive to many aspects of its environment including the attention paid by the intruder to its general nest area (defining attention in terms of direction of intruder's eye gaze). To begin to investigate the plover's knowledge/beliefs about its environment, the safe-dangerous experiments were conducted, which showed that a piping plover could learn to discriminate between two persons. These experiments are only a beginning in the exploration of whether and to what extent plovers are intentional creatures. The results so far suggest that they are. It will be important and most interesting to explore the limits of their abilities as well. They most assuredly are not the intentional creatures humans are, they are most likely far more limited than chimpanzees, and yet are probably interestingly different from snakes and blowflies. Whether critical aspects of the differences can be most profitably examined using an intentional stance to guide us remains an unanswered question.

Continuing the Dialogue

Most important is to continue the dialogue between scientists with different viewpoints and to establish more interaction with philosophers of science and of mind with whom we share concerns over similar issues. Using an intentional analysis, for example, is but one possible approach to the study of the animal and human minds. It is unlikely that any present viewpoint or theoretical orientation is totally correct. It behooves us to be open-minded, to learn from each other, and to explore.

References

Armstrong, E. A. (1947). *Bird display and behaviour*. London: Lindsay Drummond.
Bennett, J. (1976). *Linguistic behaviour*. Cambridge: Cambridge University Press.
Dennett, D. C. (1978). *Brainstorms*. Cambridge, MA: Bradford Books.

Dennett, D. C. (1983). Intentional systems in cognitive ethology: The 'Panglossian paradigm' defended. *Behavioral and Brain Sciences, 6*, 343–390.

Dennett, D. C. (1987). *The intentional stance.* Cambridge, MA: Bradford Books.

Gochfeld, M. (1984). Antipredator behavior: Aggressive and distraction displays of shorebirds. In J. Burger & B. L. Olla (Eds.), *Shorebirds: Breeding behavior and populations* (pp. 289–377). New York: Plenum.

Gould, J. L. (1982). *Ethology: The mechanisms and evolution of behavior.* New York: W. W. Norton.

Graul, W. D. (1975). Breeding biology of the mountain plover. *Wilson Bulletin, 87*, 6–31.

Grice, H. P. (1967). Logic and conversation. William James Lectures, Harvard University. In P. Cole & J. L. Morgan (Eds.), *Studies in syntax* (Vol. 3). New York: Academic Press.

Griffin, D. R. (1984). *Animal thinking.* Cambridge, MA.: Harvard University Press.

Griffin, D. R. (1985). Animal consciousness. *Neuroscience and Biobehavioral Reviews, 9*, 615–622.

Millikan, R. G. (1984). *Language, thought and other biological categories.* Cambridge, MA: Bradford Books.

Millikan, R. G. (1986). Thoughts without laws; cognitive science without content. *Philosophical Review, 95*, 47–80.

Ristau, C. A. (1988). Thinking, communicating, and deceiving: Means to master the social environment. In G. Greenberg & E. Tobach (Eds.), *Evolution of social behavior and integrative levels* (pp. 213–240). Hillsdale, NJ: Lawrence Erlbaum Associates.

Ristau, C. A. (1986). Intentional behavior by birds? The case of the "injury feigning" plovers. Unpublished manuscript.

Ristau, C. A. (Ed.) (1991). *Cognitive ethology: The minds of other animals.* Hillsdale, N.J.: Lawrence Erlbaum Associates.

Schneirla, T. C. (1972). An evolutionary and developmental theory of biphasic processes underlying approach and withdrawal I. In L. R. Aronson, E. Tobach, J. S. Rosenblatt & D. S. Lehrman (Eds.), *Selected writings of T. C. Schneirla* (pp. 297–339). San Francisco: W. H. Freeman & Company. Reprinted from *Nebraska symposium on motivation,* 1959, (pp. 1–42).

Searle, J. R. (1980). Minds, brains and programs. *Behavioral and Brain Sciences, 3*, 417–457.

Skutch, A. F. (1976). *Parent birds and their young.* Austin: University of Texas Press.

Tinbergen, N. (1969). *The study of instinct.* New York: Oxford University Press. (Original work published 1951).

Walker, J. (1955). Mountain plover. *Audobon, 57*, 210–212.

Chapter 7

Tradition in Animals: Field Observations and Laboratory Analyses

Bennett G. Galef, Jr.

A field biologist, observing a troop of rhesus monkeys in an area where they have never before been studied, discovers many troop members behaving in a way that rhesus monkeys elsewhere do not. Suppose members of our hypothetical troop eat a type of plant other rhesus ignore or, even better, suppose they use a unique method to gather food or to process it.

Discovering a behavior, particularly a complex one, exhibited by only one of the many populations comprising a species would be a significant event in the career of any behavioral scientist. Surely, before very long, our field worker will want to tell colleagues about her observations. To do so, she is going to have to decide how she will refer to the unusual behavior she has seen.

The decision as to what to call a behavior found in only one of many populations of a species may seem trivial. However, dozens of such decisions, made over decades, have had cumulative, unintentionally detrimental effects on the study of behaviors unique to particular populations.

If our hypothetical field worker makes the conventional choice, there is little doubt that she will soon be referring to the unusual behavior she discovered as "traditional" in the troop she watched. Why contemporary field workers tend to label as "traditional" any behavior unique to a population is not obvious. Whatever the origins of the practice, it poses problems for students of animal behavior in general and of animal learning in particular.

In ordinary speech, description of a behavior as traditional is understood to mean that those performing the traditional behavior have both learned it in some way from others and can pass it on to naive individuals (Gove 1971); the English word "tradition" is derived from the Latin *traditio*, meaning the action of handing something over to another, or of delivering up a possession (Lewis & Short 1969). Thus, calling a behavior traditional implies (or, at the least, may lead a listener to infer) that the user of the term believes that social learning of some sort played a role in acquisition of the "traditional" behavior.

Unfortunately for those who would call "traditional" all behaviors exhibited by the members of only one subpopulation of a species, development of behavioral differences between groups that appear to result from social transmission of behavior can sometimes be explained more parsimoniously in other ways. Consequently, by referring to all behaviors specific to local populations as traditional, important differences in their causes are obscured.

To avoid the semantic problem arising from use of the adjective "traditional" to refer to all behaviors that are unique to single populations, I shall refer to such behaviors as "locale-specific" unless I wish to indicate that social learning played some role in development of a behavior. I intend the term "locale-specific" to carry no implication as to the causes of a behavior being found in only some subpopulations of a species.

Referring to a socially learned behavior as traditional has had a second unfortunate consequence. Those with primary interest in functional analyses of behavior often assume that once it has been established that a behavior is, indeed, traditional in a population (i.e. that social learning played a role in its propagation), then the way in which the behavior spread is well understood.

Gaulin & Kurland (1976: 374) may have overstated the case in asserting that "Unless the spread of a behavioral trait is attributable to a particular diffusion mechanism, the concept of tradition is completely uninformative." They did, however, highlight an important issue. There are many different social learning processes that can result in transmission of behavior among individuals (Galef 1976, 1988). Consequently, from the perspective of those interested in understanding the development of behavior, calling a locale-specific behavior "traditional" answers few questions and raises many.

In sum, use of the term "traditional" in discussion of what I will call locale-specific behaviors has caused difficulties. Such use has led many to assume that locale-specific behaviors are socially transmitted, when no evidence of their social transmission is available. Calling behaviors traditional has also served to mask ignorance of the details of social-learning processes involved in the propagation of truly traditional, locale-specific behaviors. Below, I consider, in turn each of these problems.

Knowing if Locale-Specific Behaviors Are Traditional

Three interacting types of information can influence the course of behavioral development in an individual: (1) genetically transmitted information received from parents, (2) socially transmitted information acquired from contemporaries, and (3) individually acquired information discovered as the result of transactions with nonsocial portions of the environment (Galef 1976). Consequently, systematic differences in the behavior of two populations of a species can be the result of any of three different processes or their interactions. Behavioral differences between populations can reflect: (1) differences in the frequencies of alleles that influence, either directly or indirectly, the course of behavioral development, (2) differences in the behavior of population members that influence behavioral development in new recruits to a group, or (3) differences in the environments in which local populations are living that produce systematic differences in the reinforcement population members receive for engaging in various behaviors. Consequently, although the most easily observed result of social learning might be behavioral differences among local populations of a species, discovery of differences in the behavior of two populations does not suffice to show that social transmission processes produced those differences (Galef 1976; Nishida 1987).

Less widely appreciated is the inverse proposition: Discovery of unique properties of the ecological situation or gene pool of a population exhibiting a locale-specific behavior does not exclude the possibility that the locale-specific behavior was socially learned. The relationship between findings in population genetics and ecology and the study of social learning is sufficiently poorly understood [see, for example, the exchange between Strum (1975, 1976) and Gaulin and Kurland (1976)] that consideration of a specific instance might prove useful.

The Vampire Finches of Wolf Island

The sharp-beaked ground finches (*Geospiza difficilis*) of Wolf (Wenman) and Darwin (Culpepper) Islands in the Galápagos Archipelago are classified as a distinct subspecies (*septentrionalis*) on the basis of measurements of the body parts of adult males (Lack 1947, 1969; Schluter & Grant 1984). Members of the *septentrionalis* subspecies have, for example, longer wings and longer, more tapered beaks than do members of the other two subspecies of *G. difficilis* (Lack 1969; Schluter & Grant 1984). Presumably, such differences in morphology are heritable and reflect differences between the genotypes of members of the subspecies of *G. difficilis* found on relatively isolated Wolf and Darwin Islands (40 km apart and 100 km from the closest other island) and those subspecies of *G. difficilis* found elsewhere in the Galápagos.

The populations of *G. difficilis* on Wolf and Darwin Islands differ from those found elsewhere not only in presumably heritable, morphological characters, but also in the details of both the environment their members inhabit and the behaviors their members exhibit. For example, Wolf and Darwin Islands are not home to avian predators (owls and hawks) typically found elsewhere in the Galápagos. Possibly in consequence, *G. difficilis* on Wolf and Darwin Islands exhibit "a tameness ... that is most striking" (Bowman & Billeb 1965: 41). *G. difficilis* on Wolf Island are also the only members of their species that inhabit an island both supporting a population of *Opuntia* cactus and lacking cactus-feeding-specialist bird species [*G. scandens* and *G. conirostris* (Grant 1986)]. Perhaps because of the absence of more efficient competitors on Wolf Island, *G. difficilis* there, but not *G. difficilis* found elsewhere, feed on *Opuntia* cactus and probe *Opuntia* flowers for nectar and pollen (Lack 1969).

More startling, *G. difficilis* on Darwin and Wolf Islands, but not others of their species, perch on the tails of masked and red-footed boobies (large, white-bodied seabirds of the genus *Sula*), draw blood by pecking at the base of feathers on the boobies' wings, and feed on the blood that flows from the wounds thus created. Also, on Wolf Island but not elsewhere, *G. difficilis* use their relatively long, tapered bills to pierce and eat the contents of seabirds' eggs (Bowman & Billeb 1965; Köster & Köster 1983; Schluter & Grant 1984). In sum, the *septentrionalis* subspecies of *G. difficilis* exhibits three locale-specific patterns of behavior—cactus feeding, egg feeding and blood feeding—the last of which is frequently referred to in the literature as a tradition of the finches of Wolf Island.

The case of blood feeding in *G. difficilis* is a particularly appropriate instance of locale-specific behavior to consider because there are available in the literature both detailed descriptions of the morphology, ecology, feeding habits and biogeography of *G. difficilis* and suggestions as to the evolutionary forces responsible for the distribution of the morphological and behavioral phenotypes observed in the species [see Lack (1969) and Grant (1986) for examples]. The question before us is whether this wealth of information and theory relating to the ecology, taxonomy, natural history and evolution of sharp-beaked ground finches is of help in deciding whether the locale-specific behaviors of *G. difficilis* on Wolf Island are truly traditional. I think not.

To call a locale-specific behavior traditional is to propose an hypothesis about the factors leading to development of the locale-specific behavior in those individuals exhibiting it (Galef 1991). To test such an hypothesis, information is needed about social interactions that might increase the probability that an individual would exhibit the locale-specific behavior. Although hypotheses concerning the development of locale-specific behaviors may incorporate information about ecology or genetics, such developmental hypotheses must be at an individual, rather than an ecological or population-genetic level of analysis. For example, regarding the habit of blood feeding by *G. difficilis*, Bowman and Billeg (1965) have suggested that: (1) during the dry season, when free-living insects (the species-typical fare of *G. difficilis*) are hard to find, boobies often carry concentrations of black hippoboscid flies that are very conspicuous against the birds' white plumage and (2) finches might pursue flies onto the backs of boobies and develop the blood-feeding habit by accidentally puncturing the skin of boobies while in pursuit of flies. Although such an account fails to address the most interesting issue (why *G. difficilis* on Wolf and Darwin Islands feed on the blood of boobies, while those elsewhere do not), it is at a level of analysis appropriate for investigating that issue.

To test hypotheses about the origins of blood feeding, information is needed about the conditions associated with its development in individuals. Blood feeding by *G. difficilis* on Wolf and Darwin Islands might be the result of any of several factors: (1) heritable differences in tameness, (2) heritable differences in beak shape, (3) heritable differences in the tendency to attack seabirds, (4) differences in ecology that make blood feeding particularly energetically valuable on Wolf and Darwin Islands, (5) some sort of social transmission of the behavior of feeding on blood. Blood feeding might even develop in individuals in response to all five of these factors interacting in complex ways in the unique situation that is home to *G. difficilis septentrionalis*.

Of course field workers can often do much more than simply report the existence of locale-specific behaviors. Observation and description of social interactions during which naive individuals might acquire a traditional pattern of behavior can provide clues to the causes of the spread of a locale-specific behavior in a group of animals. Again a specific example may prove helpful in discussing general issues.

Development of Food Choices in Monkeys and Apes

Often by the time a young primate grows to adolescence, it has developed a locale-specific pattern of food selection similar to that of the adult members of its troop. How is this cross-generational convergence in acceptance and rejection of potential foods achieved? Is it, in fact, traditional?

Observations of social interactions provide useful clues. For example, as a result of study of the social situations prevailing when infant mantled howling monkeys (*Allouata palliata*) fed for the first time on seasonally available leaves and fruits in the forests of Costa Rica, Whitehead (1986) concluded that some form of socially dependent learning governed ingestion of leaves, while a learning process independent of social influence governed feeding on fruits.

Whitehead reports that when feeding on leaves, infant howling monkeys: (1) looked at a parent before eating, (2) fed only when a parent fed, (3) ate only what parents ate, and (4) were subject to parental intervention when they chose incorrectly. On the other hand, when feeding on fruit, infants: (1) only occasionally looked at parents before feeding (2) sometimes fed independently and (3) ate or sampled fruits that adults did not. Thus, feeding on fruit by infant howler monkeys was generally less coordinated with adult feeding than was infant feeding on leaves.

Like howler monkeys eating leaves, 3- to 12-month-old vervet monkeys (*Cercopithecus ascanius*) tend to feed in synchrony with their mothers, to eat only the food items she does and, consequently, never even sample some foods that could be deleterious (Hauser 1988). Similarly, mother and infant chimpanzees share food (Silk 1978) as do mother and infant rhesus macaques (Kawamura 1959) and gorillas (Watts 1985).

While failure to observe infants feeding on the same food as their mothers may exclude certain modes of social learning as explanations of intergenerational congruence in food selection, interpretation of observations of mothers and infants eating the same items is not so straightforward. Simple observation of feeding on the same foods by mothers and infants does not show that the feeding experiences of infant primates affect food selection by the young when they are grown. Common sense suggests that the food choices of adolescent primates should be affected by their feeding experiences as infants; there is even indirect evidence that infant feeding does affect adult food choice (Kawamura 1959: 45), but there is always the possibility of common sense misleading rather than enlightening. Again, an example might prove useful.

Development of Mouse Killing by Rats

Some years ago, I conducted a laboratory study of social influence on the development of predatory behavior in young Norway rats. I took pairs of mothers (both of whom reliably attacked mice), that had given birth on the same day, and cross-fostered half the litter of each mother to the other. I then placed each mother and her artificially constituted brood in a large enclosure. One mother in each pair, randomly assigned to the experimental condition, was given access to two mice a day, for 7 days, from the time that her pups were 16 days old. The other mother, assigned to the control condition, reared her young without seeing a mouse.

Once pups raised by mothers assigned to the experimental condition were old enough to wander about the enclosure, they exhibited tremendous interest in their mother's predatory behavior. Pups followed their dam to a mouse, chased the mouse, appeared to watch their mother kill it, pounced on the body of the mouse, and fed on it. When a beleaguered mother tried to carry her prey off to a secluded corner and eat in peace, her pups would often follow her, pulling vigorously at the dead mouse and acting very excited by their mother's predatory and carnivorous activities.

It seemed obvious that rat pups having such experiences, similar to those believed important in development of predatory skill by free-living domestic cats, tiger, cheetah, and meerkat (Ewer 1969), would exhibit facilitated development of their own predatory behavior. However, I could find no differences either in the probability that pups from control and experimental litters grew to be mouse predators or in the mean age at which pups from the two groups that did prey on mice made their first kills.

Common sense may suggest that early social feeding should influence development of later feeding behavior in rats or in primates. Unfortunately, observation plus common sense is not quite good enough.

Close observation of interactions between naive and knowledgeable individuals in appropriate contexts can increase the precision of hypotheses about how social transmission of behavior might occur [see Hauser (1988) for a particularly compelling example]. However, only controlled experiments can determine whether an observed, apparently relevant, social interaction actually plays a role in the development of a locale-specific behavior (whether, for example, the food eaten by an infant primate while in its mother's lap actually affects its food choices later in life). Further, as discussed below, only experimentation under controlled conditions (see for examples, Galef 1980; Sherry & Galef 1984) can determine the particular social learning processes acting in a given instance (Galef 1990).

Knowing How Behaviors Are Transmitted

Those with relatively little interest in the development of behavior frequently attribute all traditions to learning by "observation" or by "imitation" (see, for examples, Strum 1976; Bonner 1980; Goodall 1986), although a century of laboratory research suggests that a variety of simpler kinds of social learning processes can be responsible for propagation of traditions. The possibility that traditional behaviors can rest on rather humble types of social learning was first discussed at length by Edward Thorndike (1898), one of the founders of experimental, animal psychology in North America. Unfortunately, Thorndike's approach to analysis of social learning processes has not yet everywhere replaced the view, prevalent earlier in the nineteenth century, that existence of animal traditions is indicative of an ability of animals to learn by imitation.

Pre-eminent among early advocates of interpretation of the development of behavior in animals as the result of learning by imitation was George Romanes, a protégé and disciple of Darwin's. The most influential, historically, of the many purported examples of imitation learning that Romanes described in his landmark monograph, *Animal Intelligence* (1882), concerned a cat that belonged to Romanes' own coachman. This animal had learned, without formal tuition of any kind, to open a latched gate in Romanes' yard. The cat would jump up and hold the latch guard with one forepaw, depress the thumb piece with the other, and simultaneously push at the gatepost with her hind feet, thus opening the gate. Romanes argued that the cat must have observed humans grasp the latch guard, depress the thumb piece, and push open the gate. Then, said Romanes (1882: 442), the cat must have reasoned, "If a hand can do it, why not a paw?" Motivated by this insight, the cat attempted to and succeeded in opening the latched gate.

Underlying Romanes' interpretation of the observation that the cat could open the gate are two implicit assumptions concerning the role of cognition in animal behavior: first, that the idea of a behavior can produce a behavior and, second, that the idea of a behavior can arise from observing others exhibit a behavior. While it would be foolish to get bogged down in the behaviorist-cognitivist debate, it is surely true that if animals can intentionally imitate motor patterns to achieve goals, as Romanes suggested, then animals are far more cognitive creatures than behaviorists have considered them to be.

Unfortunately, Romanes' observations of the behavior of his coachman's cat provide no compelling support for his interpretation. The cat could surely open the gate. However, observing an animal behave in an uncontrolled environment provides little useful information regarding the processes responsible for the development of the behavior the animal exhibits.

In the late 1890s, Thorndike brought the gate-opening behavior of cats into the laboratory and, under controlled conditions, examined the development of animals' solutions to a variety of mechanical problems. In Thorndike's best-known study, food-deprived cats were placed individually in a cage and observed on repeated trials as they learned to escape confinement and gain access to food by depressing a treadle located in the center of the cage floor (Thorndike 1898).

Considering the results of a number of conceptually similar experiments, Thorndike proposed that cats learned to solve all such mechanical problems, presumably including the opening of garden gates, by a gradual process of trial-and-error learning. Less generally appreciated is Thorndike's (1898) explicit rejection, on both empirical and theoretical grounds, of the possibility that animals would acquire such skills by imitation.

Thorndike had found that animals of several species, cats included, did not learn to escape from cages either by watching others do so or by observing humans demonstrate solutions. Indeed, Thorndike's data suggested that observation of a trained demonstrator by a naive individual would sometimes interfere with the trial-and-error learning in which a naive animal had to engage in learning to solve a problem.

Of course, Thorndike might not have been correct in asserting that animals do not imitate; there is, in fact, some more recent data than Thorndike's suggesting that animals do sometimes imitate (e.g. Dawson & Foss 1965). However, it is surely the case, given the large number of experiments performed during the last 90 years in which learning by imitation has not been found, that the burden of proving that learning by imitation underlies any particular traditional behavior surely rests on those who suggest the possibility.

Alternatives to Learning by Imitation for Social Transmission of Behavior
Just because simple observation of a performance does not often facilitate acquisition of behavior by naive animals does not mean that other sorts of social interaction are not important in development of behavior. Thorndike himself (1898) was careful to point out that a variety of social learning processes other than imitation could shape behavioral development in animals. This notion of a multiplicity of non-imitative, social-learning processes that influence behavioral development was an important contribution to understanding of animal traditions that was largely ignored for more than 50 years in a generally unsuccessful search for evidence of learning by imitation in animals.

Only during the last two decades have students of animal, social learning begun to examine systematically in the laboratory locale-specific behaviors observed in the field to discover how social learning might shape the development of patterns of behavior exhibited by free-living animals. One of the more extensively analyzed, locale-specific behaviors involves patterns of food selection first reported in free-living Norway rats (*Rattus norvegicus*). Below, I briefly describe this program of research on social influences on diet selection in rats as an example of the level of understanding of a traditional behavior that can be achieved within the framework Thorndike first proposed.

Traditions of Food Preference in Norway Rats
Fritz Steiniger, an applied ecologist, who worked for many years on control of rodent pests, observed in 1950 that, if a single type of poison bait were used in the same place for a long time, despite great initial success, with rats eating large quantities of bait and dying in large numbers, later acceptance of the bait was surprisingly poor.

Steiniger observed that young rats, born to animals that had survived their initial encounters with a bait, never even tasted the bait that their parents had learned to avoid. Steiniger (1950) hypothesized that after learning not to eat a poisoned bait, adult rats marked the bait with their urine and feces and thus dissuaded their young from eating it.

My students and I have spent the past 20 years trying to understand the behavioral processes responsible for such locale-specific avoidance of poison baits by young rats. The first thing we learned from our experiments was that simple observation of a socially learned behavior, in this case avoidance of an adult-avoided food by juveniles, tells the observer little about the causes of that socially learned behavior.

Despite repeated attempts to demonstrate, as Steiniger had suggested, that adult rats that had learned not to eat a food would mark the food and thus cause naive others to avoid eating it, we have not been able to find any evidence consistent with that view (Galef & Clark 1971; Galef & Beck 1985). To the contrary, our results over 20 years have repeatedly suggested that, although naive young rats may appear to have learned not to eat a poison their parents are avoiding, young rats do not learn from adults to avoid a food (Galef 1985). In the laboratory, young wild rats learn through social interaction only to eat those foods that adults of their colony are eating; the young avoid a poisoned food in large part because they avoid eating any food they have not been socially induced to eat (Barnett 1958; Galef & Clark 1971).

The reason why we have been studying social transmission of food choice in Norway rats for so many years is that there is no simple answer to the question "How do young rats come to prefer foods that adults of their colony are eating?" In fact, we have uncovered four different behavioral proclivities in young rats each of which would suffice, in appropriate circumstances, to produce the phenomenon first reported by Steiniger (1950), a tendency for young rats to eat the same foods that adults of their colony are eating: (1) The milk of a mother rat contains cues reflecting the flavor of the foods she has been eating, and weaning rats select solid foods to eat that have the flavors they were exposed to in their mother's milk (Galef & Henderson 1972; Galef & Sherry 1973). (2) Young rats prefer to eat together with adult rats; consequently. if foods are distributed in patches, weanlings tend to eat the same foods that adults of their colony are eating (Galef & Clark 1971; Galef 1977). (3) Adult rats deposit attractive odors both in areas where they eat and in foods they have eaten. The odors deposited by adults bias young rats to feed both in the areas and on the foods adults have marked (Galef & Heiber 1976; Galef & Beck 1985). (4) For some hours after eating a food, a rat emits olfactory cues that allow other rats to identify and induce them to prefer the food the recently fed individual has eaten (Galef & Wigmore 1983; Galef 1989).

The Status of Laboratory Studies of Locale-Specific Food Preferences in Norway Rats
Unfortunately, just because we have found four, socially mediated, behavioral processes, each sufficient to explain Steiniger's (1950) observations of locale-specific food preference in rats, that does not mean that there are not four more waiting to be discovered. Further, data indicating that in simplified laboratory situations rats can exploit others as sources of information about where and what to eat do not show that those abilities are used (or usable) by free-living rats occupying more complex, natural habitat (Galef 1984).

Both the analysis described briefly in the preceding section (reviewed in greater detail in Galef 1977, 1986), and other laboratory analyses of traditional behaviors demonstrate that traditional patterns of behavior can be based on very simple social learning processes (see for example, Curio et al. 1978; Cook et al. 1985). Further, multiple determination of single, traditional behaviors makes it unlikely that occurrence of learning by imitation can ever be established by unobtrusive observation outside the laboratory (Galef 1984).

Unfortunately, experiments based on field observations of social interactions that might contribute to the propagation of traditional behaviors are few in number (see Marler & Tamura 1964; West et al. 1981; Curio et al. 1987 for examples). In the absence of a multitude of such experimental analyses, field reports of tradition and of learning by imitation have been accepted at face value and become part both of the textbooks and of the *Zeitgeist* of animal behavior. Below, I discuss the most widely cited example of a locale-specific behavior assumed to be traditional and to spread by imitation learning, sweet potato washing by Japanese macaques (*Macaca fascata*) living on Koshima Islet. In analyzing sweet potato washing, I consider two questions: Is sweet potato washing traditional? Is it based on imitation learning?

Sweet Potato Washing by Japanese Macaques at Koshima

In 1953, an 18 month old, female macaque (Imo) began to take pieces of sweet potato covered with sand to a stream and to wash the sand from the potato pieces before eating them. Most Japanese macaques brush sand from pieces of sweet potato with their hands, but Imo started to wash sandy pieces of potato in water and, during the next 9 years, sweet potato washing became common in her troop.

Sweet potato washing did not spread randomly through the Koshima Islet macaques; spread of the behavior followed lines of social affiliation. First, potato washing was exhibited by Imo's playmate Semushi, who began to wash potatoes a month after Imo did. Sweet potato washing was then performed by Imo's mother (Eba) and by a second playmate of Imo's (Uni), both of whom began to potato wash three months after Semushi. During the following two years (1955–1956), seven more youngsters learned to wash potatoes, and by 1958, 14 of 15 juveniles and 2 of 11 adults in the Koshima troop had started to do so (Kawamura 1959; Kawai 1965; Itani & Nishimura 1973; Nishida 1987). According to the secondary literature, the spread of sweet potato washing behavior occurred because naive monkeys observed Imo and other sweet potato washers wash potatoes and then imitated them.

It will, of course, never be known with certainty what caused sweet potato washing to spread through the Koshima Islet troop 35 years ago. Possibly, some or all of the monkeys did learn to wash potatoes by imitating Imo or others. However, as discussed below, interpretation of the spreading of washing behavior through the Koshima troop of macaques as either traditional or due to imitation is open to challenge.

One property of sweet potato washing that makes it seem a likely candidate for social propagation is the bizarreness of the behavior and the intuitive improbability of many monkeys learning independently to wash potatoes. It is, therefore, surprising to find that sweet potato washing has been observed in four other provisioned troops of Japanese macaques in addition to the troop at Koshima (Kawai 1965). Imo was not so creative a "genius" as the secondary literature suggests and potato washing is not so unlikely a behavior for monkeys to develop independently as one might imagine. Recently, Visalberghi and Fragaszy (1990) reported very rapid learning of food washing by both crab-eating macaques (*Macaca fascicularis*) and tufted capuchin monkeys (*Cebus apella*) in captivity. Apparently food-washing behaviors can be learned relatively easily by monkeys and could become common in a troop through processes other than imitation of a rare "creative genius." However, even if monkeys find it easy to learn to food wash in appropriate circumstances, it is not obvious why sweet potato washing became widespread among the macaques at Koshima, but not among other troops of macaques provisioned with sweet potatoes.

It has been suggested (Green 1975) that maintenance of sweet potato washing in the Koshima troop might not be the result of natural processes. For many years the Koshima troop has been provisioned by caretakers, local people employed to supplement the natural diet of the monkeys with sweet potatoes, wheat, and peanuts. When Green visited Koshima in the 1970s, he observed that the woman who was provisioning the macaques there, and who had been a caretaker for many years, gave sweet potatoes only to those monkeys that washed them. She thus reinforced monkeys for engaging in sweet potato washing. Green suggested that such human intervention may have maintained potato washing in the Koshima troop while it died out in other groups in which individuals initiated it. If social learning of any kind played a role in the spread of sweet potato washing at Koshima, human maintenance of washing behavior by monkeys that began to wash spontaneously could have promoted spread of the behavior. Why should caretakers at Koshima have bothered to maintain potato washing by their charges? Perhaps because some of the local income derived from visiting scientists and tourists who came to see the monkeys perform, stayed in the local inn, and gave tips to the caretakers (Green personal communication).

Green (1975) also pointed out that, while foraging, a macaque troop is spatially organized in such a way that the likelihood of individuals being close to or distant from a human reinforcing agent would vary with their age class and matriline. Hence, human intervention could produce a pattern of spread of washing behavior that would make the behavior appear traditional to an unsuspecting observer.

Of course, even if potato washing were maintained in the 1970s by caretakers, it might originally have spread by imitation learning. There are, however, a few things that make me question this conclusion. First is the fact that so many of the locale-specific behaviors observed in the Koshima troop, [e.g., sweet potato washing, wheat placer mining, caramel eating, and give-me-some behavior (Kawai 1965)], involved food provided by humans. None involved an indigenous food.

Second, some locale-specific behaviors seen in the Koshima troop, clearly not the result of social transmission, spread in a fashion strikingly similar to sweet potato washing. Consider bathing behavior. Before the summer of 1959 none of the members of the Koshima troop would do more than dip their hands and feet in the sea. That summer one of the caretakers, Mrs. Mito, induced a 2 year old male (Ego) to walk into the water of Otamari Bay by throwing peanuts (one of Ego's favorite foods) into the sea. Over a period of 3 years, Mrs. Mito induced 63 percent of the Koshima monkeys to enter the water. Japanese scientists observed and described the spread of bathing behavior. Like sweet potato washing, bathing behavior was originated by a juvenile (Ego), spread through the originator's peer group, on to their mothers, and then from those mothers to their young (Kawai 1965). Orderly spread of a behavior along social lines may not be evidence of tradition. It is surely not evidence of imitation learning.

Third, there are two parameters of the spread of sweet potato washing, generally unmentioned in published descriptions of the spread of the behavior, that lead me to suspect that social learning may have had little to do with the prevalence of sweet potato washing at Koshima. In all discussions of learning by social transmission with which I am familiar, it is assumed that an advantage of social learning over trial-and-error learning is that social learning is more rapid than trial-and-error learning. One sign of social learning should, therefore, be a relatively rapid spread of a behavior through a population.

Imo invented sweet potato washing in September of 1953, when 18 months old. At that time, there were eight members of the Koshima troop that were Imo's age or older who eventually came to wash potatoes. One of the eight, Semushi, began to wash potatoes in October of 1953. Two other troop members, Uni and Imo's mother Eba, started to do so in January of 1954. The remaining five of the eight monkeys acquiring the behavior began to wash potatoes in 1955 ($n = 1$), 1956 ($n = 2$), and 1957 ($n = 2$). Both the mean and median times to acquisition of sweet potato washing (for those who ever developed the behavior) were roughly 2 years after Imo started to demonstrate it. Such painfully slow propagation of behavior fails to provide support for the hypothesis that the behavior was learned either by imitation or by simpler forms of social learning. Wheat placer mining, a second often-cited, locale-specific behavior of the Koshima troop, spread even more slowly than did sweet potato washing (Kawai 1965; Nishida 1987)

Further, most models of social learning assume that the rate of spread of a socially transmitted behavior should increase with an increase in the number of its practitioners. In other words, the rate of recruitment to a behavior should be positively correlated with its frequency of occurrence in a population, until saturation occurs. Figure 7.1 shows, for each year from 1953 to 1958: (1) the number of monkeys in the Koshima troop old enough to sweet potato wash (i.e. >1.5 years of age), (2) the number of monkeys demonstrating sweet potato washing, and (3) the number of monkeys that learned the behavior during that year.

As can be seen in the figure, constructed from data published by Kawai (1965): (1) the pool of potential learners remained essentially constant over the years, (2) the

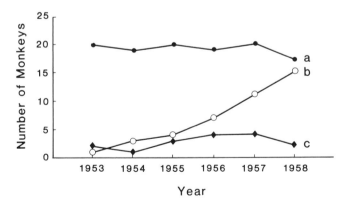

Figure 7.1
The number of monkeys at Koshima in each year from 1953 to 1958; (a) both greater than 1.5 years of age and not sweet potato washing, (b) sweet potato washing and (c) that began to wash sweet potatoes during the year. Figure prepared from data in Kawai (1965).

number of demonstrators rose dramatically, yet (3) the rate of recruitment to the behavior did not increase convincingly. These data do not suggest that social learning was responsible for the development of potato washing in the individuals that came to exhibit it.

Last, it is, perhaps, worth considering Kawai's own statement (1965: 8) of the observations that led him to suggest that social interactions were responsible for the acquisition of sweet potato washing behavior by juvenile macaques.

> Sweet potato washing monkeys eat potatoes at the edge of water. So that the potato skin is scattered around at the bottom of water. Babies, who have the experience of eating potatoes in water at the beginning of the development of feeding behavior, are conscious of the association of potato with water. In the process of learning, eating potato by picking it up out of water is to them equally on a level with eating natural food.
>
>   Being always with mothers, babies stare at their mothers' behavior while mothers are doing sweet potato washing behavior. In this manner, infants acquire sweet potato washing behavior through mothers' behavior.

The question is whether any, all, or only one of the interactions among potatoes, water, mothers, and infants mentioned by Kawai in the proceeding quotation were either necessary or sufficient for the slow spread of sweet potato washing through the Koshima troop. Simple observation does not suffice to answer the question. Surely, simple observation is not sufficient to show that imitation of one animal by another was responsible for propagation of potato-washing behavior, as so many secondary sources have suggested.

The point of all this pedantic nit-picking is not that the monkeys at Koshima did not learn to sweet potato wash either socially or by imitation. They may well have. Because the learning occurred more than 30 years ago, under conditions where the processes responsible for the spread of the behavior could not, in principle, be determined, we will never know what role social learning or learning by imitation played in the spread of potato washing at Koshima. There are, however, alternatives to social learning and imitation learning that can explain the spread of sweet potato washing through the Koshima troop: (1) each monkey acquired the behavior independently (as have monkeys elsewhere), taking an average of more than 2 years each to do so; (2) the monkeys at Koshima were individually shaped by their caretakers to wash sweet potatoes; and (3) early experience of feeding on potato scraps taken from water in some way increased the likelihood that monkeys would later bring pieces of potato to the water and wash them. Without compelling evidence that sweet potato washing was either traditional or learned by imitation, and I know of none, there is no reason to treat the behavior as a paradigmatic case both of tradition and of imitation learning, as is often done.

Conclusion

Careful observation of the behavior of many different populations of a species in the field is the only way to discover locale-specific patterns of behavior. Investigations of the ecological setting in which populations do and do not demonstrate a locale-specific behavior, physical measurements that reveal the distribution of genotypes across environments, and descriptions of social interactions that might result in propagation of a behavior are frequently the best sources of hypothesis about the causes of differences in behavior among populations. Experimentation in controlled conditions is often needed to determine whether a locale-specific behavior observed in the field can be acquired by social learning and should be considered traditional. Experimentation in the laboratory is needed to determine the types of social interaction that might permit social transmission of a traditional behavior (Galef 1990).

It is important to keep in mind that simple acquisition processes can be responsible for rather complex behavioral outcomes. Until the processes underlying the development in individuals of particular locale-specific behaviors are examined carefully, observations of locale-specific behaviors in a species, though thought-provoking, do not provide persuasive evidence either of tradition or of imitation learning. A healthy skepticism, attention to ecological detail, and a commitment to empiricism are necessary precursors to understanding of the processes leading to development of local-specific behaviors in animals.

Acknowledgements

Preparation of this manuscript was greatly facilitated by grants from the McMaster University Research Board and Natural Sciences and Engineering Research Council of Canada. I thank Mertice Clark for her help with the manuscript and Jason Kajiura for his assistance with analysis of the data from Koshima.

Literature Cited

Barnett, S. A. 1958. Experiments on "neophobia" in wild and laboratory rats. *British Journal of Psychology* 49, 195–201.

————.1968. The instinct to teach *Nature* 220, 747.

Bonner, J. T. 1980. *The Evolution of Culture in Animals.* Princeton, New Jersey: Princeton University Press.

Bowman, R. I. & Billeb, S. I. 1968. Blood-eating in a Galápagos finch. *Living Bird* 4, 29–44.

Cook, M., Mineka, S., Wolkenstein, B. & Laitsch, K. 1985. Observational conditioning of snake fear in unrelated rhesus monkeys. *Journal of Abnormal Psychology* 93, 355–372.

Curio, E., Ernst, U. & Vieth, W. 1978. Cultural transmission of enemy recognition: One function of mobbing. *Science* 202, 899–901.

Dawson, B. V. & Foss, B. M. 1965. Observational learning in budgerigars. *Animal Behaviour* 13, 470–474.

Ewer, R. F. 1969. The "instinct to teach." *Nature* 222, 698.

Galef, B. G., Jr. 1976. Social transmission of acquired behavior: A discussion of tradition and social learning in vertebrates. In: *Advances in the Study of Behavior*, Vol. 6 (ed. by J. R. Rosenblatt, R. A. Hinde, E. Shaw & C. Beer), pp. 77–99. New York: Academic Press.

————. 1977. Mechanisms for the social transmission of food preferences from adult to weanling rats. In: *Learning Mechanisms in Food Selection* (ed. by L. M. Barker, M. Best & M. Domjan), pp. 123–150. Waco, Texas: Baylor University Press.

————. 1980. Diving for Food: Analysis of a possible case of social learning in rats (Rattus norvegicus). *Journal of Comparative and Physiological Psychology* 94, 416–425.

————. 1984. Reciprocal heuristics. A discussion of the relationship of the study of learned behavior in laboratory and field. *Learning and Motivation* 15, 479–493.

————. 1985. Direct and indirect behavioral pathways to the social transmission of food avoidance. In: *Experimental Assessments and Clinical Applications of Conditioned Food Aversions* (ed. by P. Bronstein & N.S. Braveman), pp. 203–215. New York: New York Academy of Sciences.

————. 1986. Olfactory communication among rats: Information concerning distant diets. In: *Chemical Signals in Vertebrates, 4: Ecology, Evolution and Comparative Biology* (ed. by D. Duvall, D. M. Müller-Schwarze & R. M. Silverstein), pp. 487–505. New York: Plenum Press.

————. 1988. Imitation in animals: History, definition, and interpretation of data from the psychological laboratory. In: *Social Learning: Psychological and Biological Perspectives* (ed. by T. R. Zentall & B. G. Galef, Jr.), pp. 3–28. Hillsdale, New Jersey: Lawrence Erlbaum Associates.

———. 1989. Enduring social enhancement of rats' preferences for the palatable and the piquant. *Appetite* 13, 81–92.

———. 1990. An historical perspective on recent studies of social learning about foods by Norway rats. *Canadian Journal of Psychology* 44, 311–329.

———. 1991. Innovations in the study of social learning in animals: A developmental perspective. In: *Methodological and Conceptual Issues in Developmental Psychobiology* (ed. by H. N. Shair, G. A. Barr & M. A. Hofer), pp. 114–125. Oxford: Oxford University Press.

Galef, B. G., Jr. & Beck, M. 1985. Aversive and attractive marking of toxic and safe foods by Norway rats. *Behavioral and Neural Biology* 43, 298–310.

Galef, B. G., Jr. & Clark, M. 1971. Social factors in the poison avoidance and feeding behavior of wild and domesticated rat pups. *Journal of Comparative and Physiological Psychology* 75, 341–357.

Galef, B. G., Jr. & Heiber, L. 1976. The role of residual olfactory cues in the determination of feeding site selection and exploration patterns of domestic rats. *Journal of Comparative and Physiological Psychology* 90, 727–739.

Galef, B. G., Jr. & Henderson, P. W. 1972. Mother's milk: A determinant of the feeding preferences of weaning rat pups. *Journal of Comparative and Physiological Psychology* 78, 213–219.

Galef, B. G., Jr. & Sherry, D. F. 1973. Mother's milk: A medium for the transmission of cues reflecting the flavor of mother's diet. *Journal of Comparative and Physiological Psychology* 83, 374–378.

Galef, B. G., Jr. & Wigmore, S. W. 1983. Transfer of information concerning distant foods: A laboratory investigation of the "information-centre" hypothesis. *Animal Behaviour*, 31, 748–758.

Gaulin, S. J. C. & Kurland, J. A. 1976. Primate predation and bioenergetics. *Science* 191, 314–315.

Goodall, J. 1986. *The Chimpanzees of Gombe*. Cambridge, Massachusetts: Harvard University Press.

Gove, P. B. 1971. *Webster's Third New International Dictionary of the English Language Unabridged*. Springfield, Massachusetts: G. & C. Merriam Co.

Grant, P. 1986. *Ecology and Evolution of Darwin's Finches*. Princeton, New Jersey: Princeton University Press.

Green, S. 1975. Dialects in Japanese monkeys. *Zeitschrift für Tierpsychologie* 38, 305–314.

Hauser, M. D. 1988. Invention and social transmission: New data from wild vervet monkeys. In: *Machiavellian Intelligence* (ed. by R. W. Byrne & A. Whiten), pp. 327–343. Oxford: Clarendon Press.

Itani, J. & Nishimara, A. 1973. The study of infrahuman culture in Japan. *Symposium of the Fourth International Congress of Primatology: Precultural Primate Behavior*, pp. 26–50, Basel: Karger.

Kawai, M. 1965. Newly-acquired pre-cultural behavior of the natural troop of Japanese monkeys on Koshima Islet. *Primates* 6, 1–30.

Kawamura, S. 1959. The process of sub-culture propagation among Japanese macaques. *Primates* 2, 43–54.

Köster, F. & Köster, M. 1983. Twelve days among the "vampire finches" of Wolf Island. *Noticias de Galápagos* 38, 4–10.

Lack, D. 1947. *Darwin's Finches*. Cambridge: Cambridge University Press.

———. 1969. Subspecies and sympatry in Darwin's finches. *Evolution* 23, 252–263.

Lewis, C. T. & Short, C. 1969. *A Latin Dictionary*. Oxford: Clarendon Press.

Marler, P. & Tamura, M. 1964. Culturally transmitted patterns of vocal behavior in sparrows. *Science* 146, 1483–1486.

Nishida, T. 1987. Local traditions and cultural transmission. In: *Primate Societies* (ed. by B. B. Smuts, D. L. Cheney, R. M. Seyfarth, R. W. Wrangham, & T. T. Struhsaker), pp. 462–474. Chicago: University of Chicago Press.

Romanes, G. 1882. *Animal Intelligence*. London: Kegan, Paul, Tranch.

Schluter, D. & Grant, P. R. 1982. The distribution of *Geospiza difficilis* in relation to *G. fuliginosa* in the Galápagos islands: Test of three hypotheses. *Evolution* 36, 1213–1226.

———. 1984. Ecological correlates of morphological evolution in a Darwin's Finch species. *Evolution* 38, 856–869.

Sherry, D. F. & Galef, B. G., Jr. 1984. Cultural transmission without imitation: Milk bottle opening by birds. *Animal Behaviour* 32, 937–938.

Silk, J. B. 1978. Patterns of food sharing among mother and infant chimpanzees at Gombe National Park, Tanzania. *Folia Primatologica* 29, 129–141.

Steiniger, F. 1950. Beitrage zür Soziologie und sonstigen Biologie der Wanderratte. *Zeitschrift für Tierpsychologie* 7, 356–379.

Strum, S. C. 1975. Primate predation: Interim report on the development of a tradition in a troop of olive baboons. *Science* 187, 755–757.

———. 1976. Untitled. *Science* 191, 314–317.

Thorndike, E. 1898. Animal intelligence: An experimental study of the associative process in animals. *Psychological Review Monographs* 2, (Whole No. 8).

Thorpe, W. H. 1956. *Learning and Instinct in Animals.* London: Methuen.

Visalberghi, E. & Fragaszy, D. 1991. Food washing behaviour in tufted capuchin monkeys (*Cebus apella*) and crab-eating macaques (*Macaca fascicularis*). *Animal Behaviour* 40, 829–836.

Watts, D. P. 1985. Observations on the ontogeny of feeding behavior in mountain gorillas (*Gorilla gorilla beringei*) *American Journal of Primatology* 8, 1–10.

West, M. J., King, A. P. & Eastzer, D. H. 1981. The cowbird: Reflections on development from an unlikely source. *American Scientist* 69, 57–66.

Whitehead, J. M. 1986. Development of feeding selectivity in mantled howling monkeys, *Alouatta palliata*. In: *Primate Ontogeny, Cognition and Social Behaviour* (ed. by J. G. Else & P. C. Lee), pp. 105–117. *Proceedings of the 10th Congress of the International Primatological Society*, Vol. 3. Cambridge: Cambridge University Press.

Chapter 8

The Study of Adaptation

Randy Thornhill

The central problem in evolutionary biology is to elucidate the long-term process of evolution because it is this process that has produced the diversity of life. Thus it is essential to distinguish procedures that can provide direct evidence about the workings of long-term evolution from those that cannot. This essay treats teleonomy, the study of the purposeful or functional design of living systems and the directional selection pressures that have designed adaptations during long-term evolution. The study of adaptation is of fundamental importance in evolutionary biology because adaptations are information about how the long-term evolutionary process actually works; adaptations are the long-term consequences of evolution by selection and thus understanding the functional design of an adaptation is synonymous with understanding how evolution by directional selection worked over the frame of geological time to produce the adaptation. Some popular methods of analyzing adaptations cannot in themselves provide evidence useful for testing hypotheses about long-term evolution. These methods of analyzing adaptations provide information about the microevolutionary process and the action of current selection, and they yield hypotheses about long-term evolution, but when used alone they cannot elucidate the nature of long-term evolution.

The General Method of Teleonomy

The scientific study of adaptation has been called teleonomy (Pittendrigh 1958; Williams 1966) and the adaptationist program (Gould & Lewontin 1979; Symons in press). Regardless of the name attached to the study of adaptation, the field is based on the explicit recognition, elucidation and analysis of functional design in living systems. It is the complexity of functional organization of living systems and the apparent purposiveness and goal-directed nature of adaptations that attracts the attention of teleonomists. Evolutionists typically view an adaptation as any feature of an organism that performs a function or purpose "with sufficient precision, economy, efficiency, etc. to rule out pure chance as an adequate explanation" (Williams 1966: 10; also see Darwin 1859, 1874; Curio 1973; Alexander 1979; Dawkins 1982, 1986; Burian 1983; Mayr 1983; Symons 1989, 1992). Natural and sexual selection are the only scientific explanations available for the initial production and maintenance of purposeful phenotypic features, that is, adaptation. The teleonomist thus assumes that the phenotypic design that he is interested in is the long-term consequence of some type of directional selection. The hypotheses the teleonomist generates to explore the phenotypic design pertain to the nature of directional selection that may have produced it.

Teleonomic studies do not typically include analysis of the evolutionary origin of adaptations—that is, the phenotypic precursors that were modified by directional selection over long-term evolution into complex features with identifiable purposeful designs. Instead teleonomy focuses on the understanding of phenotypic design and thus the forces of selection responsible for adaptation. Both the origin and selection history of an adaptation are important to understand, but origin and selective history are different questions; the two types of questions deal with different historical causes. Many teleonomists recognize that the evolutionary purpose/function of an adaptation can be studied productively without any reference to or understanding of the adaptation's origin. However, Sherman's (1988) treatment reveals that confusion about origin versus selective history of adaptation is still a significant problem in the study of adaptation by evolutionary biologists.

The two ways by which teleonomists typically apply the hypothetico-deductive method of science (Hempel 1966) in the study of adaptation are:

1. The initial step in a very common application of teleonomic analysis is awareness of an apparent adaptation that is not understood. Recognition of an adaptation involves identification of a feature of an organism that is too complexly organized to be due to chance. The complex organization implies that the feature is not merely a byproduct of an adaptation or the product of drift; the feature is likely the product of a long evolutionary history of directional selection. (Criteria for recognizing adaptations are discussed by Sommerhoff 1950; Williams 1966; Curio 1973; Dawkins 1982, 1986; Burian 1983; Mayr 1983; Symons 1987, 1992). The recognition of an adaptation leads the teleonomist to the question "What is the adaptation's evolutionary function?" This question in turn leads to alternative hypotheses. Often detecting adaptation necessarily entails the simultaneous generation of a preliminary functional hypothesis which then leads to more specific functional questions and alternative hypotheses. The recognition of adaptation and the perception of possible function often are simultaneous events because the application of the criterion of "too complexly organized to be due to chance" frequently is based on a trait's possible purpose.

A hypothesis is a statement about presumed or possible causation. Teleonomic hypotheses attempt to identify the nature of selection that may have built an adaptation. The predictions of a hypothesis are necessary consequences of the hypothesis. By necessary consequences I mean the phenomena that must exist if the hypothesis is true, and thus if they do not exist the hypothesis is false. The predictions of a teleonomic hypothesis pertain to the functional design of an adaptation. In teleonomy each hypothesized cause, that is, each hypothesized form of directional selection (e.g. a predator of a particular type) is viewed as a potential designer of the adaptation. Functional analysis of the actual design of an adaptation tells the teleonomist which designer is most likely to have caused the evolution of the adaptation. By study of the purposeful design of an adaptation one can eliminate hypothesized designers, i.e. hypothesized selective agents. With sufficient information about the details of functional design strong conclusions can be made about the nature of historical directional selection responsible for the adaptation.

2. Another typical approach in teleonomy is similar to the first, but with the following modifications. In many cases, the investigation of phenotypic design does not begin with the observation of an adaptation that has not been explained. Instead the teleonomic study begins with the recognition of the need for an adaptation to deal with some significant ecological problem that the investigator feels is likely to have been part of the study-organism's environment for an evolutionarily relevant period of time—e.g. locating dispersed or clumped mates, or food of a particular type. The recognition of such a problem faced by an organism leads to the question, "How will the organism solve the problem?" This in turn leads to alternative hypotheses about mechanisms that might solve the ecological problem. The predictions of each hypothesis pertain to the phenotypic design that must exist if the hypothesis is correct. Tests of the predictions of alternative hypotheses result in support or falsification of the hypotheses. In this way adaptations are identified and characterized that were originally hypothetical. This form of teleonomy is typical of studies of optimal foraging (e.g. Stephens & Krebs 1986), mate searching (Parker 1984; Thornhill 1984a), sex allocation (Charnov 1982), human psychological design (Daly & Wilson 1988; Cosmides & Tooby 1989; Symons 1992) and in many other analyses of the rules organisms have evolved in solution to ecological problems that would have impinged on fitness in evolutionary history.

The long-term consequences of evolution—e.g. species, subspecies, and adaptations—hold the real facts about the pathways taken and the processes involved in evolution over geological time. If we are to understand long-term evolution, we must use Darwin's method of historical science, which he applied to problems of evolutionary causation as well as other historical *causal* issues such as the formation of coral reefs and of soil by earthworms (see Ghiselin 1969). Throughout his work Darwin used retrospective analysis of causation in order to study history scientifically. Long-term historical causes cannot be observed directly. However, the consequences of historical causation are all around us. The predictions of a hypothesis about historical cause pertain to the long-term consequences that must exist currently if the historical cause was actually in operation. Such hypotheses are falsified when their predictions are not met and are supported when their predictions are met. Application of this approach eliminates some hypothesized historical causes and provides evidence for others. Unquestionably, the actual *evidence* of how long-term evolution works can be illuminated only by examination of the long-term consequences of evolution.

The strength of teleonomic analysis, as outlined above, is that it can lead to strong inferences about the long-term process of evolution acting in nature. By "strong inference" here I mean that the two methods of teleonomy outlined above can provide actual evidence of the kind of selection that was important in long-term evolution and data that can falsify hypotheses about the kind of selection that acted over long-term evolution.

It is important to distinguish the study of the long-term outcomes of the process of natural evolution from studies of microevolution and of variation in the reproductive success of individuals. Studies of reproductive success and of microevolutionary studies may be done in the lab, the field, or in agricultural systems. By microevolutionary analysis I mean the study of phenomena such as 1) changes in the frequencies of known genes in populations, 2) genetic parameters in populations (e.g. herit-abilities of traits) and 3) artificial selection. Results from studies of microevolution and of reproductive success may provide *hypotheses* about long-term evolution (also see Betzig 1989), but results from these studies do not yield direct evidence of how the evolutionary process actually worked over the long-term to produce the diversity of life. This is why the study of adaptation is of fundamental importance in biology: teleonomic analysis provides direct evidence of how long-term evolution works because adaptations contain actual information about long-term evolution. The knowledge that we have about the kinds of directional selection that have produced adaptations represents most of our understanding of long-term evolution. I agree with Pittendrigh's (1958: 395) assessment. As he put it, "The study of adaptation is not an optional preoccupation with fascinating fragments of natural history, it is the core of biological study."

Although the two versions of teleonomy I outlined above are the typical and most productive ways to study adaptations, they are not the only ways in which adaptations are studied. I will treat other methods of teleonomy later in the paper and discuss their relationship to the two approaches outlined above. Now, I will discuss an aspect of my research in which I have applied the method of teleonomy I have emphasized. The portion of my research I have selected will serve to illustrate how the first version of the approach I have discussed is applied, and also will allow me to contrast my approach with an inappropriate teleonomic approach offered by Wade (1987).

The Abdominal Clamp of Male Scorpionflies

My analysis of functional design will focus on my study of a clamp-like structure on the dorsum of the abdomen of male, but not female, *Panorpa* scorpionflies (Mecoptera: Panorpidae) (Thornhill 1980, 1984b). The clamp is composed of two parts: a specialized section of the posterior edge of the top of abdominal segment three and a highly sclerotized spine from the anterior edge of abdominal segment four (Figure 8.1). The anterior edge of one of the female's forewings is placed in the clamp before mating. Intersegmental muscles between the third and fourth abdominal segments contract to bring the two parts of the clamp together and securely hold the female's wing during mating. Obviously, the clamp is an adaptation. It is too complexly organized for the purpose of clamping the female's wing to be a byproduct of an adaptation or the product of drift. Thus it must be the product of directional selection over the long-term of evolution. The puzzle is, "What kind of selection made it?"

Alternative hypotheses that might explain the kind of selection that produced the clamp were tested and will be discussed below. The tests favor the hypothesis that

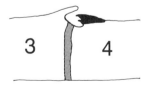

Figure 8.1
Diagram of the clamp on the top of the abdomen of male *P. latipennis*. Numbers refer to abdominal segments. The posterior portion of the clamp (inked) is more sclerotized than the anterior portion.

the evolutionary function of the clamp is forced copulation—i.e. the clamp is designed for forced mating with unwilling females. Said differently, the favored hypothesis says that variation in the clamp covaried with the fitness component, male mating success, in a specific way during the evolution of the clamp—the way being that the clamp increased male mating success via increasing the number of matings achieved by force.

Alternative Mating Tactics

Male scorpionflies have three alternative mating tactics (Thornhill 1979, 1980, 1986, 1987). Two tactics involve the feeding of the female by the male. Nuptial offerings of dead arthropods or hardened salivary masses are employed. Males with nuptial gifts release pheromone, which attracts females from a distance. The third tactic is forced copulation. In forced copulation, a male without a nuptial gift grabs a female with his genital claspers and then secures the anterior edge of one of her forewings in the abdominal clamp. The male then forcibly mates with the female. Forced copulation is not preceded by pheromone release by the male. All males are capable of using all three tactics, and adoption of each tactic is condition-dependent. Females prefer gift-giving males as mates and attempt to avoid males without gifts that will attempt forced copulation. Males must feed on dead arthropods in order to produce salivary masses. Large males have the advantage in aggressive competition for dead arthropods and therefore tend to use the alternative tactics of arthropod- and saliva-presentation more than small males. Small males primarily use forced copulation. Body size does not change after the attainment of adulthood in scorpionflies.

Tests of Hypotheses for the Clamp's Design

In a series of laboratory experiments using *Panorpa latipennis*, I studied the role of the clamp in forced and unforced copulation (Thornhill 1980, 1984b, 1987). One experiment determined whether the clamp is necessary for forced copulation (Thornhill 1980). The clamps of forty males were rendered nonfunctional by applying warmed beeswax to them. The clamps of forty control males were unaltered. All males were starved prior to the experiment so that they could not secrete saliva during the experiment. The males were not given dead arthropods to use as nuptial gifts. Thus all males were conditionally manipulated to be forced copulators. The experiment consisted of four replicates, each consisting of ten control males, ten males whose clamps were covered with beeswax, and ten receptive virgin females. The scorpionflies were individually marked. Each replicate was observed for four hours.

The results revealed that treated and control males grasped females with their genital claspers with similar frequency. However, none of the treated males secured the wing of a female in the clamp and none mated. Treated males tried to position females so as to secure their forewing in the clamp, but the females always escaped by struggling. About one-half of the control males secured the forewing of at least one female in their clamps. Eight of the forty control males succeeded in forcing copulation. Four of the eight copulating females were inseminated. (My studies indicate that females can often prevent insemination in forced copulation.) A second experiment, essentially identical to the first, provided very similar results (Thornhill 1984b). These two experiments indicate that forced copulation cannot be accomplished without an operative clamp.

Two additional experiments revealed that the clamp is not necessary for mating and insemination when males provide nuptial gifts of a salivary mass or a very small arthropod (Thornhill 1984b). The four experiments combined suggest that the clamp is designed for forced copulation.

I studied natural morphological variation in the clamp of *P. latipennis* in order to determine if males that engage in more forced copulation have clamps of a different morphology compared to males that engage in less forced copulation. Although males of all body sizes conditionally will adopt the tactic of forced copulation, small males primarily do so (Thornhill 1986, 1987). I measured the body sizes (forewing length) and the length, width and height of the posterior spine of the clamp of 60 males collected from one population over a period of a few days. The results reveal that small males have larger clamps: there are significant negative correlations between male body size and each of the three measures of size of the posterior spine of the clamp. At this time I do not know how clamp size relates functionally to the success of forced copulation by males of different size categories. Also, small males, compared to large males, possess a tooth-like structure at the base of the posterior spine (see Figure 8.1), but the role of the tooth in mating is unknown. Thus males that primarily use forced copulation, i.e. small males, have significantly different clamps than males that use forced copulation less often. This analysis of natural variation in the size and structure of the clamp provides additional evidence to that of the experiments that the clamp's evolutionary function is forced copulation.

I examined four additional hypotheses that might explain the reason the clamp evolved. I have suggested that the clamp functions to prevent disruption of copulating pairs and the insemination of the female of the pair by an intruding male (Thornhill 1974). A fundamental prediction about the functional design of the clamp from this hypothesis was not supported: In a lab experiment, copulating males with treated clamps and copulating males with normal clamps experienced equal rates of copulation disruption and mate take over by intruding males (Thornhill 1984b). Apparently, the clamp does not reduce the probability of a copulating pair being disrupted by intruders.

The clamp is not a source of a male pheromone, as suggested by Felt (1895). Histological studies I have conducted reveal no glandular tissue in the vicinity of the clamp (Thornhill 1984b). It might be suggested that the clamp functions in sexual or species visual recognition. However, the clamp does not show the design features that the sexual or species recognition hypotheses require. The clamp typically is not visible to females during courtship, because the males' wings are held roof-like over the abdomen. Also, in addition to the male-produced pheromone, male scorpionflies have numerous sexually differentiated and very visible morphological features that are species-specific and thus could serve as features that identify sex and species (see Thornhill 1984b).

The results of my studies of the clamp support the hypothesis that its evolutionary purpose is forced copulation.

Wade's Alternative Method of Teleonomy

Wade (1987) recently has criticized my interpretation of the results from the first experiment (Thornhill 1980) I described above in which I concluded that the clamp is essential for forced copulation and may be designed for forced copulation. His critique also applies to my repetition of the experiment (Thornhill 1984b) because techniques and results were virtually identical. Using techniques for measuring current selection acting in populations that he and his colleagues have developed (Wade

& Arnold 1980; Lande & Arnold 1983; Arnold & Wade 1984), Wade calculated from the data of the first experiment that only 11% of "the total opportunity for selection" on males is focused on the presence or absence of the abdominal clamp. He concluded that there is weak selection on the presence vs. the absence of the clamp in *Panorpa*. Wade's calculation of weak selection derives from the fact that there was great variation in copulation-success among the males with functionally normal clamps. If the data from the two experiments are combined only nineteen of eighty males (24%) with normal clamps mated. Wade (1987: 204) uses this example to emphasize that, "Hypothesis testing [what I did] and parameter measurement [measuring the strength of current selection] on the same data set do not always lead to the same evolutionary inferences." Apparently, Wade feels that the magnitude of current selection on a trait determines the inferences that can be made about evolutionary function.

The research Wade criticizes was done as part of a research program to determine the functional design of the clamp. Specifically, the part he criticized was done to determine if males without a functional clamp could mate when they did not have resources to offer females, but employed forced copulation behavior. The answer is no. In thirty-two hours (the results of the two experiments combined) not a single male of eighty males with nonfunctional clamp's mated; however, nineteen of eighty normal males mated. Clearly, the clamp is necessary for mating when males do not possess nuptial gifts.

For the following reasons, I feel the tentative conclusion that the clamp's evolutionary function is forced copulation is warranted: a) the results showing that the clamp *per se* (and not a correlated trait) is necessary for mating when males do not provide a resource and use forced copulation behavior, b) the results showing that the clamp is unnecessary for mating and insemination when males provide resources to mates, c) the results revealing the correlation between use of the clamp and the clamp's structure within a species and d) the results that seriously question the alternative functional hypotheses not involving forced copulation.

Note that a) demonstrates the existence of current selection on the clamp in the context of the artificial variation in the lab experiments. That is, the presence versus absence of the clamp causally influences male mating success. The demonstration of current selection associated with artificial experimental variation was only an incidental aspect of my study of the design of the clamp.

Wade's approach of inferring evolutionary function from the *strength* of current selection is problematic. The strength of current selection on the clamp (and other adaptations) will be variable, sometimes relatively weak or nonexistent and sometimes relatively strong. My research on the mating system of *Panorpa* has revealed that small females are the primary targets of forced copulations (Thornhill 1987), and the abundance of small females is variable in space and time. Also, the success of forced copulation, compared to unforced copulation, depends on the extent of competition within and between *Panorpa* species for dead arthropods (Thornhill 1979, 1986, 1987), which varies considerably within seasons and between seasons and populations. Wade's approach would only allow forced copulation as the evolutionary function of the clamp when current selection on the clamp is strong in some arbitrarily defined sense. If it were shown that the current selection on visual ability in humans in the USA is weak, because of the availability of eyeglasses and other ophthalmic technology, it would be ludicrous to conclude that the evolutionary function of the human eye in the USA is not vision.

My most fundamental criticism of Wade's approach is that it totally misunderstands the problem in the study of adaptation. The problem that the teleonomist strives to solve is the evolutionary purpose of complexly organized traits of individual organisms. The problem of the evolutionary purpose of an adaptation is solved only when its true functional design is elucidated. Such elucidation demonstrates how the trait covaried with fitness in the environment of evolutionary adaptation and thus the nature of directional selection that produced the adaptation. It is usually inappropriate to make conclusions about evolutionary function solely on the basis of information about the mere presence or nature of current selection on an adaptation. Because of changed current environments, compared to the environment in which an adaptation evolved, the variation (natural or experimentally-induced) of an adaptation may be unrelated to variation in either total fitness or any fitness component, or the adaptation may be related to an evolutionarily novel fitness component. Even if human visual ability in the USA were unrelated to survival and all other fitness components, the physiology, biochemistry and morphology of the human eye would demonstrate that its evolutionary purpose is vision. (Incidentally, this means that the presence or absence of current selection on an adaptation cannot be used to distinguish effects of adaptations [byproducts of adaptations, Williams 1966] from actual adaptations.) It is never appropriate to make inferences about evolutionary function on the basis of the strength of selection on an adaptation. In current environments the variation in an adaptation may show a correlation with a fitness component that was not the important fitness correlation during the evolution of the adaptation. Thus, regardless of how strong a form of current selection on an adaptation may be, that form of selection may have had nothing to do with the production of the adaptation during evolutionary history.

The study of the current selection on an adaptation and the study of the evolutionary function of the adaptation are philosophically different endeavors in terms of how results from each bear on the elucidation of long-term evolution. I will explore this in some detail later in this essay. Here I want to emphasize that the kind of directional selection that designed an adaptation can only be addressed directly via tests of alternative hypotheses about the functional design of the adaptation-elucidating by hypothesis testing the details of how the adaptation works to allow its bearers to cope with an environmental problem. The nature of current selection on an adaptation (but never the magnitude of selection) can be an important piece of evidence about an adaptation's design, but more information than current selection is needed because of the problems in interpretation of data on current selection mentioned in the previous paragraph.

This framework for studying historical directional selection is especially productive when coupled with analysis of functional design using the comparative method to test hypotheses about the evolved diversity in adaptation. (For discussion of the strengths and weaknesses of the comparative method, and other methods such as experimentation, see Thornhill 1984c; also for discussion of the comparative method see Ridley 1983; Pagel & Harvey 1988.) Both the analysis of the phenotypic design of an adaptation and the study of the diversity of adaptation yield actual evidence about historical selection, because these approaches characterize the long-term phenotypic consequences of selection.

Direct Methods of Teleonomic Analysis

Teleonomy is the study of evolutionary purpose. Each of the methods discussed in this section can falsify hypotheses about long-term evolution and provide actual evidence about the nature of directional selection that has been important in long-term evolution because the methods are focused on illuminating phenotypic design. I refer to such methods as direct.

Modern teleonomists realize the important role of selection theory in directing them to observations that would be overlooked in the absence of the theory. Some understanding of sexual selection theory, for example, is essential for deriving the hypothesis that the clamp of male *Panorpa* is an adaptation to forced copulation. This hypothesis has led to some unique discoveries about the clamp. The primary value of theory in evolutionary science, as in any other science, is to render phenomena discoverable that otherwise would not be. Thus the usefulness of a scientific theory can be measured by the discoveries it provides. Evolution by selection is a very useful theory by this criterion: It continually leads biologists to new findings about life (e.g. see recent issues of *The American Naturalist, Animal Behaviour, Ethology,* or *Evolution*).

In general the theory of evolution by selection is used in the study of adaptations in the two ways outlined earlier in the essay, coupled with comparative analysis of the distribution of adaptations across taxa in relation to hypothesized selective agents. These ways of using selection theory to study adaptations might be called the standard approach of teleonomy, because it is the most commonly employed form of teleonomic analysis. For example, about 75% of the papers in the issue of the journal *Animal Behaviour* that happens to be beside my computer (Volume 36, 6, Nov./Dec. 1988) use what I have called the standard teleonomic approach. This is the approach that C. Darwin (e.g. 1859, 1874) developed: It involves analysis of phenotypic design in order to elucidate a predicted evolutionary function and thus support the expected selection responsible for the design. Darwin's approach combined testing hypotheses about the functional design of adaptations with comparative analysis of the taxonomic distribution of adaptations. (See for example Darwin's [1874] discussion of evidence that male ornamental features function in sexual competition among males; also see Ghiselin's 1969 discussion of Darwin's approach in studying evolution.)

This standard approach to teleonomy has been used as the basis for developing other very important direct methods for analyzing adaptations. As mentioned earlier, the study of current selection can provide evidence of functional design and thus evidence of the historical selection responsible for the design. The evidence that identifies causal current selection on an adaptation is the evidence for the adaptation's functional design. For example, the experimental evidence that the clamp of male scorpionflies itself causes variation in male mating success in the context of forced copulation is part of the evidence for the clamp's design for forced copulation. However, for reasons mentioned above, more information than current causal selection on a trait is necessary to identify adaptation and to elucidate the evolutionary purpose of adaptation. Furthermore, the identification of causal selection on a trait can be extremely difficult. Most commonly, the results of studies of current selection demonstrate selection but do not demonstrate the trait upon which selection is focused (e.g. most chapters in Clutton-Brock 1988); such studies do not provide evidence of functional design. I will treat the study of current selection in general in the next section, which deals with indirect methods of teleonomic analysis—that is, methods that in themselves do not provide direct evidence of functional design. I delay the discussion because a somewhat lengthy evaluation is needed to distinguish the analysis of causal selection on a trait, a direct method of teleonomic analysis, from the study of variation in individual reproduction in general.

The evolutionarily stable strategy (ESS) approach (reviewed in Maynard Smith 1982) is a direct method for study of adaptation. It is specifically formulated to provide hypotheses for the evolution of adaptations by frequency-dependent selection. Said differently, ESS hypotheses attempt to identify and characterize the phenotypic design that has arisen due to long-term frequency-dependent selection. A set of strategies (phenotypes) is envisioned and their relative fitness depends on the use of the strategies in the population. This approach is based on optimality. It determines the theoretical solution, the evolutionarily stable strategy or mixture of stable strategies, i.e. the "optimum" or best, under frequency-dependent selection.

The ESS approach in studies of adaptations may or may not involve mathematics as an accessory tool. Fisher's (1958) hypothesis about the evolution by selection of the equal investment by parents in sons and daughters is an example of a non-mathematical evolutionary hypothesis based on ESS reasoning (see Parker 1984). Fisher envisioned the hypothetical circumstance of numerical disparity of the sexes of offspring as a phenotype of parental reproduction that was an alternative to the parental strategy of production of equal numbers of sons and daughters. Later Hamilton (1967) used ESS reasoning to formulate his successful hypothesis for the evolution of female-biased sex ratios under inbreeding. The ESS approach was made highly mathematical in the 1970s by the application of game theory to evolutionary problems involving frequency-dependent selection (Maynard Smith & Price 1973). The ESS approach has been especially valuable in providing useful hypotheses about phenotypic design associated with contesting resources (e.g. Austad 1983) and mating (see Parker 1984).

Another important direct method of teleonomy also incorporates a mathematical optimality approach in the study of adaptations (e.g. MacArthur & Pianka 1966; Charnov 1976; Stephens & Krebs 1986). This approach, sometimes called optimality theory, provides hypotheses that attempt to elucidate the kind of selection that has produced adaptations for coping with fixed environmental problems, that is, when the fitness of hypothetical phenotypes under selection is not frequency-dependent. It has proven its value, especially in successful prediction of foraging adaptations (Stephens & Krebs 1986).

The standard teleonomic approach, the analysis of current selection on an adaptation, and the two versions of optimality mentioned above typically ignore the nature of genetic control of phenotypic design. Although the ignoring of the genetic control of adaptations by teleonomists has been criticized by Lewontin (1978), this is not a general problem in teleonomy (e.g. see Grafen 1984; Stephens & Krebs 1986). Cases where genetics might make a difference in the teleonomist's hypothesizing (e.g. overdominance) probably are rare (Maynard Smith 1982; Grafen 1984). Of course, any time a phenotypic feature meets the criteria of an adaptation (see above), the very existence of the feature demonstrates that there was heritability in the trait in the evolutionary past.

The final direct teleonomic approach is based explicitly on genetics. This approach provides hypotheses based on the dynamics of gene frequencies that may be brought about by selection. Genetical modeling of the evolution of phenotypes continues to make important contributions to the understanding of the evolved design of living systems. For example, Hamilton & Zuk's (1982) parasite hypothesis of sexual selection, which is based on the dynamics of gene frequencies in parasites and their hosts under frequency-dependent selection, has led to a number of novel findings about the signal content and thus the design of sexual displays of birds (Hamilton & Zuk 1982; Read 1987; Zuk 1991; Zuk et. al. 1990) and fish (Ward 1988; McMinn 1990).

In sum, each of the teleonomic procedures discussed above are direct methods for study of evolutionary purpose, because each can characterize phenotypic design and thereby can yield actual evidence that can be used to refute or support hypotheses about the kind of selection that was important in long-term evolution. Unquestionably, these methods work in the sense that matters in science—that is, they lead to discoveries about phenotypic design and thus about the selection responsible for the design. Just because the procedures work, it does not follow that they are perfect and not in need of refinement. As Williams (1966: 260) pointed out over 20 years ago:

> How, ultimately, does one ascertain the function of a biological mechanism? ... I have assumed, as in customary, that functional design is something that can be intuitively comprehended by an investigator and convincingly communicated to others. Although this may often be true, I suspect that progress in teleonomy will soon demand a standardization of criteria for demonstrating adaptation, and a formal terminology for its description.

It would seem that a formal system for recognizing and describing phenotypic design is urgently needed in biology given that the concept of adaptation is fundamental for understanding long-term evolution.

Indirect Methods of Teleonomy

There are other methods used in the study of adaptation. I emphasize that I am not saying that the methods discussed in this section are unscientific. They are used with the hypothetico-deductive model and thus meet scientific standards. Nor am I saying that the methods do not provide interesting and valuable information about organisms. Our understanding of natural history has been advanced significantly by each of the methods discussed below. Nor am I saying that the methods below do not yield hypotheses that lead to better understanding of long-term natural evolution; they do. My point about the so-called indirect methods is that, without the assistance of the direct methods discussed above, they do not allow quality inferences about long-term evolution. In contrast, each of the direct methods can provide actual evidence for or against a hypothesis about long-term evolution. All the indirect teleonomic methods comprise studies of microevolution or reproductive success.

Artificial Selection

As Williams (1985) has pointed out with respect to studies of artificial selection, the findings of such studies—Williams mentioned Wade's (1976) lab research on artificial group selection in flour beetles as an example—can provide only hypotheses of how evolution might have worked over geological time but never actual evidence of the action of long-term evolution in nature. Williams' point applies to Wade's results because Wade studied artificial selection and not because the research was done in the lab. Evolution in nature proceeds in an open system over the long-term. The openness of gene pools means that the events that would be necessary for foretelling the future long-term course of evolution are unpredictable. Which mutations will occur is not predictable; nor is the nature of the environment that will impinge on any population in the long-term future predictable. Thus we cannot know the future availability of genetic raw material or future adaptations and evolutionary constraints that would be necessary for predicting future long-term evolution. Similarly, because evolution proceeds in an open system it is impossible to determine if the specific events that contribute to the occurrence of a particular form of current evolution (e.g. evolution by group selection in flour beetles in the lab) held in the evolutionary past.

Wade's (1976) results suggest how long-term evolution might work to provide a hypothesis about long-term evolution. The hypothesis that group selection has been effective in producing adaptations during long-term evolution is testable only by determination of whether the long-term phenotypic consequences of such a process are present in nature. That is, do we see the stamp of a history of group selection in the phenotypes of organisms? Examination of organisms for evidence of phenotypic design indicative of effective group selection reveals that the process has not been important in shaping adaptation (see especially Williams 1985; also Williams 1966; Dawkins 1982, 1986; Alexander 1979, 1987; Thornhill & Alcock 1983; and many others).

I'm not arguing that knowledge about artificial selection is unimportant for our general understanding of long-term evolution. For example, knowledge of artificial selection apparently helped Darwin clarify his ideas about the role of natural and sexual selection in long-term evolution. Darwin argued that the phenotypic consequences of artificial selection are analogous to the phenotypic consequences of selection generated by nonhuman agents during long-term evolution. Also, the results from studies of artificial selection since Darwin's time demonstrate that microevolution occurs by selection. (Darwin's "demonstration" of selection was by deduction from the fact of high reproductive output and the inevitability of nonrandom mortality of individuals that must follow given the stability of populations.) Thus work on artificial selection has been essential in clarifying the general conceptual connection between the microevolutionary process of evolution and the long-term historical process of evolution.

I am arguing that results from studies of artificial selection that demonstrate or falsify a particular microevolutionary process cannot be viewed as evidence for or against the same process in long-term evolution. However, such results may lead to valuable hypotheses about long-term evolution.

The work on senescence in *Drosophila* by Rose & Charlesworth (1980) can be used to clarify points about artificial selection touched on above. Williams (1957) hypothesized that senescence is the inevitable evolutionary consequence of the pleiotropic effects of alleles with positive fitness effects early in life and negative effects late in life. Genes may have many effects, some positive and some negative. Selection favors alleles whose net effect is more positive than alternative alleles. Williams argued that senescence is the maladaptive result of selection of alleles whose negative effects are expressed late in life. The *Drosophila* study revealed an evolutionary response to artificial selection for later high rates of reproduction and a correlated evolutionary response in delay of onset of senescence. This result suggests that the kind of pleiotropic genes Williams' hypothesis requires do indeed exist. There is a genetic correlation, apparently due to pleiotropy, between late reproduction and delayed senescence. However, the evolutionary response in the study was a micro-evolutionary response, and therefore cannot be viewed as providing evidence for William's view of the evolution of senescence in long-term evolution. The evolutionary response in the study however does suggest that the hypothetical scenario envisioned by Williams possibly could apply to long-term evolution.

Williams' hypothesis can best be tested by deriving the predicted long-term phenotypic consequences of the evolutionary process that the hypothesis contains and then determining if these consequences are actually manifested in senescence. Senescence is not an adaptation but it is a product of long-term evolution, and therefore the evolutionary process that produced it can be understood by detailed analysis of the nature of the phenotypic responses that occur during senescence (for discussion of the kind of evidence most useful for testing Williams' hypothesis see Williams 1957; Hamilton 1966; Bell 1984; Alexander 1987).

Reproductive Success

A currently popular form of evolutionary study involves measurement of the extent of current variation in reproductive performance among individuals. This approach was the basis of Wade's analysis of the selection acting on the abdominal clamp of male scorpionflies discussed above. Another example is the collection of papers, edited by Clutton-Brock (1988), reporting measurement of variation in reproductive success of individuals of numerous animal species over a large part of their lives. Grafen (1988) pointed out in his paper in Clutton-Brock's edited collection that the contributors to the book are interested to an important extent in understanding adaptations of the animals whose lives they are studying. Grafen's paper provides a detailed critique of analyzing adaptation by study of individual variation in reproduction. Symons (1989; 1992) has provided important papers dealing with the erroneous notion that human adaptations can best be understood by study of current variation in individual reproductive success. Williams (1966) and Stephens & Krebs (1986) also have criticized briefly this approach in the study of adaptation. I will briefly cover some of the points discussed in these critiques and raise some additional problems associated with teleonomic studies that are based on individual variation in reproduction.

Studies of individual variation in reproduction take two forms:

1. Mere differential reproduction among individuals does not demonstrate the action of current selection, because selection is *nonrandom* differences in reproduction (see below). Reproductive variance among individuals may be random with regard to phenotypic differences and thus due to drift rather than selection. Sutherland (1985) has shown that the data from Bateman's well known study of variation in reproductive success in *Drosophila melanogaster* cannot be distinguished from a random pattern. Also, studies of mere differentials in reproduction say nothing about phenotypic design and therefore nothing about adaptation and long-term evolution. As Williams (1966: 159) so appropriately put it, "measuring reproductive success focuses attention on the rather trivial problem of the degree to which an organism actually achieves reproductive survival. The central biological problem is not survival as such, but design for survival."

2. Data on individual variance in reproductive performance may identify selection in action—that is, the occurrence of nonrandom differential reproduction of individuals. Note that my definition of selection does not include an evolutionary response to selection. Evolution typically is defined as any change in the frequency of genes in a population. Evolution may result from any agent of evolution (drift, mutation, migration, or selection). Defining selection in terms of changes in gene frequency resulting from nonrandom individual reproduction (e.g. Endler 1986) confuses selection, a phenotypic event, with evolution, a genetic event. As pointed out by Fisher (1958) selection is not evolution (also see Arnold 1983; Lande & Arnold 1983; Wade 1987).

The action of current selection is demonstrated: 1) by a correlation between trait variation and some fitness-related measure such as mating success or survival, or 2) when there is repeatability in the performance of individuals in some fitness-related measure in the absence of a detectable correlation between phenotypic trait variation and individual performance. An example of 2) is McVey's (1988) demonstration that males of a dragonfly species when experimentally forced to reestablish a territory obtain a territory that yields a positive correlation with their original territory in terms of reproductive success. Thus variance in male reproductive success was due to variance in male competitive ability, even though McVey could not determine which aspects of male phenotype were important. Either 1) or 2) is sufficient to demonstrate nonrandom variation in the reproductive performance of individuals.

A demonstration of selection by 1), however, does not identify the trait that correlates with fitness-related variation as the actual focus of selection, because other traits that may correlate with the trait may be the causal source of variation in nonrandom individual reproduction. Grafen's (1988) paper mentioned above deals in detail with the important problem of correlated traits in the study of current selection (also see Arnold 1983; Lande & Arnold 1983; Endler 1986: 162–165; Mitchell-Olds & Shaw 1987; Crespi & Bookstein 1989). Grafen emphasizes the important role of experimentation in untangling a trait that is thought to correlate with fitness from known or unknown correlations with other traits.

This is why I created experimentally a category of male scorpionflies without functional clamps. This manipulation allowed examination of the role of the clamp itself in forced copulation, uncomplicated by variation in other features (behavioral, morphological, physiological, etc.) that might correlate with natural variation in the clamp and confound my results on the functional design of the clamp for use in forced mating. Note that my reason for manipulating the clamp was to provide evidence of its evolutionary function, and in the course of the experiment, causal sexual selection on the clamp was demonstrated incidentally; that is, variation in the clamp (functional versus nonfunctional in the experiments) caused a difference in male mating success. Indeed any time an adaptation is experimentally manipulated the real question is evolutionary purpose/functional design and not current selection.

Some traits are very hard to manipulate experimentally. In these cases, only by detailed functional analysis, characteristic of the field of functional morphology (e.g. Altenbach 1979), can it be demonstrated that a trait is causally related to selection. The primary question in such analyses pertains to phenotypic design and not the action of current selection.

The demonstration of causal current selection on an adaptation, by experimental manipulation or detailed functional analysis, can identify phenotypic design and thus results from such studies bear directly on the kind of selection that produced the adaptation. Studies of current selection become relevant to the issue of adaptation only when functional design is analyzed—that is, only when causal current selection is detected. Otherwise, a study of current selection has limited significance: such information alone does not contribute to a better understanding of the long-term process of evolution in nature although it may lead to hypotheses that can be tested. As Symons (1989: 132) put it "In modern evolutionary biology, an adaptation is usually considered to be an aspect of a phenotype ... that was designed by natural selection to serve a specific function ... hence, to the extent that one fails to describe or characterize phenotypic design, one fails to describe or characterize adaptation."

The issue in teleonomy is not the existence of current selection in natural populations; nor the magnitude of current selection in natural populations; nor the extent of causal current selection on adaptations; nor whether adaptations are related causally to current selection. Clearly, evidence of a causal relationship of a trait to selection may provide evidence of phenotypic design and thus evidence of historical directional selection. However, for reasons mentioned above, this evidence is not the only evidence of interest, nor is it the most informative of historical selection. Other information about the adaptation's design beyond the existence and nature of current selection on the adaptation is essential for determining whether the adaptation evolved in the selective context indicated by data on its current covariation with fitness.

Thus I would disagree with the emphasis in Arnold's (1983: 347) interesting paper on the measurement of current selection acting on adaptations. He states:

> My thesis in this paper is that it is possible to measure adaptive significance directly. In particular it is possible to characterize statistically the relationship between fitness and morphology in natural populations. One can argue that this statistical approach constitutes the highest grade of evidence for selection and adaptation.

I have argued that methods other than measurement of selection on adaptations address adaptive significance directly. Also, I have argued that measurement of selection on adaptations does not "constitute the highest grade of evidence for ... adaptation." Finally, I have argued that measurement of selection on adaptations may not provide any evidence at all for adaptations.

I would agree completely however with the following point made by Arnold (1983: 347):

> Despite its virtues measurements of selection should not be considered a substitute for other modes of attack on adaptive significance. Direct analysis of selection will be most valuable when it is combined with analytical studies of function and with comparative studies that describe the scope of evolution. Likewise, inferences from functional and comparative studies will be strengthened by companion studies of selection....

The fundamental issue in teleonomy is, "How did an adaptation of interest relate to fitness during the evolution of the adaptation?" This question is the same as "What is the evolutionary purpose of an adaptation?" The answer can be determined directly only by analysis of the functional design of an adaptation, and such analyses may include measurement of current selection on an adaptation.

Although evidence of causal current selection on an adaptation can provide evidence of the adaptation's evolutionary purpose, I suggest that studies in evolutionary biology that emphasize the identification and characterization of current selection are important primarily for the following two reasons. First, the demonstration of current selection of a particular form suggests the possibility that the same selection may have operated in long-term evolution. Such a demonstration then may give some credibility to a hypothesis about long-term evolution resulting from the same selection. This is useful because the relative credibility of alternative hypotheses about the selection that acted in long-term evolution is important to assess in determining research priorities for testing alternative hypotheses. For example, many hypotheses have been proposed to explain how sexual selection works in long-term evolution (review in Bradbury & Andersson 1987). Studies of the current action of sexual selection may be helpful in determining how evolutionary biologists should proceed in prioritizing for testing the numerous hypotheses for long-term evolution by sexual selection. Second, studies of current selection sometimes yield hypotheses about the effective selection that may have operated in long-term evolution that might not be realized otherwise (see e.g. Howard 1988; also Chapter 29 by Clutton-Brock in Clutton-Brock 1988).

Genetic Parameters

The final category of indirect analysis of adaptation I will discuss is the empirical evaluation of genetic parameters of populations. Recently this approach has focused on the measurement of the genetic basis of life history characters (e.g. Rose & Charlesworth 1980; Dingle & Hegmann 1982) and traits related to sexual selection (e.g. Majerus et al. 1982). I will not argue here that evolutionary ideas that are explicitly genetical are all indirect analyses of adaptation. Recall that I emphasized earlier that hypotheses for long-term evolution that are based on the dynamics of hypothetical genetic alternatives represent a direct approach in teleonomy. I do feel that although the measurement of genetic parameters of populations is a useful tool in the overall effort to solve the problems of long-term evolution, it is not the panacea. Thus I disagree with Lande's (1987: 83) statement that "Salient features of sexual selection and the evolution of sexual dimorphism can be understood *only* through the study of genetic mechanisms." (emphasis added) Genetic correlations between the sexes are the genetic mechanisms that Lande argues will elucidate sexual selection and sexual dimorphism. Lande is a geneticist and it is not surprising that he is enthusiastic about genetics. Lewontin is also a geneticist, and he (1978) apparently feels that it is essential for teleonomists to become geneticists. Enthusiasm about one's own field usually is a good thing. However, the view that the field of genetics is synonymous with modern evolutionary science is erroneous and ignores many excellent evolutionary studies.

I suggest that the major empirical contribution of geneticists to the understanding of evolution will not derive from measuring genetic parameters such as genetic correlations or heritabilities of traits or from measuring changes in the frequencies of genes in populations. Such studies do provide interesting information about the natural history of organisms, and we are much better off with this information than without it. The same can be said about all facts of natural history. Information about the genetic parameters of traits and microevolution in a species is as interesting as information about what the species eats, season of breeding, etc.; any fact of natural history may lead to useful hypotheses about long-term natural evolution and can falsify or support these hypotheses if studied to test their predictions.

My guess is that the major empirical contribution of genetics to the understanding of long-term evolution will derive from teleonomic analysis of the functional design of genetic adaptations. Genetic adaptations are as important to understand as other categories of adaptations, because all adaptations are the long-term consequences of selection in nature. The only way to understand the way selection has worked on genetic systems is by discovery of the nature of the design of genetic systems.

Consider the following example. Lande (1987) argues that variation in sexual dimorphism in sexually-selected traits across species should coincide with the degree of pleiotropic genetic correlation of the traits. He offers this as an explanation for the pattern of "transference" of male secondary sexual characters to females discovered by Darwin (1874). Empirically this idea can be tested by measuring, in a group like the Phasianidae (pheasants), the degree of genetic correlation between the sexes in features such as morphological ornaments that may be expressed in both sexes. Lande would expect that the magnitude of the genetic correlation will correlate positively with the similarity of the sexes in ornamentation, because his hypothesis for transference assumes limited or ineffective selection on the postulated genetic mechanisms. The view that genetic systems reflect fine-tuned adaptation to the same degree as the morphological and physiological features of individuals (also see Trivers 1988: 271–272) would suggest a different and more encompassing line of research on sexual dimorphism than Lande's perspective: If the empirical finding was against Lande's hypothesis, more research would be needed to determine how the genetic systems across species of phasianids proximately regulate the expression of genes for ornaments in relation to the sex of the individual. If the empirical finding favored Lande's hypothesis, the same research just mentioned would be needed. That is, viewing genomes as highly evolved adaptive systems would lead to questions about the design of the genetic adaptations for sexual dimorphism.

The diversity in the phenotypic expression of features in both sexes in groups like the phasianids ranges from sexual uniformity to restricted to only one sex. Even within single species certain features are "transferred" and others are not. The question is why? (For example, the red jungle fowl, *Gallus gallus*, hen has a small comb compared to the large comb of the rooster. The hen lacks the other ornaments of males.) I suggest that this diversity in sex-limited control of traits reflects the diversity of adaptations of the genetic systems involved.

Genetic correlations are often viewed by geneticists as mere constraints on long-term evolution (e.g. Lande 1987). In its most naive form this view confuses proximate and ultimate levels of causation. Genetic correlations, indeed all properties of living systems, are constraints on long-term evolution in only one sense: Selection will act on what evolution in the past has produced. Genetic correlations and other complex genetic properties may be most appropriately viewed as an aspect of the evolved design of genetic systems, a perspective that suggests very different questions about genetic features than would be asked in descriptive quantitative genetics.

I will make one final comment on the recent flurry of interest in quantitative genetics among evolutionary biologists. Some evolutionary biologists that I have discussed the matter with apparently feel that if all the genetic parameters and current selective forces in a natural system are empirically documented, future evolution in the system should be predictable. It is conceivable that such an approach may sometimes work over the short-term, although the thorough understanding of all the forces of selection, heritabilities, genetic correlations. etc. that would be necessary is mind-boggling. However, it would not be wise to attempt to predict long-term future evolution from knowledge of current genetic parameters and selection for the reasons mentioned earlier.

Conclusions

The central problem in evolutionary biology is to understand the long-term process of evolution in nature. Thus it is essential to distinguish the direct from the indirect methods of analyzing long-term evolution. There are several methods used in teleonomy, the study of adaptations. The functional design of an adaptation provides the relevant evidence of the kind of directional selection responsible for the adaptation. Methods that do not elucidate the purposeful design of phenotypic traits do not provide direct evidence of the ultimate causation of adaptation. The standard approach used in teleonomy today, the Darwinian approach, has been modified to form the basis of optimality theory, evolutionarily stable strategy theory, genetic modelling of the evolution of adaptation, and the study of causal current selection acting on adaptation. All these approaches analyze phenotypic design and thus yield evidence directly relevant to illuminating long-term evolution, specifically the selection that produced phenotypic design.

Some popular methods of analyzing adaptation do not focus on phenotypic design and therefore do not actually address adaptation directly. These indirect methods of analyzing adaptation focus on microevolution and on variation in reproductive performance of individuals, as opposed to long-term outcomes of evolution. Microevolutionary questions are addressed by studies involving: artificial selection; tallies of changes in the frequencies of identifiable genes in populations; and measures of the genetic parameters of populations. Microevolutionary analyses and studies characterizing the current selection acting in populations may lead to testable hypotheses about long-term evolution, but alone they cannot provide evidence of how evolution actually works over the long-term.

I suggest that the major empirical contribution of the field of genetics to the understanding of long-term evolution will derive from teleonomic analysis of the functional design of genetic adaptations.

Acknowledgements

I am grateful to M. Daly, M. Bekoff, L. Betzig, D. Jamieson, W. Kuipers, R. Pierotti, P. Stacey, D. Symons, F. Taylor and an anonymous reviewer for useful comments on the manuscript. Discussion about methodology with M. Daly, W. Kuipers, P. Stacey, D. Symons, F. Taylor, P. Watson, M. Wilson, M. Zuk, and especially N. W. Thornhill were helpful. My research on scorpionflies discussed in this essay was supported by grants from the National Science Foundation. I also acknowledge support from NSF grant BSR-8515377, the H. F. Guggenheim Foundation, and Paul Risser, Vice President of Research, University of New Mexico.

Literature Cited

Alexander, R. D. 1979. *Darwinism and Human Affairs.* Seattle, Washington: University of Washington Press.

————. 1987. *The Biology of Moral Systems.* New York: Aldine de Gruyter.

Altenbach, J. S. 1979. *Locomotion Morphology of the Vampire Bat, Desmodes rotundus. Special Publications of the American Society of Mammalogists* Number 6.

Arnold, S. J. 1983. Morphology, performance and fitness. *American Zoologist* 23, 347–361.

Arnold, S. J. & Wade, M. J. 1984. On the measurement of natural and sexual selection: Theory. *Evolution* 38, 709–719.

Austad, S. N. 1983. A game theoretical interpretation of male combat in the bowl and doily spider, *Frontinella pyramitela. Animal Behaviour* 31, 59–73.

Bell, G. 1984. Evolutionary and nonevolutionary theories of senescence. *American Naturalist* 124, 600–603.

Betzig, L. 1989. Rethinking human ethology: A response to some recent critiques. *Ethology and Sociobiology* 10, 315–324.

Bradbury, J. W. & Andersson, M. B. (eds.) 1987. *Sexual Selection: Testing the Alternatives.* New York: John Wiley and Sons.

Burian, R. M. 1983. Adaptation. In: *Dimensions of Darwinism: Themes and Counterthemes in 20th Century Evolutionary Theory* (ed. by M. Grene). pp. 287–314. Cambridge: Cambridge University Press.

Charnov, E. L. 1976. Optimal foraging: the marginal value theorem. *Theoretical Population Biology* 9, 129–136.

————. 1982. *The Theory of Sex Allocation.* Princeton, New Jersey: Princeton University Press.

Clutton-Brock, T. H. (ed.) 1988. *Reproductive Success: Studies of Individual Variation in Contrasting Breeding Systems.* Chicago, Illinois: University of Chicago Press.

Cosmides, L. & Tooby, J. 1989. Evolutionary psychology and the generation of culture, Part II: Case study: A computational theory of social exchange. *Ethology and Sociobiology* 10, 51–98.

Crespi, B. J. & Bookstein, F. L. 1989. A path-analytic model for the measurement of selection on morphology. *Evolution* 43, 18–28.

Curio, E. B. 1973. Towards a methodology of teleonomy. *Experientia* 29, 1045–1058.

Daly, M. & Wilson, M. 1988. *Homicide.* New York: Aldine de Gruyter.

Darwin, C. R. 1859. *The Origin of Species.* London: Dent.

————. 1874. *The Descent of Man and Selection in Relation to Sex.* New York: Rand McNally.

Dawkins, R. 1982. *The Extended Phenotype.* Oxford: Oxford University Press.

————. 1986. *The Blind Watchmaker.* New York: W. W. Norton and Company.

Dingle, H. & Hegmann, J. P. (eds.) 1982. *Evolution and Genetics of Life History.* New York: Springer-Verlag.

Endler, J. A. 1986. *Natural Selection in the Wild.* Princeton, New Jersey: Princeton University Press.

Felt, E. P. 1895. The scorpionflies. In: *Tenth Report of the State Entomologist on the Injurious and Other Insects of the State of New Mexico.*

Fisher, R. A. 1958. *The Genetical Theory of Natural Selection,* 2nd Edition. New York: Dover.

Ghiselin, M. T. 1969. *The Triumph of the Darwinian Method.* Berkeley, California: University of California Press.

Gould, S. J. & Lewontin, R. C. 1979. The spandrels of San Marco and the panglossian paradigm: A critique of the adaptationist program. *Proceedings of the Royal Society London* B205, 581–598.

Grafen, A. 1984. Natural selection, kin selection and group selection. In: *Behavioral Ecology: An Evolutionary Approach,* 2nd Edition (ed. by J. R. Krebs and N. B. Davies), pp. 62–89. Sunderland, Massachusetts: Sinauer.

————. 1988. On the uses of data on lifetime reproduction. In: *Reproductive Success: Studies of Individual Variation in Contrasting Breeding Systems* (ed. by T. H. Clutton-Brock), pp. 454–471. Chicago, Illinois: University of Chicago Press.

Hamilton, W. D. 1966. The molding of senescence by natural selection. *Journal of Theoretical Biology* 12, 12–45.

————. 1967. Extraordinary sex ratios. *Science* 156, 477–488.

Hamilton, W. D. & Zuk, M. 1982. Heritable true fitness and bright birds: A role for parasites? *Science* 218, 384–387.

Hempel, C. G. 1966. *Philosophy of Natural Science.* Englewood Cliffs, New Jersey: Prentice Hall.

Howard, R. D. 1988. Reproductive success in two species of anuarans. In: *Reproductive Success: Studies of Individual Variation in Contrasting Breeding Systems* (ed. by T. H. Clutton-Brock), pp. 99–113. Chicago, Illinois: University of Chicago Press.

Lande, R. 1987. Genetic correlations between the sexes in the evolution of dimorphism and mating preferences. In: *Sexual Selection: Testing the Alternatives* (ed. by J. W. Bradbury and M. B. Andersson), pp. 83–94. New York: John Wiley and Sons.

Lande, R. & Arnold, S. J. 1983. The measurement of selection on correlated characters. *Evolution* 37, 1210–1226.

Lewontin, R. C. 1978. Adaptation. *Scientific American* 239, 156–169.

MacArthur, R. H. & Pianka, E. R. 1966. On optimal use of a patchy environment. *American Naturalist* 100, 603–609.

Majerus, M. E. N., O'Donald, P. & Weir, J. 1982. Female mating preference is genetic. *Nature* 300, 521–523.

Maynard Smith, J. 1982. *Evolution and the Theory of Games*. Cambridge: Cambridge University Press.

Maynard Smith, J. & Price, G. R. 1973. The logic of animal conflict. *Nature* 246, 15–18.

Mayr, E. 1983. How to carry out the adaptationist program? *American Naturalist* 121, 324–334.

McMinn, H. 1990. Effects of the nematode parasite *Camallanus cotti* on sexual and non-sexual behaviors in the guppy (*Poecilia reticulata*). *American Zoologist* 30, 245–249.

McVey, M. E. 1988. The opportunity for sexual selection in a territorial dragonfly, *Erythemis simplicicollis*. In: *Reproductive Success: Studies of Individual Variation in Contrasting Breeding Systems* (ed. by T. H. Clutton-Brock), pp. 44–58. Chicago, Illinois: University of Chicago Press.

Mitchell-Olds, T. & Shaw, R. G. 1987. Regression analysis of natural selection: Statistical inference and biological interpretation. *Evolution* 41, 1149–1161.

Pagel, M. D. & Harvey, P. H. 1988. Recent developments in the analysis of comparative data. *The Quarterly Review of Biology* 63, 413–440.

Parker, G. A. 1984. Evolutionarily stable strategies. In: *Behavioural Ecology: An Evolutionary Approach* (ed. by J. R. Krebs & N. B. Davies), pp. 30–61. Oxford: Blackwell.

Pittendrigh, C. S. 1958. Adaptation, natural selection, and behavior. In: *Behaviour and Evolution* (ed. by A. Roe & G. G. Simpson), pp. 390–416. New Haven, Connecticut: Yale University Press.

Read, A. F. 1987. Comparative evidence supports the Hamilton and Zuk hypothesis on parasites and sexual selection. *Nature* 327, 68–70.

Ridley, M. 1983. *The Explanation of Organic Diversity*. Oxford: Clarendon Press.

Rose, M. & B. Charlesworth. 1980. A test of evolutionary theories of senescence. *Nature* 287, 141–142.

Sherman, P. W. 1988. The levels of analysis. *Animal Behaviour* 36, 616–618.

Sommerhoff, G. 1950. *Analytical Biology*. Oxford: Oxford University Press.

Stephens, D. W. & Krebs, J. R. 1986. *Foraging Theory*. Princeton, New Jersey: Princeton University Press.

Sutherland, W. J. 1985. Chance can produce a sex difference in variance in success and explain Bateman's data. *Animal Behaviour* 33, 1349–1352.

Symons, D. 1987. If we're all Darwinians, what's the fuss about? In: *Sociobiology and Psychology: Ideas, Issues and Applications* (ed. by C. Crawford, M. Smith & D. Krebs), pp. 121–146. Hillsdale, New Jersey: Lawrence Erlbaum Associates.

———. 1989. A critique of Darwinian anthropology. *Ethnology and Sociobiology* 10, 131–144.

———. 1992. On the use and misuse of Darwinism in the study of human behavior. In: *The Adapted Mind: Evolutionary Psychology and the Generation of Culture* (ed. by J. Barkow, L. Cosmides, & J. Tooby). Cambridge: Cambridge University Press.

Thornhill, R. 1974. *Evolutionary Ecology of Mecoptera* (Insecta). Ph.D. Dissertation, University of Michigan, Ann Arbor, MI.

———. 1979. Male and female sexual selection and the evolution of strategies in insects. In: *Sexual Selection and Reproductive Competition in Insects* (ed. by M. S. Blum & N. A. Blum), pp. 81–121. New York: Academic Press.

———. 1980. Rape in *Panorpa* Scorpionflies and a general rape hypothesis. *Animal Behaviour* 18, 52–59.

———. 1984a. Alternative female choice tactics in the scorpionfly *Hylobittacus apicalis* (Mecoptera) and their implications. *American Zoologist* 24, 367–383.

———. 1984b. Alternative hypotheses for traits believed to have evolved by sperm competition. In: *Sperm Competition and the Evolution of Animal Mating Systems* (ed. by R. L. Smith), pp. 151–178. New York: Academic Press.

———. 1984c. Scientific methodology in entomology. *Florida Entomologist* 67, 74–79.

———. 1986. Relative parental contribution of the sexes to their offspring and the operation of sexual selection. In: *Evolution of Animal Behavior* (ed. by M. H. Nitecki & J. A. Kitchell), pp. 113–136. Oxford: Oxford University Press.

———. 1987. The relative importance of intra-and interspecific competition in scorpionfly mating systems. *American Naturalist* 130, 711–729.

Thornhill, R. & Alcock, J. 1983. *The Evolution of Insect Mating Systems*. Cambridge, Massachusetts: Harvard University Press.

Trivers, R. L. 1988. Sex differences in rates of recombination and sexual selection. In: *The Evolution of Sex* (ed. by R. E. Michod & B. R. Levin), pp. 270–286. Sunderland, Massachusetts: Sinauer.

Wade, M. S. 1976. Group selection among laboratory populations of *Tribolium*. *Proceedings of National Academy of Sciences* 73, 4604–4607.

———. 1987. Measuring sexual selection. In: *Sexual Selection: Testing the Alternatives* (ed. by J. W. Bradbury & M. B. Andersson), pp. 197–207. New York: John Wiley and Sons.

Wade, M. J. & Arnold, S. J. 1980. The intensity of sexual selection in relation to male sexual behaviour, female choice and sperm precedence. *Animal Behaviour* 28, 446–461.

Ward, P. I. 1988. Sexual dichromatism and parasitism in British and Irish freshwater fish. *Animal Behaviour* 36, 1210–1215.

Williams, G. C. 1957. Pleiotropy, natural selection, and the evolution of senescence. *Evolution* 11, 398–411.

———. 1966. *Adaptation and Natural Selection*. Princeton, New Jersey: Princeton University Press.

———. 1985. A defense of reductionism in evolutionary biology. In: *Oxford Surveys in Evolutionary Biology*, Volume 2 (ed. by R. Dawkins and M. Ridley), pp. 1–27. Oxford: Oxford University Press.

Zuk, M. 1991. Parasites & bright birds: New data and a new prediction. In: *Bird-parasite Interactions: Ecology, Evolution, and Behavior* (ed. by J. Loy & M. Zuk). Oxford University Press.

Zuk, M., Thornhill, R., Ligon, J. D. & Johnson, K. 1990. Parasites and mate choice in red jungle fowl. *American Zoologist* 30, 235–244.

Chapter 9

The Units of Behavior in Evolutionary Explanations

Sandra D. Mitchell

Sociobiology is that branch of evolutionary biology which aims at providing biological explanations of social behavior. Sociobiology invokes no new general theories. Rather, it is characterized by its special domain. Given the assumption that natural selection has been the most significant force operating in evolutionary history, the explanation of the presence of a given behavior in a population is most often couched in terms of its adaptive significance. That is, given recent developments in evolutionary biology, the explanation of a behavior can employ any of a variety of analyses (including game-theoretic models, optimality models, kin selection models and reciprocal altruism models) to show how a given behavior, in a particular environment, affects the reproductive success of individuals who display that behavior. In this regard, sociobiological investigations of adaptive behaviors require the same evidence as other evolutionary inquiries, including measures of the consequences of trait possession on relative reproductive success, the genetic basis of the behavior, the historically available alternatives and the level at which selection is operating.

Though detailed evidence for all the parts of a justification of adaptive significance is difficult for any evolutionary explanation, sociobiological explanations are subject to further, domain specific, complications. While behavior is unquestionably part of an organism's phenotype (or gene's "extended phenotype") (Dawkins 1982), I will argue that special concerns regarding the target of selection in sociobiological explanations, i.e. individuating evolutionarily significant behaviors, are problematic. In this paper I will consider two such problems; the difficulties of individuating evolutionarily significant behaviors, and the collateral problem of recognizing similarity of behaviors across species. After a general discussion of these issues, I will turn to some recent studies of the adaptive significance of rape for illustration.

Causal Explanation in Evolutionary Biology

To claim that this or that behavior is an adaptation, rather than an aberration, or present just by chance, is to invoke a particular causal history. Here "adaptation" refers to a result of the historical process of evolution by natural selection. This usage of the term is common, although there are instances where "adaptation" is taken to refer generally to the "fit" of organism to its environment whatever the causal process that generated it. According to the second sense the chameleon "adapts" to the change of color of the background by the chemical process leading to a change in skin color, as well as peppered moths adapting to environmental pollution by changes over time in frequencies of melanism in the population. In this paper I will follow the first interpretation (Williams 1966; Gould & Vrba 1982; Burian 1983; Brandon 1985a; Mitchell 1987a) and embrace the historical connotation. Identifying a behavior as an adaptation then can be taken to offer an answer to the question "Why is this behavior, rather than another, present in the population?" Correctly identifying a behavior as an adaptation entails that this behavior, rather than some historically available alternatives, has evolved by means of natural selection because of its consequences on reproductive success in a specified environment. Of course, cases other than fixation of a single trait in a population can result. For example, frequency dependent selection issues in a population maintaining a variety of traits which are adaptive at specific frequencies.

B_1 is an adaptation entails:

B_1 is present in a population because, relative to historically available alternatives, $B_2, B_3 \ldots B_n$, in environment E, B_1 yielded, on average, greater net inclusive fitness than $B_2, B_3 \ldots B_n$.

We can separate the required evidence into three parts:

1. showing differential reproductive success results from having or not having B_1;
2. showing the proximate mechanisms of the behavior/environment interactions on reproductive success;
3. showing differential genetic transmission of B_1 results (and hence leads to differential expression of the phenotype).

Meeting conditions 1 and 3 ensures that B_1 will increase in frequency in the population over time, i.e. it will evolve. Condition 2 is required in order to distinguish selection *for* B_1 from mere selection *of* B_1. This extremely useful distinction was drawn by Elliott Sober (1984) in order to clarify the nature of the causal process generating a particular trait. It allows us to distinguish mere evolution of a trait from evolution by natural selection for the trait. To be an adaptation, the behavior must be a direct result of evolution by natural selection. It must be B_1's relation to environmental conditions that results in relatively higher reproductive success, rather than its being associated with reproductive success by means of either an indirect selective process, such as chance (by drift) or by means of an indirect selective process (B_1's being genetically linked to another trait and then increasing in frequency when the linked trait is directly selected for its consequences in that environment). In short, the explanandum behavior must result in the alleged consequence on reproductive success, and that consequence must be directly causally relevant to the presence of that very behavior.

The difficulties in directly justifying an adaptation explanation are legion (Endler 1986). Indirect arguments for adaptive significance are also offered. Two types of indirect argument, comparative analysis and the bypassing of proximate causal mechanisms, are common in extending sociobiological explanations from the nonhuman to the human realm. Comparative analysis or analogical arguments are proposed to allow inference about the evolutionary significance of a trait from evidence gleaned from multiple populations or species. Sometimes the adaptive significance of a trait is inferred from the correlation between repeated instances of it and a specific ecological condition. Given the correlation it is inferred that the trait has evolved as an adaptation in response to that ecological condition. This inference assumes that similar selection pressures produce similar responses, divergent pressures produce divergent responses. (See Bock 1977 for a detailed account of the assumptions of this type of argument.) On other occasions, direct evidence of the adaptedness of a trait to certain environmental conditions obtained for one species is generalized to other species sharing the same trait and conditions. All such comparative arguments are based on the presumption of similarity of traits, ecological conditions, and selection pressures.

A second type of indirect argument is found almost exclusively in human sociobiology. It allows evidence of the reproductive consequences of alternative behaviors to justify ascription of adaptive significance by presuming that there must be some genetic basis for all phenotypes and hence whatever developmental sequence or environmental trigger directly causes the phenotype can be ignored. That is, the "ultimate" causes for any trait are based in the genetic substrate so "ultimately evolutionary explanations can ignore the proximate mechanisms" (Durham 1979; Irons 1979).

Clarifications of the evidence required "ideally" for justifying a claim that a trait is an adaptation have been developed, in part, in the context of distinguishing between different *levels* at which selection may operate. For example, describing the benefits as accruing at the group level, and the differential transmission of the traits by means of differential group propagation gives grounds for claiming the trait is a group adaptation and hence that selection has operated at the group level. This paper is not concerned with questions of the level of selection but rather with the *target* of selection. What behaviors are candidates for explanation by appeal to the process of evolution by natural selection (at whatever level)? In the case of direct experimental evidence, one may ask what counts as a behavioral "unit" which could be an adaptation. For indirect inference one must consider what counts as the "same" behavior in different species. I will consider these two questions in turn.

Individuating Behaviors

The "Adaptationist Program" has been criticized for accepting evolutionary explanations that presume every observable trait is adaptive and then conjure a story which justifies that assumption. One objection to this strategy concerns the "atomization" of traits. By assuming every conceptually distinct trait is an adaptation, the argument goes, we have made errors in identifying the actual objects of biological processes. Gould & Lewontin (1979) have argued that what appears to us as an individual trait may not always appear so to the forces of evolution. We intuitively begin by suggesting that what is perceptually distinct to us (like the height of an individual, or its color) is a trait that has evolved by means of natural selection. But this may fail to explain the presence of the trait, because what we have identified is not an adaptable unit. One example they offer is the change in accepted explanation for the shape of the human chin. While we can designate a portion of the anatomy of the face as "the chin" and can see variety in this feature within a population or over evolutionary time, it does not operate as an integral whole in the process of evolution by natural selection. What we see as "the chin," the process of evolution "sees" as the necessary consequence of two distinct growth fields. Gould & Lewontin claim that the chin is a developmental artifact of evolution operating on other discrete traits and not itself the object of the joint process of selection and evolution. Since adaptations result only when both processes operate on the same object, the chin fails to be an adaptation.

This example challenges the strategy of producing adaptation explanations for ignoring developmental constraints. We cannot tell an adaptation story about the chin, it is claimed, because selection cannot weld together what development has torn asunder. (But see Gould 1987a,b; and Alcock 1987 for a disagreement about the significance of this type of claim.) I would like to suggest that adaptation explanations of social behavior may suffer a related hazard. In this context adaptive status is conferred onto individual behaviors which may, in fact, not be individually transmitted. An isolated behavior, like rape, may not be the correct subject of an adaptation story if it is an integral part of a complex behavioral strategy, or the outcome of a learning process. While isolated behaviors may be shown to have the requisite differential consequences for reproductive success, the genetic transmission of the behaviors may take a more complex route.

The possible relationships between genetic replicators and individual behaviors increases in number and complexity when we consider the role of learning in generating specific human behaviors. For the purposes of this discussion I am not concerned with the complexities occurring in the genome, i.e. whether a single allelic pair, multiple alleles closely aligned on the chromosome or a more complex interplay among disparate sections of the chromosome control phenotypic expression of a given trait. Rather it is the complexities at the phenotypic level and the path from whatever the relevant replicating structure in the genome that is central. Thus "gene" or "genetic replicator" is used in the sense employed by Dawkins (1982) and Hull (1981). Direct evidence of the genetic basis of many behavioral traits has been difficult to obtain. Given the variety of pathways from genetic replicators to behaviors, evidence of reproductive consequences alone will not be sufficient to endorse claims of adaptedness.

From Genes to Behavior

In order to evaluate the legitimacy of such explanations it is, thus, necessary to explicate the variety of possible causal pathways connecting genetic replicators and social behaviors. If phenotypic variation is the direct object of natural selection, one must understand the underlying relationship between the phenotypic expression and genetic replicators to argue that any such phenotypic trait is, or can be, an adaptation.

One-one Relationship: $g \leftrightarrow b_1$ and $g' \leftrightarrow b_2$

If it is plausible to assume that specific behaviors are genetically determined directly with little environmentally induced variability, then, given a history of genetic variation, the presence of a behavior in a population can be unproblematically explained by its effect of maximizing inclusive fitness. Obviously, traits are neither completely genetically determined nor completely environmentally determined. Everything always has genetic and environmental components. The question is rather when should we appeal to a genetic component to explain the presence of the trait, and when to an environmental component. If specific behavior b_1 is directly tied to a replicator, g, and b_2 tied to g' in a one-one relationship, then it is clear that the differential consequences of having b_1 relative to b_2 on an organism's reproductive success will cause one, say b_1, to be present in a population via evolution by natural selection. (See Figure 9.1, pathway I.) In this case, the explanation of a behavior can be identified by its consequence on reproductive success, and hence the adaptation claim is justifiable.

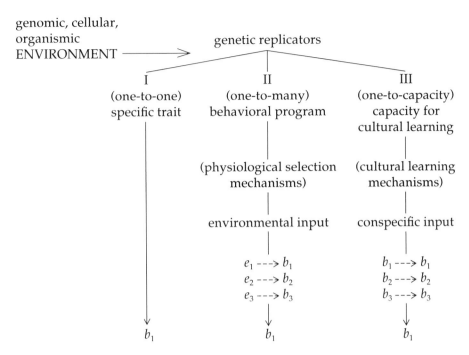

Figure 9.1
Causal paths from genes to behaviors.

A one-one relationship is found in traits like wing color in peppered moths. Any trait will have a range of expression depending on the range of environments experienced during development, i.e. the norm of reaction of the trait. Phenotypic expressions are the result of both the genetic coding and the environment of development and expression. The same genotype developing in two different environments can have very different corresponding phenotypes. (See Ricklefs' 1973 discussion of the arrowleaf plant for an illustration.) Once the organism is developed, the trait will no longer vary substantially with variation in the environment. (See Figure 9.1, environmental input between g and b_1.) This category, however, cannot be applied to social behaviors. It is in the very nature of what it is to be a social behavior, rather than a fixed trait, that the action involves a relationship with at least one other individual and is in part environmentally induced. The behavior will vary at least with respect to the presence or absence of relevant environmental input after development. This seems a plausible necessary condition even given our lack of detailed information of exact causal pathways from genetic replicator to behavior. "Our ignorance of the pathways from genes to morphology is great. Our ignorance of the pathways from genes to behavior, pathways which surely vary with differences in the achieved morphology, is even greater" (Burian 1981–2: 54–5).

One-many Relationship: $g \rightarrow b_1$ or b_2 or b_3 and $g' \rightarrow b'_1$ or b'_2 or b'_3
Suppose that specific behaviors are not tied directly to specific genetic counterparts, but are rather the result of environmental inputs via a genetically determined proximate mechanism. (See Figure 9.1, pathway II.) Thus behaviors are facultative, rather

than obligate, or are governed by a "closed program." Here a particular g codes for a range of possible behaviors. Which behavior is expressed requires additional environmental input. Such environmental information is then mediated through proximate physiological mechanisms to generate a specific behavioral output.

$$g \rightarrow \text{if } e_1 \rightarrow b_1$$
$$\text{if } e_2 \rightarrow b_2$$
$$\text{if } e_3 \rightarrow b_3$$

$$g' \rightarrow \text{if } e_1 \rightarrow b'_1$$
$$\text{if } e_2 \rightarrow b'_2$$
$$\text{if } e_3 \rightarrow b'_3$$

A specific behavior is expressed only by having both the genetic capacity that codes for the environment/behavior pair and having the appropriate environmental input. Thus behavioral variation within a population may be the result of either the variation in experiential histories of different individuals, i.e. differences in e, or may be due to similar environmental experiences and differences in the genetic replicator. If there is (or was) genetic variation (one of the prerequisites for evolution by natural selection), then the adaptive significance of a strategy including a set of behaviors can be identified with that set's consequence on reproductive success, and contributes to the justification of identifying the complete strategy as adaptive.

Since each individual acquires a behavior via the appropriate gene/environment conditions, the only means of transmission of traits across generations is the genetic pathways through differential replication. Thus evolution by natural selection is the appropriate causal history. Since that process takes consequences on reproductive success to be causally relevant, those consequences are explanatorily relevant.

The behavioral response in this case is "hard wired" by the genetic program—what Mayr calls a "closed program" in which "the program is contained completely in the fertilized zygote" (Mayr 1974: 652). Evidence for the genetic component of the behaviors in category II can be obtained from studies involving artificial selection. For example, it was noticed that there are two mating strategies adopted by male field crickets (*Gryllus integer*). A male will either call frequently or infrequently. A breeding program was developed to test for the genetic component to these alternate behaviors (there might clearly be environmental components having to do with the density of crickets in the area). Intense artificial selection effected a change in the frequency of the calling trait very quickly and hence provided evidence of a genetic component. (This case was reported in Trivers 1985: 95–98.)

Environmental Learning Plus Cultural Transmission: $g \rightarrow (e_1 \rightarrow b_1)$ *or* $(e_2 \rightarrow b_2)$ *or*
$(e_3 \rightarrow b_3)$ *or* $(b_1 \rightarrow b_1)$ *or* $(b_2 \rightarrow b_2)$ *or* $(b_3 \rightarrow b_3)$
Consider yet another way in which a specific behavior can be acquired. This is what some have called an open program, cultural learning or cultural transmission. Here the genome determines a capacity for learning from the environment or conspecifics. One manner in which learning occurs, allows an individual to adopt behavior b_1 by imitation of another instance of b_1 expressed by a conspecific. There clearly are genetic constraints even on such an open behavioral program. "An open program is by no means a *tabula rasa*, certain types of information are more easily incorporated than

others" (Mayr 1974: 652). Here the informational input (a subset of general environmental input, namely that which is specifically from the behavior of another conspecific) is mediated through some proximate learning mechanism that selects a behavior as preferential to others based on some specified selection criteria (See Figure 9.1, Pathway III.). The specification of how this mechanism operates is the domain of learning theory. Some suggested proximate selection criteria include avoidance of pain and maximization of "satisfaction."

As outlined above, for a trait to be an adaptation two processes must occur and be appropriately connected. The first is that interaction of variants in a given environment resulted in differential reproduction. Whether it be through an individual trait bearer's own reproduction or that of genetic relatives, to be an adaptation the trait must have such an effect on reproductive success. The second is that the trait be differentially transmitted, which will occur if the trait is genetically produced and there is differential reproduction. That effect on reproductive success must cause the differential transmission of genetic replicators. And the differential replication of genes must in turn be responsible for the consequent frequencies of the behaviors.

It is obvious that different behaviors can have varying effects on the reproductive success of an individual and his/her genetic relatives. Abstaining from reproduction and not aiding in the survival and reproduction of kin is a behavioral trait that will fare ill on this test compared to having lots of offspring and helping kin. But the celibate hermit's behavior would be maladaptive in the biological sense only if the genetic replicators that get transmitted differentially as a result of differential reproductive success are responsible for the behavioral trait in question.

In the case of cultural learning, the step of selection for increased reproductive success may be severed from the step of transmission necessary for the evolution of the selected trait. No matter how greatly the trait enhances genetic reproductive success, that factor may have no role in the presence of the trait in future generations—transmission follows a different path. Indeed, not only is increased fitness not sufficient for explaining the presence of the trait, it may not be necessary. (For a detailed argument, see Boyd & Richerson 1985; Brandon 1985b; Mitchell 1987b.)

When we observe or presume changes in behavioral traits, the inclination to treat those changes as adaptively significant requires strong assumptions about both reproductive consequences and the pathway from genetic replicators to behavior. In sum, for an individual behavior to be an adaptation it must be the direct cause of differential reproductive success and it must be directly transmitted as a result. In the case of complex strategies (the one-many relationship), an individual component behavior is not the unit of adaptation. Since adaptations involve both selection and evolution, the correct unit is the complete strategy, for it is the unit that gets transmitted as an integral whole. In the case of a learned behavior, it is the proximate learning mechanisms themselves that have been the object of evolution, and not any one or complex set of behaviors. Having identified the criteria for a unit of adaptation, one can then garner direct evidence that a given behavior (or behavioral strategy) is in fact an adaptation. Artificial selection experiments may be designed to justify the genetic underpinnings of a behavior and field and lab studies used for determining the effects on reproductive success. Appropriate alternatives (either individual behaviors, strategies, or proximate cultural learning mechanisms) may then be proposed and discerned.

Classifications of Similarity

Up to now I have been concerned with what counts as an individual behavioral trait. Once the unit of adaptive behavior has been clarified, a derivative problem arises in comparing behaviors in one population or species with those found in another. This issue becomes especially relevant in the employment of the comparative method. The new question is what are the criteria for similarity across populations or species or even taxa, that justify ascribing the same name to two behaviors? That is, what are the criteria for similarity which allow the same evolutionary explanation to be inferred. The problems surrounding the link between behavior and genetic determinant might be hidden if the descriptions of significant social behaviors are cavalierly attached to correlative genetic replicators. For behaviors to be explained by their adaptive significance, the very same item which results in relatively higher reproductive success must be present because of that consequence. Sociobiological explanations often leave this presupposition ungrounded.

Burian argues that one of the problems with establishing the genetic determinism of social behaviors arises, in part, from the use of two different descriptive paradigms or "units of behavior" (Burian 1981–2: 53). We describe social behaviors from the perspective of their human significance using terms like "aggressiveness" or "rape." But these do not necessarily correspond directly to the genetic units of behavior, namely particular genetic replicators or gene complexes that both operate as coherent wholes in transmission and are responsible for the development of the behavior. Since adaptation explanations require the operation of both selection of phenotypes and transmission of corresponding replicators, there needs to be an account of how socially significant behaviors are mapped onto biologically significant units.

The blurring of descriptive categories is most likely to occur in indirect sociobiological arguments. The "comparative method" is often employed in order to justify sociobiological explanations of human behavior. That is, the "same" or similar behavior is studied in a variety of species who share certain environmental or structural similarities. Evidence is obtained for explaining the behavior's presence in one (or some) species and, by analogy, is extended to account for the presence of the "same" behavior in humans (Kitcher 1985: 184).

The Case of Rape
An example of the illegitimate grouping together of disparate behaviors under one descriptive category is found in Thornhill's work on rape in scorpionflies and humans (Thornhill 1980, 1984; Thornhill & Thornhill 1983). Thornhill's initial study of "rape" in scorpionflies suggested a generalized hypothesis about rape as an adaptive copulation strategy in any population where females exhibit choice of mates and males can secure material assets. He observed "rape" in the scorpionflies, and tested to determine the reproductive consequences of the behavior as well as describing the associated ecological conditions. On the basis of direct investigation of the different copulation behaviors of scorpionflies (including copulation with and without the presentation by the male of a "nuptial gift" of a dead insect or salivary mass to the female), combined with information gleaned from studies of territorial fish and mallard ducks, Thornhill formulated a general hypothesis about the conditions under which "rape" as a copulation strategy would evolve by natural selection in any population. Humans were explicitly included in the scope of the hypothesis. He later (Thornhill &

Thornhill 1983) was involved in a more direct consideration of the evolutionary significance of human rape; that is, he tested the predictions of the hypothesis he developed from his scorpionfly studies. To endorse a general hypothesis and be compelled
to further test applications of it for humans presumes that "rape" in scorpionflies and
"rape" in humans is a similar behavioral strategy, that the necessary ecological conditions are shared, that the causal history which generated "rape" in each case would
be the same and hence has the same adaptive significance for both.

Is it uncontroversial in the case of the flies, that their behavior is genetically controlled, and hence explicable by consequences on reproductive success? The "unit" of
behavior question is not entirely straightforward even in this case. No individual
male adopts a single copulation behavior obligately. Rather, the evidence from
Thornhill's own experiments is that any male will "rape" under the correct triggering
environmental conditions. Similarly any will, under appropriate conditions, send out
a long distance pheromone when either guarding a dead insect or after producing a
salivary mass. Hence "rape" is not an isolated behavioral alternative subject to
selection, but rather part of a complex strategy for copulation that includes a set of
outcome behaviors that depend on environmental triggers. In short, it is a component
of a conditional male reproductive strategy composed of behavioral alternatives. It
might be better represented as the ordered sequence: 1. If possessing dead arthropod,
emit long distance pheromone, then copulate. 2. If no dead arthropod, produce salivary mass, emit long distance pheromone, then copulate. 3. If no dead arthropod and
unable to produce salivary mass, and female is present, secure female with physical
force, then copulate. Understanding it thus it is clear that identifying "rape" as an
adaptation is shorthand for claiming that the complex conditional strategy which includes "rape" is adaptive. One must then make a case for variant copulation strategies
being present in the evolutionary history of the scorpionflies such that some included
the "rape" component and others did not. It should be pointed out that in more recent writings (Thornhill & Thornhill 1983, 1987) the conditional, facultative nature of
copulation strategies is explicitly acknowledged. However, the evolutionary hypothesis is still framed in terms of *rape* being adaptive or maladaptive.

Clarifying what are alternative strategies subject to evolutionary explanation is
important in the context of game-theoretic analysis as well. Those studies focus on
explaining the maintenance of behavioral variation in a population by means of frequency dependent or disruptive selection processes. Austad has pointed out that
confusion resulted from the absence of common terminology for describing behavioral alternatives. The use of both "tactic" and "strategy" indiscriminately in referring
to behavioral components of complex strategies and obligate behaviors as well as the
complex strategy as a whole produced the ambiguity (Austad 1984). Clearly if the
unit of behavior is ambiguous, identifying alternative behaviors will be hopeless.

Suppose the evidence is convincing that copulation strategies which include "rape"
are adaptive for the scorpionflies. Can we then infer that human rape is similarly explained? For an analogical argument to support an explanation of human behavior as
adaptive, the properties appealed to as shared must be relevantly similar. Serious
doubts can be raised to the successful grouping together of human behavior and fly
behavior as "rape." If this similarity fails, then the evidence that the behavior in the
one species is adaptive lends little credence to the claim that it is so for the other
species as well.

Let us look more closely then, at the identification and explanation of "rape" in scorpionflies in order to see if evolutionary explanations of its adaptive nature are justified there, and if so, if they can be extended to explain rape in humans as well. Thornhill describes the observable sequence of events that constitute "rape" in scorpionflies.

> A rape attempt involves a male without a nuptial offering (i.e. dead insect or salivary mass) rushing toward a passing female and lashing out his mobile abdomen at her. On the end of the abdomen is a large, muscular genital bulb with a terminal pair of genital claspers. If the male successfully grasps a leg or wing of the female with his genital claspers, he slowly attempts to reposition the female. He then secures the anterior edge of the female's right forewing in the notal organ.... Females flee from males without nuptial gifts. If grasped by such a male's genital claspers, females fight vigorously to escape. When the female's wings are secured, the male attempts to grasp the genitalia of the female with his genital claspers. The female attempts to keep her abdominal tip away from the male's probing claspers. The male retains hold of the female's wing with the notal organ during copulation, which may last a few hours in some species. (Thornhill 1980: 53)

Is what is described an instance of "rape?" In order to demonstrate that it is Thornhill suggests two criteria which must be met '... it is necessary to (1) clearly distinguish female coyness from rape and (2) show that males that rape enhance their own fitness" (Thornhill 1980: 52). What is the motivation for these criteria? The descriptive content of the term "rape" must be derived from its use in human social contexts. For humans, purely behavioral information is insufficient to determine that a social interaction counts as rape (throughout rape will mean only heterosexual rape). There is an essential intentional component. For it to be rape two psychological conditions must be true, the female must be unwilling to engage in sexual intercourse, and the male must be willing. No behavioral expression is either necessary or sufficient to characterize this behavior.

This definition is unassailable if you consider a set of behavioral observations and ask yourself if any count as cases of rape. Consider a case of copulation where there is physical struggle between male and female. On the face of it, this can be either consenting sadist-masochistic behavior or it could truly be rape. What makes the difference is the intentional attitudes of the participants—not the behavioral counterparts. What if there is no physical struggle associated with intercourse? That behavioral set does not guarantee that what is going on is not rape. Fear of physical harm induced by threats can easily account for cases when the female is not consenting and yet not physically struggling. Again, what makes it genuine rape has to do with intentional attitudes. Since all such cases are male induced actions, the assumption of male willingness is unproblematic.

It is crucial to separate ontological from epistemological or evaluative judgments. The legal definition of rape involves assigning culpability and degree of punishment appropriate to a given case. Here the kind of behavioral evidence I have claimed to be inessential in defining rape may well come into play. But this is not a question of whether or not the action *is* rape, but whether or not the parties involved had good evidence for knowing that. For purposes of evaluation, one must first be able to identify the behavior.

How do the criteria for human rape correspond to the criteria used in Thornhill's study? In order to apply a concept like "rape" which is essentially intentional, not just correlated with intentions, an analog to unwillingness must be found. Thornhill's first criterion, distinction from female coyness, presumably plays that role. But what is packed into this distinction? Female coyness is taken to be a way for the female to exercise a discriminating role in interactions. By not engaging immediately in copulation behavior, the female may be able to elicit information about the male's fitness. Thus, in the case of the scorpionfly behavior Thornhill described above, it is plausible that the female by struggling to free herself from the grasp of the male, is in fact determining if he is strong enough to hold her, and hence likely to have those features which make him well adapted to a hazardous environment. Thornhill points out that 65% of adult mortality is due to predation by web-building spiders (Thornhill 1980: 54.). If the female is using the struggle to evaluate male fitness, then the behavior described is not "rape." What Thornhill argues, however, is that given his studies which show an ordered preference of females for males with large, rather than small dead arthropods as nuptial gifts, and dead arthropods rather than salivary masses, that there is no reproductive advantage for the female to copulate with a male who fails to present a nuptial gift (Thornhill 1984: 91). To be fair, Thornhill has refined his hypotheses regarding scorpionfly preferences, testing the contributions of body size, prey size, and frequency of males on female choice (see Thornhill 1984 for a list of his relevant studies). By receiving a gift, the female acquires nourishment which otherwise she would have to obtain by means of risky foraging in a hostile environment. Both the fact that a male offering a gift displays his ability to acquire food in that environment (producing a salivary mass is only possible after a male has recently fed) and the fact that she directly benefits materially from the food, make copulation with a "rapist" less beneficial. So to defend the view that the behavior is "rape" Thornhill must presuppose that to distinguish it from coyness the behavior must be clearly *not* in the reproductive interests of the female. Thus the analog to unwillingness is reproductive disadvantage.

This interpretation is consistent with the other half of the set of criteria. A male's fitness is enhanced, so Thornhill argues, by inseminating a female without having to put himself at risk foraging to acquire a dead arthropod to present or as a means of producing a salivary mass. What makes the incidence of "rape" in the flies so rare is the lower frequency of successful insemination for that behavior. Thus for a behavior to be "rape" it has to be, at the same time, in the reproductive interests of the male and against the reproductive interests of the female.

There are two criticisms to be raised to this analysis of "rape" in scorpionflies. The first is that it is not clear that the two criteria that Thornhill has set out are met. That is, it is not clear that the behavior is really "rape." The behavior of the female in struggling to free herself from the grasp of the male has not been sufficiently distinguished from coyness. Her behavior may elicit just the sort of fitness information she requires to make copulation in her reproductive interests. Furthermore, given the aggressive nature of the interactions with conspecifics, heterospecifics, and predators in that environment, the female's behavior may have nothing whatsoever to do with her willingness or unwillingness to copulate with a given male. Rather than struggle indicating an instinct to avoid copulation, it may be part of a different behavioral set. She may be avoiding being grasped in general, a behavior much to her advantage. Supporting this view are the following facts: there is no pheromone release from the "rapist" male, pheromones are used for species recognition, there is aggressive behavior over food between conspecific males, heterospecific pairs of any sex and with predatory spiders (Thornhill 1984: 81–83). Given this, it is plausible that the female's struggle with the "rapist" has nothing to do with copulation at all.

The second criticism is more global. If, in fact, the criteria are met, and the behavior is thus classified as "rape," by so doing Thornhill cannot ask the further question, "Is 'rape' adaptively significant?" That is because to be rape in the first place, by definition entails that the behavior is in the reproductive interests of the male and contrary to the reproductive interests of the female. A more neutral classification of the behavior would allow the question of adaptive significance to be raised, tested and disputed.

With respect to the extension of the adaptive significance of "rape" in scorpionflies to rape in humans, two points must be made. The first has to do with the analog of unwillingness. In the case of humans, unwillingness refers to some proximate psychological mechanism that, while itself having an evolutionary history, can generate behaviors that are not directly subject to the process of evolution by natural selection. That means that, for humans, unwillingness is not directly correlated with consequences of reproductive failure. This is just the point of the distinction drawn above between behaviors that are part of a closed behavioral program and behaviors that are generated by cultural learning mechanisms. The relevant causal processes for these two categories are distinguishable. For that reason, the adaptive significance for what we may describe as "rape" in one case cannot be generalized to cover a behavior with a different, and not necessarily complimentary, causal history in the other case.

This slide between components of closed and open behavioral programs is made by those who believe that because a cultural learning program has itself evolved by means of natural selection, particular behaviors proximately generated by it must necessarily be in the reproductive interests of the actors. Thornhill and Thornhill (1983: 139) while recognizing the different causal routes involved in the evolution of human behavior—i.e. evolution via natural selection and learning via cultural selection models, nevertheless insist that "Both ... routes are expected to result in behavior that promotes inclusive fitness (number of descendent and nondescendent kin) of individuals" (see also Durham 1979; Irons 1979; Shields & Shields 1983). However, Boyd & Richerson have convincingly argued that there is a consistent evolutionary account of how a cultural learning model can arise by natural selection and yet generate behaviors which do not promote the genetic fitness interests of the actors who express them (Boyd & Richerson 1985; Brandon 1985b; Mitchell 1987b). Once that inexorable relationship between behaviors generated by a proximate learning mechanism and consequences which increase the reproductive fitness of actors is given up, then all the statistical evidence that Thornhill and Thornhill provide on the reproductive consequences for rapists and raped women are beside the point.

Sociobiologists attempt to explain human behavior as biologically adaptive. Why a social behavior is present in a specific human society is answered by appeal to the consequences of that behavior for maximizing inclusive fitness. To be adequate to the task, such explanations require that there be an appropriate connection between the causal background processes. While it may be shown that a behavior confers a relative advantage for reproductive success onto the actor, for the behavior to be an adaptation, that advantage must be the cause of the behavior being present in the population. Such is the case when a trait is genetically determined since the advantage in reproductive success directly corresponds to an increase in genetic replication. However, when the direct connection between behavior and genetic replicators is severed, then the causal significance of the consequence of a behavior on reproductive success becomes questionable.

Whereas some types of behavioral variability are indeed the result of evolution by natural selection, namely those that are generated and transmitted by genes, other types of behavioral variability have a different etiology. The consequences on inclusive fitness of behaviors of the first type of variability can indeed explain why such behaviors are present in a population, even though there is no direct link between genetic replicator and specific behavior. The consequences on inclusive fitness will not, however, explain why a behavior is present that is learned and transmitted by imitation. Neither direct nor indirect arguments for the adaptive significance will help explain behaviors which are the result of a causal history independent of the combined processes of natural selection and evolution. (Thornhill and Thornhill's most recent collaboration (1989) shifts the focus of explanation of human rape to the psychological mechanisms generating male rape behavior and away from the behavior itself.)

In launching an investigation into the adaptive significance of a trait, it is advantageous to clearly identify the target of evolution by natural selection. Making explicit the assumptions concerning the relationship of the target to the genetic substrate, the specification of phenotypic alternatives, and the environmental conditions and reproductive consequences of the alternatives will aid in avoiding the comparison of incommensurable traits across species. Inferences of the same adaptive significance for similar targets of selection involve justification that the same causal forces are at work. Ultimately it is the causal history of the trait that determines whether it is an adaptation and the nature of its adaptiveness.

Acknowledgements

I wish to thank the following people for helpful discussions of the topics in this paper: James Bogen, Michael Dietrich, Jerry Downhower, Philip Kitcher, Peter Machamer, and Rob Page. Thanks also to Randy Thornhill for sending me his recent manuscripts.

Literature Cited

Alcock, J. 1987. Ardent adaptationism. *Natural History* 96, 4.

Austad, S. N. 1984. A Classification of Alternative Reproductive Behaviors and Methods for Fieldtesting ESS Models. *American Zoologist* 24, 309–19.

Bock, W. J. 1977. Adaptation and the comparative method. In: *Major Patterns in Vertebrate Evolution* (ed. by M. K. Hecht, P. C. Goody & B. M. Hecht), pp. 57–81. New York: Plenum Press.

Boyd, R. & Richerson, P. J. 1985. *Culture and the Evolutionary Process*. Chicago, Illinois: University of Chicago Press.

Brandon, R. N. 1985a. Adaptation explanations: Are adaptations good for interactors or replicators? In: *The New Biology and the New Philosophy of Science* (ed. by D. Depew & B. Webber), pp. 81–96. Cambridge, Massachusetts: MIT Press.

———. 1985b. Phenotypic plasticity, cultural transmission and human sociobiology. In: *Sociobiology and Epistemology* (ed. by J. H. Fetzer), pp. 57–74. Dordrecht: Reidel.

Burian, R. M. 1981–2. Human sociobiology and genetic determinism. *The Philosophical Forum* 13, 43–66.

Burian, R. 1983. "Adaptation." In *Dimensions of Darwinism: Themes & Counterthemes in Twentieth-century Evolutionary Theory* (ed. by M. Grene), pp. 287–314. Cambridge: Cambridge University Press.

Dawkins, R. 1982. *The Extended Phenotype: The Gene as the Unit of Selection.* Oxford: Oxford University Press.

Durham, W. H. 1979. Towards a coevolution theory of human biology and culture. In: *Evolutionary Biology and Human Social Behavior: An Anthropological Perspective.* (ed. by N. A. Chagnon & W. Irons), pp. 39–59. North Scituate, Massachusetts: Duxbury Press.

Endler, J. A. 1986. *Natural Selection in the Wild.* Princeton, New Jersey: Princeton University Press.

Gould, S. J. 1987a. Freudian Slip. *Natural History* 96, 14–21.

———. 1987b. Stephen Jay Gould replies. *Natural History* 96, 4–6.

Gould, S. J. & Lewontin, R. C. 1979. The spandrels of San Marco and the Panglossian paradigm: A critique of the adaptationist programme. *Proceedings of the Royal Society of London* 8, 205–258.

Gould, S. J. & Vrba, E. S. 1982. Exaptation—a missing term in the science of form. *Paleobiology* 8, 4–15.

Hull, D. L. 1981. Units of evolution: A metaphysical essay. In: *The Philosophy of Evolution* (ed. by U. L. Jensen & R. Harre), pp. 2–44. Brighton: Harvester Press.

Irons, W. 1979. Cultural and biological success. In: *Evolutionary Biology and Human Social Behavior: An Anthropological Perspective* (ed. by N. A. Chagnon & W. Irons), pp. 257–272. North Scituate, Massachusetts: Duxbury Press.

Kitcher, P. 1985. *Vaulting Ambition.* Cambridge, Massachusetts: MIT Press.

Mayr, E. 1974. Behavior programs and evolutionary strategies *American Scientist* 62, 650–659.

Mitchell, S. D. 1987a. Competing units of selection?: A case of symbiosis. *Philosophy of Science* 54, 351–367.

———. 1987b. Can evolution adapt to cultural selection? *PSA 1986*, Volume 2 (ed. by A. Fine & P. Machamer), pp. 87–96. East Lansing, Michigan: Philosophy of Science Association.

Ricklefs, R. 1973. *The Economy of Nature*, 2nd Edition. New York: Chiron Press.

Shields, W. M. & Shields, L. M. 1983. Forcible rape: An evolutionary perspective. *Ethology and Sociobiology* 4, 115–136.

Sober, E. 1984. *The Nature of Selection.* Cambridge: MIT Press.

Thornhill, R. 1980. Rape in panorpa scorpionflies and a general rape hypothesis. *Animal Behavior* 28, 52–59.

———. 1984. Scientific methodology in entomology. *Florida Entomologist* 67(1) 74–96.

Thornhill, R. & Thornhill, N. W. 1983. Human rape: An evolutionary analysis. *Ethology and Sociobiology* 4, 137–173.

———. 1987. Human rape: The strengths of the evolutionary perspective. In: *Sociobiology and Psychology: Ideas, Issues and Applications* (ed. by C. Crawford, M. Smith, & D. Krebs), pp. 269–292. Hillsdale, New Jersey: Lawrence Erlbaum Associates.

———. 1989. The evolutionary psychology of rape. Unpublished manuscript.

Trivers, R. L. 1985. *Social Evolution.* Menlo Park, California: Benjamin/Cummings Publishing Company, Inc.

Williams, G. C. 1966. *Adaptation and Natural Selection.* Princeton, New Jersey: Princeton University Press.

Chapter 10

Levels of Analysis and the Functional Significance of Helping Behavior

Walter D. Koenig and Ronald L. Mumme

Introduction

The field of behavioral ecology includes a diverse range of problems having to do with the developmental, physiological, genetical, and ecological bases of behavior. Partly as a result of this diversity, it is not unusual for controversies to arise from a failure to place hypotheses within their appropriate context. When this happens, advances can sometimes best be made by combining a critical evaluation of the available data with a more philosophical analysis of the questions involved.

In this chapter we pursue such an approach to the question of the evolution of helping behavior in cooperative (or communal) breeders: species in which individuals other than a male-female pair cooperate in rearing offspring. Because it involves apparently altruistic behaviors in the absence of parent-offspring relatedness, cooperative breeding is of interest both to behavioral ecologists and evolutionary biologists. Recent reviews include Brown (1987) and Stacey & Koenig (1990) for birds, Gittleman (1985) for mammals, Emlen (1984) for birds and mammals, and Taborsky & Limberger (1981) for fishes.

Much of the literature on cooperative breeding is devoted to the search for adaptive explanations of helping behavior. Recently, however, Jamieson (1986, 1989a) and Jamieson & Craig (1987) have presented a critique of functional explanations of helping behavior in birds, suggesting instead that this phenomenon might be an unselected consequence of the delayed dispersal and group-living that characterizes cooperative breeders. Our goal here is to provide a reconsideration of this issue. First, we define what helpers are and the kinds of aid they appear to offer. Second, we discuss levels of analysis (Sherman 1988, 1989; Jamieson 1989b) as it applies to the question of why some individuals care for offspring that are not their own. Third, we briefly clarify how Jamieson & Craig's (1987) alternative explanation for the evolution of helping behavior combines different levels of analysis, and therefore obfuscates the issue of whether helping behavior has current adaptive utility. Finally, we focus on the kinds of data relevant to hypotheses that helping behavior is selectively advantageous and assess the current status of our ability to reject the alternative hypothesis that it is not. Parallel papers by Ligon & Stacey (1989) and Emlen et al. (1990) discuss some of these same issues and reach conclusions similar to ours.

What Are Helpers and What Do They Do?

A helper, as originally defined by Skutch (1961: 198), is an individual that "assists in the nesting of an individual other than its mate, or feeds or otherwise attends a bird of whatever age which is neither its mate nor its dependent offspring." A more recent definition by Brown (1987: 300–301) is similar: "An individual that performs parent-like behavior toward young that are not genetically its own off-spring…. Helpers may be altruistic, cooperative, or selfish. Note that breeding status and conferral of benefit or harm to recipient or helper are irrelevant to the definition."

Provisioning of dependent young is the most conspicuous form of helping be-havior, but helpers may also perform a variety of other alloparental duties, including building the nest (e.g. white-winged choughs *Corcorax melanorhamphos*; Rowley 1978), incubating eggs and brooding young (e.g. acorn woodpeckers *Melanerpes formicivorus*; Koenig et al. 1983), defending young against predators (e.g. bicolored wrens *Camphylorhynchus griseus*; Austad & Rabenold 1985), and cleaning or groom-ing young (e.g. *Lamprologus brichardi*; Taborsky 1984).

Although Brown's (1987) definition indicates that helpers can provide alloparental care without necessarily conveying fitness benefits to recipients, it is equally impor-tant to note that the converse is also true: helpers can convey important fitness bene-fits to recipients in ways that are not directly attributable to the alloparental care they provide. For example, in addition to caring for nondescendant young, helpers in a number of species also contribute to the defense of group territories (e.g. Hunter 1985; Mumme & de Queiroz 1985), which can reduce the amount of time breeders must spend in territorial defense (e.g. Kinnaird & Grant 1982; Taborsky 1984). Helpers can also improve anti-predator defenses in ways unrelated to alloparental care. Family groups of Florida scrub jays (*Aphelocoma coerulescens*), which typically contain one or more nonbreeding helpers, have a coordinated sentinel system that serves primarily to detect aerial predators during the fall and winter (McGowan & Woolfenden 1989). The improved sentinel performance in larger groups may be responsible for the higher annual survivorship observed among breeders assisted by helpers in this species (Woolfenden & Fitzpatrick 1984).

Similarly, the presence of nonbreeders in the acorn woodpecker significantly in-creases annual survivorship of male breeders, but this increase in survivorship does not appear to be attributable to the alloparental care that nonbreeders provide (Koenig & Mumme 1987). Thus, not all the effects of helpers on fitness is neces-sarily attributable to alloparental behavior *per se*. This issue is discussed in further detail below.

Helping Behavior and Levels of Analysis

Following Tinbergen (1963), Sherman (1988, 1989) proposed the existence of four different levels of analysis in behavioral research: evolutionary origins, functional consequences, ontogenetic process, and mechanisms, the latter including both cogni-tive and physiological processes. Any behavior can be explained at each of these levels (e.g. Holekamp & Sherman 1989), but only hypotheses within a particular level are legitimate alternatives. Although we recognize the existence of several alternative philosophical frameworks by which behavioral hypotheses may be categorized (c.f. Dwyer 1984; Horn 1990), we believe that Sherman's levels provide a relatively straightforward and heuristically useful scheme for organizing many ideas in this field. Below we discuss some of the hypotheses at each level that address the ques-tion: Why do some individuals feed offspring not their own?

Evolutionary Origins

Of interest here is the context in which helping behavior evolved. One plausible hypothesis is that helping arose as a byproduct of selection in some other context, such as on parents to feed begging offspring (e.g. Williams 1966: 208; Jamieson 1989a). Second, helping might be present in a particular species as a consequence of phylogenetic inertia (Edwards & Naeem 1990). Note, however, that this explanation only shifts the question of the ultimate evolutionary origin of the trait from the species of interest to the one from which it phylogenetically "inherited" the trait. Alternatively, helping behavior could have arisen directly as an adaptive response to natural selection reflecting the particular ecological and demographic conditions of the population or species under consideration.

Discriminating among hypotheses at this level is notoriously difficult. It is usually impossible to obtain a clear glimpse of the evolutionary origin of a trait much less to examine those origins experimentally. However, we can envision two approaches that are potentially productive. The first is to search for probable evolutionary origins by comparing the behavior and phylogeny of closely related species. An example is the recent cladistic analysis of the distribution of cooperative breeding in passerine birds by Edwards & Naeem (1990). By providing evidence that phylogeny plays a role in determining the presence of cooperative breeding, these authors demonstrate that this phenomenon may not be an independently evolved adaptation in some species (see also Russell 1989). Their analyses, however, also demonstrate that helping behavior is frequently lost from a clade, contrary to the suggestion that, once present, helping is difficult to eliminate. The resulting patchwork pattern in the presence of this trait is consistent with the hypothesis that selection is acting within at least some lineages to maintain or eliminate this behavior, depending on the ecological conditions faced by each species.

A second approach that addresses the issue of whether helping could have originated as a byproduct of selection in some other context is to determine the correlation between helping behavior and other behaviors hypothesized to be the direct agents of selection. For example, one might examine the correlation between the quantity and quality of alloparental care given by individuals when they are helpers and the parental care they provide as parents. No correlation (or an inverse correlation) would effectively reject Jamieson & Craig's (1987) hypothesis that helping behavior arose as a byproduct of selection on parents to feed begging offspring, while a positive correlation would be consistent with this hypothesis (as well as others, including that nonbreeders gain experience by helping that makes them better parents later in life).

This latter approach does not directly address evolutionary origins: Knowing the correlation between two traits does not tell us how closely they were linked when they arose. Nonetheless, such analyses, using both interspecific and intraspecific data, may provide the least ambiguous test possible of Jamieson and Craig's unselected hypothesis for the origin of helping behavior.

Functional Consequences

At this level, the question of interest is whether helping confers selective advantages to the individuals involved or whether it is selectively neutral, or even maladaptive. Answering this question involves determining not only whether helping behavior correlates with fitness, but whether it is the direct target of selection rather than a byproduct of selection for a correlated trait (e.g. Lande & Arnold 1983).

There are three general ways in which the fitness benefits of helping behavior can accrue to helpers: (1) kinship or indirect fitness benefits (*sensu* Brown & Brown 1981), (2) any of several direct (or Darwinian) fitness advantages to the helper, such as increased experience, and (3) reciprocal benefits. If helping has no direct fitness benefit, it could still be present for at least three reasons: (1) selection on a correlated character, (2) phylogenetic inertia, or (3) drift. Evidence for the functional significance of helping behavior is discussed and critically evaluated in detail below.

Ontogenetic Processes

Hypotheses at this level concern the development of helping behavior in individuals, particularly in reference to age, sex, social environment, and previous experience. Virtually all research on the ontogeny of helping behavior has been descriptive in nature (e.g. Stallcup & Woolfenden 1978; Lawton & Guindon 1981; Jamieson & Craig 1987; Jamieson 1988); there has been little general theory concerning the ontogeny of helping behavior and virtually all hypotheses have been *ad hoc* and species-specific.

Physiological Processes

The fourth level of analysis is that of mechanisms, including both cognitive and physiological processes (Sherman 1988). There is little discussion in the cooperative breeding literature of the former. Two plausible physiological explanations of helping behavior are that it is (1) an expression of the same stimulus-response that produces feeding of young by parents (e.g. Jamieson & Craig 1987; Jamieson 1989; Ligon & Stacey 1989) and (2) a byproduct of seasonal hormonal changes in nonbreeders.

Levels of Analysis: Jamieson & Craig's Critique

Jamieson & Craig (1987) and Jamieson (1986, 1989a) offer an alternative to the hypothesis that helping behavior is a direct product of natural selection. They propose that helping behavior originated and is currently maintained nonadaptively as a result of its tight linkage with the clearly adaptive behaviors associated with normal parental care. Viewed in this context, helping behavior is an unselected consequence of delayed dispersal, group living, and the physiological processes that normally lead individuals to feed begging offspring.

Examined in the framework of levels of analysis, Jamieson & Craig's hypothesis actually consists of sub-hypotheses on all four of the levels discussed above. First, at the level of evolutionary origins, helping behavior originated as an unselected consequence of group living. Second, at the level of functional consequences, helping behavior presently has no selective value but is maintained indirectly by virtue of its genetic correlation with provisioning behavior of parents. Third, on the level of ontogenetic processes, helping behavior develops as a neotenic shift in the timing of the expression of provisioning behavior. Fourth, at the level of physiological processes, provisioning behavior is elicited from potential helpers by begging juveniles via a stimulus-response mechanism.

Knowledge at any one level of analysis may provide important clues, but cannot supercede, hypotheses at other levels. For example, consider the possibility that there is a phylogenetic component to helping behavior in some taxa (Edwards & Naeem 1990). This hypothesis specifically addresses evolutionary origins. However, consider species A in taxon B, and imagine that we know, from an analysis using appropriate null models, that helping behavior occurs more frequently in taxon B than expected by chance. This knowledge of the possible importance of phylogenetic inertia in taxon B would then make it more plausible that helping behavior might be of no current adaptive utility in species A, at least compared to a species in a taxon in which helping behavior is not found more frequently than expected.

In this example, information at the level of evolutionary origins provides clues about possible functional consequences or the lack thereof. However, helping behavior could still be of current functional significance regardless of its evolutionary origin or its developmental and physiological bases (Greene 1986; Sherman 1988).

Jamieson & Craig's failure to distinguish clearly between hypotheses at different levels of analysis leads to considerable confusion. For example, Jamieson & Craig (1987: 80) suggest as an alternative to "increased fitness" type arguments (level of functional consequences) that feeding of nestlings in cooperative breeders is "maintained by the same stimulus-response mechanism that results in parents feeding their own young or host species feeding parasitic young" (level of physiological processes). In an earlier paper, Jamieson (1986; 203) suggests that if helping behavior is an elicited response to the presence of nestlings, then "the functional question 'What is the selective advantage of helping behavior' could be replaced by a developmental question, 'How does parenting behavior develop in nonbreeders of cooperative species?'"

In fact, neither the stimulus-response subhypothesis nor the ontogeny of helping behavior in cooperative species can supersede explanations at other levels of analysis. The hypothesis that helping behavior is explained at the physiological level by a stimulus-response mechanism is entirely consistent with functional hypotheses proposing that helping behavior is maintained as a direct result of natural selection. Similarly, helping behavior may confer a selective advantage regardless of its ontogeny.

This mixing levels of analysis is particularly dangerous when evaluating alternative, testable hypotheses for helping behavior. For example, Jamieson (1989a: 403) proposes that if helping behavior has been the direct product of selection, then there should be a greater predisposition of naive juveniles to provision nestlings in cooperative species than in closely related, noncooperative species. Results of such a test, if positive, would indeed reject Jamieson's subhypothesis that helping behavior is the result of the same stimulus-response mechanism responsible for parental behavior. However, the test does not reject alternatives consistent with the hypothesis that helping behavior is an unselected trait; for example, the increased predisposition for provisioning could still be a side effect of the hormonal state of individuals which, purely as a side effect of group living, is different in naive juveniles of cooperative compared to noncooperative breeders. Jamieson's (1989a) proposed test therefore cannot reject hypotheses concerning current utility of helping behavior; such behavior may or may not be of adaptive utility regardless of the outcome.

To avoid the fruitless debate and semantic confusion that arise when levels of analysis are mixed (Sherman 1988), we will devote the rest of this chapter to a detailed consideration of the functional consequences of helping behavior. First we critically evaluate evidence suggesting that helping behavior results in selective benefits for helpers and/or recipients. We then briefly discuss some of the evidence for the hypothesis that helping behavior does not have current selective utility.

Fitness Consequences of Helping Behavior

The Evidence

For a trait to have current adaptive utility, it must have an overall positive effect on fitness. Here we evaluate the empirical evidence that individuals increase their fitness by acting as helpers. A summary is provided in Table 10.1. Another classification of the potential fitness effects of helpers with a somewhat different philosophical orientation is presented by Emlen & Wrege (1989).

Helpers Increase the Reproductive Success of Related Breeders   Groups with helpers have been shown to produce significantly more young than groups without helpers in at least five species of mammals (Gittleman 1985) and ten species of birds (Brown 1987). In a few of these, such as the white-fronted bee-eaters (*Merops bullockoides*) studied by Emlen & Wrege (1988, 1989) and the bicolored wrens studied by Austad & Rabenold (1985), the effect is so pronounced that it is unlikely to be due to confounding variables. Helping in these species yields significant fitness benefits both to the individuals helped, who are able to raise more offspring, and to their closely related helpers, who gain indirect fitness benefits.

However, in many species the apparent helper effect, if present at all, is modest and could occur because helpers are associated with groups which are reproductively superior for other reasons (Lack 1968). For example, because helpers are usually the offspring of breeders from prior years, breeders with helpers are almost always more experienced and often on territories of higher quality than breeders without helpers. Hence, increased reproductive success of groups with helpers could be due to their experience or better territories rather than helpers *per se*.

There are at least three approaches toward resolving this difficulty. The first is to restrict analyses to sets of birds with comparable prior histories and living on similar territories. For example, Gibbons (1987), studying helping by juvenile moorhens (*Gallinula chloropus*), restricted analyses to experienced pairs, to pairs attempting renests or second nests during different parts of the season, to pairs with territories of a particular size class, and pairs breeding in each of the three years of his study in order to control for the potentially confounding effects of experience, season, territory quality, and yearly variation, respectively. Based on these analyses, Gibbons (1987) concluded that helpers resulted in an increase in the number of young fledged.

With longer-term data it is even possible to control for individual variation, rendering this approach as robust as the best experimental studies. An excellent example is the analysis of the Florida scrub jay by Woolfenden & Fitzpatrick (1984). They restricted their analysis to resident breeders that had attempted reproduction on the same territories at least twice with and without helpers and found a significant increase in reproductive success due to helpers. When further restricting the analysis to pairs (either previously successful or not) breeding on the same territory with and without helpers, a difference still emerged, but was no longer significant.

A second approach is to control statistically for the effects of experience and territory quality. This approach is particularly useful in species whose group composition

Table 10.1
Evidence for the hypothesis that helping behavior has current adaptive utility

Observation	Species	References
A. Fitness consequences of helping behavior		
1. Helpers increase the reproductive success of related breeders (current indirect fitness benefits)	Many (descriptive) Grey-crowned babbler Florida scrub jay *Lamprologus brichardi*	Gittleman 1985; Brown 1987 Brown et al. 1982 R. L. Mumme unpubl. data Taborsky 1984
2. Helpers increase the survival of related breeders (future indirect fitness benefits)	Groove-billed anis (male) Florida scrub jay (male and female) Pied kingfisher (female) Bicolored wren (male and female) Acorn woodpecker (male) Splendid fairy-wren (female)	Vehrencamp 1978 Woolfenden & Fitzpatrick 1984 Reyer 1984 Austad & Rabenold 1986 Koenig & Mumme 1987 Russell & Rowley 1988
3. Helpers lighten the load of breeders	Dwarf mongoose Grey-crowned babbler Green woodhoopoe White-browed sparrow weaver Galápagos mockingbird Stripe-backed wren Pied kingfisher Bicolored wren Beechey jay Moorhen	Rood 1978 Brown et al. 1978 Ligon & Ligon 1978b Lewis 1982 Kinnaird & Grant 1982 Rabenold 1984 Reyer 1984 Austad & Rabenold 1985 Raitt et al. 1984 Eden 1987; Gibbons 1987
4. Helpers gain direct fitness benefits		
a. Increased access to breeding space	Florida scrub jay	Woolfenden & Fitzpatrick 1984
b. Increased experience	Brown jay White-winged chough Florida scrub jay Spendid fairy-wren Purple gallinule	Lawton & Guindon 1981 Heinsohn et al. 1988 Woolfenden & Fitzpatrick 1984 Rowley & Russell 1989 Hunter 1987
c. Forming associations leading to increased future reproductive success	Arabian babbler Green woodhoopoe Bell miner Galápagos mockingbird Brown hyena Gray-breasted jay Pied kingfisher	Carlisle & Zahavi 1986 Ligon & Ligon 1978 Clarke 1989 Curry 1988a Owens & Owens 1984 Brown & Brown 1980; Caraco & Brown 1986 Reyer 1984
d. Gaining access to group resources	*Lamprologus brichardi*	Taborsky 1985
B. Functional patterns of helping behavior		
1. Differential feeding of relatives	Bell miner White-fronted bee-eater Galápagos mockingbird Brown hyena Pied kingfisher	Clarke 1984 Emlen & Wrege 1988 Curry 1988a Owens & Owens 1984 Reyer 1984, 1986

is complex. For example, Koenig & Mumme (1987) performed an analysis of variance of reproductive success in the acorn woodpecker including four variables: (1) whether or not a turnover in breeders had occurred in the prior year, (2) number of breeder males, (3) number of breeder females, and (4) number of nonbreeding helpers. They found no significant effect of nonbreeding helpers on group reproductive success when the other three variables were controlled, contrary to the results of univariate analyses. Similarly, Zack & Ligon (1985) found no influence of group size on reproductive success of gray-backed fiscal shrikes (*Lanius excubitorius*) controlling for cover and Nias (1986) found no effect of number of helpers on reproduction in superb fairy-wrens (*Malurus cyaneus*) controlling for a suite of vegetational characters. Such studies reinforce the hypothesis that apparent helper effects in many species may be due to confounding variables.

A third approach to this problem is experimental. We are aware of four such studies. First, Brown et al. (1982) compared the number of young fledged in second nests by groups of grey-crowned babblers (*Pomatostomus temporalis*) with multiple helpers to groups that had been reduced to trios (presumably the breeding pair and one helper), and found that subsequent reproductive success of the experimental groups was one-third times that of the controls. Second, Taborsky (1984), studied the cichlid fish *Lamprologus brichardi* in the laboratory under controlled conditions. Although helpers in this species do not feed offspring, they do engage in a variety of parental duties including cleaning of eggs, larvae, and fry. He found that pairs with helpers produced larger clutches and that egg survival was possibly enhanced when helpers were present. Third, Mumme (in preparation) removed helper Florida scrub jays and was able to demonstrate that helpers help by reducing nest predation, as suggested by Woolfenden & Fitzpatrick (1984).

In contrast to the results of these three studies, which support the hypothesis that helping behavior increases the reproductive success of breeders, is the work of Leonard et al. (1989) who removed moorhen juvenile helpers and observed no effect on subsequent survival or reproductive success of the breeding pair. This suggests that the enhanced reproductive success observed in groups with helpers by Gibbons (1987) was due to interactions with confounding variables, despite his attempt to control for such interactions by restricting his analyses to comparable subsets of groups.

Unfortunately, the experimental approach is not without its shortcomings. There are at least three potential difficulties. First, experimental removals of potential helpers from social groups usually will affect both group size and alloparental behavior, thereby confounding estimates of the fitness effects of alloparental behavior *per se*. This point is discussed further below. Second, the social disruption of removing helpers from experimental groups is not easily controlled. For example, most experimental groups in Brown et al.'s (1982) study simply stopped breeding after three to five nonbreeding group members (potential helpers) were removed, while most unmanipulated control groups attempted to raise additional broods. Although the analysis of Brown & Brown (1981) suggests that the cessation of reproductive activities in experimental groups was due to the loss of potential helpers, their data are also consistent with the alternative hypothesis that the reproductive failure of experimental groups was caused by the social disruption resulting from the removal of a substantial fraction of the social unit. The only solution to this difficulty may be a combination of experimental studies and exhaustive nonmanipulative work.

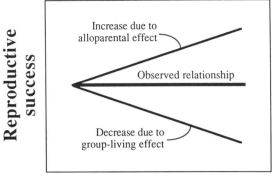

Group size

Figure 10.1
Potential opposing relationship between alloparental and group-living effects in cooperative breeders. In this hypothetical example, helpers have a significantly positive effect on fitness (the alloparental effect) which is cancelled by the adverse effect of group size; the resulting relationship between group size and group reproductive success is flat. It is equally possible that the alloparental effect could be negative, but the relationship between group size and group reproductive success could be positive as a consequence of a beneficial group-living effect.

Third, it is possible that helpers help and yet result in no increase in reproductive success (or survivorship) compared to groups without helpers. Group living incurs several automatic disadvantages and entails no automatic advantage (Alexander 1974; Hoogland & Sherman 1976). Consequently, it is entirely plausible that the aid provided by helpers (the "alloparental effect") may in some species simply counter the otherwise negative effect of larger group size (the "group-living effect") on reproductive success (Figure 10.1). This would be the case if, for example, larger groups depleted their resources more quickly or thoroughly than smaller groups and thus had less food for reproduction. In such a system, neither detailed empirical work nor experimental studies would reveal an increase in reproductive success in groups with helpers, yet helpers are significantly enhancing reproductive success compared to groups of similar size in which helpers do not help. Indeed, groups in such a system might even experience *lower* reproductive success than pairs without helpers, despite the aid-giving behavior of helpers. Separating the alloparental and group-living effects could only be accomplished by careful study of the relationship between group size, reproductive success, and variation in the degree of help provided by individual helpers, or by manipulating helping behavior without altering group size. Such analyses have yet to be performed. We will discuss this problem in further detail below.

Helpers Increase the Survival of Related Breeders
The majority of workers have focused on the effects of helpers on current reproduction. However, helpers may also influence the survivorship of breeders. When helpers are related to the breeders, as is usually the case, increased survival of breeders augments the fitness of both parties. Increased survivorship of breeders as a consequence of helpers has been documented in at least six species (Table 10.1).

The effect of helpers on breeder survivorship may seem slight yet still contribute substantially to the indirect fitness benefits of helping behavior (Mumme et al. 1989). For example, annual survivorship of Florida scrub jay breeders with helpers is only 8% greater than those without helpers (Woolfenden & Fitzpatrick 1984). Yet this difference is sufficient to provide 46% of the estimated indirect fitness benefits of helping. In four other species for which data are available, future indirect fitness benefits arising from increased survivorship are estimated to provide between 29% and 49% of the total gain in indirect fitness accruing to helpers (Mumme et al. 1989).

These results indicate that increased survivorship of breeders may yield important fitness benefits to helpers by increasing their future indirect fitness. However, as with the relationship between helpers and reproductive success, the apparent increased survivorship of breeders when helpers are present could be due largely or in part to confounding variables such as territory quality. Unfortunately, the experimental studies necessary to reject this alternative have yet to be attempted. Thus, direct experimental evidence that helping behavior increases breeder survivorship is thus far lacking.

Helpers Lighten the Load of Breeders   In at least ten species, breeders reduce their feeding rates when assisted by helpers (Table 10.1). This "lightening of the load" of breeders will have fitness consequences only if it increases breeder survival, reproductive success, or both. For example, lightening of the load by helpers correlates with a higher incidence of renesting (increasing annual reproductive success) in several species (e.g. white-browed sparrow weavers *Plocepasser mahali* [Lewis 1982], grey-crowned babblers [Brown & Brown 1981], stripe-backed wrens *Campylorhynchus nuchalis* [Rabenold 1984], and bicolored wrens [Austad & Rabenold 1985]) and with increased breeder survival in the pied kingfisher *Ceryle rudis* (Reyer 1984).

Helpers Gain Direct Fitness Benefits   By increasing the reproductive success or survivorship of a breeder, helpers increase the breeder's direct fitness and their own indirect fitness. There is also considerable evidence to suggest that helpers may increase their own direct fitness; that is, improve their own survivorship or future reproductive success. A variety of different mechanisms for this have been suggested. These are discussed below.

Helpers Gain Access to Breeding Space   Woolfenden & Fitzpatrick (1984) have shown that helpers in the Florida scrub jay, by augmenting reproductive success and thus the size of their group, increase the size of their group's territory. This in turn enables male helpers to "bud off" and inherit a portion of the territory for their own reproduction.

Helpers Gain Experience   By helping, helpers may acquire experience which increases their direct fitness by allowing them to be more successful breeders later in life. First suggested by Skutch (1961), this hypothesis implies that, for whatever reason, young birds in cooperative breeders are unable to acquire the skills necessary to successfully raise young, and was thus dubbed the "skill hypothesis" by Brown (1987). Brown (1987) also discusses several lines of circumstantial evidence for this hypothesis, including reduced foraging efficiency of birds with recognizable immature plumage, a character observed in many helpers, and smaller body mass in birds of normal helper age in many cooperative breeders.

Better evidence for this hypothesis comes from the brown jay (*Psilorhinus morio*) and the purple gallinule (*Porphyrula martinica*) in which the effectiveness of helping behavior increases with helper age and with experience, even within a season (Lawton & Guindon 1981; Hunter 1987), and the white-winged choughs, in which foraging success and feeding rates increase with age (Heinsohn et al. 1988). Brown jays and white-winged choughs, but not purple gallinules, have immature plumages and may require several years to attain full adult characters.

The definitive test for this effect is to compare the reproductive success of birds as a function of the help they provided as auxiliaries. Such a test has yet to be performed. However, several workers have tested for an effect of the number of years that individuals spent as auxiliaries on their subsequent reproductive success. The results are equivocal. No difference between the subsequent reproductive success of helpers and nonhelpers was found in white-fronted bee-eaters (Emlen & Wrege 1989) or in acorn woodpeckers (Koenig & Mumme 1987). Male Florida scrub jays with three or more years of helping experience were reported to reproduce more successfully than those with one or two years of experience (Woolfenden & Fitzpatrick 1984), but additional data have failed to support this trend (G. E. Woolfenden personal communication). Female splendid fairy-wrens (*Malurus splendens*) with prior helping experience tended to reproduce slightly better than those without experience, but the difference was not significant (Rowley & Russell 1990).

Helpers Establish Social Relationships   By caring for dependent offspring, helpers may form associations that improve their own reproductive success later in life. A variety of different mechanisms has been proposed, hypothesizing the critical association to be (1) among the helpers, (2) between the helpers and the nestlings being fed, and (3) between the helpers and the breeders being helped.

The first of these mechanisms was suggested for Arabian babblers (*Turdoides squamiceps*) by Carlisle & Zahavi (1986). These authors detailed various interactions and interference between helpers which they interpreted as efforts to establish their status vis-à-vis other helpers. They suggested, with little supporting documentation, that the probability of a helper obtaining the collaboration of other helpers in establishing and defending territories later in life increases with the enhanced dominance that comes from helping.

Better supported is the hypothesis that helping forges reciprocal associations between the helpers and the recipient nestlings. Ligon & Ligon (1978a, 1983), for example, proposed that recipients of aid in green woodhoopoes (*Phoeniculus purpureus*) may later cooperate with donors (helpers) to compete for vacant breeding territories and even, through a process of delayed reciprocity or generational mutualism (Brown 1983), serve as helpers during a donor's own breeding attempts. Wiley & Rabenold (1984) proposed that such delayed reciprocity might be important in any cooperative breeder in which helpers queue for succession to breeding status within groups. Their suggestion that this occurs regularly in stripe-backed wrens has not been confirmed (Rabenold 1985), but reciprocation of help to donors occurs regularly in Galápagos mockingbirds *Nesomimus parvulus* (Curry 1988a), brown hyenas *Hyaena brunnea* (Owens & Owens 1984), and bell miners *Manorina melanophrys* (Clarke 1989). Clarke (1989) further shows reciprocation to be independent of genetic relatedness, thereby strengthening the hypothesis that some direct fitness benefit is derived from helping behavior in this species.

A similar "helper-resource" hypothesis was suggested as a possible explanation for the apparently indiscriminate feeding of young within a social unit observed in gray-breasted jays (*Aphelocoma ultramarina*) by Brown & Brown (1980). The proposed benefit of reciprocal feeding in this species is to decrease the variance in time between feedings for nestlings (Caraco & Brown 1986) rather than to increase the probability of helpers gaining breeding status, as in the green woodhoopoe.

The third social relationship that may be established by helping behavior is that between the helper and the breeders whose offspring are fed. An excellent example of this effect has been documented in the pied kingfisher by Reyer (1980, 1984, 1986). This species is unique in having two categories of male helpers: "primary" helpers, which are closely related to the breeders, and "secondary" helpers, which are not. Reyer (1984) showed that secondary helpers were more likely to be mated in the subsequent year, usually with the female they had helped, than were birds that did not choose to become secondary helpers. Reyer (1986) also showed that by bringing fish to the nest, secondary helpers reduced the probability of being attacked by the breeding pair and that secondary, but not primary, helpers tend to concentrate on feeding the breeding female rather than the nestlings. These observations support the interpretation that secondary helpers assist the breeding female in order to increase their chances of mating with her in subsequent years (Reyer 1980, 1986).

Reyer's (1986) observations are also consistent with the hypothesis that feeding by secondary helpers is "payment" for being accepted as a group member. This possibility, first proposed as an explanation of helping by Gaston (1978), is also supported by Taborsky's (1985) work on a fish, *Lamprologus brichardi*, discussed next.

Helpers Gain Access to Group Resources   Numerous studies have proposed that auxiliaries, by remaining on their natal territory, gain access to critical group resources which afford them increased survival. As in the secondary helpers of pied kingfishers, helping by such auxiliaries might be payment for being allowed access to these resources (Gaston 1978).

Only one study thus far has demonstrated a direct relationship between helping behavior and increased survival of helpers. In the territorial fish *Lamprologus brichardi*, Taborsky (1984, 1985) experimentally demonstrated that large helpers, generally expelled by breeders, are tolerated when a pair is exposed to predators or conditions of severe inter- or intra-specific competition for space, conditions under which helpers are especially important to the survival and success of a pair. Helpers in this species benefit significantly by having access to shelter sites, and thus the interpretation that helping is payment for access to these sites, which have a strong influence on survival, appears reasonable.

A Caveat: Distinguishing between Group-living and Alloparental Effects
As should now be evident, helpers appear to have a variety of effects on their own fitness and on the fitnesses of other individuals. It is thus tempting to conclude that helping behavior is generally not a neutral trait. Unfortunately, virtually all of the studies summarized above are vulnerable to an important criticism: Many (or even all) of the purported effects of helpers on fitness that have been documented may merely be a consequence of living in groups ("group-living" effects) rather than help-

ing behavior ("alloparental" effects) *per se* (Figure 10.1). This criticism is not trivial. If we wish to demonstrate an adaptive function to helping behavior independent of the benefits of living in groups, we must be certain that the alloparental behavior performed by helpers has a direct effect on fitness and that this effect is not due simply to the presence of additional individuals within the social unit.

The main problem in separating these two effects is that in most cooperatively breeding species, all helpers at a particular nest are members of a cohesive social unit and virtually all nonbreeding members of that social unit act as helpers. As a result of this close linkage, it is extremely difficult to disentangle the effects of the two phenomena. This is the major criticism leveled by Jamieson (1989a) of studies purporting to demonstrate that helping behavior results in significant fitness benefits. As a simple example, consider a monogamous, permanently territorial species of cooperative breeder in which each breeding pair shares its territory with one or more mature, nonbreeding offspring from previous seasons. Nonbreeders assist their parents by participating in territory defense and by feeding dependent nestlings and fledglings. By helping to defend the territory, nonbreeders lighten the load on the breeders, thereby allowing them to devote more time to finding food for their dependent young. The extra food provided to dependent young by breeders and nonbreeding helpers results in reduced nestling starvation and increased reproductive success.

The nonbreeding helpers in this example influence food delivery to dependent young, and hence reproductive success, in two ways: directly, by feeding dependent young themselves, and indirectly, by helping to defend the group territory. Only the former, alloparental effect can be marshalled as evidence for the adaptive significance of helping behavior, while the latter, group-living effect cannot.

The problem of distinguishing between group-living and alloparental effects deserves considerably more attention than it has thus far received. Removal experiments do not circumvent this difficulty: The removal of potential helpers confounds group-living and alloparental effects just as surely as do nonmanipulative descriptive studies. Similarly, nonbreeders could conceivably lighten the load of related breeders, gain access to group resources and breeding sites, gain experience, and form reproductively valuable relationships simply by living and interacting within their social unit without performing any alloparental behavior *per se*.

At least four types of evidence potentially address this problem. First are data from species, such as the pied kingfisher (Reyer 1984), bell miner (Clarke 1984), white-fronted bee-eater (Emlen & Wrege 1988), and Galápagos mockingbird (Curry 1988b), where group size and helping behavior are not closely linked. In these species, positive effects of helpers on fitness are much more likely to be due to alloparental behavior rather than benefits associated with living in groups (Reyer 1984; Emlen & Wrege 1988). A second approach would be to perform removal experiments in species where young birds remain on their natal territories as nonbreeding territorial auxiliaries but do not act as helpers, such as in the green jay *Cyanocorax yncas* (Gayou 1986), or only rarely act as helpers, as in the northwestern crow *Corvus caurinus* (Verbeek & Butler 1981).

A third approach would be to undertake detailed analyses of the mechanisms by which helpers may enhance fitness (Brown & Brown 1981; Mumme in preparation). If such studies are sufficiently detailed, they should facilitate efforts to disentangle group-living effects from alloparental effects on fitness. Finally, one could manipulate helping behavior without simultaneously altering group size, possibly by careful use of hormonal implants. Such experiments would be very difficult to perform, but would nonetheless be the most powerful and unambiguous means of examining the effects of alloparental behavior on fitness.

Functional Patterns of Helping Behavior

Patterns of helping behavior that appear to have been modified or "fine-tuned" by selection suggest adaptation by design and thus that helping is a direct product of natural selection (Emlen et al. 1990). Here we discuss four ways in which helpers appear to alter their behavior in adaptive ways; Emlen et al. (1990) discuss several additional patterns.

Differential Feeding of Relatives

Bell miners, white-fronted bee-eaters, and Galápagos mockingbirds all have flexible breeding systems in which birds may act as helpers, breeders, both, or neither simultaneously within a season. Further, individuals often have the opportunity to help at more than one concurrent nest. These characteristics allow for tests of kin discrimination by helpers which would be difficult or impossible in most cooperative breeders.

Evidence for differential feeding of kin in bell miners (Clarke 1984) is suggestive but equivocal on account of small sample size and the inclusion of breeders provisioning their own offspring (Payne et al. 1985; Emlen & Wrege 1988). More conclusive are data from from the white-fronted bee-eater, where Emlen & Wrege (1988) found that kinship between potential donors and recipients was a highly significant predictor of whether or not birds acted as helpers and that helpers preferentially chose to aid their closest genetic relatives within their social unit 94% of the time. Equally good is the evidence from Galápagos mockingbirds, where Curry (1988a) showed that auxiliaries are more likely to become helpers when they are able to aid close relatives compared to distant or unrelated nestlings and that, when a choice was available, helpers invariably fed nestlings to which they were more closely related.

Two other studies yield data relevant to differential feeding of relatives by helpers. In the brown hyena, Owens & Owens (1984) found that potential male helpers fed infant half-siblings but not more distantly related cubs. Finally, in the pied kingfisher, the higher feeding rates of primary compared to secondary helpers correlates with their closer genetic relatedness to recipients (Reyer 1984, 1986).

Evidence that helping behavior is influenced by genetic relatedness provides strong support for the hypothesis that helping behavior has current adaptive function. These data are also relevant to at least two other hypotheses of general interest in behavioral ecology. First, they support the hypothesis that indirect fitness benefits have had a strong influence on the evolution of helping behavior in these species (e.g. Emlen & Wrege 1989). Second, they address the issue of how donors should dispense aid among potential recipients. Despite the importance of kinship to the decision of whether or not to help shown by white-fronted bee-eaters and Galápagos mockingbirds, degree of genetic relatedness was not found to influence the amount of aid offered in either these species or two others in which the possibility of such a correlation was tested (stripe-backed wrens [Rabenold 1985] and splendid fairy-wrens [Payne et al. 1985]). As discussed by Emlen & Wrege (1988), these findings are generally in accord with a "diminishing returns model," which predicts that helping should be an all-or-none response.

Helping Behavior Is Influenced by Specific Ecological Conditions
The considerable data indicating that cooperative breeding occurs under specific eco-logical conditions (Koenig & Pitelka 1981; Emlen 1982, Stacey & Ligon 1987; Ford et al. 1988) cannot be used as evidence for an adaptive basis of helping behavior be-cause of the high concordance between group living and the expression of helping behavior by auxiliaries (Jamieson 1989a). However, at least three studies indicate that the manifestation of helping behavior by auxiliaries is influenced by ecological con-ditions, and thus provide evidence for an adaptive basis of helping behavior.

Emlen (1984) found a correlation between the degree of environmental harshness, as measured by rainfall, and the proportion of the population of white-fronted bee-eaters that act as nonbreeding helpers. Although indirect, these data suggest that in-dividual bee-eaters may assess the ecological potential for independent breeding and act as helpers when conditions are poor (Emlen 1981). Evidence for a more drastic in-teraction providing less ambiguous support for an adaptive value of helping was de-scribed by Curry (1988b), who found evidence that in dry years dominant breeders may recruit helpers by interfering with, and ultimately causing the failure of, the breeding efforts of competing subordinates within their group.

Direct evidence of a relationship between energetic stress and helping behavior is available from the pied kingfisher, where the use of doubly-labeled water revealed that energetically stressed male breeders were more likely to accept unrelated helpers than nonstressed birds (Reyer & Westerterp 1985). Their work thus provides ex-cellent evidence that helping behavior in this species confers fitness benefits to breeders.

Sex Ratio of Nestlings Influenced by Helpers
In the red-cockaded woodpecker (*Picoides borealis*), as in several species of cooperative breeders, helpers are almost exclusively young males aiding their parents. Gowaty & Lennartz (1985) presented evidence that the nestling sex ratio in this species is biased toward males and that "nontenured" females (those not having bred previously in the study area) were more likely to produce sons than daughters.

This finding has led to considerable discussion concerning the possibility of local resource enhancement (Clark 1978) influencing the sex ratio of species with helpers (Gowaty & Lennartz 1985; Emlen et al. 1986; Lessells & Avery 1987). Emlen et al. (1986), for example, hypothesized that, by helping, nonbreeders can be thought of as repaying breeders, thereby rendering their own production less costly than that of the nonhelping sex. In the case of red-cockaded woodpeckers, this means that a son is cheaper to produce than a daughter, and therefore, because parents should invest equally in the production of sons and daughters (Fisher 1930), the sex ratio should favor sons.

The repayment model yields specific predictions concerning the sex ratios of species with helpers: in particular, in species in which helpers are males, the sex ratio bias should be proportional to the fitness enhancement (e.g. increase in reproductive success and survivorship) accruing to breeders as a consequence of having a helper, while in species in which both males and females act as helpers, there should be no such correlation. These and other predictions have yet to be tested. However, the apparently biased sex ratio in red-cockaded woodpeckers provides evidence that helping behavior may be an important evolutionary force. Certainly no interpretable relationship between helping behavior and nestling sex ratio is predicted if helping behavior has no functional basis.

Relationship between Helping and Reproductive Opportunities

In most of the species discussed thus far helpers are nonbreeders. In such species, provisioning of young is decoupled from the reproductive opportunities of helpers at that nest, which are small or nonexistent. In some species, however, more than a single individual of one sex may contribute genetically to the offspring in a communal nest. Because breeders later cooperate in raising the communal offspring, only some of which may be their own, individuals in such plural breeding species are "breeding" helpers (Brown 1987).

The variations on this theme are remarkably diverse. In the cooperatively polyandrous Galápagos hawk *Buteo galapagoensis* and Harris' hawk *Parabuteo unicinctus* (Mader 1979; Faaborg & Bednardz 1990) up to five males may consort and possibly mate with a single female. In the groove-billed ani *Crotophaga sulcirostris*, up to four pairs of birds may nest jointly in a communal nest (Vehrencamp 1978). In the dunnock *Prunella modularis*, two males may share a single female or more than one female, but the females nest solitarily (Davies 1985). The lack of a traditional pair bond and the mate-sharing by both sexes results in a mating system known as polygynandry. Finally, in the acorn woodpecker (Koenig et al. 1984) and pukeko *Porphyrio porphyrio* (Craig 1980), several cobreeding males may share several joint-nesting females. These mating systems are among the most complex known.

The benefits of provisioning offspring for a breeder are dependent on a variety of factors (Winkler 1987). The variable most relevant here is an individual's probability of having parented offspring (opportunity of parentage). Several studies have focused specifically on the relationship between provisioning rate and opportunity of parentage in species in which more than one male share a female and/or more than one female nest jointly.

The most complete of these is recent work on the dunnock by Burke et al. (1989). These authors were able to correlate the degree of reproductive access mate-sharing males enjoyed with a particular female with not only the degree to which the males subsequently fed nestlings but also, by use of DNA fingerprinting, with the actual number of offspring fathered by the male in the nest. Their results indicated a high correlation among these three variables; that is, males that had relatively great access to a female during her fertile period parented a high proportion of offspring in her nest and fed relatively often, while those with little or no access to a female neither parented offspring nor fed at her nest.

Less definitive data are available for the acorn woodpecker. In New Mexico, Stacey (1979) showed that males joining groups prior to egg laying subsequently helped provision offspring, while those joining after egg-laying did not. In California, Koenig (1990) performed experiments whose results suggest that males experimentally denied opportunity of parentage may either destroy the nest of their cobreeders or help provision the offspring depending, in part, on their dominance status vis-à-vis their cobreeders: Dominants, with a presumably high probability of parenting offspring in a renest, destroy the nest, while subordinates do not and instead assist in raising the nondescendant, but related, offspring in the nest.

A third relevant study is that of Gibbons (1986) on the moorhen, in which females may either nest jointly or parasitize the nests of other females. Joint-nesting females, which were usually close relatives, cooperated in parental care, while parasites, which were unrelated, did not. Similar results have been reported for the white-fronted bee-eater (Emlen & Wrege 1986). The coexistence of these behaviors indicates that helping is not simply a byproduct of laying eggs in a nest, but is part of an overall reproductive strategy fundamentally different from intraspecific nest parasitism.

These studies all support the hypothesis that provisioning behavior in mate-sharing and joint-nesting species has functional significance. This conclusion is most strongly supported in the dunnock, where helping behavior by breeders is correlated both with opportunity of parentage and actual genetic contribution to a particular nesting attempt.

Nonadaptive Helping Behavior?

In the previous section we discuss cases in which helping may confer fitness advantages to helpers and recipients. In other cases, however, helping behavior may have no effect on fitness or even be maladaptive. A widely-cited example of helping behavior proposed to not be adaptive is Price et al.'s (1983) report of helpers in the cactus finch (*Geospiza scandens*) and the medium ground-finch (*G. fortis*) in the Galápagos. Helpers in these species occurred on only one island and were found only following a particularly dry year. All were unpaired and usually held the territory adjacent to the offspring they fed. Helpers were apparently unrelated to the offspring they fed, in many cases had bred in prior years (hence reducing the probability that essential experience was gained), and did not appear to be likely to mate with the breeding female whose offspring they fed in the following season. Having rejected these potential advantages to helping, Price et al. (1983) concluded that helping was misdirected parental care and not adaptive.

There are, however, reasons to be cautious concerning this conclusion. Helpers contributed a substantial proportion (up to 24.9%) of regurgitations at some nests; it seems reasonable that this amount might either increase reproductive success or lighten the load of breeders. Benefits to the helpers might also include increasing their probability of acquiring a mate, as found in the pied kingfisher (see above). Although Price et al. (1983) found no significant difference in the probability that helpers and nonhelpers obtained mates within a year, the difference (91% of helpers obtained mates compared to 69% of nonhelpers) is suggestive. Only a great deal of additional data could conclusively reject this possibility. Given the rarity of helping in these populations, such data are unlikely to be forthcoming.

The equivocal nature of Price et al.'s (1983) conclusion reflects an important asymmetry between the data necessary to accept the hypothesis that helping behavior has a positive effect on fitness compared to that necessary to reject this hypothesis. One cannot directly test the hypothesis that helping behavior is selectively neutral. To accomplish this goal it would be necessary to eliminate all of the ways in which helping may confer fitness benefits to the donor or recipients. This is clearly a difficult undertaking.

Thus, just as one should not automatically assume that a behavior has an adaptive explanation (Gould & Lewontin 1979), one must be equally circumspect in concluding that no adaptive explanation exists. This is well illustrated by brood parasitism (Payne 1977) and interspecific helping behavior (Shy 1982). Both involve parent-like behavior expressed in contexts where it may appear that any benefit to the helper is exceedingly unlikely. However, to always assume that this is true would run the risk of missing rare but biologically interesting and instructive cases in which these phenomena may confer fitness advantages to helpers (Smith 1968; McKaye 1977). Right or wrong, adaptive hypotheses promote valuable empirical testing and should not be dismissed out of hand (see also Alcock 1987).

Conclusion

A characteristic feature of cooperatively breeding species is helping behavior: parent-like behavior directed toward young other than one's own genetic offspring. In the past two decades, a large literature has developed focusing on the search for adaptive explanations of helping behavior. A variety of mechanisms by which helping may increase fitness have been proposed, all leading to increased lifetime inclusive fitness of individuals, usually nonbreeders, that help compared to those that do not help. The data supporting this contention are widespread. Unfortunately, many of the relevant studies fail to control for the effects of potentially confounding variables. The most important of these is that enhanced fitness of helpers may in many cases result from living in social groups rather than from performing alloparental care *per se*. These studies thus do not provide unambiguous support for the hypothesis that helping behavior is of current adaptive utility.

More convincing evidence for this hypothesis comes through "argument by design": examples in which helping behavior has apparently been "fine-tuned" by selection (Williams 1966; Emlen et al. 1990). Four such functional patterns of helping behavior are discussed, including differential feeding of relatives, cases in which the propensity to help is apparently influenced by specific ecological conditions, cases in which the sex ratio of nestlings is apparently influenced by helpers, and cases in which there is a clear, interpretable relationship between helping and reproductive opportunities. These examples provide sound evidence for the current selective utility of helping behavior in a variety of species.

Jamieson (1986, 1988, 1989a) and Jamieson & Craig (1987) have recently challenged this conclusion. Their critique of helping behavior consists of a series of sub-hypotheses addressing the significance of helping behavior on four different levels of analysis (Tinbergen 1963; Sherman 1988): evolutionary origins, functional consequences, ontogeny, and physiological processes. They propose that helping behavior arose "epigenetically" in communal-living species as a byproduct of selection for normal parental behavior, and suggest a physiological mechanism (the normal expression of a stimulus-response link between begging offspring and provisioning behavior) by which helping behavior could be maintained in the absence of any current adaptive utility.

We agree with several aspects of Jamieson & Craig's (1987) arguments. It is quite possible that helping behavior has originated, in at least some cases, as a byproduct of selection in some other context. Brown & Brown (1980), for example, suggested that cooperative breeding, by allowing birds to coexist within social units, enables and ultimately capitalizes on the "mistake" of feeding unrelated offspring. Helping behavior might very well persist only in species where the initial "mistake" can be turned into a selective benefit for the helper, the individuals helped, or both. Jamieson & Craig (1987) are also correct to suggest that phylogenetic factors may have played a role in determining the potential for some species to exhibit cooperative breeding

(Edwards & Naeem 1990). Furthermore, the physiological mechanism which they propose as leading to the expression of helping behavior may be accurate, at least for some species.

Where we differ from Jamieson & Craig is in how we view the relevance of these hypotheses to the current functional utility of helping behavior. Jamieson (1989a) and Jamieson & Craig (1987), stress that the evolutionary origin, ontogeny, and physiological basis of helping behavior are critical pieces of information needed to discern its functional utility. Such information, however, explains helping behavior at different levels of analysis and thus may complement, but does not compete with, adaptive hypotheses for the functional utility of helping behavior. Even if it were possible to know that helping behavior in a particular species was present due to phylogenetic constraints (that is, was "inherited" from an ancestral population rather than originated *de novo*) and that helping behavior was expressed through a stimulus-response mechanism, it would still be necessary to test hypotheses for the current functional utility of helping behavior before accepting the hypothesis that it is an "unselected" trait.

Where do we go from here? First, we recommend that researchers keep in mind that problems can be profitably addressed at more than one level, no one of which is inherently better than the others. Second, researchers must be careful to recognize which level they are addressing. In our view, the substantive criticisms of "functional explanations" for helping behavior presented by Jamieson (1986, 1989a) and Jamieson & Craig (1987) run the risk of being overlooked or dismissed out of hand as a result of Jamieson's (1989b) refusal to accept that hypotheses at one level do not compete with or exclude hypotheses at other levels (Sherman 1988, 1989).

Finally, there is considerable need for rigorous work addressing the significance of helping behavior at all levels of analysis. Very little is known about the hormonal and physiological mechanisms of helping behavior and the importance of phylogeny has only recently been rigorously considered. At the level of functional consequences, the evidence for helping behavior being the direct product of selection is strong in some species but in general is not sufficiently unimpeachable that workers in this area can afford to blithely ignore the alternatives proposed by Jamieson (1989a) and Jamieson & Craig (1987). Only by careful analyses at all levels will we eventually understand the evolutionary bases of this intriguing biological phenomenon.

Acknowledgements

We thank Marc Bekoff, Nick Davies, Janis Dickinson, Steve Emlen, Andy Horn, Dale Jamieson, Ian Jamieson, Marty Leonard, Frank Pitelka, Paul Sherman, and Mark Stanback for comments on the manuscript, and Scott Edwards, Steve Emlen, Andy Horn, Ian Jamieson, Marty Leonard, Dave Ligon, Paul Sherman, and Pete Stacey for access to unpublished manuscripts. Our work on cooperative breeding has been supported by the NSF, most recently through grants DEB87-04992 to WDK and BSR86-00174 to RLM.

Literature Cited

Alcock, J. 1987. Ardent adaptationism. *Natural History* 96, 4.
Alexander, R. D. 1974. The evolution of social behavior. *Annual Review of Ecology & Systematics* 5, 325–383.

Austad, S. N. & Rabenold, K. N. 1985. Reproductive enhancement by helpers and an experimental inquiry into its mechanism in the bicolored wren. *Behavioral Ecology & Sociobiology* 17, 19–27.

———. 1986. Demography and the evolution of cooperative breeding in the bicolored wren, *Campylo-rhynchus griseus*. *Behaviour* 97, 308–324.

Brown, J. L. 1983. Cooperation—a biologists' dilemma. *Advances in the Study of Behavior* 13, 1–37.

———. 1987. *Helping and Communal Breeding in Birds: Ecology and Evolution*. Princeton, New Jersey: Princeton University Press.

Brown, J. L. & Brown, E. R. 1980. Reciprocal aid-giving in a communal bird. *Zeitschrift für Tierpsychologie* 53, 313–324.

———. 1981. Kin selection and individual selection in babblers. In: *Natural Selection and Social Behavior: Recent Research and New Theory*. (ed. by R. D. Alexander and D. W. Tinkle), pp. 244–256. New York: Chiron Press.

Brown, J. L., Brown, E. R., Brown, S. D. & Dow, D. D. 1982. Helpers: Effects of experimental removal on reproductive success. *Science* 215, 421–422.

Brown, J. L., Dow, D. D., Brown, E. R. & Brown, S. D. 1978. Effects of helpers on feeding of nestlings in the grey-crowned babbler *(Pomatostomus temporalis)*. *Behavioral Ecology & Sociobiology* 4, 43–59

Burke, T., Davies, N. B., Bruford, M. W. & Hatchwell, B. J. 1989. Parental care and mating behaviour of polyandrous dunnocks *Prunella modularis* related to paternity by DNA fingerprinting. *Nature* 338, 249–251.

Caraco, T. & Brown, J. L. 1986. A game between communal breeders: When is food-sharing stable? *Journal of Theoretical Biology* 118, 379–393.

Carlisle, T. R. & Zahavi, A. 1986. Helping at the nest, allofeeding and social status in immature Arabian babblers. *Behavioral Ecology & Sociobiology* 18, 339–351.

Clark, A. B. 1978. Sex ratio and local resource competition in a prosimian primate. *Science* 208, 163–165.

Clarke, M. F. 1984. Co-operative breeding by the Australian bell miner *Manorina melanophrys* Latham: A test of kin selection theory. *Behavioral Ecology & Sociobiology* 14, 137–146.

———. 1989. The pattern of helping in the bell miner *(Manorina melanophrys)*. *Ethology* 80, 292–306.

Craig, J. L. 1980. Pair and group breeding behaviour of a communal gallinule, the pukeko, *Porphyrio p. melanotus*. *Animal Behaviour* 28, 593–603.

Curry, R. L. 1988a. Influence of kinship on helping behavior in Galápagos mockingbirds. *Behavioral Ecology & Sociobiology* 22, 141–152.

———. 1988b. Group structure, within-group conflict and reproductive tactics in cooperatively breeding Galápagos mockingbirds, *Nesomimus parvulus*. *Animal Behaviour* 36, 1708–1728.

Davies, N. B. 1985. Cooperation and conflict among dunnocks, *Prunella modularis* in a variable mating system. *Animal Behaviour* 33, 628–648.

Dwyer, P. D. 1984. Functionalism and structuralism: Two programs for evolutionary biologists. *American Naturalist* 124, 745–750.

Eden, S. F. 1987. When do helpers help? Food availability and helping in the moorhen, *Gallinula chloropus*. *Behavioral Ecology & Sociobiology* 21, 191–195.

Edwards, S. V. & Naeem, S. 1990. The phylogenetic component of cooperative breeding in passerine birds. Unpublished manuscript.

Emlen, S. T. 1981. Altruism, kinship and reciprocity in the white-fronted bee-eater. In: *Natural Selection and Social Behavior: Recent Research and New Theory*. (ed. by R. D. Alexander & D. W. Tinkle), pp. 217–230. New York: Chiron Press.

———. 1982. The evolution of helping. I. An ecological constraints model. *American Naturalist* 119, 29–39

———. 1984. Cooperative breeding in birds and mammals. In: *Behavioural Ecology: An Evolutionary Approach*, 2nd Edition. (ed. by J. R. Krebs & N. B. Davies), pp. 305–339. Oxford: Blackwell.

Emlen, S. T., Emlen, J. M. & Levin, S. A. 1986. Sex-ratio selection in species with helpers-at-the-nest. *American Naturalist* 127, 1–8.

Emlen, S. T., Reeve, H. K., Sherman, P. W., Wregge, P. H., Ratnieks, F. L. W., and Shellman-Reeve, J. (1991). Adaptive versus non-adaptive explanations of behavior: The case of alloparental helping. *American Naturalist* 138, 259–270.

Emlen, S. T. & Wrege, P. H. 1986. Forced copulation and intraspecific parasitism: Two costs of social living in the white-fronted bee-eater. *Zeitschrift für Tierpsychologie*, 71, 2–29.

———. 1988. The role of kinship in helping decisions among white-fronted bee-eaters. *Behavioral Ecology & Sociobiology* 23, 305–315.

————. 1989. The role of direct and indirect selection in the evolution of helping behavior in white-fronted bee-eaters of Kenya. *Behavioral Ecology & Sociobiology* 25, 303–319.

Faaborg, J. & Bednarz, J. C. 1990. Galápagos and Harris' hawks: Divergent causes of sociality in two raptors. In: *Cooperative Breeding in Birds: Long-term Studies of Ecology and Behavior* (ed. by P. B. Stacey & W. D. Koenig), pp. 357–383. Cambridge: Cambridge University Press.

Fisher, R. A. 1930. *The Genetical Theory of Natural Selection*, 2nd Edition Oxford: Clarendon.

Ford, H. A., Bell, H., Nias, R. & Noske, R. 1988. The relationship between ecology and the incidence of cooperative breeding in Australian birds. *Behavioral Ecology & Sociobiology* 22, 239–249.

Gaston, A. J. 1978. The evolution of group territorial behavior and cooperative breeding. *American Naturalist* 112, 1091–1100.

Gayou, D. C. 1986. The social system of the Texas green jay. *Auk* 103, 540–547.

Gibbons, D. W. 1986. Brood parasitism and cooperative nesting in the moorhen, *Gallinula chloropus*. *Behavioral Ecology & Sociobiology* 19, 221–232.

————. 1987. Juvenile helping in the moorhen *Gallinula chloropus*. *Animal Behaviour* 35, 170–181.

Gittleman, J. L. 1985. Functions of communal care in mammals. In: *Evolution: Essays in Honour of John Maynard Smith* (ed. by P. J. Greenwood, P. H. Harvey & M. Slatkin), pp. 187–205. Cambridge: Cambridge University Press.

Gould, S. J. & Lewontin, R. C. 1979. The spandrels of San Marco and the Panglossian paradigm: A critique of the adaptationist programme. *Proceedings of the Royal Society of London* B205, 581–598.

Gowaty, P. A. & Lennartz, M. R. 1985. Sex ratios of nestlings and fledgling red-cockaded woodpeckers (*Picoides borealis*) favor males. *American Naturalist* 126, 347–353.

Greene, H. W. 1986. Diet and arborality in the emerald monitor, *Varanus prasinus*, with comments on the study of adaptation. *Fieldiana (Zoology) New Series* 31, 1–12.

Heinsohn, R. G., Cockburn, A. & Cunningham, R. B. 1988. Foraging, delayed maturation, and advantages of cooperative breeding in white-winged choughs, *Corcorax melanorhamphos*. *Ethology* 77, 177–186.

Holekamp, K. E. & Sherman, P. W. 1989. Why male ground squirrels disperse. *American Scientist* 77, 232–239.

Hoogland, J. L. & Sherman, P. W. 1976. Advantages and disadvantages of bank swallow (*Riparia riparia*) coloniality. *Ecological Monographs* 46, 33–58.

Horn, A. G. 1990. The levels of confusion. Unpublished manuscript.

Hunter, L. A. 1985. The effects of helpers in cooperatively breeding purple gallinules. *Behavioral Ecology & Sociobiology* 18, 147–153.

————. 1987. Cooperative breeding in purple gallinules: The role of helpers in feeding chicks. *Behavioral Ecology & Sociobiology* 20, 171–177.

Jamieson, I. G. 1986. The functional approach to behavior: is it useful? *American Naturalist* 127, 195–208.

————. 1988. Provisioning behaviour in a communal breeder: an epigenetic approach to the study of individual variation in behaviour. *Behaviour* 104, 262–280.

————. 1989a. Behavioral heterochrony and the evolution of birds' helping at the nest: An unselected consequence of communal breeding? *American Naturalist* 133, 394–406.

————. 1989b. Levels of analysis or analyses at the same level. *Animal Behaviour* 37, 696–697.

Jamieson, I. G. & Craig, J. L. 1987. Critique of helping behaviour in birds: A departure from functional explanations. In: *Perspectives in Ethology*, volume 7 (ed. by P. P. G. Bateson & P. H. Klopfer), pp. 79–98. New York: Plenum Press.

Kinnaird, M. F. & Grant, P. R. 1982. Cooperative breeding by the Galápagos mockingbird, *Nesomimus parvulus*. *Behavioral Ecology & Sociobiology* 10, 65–73.

Koenig, W. D. 1990. Opportunity of parentage and egg destruction in polygynandrous acorn woodpeckers: An experimental study. Unpublished manuscript.

Koenig, W. D. & Mumme, R. L. 1987. *Population Ecology of the Cooperatively Breeding Acorn Woodpecker*. Princeton, New Jersey: Princeton University Press.

Koenig, W. D., Mumme, R. L. & Pitelka, F. A. 1983. Female roles in cooperatively breeding acorn woodpeckers. In: *Social Behavior of Female Vertebrates*, (ed. by S. K. Wasser), pp. 235–261. New York: Academic Press.

————. 1984. The breeding system of the acorn woodpecker in central coastal California. *Zeitschrift für Tierpsychologie* 65, 289–308.

Koenig, W. D. & Pitelka, F. A. 1981. Ecological factors and kin selection in the evolution of cooperative breeding in birds. In: *Natural Selection and Social Behavior: Recent Research and New Theory* (ed. by R. D. Alexander & D. W. Tinkle), pp. 261–280. New York: Chiron Press.

Lack, D. 1968. *Ecological Adaptations for Breeding in Birds.* Methuen: London.

Lande, R. & Arnold, S. J. 1983. The measurement of selection on correlated characters. *Evolution* 37, 1210–1226.

Lawton, M. F. & Guindon, C. F. 1981. Flock composition, breeding success, and learning in the brown jay. *Condor* 82, 27–33.

Leonard, M. L., Horn, A. G. & Eden, S. F. 1989. Does juvenile helping enhance breeder reproductive success? A removal experiment. *Behavioral Ecology & Sociobiology* 25, 357–361.

Lessells, C. M. & Avery, M. I. 1987. Sex-ratio selection in species with helpers at the nest: some extensions of the repayment model. *American Naturalist* 129, 610–620.

Lewis, D. M. 1982. Cooperative breeding in a population of white-browed sparrow weavers *Plocepasser mahali. Ibis* 124, 511–522.

Ligon, J. D. & Ligon, S. H. 1978a. Communal breeding in green woodhoopoes as a case for reciprocity. *Nature* 276, 496–498.

———. 1978b. The communal social system of the green woodhoopoe in Kenya. *Living Bird* 17, 159–198.

———. 1983. Reciprocity in the green woodhoopoe (*Phoeniculus purpureus*). *Animal Behaviour* 31, 480–489.

Ligon, J. D. & Stacey, P. B. 1989. On the significance of helping behavior in birds. *Auk* 106, 700–705.

Mader, W. J. 1979. Breeding behavior of a polyandrous trio of Harris' hawks in southern Arizona. *Auk* 96, 776–788.

McGowan, K. J. & Woolfenden, G. E. 1989. A sentinel system in the Florida scrub jay. *Animal Behaviour* 37, 1000–1007.

McKaye, K. R. 1977. Defense of a predator's young by a herbivorous fish: an unusual strategy. *American Naturalist* 111, 301–315.

Mumme, R. L. & de Queiroz, A. 1985. Individual contributions to cooperative behaviour in the acorn woodpecker: Effects of reproductive status, sex, and group size. *Behaviour* 95, 290–313.

Mumme, R. L., Koenig, W. D. & Ratnieks, F. L. W. 1989. Helping behaviour, reproductive value, and the future component of indirect fitness. *Animal Behaviour* 38, 331–343.

Nias, R. C. 1986. Nest-site characteristics and reproductive success in the superb fairy-wren. *Emu* 86, 139–144.

Owens, D. D. & Owens, M. J. 1984. Helping behaviour in brown hyenas. *Nature* 308, 843–845.

Payne, R. B. 1977. The ecology of brood parasitism in birds. *Annual Review of Ecology & Systematics* 8, 1–28.

Payne, R. B., Payne, L. L. & Rowley, I. 1985. Splendid wren *Malurus splendens* response to cuckoos: An experimental test of social organization in a communal bird. *Behaviour* 94, 108–127.

Price, T., Millington, S. & Grant, P. 1983. Helping at the nest in Darwin's finches as misdirected parental care. *Auk* 100, 192–194.

Rabenold, K. N. 1984. Cooperative enhancement of reproductive success in tropical wren societies. *Ecology* 63, 871–885.

———. 1985. Cooperation in breeding by nonreproductive wrens: Kinship, reciprocity, and demography. *Behavioral Ecology & Sociobiology* 17, 1–17.

Raitt, R. J., Winterstein, S. R. & Hardy, J. W. 1984. Structure and dynamics of communal groups in the Beechey jay. *Wilson Bulletin* 96, 206–227.

Reyer, H.-U. 1980. Flexible helper structure as an ecological adaptation in the pied kingfisher (*Ceryle rudis rudis* L.). *Behavioral Ecology & Sociobiology* 6, 219–227.

———. 1984. Investment and relatedness: A cost/benefit analysis of breeding and helping in the pied kingfisher (*Ceryle rudis*). *Animal Behaviour* 32, 1163–1178.

———. 1986. Breeder-helper-interactions in the pied kingfisher reflect the costs and benefits of cooperative breeding. *Behaviour* 96, 277–303.

Reyer, H.-U. & Westerterp, K. 1985. Parental energy expenditure: a proximate cause of helper recruitment in the pied kingfisher (*Ceryle rudis*). *Behavioral Ecology & Sociobiology* 17, 363–369.

Rowley, I. 1978. Communal activities among white-winged choughs *Corcorax melanorhamphus. Ibis* 120, 178–197.

Rowley, I. & Russell, E. 1990. Splendid fairy-wrens: demonstrating the importance of longevity. In: *Cooperative Breeding in Birds: Long-term Studies of Ecology and Behavior.* (ed. by P. B. Stacey & W. D. Koenig), pp. 1–30. Cambridge: Cambridge University Press.

Russell, E. M. 1989. Co-operative breeding—a Gondwanan perspective. *Emu* 89, 61–62.

Russell, E. & Rowley, I. 1988. Helper contributions to reproductive success in the splendid fairy-wren (*Malurus splendens*). *Behavioral Ecology & Sociobiology* 22, 131–140.

Sherman, P. W. 1988. The levels of analysis. *Animal Behaviour* 36, 616–619.

————. 1989. The clitoris debate and the levels of analysis. *Animal Behaviour* 37, 697–698.

Shy, M. M. 1982. Interspecific feeding among birds: A review. *Journal of Field Ornithology* 53, 370–393.

Skutch, A. F. 1961. Helpers among birds. *Condor* 63, 198–226.

Smith, N. G. 1968. The advantage of being parasitized. *Nature* 219, 690–694.

Stacey, P. B. 1979. Kinship, promiscuity, and communal breeding in the acorn woodpecker. *Behavioral Ecology & Sociobiology* 6, 53–66.

Stacey, P. B. & Koenig, W. D. (eds.) 1990. *Cooperative Breeding in Birds: Long-term Studies of Ecology and Behavior*. Cambridge: Cambridge University Press.

Stacey, P. B. & Ligon, J. D. 1987. Territory quality and dispersal options in the acorn woodpecker, and a challenge to the habitat-saturation model of cooperative breeding. *American Naturalist* 130, 654–676.

Stallcup, J. A. & Woolfenden, G. E. 1978. Family status and contribution to breeding by Florida scrub jays. *Animal Behaviour* 26, 1144–1156.

Taborsky, M. 1984. Broodcare helpers in the cichlid fish *Lamprologus brichardi*: Their costs and benefits. *Animal Behaviour* 32, 1236–1252.

————. 1985. Breeder-helper conflict in a cichlid fish with broodcare helpers: an experimental analysis. *Behaviour* 95, 45–75.

Taborsky, M. & Limberger, D. 1981. Helpers in fish. *Behavioral Ecology & Sociobiology* 8, 143–145.

Tinbergen, N. 1963. On aims and methods of ethology. *Zeitschrift für Tierpsychologie* 20, 410–433.

Vehrencamp, S. L. 1978. The adaptive significance of communal nesting in groove-billed anis (*Crotophaga sulcirostris*). *Behavioral Ecology & Sociobiology* 4, 1–33.

Verbeek, N. A. M. & Butler, R. W. 1981. Cooperative breeding of the northwestern crow *Corvus caurinus*. *Ibis* 123, 183–189.

Wiley, R. H. & Rabenold, K. N. 1984. The evolution of cooperative breeding by delayed reciprocity and queuing for favorable social positions. *Evolution* 38, 609–621.

Williams, G. C. 1966. *Adaptation and Natural Selection*. Princeton, New Jersey: Princeton University Press.

Winkler, D. W. 1987. A general model for parental care. *American Naturalist* 130, 526–543.

Woolfenden, G. E. & Fitzpatrick, J. W. 1984. *The Florida Scrub Jay: Demography of a Cooperative-breeding Bird*. Princeton, New Jersey: Princeton University Press.

Zack, S. & Ligon, J. D. 1985. Cooperative breeding in *Lanius* shrikes. II. Maintenance of group-living in a nonsaturated habitat. *Auk* 102, 766–773.

Recognition, Choice, Vigilance, and Play

Chapter 11

The Ubiquitous Concept of Recognition with Special Reference to Kin

Andrew R. Blaustein and Richard H. Porter

"It takes a wise man to recognize a wise man."
—Diogenes Laertius

The concept of recognition is crucial to understanding biological systems from the molecular to the population level. Yet, in many instances, the usefulness of this concept suffers from a lack of clear definitions. Thus, the biological significance of recognition is not always readily apparent. In this paper, we attempt to provide an assessment of the word "recognition" by briefly reviewing its application and relevance to diverse biological phenomena, with a particular emphasis on "kin recognition." We hope that explication of the fundamental nature of recognition across life-forms, and discussions of unambiguous applications of the concept of recognition, will enhance its utility and be of interest to those who study behavior in various subdisciplines. After reviewing the literature on kin recognition, we conclude, as do others, that we must be careful about what can be inferred from observations.

According to common usage, the term "recognition" can convey a variety of different meanings. Included among the various definitions of recognition listed in the *Oxford English Dictionary* are the following:

1) "Knowledge or consciousness"
2) "To know again or further"
3) "The action or fact of perceiving that something, person, etc., is the same as one previously known"
4) "The action or fact of apprehending a thing under a particular category, or as having a certain character"

Despite the (sometimes subtle) differences between the above definitions, in each case, recognition refers to abstract (neural) processes that are difficult to study. For example, one cannot specify, nor therefore measure, the precise physical/chemical events in the central nervous system that are involved in perceiving that a person "is the same as one previously known."

In practice, recognition is typically defined operationally as discriminative responsiveness to particular stimuli—including discriminative interactions between individual elements, ranging from sub-cellular particles to whole organisms and social groups (e.g. Colgan 1983; Fletcher & Michener 1987; Grosberg et al. 1988; Klein 1982; Roitt 1988).

Defining recognition as discriminative interactions is generally consistent with the fourth conceptualization of recognition listed above, i.e. "the action or fact of apprehending a thing under a particular category, or as having a certain character." That is, if individual A habitually responds to B differently than to others of their own kind (e.g. conspecifics) found in the same area, B must possess a discernibly unique phenotype, and A the capacity for mediating discrimination of those traits. Discriminable phenotypic "signatures" could include characteristic physical features as well as idiosyncratic behavioral patterns.

It should be pointed out, however, that this operational definition of "recognition" is not fully compatible with dictionary definitions 2 and 3 above, which are restricted to instances where something is discriminated as a function of prior knowledge or familiarization with that same stimulus. The latter use of the term is in keeping with the etymological roots: *re* (again) + *cognoscere* (to know)—thus, Re-cognition (Bekoff personal communication). When conceptualized in this manner, recognition implies some manner of information storage or memory of earlier events, but neither the involvement of complex cognitive processes nor conscious awareness. As will be discussed more fully below, several developmental mechanisms could result in an ability to distinguish accurately between individual stimuli, and not all of these need involve earlier exposure and familiarity. Such ontogenetic mechanisms are not to be confused with the neural and sensory processes underlying recognition. Rather, the former mechanisms refer to the particular experiential and genetic factors that contribute to discrimination; how an individual develops the ability to discriminate others (or their characteristic phenotypic signatures). This question is at a different level of analysis (see Koenig & Mumme chapter 10 of this reader) than that concerning the physiological basis of recognition and has been the subject of a greater number of recent empirical investigations.

The Fundamental Nature of Recognition

Discriminative interactions among individuals, animals, cells, or classes of individuals (e.g. like-sexed conspecifics, agemates), hence recognition in the broad sense of the term, is a fundamental biological phenomenon. Indeed, the physical structure of the basic unit of life, the DNA molecule, is a function of specific pairings of complementary bases on the two strands of the double helix (viz. Adenine with Thymine, Guanine with Cytosine). Moreover, as pointed out by Watson (1970: 395), "The overall accuracy of protein synthesis can ... be no greater than the accuracy with which the activating enzymes can selectively recognize the various amino acids" and the adaptors that attach them to the RNA templates.

Historecognition, or the ability to discriminate between "self" and "nonself," is a universal characteristic of metazoan animals, and is even found in some primitive sponges (Porifera) (e.g. Roitt 1988; Van de Vyver 1988). Two categories of historecognition have been described (Grosberg 1988a,b): Allogenic—discrimination between self and genetically dissimilar conspecifics (or conspecific tissue); and Xenogenic—recognition of heterospecific nonself. It has been argued that self/nonself discrimination is a "basic prerequisite" for specific cell adhesion and therefore the development of multicellular organisms (Coombe & Parish 1988). Moreover, the vertebrate immune system, which protects an individual against invasion by foreign (nonself) substances, is believed to have evolved from primitive cellular recognition mechanisms that functioned to maintain both self-integrity and symbiotic interactions between different organisms (Thomas 1975; Boyse & Cantor 1978; Van de Vyver 1988). In our own species, the likelihood of rejection of a tissue graft or transplanted organ depends upon whether that material is recognized as foreign by the recipient's immune system, or more specifically, by that person's major histocompatibility complex.

Conspicuous manifestations of recognition are readily apparent in the social behavior of animals. Thus, interactions among members of the same species generally differ from the behavior displayed during heterospecific encounters (e.g. Roy 1980; Colgan 1983). For many sexually reproducing organisms, mating success depends on accurate identification of a conspecific of the opposite sex, in the appropriate physiological condition. Maintenance of the complex social systems characteristic of numerous vertebrates and invertebrates, may entail discrimination between individuals on the basis of age, sex, or dominance status, and differential treatment of members of one's own group versus outsiders. Territorial birds, for example, often recognize the calls of their neighbors and thereby avoid recurring agonistic encounters with those same individuals (Falls 1978).

The remainder of this chapter will focus on kin recognition, a category of social discrimination that has recently been the topic of considerable theoretical interest and empirical research. Although it is clear that numerous species from a wide array of taxa can discriminate between related and unrelated individuals, the adaptive value of the behavior is poorly understood (Blaustein et al. 1987a,b; 1991). Furthermore, there seem to be limits to the recognition abilities of certain species and there is increasing evidence that many species are not capable of discriminating between kin and nonkin, although the potential benefits of doing so appear to humans to be large.

Kin Recognition: What Have We Learned?

Hamilton's (1964a,b) model of inclusive fitness provided a seminal theoretical breakthrough for an understanding of the evolution of social behavior. His model predicts, all things being equal and depending upon relative costs and benefits, that individuals will behave differently toward one another depending upon genetic relatedness. Thus, close relatives are more likely to cooperate with or aid one another (nepotism) than are distant relatives or unrelated individuals. Furthermore, characteristics that may decrease the fitness of an individual may persist in a population if a sufficient number of kin are thereby aided.

An ability to discriminate between kin and nonkin is not necessary for kin selection to operate. For example, if dispersal from a birth place is relatively infrequent, then it is probable that a relatively large proportion of interacting individuals within the population are kin (Bekoff 1981a; Holmes & Sherman 1982). Therefore, probabilistically, cooperation and aid-giving behavior would be nepotistic and these behaviors could be maintained within a population through kin selection without a mechanism of discriminating between kin and nonkin. In other contexts, however, effective nepotism may indeed require that individuals are capable of such discrimination. This is most obvious when kin and nonkin occur within the same area, so that indiscriminate investment would not result in a net relative advantage to one's kin (and thereby fail to enhance one's own inclusive fitness).

Besides obvious gains in inclusive fitness, there are other potential functions of kin recognition. For example, individuals may achieve optimal outbreeding by assessing genetic affinities of conspecifics when choosing mates (Bateson 1983). Moreover, important ecological phenomena may be influenced by kin recognition (e.g. Bekoff 1981b; Blaustein et al. 1987a,b; Anderson 1989). For example, individuals may compete more intensely with or selectively prey upon unrelated conspecifics (Blaustein et al. 1987b; Porter & Blaustein 1989).

Experimental analyses of special cases of kin recognition, such as those involving parent-offspring relationships in vertebrates and nestmate recognition in social insects, had been conducted prior to the appearance of Hamilton's (1964a,b) papers (e.g. reviews by Hölldobler & Michener 1980; Colgan 1983). However, experimental studies concerned with recognition of collateral (nonparent/offspring) kin were not common at the time Hamilton formulated his kinship model (see discussion in Hamilton 1987).

Except for studies of social insects (see papers in Fletcher & Michener 1987 and references therein) and desert isopods (Linsenmair 1987), experimental papers investigating collateral kin recognition (hereafter collateral kin recognition = kin recognition) did not begin to appear prominently in the literature until more than 10 years after Hamilton's (1964a,b) model was published. In fact, as Hamilton (1987: 426) states, "the first recent papers about actual cases [of kin recognition were] reviewed with almost open hostility and suspicion." Hamilton (1987: 246) suggests that the relationship between nepotism and kin recognition may have been a major factor contributing to a lack of kin recognition studies because nepotism, "at least in civilized cultures, has become an embarrassment." Crozier (1987) points out that the prevailing environmentalist-determinist views at the time Hamilton conceived his theory may have halted the development of quantitative genetic models of recognition. Perhaps the lag was so long because it took more than a decade to understand the overall importance of kinship theory to evolutionary biology (see discussion in Crozier 1987).

Regardless of the reasons, this lag is especially perplexing because Hamilton (1964a,b) explicitly discussed the implications of kin recognition to his kinship theory. Moreover, before papers on kin recognition began to appear *en masse* in the late 1970s there were published reports illustrating interest in the phenomenon. For example, a statement made by Richard Wassersug at a symposium held in 1970 was one particularly early, but still relatively unknown, insight into the kin recognition phenomenon. Nevertheless, it provided the impetus for the extensive research on kin recognition in anuran larvae (reviewed in Blaustein 1988). In discussing the schooling characteristics of toad tadpoles Wassersug (1973: 289) wrote:

> Many aspects of the *Bufo* pattern—conspicuousness, unpalatability, and gregariousness—suggest that kin selection may be operative. The degree of genetic similarity among proximal individuals could be determined in *Bufo* because the eggs adhere in strands. Clutches could be individually stained with vital dyes to determine the amount of sibling relationship in schools that form once the eggs hatch.

The lag in empirical work on kin recognition also coincided with a lag in theoretical models. Although Alexander & Borgia (1978) discussed several aspects of the mechanisms of kin recognition in some detail, the first quantitative model of kin recognition appeared in 1979 (Crozier & Dix, 1979) and was followed by several others in rapid succession (e.g. Getz 1981; Beecher 1982; Lacy & Sherman 1983).

For the past 10 years there has been an incredible flurry of empirical research in the field. This can best be appreciated by the numerous review articles and volumes on kin recognition that have recently been published (e.g. Gadagkar 1985; Sherman & Holmes 1985; Hepper 1986; Fletcher & Michener 1987; Waldman 1987; Blaustein et al. 1987a,b, 1988; Holmes 1988; Porter & Blaustein 1989). It is time to reflect on this body of research and evaluate what we have learned. Perhaps the best way to do this is to relate it to the four basic questions of animal behavior posed by Tinbergen (1963). In the context of kin recognition, these questions would be 1) What is the proximate (sensory) basis of kin recognition behavior?; 2) How does kin recognition behavior develop? 3) What is the evolutionary history of the behavior? 4) What is the function of the behavior?

Early experimental work on kin recognition dealt primarily with the ontogeny of the behavior and the processes used in discriminating between kin and nonkin (e.g. Porter et al. 1978; O'Hara & Blaustein 1981; Waldman, 1981; Buckle & Greenberg 1981; Holmes & Sherman 1982; Kareem 1983; see reviews by Michener & Smith 1987; Breed & Bennett 1987). Many of these studies included analyses of the proximate (sensory) bases of kin recognition. Therefore, questions 1 and 2 have been addressed in some detail as is discussed below.

Ontogeny and Proximate Basis of Kin Recognition

Familiarity and Recognition

Attributes of a stimulus complex may be learned and remembered even though they have never been associated with a conventional reinforcer (or unconditioned stimulus, in the case of classical conditioning). Familiarization resulting from such mere exposure or from reinforced learning (or both), is perhaps the most obvious means by which animals develop the ability to discriminate individuals or members of a particular social category, such as close kin (Bekoff 1981a).

There are numerous accounts of preferential interactions among littermate or broodmate siblings that had been raised together, but isolated from other conspecific agemates, during early development (e.g. O'Hara & Blaustein 1981; Waldman 1981; Halpin & Hoffman 1987; Porter et al. 1978; Wilson 1982; Kareem 1983; Hepper 1983; Holmes & Sherman 1982). To assess the relative importance of rearing association versus genetic relatedness in the ontogeny of kin recognition, neonates are exchanged between different litters or sibling aggregations. Although the data are not generally consistent across species, such fostering experiments generally reveal that early association markedly influences the development of sibling recognition. Among wood frog (*Rana sylvatica*) tadpoles (Waldman, 1984), thirteen-lined ground squirrels (*Spermophilus tridecemlineatus*) (Holmes 1984), and white-footed mice (*Peromyscus leucopus*) (Halpin & Hoffman 1987), siblings that are reared together interact differently than such kin that have been raised apart. In addition, several ground squirrel species (see Schwagmeyer 1988), Townsend's chipmunk (*Tamias townsendii*), spiny mice (*Acomys cahirinus*) and white-footed mice discriminate agemates with which they had been reared—regardless of whether those conspecifics are full-siblings or nonkin (Halpin & Hoffman 1987; Holmes 1984; Schwagmeyer 1988; Porter et al. 1981; Fuller & Blaustein 1990). Actual bodily contact and physical interactions are not always necessary for the development of social familiarity and discrimination provided that there is access to, and perception of, individuals' salient phenotypic signatures. As but one illustration of this point, spiny mouse weanlings whose only exposure to one another was across a double wire-mesh barrier separating their two cages, nonetheless huddled together preferentially during subsequent test sessions (Porter et al. 1984). Neighbors were presumably discriminated by their familiar odor signatures since previous studies with this species found no evidence of social discrimination among animals with olfactory deficits—including littermate siblings that had been housed together since birth (Porter et al. 1978).

It should not be concluded from the sibling-recognition "errors" discussed above (e.g. unrelated foster littermates interacting like biological siblings) that direct individual familiarization is an unreliable mechanism for discriminating kin. In nature, if members of a sibship are unlikely to encounter unrelated conspecifics (at least during certain stages of development), individual agemate recognition based on direct association and familiarity would indeed be equivalent to sibling recognition. On the other hand, discriminative interactions among kin have also been documented among animals that have not previously encountered one another, or when related and unrelated conspecifics co-exist throughout the life cycle. Although such observations cannot be explained by direct prior contact with the recognized individuals, familiarity of an *indirect* sort could still mediate the development of kin discrimination in these contexts. If genotypic relatedness is correlated with phenotypic resemblance, close kin should be more similar than nonkin on those traits. Once an animal becomes acquainted with the salient signature(s) of particular kin (or even with its own signature), other individuals whose phenotypes approximate those that are already familiar, might also be discriminated—i.e. the previously learned signature would be used as a standard against which unknown others are compared. Kin recognition as a function of such *indirect familiarization*, commonly referred to as "phenotype-matching" (Holmes & Sherman 1982) or the "armpit effect" (Dawkins 1982), is not distinctly different from recognition through direct association and familiarity. In both instances, kin recognition is based upon learned familiarization with salient phenotypic signatures and a correspondence between those templates and the current phenotype of the "familiar" animal (e.g. Porter 1988).

Indirect familiarization has been implicated as a likely kin recognition mechanism in organisms across a wide range of taxa, including social insects (Buckle & Greenberg 1981; Gamboa et al. 1986), frog and toad tadpoles (Blaustein & O'Hara 1981, 1982; Waldman 1981), rodents (Holmes 1986; Porter et al. 1983) and humans (Porter et al. 1985; Wells 1987). To test nestmate recognition in sweat bees (*Lasioglossum zephyrum*), Buckle & Greenberg (1981) observed the responses of guard bees to nonresident intruders. Experimental colonies were composed either entirely of sisters from the same source nest, or mixtures of equal numbers of bees from two unrelated nests. Guards in the mixed colonies accepted sisters of their nonkin nestmates more frequently than unrelated bees were permitted to enter the all-sister nests. Mixed-nest guards did not discriminate between their own sisters and sisters of their unrelated nestmates—i.e., the acceptance rates for both types of intruders were similarly high. In a second experiment, each mixed colony contained several nestmate sisters plus one unrelated "odd" bee. The acceptance rate by odd-bee guards was significantly less when confronted with their own (nonresident) sisters than with intruding sisters of their unrelated nestmates. Buckle and Greenberg (1981) concluded that the guard bees learn their nestmates' odor and afterwards accept nonresidents who have similar scents.

Results analogous to those for sweat bees were obtained in a series of similar studies with Belding's ground squirrels (Holmes 1986) and spiny mice (Porter 1988; Porter et al. 1983). For both species, individuals that had been raised apart from one another but with one another's sibling(s), interacted discriminatively during subsequent recognition tests—regardless of whether they were kin or nonkin. It therefore appears that phenotypic resemblance of siblings was discernible even to conspecifics who were not themselves close relatives of the stimulus animals. Correlations between genetic relatedness and phenotypic resemblance are likewise evident among members of our own species. Siblings, parents and offspring, and other classes of close kin, frequently share similar facial features and audible voice qualities. Noticeable similarities in individual odors emanating from kin also exist, presumably as a result of genetically influenced biochemical pathways. This is reflected in the behavior of trained tracking dogs who more often confuse the odors of identical twins than scents from fraternal twins or nontwin siblings (Kalmus 1955; Hepper 1988). Humans may not possess the olfactory prowess of dogs, but those tested in a recent experiment accurately matched the body odors of mothers and their offspring at a rate significantly greater than that expected by chance alone (Porter et al. 1985).

Indirect familiarization has also been evoked as a possible ontogenetic mechanism enabling animals to discriminate between kin of differing degrees of relatedness. In laboratory colonies of sweat bees, a strong linear relationship was observed between the likelihood that a guard would accept a nonnestmate and the coefficient of genetic relatedness of the tested individuals (Greenberg 1979). Furthermore, Cascades frog tadpoles that had been reared with siblings or in isolation associated preferentially with full-siblings over half-siblings, but nonetheless preferred half-siblings over nonsiblings (Blaustein & O'Hara 1982). Kin discrimination by isolation-reared tadpoles could be accomplished by those individuals using their own familiar signatures as templates against which others are compared (i.e. self-matching).

Familiarity and Re-Cognition
As mentioned in the Introduction, one of the common definitions of "recognition" is to know or perceive that something "is the same as one previously known." Recognition according to this meaning, can be more precisely operationalized as discriminative responses to particular stimuli as a function of prior exposure. Once again, one can turn to immunology for a relevant example. Immune responses to specific micro-organisms develop through initial exposure to their antigens. Such preliminary contact alters the functioning of the immune system so that subsequent encounters with those same antigens elicit a more intense and rapid antibody response (Roitt 1988). Acquired specific immunity therefore entails the memory of earlier exposure to particular antigens and later discrimination of them.

Arguably, all occurrences of kin discrimination that involve familiarity as an ontogenetic mechanism fit under the definition of "recognition" as "knowing again." This is no doubt most obvious for direct familiarization, where particular conspecifics are discriminated as a result of prior contact with them. In these instances, the recognized individuals would indeed be ones that were previously known.

While kin recognition resulting from indirect familiarization does not entail prior interactions with the discriminated individuals, the salient phenotypic traits of those

animals (or at least close approximations of those signatures) would have been encountered previously. The signatures *per se* would therefore be known, but in a different social context; i.e. in association with different conspecifics or as a discernible
characteristic of the recognizing individual itself. As seen above, the correspondence
in the signatures of familiar and unfamiliar kin need not be one-hundred percent for
the latter to be discriminated. Animals that become well-acquainted with the salient
phenotypes of particular relatives might then display generalized recognition of
signatures of other kin that resemble, but are not identical to the already familiar
standards.

Genetic Recognition Systems

Perhaps the most controversial issue in the kin recognition literature concerns the
possibility of a "genetic recognition system," where the unique phenotypic signature
does not have to be learned. Theoretically, as Hamilton (1964a,b) originally suggested, a supergene (or "recognition alleles" = green beard recognition; Dawkins
1976) would express a unique signature phenotypically, cause the recognition of the
signature, and enable those individuals carrying copies of these alleles to favor other
individuals also carrying these alleles.

The controversy over the existence of recognition alleles stems from theoretical
discussions suggesting that such a system is too complex to evolve (e.g. Alexander &
Borgia 1978; Sherman & Holmes 1985) and that recognition alleles may be "outlaws"
that favor themselves at the expense of all other alleles in the genome (including
those at other gene loci) (Alexander & Borgia 1978). Thus, they may act like segregation distorters or meiotic drive genes that are favored at their own locus and
appear in more than 50% of the gametes produced. In some animals, heterozygous
individuals fail to produce equal proportions of their two different alleles because of
meiotic drive, which is believed to be a result of the interaction of the different chro-
mosomes when they are synapsed during meiosis (Hedrick 1984). As discussed by
Rothstein & Barash (1983), meiotic drive may harm the genome as a whole when it is
achieved by the selective destruction of gametes lacking the driving allele. This results in fewer gametes and lowered fertility in males but not in females where only
one of the four products of meiosis becomes a functional gamete. Such reduced fertility has been demonstrated in male fruit flies (*Drosophila*, Crow 1979).

The theoretical arguments concerning the improbability of recognition alleles have
been generally accepted even though Hamilton (1964b: 25) suggested that the same
a priori objections may be argued against positive assortative mating which has
evolved "despite its obscure advantages." Moreover, it is questionable that recognition alleles are outlaws (Ridley & Grafen 1981; Rothstein & Barash 1983; Guilford
1985).

Nevertheless, if one carefully reads the literature concerning recognition alleles,
there should be no controversy. To wit, while several authors have suggested that
the results of some kin preference experiments *are consistent with* both recognition
alleles and indirect familiarization through self matching, they also point out that it
may not be possible to distinguish experimentally between these two mechanisms
(Blaustein 1983; Crozier 1987). Both mechanisms allow an individual to recognize
others with whom they have never had contact and lead to the same evolutionary
predictions (Blaustein 1983). Unequivocal support for the recognition allele hypothesis could only be achieved by experimentally masking the ability of an individual to

perceive the phenotypic signature in question throughout ontogeny. For most species this would be extremely difficult. Thus, to argue exclusively that either indirect familiarity or recognition alleles are involved in those cases where it is impossible to distinguish between them is pointless (see Bekoff's discussion, 1988). Importantly, the most extreme proponents of recognition alleles only suggest their *possibility* even though they "do not necessarily endorse their existence" (Blaustein et al. 1987b: 339).

Another point of controversy seems to have sprung from "nature/nurture paranoia" and the red flag that the terms "genetic" and "innate" convey (Bekoff 1988; Holmes 1988). In the context of kin recognition, the term "genetic" has been used in several ways. As stated above, Hamilton (1964a,b) used a supergene model to explain the theoretical possibility of a recognition system where the perception of the signature occurs without learning. Others have used the term to denote genetically based signatures such as odors and the term "genetic" does not in any way relate to the *perception* of the signature (e.g. Greenberg 1979; Getz & Smith 1983; see discussion by Holmes 1988).

Theoretical discussions of "genetic recognition systems" are usually very clear about defining terms. For example, Crozier (1987, 1988) distinguishes between green beard alleles that convey all the characteristics formulated by Hamilton (1964a,b) in his supergene model and recognition alleles that do not encode behavioral characteristics but do confer the bearing of the phenotypic marker and the ability to recognize the marker in others. As Alcock (1988) suggests, the general use of the terms "genetic" or "innate" for "developmentally resilient" performs a useful service. Burghardt (1988) points out that "innate" in reference to behavior is a shorthand way of referring to a phenomenon that may be shaped or influenced strongly but not solely by genetic information. Clearly, the realization with regard to kin recognition is that "virtually no complicated behavior is totally impervious to learning" (Blaustein 1983: 753).

An often discussed potential example of a "genetic recognition" system in the sense of Hamilton (1964a,b) is the H-2 major histocompatibility complex (MHC) in house mice (*Mus musculus*) (Beauchamp et al. 1988; Lenington et al. 1988). This system is involved in the production of antigens responsible for self/nonself recognition (Beauchamp et al. 1985, 1988). Moreover, the MHC is the most variable gene complex known, has a high rate of mutation and is involved in the production of discernible olfactory signatures characteristic of the animal's genotype (Beauchamp et al. 1988 and references therein). Early experiments showed that male mice associated preferentially with females that differed in H-2 type (most comparisons) or that were the same in H-2 type (Yamazaki et al. 1976). A theoretical genetic model based on these data suggested that mating preference may be controlled by two linked genes in the H-2 region, one for the signal and one for the receptor (Yamazaki et al. 1976).

More recent evidence from cross-fostering experiments, however, suggests that although the signature (odor) may be under the control of alleles at the H-2 region, preferences for those cues are influenced by rearing experience (Beauchamp et al 1988; Yamazaki et al. 1988). It appears that males are biased towards females that differ from their parental MHC types (Beauchamp et al. 1988; Yamazaki et al. 1988). Thus, at present there is little evidence that the MHC in house mice functions as a genetic recognition system in the sense of Hamilton (1964a,b).

Perhaps, a more plausible possibility of a genetic recognition system is found in marine invertebrates (Grosberg et al. 1986). Under experimental conditions, the larvae of at least two species (a tunicate and a bryozoan) have been shown to settle near siblings (Keough 1984; Grosberg & Quinn 1986). In many clonal species, clone-mates and close kin can be distinguished from nonclonemates with remarkable specificity (Grosberg & Quinn 1986). As suggested by Grosberg & Quinn (1986), this ability requires a recognition system that can detect small differences among individuals and contains sufficient genetic variation at loci conferring allotypic specificity so that relatedness can be inferred from shared alleles.

In laboratory experiments, tunicates (*Botryllus schlosseri*) that have been shown to settle near siblings in the field, distinguish between kin and nonkin on the basis of shared alleles at the highly polymorphic histocompatibility locus that regulates fusion between colonies (Grosberg & Quinn 1986). Thus, Grosberg & Quinn (1986) suggest that kin recognition in this species enhances the settlement of histocompatible colonies and the restriction of fusion to closely related genotypes may be beneficial to the colony as a whole. Fusion among kin may decrease mortality and enhance reproduction in the colony (Grosberg & Quinn 1986). Unfortunately, currently it is not known for certain if the histocompatibility alleles influence settlement behavior or just the phenotypic signature. In summary, to date, there is no clear cut case of a recognition allele system in any species, vertebrate or invertebrate.

Phylogeny and Adaptive Value
It is obviously not possible to know the precise selective pressures influencing how a particular behavior first originated. Yet, from the fossil record and through comparative studies, we can sometimes trace the evolutionary pathway of a particular behavior and speculation concerning its evolutionary history can be put forth (e.g. Foster & Gamboa 1989). Comparing differences in how kin recognition is manifested in closely related species that differ in key ecological characteristics is one way that has been used to address the evolution of kin recognition and to track its possible antiquity within a group. However, until recently, most of the available comparative information was on eusocial insects (e.g. Gamboa et al. 1986; Breed & Bennett 1987; Michener & Smith 1987). We are just beginning to build a solid foundation of comparative information in other groups such as amphibian larvae (reviewed by Blaustein 1988) and ground squirrels (reviewed by Schwagmeyer 1988).

There is certainly evidence from field observations in which no experimental manipulations were performed, that is consistent with the hypothesis that kin recognition may function in promoting optimal outbreeding (e.g. Berger & Cunningham 1987) and may be used as a mechanism enhancing cooperation among kin (e.g. Emlen 1984; Gouzoules 1984; Brown 1987). However, few species for which there are good data on kin relationships in the field have been experimentally investigated for kin recognition. Furthermore, except for social insects and some subsocial arthropods (see Fletcher & Michener 1987; Page et al. 1989), we know very little about the function of kin recognition in those species that have been the subject of intensive *experimental* investigations. This stems from 1) a lack of knowledge of the natural history of the species and 2) an almost total reliance on laboratory experiments.

In vertebrates, comprehensive field experiments have been conducted only on Belding's ground squirrels (*S. beldingi*) (Holmes & Sherman 1982) and two species of larval amphibians (Waldman 1982; O'Hara & Blaustein, 1985). Among ground squirrels, kin recognition may function to facilitate cooperation among certain classes of kin (Holmes & Sherman 1982) and in directing alarm calls toward kin (Sherman

1980). Similarly, nepotistic cooperation and warning have been suggested as functions for kin recognition in larval anurans (e.g. Waldman & Adler 1979; Hews & Blaustein 1985; see also Jasienski 1988). However, even in species for which field experiments were conducted, the ultimate functional significance of kin recognition is not well understood (see discussions in Blaustein 1988; Guilford 1988), despite what is often implied (West-Eberhard 1989; Blaustein et al. 1991).

To understand the function of kin recognition, we must know key aspects of the ecology and social behavior of the species being investigated before a coherent set of testable hypotheses are constructed. For many species that have been investigated, it is not even known if kin come in contact with one another in nature (see review by Blaustein et al. 1987a and discussion by Holmes 1988: 407). Yet, it has become conventional to invoke kin selection scenarios to explain the evolution of kin recognition systems.

What Have We Learned about Kin Recognition?

Numerous species across many taxa can discriminate between kin and nonkin (Fletcher & Michener 1987). We know a good deal about the ontogeny and proximate bases of kin recognition behavior (see papers in Fletcher & Michener 1987 for information on the sensory bases of kin recognition). However, other than for eusocial insects and a very small number of vertebrates (e.g. Holmes & Sherman 1982), we know practically nothing about the adaptive value of kin recognition in nature (Blaustein et al. 1991). Furthermore, there are important questions that must be addressed for a thorough understanding of the interrelationships among social behavior, behavioral ecology, kin selection and kin recognition. For example, is there an opportunity for kin to interact in nature? Are the results of laboratory experiments ecologically meaningful? What are the genetic affinities of animals in natural social groups? We need additional studies of closely related species and the use of field experiments to assess the evolutionary and ecological significance of kin recognition behavior. Field experiments can corroborate results of laboratory tests and make them more meaningful.

The vast amount of data generated from kin recognition studies indicate a statistically significant trend in which kin are distinguished from nonkin most of the time. But are these trends biologically significant? Perhaps, only after numerous individuals of a particular species have been observed in nature and many experimental replicates have been performed in both the laboratory and the field, should we state that the statistically significant results are also biologically significant.

Adaptationist Views, "Recognition Errors," Human Inference, and Limits to Knowledge

There are numerous examples in the literature implicating limits to the recognition abilities of various organisms. For example, in natural populations of Belding's ground squirrels, yearlings may cooperate with unrelated foster sisters or treat genetic sisters as if they are unrelated (Sherman 1980). Young colonial nesting birds may enter the "wrong" nest and be fed by unrelated parents before they are expelled (e.g. Hoogland & Sherman, 1976; Beecher et al. 1981). Many species are often reared by foster parents that may even be of a different species (Riedman 1982). Hosts of the parasitic Brown-headed cowbird (*Molothrus ater*) may accept the egg of the brood parasite which may result in a great potential loss in fitness (Rothstein 1982). In kin recognition studies, certain species fail to discriminate between kin and nonkin even though they have been tested under experimental regimes identical to those in which other closely related species made these discriminations (e.g. O'Hara & Blaustein 1988; Crosland 1988).

It is possible that many of the limits exhibited by animals in laboratory experiments may actually be the results of procedures that are not sensitive enough to detect subtle behaviors that may indicate that recognition was achieved (Blaustein et al. 1987b). Moreover, many of the errors may stem from our own expectations as scientists. We may consider them "errors" but it is possible that animals are not making mistakes in the ways they direct their behaviors toward other individuals. Perhaps, the animals were not motivated under the experimental conditions used (Blaustein et al. 1987b). Recognition may also be a polymorphic trait (Blaustein et al. 1987b). Thus, not all individuals within a population or experimental group may exhibit kin recognition. This behavioral polymorphism could be maintained by fluctuating environmental conditions and varying selective pressures. Some individuals may exhibit kin recognition behavior under certain conditions but not in other situations. As Beecher (1988) has pointed out, selective pressures and costs and benefits to the sender and the receiver may not coincide. Under certain conditions the sender does not benefit by reliably identifying itself (Beecher 1988). Perhaps individuals can turn their signatures off and on depending upon the social and ecological circumstances. Of course, while intermittent signature-onset of this nature is possible within certain phenotypic traits (e.g. calls), other discriminable traits (e.g. whole-body odors, conspicuous visual features) are continuously accessible.

Importantly, not all behaviors are optimal even though biologists usually expect them to be (Rothstein 1982, 1986; Bekoff et al. 1989). Several authors have cautioned investigators in their quest for "adaptive value" explanations (e.g. Curio 1973; Gould & Lewontin 1979; Rothstein 1982). There are many good reasons why natural selection may fail to provide optimal solutions (in humans' opinions) to particular problems and why seemingly nonadaptive traits may persist in a population (Rothstein 1982; Gould & Lewontin 1979). Bekoff (1988: 631) points out one of the major problems "when humans study nonhumans, [is that] they inevitably incompletely understand them and their inferences cannot be perfect" (see also Byers & Bekoff 1986). Thus, questions concerning optimality must be considered cautiously in light of our observational and experimental limitations.

Acknowledgements

Discussions with Mike Beecher, Warren Holmes, Marvin K. Mooney, Rick O'Hara and Steve Rothstein were extremely helpful. The manuscript was critically reviewed by Mike Beecher, Marc Bekoff, Dale Jamieson, Rick O'Hara, Kathy Moore, Steve Rothstein, and an anonymous reviewer. We wish to thank Marc Bekoff for calling our attention to the etymology of "recognition" and Kathy Moore for helping us with some of our definitions. ARB wishes to thank Steve Rothstein for providing the initial stimulus of interest in problems concerning recognition. We thank Karen Chang for conducting library research and other important duties that helped to get this manuscript completed. Preparation of this manuscript was supported in part by NSF grant BNS-8718536 to ARB and grant HD-15051 from the National Institute of

Child Health & Human Development to RHP. Research on tadpole kin recognition was generously supported by NSF and the National Geographic Society. ARB wishes to especially thank Travis Bickle for his unusual insight into problems of recognition.

Literature Cited

Alcock, J. 1988. Singing down a blind alley. *Behavioral and Brain Sciences* 11, 630.

Alexander, R. D. & Borgia, G. 1978. Group selection, altruism, and the levels of organization of life. *Annual Review of Ecology and Systematics* 9, 449–474.

Anderson, P. K. 1989. *Rodent Dispersal: A Resident Fitness Hypothesis.* Special Publication No. 9. American Society of Mammalogists.

Bateson, P. (ed.) 1983. *Mate Choice.* New York: Cambridge.

Beauchamp, G. K., Yamazaki, K., Bard, J., & Boyse, E. A. 1988. Preweaning experience in the control of mating preferences by genes in the major histocompatibility complex of the mouse. *Behavior Genetics* 18, 537–547.

Beauchamp, G. K., Yamazaki, K., & Boyse, E. A. 1985. The chemosensory recognition of genetic individuality. *Scientific American* 253, 86–92.

Beecher, M. D. 1982. Signature systems and kin recognition *American Zoologist* 22, 477–490.

———. 1988. Kin recognition in birds. *Behavior Genetics* 18, 465–482.

Beecher, M. D., Beecher, I. M. & Lumpkin, S. 1981. Parent-offspring recognition in Bank swallows (*Riparia riparia*): I. Natural history. *Animal Behaviour* 29, 86–94.

Bekoff, M. 1981a. Mammalian sibling interactions: Genes, facilitative environments, and the co-efficient of familiarity. In: *Parental Care in Mammals* (ed. by D. J. Gubernick & P. H. Klopfer), pp. 307–346. New York: Plenum.

———. 1981b. Vole population cycles: kin selection or familiarity? *Oecologia* 48, 131.

———. 1988. Birdsong and the "problem" of nature and nurture: Endless chirping about inadequate evidence or merely singing the blues about inevitable biases in, and limitations of, human inference? *Behavioral and Brain Sciences* 11, 631.

Bekoff, M., Scott, A. C., & Conner, D. A. 1989. Ecological aspects of nesting success in Evening Grosbeaks. *Oecologia* 81, 67–74.

Berger, J. & Cunningham, C. 1987. Influence of familiarity on frequency of inbreeding in wild horses. *Evolution* 41, 229–231.

Blaustein, A. R. 1983. Kin recognition mechanisms: Phenotypic matching or recognition alleles? *American Naturalist* 121, 749–754.

———. 1988. Ecological correlates and potential functions of kin recognition and kin association in anuran larvae. *Behavior Genetics* 18, 449–464.

Blaustein, A. R. & O'Hara, R. K. 1981. Genetic control for sibling recognition? *Nature* 290, 246–248.

———. 1982. Kin recognition in *Rana cascadae* tadpoles: Maternal and paternal effects. *Animal Behaviour* 30, 1151–1157.

Blaustein, A. R., Bekoff, M., & Daniels, T. J. 1987a. Kin recognition in vertebrates (excluding primates): Empirical evidence. In: *Kin Recognition in Animals* (ed. by D. J. C. Fletcher & C. D. Michener), pp. 287–331. New York: Wiley.

———. 1987b. Kin recognition in vertebrates (excluding primates): Mechanisms, functions, and future research. In: *Kin Recognition in Animals* (ed. by D. J. C. Fletcher & C. D. Michener), pp. 333–357. New York: Wiley.

Blaustein, A. R., Bekoff, M., Byers, J. A., & Daniels, T. J. 1991. Kin recognition in vertebrates: What do we really know about adaptive value? *Animal Behaviour* 41, 1079–1083.

Blaustein, A. R., Porter, R. H., & Breed, M. D. (eds.) 1988. Special issue: Kin recognition in animals. *Behavior Genetics* 18, 405–564.

Boyse, E. A. & Cantor, H. 1978. Immunogenetic aspects of biologic communication: A hypothesis of evolution by program duplication. In: *Birth Defects: Original Article Series, Vol. XIV* (ed. by R. A. Lerner & D. Bergsma), pp. 249–283. New York: Alan R. Liss.

Breed, M. D. & Bennett, B. 1987. Kin recognition in highly eusocial insects. In: *Kin Recognition in Animals* (ed. by D. J. C. Fletcher & C. D. Michener), pp. 243–285. New York: Wiley.

Brown, J. L. 1987. *Helping and communal brooding in birds: Ecology and evolution.* Princeton: Princeton.

Buckle, G. R. & Greenberg, L. 1981. Nestmate recognition in sweat bees (*Lasioglossum zephyrum*): Does an individual recognize its own odour or only odours of its nestmates? *Animal Behaviour* 29, 802–809.

Burghardt, G. M. 1988. Developmental creationism. *Behavioral and Brain Sciences* 11, 632.

Byers, J. A. & Bekoff, M. 1986. What does "kin recognition" mean? *Ethology* 72, 342–345.

Colgan, P. 1983: *Comparative Social Recognition*. New York: Wiley.

Coombe, D. R. & Parish, C. R. 1988. Sulfated polysaccharide-mediated sponge cell aggregation: The clue to invertebrate self/nonself-recognition? In: *Invertebrate Historecognition* (ed. by R. K. Grosberg, D. Hedgecock & K. Nelson), pp. 31–54. New York: Plenum.

Crosland, M. W. J. 1988. Inability to discriminate between related and unrelated larvae in the ant *Rhytidoponera confusa* (Hymenoptera: Formicidae). *Annals of the Entomological Society of America* 81, 844–850.

Crow, J. F. 1979. Genes that violate Mendel's rules. *Scientific American* 240, 134–146.

Crozier, R. H. 1987. Genetic aspects of kin recognition: Concepts, models, and synthesis. In: *Kin Recognition in Animals* (ed. by D. J. C. Fletcher & C. D. Michener), pp. 55–73. New York: Wiley.

————. 1988. Kin recognition using innate labels: A central role for piggy-backing? In: *Invertebrate Historecognition* (ed. by R. K. Grosberg, D. Hedgecock & K. Nelson), pp. 143–156. New York: Plenum.

Crozier, R. H. & Dix, M. W. 1979. Analysis of two genetic models for the innate components of colony odor in social hymenoptera. *Behavioral Ecology and Sociobiology* 4, 217–224.

Curio, E. 1973. Towards a methodology of teleonomy. *Experientia* 29, 1045–1058.

Dawkins, R. 1976. *The Selfish Gene*. Oxford: Oxford.

————. 1982. *The Extended Phenotype*. San Francisco: Freeman.

Emlen, S. T. 1984. Cooperative breeding in birds and mammals. In: *Behavioural Ecology: An Evolutionary Approach* (Second Edition) (ed. by J. R. Krebs & N. B. Davies), pp. 305–339. Sunderland: Sinauer.

Falls, J. B. 1978. Bird song and territorial behavior. *Advances in the Study of Communication of Affect* 4, 61–89.

Fletcher, D. J. C. & Michener, C. D. 1987. *Kin Recognition in Animals*. New York: Wiley.

Foster, R. L. & Gamboa, G. J. 1989. Nest entrance marking with colony specific odors by the Bumble bee *Bombus occidentalis* (Hymenoptera: Apidae). *Ethology* 81, 273–278.

Fuller, C. A. & Blaustein, A. R. 1990. An investigation of sibling recognition in a solitary sciurid, Townsend's chipmunk, *Tamias townsendii*. *Behaviour*, in press.

Gadagkar, R. 1985. Kin recognition in social insects and other animals—A review of recent findings and a consideration of their relevance for the theory of kin selection. *Proceedings Indian Academy of Sciences (Animal Science)* 94, 587–621.

Gamboa, G. J., Reeve, H. K., & Pfennig, D. W. 1986. The evolution and ontogeny of nestmate recognition in social wasps. *Annual Review of Entomology* 31, 431–454.

Getz, W. M. 1981. Genetically based kin recognition systems. *Journal of Theoretical Biology* 92, 209–226.

Getz, W. M. & Smith, K. B. 1983. Genetic kin recognition: honey bees discriminate between full and half sisters. *Nature* 302, 147–148.

Gould, S. J. & Lewontin, R. F. 1979. The spandrels of San Marco and the Panglossian paradigm: A critique of the adaptationist programme. *Proceedings of the Royal Society of London B* 205, 581–598.

Gouzoules, S. 1984. Primate mating systems, kin associations and cooperative behavior: Evidence for kin recognition? *Yearbook of Physical Anthropology* 27, 99–134.

Greenberg, L. 1979. Genetic component of bee odor in kin recognition. *Science* 206, 1095–1097.

Grosberg, R. K. 1988a. Preface. In: *Invertebrate Historecognition* (ed. by R. K. Grosberg, D. Hedgecock & K. Nelson), pp. v–vi. New York: Plenum.

————. 1988b. The evolution of allorecognition specificity in clonal invertebrates. *Quarterly Review of Biology* 63, 377–412.

Grosberg, R. K., Hedgecock, D. & Nelson, K. 1988. *Invertebrate Historecognition*. New York: Plenum.

Grosberg, R. K. & Quinn, J. F. 1986. The genetic control and consequences of kin recognition by the larvae of a colonial marine invertebrate. *Nature* 322, 456–459.

Guilford, T. 1985. Is kin selection involved in the evolution of warning coloration? *Oikos* 45, 31–36.

————. 1988. The evolution of conspicuous coloration. *American Naturalist* 131 (Supplement), S7–S21.

Halpin, Z. T. & Hoffman, M. D. 1987. Sibling recognition in the white-footed mouse, *Peromyscus leucopus*: association or phenotype matching? *Animal Behaviour* 35, 563–570.

Hamilton, W. D. 1964a. The genetical evolution of social behaviour. I. *Journal of Theoretical Biology* 7, 1–16.

————. 1964b. The genetical evolution of social behaviour. II. *Journal of Theoretical Biology* 7, 17–52.

————. 1987. Discriminating nepotism: Expectable, common, overlooked. In: *Kin Recognition in Animals* (ed. by D. J. C. Fletcher & C. D. Michener), pp. 417–437. New York: Wiley.

Hedrick, P. W. 1984. *Population Biology: The Evolution and Ecology of Populations*. Boston: Jones and Bartlett.

Hepper, P. G. 1983. Sibling recognition in the rat. *Animal Behaviour* 31, 1177–1191.

———. 1986. Kin recognition: functions and mechanisms. A review. *Biological Reviews* 61, 63–93.

———. 1988. The discrimination of human odour by the dog. *Perception* 17, 549–554.

Hews, D. K. & Blaustein, A. R. 1985. An investigation of the alarm response in *Bufo boreas* and *Rana cascadae* tadpoles. *Behavioral and Neural Biology* 43, 47–57.

Hölldobler, B. & Michener, C. D. 1980. Mechanisms of identification and discrimination in social hymenoptera. In: *Evolution of Social Behavior: Hypotheses and Empirical Tests* (ed. by H. Markl), pp 35–57. Verlag Weinheim: Chemie.

Holmes, W. G. 1984. Sibling recognition in thirteen-lined ground squirrels: Effects of genetic relatedness, rearing association, and olfaction. *Behavioral Ecology & Sociobiology* 14, 225–233.

———. 1986. Kin recognition by phenotype matching in female Belding's ground squirrels. *Animal Behaviour* 34, 38–47.

———. 1988. Kinship and development of social preferences. In: *Handbook of Behavioral Neurobiology.* Volume 9. *Developmental Psychobiology and Behavioral Ecology* (ed. by E. M. Blass), pp. 389–413. New York: Plenum.

Holmes, W. G. & Sherman, P. W. 1982. The ontogeny of kin recognition in two species of ground squirrels. *American Zoologist* 22, 491–517.

Hoogland, J. L. & Sherman, P. W. 1976. Advantages and disadvantages of bank swallow (*Riparia riparia*) coloniality. *Ecological Monographs* 46, 33–58.

Jasienski, M. 1988. Kinship ecology of competition: Size hierarchies in kin and nonkin laboratory cohorts of tadpoles. *Oecologia* 77, 407–413.

Kalmus, H. 1955. The discrimination by the nose of the dog of individual human odours and in particular of the odours of twins. *British Journal of Animal Behaviour* 5, 25–31.

Kareem, A. M. 1983. Effect of increasing periods of familiarity on social interactions between male sibling mice. *Animal Behaviour* 31, 919–926.

Keough, M. J. 1984. Kin recognition and the spatial distribution of larvae of the bryozoan *Bugula neritina* (L). *Evolution* 38, 142–147.

Klein, J. 1982. *Immunology: The Science of Self Nonself Discrimination.* New York: Wiley.

Lacy, R. C. & Sherman, P. W. 1983. Kin recognition by phenotype matching. *American Naturalist* 121, 489–512.

Lenington, S., Egid, K., & Williams, J. 1988. Analysis of a genetic recognition system in wild house mice. *Behavior Genetics* 18, 549–564.

Linsenmair, K. E. 1987. Kin recognition in subsocial arthropods, in particular in the desert isopod *Hemilepistus reaumuri*. In: *Kin Recognition in Animals* (ed. by D. J. C. Fletcher & C. D. Michener), pp. 121–208. New York: Wiley.

Michener, C. D. & Smith, B. H. 1987. Kin recognition in primitively eusocial insects. In: *Kin Recognition in Animals* (ed. by D. J. C. Fletcher & C. D. Michener), pp. 209–242. New York: Wiley.

O'Hara, R. K. & Blaustein, A. R. 1981. An investigation of sibling recognition in *Rana cascadae* tadpoles. *Animal Behaviour* 29, 1121–1126.

———. 1985. *Rana cascadae* tadpoles aggregate with siblings: an experimental field study. *Oecologia* 67, 44–51.

———. 1988. *Hyla regilla* and *Rana pretiosa* tadpoles fail to display kin recognition behaviour. *Animal Behaviour* 36, 946–948.

Page, P. E., Robinson, G. E. & Fondrk, M. K. 1989. Genetic specialists, kin recognition and nepotism in honey-bee colonies. *Nature* 338, 576–579.

Porter, R. H. 1988. The ontogeny of sibling recognition in rodents: Super-family Muroidea. *Behavior Genetics* 18, 483–494.

Porter, R. H. & Blaustein, A. R. 1989. Mechanisms and ecological correlates of kin recognition. *Science Progress* 73, 53–66.

Porter, R. H., Cernoch, J. M. & Balogh, R. D. 1985. Odor signatures and kin recognition. *Physiology & Behavior* 34, 445–448.

Porter, R. H., Matochik, J. A. & Makin, J. W. 1983. Evidence for phenotype matching in spiny mice (*Acomys cahirinus*). *Animal Behaviour* 31, 978–984.

———. 1984. The role of familiarity in the development of social preferences in spiny mice. *Behavioral Processes* 9, 241–254.

Porter, R. H., Tepper, V. J. & White, D. M. 1981. Experiential influences on the development of huddling preferences and "sibling" recognition in spiny mice. *Developmental Psychobiology* 14, 375–382.

Porter, R. H., Wyrick, M. & Pankey, J. 1978. Sibling recognition in spiny mice (*Acomys cahirinus*). *Behavioral Ecology & Sociobiology* 3, 61–68.

Ridley, M. & Grafen, A. 1981. Are green beard genes outlaws? *Animal Behaviour* 29, 954–955.

Riedman, M. L. 1982. The evolution of alloparental care and adoption in mammals and birds. *Quarterly Review of Biology* 57, 405–435.

Roitt, I. 1988. *Essential Immunology* (6th Edition). Blackwell Scientific: Oxford.

Rothstein, S. I. 1982. Successes and failures in avian egg and nestling recognition with comments on the utility of optimality reasoning. *American Zoologist* 22, 547–560.

———. 1986. A test of optimality: egg recognition in the eastern phoebe. *Animal Behaviour* 34, 1109–1119.

Rothstein, S. I. & Barash, D. P. 1983. Gene conflicts and the concept of outlaw and sheriff alleles. *Journal of Social and Biological Structures* 6, 367–379.

Roy, M. A. 1980. *Species Identity and Attachment*. New York: Garland.

Schwagmeyer, P. L. 1988. Ground squirrel kin recognition abilities: Are there social and life-history correlates? *Behavior Genetics* 18, 495–510.

Sherman, P. W. 1980. The limits of ground squirrel nepotism. In: *Sociobiology: Beyond Nature/Nurture?* (ed. by G. W. Barlow & J. Silverberg), pp. 505–544. Boulder: Westview.

Sherman, P. W. & Holmes, W. G. 1985. Kin recognition: Issues and evidence. *Fortschritte der Zoologie* 31, 437–460.

Thomas, L. 1975. Symbiosis as an immunological problem. In: *The Immune System and Infectious Diseases* (ed. by E. Neter & F. Milgrom), pp. 2–11. Basel: Karger.

Tinbergen, N. 1963. On aims and methods of ethology. *Zeitschrift für Tierpsychologie* 20, 410–433.

Van de Vyver, G. 1988. Histocompatibility responses in freshwater sponges: A model for studies of cell-cell interactions in natural populations and experimental systems. In: *Invertebrate Historecognition* (ed. by R. K. Grosberg, D. Hedgecock & K. Nelson), pp. 1–14. New York: Plenum.

Waldman, B. 1981. Sibling recognition in toad tadpoles: The role of experience. *Zeitschrift für Tierpsychologie* 56, 341–358.

———. 1982. Sibling association among schooling toad tadpoles: field evidence and implications. *Animal Behaviour* 30, 700–713.

———. 1984. Kin recognition and sibling association among wood frog (*Rana sylvatica*) tadpoles. *Behavioral Ecology & Sociobiology* 14, 171–180.

———. 1987. Mechanisms of kin recognition. *Journal of Theoretical Biology* 128, 159–185.

Waldman, B. & Adler, K. 1979. Toad tadpoles associate preferentially with siblings. *Nature* 282, 611–613.

Wassersug, R. J. 1973. Aspects of social behavior in anuran larvae. In: *Evolutionary Biology of the Anuran* (ed. by J. L. Vial), pp. 273–297. Columbia: Missouri.

Watson, J. D. 1970. *Molecular Biology of the Gene* (2nd Edition). New York: W. A. Benjamin.

Wells, P. A. 1987. Kin recognition in humans. In: *Kin Recognition in Animals* (ed. by D. J. C. Fletcher & C. D. Michener), pp. 395–415. New York: Wiley.

West-Eberhard, M. J. 1989. Kin recognition in animals. *Evolution* 703–705.

Wilson, S. C. 1982. The development of social behaviour between siblings and non-siblings of the voles *Microtus ochrogaster* and *Microtus pennsylvanicus*. *Animal Behavior* 30, 426–437.

Yamazaki, K., Beauchamp, G. K., Kupniewski, D., Bard, J., Thomas, L., & Boyse, A. 1988. Familial imprinting determines H-2 selective mating preferences. *Science* 240, 1331–1332.

Yamazaki, K., Boyse, E. A., Mike, V., Thaler, H. T., Mathieson, B. J., Abbott, J., Boyse, J., Zayas, Z. A., & Thomas, L. 1976. Control of mating preferences in mice by genes in the major histocompatibility complex. *Journal of Experimental Medicine* 144, 1324–1335.

Chapter 12

Do Animals Choose Habitats?

Michael L. Rosenzweig

Habitats differ in space and time. Such differences are a fundamental ecological phenomenon.

Individuals of different species often tend to be found in different habitats, or they utilize distributions of habitats which overlap but are not identical. Ecologists have accepted such dissimilarities among species as one of the two important properties of ecological communities which allow life's diversity to persist.

Hutto (1985) has noted that although different species use different habitats, they may not necessarily choose different habitats. He proposes the term "habitat selection" be reserved for instances in which "organisms consciously choose among alternative habitats" (p. 457).

Actually, the term "habitat selection" as taught by its originator, Robert H. Mac-Arthur, did not imply choice. It referred instead to habitat differences which play a significant role in preventing competitive extinction. Not all habitat use differences need be engines of competitive coexistences, so MacArthur had a point. But Hutto's point is equally valid; not all habitat use differences need be the products of choice.

Peirce's ethics of scientific terminology (Ketner 1981) provides a good reason for preferring Hutto's definition to MacArthur's. Peirce pointed out that it could only lead to confusion if scientists used perfectly well-defined, common words to mean something quite different in a scientific context from what they usually mean. In plain English, "selection" surely implies "choice." So MacArthur's "habitat selection" ought to be called something else. I shall use "habitat allocation" (in parallel to MacArthur's "resource allocation") in order to express his idea.

The purposes of this chapter are now easier to explain. First, I wish to lay out a spectrum of habitat allocation modes. One of the principal differences among them will be whether habitat selection is involved. Then I wish to examine to what extent and how it is possible to determine which mode applies to any particular situation. Finally, I want to inquire whether it is possible to determine (or at least hypothesize) the attributes of cases in which habitat selection will be favored by natural selection.

From the ecologist's point of view, it is perhaps secondary to wonder about the presence of choice in habitat allocation. The work of supporting biodiversity will be done in any case. Yet it is my experience that the question has a fascination all its own. To make it scientifically approachable, however, one needs straightaway to put two cards face up on the table.

Hutto uses the word "conscious." I do not know what that means and will not explore it in this contribution. Instead, I shall define "choice," Thus: if an animal with a central nervous system encounters alternatives, and the information needed to distinguish the alternatives can be shown to be processed by that central nervous system, and the animal behaves non-randomly in following one of the alternatives more than the other, then that animal is choosing.

That definition becomes important because it will soon force us to admit that insects choose. The definition is also important because it does exclude a number of phenomena which, no doubt, function ecologically just like habitat selection. Most of these are physiological, such as hibernation in vertebrates and hostorium formation in parasitic plants (more about this below). But the definition may fail to be useful in dealing with unicellular animals. Requiring a central nervous system for acceptance of the possibility of choice in a paramecium is undoubtedly just an anthropocentric bias.

The second point is not unrelated to the first. The solipsists convinced me long ago that I cannot prove the existence of any other being but myself. For all I know, the entire external world is a figment of my imagination. It follows rather trivially that if I cannot prove the independent existence of the black-chinned hummingbird now feeding near my window, I certainly cannot prove it is collecting information and choosing to feed in the *Tecoma* flowers in which I see it. Furthermore, I cannot prove you are reading this page in the same way I understand that process for myself. So be it. I believe you are. I believe the hummingbird also exists and is experiencing a sensation we call sweetness, though I guess it may be quite different from what we experience when we drink a glass of fruit juice. Similarly, if the evidence indicates that an animal is faced with alternatives which transmit information, information I can sense or measure, and which the animal appears able to sense and transfer to its central nervous system, and the animal non-randomly accepts or rejects one alternative, I believe it is appropriate to project that very human word "choose" onto its behavior. But I admit that projection is an act of faith.

Modes of Habitat Allocation

Levins (1968) introduced the terms "fine grained" and "coarse grained" to ecology. He meant us to understand by them that environments of similar heterogeneity might be arranged quite differently: the coarse grained has its similar habitat patches clustered into large patches; the fine grained has them interspersed among all sorts of habitats. From the outset, it was clear that these terms—although ostensibly describing the environment—actually described an interaction between the environment and its users. A fine-grained environment is one used as it comes. A coarse-grained environment is used in proportions other than those in which it occurs. Yet I urge those who think those two sentences settle anything to reread them.

First, there is the matter of scale. An environment may be finely used at a scale large enough to support a whole population, but coarsely used within a home range. Morris (1987) demonstrates this phenomenon in small mammals. They are very restricted as to major habitat type—some in fields, some in forests—but use their home ranges coarsely.

At more startling example is the opposite. Mountain quail in northern California use major vegetative cover types in proportion to their area. But within each cover type, quail are most likely to be found near water and tall, dense shrubs (Brennan et al. 1987).

After scale, other specifications remain. Perhaps the most obvious is body size. A small mammal may treat an environment coarsely; a large one may treat it finely. And there is season: the same animal may alter its strategy from coarse to fine and back again depending on the time of year. I do not mention these things to be cautious, but to emphasize the interactive nature of the designations "coarse" and "fine." The animal is playing the ultimate game, survival, and its strategies ought to be honed as nearly as possible to its opportunities and constraints (Brown & Vincent 1987). In this context, we must carefully define the scale and the setting in which we ask our question. It must be of the form "Is this animal choosy at this scale and in this place at this time?" It can never be "Is this a choosy species?" nor "Is this a coarse or fine-grained environment?" Moreover, negative evidence—according to Popper (1972) the best sort to have in science—may not mean much here. Unless we have a theory of how an individual ought to be playing the game—a theory, mind you, in which we have considerable confidence—and the theory predicts choosiness when and where we find none, it will be very difficult to say, "This species is not able to be choosy." Without such a theory, lack of choice may simply mean tests were run in an inappropriate space-time environment.

Be that as it may, the first mode on our spectrum must be a non-choosy organism. More particularly, it must be one which uses whatever patch type it encounters, and is not biased to encounter any type more than any other. Both these attributes are actually required for true fine-grainedness. Chesson's models (Chesson & Huntly 1988) are remarkable in showing that different species of such organisms can actually coexist owing to habitat heterogeneity despite their total passiveness toward the opportunities of heterogeneity. Let us call this mode the fine-grained mode of habitat allocation.

The second mode remains passive but is associated with non-random habitat use. The animal uses whatever it encounters in the proportions encountered, but the encounters are biased. The biases may be anatomically or physiologically produced but it is also likely that behavior could cause them. Here are some examples.

Some homeothermic vertebrates go into torpor regularly or irregularly. Torpor in winter is called hibernation. It is a physiological mechanism for allowing the hibernator to come disproportionately into foraging contact with warm, productive seasons (Brown 1989). Choosiness has nothing to do with such habitat allocation. Another example has a variety of causes. A forest floor often has a soil layer and a leaf litter layer. Some animals such as kiwis and snipes make their livings probing for invertebrates in these layers. Others such as shrews, plunge right in (body and soul?) in their hunt for food. Now I cannot believe a kiwi ever chooses not to plunge in, anymore than I choose not to when I am in the forest. Instead, it must be "hard wired" to use the forest as it does. Nevertheless, it is reasonable to expect that the resources and microhabitat patches it senses will differ from those sensed by the shrew. Is it coarse-grained because of such a biased encounter? It must be, but it is not choosy. (By the way, at least one bird does plunge in; the eastern scrub bird, *Atrichornis rufescens*, of Australia's temperate rainforests, forages *under* the leaf litter. This emphasizes that one must be very careful about ascribing encounter biases to anatomy alone.)

In sum, the second mode is coarse-grained, but without choice. The organism uses whatever it encounters, but is so constituted that it encounters a non-random distribution of habitats.

The demarcation of the first two modes leads obviously to the third. If an organism does not use what it encounters in the encounter proportions, then it is in mode three. But mode three actually covers two subcases which relate to the question of choice: The non-random use may or may not involve a central nervous system.

The clearest cases without nervous coordination probably are those involving plants. Dodder is a parasitic, viny member of the milkweed family. It grows along in the aboveground parts of potential hosts going from plant to plant. When it arrives at some plants, it grows many coils and sends out hostoria which penetrate the host and deprive it of resources. When it arrives at most hosts, it grows a few hostoria and quickly grows onward as if to reject the potential host (Kelly 1988). I would rather not be forced to conclude that dodder chooses. Probably instead, it is growing differentially in response to physico-chemical cues, all of which it does mechanically. Yet is achieves the same results—and probably for the same ultimate reasons—as, say, a butterfly which lays its eggs on a particular host plant (e.g. Rauscher 1979). The butterfly has a nervous system. How can one tell whether such an animal chooses? This will be the topic of the next section.

Methods for Determining Whether Choice Occurs

Proportional Use

The definition of "coarse-grainedness" has suggested the most popular test for choice. Investigators compare the proportional use of habitat types with their proportional availability. If there is no significant difference, they conclude fine-grainedness exists. If there is, they attribute it to coarse-grainedness. Both Morris (1987) and Brennan et al. (1987) provide examples, although the literature is extensive on this topic. This method, unfortunately, will not help us much in recognizing choice.

First, it is meant only to separate fine-grainedness from coarse-grainedness, and not to identify choice. We have already seen that a non-random distribution of habitat use could arise from biased encounter rates and have nothing to do with choice.

Second, it is really a comparison of an organism's habitat use with a human's ability to measure habitat availability. How can we know whether our definitions of habitat types are meaningful to the species being studied? How can we know whether our evaluation of the natural distribution is taken at a correct scale?

Third, this method is applied to population averages. But choice requires one to look at individuals. Density-dependence will force individuals to spread out among the habitats available and achieve an evenness of habitat use far greater than that which would obtain at low densities (Fretwell 1972; also, for examples, Rosenzweig & Abramsky 1985; Rosenzweig 1986). In other words, when a species is common, choice may be used to achieve a more even use of habitats, a use which is fairly similar to the proportions at which they occur naturally.

Proportional use has its most powerful application in the formulation of hypotheses. Knowing which habitats are 'overused' and which are rarely used yields clues as to the habitat variable(s) which may underlie habitat allocation and habitat choice. Occasionally, this knowledge is then used in a habitat tailoring experiment to check up on the identification of the variable(s).

A habitat tailoring experiment is really a set of experimental proportional use studies. Species with known distributions of habitat use are tested to see what varia-

bles can alter that use. For example, small desert rodent species vary in the proportion of time they use open habitat versus sheltered habitat. That fact has been
concluded again and again from live-trapping records (e.g., Rosenzweig & Winakur
1969), from snap-trapping records (e.g., Brown & Lieberman 1973), and from studies
which trace where seeds are being collected (e.g. Lemen & Rosenzweig 1978). But
what is at the root of such disproportionate use? Is it warmer under shrubs owing to
the fact that animals are shielded from radiation of their heat to the generally clear,
nighttime desert sky? Are animals actually responding to the presence of vegetation?
Or is the vegetation merely correlated with the true, underlying proximate variable
(perhaps soil type)? After obtaining baseline data, and in the presence of appropriate
controls, one can alter the vegetation structure in various ways, and study the immediate effects on the different species. Whitford et al. (1978) did it by removing shrubs
with herbicide. I did it by clearing patches of the desert floor, or piling up extra plant
parts in patches (Rosenzweig 1973). Indeed, some species, as predicted, tended to
alter their use of such patches after treatment. A lucky outcome was that some species did not alter their use when a patch was made clear for a distance of 4m from
cover, but did when the same patch was cleared so that its resources were 8m from
cover. This told us that radiational cooling was not behind the proportional use pattern. Kotler's (1984) experiments are the most subtle examples of tailoring in this
system. He did not touch the plants, but put up lanterns on moonless nights in some
of his plots. Thus he altered the difference in darkness between covered and open
patches. Sure enough, when he compared proportional use in lantern-lit plots with
control plots, several species exhibited a difference. They tended to use the covered
patches even more disproportionately if plots were lit than if plots were left dark.
That experiment not only implicates cover as the proximate variable, it implicates
vigilance as the ultimate variable in the habitat allocation (see Lima, chapter 13 of this
reader). In a habitat tailoring experiment with grassland finches, Lima & Valone
(1991) implicate cover and vigilance in the same way.

Yet, no habitat tailoring experiment nails down the issue of habitat choice. After
the experiment, all we know is whether the individuals (or species) altered their proportional uses. That is important, but it tells us no more about choice than non-
experimental studies of proportional use. In sum, proportional use tests are valuable
to identify likely habitat allocations and formulate hypotheses, but they are never
conclusive about choice. Reliance on them to determine choice is precisely what
bothered Hutto (1985). He was right.

Presentation of Alternatives
Once hypotheses are formulated by the method of proportional use they must
be tested experimentally. All other methods share the property that they are
experimental.

The simplest such experiment is the presentation of alternatives in a laboratory
setting where the proportion of what is available is known because it is controlled
(usually at 50%). Among the earliest such experiments which were ecologically motivated are those of Morisita (1952) and his colleagues (e.g. Kosaka 1956) in Japan.
Morisita gave antlions (a predatory insect larva) the alternatives of building their
funnel-shaped pit traps in fine or coarse sand. He placed them in an arena on the border of two equal area patches of each substrate. The antlions constructed their pits in
fine sand 89% of the time. Kosaka performed experiments in sand and gravel with

flatfish of two different species with similar results: one settled 97% of the time on sand; the other, 90%.

Such "choice" experiments are not rare. What do they really tell us about choice? Suppose, for example, that an animal's movement follows a simple rule: speed in direct proportion to a certain habitat variable. Then it would tend to stay in habitats with low values of the variable. This model of habitat mobility, called kinesis, is actually quite old and respectable (e.g. Marler & Hamilton 1966: 539). So the missing ingredient in demonstrating choice remains. How does one know the animals actually know of the alternatives?

We could eliminate the differential mobility hypothesis by measuring speed in the alternative patches. That would help, but I am not aware of its ever having been tried. Perhaps it should be.

We could also design the experiment to ensure that the animal is acquainted with its choices. That has, in fact, been the strategy. Morisita's and Kosaka's arenas, for example, had patches that were sharply divided from each other. The patches were each more than large enough to house the entire animal. And finally, animals were introduced right on a border so that, presumably, they began their experience in the arena by sensing both patch types. Such a design hardly amounts to a conclusive proof of choice, but it is much more suggestive than proportional use differences. It also gets to a real crux: we should like very much to know that the animal's central nervous system contains information about both alternatives simultaneously. In the absence of a 10^9 CRT display of the simultaneous contents of all the memory registers of a brain, one might think that to be an impossible goal. But, as I shall point out later, it has actually been achieved, albeit with simplicity and elegance. Meanwhile, we must consider a variation on the method of presentation of alternatives.

Sometimes the alternatives are presented in a variety of background environments and the investigator asks, "What is the effect of that background variable on habitat use?" Often, there is an effect. One might interpret such a result to mean that choice must have been demonstrated, because flexibility had been shown. However, it is not clear to me what choice and flexibility have to do with each other. Some examples should convince the reader that I am not just being perverse.

Both Morisita and Kosaka were really interested in the effect of population size on habitat use. Their experiments consequently progressed from the results I have already cited, which involved one antlion or one fish at a time, to experiments in which more and more individuals were present in the arena at the same time. As the number of individuals was increased, a smaller and smaller proportion used the "preferred" habitat type. Such a result clearly shows flexibility of habitat use proportions. Moreover, that flexibility is probably quite adaptive (Fretwell 1972). But what is the proximate mechanism of the flexibility? If the individuals are going around sampling the habitats and the density of their residents, OK, they are choosing. But suppose they are just using a hierarchy of movement cues? Suppose their rule is: Move regardless of your habitat if you sense someone else or if you are attacked by a territorialist. That is not habitat selection. We know of many cases of such density-dependent habitat use. And we know that at least some involve aggressive displacement from preferred habitats. For example, Bovbjerg (1970) showed that a more docile crayfish (*Oronectes immunis*) is displaced from preferred substrate in the laboratory (and probably in the field, too) by a more aggressive congener (*O. virilis*).

We also know of some fairly simple creatures showing density-dependent habitat use. It is hard to imagine that choice has anything to do with where they live. For example, Holmes (1961) studied the gut parasites of rats. Along a mammal's gut, there is a substantial variation in ambient conditions, especially pH and nutrient availability. Both tapeworms and acanthocephalans use the region about 15% to 20% down from the stomach more than any other region. But the tapeworms spread out in the presence of either lots of tapeworms or lots of acanthocephalans (or both). That shows flexibility. Do we want to conclude it also shows choice?

The opposite phenomenon may further clarify the difficulty. Sometimes species cling to their characteristic nonrandom habitat distributions despite large and seemingly crucial changes in environment. Does that mean they are not choosy? Does rigidity reveal a lack of ability to choose?

For example, Broadhead & Wapshere (1966) studied two species of wood lice (fungus-eating insects of the family Psocidae, genus *Mesopsocus*). They co-occur in large areas of British woodland below 800m elevation. They eat the same food, are attacked by the same predators and are so similar in size and appearance that they can be distinguished only by details of their genitalia. *M. unipunctatus* tends to lay its eggs on fine twigs (i.e. those 0.2cm diameter or less). *M. immunis* lays its eggs mostly on twigs thicker than 0.2cm. Evidence strongly indicates that the two species are each limited by lack of available oviposition sites. Yet neither changes its oviposition strategy in the absence of the other. They are rigid in their habitat use despite the fact that this rigidity seems to waste great opportunity. Does that rigidity mean they are not each choosing twigs of a certain diameter?

In another case, Schroder and I (1975) removed a large number of Ord kangaroo rats (*Dipodomys ordii*) from an arid field partly shared with *D. merriami*. The Merriam kangaroo rats clung to their previous habitats; they did not move into the vacated *D. ordii* habitat. Even newly-introduced *D. merriami* refused to settle there. Again, we saw rigidity in the face of opportunity. But how could anyone interpret such results to mean that the *D. merriami* were not choosing their restricted habitat distribution? An evolutionary theory of mine (Rosenzweig 1987) actually predicts the evolution of such rigidity and it could easily be enforced by habitat choice.

All in all, the presentation of alternatives in the laboratory or the field in controlled experiments is a very powerful way to show habitat use differences. It is also able to show us their flexibility. But unless the individual subjects are presented with the experimental arena so that it is hard to believe they haven't sensed the alternatives simultaneously, we cannot use such experiments to demonstrate choice. Moreover, even in such cases, our conclusion of choice is weak, depending as it does on our projection of our own sensory experiences onto those of the subjects. Just because we see the sand and the gravel simultaneously does not mean the fish does.

Exploratory Behavior

Demonstrating that information about habitats is actually stored in a central nervous system would go a long way to convincing me that the animal which does it also chooses its habitats. If individuals can be shown to investigate new habitats for the purpose of collecting such information, I would have to conclude they must be storing it too. (Yes, that is an adaptationist's bias.)

Investigation of new habitat patches (in space or time) is a form of exploratory behavior. Natural historians, behavioral ecologists and others have long interpreted some of the things they see in wild vertebrates as exploratory behavior (e.g. Orians 1980; Cowan 1983; Lidicker 1985). But my impression is that the phenomenon is being taken for granted and the efforts of the biologists restricted to questions like: "Given that there is exploratory behavior in this species, what activities that we have observed in the field are most likely to be attributed to it?" Or, "Given that there is exploratory behavior, what circumstances lead to a higher proportion of it?" Yes, vertebrates in the laboratory have repeatedly been shown to explore new habitats, but I could not uncover a single case where this had been demonstrated in the field.

Perhaps because they are not vertebrates, bees have been treated more skeptically. Honeybees, of course, communicate the direction and distance of nectar sources by dancing in the hive. It is also known that at any one time a hive has workers which are going back and forth to established sources (recruits) and workers which are flying out to seek new sources (scouts) (Seeley 1983). That is an important distinction, because it demonstrates the division between information collection and information use—a demonstration much more difficult to accomplish in vertebrates. But it does not yet show choice because it does not show that the recruits are sampling information from different scouts and choosing one source over another. Recently, however, that problem has also been solved.

There is a third class of workers called receivers. These bees stay in the hive and do sample the information (i.e. sugar concentrations) coming in from the scouts. Then they allocate recruits to the various sources in proportions which will take good advantage of the opportunities (Nowogrodzki 1981, quoted in Seeley 1985). The receivers are choosing. In fact, they do nothing else. It is ironic that they themselves never see the habitats they choose.

I can imagine an experiment which would help to demonstrate exploratory behavior in vertebrates, but I do not know whether it has ever been performed. It would take advantage of the conjecture that a naive animal should spend more time exploring than an experienced one. Naive animals would be introduced to a field enclosure set up to record where and when they were active. If they engage in exploratory behavior, the variance in their position should decline. The experiment could even be run as a series, with patches in the enclosure set up to conform to any one of a number of optimal foraging theories so that the asymptotic behavior of the individuals could be predicted. Krebs et al. (1978) performed an experiment with great tits (*Parus major*) which comes fairly close to the latter. They showed that birds encountering two habitats spend more time exploring them when the habitats are more similar in their payoffs.

Demonstrating Memory of Habitats
Another possible way to show that information about habitats is present in a vertebrate's brain (and thus available for comparisons) is to show an animal is engaging in obsolete behavior. In other words, show that the animal's behavior is appropriate to habitats of a previous time rather than the time at which the behavior is performed.

Presumably, experiments to expose obsolete behavior would require knowing a great deal about optimal responses to a habitat structure, allowing an animal to approach an optimum, and then changing the habitat structure to make the former optimum nonadaptive. While that may be ideal, it is also very difficult to achieve. Meanwhile, there are cruder methods, almost as convincing, which do not depend on a precise knowledge of optimal foraging equations.

Bené (1945) performed a series of experiments on a single blackchinned humming-bird (*Archilochus alexandri*). The bird learned to come to a feeder in a particular location and then the feeder was moved a short distance. The bird returned to the original spot and hovered as if to begin feeding. Investigators of hummingbirds (including me) have seen this behavior again and again. Bené went further, however. He moved the feeder to a third location. The bird went to spot 2, hovered awhile, then went to spot 1 and repeated the hovering. The bird retraced its flight despite the fact that the backward direction was novel.

Bené repeated this procedure with a fourth spot after the third had been learned and the bird retraced from 3 to 2 to 1. Locations were not in a straight line, nor were they equidistant. Bené continued this establishment of new spots until nine had been established. Beyond four, a new phenomenon appeared. The bird began to take shortcuts. All in all, the evidence was overwhelming that this wild bird had a mental map of the feeder locations.

Demonstrations of a mental (or cognitive) map by the method of evoking obsolete behavior has, in my opinion, not been often enough taken advantage of. But short-cuts are quite another matter. They are almost always invoked (e.g. Peters 1978, for wolves).

Occasionally, some special feature of the natural history of a taxon allows an unusual demonstration of the existence of mental maps. For example, jays of several species store seeds in scattered caches. They retrieve them much more accurately than can be explained by random search (Balda & Kamil 1989). One of the most extraordinary of these demonstrations was made in wild chimpanzees. Chimps carry scarce, large stones to use as hammers in cracking *Panda* nuts. Boesch and Boesch (1984) marked the stones and showed that the chimps were generally carrying them to the closest *Panda* trees although those trees were not visible from the spot the stones were picked up.

Demonstrating the existence of mental habitat maps proves that animals do store information relating to habitat location and contents. Knowing this to be so, and knowing also that the information is used to determine pathways of movement, is compelling evidence in favor of interpreting those movements as a result of choice.

Harnessing Optimal Foraging Theory

I have twice hinted that theoretical predictions could play an important role in deciding what is happening inside an animal's head. If we know something about optimal habitat use, we can observe naive foragers approaching such an optimum behavior and thereby exhibiting their exploratory behavior. If we know something about optimal behavior in a given setting, we can change the setting so that another behavior is appropriate, and observe the forager doing the obsolete thing, thereby exhibiting its memory. In neither case does it matter whether the animal is picturing trees and flowers. It might instead be storing a kinetic program, because that particular pattern of movements brought it a higher reward than alternatives. Even so, it would be storing information about a restricted mode of habitat use culled after experience with alternatives. From the following experiment, however, the conclusion must be that birds actually do choose among the habitats themselves.

The most sophisticated use of optimal foraging to study habitat selection concerns neither exploratory behavior nor obsolete behavior. Instead, it concerns route planning and was performed by Mitchell (1989) on wild hummingbirds in the field.

Mitchell's theory is an example of the use of the optimal foraging paradigm at its best.

Suppose an animal sees only one habitat patch at a time. Any optimal foraging it does will involve comparison of the patch to an abstract distribution of patches which the forager could hope to encounter in the future. But the forager will not yet have sensed any of these future patches. Mitchell calls such a model "myopic foraging" because the forager senses only what is nearby.

An alternative to myopic foraging Mitchell calls periscopic. A periscopic forager senses (or knows of the existence and location of) numerous patches simultaneously. Periscopic optimal foragers have an added opportunity or problem. If they can solve a version of the traveling salesman problem and plot an optimal course from patch to patch, they can improve upon one-at-a-time strategies.

The traveling salesman problem is so difficult that mathematicians have solved only bits of it and special cases of it. Nevertheless, certain comparative properties of a traveling salesman vs. a myopic forager seem clear. For example, a myopic forager will accept or reject whole classes of habitat types. But a periscopic one ought sometimes to accept some secondary habitat patches but not others of the same type: Imagine a secondary patch near a primary one. It can be picked up with little travel cost. But if the secondary patch is far, it will involve substantial extra traveling and needs to be ignored by an optimal forager.

Another of Mitchell's predictions is that the likelihood of a periscopic forager's using a patch increases with the value of nearby patches. This is similar to the previous prediction, but differs in that it also applies to richer patches. An isolated rich patch may be ignored because of high travel costs compared with a similar one near others.

Mitchell made a number of such predictions and tested them with several species of hummingbirds. His experimental technique involved setting up an array of tiny, easily-depleted feeders to mimic flowers. Some of these had 1.0M sucrose solution, some more dilute sucrose solution. When he wished to run a periscopic trial, the feeders were set out with color coding, i.e. the 1.0M sucrose solution was coded by a blue ribbon, the weaker concentration by an orange ribbon. In the same places, with the same populations of hummingbirds, myopic trials were run simply by leaving out the color coding. Then a bird could determine the nature of a patch only by visiting it and probing it. (Of course, appropriate randomization of feeder locations deprived birds of spatial cues.)

The hummingbirds responded unequivocally to the difference between myopic trials and color-coded trials. Moreover, they responded in just the ways optimal foraging theory had predicted. For example, periscopic foragers were more likely to use a rich patch near another rich patch than near a poor patch. And they were more likely to use a poor patch near a rich patch than near another poor patch.

Mitchell's experiments demonstrate more than choice. They show the birds were planning their foraging. A wag might object that the optimal foraging theories Mitchell used produced insufficiently precise predictions to distinguish whether the birds were actually plotting a route through the array of feeders or merely seeing the nearest neighbor(s) to each current feeding station. Perhaps. The traveling salesman problem is sufficiently complex that even human minds have not solved it. Even so, demonstrating that a wild, free-living bird is seeing a habitat from a distance, taking account of its likely resource qualities and distance away, and then deciding whether to visit it is a remarkably significant experimental feat. It demonstrates anticipation rather than mere reaction. And that, I believe, is the essence of choice.

Evolution

One may imagine a dodder vine equipped with eyes, a brain and the power to choose. It would undoubtedly do a better job of plotting a course to its nearest preferred host than it could do by growing reactively. Why does dodder not evolve the paraphernalia required? What are the circumstances in which choice does evolve? In my opinion, this question is virtually unexplored.

It is possible to outline the question in more detail and to explore some issues that ought to be included in the contributions that supplant this one. Anyone's list ought to include 1) evolutionary constraints; and 2) environmental variability and the need for flexibility or rigidity in behavior.

Evolutionary Constraints

There are a number of classifications of evolutionary constraint (e.g. Rosenzweig et al. 1987). For purposes of this question, however, only two kinds of constraint seem important to me: choice may not have evolved in some taxa because there has not yet been enough time. Or it may not have evolved because it is, in balance, not actually a good idea.

I have no idea how to assess whether dodder (say) has lacked adequate time to evolve choice. Presumably an answer for this question would in turn require working out the time scale for the evolution of choice. That would require two things. First, some plants would have to be shown to have evolved choice. Second, we should have to figure out how to determine the presence of choice in fossil plants. The first is possible if we change the word "plants" to "animals." The second is outrageous for both. Lacking the answer, however, leaves us with no idea of the time scales at which a dynamical theory must operate. So I shall drop further discussion of this constraint. If it is operating, we do not have the ability to discover it.

The second constraint is more tractable. It implies the existence of one of two sorts of tradeoff. Either the cost of choice would more than counterbalance its benefits, or benefits would not even accrue until after a considerable interval of costly evolution. In the first case, choice is not truly beneficial. In the second, choice would be beneficial, but cannot evolve owing to maladaptedness of intermediate forms. In Wright's terms (1931), the species is marooned on an adaptive peak although another one, not too far away, is even higher.

In theory, tradeoffs can be analyzed. But in practice, we know far too little about choice to accomplish the analysis. What are the developmental costs of choice? The energetic? What neurons does it occupy which might otherwise be employed? We are in the stone age with regard to describing the mechanisms of choice, so how can we be expected to analyze their costs? We shall have to leave this issue of constraint to our children and grandchildren.

Environmental Variability

The ability to choose has zero selective value to individuals in a homogeneous environment. But is it likely that some sorts of heterogeneity will be handled with choice and some without?

Choice seems to govern movements, that is, relationships in space. Habitat allocation which occurs in time is accomplished physiologically (torpor, germination inhibition, etc.). Yet that generalization may not be 100% valid.

A desert mouse may be choosing to remain in its burrow when there is high short-term risk of predation because the moon is out. If so, it would be choosing not to move into a certain set of microhabitats, so space would be involved. But primarily it would be avoiding certain risky times because eventually it must come out into the risky habitats to get its food. Of course, we do not know whether moonlight-avoiding desert rodents are choosing; the data are only of the proportional use type. But the point remains. Choice may well evolve if the heterogeneity is temporal with a spatial component, i.e. if it involves appropriate matching of times and places. But choice is probably not worth looking for in situations where the heterogeneity is purely temporal.

Howard & Harrison (1984) performed an interesting set of experiments on two closely-related species of meadow crickets (*Allonemobius* species) in Connecticut. In the wettest part of the meadow, crickets are virtually all *A. fasciatus*; in the driest, *A. allardi*. The proportion of the two species changes gradually along the moisture gradient. Long enclosures running from wet to dry were constructed and cleared of crickets. Then new crickets were introduced in the middle of the gradient. In some enclosures, both species were introduced; in others, only one species. After a few weeks, cricket distribution was sampled. Perhaps there was inadequate time because the crickets in the mixed species enclosures did not achieve their natural distributions. But habitat allocation was already becoming apparent. And one thing was surely clear: *A. fasciatus* was piling up on the wet side of the gradient whether or not *A. allardi* was present. These crickets appeared inflexible in their habitat use.

One might hypothesize that the environment of the crickets is temporally so stable that the crickets need not evolve choice. But that hypothesis is flawed. As I said above, there is no reason to exclude the possibility that choice could be used to maintain a rigidly restricted habitat use. Even if there is zero temporal variation, individuals may need to choose in order to maintain a single optimal strategy. The need for flexibility is not the same as the need for choice.

The scale of the heterogeneity may be a more fruitful question than the degree of temporal heterogeneity. An animal with a cognitive map of the habitat in its own ambit will be a more efficient user of space if such heterogeneity is substantial. On the other hand, an animal in a habitat of similar heterogeneity but with much, much larger patches may need only to find one appropriate patch and settle in. A cognitive map of habitat types within its home range would be useless. Reactive settlement is probably the optimal strategy. Bumble along until things seem right and then settle. But even here we cannot be sure choice will not be the tool used.

Although a cognitive map of habitats may be good evidence for choice, it is not required for choice. The central question will be: Is the neurological cost of providing the ability to choose too much to pay for the one time task of finding an appropriate patch? How expensive is the provision of choice compared with "hard-wiring" the movement? Is one better than the other? We do not know. What we do know is that the significance of proper settlement can be ultimate. Desert isopod females, for example, march along for up to thirty days in search of a burrow site. If they settle in a place which will have 6% or more soil moisture 50cm below the surface and six months in the future (neither a time nor a space they experience before settlement), then they and their families survive. Otherwise they are dead (Shachak et al. 1979; Shachak & Brand 1988). So even though the event happens but once in a lifetime, it is so important that natural selection should not stint on the tool used. If choice does a better job of seeing the isopods in suitable nests, then choice they should have.

So far we have not learned much from evolutionary considerations. It is unlikely that they will be useful in the near future for helping the investigator decide whether a particular habitat allocation is arrived at by choice. Nevertheless they remain fascinating in their own right.

Summary Discussion

Few ecologists have been careful about using the term "habitat selection." It seems reasonable, however, to follow Hutto (1985) and restrict its use to cases of actual choice. The more common use, meaning a differential use of space-time which aids in competitive coexistence, should be termed "habitat allocation."

Habitat allocation can occur passively. It can also occur actively, but without choice. The latter is probably true in plants and in physiological responses to pure temporal variation such as hibernation. Yet there is much field evidence which identifies real choice at work in some instance of habitat allocation.

The most common type of field evidence is not convincing. The demonstration of differential use of habitat by various species serves the purposes of formulating hypotheses and providing ecologically relevant data on habitat allocation. But it says nothing about choice.

Even when non-randomness of use is demonstrated in the laboratory, it is only the weakest sort of evidence for choice. It argues for choice only because animals are usually carefully introduced to an experimental arena at a habitat border, thus causing the presumption that the animal actually senses the alternatives.

Much stronger evidence of choice comes from studies which show the sort of information being collected and sometimes stored and then used in exploiting habitats non-randomly. Showing that there is exploratory behavior is an excellent example of what would work, but exploratory behavior in wild vertebrates has generally been taken for granted. There is superb evidence for exploratory behavior in bees, however. A group of workers has the job of receiving the novel information from scouts and using it to allocate recruits to forage appropriately.

One form of strong evidence in vertebrates comes from the demonstration of mental (cognitive) habitat maps. The most often used argument for these is the observation of shortcuts. Another, much rarer but equally elegant, is the display of obsolete foraging behavior. The animal forages as if stimuli formerly present at specific sites were still there. This is especially convincing when an animal follows novel pathways to exploit the stimuli which used to be present. Other demonstrations of mental maps in vertebrates have taken advantage of special opportunities afforded by special species.

A new form of evidence for choice is emerging from the marriage of optimal foraging theory with simple, powerful field experiments. Foraging theory can predict the alternate consequences of having or not having information about the spatial distribution of habitats. Mitchell's (1989) field experiments with hummingbirds show that they can and do change their foraging behavior appropriately when they are permitted to gain such information. I predict this approach will become increasingly important in discovering the kinds of information that animals acquire about their world.

Two disappointments emerged as I wrote this essay. First, evolutionary principles do not yet promise much help. Except for conjecturing that heterogeneity which is purely temporal is not likely to produce choice, there was little I could do except ask questions. Second, and really quite a shock to me, the demonstration of behavioral flexibility does nothing to establish choice. I must admit my bias was otherwise at first. But I could not generate a single logical argument to link flexibility to choice, nor could I muster any data to do it. There is a lesson in that.

Flexibility or rigidity of habitat use is a crucial ecological distinction. It bears on fundamental ecology and conservation biology. Similarly, nonrandom patterns of habitat use are weighty matters for the community ecologist, but also resist linkage to choice. A choosing individual may (and sometimes should) cause its spatial habitat use to approximate randomness. The lesson then is that the whole issue of choice may not be of much significance to the ecologist. Granted it is of deep interest in its own right; it may not much matter ecologically how each species achieves its own particular spatio-temporal distribution. Yet the techniques of the ecologist are proving and will continue to prove of service to the investigation of choice.

Acknowledgements

Discussions with a number of people were instrumental in helping me think about choice. They are Jeff Galef, Mike Kaspari, Wayne Spencer, Tom Valone and especially Marc Bekoff. My research is supported by the National Science Foundation, BSR89-05728.

Literature Cited

Balda, R. P. & Kamil, A. C. 1989. A comparative study of cache recovery by three corvid species. *Animal Behaviour* 38, 486–495.

Bené, F. 1945. The role of learning in the feeding behavior of black-chinned hummingbirds. *Condor*, 47, 3–22.

Boesch, C. & Boesch, H. 1984. Mental map in wild chimpanzees: an analysis of hammer transports for nut cracking. *Primates* 25, 160–170.

Bovbjerg, R. V. 1970. Ecological isolation and competitive exclusion in two crayfish (*Orconectes virilis* and *Orconectes immunis*). *Ecology* 51, 225–236.

Brennan, L. A., Block, W. M. & Gutiérrez, R. J. 1987. Habitat use by mountain quail in northern California. *Condor* 89, 66–74.

Broadhead, E. & Wapshere, A. J. 1966. Mesopsocus populations in larch in England—the distribution and dynamics of two closely-related coexisting species of Psocoptera sharing the same food resource. *Ecological Monographs* 36, 327–388.

Brown, J. H. & Lieberman, G. A. 1973. Resource utilization and coexistence of seed-eating desert rodents in sand dune habitats. *Ecology* 54, 788–797.

Brown, J. S. 1989. Coexistence on a seasonal resource. *American Naturalist* 133, 168–182.

Brown, J. S. & Vincent, T. L. 1987. Coevolution as an evolutionary game. *Evolution* 41, 66–79.

Chesson, P. & Huntly, N. 1988. Community consequences of life history traits in a variable environment. *Annales Zoologica Fennici* 25, 5–16.

Cowan, P. E. 1983. Exploration in small mammals, ethology and ecology. In: *Exploration in Animals and Humans* (ed. by J. Archer & L. I. A. Birke), pp. 147–175. New York: Van Nostrand Reinhold.

Fretwell, S. D. 1972. *Populations in a Seasonal Environment*. Princeton, New Jersey: Princeton University Press.

Holmes, J. C. 1961. Effects of concurrent infections on *Hymenolepis diminuta* (Cestoda) and *Moniliformis dubius* (Acanthocephala) I. General effects and comparison with crowding. *Journal of Parasitology* 47, 209–216.

Howard, D. J. & Harrison, R. G. 1984. Habitat segregation in ground crickets: the role of interspecific competition and habitat selection. *Ecology* 65, 69–76.

Hutto, R. L. 1985. Habitat selection by nonbreeding: migratory land birds. In: *Habitat Selection in Birds* (ed. by M. L. Cody), pp. 455–476. Orlando, Florida: Academic Press.

Kelly, C. 1988. *Host Use and Foraging in the Parasitic Plant, Cuscuta subinclusa (Convolvulaceae)*. Ph.D. Dissertation, University of Arizona, Tucson.

Ketner, K. L. 1981. Peirce's ethics of terminology. *Charles S. Peirce Society* 17, 327–347.

Kosaka, M. 1956. Experimental studies on the habitat preference and evaluation of environment by flatfishes, *Limanda yokohamae* (Gunthek) and *Kareius bicoloratus* (Basilewsky), In Japanese with English summary. *Bulletin Japanese Society of Scientific Fisheries* 22, 284–288.

Kotler, B. P. 1984. Risk of predation and the structure of desert rodent communities. *Ecology* 65, 689–701.

Krebs, J. R., Kacelnik, A. & Taylor, P. 1978. Test of optimal sampling by foraging great tits. *Nature* 275, 27–31.

Lemen, C. & Rosenzweig, M. L. 1978. Microhabitat selection in two species of heteromyid rodents. *Oecologia* 33, 127–135.

Levins, R. 1968. *Evolution in Changing Environments*. Princeton, New Jersey: Princeton University Press.

Lidicker, W. Z. 1985. An overview of dispersal in non-volant small mammals. In: *Migration mechanisms and adaptive significance* (ed. by M. A. Rankin), pp. 359–375. Austin, Texas: University of Texas Press.

Lima, S. L. & Valone, T. J. 1991. Predators and avian community organization: An experiment in a desert grassland. *Oecologia* 86, 105–112.

Marler, P. & Hamilton, W. J. III. 1966. *Mechanisms of Animal Behavior*. New York: John Wiley & Sons.

Mitchell, W. A. 1989. Information constraints on optimally foraging hummingbirds. *Oikos* 55, 145–154.

Morisita, M. 1952. Habitat preference and evaluation of environment of an animal. Experimental studies on the population density of an ant-lion, *Glenuroides japonicus* M'L. I. (in Japanese with English summary). *Physiology and Ecology* 5, 1–16.

Morris, D. W. 1987. Ecological scale and habitat use. *Ecology* 68, 362–369.

Nowogrodzki, R. 1981. *Regulation of the Number of Foragers on a Constant Food Source by Honeybee Colonies*. M. S. thesis, Cornell University, Ithaca, New York.

Orians, G. H. 1980. Foraging behavior and the evolution of discriminatory abilities. In: *Foraging Behavior, Ecological, Ethological and Psychological Approaches* (ed. by A. C. Kamil & T. D. Sargent), pp. 389–405. New York: Garland STPM.

Peters, R. 1978. Communication, cognitive mapping and strategy in wolves and hominids. In: *Wolf and Man: Evolution in Parallel* (ed. by R. Hall & H. S. Sharp). pp. 95–107. New York: Academic Press.

Popper, K. R. 1972. *The Logic of Scientific Discovery*. Third ed. London: Hutchinson.

Rausher, M. D. 1979. Larval habitat suitability and oviposition preference in three related butterflies. *Ecology* 60, 503–511.

Rosenzweig, M. L. 1973. Habitat selection experiments with a pair of coexisting heteromyid rodent species. *Ecology* 54, 111–117.

———. 1986. Hummingbird isolegs in an experimental system. *Behavioral Ecology and Sociobiology* 19, 313–322.

———. 1987. Habitat selection as a source of biological diversity. *Evolutionary Ecology* 1, 315–330.

Rosenzweig, M. L. & Abramsky, Z. 1985. Detecting density-dependent habitat selection. *American Naturalist* 126, 405–417.

Rosenzweig, M. L., Brown, J. S. & Vincent, T. L. 1987. Red Queens and ESS: The coevolution of evolutionary rates. *Evolutionary Ecology* 1, 59–96.

Rosenzweig, M. L. & Winakur, J. 1969. Population ecology of desert rodent communities: habitats and environmental complexity. *Ecology* 50, 558–572.

Schroder, G. & Rosenzweig, M. L. 1975 Perturbation analysis of competition and overlap in habitat utilization between *Dipodomys ordii* and *Dipodomys merriami*. *Oecologia* 19, 9–28.

Seeley, T. D. 1983. Division of labor between scouts and recruits in honeybee foraging. *Behavioral Ecology and Sociobiology* 12, 253–259.

———. 1985. The information-center strategy of honeybee foraging. In: *Experimental Behavioral Ecology* (ed. by B. K. Hölldobler & M. Lindauer), pp. 75–90. Stuttgart and New York: G. Fischer-Verlag:

Shachak, M. & Brand, S. 1988. Relationship among settling, demography and habitat selection: an approach and a case study. *Oecologia* 76, 620–627.

Shachak, M., Steinberger, Y. & Orr, Y. 1979. Phenology, activity and regulation of radiation load in the desert isopod, *Hemilepistus reaumuri*. *Oecologia* 40, 133–140.

Whitford, W. G., Dick-Peddie, S., Walters D. & Ludwig, J. 1978. Effects of shrub defoliation on grass cover in a Chihuahuan desert ecosystem. *Journal of Arid Environments* 1, 237–242.

Wright, S. 1931. Evolution in mendelian populations. *Genetics* 16, 97–159.

Chapter 13

The Influence of Models on the Interpretation of Vigilance

Steven L. Lima

Foraging animals are usually simultaneously both predator and prey. This simple truism dictates that many animals face a profound conflict between predator avoidance and efficient food intake, because behavioral decisions minimizing the risk of predation are often antithetical to efficient food intake. Such a conflict may exist at several levels of decision-making, from broad-scale habitat selection to diet selection (Lima & Dill 1990). Here, I will focus on a conflict faced by many higher vertebrates that arises from the simple act of ingesting food itself.

The nature of this conflict is illustrated in Figure 13.1. An animal with its head up and eyes scanning for predators is relatively safe, but it cannot feed. An animal with its head down can feed, but its ability to detect predators is severely compromised because its attention is narrowly focused on food items. Thus an animal faced with this conflict must decide how to trade-off vigilance against feeding in order to maximize its Darwinian fitness (i.e. survival for present purposes).

This conflict and ensuing tradeoff have been the subject of several behavioral studies over the last 20 years (Lima & Dill 1990). My goal here is to critically examine these studies and the conclusions drawn from them; a major theme throughout is that our present interpretation of antipredatory vigilance is perhaps more a function of human intuition than of a critical examination of the processes thought to underlie observed behavior. I will focus on four main areas in the study of antipredatory vigilance: the effect of group size, cooperative vigilance, the scanning process itself, and the role of mathematical modelling. I begin with the effect of group size, the early studies of which set the stage for all subsequent work.

The Effect of Group Size

Many animals forage in groups, and group size may have a strong influence on how individuals tradeoff vigilance against feeding. The reason is simple. As group size increases, there are more eyes to scan for approaching predators. Thus, each individual in the group can devote less time to vigilance and more time to feeding as group size increases, without seriously affecting the group's ability to detect predators (assuming that predator detection is somehow rapidly transmitted to all group members). This effect was mentioned long ago (Allee 1938) but was not examined in detail until the 1970s. At this point in time, there was much discussion of the costs and benefits of sociality, and several researchers independently converged on the vigilance benefits of sociality. For instance, Powell (1974) showed that a group of starlings (*Sturnus vulgaris*) detected predators sooner than solitary individuals. This result held despite

Figure 13.1
Representative forager in a nonvigilant feeding position (head down) and vigilant, nonfeeding position (head up). (Figure kindly drawn by K. L. Wiebe.)

the fact that individuals decreased their vigilance as group size increased. Dimond & Lazarus (1974) independently confirmed the "group size effect" on individual vigilance in flocks of geese. Since this early work, the group size effect has been demonstrated in many studies, mostly on birds (see Lima & Dill 1990). Some representative examples are shown in Figure 13.2a–c.

Perhaps the most influential work on antipredatory vigilance was a brief model of group predator detection developed by Pulliam (1973). This seminal model provided a simple and elegant statement of the many-eyes hypothesis and served as a focus for the great majority of studies on the group size effect. For purposes of discussion, I will develop a simple model of vigilance which expresses the essence of the ideas in Pulliam (1973).

A Model of Vigilance Behavior

Assume that vigilance and feeding are mutually exclusive activities. Following Parker & Hammerstein (1985), let $V(n)$ be the probability that at least one member of a group of size n is vigilant when an attack occurs. $V(n)$ is essentially the probability that every group member escapes from the predator, thus $1 - V(n)$ is the probability that the predator is successful. The probability of escape during a successful attack is $(n - 1)/n$, assuming only one death. Thus a given animal's probability of surviving an attack is $[1 - V(n)](n - 1)/n + V(n)$, which can be rearranged to $(n - 1)/n + V(n)/n$.

Note that $V(n)$ incorporates the many-eyes hypothesis. Following the assumptions in Pulliam (1973), $V(n) = 1 - (1 - v)^n$ where v is the proportion of time spent vigilant by a given group member. This form of $V(n)$ assumes independent scanning by the n group members. Let p be the probability of the group being attacked by a predator, and let S be an individual's probability of avoiding starvation. A group member thus has the following probability of surviving the time period in question:

$$P(\text{survival}) = (1 - p)S + p\{(n - 1)/n + V(n)/n\}S. \tag{1}$$

Assuming that S has the reasonable form of $S = 1 - v^2$, and substituting the above relationship for $V(n)$ into (1), we have (after simplification):

$$P(\text{survival}) = [1 - p(1 - v)^n/n][1 - v^2]. \tag{2}$$

The optimal level of vigilance (v^*) is that which maximizes the probability of survival.

Figure 13.2d shows the relationship between group size (n) and v^*. Regardless of

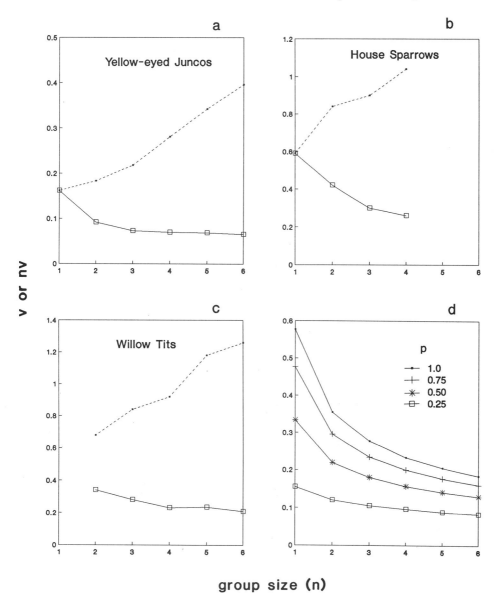

Figure 13.2
(a)–(c) Representative examples of individual vigilance as a function of group size in yellow-eyed juncos (Pulliam et al. 1982), willow tits (Ekman 1987), house sparrows (Lima 1987a). Shown are v (———), the average proportion of time spent vigilant by individuals, and "total group vigilance" given by the quantity NV (- - - -). (d) Individual vigilance (v) predicted by Eq. (2) for the indicated probabilities of predatory attack.

the probability of attack (p), v^* decreases at a decelerating rate as n increases. When compared to actual vigilance behavior (Figure 13.2a–c), the heuristic power and appeal of this model is apparent: It readily explains the "classical" response of vigilance to group size. Several variants of this simple model that explicitly consider scanning rates, etc. (e.g. Pulliam et al. 1982; Lima 1987b), produce similarly striking correspondences between theory and observation.

There have been no major challenges to the basic view of predation and vigilance embodied in Eq. (2), nor is it really my goal here to do so. I will, however, raise some concerns stemming from a simple fact: Models of vigilance behavior have rarely been tested quantitatively. While it is possible to test certain assumptions of the model (e.g. independent scanning in group members), the difficulty in testing the model's numerical predictions stems from the difficulty in measuring many parameters, such as the probability of being attacked, and a host of other parameters (regarding the process of attack and escape, etc.) in more realistic models (e.g. Pulliam et al. 1982; Lima 1987b). With this in mind, I will probe a bit more deeply into the group size effect. A main theme is that simple models such as that developed above are such powerful heuristics that they have "channelled" our interpretation of vigilance away from some potentially important matters.

Simple Models and Reality

Perception of Group Size   One major reason for the strong appeal of Eq. (2) is its emphasis on group size (n), the parameter most easily measured. However, even the nature of n is not clear. For instance, Metcalfe (1984) and others report that vigilance responds to forager density rather than group size *per se*. Furthermore, Elgar et al. (1984) found that a house sparrow separated from others by as little as 1.2 m (but in visual contact) scans as if it were alone. The bottom line here is that we have remarkably little understanding of the way in which group size is perceived by various animals. More troubling is the possibility that the effects of forager density on vigilance may imply a process fundamentally different from the many-eyes hypothesis in Eq. (2), perhaps one involving antipredatory tactics other than group vigilance.

On the Awareness of Vigilance   Since it is not clear how various animals perceive n, it may come as no surprise that it is not clear whether social foragers have any regard for the vigilance of their group mates. In fact, I can cite no studies which directly examine this question. Information about the vigilance of group mates is presumably acquired visually in most animals (especially birds). However, Sullivan's (1984) observation that downy woodpeckers' (*Picoides pubescens*) lower vigilance in response to titmice (*Parus* spp.) that they can only hear and not see suggests that these woodpeckers reduce vigilance in situations where they cannot possibly be aware of the vigilance of flock mates.

This point concerning the awareness of vigilance means that there is no solid evidence for the $(1 - v)^n$ factor in Eq. (2), which is the crux of the many-eyes hypothesis. Just for fun, let's say that the forager is aware of n but only its own level of vigilance. Therefore the exponent n in Eq. (2) is set equal to 1, and Eq. (2) reduces to

$$P(\text{survival}) = [1 - p(1 - v)/n][1 - v^2]. \tag{3}$$

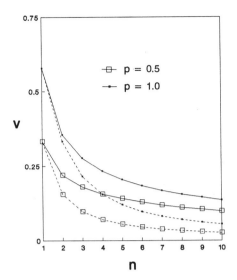

Figure 13.3
Individual vigilance predicted by Eq. (2) with the many-eyes hypothesis included (———) and excluded
(- - - -). These relationships are shown for two values of p.

The n remaining in (3) represents the dilution of risk with increasing group size
(again, assuming one death in a successful attack). Taking the derivative of (3) with
respect to v and setting it equal to zero shows that optimal vigilance is given by

$$v^* = [\sqrt{z^2 + 3y^2} - z]/3y$$

where $y = p/n$ and $z = 1 - y$. As seen in Figure 13.3, Eq. (3) produces optimal behavior very similar in form to Eq. (2), which incorporates the many-eyes hypothesis.
An overall greater level of vigilance is predicted by the many-eyes model, but this
difference cannot be exploited empirically unless confidence can be placed in quantitative predictions and the models themselves. In any case, the point of this exercise is
clear: the dilution of risk with increasing group size may account for much of the
group size effect, even if a forager *is* aware of the vigilance of others (see also Packer
& Abrams 1990).

Group Size and Attack   A further point on interpreting the group size effect is the
possibility that the probability of being attacked (p) is group-size-dependent (e.g.
Caraco 1979a). For instance, if larger flocks detect predators with greater certainty,
then perhaps predators avoid attacking larger groups. Such an effect could add
greatly to the decrease in vigilance with group size. There is not much evidence from
field work that p is a function of n (but see Lindström 1989), which partly reflects the
lack of our ability to determine p itself.

Competition for Limited Food Resources   Virtually all models of vigilance implicitly assume unlimited food resources. This essentially ensures that the group size parameter
n appears only in the many-eyes factor (e.g. $(1 - v)^n$ in Eq. [2]) and the dilution factor
(e.g. $1/n$ in Eq. [2]) of a given model. With limited food resources, however, n may

strongly influence vigilance not only by decreasing the risk of predation, but also by increasing competition for food.

One way to approach this "competition effect" is to view antipredatory vigilance as a component of food handling time. If *n* animals are competing for a limited amount of food, then there is a premium on consuming food as quickly as possible (c.f. Barnard et al. 1983). One obvious way to achieve this end is to decrease vigilance. Since competition will increase with increasing group size, it may account for a major portion of the group size effect traditionally ascribed to antipredatory effects.

Very few studies have seriously considered competition as a possible factor in vigilance (but see Bertram 1980). Furthermore, no studies to date have examined the problem directly through experimentation. Thus, it is currently impossible to assess the extent to which the group size effect is dominated by competition for food, although many studies effectively side-stepped the problem by eliminating (short-term) competition through the use of superabundant food (e.g. Lima 1987a). Surprisingly, studies suggesting that competition is not necessarily an overriding factor in the group size effect deal with sleeping animals; the observation that animals interrupt their sleep (to scan their environment) less frequently with increasing group size (Lendrem 1984b; da Silva & Terhune 1988) cannot easily be construed as evidence of competition for sleep.

Object of Vigilance   So far, I have accepted the premise that vigilance is antipredatory in nature. What is the evidence for such a premise? A few studies have demonstrated that recent sightings of predators, etc., actually lead to higher vigilance in birds (Caraco et al. 1980a; Lendrem 1984a; Sullivan 1984; Glück 1987). Predation is also strongly implicated by observations that foragers adjust vigilance in response to the distance to safe refuge or the presence of visual obstructions (see Lima 1987b). However, it is probably fair to say that the group size effect itself is the main support for this predation premise. Clearly, the logical problems not withstanding, a forager with its head down (e.g. Figure 13.1) has compromised not only its ability to detect predators, but also its ability to detect a host of lesser threats (Dimond & Lazarus 1974). How might such considerations alter our interpretation of the ubiquitous group size effect?

A few recent studies have begun to address the possibility of nonantipredatory vigilance. For instance, Thompson & Lendrem (1985; see also Barnard & Thompson 1985) found that vigilance in certain shorebirds may be directed towards food-robbing gulls. A few studies also suggest that vigilance may be directed toward other, potentially aggressive group members in social birds (Waite 1987a,b; Withiam et al. 1990; Knight & Knight 1986) and mammals (Caine & Marra 1988; Roberts 1988).

The extent to which our present interpretation of the group size effect should be influenced by nonpredatory factors is not clear. Of particular concern is the role of intragroup aggression, which can be considerable (e.g. Caraco 1979b). Overall, however, it is unlikely that antiaggression vigilance is of overriding importance in the group size effect for two main reasons. First. experimental studies (Waite 1987a,b; Withiam et al. 1990) induced unusually high rates of aggression by forcing birds to feed in highly constrained situations uncharacteristic of most natural situations. Second, since aggression often increases with group size (e.g. Caraco 1979b), one might generally expect vigilance to increase with group size (Bertram 1980). However, only Knight & Knight (1986) report such an effect.

In summary, while the foregoing discussion is largely critical of studies on vigilance and the group size effect, my main point is really that the interpretation of vigilance in social animals may reflect more the elegance of simple heuristic models than experimentation examining key behavioral postulates. I suspect, however, that the simple many-eyes hypothesis embodied in Eq. (2) will survive as an important heuristic tool even in the face of more critical experimentation. I can cite two main reasons for this optimism. First, an increase in predation risk has demonstrable effects on vigilance (see above and Lima 1987b). Second, larger groups do in fact detect predators sooner than smaller ones (Powell 1974; Kenward 1978; Lazarus 1979), and I find it difficult to believe that natural selection has not molded animals to take this into account and be less vigilant with increasing group size.

Cooperation in Vigilance

All models of social vigilance assume (implicitly or explicitly) that natural selection has molded animals to take into account the vigilance of other group members when deciding upon their own level of vigilance. This assumption, however, actually presents a major problem for the vigilance model developed above. The reason is basic to the evolutionary process: natural selection should produce inherently selfish animals. In terms of vigilance, what will stop a selfish individual from "parasitizing" the vigilance of its group mates by decreasing its vigilance (and thereby increasing its time spent feeding)? In the absence of human conventions such as legally-binding contracts between individuals, nothing will stop attempts at "cheating." Because the simple model developed above does not consider the possibility of such cheating, it implicitly assumes a level of intragroup cooperation that may not be evolutionarily stable to cheating (i.e. cheaters should enjoy a relative advantage over cooperators and thus be favored by natural selection). A game-theoretical modelling approach is necessary to determine evolutionarily stable optimal behavior in such situations (see Maynard Smith 1982; Parker 1984).

Pulliam et al. (1982) recognized the possibility of cheating as a major problem for the many-eyes hypothesis, and developed a game-theoretical model of vigilance behavior to compare and contrast selfish and cooperative vigilance. Their model, based on scanning rates as per Pulliam (1973), showed that scanning rates in selfish groups are lower than those in cooperative groups. Furthermore, they found that vigilance observed in socially foraging yellow-eyed juncos (*Junco phaeonotus*) was close to that predicted for cooperative groups (see Table 13.1). To explain the existence of this presumably unstable vigilance pattern, Pulliam et al. tentatively proposed that juncos employ a "judge" strategy, where each flock member remains cooperative as long as others do so. This strategy is functionally equivalent to the Tit-for-Tat strategy proposed for stable cooperation in other behavioral contexts (Axelrod & Hamilton 1981).

Further theoretical work by Parker & Hammerstein (1985) confirmed these basic results on social vigilance using Eq. (4), which is essentially a game-theoretical version of Eq. (2).

$$P(\text{survival of } v \text{ in group using } \hat{v}) = [1 - p(1 - v)(1 - \hat{v})^{n-1}/n][1 - v^2] \qquad (4)$$

Here, v represents the vigilance of a potential cheater, and $\hat{v}$ is the (evolutionarily stable) vigilance of the remaining $n - 1$ individuals. The selfish optimum is deter-

Table 13.1
Observed scanning rates of yellow-eyed juncos vs. predicted cooperative and selfish scanning optima (from Pulliam et al. 1982)

Flock size	Scanning rate (per min.)		
	Observed	Cooperative	Selfish
1	13.9	15.9	15.9
2	7.85	6.2	0.0
3	6.22	5.9	0.0
4	6.02	5.5	0.0
5	5.87	5.2	0.0
6	5.66	4.9	0.0
7	5.58	4.7	0.0
8	5.59	4.5	0.0
9	4.88	4.4	0.0
10	4.65	4.0	0.0

mined by taking the derivative of (4) with respect to v, setting it equal to zero, and solving for v after setting $\hat{v} = v$; setting $\hat{v} = v$ in (4) before performing this mathematical procedure yields the cooperative optimum. Assuming $p = 1$, Parker & Hammerstein also found that selfish groups are less vigilant than cooperative ones (Figure 13.4). In addition, because vigilance decreases with group size regardless of selfish or cooperative strategies, Parker & Hammerstein proposed that the two might be distinguished by the quantity nv. As seen in Figure 13.4, nv increases with group size for cooperative groups, and decreases for selfish groups. A survey of empirical results often suggests cooperation in vigilance; some real-world examples of increasing nv are illustrated in Figure 13.2a–c.

These results are remarkable. They suggest widespread cooperative vigilance among largely nonrelated animals (at least in birds), even though such cooperation has been difficult to demonstrate elsewhere (see Packer 1986).

Before accepting cooperation as fact, however, I must stress some important points concerning the interpretation of vigilance. First, all of the above-mentioned problems in interpreting the basic group size effect apply to cooperation. In particular, the complete lack of direct evidence that social animals have any regard for the vigilance of others (beyond the group size effect itself) leaves the "judge" strategy in question.

Furthermore, consider the implications of previous work concerning the perception of group size (see above). This work suggests that animals perceive only a fraction of the n animals in a group. For simplicity, assume that the perceived group size (m) is given by $m = 1 + k(n - 1)$ where k indicates the fraction of the group perceived by the animal in question; $m = n$ if $k = 1$. Substituting m for n in Eq. (4), and solving for selfish optima, significantly alters the above results regarding cooperation. As seen in Figure 13.5a, the basic group size effect holds over several values of k. However, as k decreases, the quantity nv may increase with n (but not m), even though these are selfish optima (Figure 13.5b). Does this explain the real-world cases of increasing nv (Figure 13.2a–c)? It is presently impossible to say given our lack of understanding of the perception of group size.

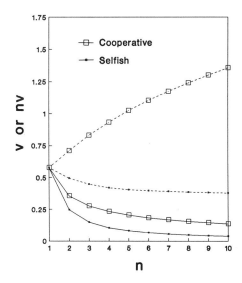

Figure 13.4
Selfish and cooperative vigilance levels predicted by Eq. (4). Individual vigilance v (———) and nv (- - - -) are shown. The parameter p is set at 1.0.

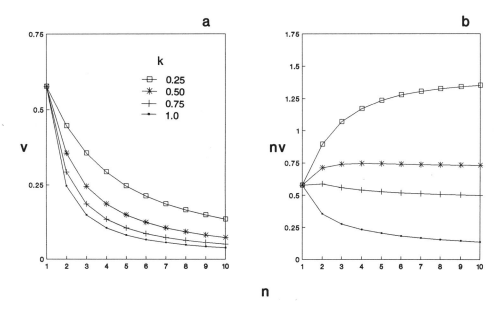

Figure 13.5
Selfish vigilance and the "incomplete" perception of group size. (a) Individual vigilance as a function of actual group size (n) for the indicated values of k. (b) The quantity nv for the values of k as per (a).

Recent theoretical work shows further how conclusions regarding cooperation depend critically on the way in which the overall predator-prey interaction is modelled. For instance, Packer & Abrams (1990) point out that Parker & Hammerstein's model (the "PH model") applies only when a successful predator kills randomly within the group of n foragers. By realistically relaxing several implicit assumptions in the PH model, Packer & Abrams identified several situations where cooperative groups should be *less* vigilant than selfish groups. For instance, this result may hold if predators preferentially attack the least vigilant members of foraging groups, as suggested by FitzGibbon (1989). Selfish vigilance may also exceed cooperative vigilance if the chances of escape depend upon the vigilance of other group members at the time of attack. Such an effect of vigilance on escape is suggested by Elgar (1986), who found that nonvigilant house sparrows react more slowly to attack than vigilant sparrows.

There are other reasons for expecting similarities in selfish and cooperative behavior. All of the models of selfish/cooperative vigilance mentioned above assume that the group is concerned with surviving only one attack or one short period of time (e.g. one day). Clearly, most animals will be concerned with multiple attacks or longer periods of time. I have shown (Lima 1989) that apparent cooperation may be evolutionary stable in such situations; essentially, cheating only leads to the death of groupmates, who may be essential to long-term survival. Kaitala et al. (1989) independently came to a similar conclusion in re-analyzing Pulliam et al.'s (1982) model. In particular, they found that the very low levels of selfish vigilance predicted by Pulliam et al. (see Table 13.1) are not to be expected when considering behavior over the long-term.

Overall, despite a promising start based upon simple, heuristically elegant models, I must conclude that there is little unambiguous empirical support for cooperative vigilance in social foragers. In fact, the many "selfish" ways of achieving apparent cooperation may make selfish and cooperative strategies virtually impossible to distinguish empirically without great confidence in quantitative tests of various models. Perhaps future studies should focus on simple, well-defined situations where unambiguous qualitative tests may be possible.

I conclude this section by noting that the study of cooperation may have been side-tracked somewhat by the historical development of the study of vigilance. The assumption of many-eyes independently vigilant for predators has been carried through all empirical and theoretical studies since Pulliam (1973) and earlier, including those concerned with cooperative vigilance. However, perhaps truly cooperative vigilance involves sentinels; i.e. highly vigilant, nonfeeding individuals which stand guard over the remaining $n - 1$ feeding individuals (e.g. Rasa 1987). I have shown that n group members alternately sharing $1/n$ of the total vigilance burden achieve a higher level of survival than n independently scanning individuals. In fact, independent scanning may itself represent a lack of cooperation. The obvious problem with cheating in sentinel vigilance is that there is no guarantee that other group members will take their watch after a given sentinel wishes to feed. It is perhaps no coincidence that sentinels are often observed in stable, family groups (e.g. Ferguson 1987; Rasa 1987) which are presumably favorable situations for the evolution of cooperation (Hamilton 1964; Trivers 1971).

Patterns in Individual Vigilance

The process of vigilance involves a repeating sequence of head lifts, scans of the environment, and nonvigilant inter-scan intervals where actual feeding takes place. As with other subjects, the early models of vigilance played a major role in shaping the study of patterns in the vigilance of individuals.

Scan Initiation

Pulliam (1973) assumed that individual foragers initiate scans of constant length according to an exponential probability distribution $re\text{-}rt$, where r is the overall rate of scan initiation, and t is the time since terminating the last scan. This distribution implies that a scan is initiated with constant probability in any small time interval, regardless of t. Hence, the logical basis for this "exponential" assumption is that a predator cannot easily time an attack against such a forager.

This assumption is intuitively reasonable, but there are overriding mathematical needs for it as well. First, it implies that the forager has control over a single variable r, which completely specifies the probability distribution. The exponential assumption also yields very simple probabilities concerning predator detection. For instance, let "a" represent the time a forager has to detect an attack once the predator is no longer concealed by vegetation, etc. The probability that the forager fails to detect the attack is therefore e^{-ra}. With n independently scanning individuals, this probability is e^{-nra}. Most other probability distributions would yield much more "messy" probabilities (c.f. Hart & Lendrem 1984) that may involve more than one parameter under a forager's control; such multi-parameter optimization models are mathematically more difficult.

This exponential assumption has evoked several tests, all with birds. Bertram (1980), Caraco (1982), and Studd et al. (1983) showed that the lengths of interscan intervals fit nicely to exponential distributions. Lendrem (1983) found interscan intervals in blue tits (*Parus caeruelus*) became more exponentially distributed as the risk of predation increased. The exponential assumption was largely unsupported by Elcavage & Caraco (1983), Sullivan (1985), and Pöysä (1987); Hart & Lendrem (1984) re-analyzed Bertram's (1980) data in detail and also found a lack of support. Lendrem et al. (1986) suggested that a slightly more complicated exponential distribution, where r is a time-dependent function, can help explain some of these discrepancies. More recently, Desportes et al. (1989) used spectral analysis to suggest that scanning patterns are random in appearance, but underlaid by regular patterns nonetheless.

These studies represent one of the few areas where the behavioral processes underlying vigilance have been examined critically. They also, however, demonstrate the power of the simple many-eyes hypothesis to channel research into perhaps overly-narrow areas of discourse. With respect to understanding patterns in vigilance behavior, perhaps a more fruitful approach would also have addressed the simple question of what pattern should we expect to observe. In this regard, Desportes et al. (1989) correctly suggest that when predators attack without regard to prey behavior, regular (i.e. constant) interscan intervals are superior to exponential scanning in detecting predators. I suggest that even if predators time their attacks relative to prey vigilance (c.f. Hart & Lendrem 1984), an exponential pattern might not be expected, particularly if the parameter "a" is known with certainty. Overall, because so much work has focused on a mathematically convenient assumption, relatively little is understood about this aspect of the scanning process.

Scan Length

Two further assumptions in simple scanning-rate models of vigilance (e.g. Lima 1987b) are worthy of mention: (i) scan length, s, is appreciable and constant; and (ii) predator detection is instantaneous. These assumptions are, in fact, somewhat contradictory, for why would scans be of appreciable length if predator detection is instantaneous? It turns out that assumption (i) is necessary because assumption (ii) dictates that the optimal scanning rate approaches infinity as s becomes smaller. Clearly, a forager has control over s, and the fact that scans are appreciable in length probably means that there are differing consequences for one s over another.

Relatively little work has examined scan lengths, perhaps because the above two assumptions seem rather innocuous. The assumption of constant s has some support (Pulliam et al. 1982), while other studies show that s decreases markedly with group size (Metcalfe 1984). Glück (1987) found that s increases in solitary birds which have recently sighted a predator, while Pöysä (1987) found foraging constraints may affect scan length. McVean & Haddlesey (1980) and Elcavage & Caraco (1983) provide evidence for variable and constant s, respectively, in the same species (house sparrows).

The adaptive value of altering vigilance via scan length (in addition to scanning rate) is not clear. It seems reasonable that longer scans yield more information about the immediate risk of predation. Perhaps this is why solitary individuals may exhibit longer scans than grouped foragers (Metcalfe 1984). However, longer scans may actually prevent attack (e.g. FitzGibbon 1989). Furthermore, does a decrease in scan length with increasing group size mean each individual requires less information, or does it reflect competition for food?

I must once again caution that in interpreting the fine-scale patterns in vigilance, care should be taken not to equate vigilance solely with predator detection (which is the strong tendency). A particular problem to avoid is the violation of the assumption of mutually exclusive food ingestion and vigilance; in some cases, scan lengths may strongly reflect food handling times if scanning and handling are not mutually exclusive (e.g. Lima 1988). In other cases, scanning may be influenced by multiple objects of vigilance (e.g. predators, aggressors, food-robbers, etc.).

Models and the Study of Vigilance Behavior

I have argued that simple heuristic models have played a major role in the study of vigilance behavior. At the risk of promoting the abandonment of such modeling, I have focused mainly on its more negative effects on the interpretation of vigilance behavior. In this section, however, I wish to elaborate more on the role of modeling, and suggest that it has played, and will continue to play, an important and positive role.

It is something of a theoretician's cliché to state that models act to clarify the important issues at hand, and thus stimulate meaningful research. However, I believe this is precisely what the early models have done. Pulliam (1973), in particular, stimulated a great deal of relatively well-focused research that has identified a genuine phenomenon (the group size effect) in many taxa (Lima & Dill 1990). Perhaps a more important need for models relates to a simple fact: Human intuition has not always been the best guide to interpreting vigilance.

Consider first the idea of cheating and cooperation in vigilance. It is highly intuitive that selfish animals should be less vigilant than cooperative ones (Pulliam et al. 1982; Parker Hammerstein 1985). However, modeling that exposed the hidden assumptions in the early models (Packer & Abrams, 1990; Kaitala et al. 1989) showed that intuition is less than adequate in many reasonable situations (see above). This theoretical discourse on the problem of cheating/cooperation in vigilance, at the very least, should give the empiricist reason to tread carefully in this matter.

The same may be said for intuition and the influence of environmental factors on vigilance. For instance, sparrows may be more vigilant the farther they must feed from the safety of dense brushy cover (e.g. Barnard 1980). This result is intuitively clear: the increase in risk with increasing distance to the refuge leads to an increase in vigilance. However, a simple model (Lima 1987b) indicates that the opposite result is also a reasonable expectation (see also Lima 1987a). This model makes clear two nonintuitive main points regarding the interpretation of vigilance: (i) that vigilance need not always increase with increasing risk, and (ii) a behavioral response to one factor may actually reflect a response to one or more correlated factors (e.g. an increase in the likelihood of attack with increasing distance to cover).

Overall, I believe that models will be essential to the proper interpretation of vigilance behavior. However, I again must stress a few points concerning the use of such models. First, most models are quantitatively untestable given our current inability to measure many parameters. Second, little is known about the perceptions of the animals being studied, thus our models reflect mainly the perceptions of the modelers themselves. Finally, all models are gross caricatures of reality. For instance, consider Eq. (2). There is no explicit consideration of scan lengths or scanning rates, nor is there any mention of the relationship between the latter and time exposed to attack. There is no consideration of perceived group size, competition for food, aggression, or the fact that groups size is rarely constant over time. Thus, the quantitative predictions derived from such models may be meaningless and even misleading. Models of vigilance behavior are merely heuristic devices to be used as guides to research. As such, their use should be accompanied by a healthy dose of skepticism.

Conclusion

A great many studies have established the generality of the group size effect in the vigilance of several taxa (see Lima & Dill 1990). In fact, the many-eyes hypothesis interpretation of the group size effect may be approaching the status of dogma. However, I have argued here that our current interpretation of this effect is related more to the power of simple models to mimic observed behavior rather than experimentation examining critical behavioral processes. The same can be said for other aspects of vigilance behavior.

Future empirical and theoretical work must be more focused and critical if further progress is to be made in the study of vigilance behavior; in my view, the halcyon "Golden Age" is over. I have outlined several topics in need of further research, many of which can be approached experimentally. In pursuing these and other topics, researchers should take care to: (i) allow for nonpredatory interpretations of vigilance; (ii) explicitly consider the perceptions of the animals themselves; (iii) stay within the realm of ecological reason; and (iv) understand the influence, importance, and limitations of models in the study of vigilance behavior.

Literature Cited

Allee, W. C. 1938. *The Social Life of Animals*. New York: Norton and Company.

Axelrod, R. & Hamilton, W. D. 1981. The evolution of cooperation. *Science* 211, 1390–1396.

Barnard, C. J. 1980. Flock feeding and time budgets in the house sparrow (*Passer domesticus* L.). *Animal Behaviour* 28, 295–309.

Barnard, C. J. & Thompson, D. B. A. 1985. *Gulls and Plovers*. New York: Columbia University Press.

Barnard, C. J., Brown, C. A. J. & Gray-Wallis, J. 1983. Time and energy budgets and competition in the common shrew (*Sorex araneus* L.). *Behavioral Ecology and Sociobiology* 13, 13–18.

Bertram, B. C. R. 1980. Vigilance and group size in ostriches. *Animal Behaviour* 28, 278–286.

Caine, N. G. & Marra, S. L. 1988. Vigilance and social organization in two species of primates. *Animal Behaviour* 36, 897–904.

Caraco, T. 1979a. Time budgeting and group size: a theory. *Ecology* 60, 611–617.

———. 1979b. Time budgeting and group size: a test of theory. *Ecology* 60, 618–627.

———. 1982. Flock size and the organization of behavioral sequences in juncos. *Condor* 84, 101–105.

Caraco, T., Martindale, S. & Pulliam, H. R. 1980. Avian time budgets and distance to cover. *Auk* 97, 872–875.

———. 1982. Avian flocking in the presence of a predator. *Nature* 285, 400–401.

da Silva, J. & Terhune, J. M. 1988. Harbour seal grouping as an antipredator strategy. *Animal Behaviour* 36, 1309–1316.

Desportes, J. -P., Metcalfe, N. B., Cezilly. F., Lauvergeon, G & Kervella, C. 1989. Tests on the sequential randomness of vigilant behaviour using spectral analysis. *Animal Behaviour* 38, 771–777.

Dimond, S. & Lazarus, J. 1974. The problem of vigilance in animal life. *Brain, Behavior, and Evolution* 9, 60–79.

Ekman, J. 1987. Exposure and time use in willow tit flocks: The cost of subordination. *Animal Behaviour* 35, 445–452.

Elcavage, P. & Caraco, T. 1983. Vigilance behaviour in house sparrow flocks. *Animal Behaviour* 31, 303–304.

Elgar, M. A. 1986. Scanning, pecking, and alarm fights in house sparrows. *Animal Behaviour*. 34, 1892–1894.

Elgar, M. A., Burren, P. J. & Posen, M. 1984. Vigilance and perception of flock size in foraging house sparrows (*Passer domesticus* L.). *Behaviour* 90, 215–223.

Ferguson, J. W. H. 1987. Vigilance behavior in white-browed sparrow-weavers, *Plocepasser mahali*. *Ethology* 76, 223–235.

FitzGibbon, C. D. 1989. A cost to individuals with reduced vigilance in groups of Thomson's gazelles hunted by cheetahs. *Animal Behaviour* 37, 508–510.

Glück, E. 1987. An experimental study of feeding, vigilance, and predator avoidance in a single bird. *Oecologia* 71, 268–272.

Hamilton, W. D. 1964. The genetical evolution of social behavior. *Journal of Theoretical Biology* 7, 1–52.

Hart, A. & Lendrem, D. W. 1984. Vigilance and scanning patterns in birds. *Animal Behaviour* 32, 1216–1224.

Kaitala, V., Lindström, K. & Ranta, E. 1989. Foraging, vigilance, and risk of predation in birds—a dynamic game study of ESS. *Journal of Theoretical Biology* 138, 329–345.

Kenward, R. E. 1978. Hawks and doves: Attack success and selection in goshawk flights at wood-pigeons. *Journal of Animal Ecology* 47, 449–460

Knight, S. K. & Knight, R. L. 1986. Vigilance patterns in bald eagles feeding in groups. *Auk* 103, 263–272.

Lazarus, J. 1979. The early warning function of flocking in birds: An experimental study with captive quela. *Animal Behaviour* 27, 855–865.

Lendrem, D. W. 1983. Predation risk and vigilance in the blue tit (*Parus caeruleus*). *Behavioral Ecology and Sociobiology* 14, 9–13.

———. 1984a. Flocking, feeding and predation risk: Absolute and instantaneous feeding rates. *Animal Behaviour* 32, 298–299.

———. 1984b. Sleeping and vigilance in birds. II. An experimental study of the Barbary dove (*Streptopelia risoria*). *Animal Behaviour* 32, 243–248.

Lendrem, D. W., Stretch, D., Metcalfe, N. & Jones, P. 1986. Scanning for predators in the purple sandpiper: A time-dependent or time-independent process? *Animal Behaviour* 34, 1577–1578.

Lima, S. L. 1987a. Distance to cover, visual obstructions, and vigilance in house sparrows. *Behaviour* 102, 231–238.

———. 1987b. Vigilance while feeding and its relation to the risk of predation. *Journal of Theoretical Biology* 124, 303–316.

———. 1988. Vigilance and diet selection: a simple example in the dark-eyed junco. *Canadian Journal of Zoology* 66, 593–596.

———. 1989. Iterated prisoner's dilemma: An approach to evolutionarily stable cooperation. *American Naturalist* 134, 828–838.

Lima, S. L. & Dill, L. M. 1990. Behavioral decisions made under the risk of predation: A review and prospectus. *Canadian Journal of Zoology* 68.

Lindström, A. 1989. Finch flock size and risk of predation at a migratory stopover site. *Auk* 106, 225–232.

Maynard Smith, J. 1982. *Evolution and the Theory of Games*. New York: Cambridge University Press.

McVean, A. & Haddlesey, P. 1980. Vigilance schedules among house sparrows *Passer domesticus*. *Ibis* 122, 533–536.

Metcalfe, N. B. 1984. The effects of mixed-species flocking on the vigilance of shorebirds. Who do they trust? *Animal Behaviour* 32, 986–993.

Packer, C. 1986. Whatever happened to reciprocal altruism? *Trends in Ecology and Evolution* 1, 142–143.

Packer, C. & Abrams, P. 1990. Should cooperative groups be more vigilant than selfish groups? *Journal of Theoretical Biology* 142, 341–357.

Parker, G. A. 1984. Evolutionarily stable strategies. In: *Behavioral Ecology: An Evolutionary Approach*, 2nd Edition. (ed. by J. R. Krebs & N. B. Davies), pp. 30–61. London: Blackwell.

Parker, G. A. & Hammerstein, P. 1985. Game theory and animal behaviour. In: *Evolution: Essays in Honour of John Maynard Smith*. (ed. by P. J. Greenwood, P. H. Harvey, & M. Slatkin) pp. 73–94. New York: Cambridge University Press.

Powell, G. V. N. 1974. Experimental analysis of the social value of flocking by starlings (*Sturnus vulgaris*) in relation to predation and foraging. *Animal Behavior* 22, 501–505.

Pöysä, H. 1987. Feeding-vigilance trade-off in the teal (*Anas crecca*): Effects of feeding method and predation risk. *Behaviour* 103, 108–122.

Pulliam, H. R. 1973. On the advantages of flocking. *Journal of Theoretical Biology* 38, 419–422.

Pulliam, H. R., Pyke, G. H. & Caraco, T. 1982. The scanning behavior of juncos: a game-theoretical approach. *Journal of Theoretical Biology* 95, 89–103.

Rasa, O. A. E. 1987. Vigilance behavior in dwarf mongooses: selfish or altruistic? *South African Journal of Science* 83, 587–590.

Roberts, S. C. 1988. Social influences on vigilance in rabbits. *Animal Behaviour* 36, 905–913

Studd, M., Monlgomerie, R. D., & Robertson, R. J. 1983. Group size and predator surveillance in foraging house sparrows (*Passer domesticus*). *Canadian Journal of Zoology* 61, 226–231.

Sullivan, K. A. 1984. Information exploitation by downy woodpeckers in mixed-species flocks. *Behaviour* 91, 294–311.

———. 1985. Vigilance patterns in downy woodpeckers. *Animal Behaviour* 33, 328–330.

Thompson, D. B. A. & Lendrem, D. W. 1985. Gulls and plovers: Host vigilance, kleptoparasite success and a model of kleptoparasite detection. *Animal Behaviour* 33, 1318–1324.

Trivers, R. L. 1971. The evolution of reciprocal altruism. *Quarterly Review of Biology* 46, 35–57

Waite, T. A. 1987a. Dominance-specific vigilance in the tufted titmouse: Effects of social context. *Condor* 89, 932–935.

———. 1987b. Vigilance in the white-breasted nuthatch: Effects of dominance and sociality. *Auk* 104, 429–434.

Withiam, M. L., Lemmon D. & Barkan, C. P. L. 1990. Scanning and social dominance in black-capped chickadees (*Parus atricapillus*). Unpublished manuscript.

Chapter 14

Is There an Evolutionary Biology of Play?

Alexander Rosenberg

Some evolutionary biologists and sociobiologists seem to think so. That is, they believe that there is a single unified selectionist explanation for the emergence and persistence of play as a behavioral phenotype. E. O. Wilson (1977) lists play, along with four other areas of animal behavior as warranting detailed sociobiological explanation, and Bekoff & Byers (1985: 247) insist that "detailed analysis of play could further our understanding of the evolution of social behavior, developmental processes (neural and behavioral) and learning." They go on to say that "study of the function of play is a study of the process through which natural selection shaped this aspect of the behavioral phenotype" (p. 255). In this paper I wish to explore whether Bekoff, Byers, and Wilson are right about the evolutionary significance of play, and if so, what an evolutionary biology of play would have to be like.

First, we need to consider the concept of play, for it has features that make a theory of play difficult to envision right from the start. Like the concept of "clock" or "hammer," "play" is an functional or "etiological" one. To call something a clock is to make no claim about its structure. Clocks can come in a vast range of different mechanisms—cogs and wheels, sand and glass, pulsing arteries, microprocessors, and they can keep different units of time. For something to be a clock what is required is that it bear certain causal relations to the activities of the agents who measure units of time. To be a clock is to enter into a network of causes and effects, not to have a certain structure, or composition. For this reason the notion of "clock" is a functional one, defined in terms of its functional role, and the etiology that brought it about. For the same reason there is no theory of clocks. There are too many different causes and consequences of something's being a clock for us to provide a single general explanatory theory that really explains what clocks do, how and why they do it.

Similarly, "play" characterizes behavior in terms of its causes and effects, which contrast with the causes and effects of behavior we decline to call play. The difference between a play-fight and a real one may not reflect differences in the blows struck or the pain inflicted, or even in how the bodies of the fighters roll on the floor, and shout abuse at one another. The difference is between their causes—say animosity versus friendly competitiveness, and their effects—the loser's desire for revenge versus his admiration for the winner. But if the behaviors we identify as play do not have a manageable set of broadly similar causes and consequences, then there can be no single evolutionary theory of play. For there will be no small number of effects of play that might be part of a causal basis for its evolutionary selection.

In general, the evolutionary biologist aims to explain dispositions, capacities, abilities, not the particular occasions when these dispositions are actually exercised by an organism. It's not individual acts of altruism the sociobiologist is out to explain by a theory of inclusive fitness; it's the disposition to engage in such acts. But, the disposition to play is much harder to identify than other behavioral dispositions of interest to the behavioral biologist, because the activity of play is itself harder to identify than other behaviors whose dispositions are given sociobiological explanation. Compare the other phenomena Wilson says demand sociobiological explanation along with play: kin-selection, parent-offspring conflict, territoriality, homosexuality. These are all phenomena whose occurrence we can establish without embracing much controversial theory. There are observational tests for whether a sexual encounter is homosexual—examine the organism's sexual organs, or whether two competing or cooperating organisms are kin or not—trace their geneology. There is no such test for whether some bit of behavior is "play."

Of course biologists and nonbiologists for that matter are convinced that they can tell play when they see it: Surely a kitten treating the trailing end of a string the way a cat treats a mouse is playing. No one who has observed red deer calves fighting to be king of the hill can doubt they are playing. But despite the naturalness of such descriptions, evolutionary biologists had better not be irrevocably committed to them. For if they are, they are also committed to providing the same explanation for the kitten's behavior and the calves, and if they have quite different causes, the biologist is bound to be frustrated in the search for such a univocal theory that identifies a common selection mechanism behind different dispositions to play. To assert that play needs evolutionary explanation is to commit yourself to a single or small number of dispositions subject to selection, that stand behind the variety of behaviors we describe as play. For without a single disposition across species to be selected, there isn't a subject for an evolutionary theory here. Play thus turns out to be treated as a natural kind, like reproduction, or respiration, of which the theory of natural selection owes us an account.

If evolutionary biologists are not confident that they can give a selectionist explanation of play, they had better remove it from the priority agenda of their discipline, and put it on the back-burner. Unless of course, the mere *possibility* of play threatens the theory.

Compare altruism. The reason the sociobiologist identifies altruism as a crucial explanandum-phenomenon for his theory is not the undebatable agreement that it occurs. For even the claim that people are at least sometimes altruistic is open to dispute. What seems indisputable is that people and animals *can* be altruistic. And the mere possibility seems incompatible with the thesis that evolution selects for individual fitness-maximization. So, the possibility of altruism is a real challenge, regardless of whether altruism is more than a possibility. If the possibility of play is a challenge to the theory of natural selection, then explaining that possibility will be as high on the explanatory agenda of sociobiology as altruism has rightly been.

What features of play might make it a challenge to sociobiology? If play reduces fitness, then in the long run the disposition to play should be eliminated. There is some reason to suppose that play may reduce fitness, for it increases the risk of injury, wastes energy, increases exposure to predators, and in the case of young organisms removes them from the supervision and protection of adults (see Fagen 1981). So, unless a counter-balancing fitness-raising property of play is found, its very possibility must be ruled out by a strictly adaptational approach to behavior. To the extent that we do not wish evolutionary biology to make play impossible *a priori*, we need either to deny that these immediate consequences for the individual reduce fitness to an evolutionarily significant degree, or else identify other consequences that counterbalance these deleterious ones. Or else we can take a less than strictly adaptational approach to behavior, and seek non-selective explanations for play, which do not explain it by appeal to fitness. But this last alternative is in effect the denial that there is a single disposition to play that is sensitive to selection.

About the first thing that students of the problem of play report is the difficulty of defining play. Wilson writes, "No behavioral concept has proved more ill-defined, elusive, controversial and unfashionable" (1975: 164). This difficulty bedevils the collection of data that might test theories about play. Without a definition, we can't tell what sort of behavior counts as play and what doesn't; and without this sorting, we can't test theories against relevant data. But the difficulty can't be resolved, because finding a definition for any functional term like play is identifying its causes and effects, and this is nothing more or less than finding a theory that explains why organisms play. If there is no such theory, there is no such scientifically interesting definition.

The trouble is not just that play is an functional concept, one which characterizes behavior in terms of its causes and effects. It is also an intentional concept. That is, the causes that make a piece of behavior an instance of play must be intentional, in the philosopher's sense of this term. And for reasons I will sketch, we have lots of reasons to fear that there can be no evolutionary theory of intentionality. For there can be no scientific theory of intentionality.

Consider Wilson's (1975: 164) definition of play: "a set of pleasurable activities ... that imitate the serious activities of life without consummating serious goals." There are grave difficulties with several terms in this definition, terms like "pleasurable" and "serious", but the most important term to focus on for our purposes is "imitate."

When an animal plays at fight or flight it is imitating "real" fighting or flight—though we need not suppose it is doing so consciously. Nevertheless, we recognize that the organism is merely playing at these activities, because the behavior is reasonably similar to them, but the circumstances do not make such behavior appropriate. However, inappropriateness is clearly not sufficient for play. When one of Pavlov's dogs salivates at the ringing of a bell, the behavior is inappropriate—no food is present, but it's not play. What's missing in Pavlov's dogs is some sort of *representation* in the organism's cognitive economy: again, perhaps not conscious, but a representation of the behavior to be imitated, together with the recognition that it will be produced as a *pretence*, to be responded to as such by interacting organisms, for instance. This is what imitation comes to.

The trouble is we are reluctant to credit many organisms that play with such cognitive powers as representing an activity to themselves, still less bringing it under the description of a pretense. Does a cat have the concept of mouse-hunting? Does it have the concept of mouse, *Mus musculus* in Linnaean terms? Surely not. It responds differentially and appropriately to the presence of mice, but this is not the same thing as recognizing a perceived object as falling under a concept.

We should be even more reluctant to say that it has the concept of pretending, under which it brings the notion of mouse-hunting. The reason we are reluctant to credit the cat with such concepts is that there seems to be no behavior it could engage in that is discriminating enough for us to attribute the concept of mouse, as opposed to the concept of suitable prey, or fast moving food, or edible toy, etc. This leads the tender-hearted among students of animal behavior to insist that though the animal may not have our concept, it has some concept or other, for the behavior animals engage in is just too complicated and discriminating to be explained without attributing some representations or others. The kill-joy argues that short of behavior discriminating enough from which to infer a conceptual system, attributing concepts at all is gratuitous anthropomorphism (the expression kill-joy here comes from Dennett, 1983; see also Fisher 1990 [chapter 1 in this reader). When it comes to such abstract concepts as those required to attribute playfulness, in the literal sense, to mammals much below that of the monkey, the kill-joy's position seems hard to deny. But if we insist that animals *really* play, we must make such attributions.

And if we hold that animals play with one another, the intellectual powers we must accord them are at least as strong as those sufficient for language. Consider what's involved in animal a doing act d to animal b *playfully*, as we ordinarily understand the term: a does d with the intention of b's recognizing that a is doing d not seriously but playfully, that is with the intention of playing. So, a wants b to believe that a wants to do d not seriously but with other goals or aims. This is *third* order intentionality: For a to play with b requires a have the cognitive power to conceive of b's having beliefs about a's thoughts. That, on the view of some philosophers, is enough to endow an organism with language, or at least the power to produce it (c.f. Dennett, 1983). How much of the intentional content of "play" can we pare away, and still be talking about the same thing? How much do we have to pare away to produce a selectionist explanation for the emergence of play?

An evolutionary biology of the disposition to play must be an evolutionary biology of the disposition—consciously accessible or not—to bring certain behavior under certain concepts, including the concept of pretence, a pretty complicated one. When two or more animals are playing with one another, the amount of cognitive power we need to attribute in order to describe the behavior as play becomes staggering. I think few sociobiologists want to burden their theory with the obligation of accounting for the adaptiveness of a general mammalian disposition to bring some behavior under the concept of pretending.

Of course, behavioral biologists are aware of the difficulties of an intentional definition of play behavior. And when pressed to offer a definition of play they avoid such intentional characterizations, in favor of behavioral ones. But, as with other attempts to thoroughly behaviorize mentalistic concepts, it is not clear that such definitions really escape the intentionality of play. Here is a list of characteristics of play offered by Bekoff & Byers (1985). Presumably the list should help us identify examples of play behavior, even if it is offered as at most a part of the definition of play. The trouble with it is that though it doesn't mention any intentional dimensions to play, the only plausible way of uniting the features of play it does cite seems to me to be through intentional powers of organisms.

Some defining characteristics of play include:

1. activities from a variety of contexts are linked together sequentially;
2. specific sets of signals (visual, vocal, chemical, tactile), including gestures, postures, facial expressions, and gaits, are important in its initiation;
3. certain behaviors, such as threats and submission, are absent or occur infrequently;

4. there are breakdowns in dominance relationships, role reversals, changes in chase-flee relationships and contact time, and individuals engage in self-handicapping; and

5. there are detectable changes in individual motor acts and differences in sequencing when compared to non-play situations.

It's hard to see how animals could engage in such behavior without a good deal of cognitive processing, at least some of which will have to be richly representational. Go down the list.

When activities from a wide variety of contexts are linked, the pressing question is why these activities? Taken from their context, that is, the circumstances in which they are "normal" adaptive responses, and placed together out of context, what do they have in common? Answer: the organism *recognizes* that they are appropriate to its immediate aim, an aim different from its aims in the original contexts.

If signals are important in the initiation of activities we describe as play, then presumably these behaviors, "gestures, postures, facial expressions, gaits" are both transmitted because they have "meaning"—i.e. express the desire of the animal to communicate an intention, and they are received and decoded as having these meanings. Short of such assumptions, the use of the word "signal" must be metaphorical or gratuitous.

The absence of certain natural end-states of behavior, like submission, or threat can most naturally be explained by treating the organisms engaged in the behavior as recognizing their inappropriateness, i.e. engaging in the behavior with a different aim or goal from its usual one, which requires "submission" or "threat."

"Role-reversal" and "self-handicapping" are hard to understand unless we credit recognition to animals of the roles to be reversed, and the behaviors to be "reigned in" and not carried out in full measure. The same must be said about the sequencing of "motor acts when compared to non-play situations." It's not just that the observer compares the sequencing differences, the organism too presumably performs a sequence which it somehow recognizes to be different in its order, from normal.

If these are the features of play, then it is hard to avoid the conclusion that the behavior we so label is always highly cognitive in its proximate causes. As such, the disposition to play is the disposition to engage in certain cognitive processes. Thus, it differs radically from other behavioral dispositions for which an evolutionary account is sought. Individual instances of altruism are certainly sometimes the result of deliberation, as are decisions about whether to have sexual relations with kin, or other organisms of the same sex. But they are not always the proximal effects of ratiocination or calculation in species capable of such activities. Indeed altruism or incest in our species may rarely be the result of calculation or reflection, even though it is often rationalized away by *ex post facto* deliberation. But if there is a disposition to be altruistic, or engage in optimal inbreeding, or homosexual relations, which is common to several species, and which shares a single selectionist explanation, it is one that *can* be utterly free of a cognitive base, or an intentional proximal release or cause when it is exercised. But this will be no more true of play than it is of language. Both must be dispositions whose existence rests on complex cognitive capacities in whatever species manifests it. If highly cognitive activities, like the use of language, are not behaviors for which it is useful to seek (even poly-) genetic control, then play is in the same boat.

If we are to have a *behavioristic* biology of play it will have to be the study of play under a quite different definition, one only metaphorically connected to our ordinary conception. It will have to be much more metaphorically connected to it than, say, the sociobiological conception of (behavioral) altruism is related to the literal conception. The sociobiological conception is defined in terms of the effects of an action: An action is altruistic, no matter its causes, just in case it increases the fitness of another organism. Thus, what we call altruism (advantaging others with nonselfseeking causes, i.e. motives) in ordinary contexts is a (small) subclass of behaviors that are altruistic in the sociobiologist's sense. The same will not be said for the ordinary conception of the disposition to play. Every exercise of the disposition to play will be an activity caused by some intentional cause. So the disposition is the disposition to engage in some cognitive process which eventuates in behavior meeting one or more of the five characteristic features Bekoff & Byers cite.

The sociobiologist's redefinition of play will have to be purely *behavioral*. That is, it will have to be one in terms of either the observable behavior—the "choreography" of the play behavior, or the observable *effects* of play, not its hidden neural causes. This is so, because we must be neutral about its causes if we wish to classify together the complex activities of apes, and the much simpler behavior of the red squirrel as both instances of the same functional kind: play. What ape play and squirrel play share can only be their effects, and not the level of cognitive complexity in their immediate causes.

But which effects should we focus on as a basis for identifying play behavior, under its new purely behavioral definition. Obviously the only effects that are relevant will be those that might be selected for, that is, the *functions* of play.

The trouble with this strategy will be obvious to those who have wrestled with a definition of play. For it is very tempting to say that play is any postnatal activity performed in nondeprived settings that *appears* functionless. If the appearance proves to be the reality, then of course, the search for a selectionist explanation of play will come up against a dead end. What is worse, to the extent that the disposition to play is a widespread and hardwired one, the conclusion that it has no function places an evolutionary theory of behavior in jeopardy. To preserve it from falsification we would have to reject the idea that the disposition to play is hereditary, or "hardwired." Or to save the hypothesis we will have to reject the appearance of purposelessness. Clearly, the second option is to be preferred. Our preference for it reflects the "Panglossianism" of evolutionary biology. If we can't find a function for a widespread apparently hardwired disposition, we tend to blame ourselves: we haven't looked hard enough.

Of course, it will not do to simply insist that the disposition to play is a disposition to produce behavior with no apparent function that nevertheless increases fitness. Such a characterization would be Panglossian in the worst sense of that term. It would trivialize the search for an evolutionary explanation of play, and beg the question of why animals engage in such behavior. Even Voltaire's Dr. Pangloss was innocent of so egregious an error. When Dr. Pangloss explained the existence of the bridge of the nose by noting its suitability for the bearing of glasses, even he recognized that a reason had to be given for something's being adaptive. Nothing is intrinsically adaptive. If play increases fitness it must do so indirectly, because it has some immediate effect which raises reproductive rates. It can hardly do so directly. Not all play is foreplay.

On the other hand, just because a bit of behavior *appears* functionless, of course, it doesn't follow that it *is* functionless. But if the definition of play as apparently functionless is appealing it is because identifying one or a small number of functions that all or most instances of play behavior share is a daunting task, indeed one that at least appears impossible at first blush. Moreover, suppose the number of functions, detectable or not, that play could or does serve in different species, is very large and heterogeneous. If this assumption is right, then different instances of behavior we label "play" will have quite diverse and heterogeneous functions for differing species at different times and places. But then not only will it be difficult to enumerate these functions, but when enumerated they will not enable us to produce a uniform selectionist explanation of play. At best we will have a set of narrow selectionist explanations of each of the vast number of types of behaviors that fulfill one or another of these functions on some occasion or another.

There will be a collection of selectionist explanations for the persistence and spread of several different dispositions each distinct and individuated from the rest by the distinctive function it subserves. There will be no such thing as "play," except perhaps to the extent that we use the term in a metaphorical sense as a convenient *portmanteau* for a congeries of different things.

In a way, this is not news to the student of the evolutionary biology of "play." For though they use the term "play," they have long been thinking about the phenomena so labelled in ways that have little to do with the ordinary meaning of the term. Behavioral biologists find it tempting to connect the apparently purposeless behavior of young animals to apparently purposeless prenatal behavior. Thus, Bekoff & Byers (1985: 249) report that "it has been found that there is a strong resemblance in covert patterns of muscle activation and coordination between (prenatal) and (post-natal) motility and between hatching and walking, as demonstrated by electromyographic recordings."

Prenatal motility is a prime candidate for hard-wired, genetically coded behavior, likely to be emitted independent of an environmental elicitation. Its immediate causes are probably to be found in the interaction of muscle and nerve proteins with enzymes and hormones, all produced, and organized in accordance with genetic instructions. Moreover, there seems a very appealing adaptive explanation for such prenatal behavior. Organisms that develop muscular control before birth are likelier to be better able to cope with their immediate post-natal environments than ones which do not. Accordingly such prenatal apparently purposeless activity has the function of facilitating neuromuscular development. From this conclusion to an evolutionary explanation of play *seems* but a short step:

> The perspective provided by consideration of prenatal development is that outwardly purposeless motor activity is a regular feature of vertebrate ontogeny that seems to have reached the peak of its expression in mammals, in which it is continued, long after birth as play.
>
> Therefore, the phylogenetically oldest function of postnatal outwardly purposeless motor behavior (play) was probably the facilitation of neuromuscular development (Bekoff & Byers 1985: 249).

Here a concept of "play" is in action that has very little to do with the five dimensions Bekoff & Byers cite as characteristic of play. That a bit of behavior facilitates neuromuscular development is neither causally necessary nor causally sufficient for its having any of these five characteristics. Doubtless behavior that does have the characteristics of play will facilitate such development. But it is plain that prenatal motility is innocent of the five features mentioned, and that if postnatal behavior is viewed as a *continuation* of prenatal behavior, and functionally explained on the same basis, then these five characteristics that might lead us to call it play have nothing to do with its functional and ultimately adaptational explanation. Postnatal play, in the sense these characteristics define, has not been provided an evolutionary explanation. There has been selection of play, but not *for* it.

In this sense we still don't have an explanation of why animals "play." We only have an explanation of why they engage in behavior that facilitates neuromuscular coordination. What we need is a further account of how and why such coordination-facilitating behaviors should take the form of play. Either that or we are implicitly defining "play" as the postnatal continuation of prenatal activity that no one would consider play. That is, we are implicitly redefining "play" in a way that deletes its cognitive component. We're still using the word "play," but we're not talking about play any more.

The picture is roughly this. Prenatally, a variety of genetically controlled macromolecules act on neuromuscular architecture, setting it in motion, which has feedback effects on improvements in the coordination of these motions. This sequence has adaptive value for postnatal coordination of the organism. Accordingly it has been selected for. Postnatally, the same macromolecular releasers, now produced also as a result of environmental influences, mainly mediated by the sensory apparatus, continue to trigger such movements. And in turn they continue to be subject to feedback improvements in coordination through use during the entire animal's life.

As the animal reaches maturity, these movements are further smoothed out and packaged together into plainly adaptive behavior: the famous four Fs feeding, fighting, flight, and reproduction. But, during infancy and childhood, when the occasions for these behaviors do not arise, and when the organism is not yet sufficiently developed to engage in them, the released muscle movement is packaged and channelled by the young animal's environment into combinations we call "play." And this packaging into behavior we call play has no adaptive explanation, for two reasons: first, its display is too variable, too sensitive to environmental factors, and not distinctive enough in observable character to be an easily identified phenotype; second, and more important, there is nothing left to explain adaptationally. What we identify as play-behavior is just the packaging by the environment of movements already adaptively explained by the adaptiveness of the prenatally manifested dispositions of embryonic development that is responsible for them. There is no further disposition to play which requires an additional adaptational explanation.

Bekoff & Byers (1985: 249) write, "the phylogenetically oldest function of postnatal outwardly purposeless motor behavior (play) was probably the facilitation of neuromuscular development." If this is its only function as well as its oldest one, then there is nothing about play qua play that needs or admits of evolutionary explanation. If there is something about play to be explained by evolutionary theory, it can only be because play has other functions besides facilitating neuromuscular development.

It is of course quite possible that a pattern of behavior which results from the selection of some group of other dispositions can itself come under the influence of natural selection, now operating on some other effect besides the one originally selected for.

There is something about play that has led behavioral biologists to search for such further functions that will give it a distinctive adaptational explanation. It is the fact that while prenatal motility is ubiquitous in the vertebrates, postnatal behavior of the sort we are likely to call play is not. In fact it is characteristic only of birds and mammals. The argument goes, if all there is to play is facilitating neuromuscular development, then since this is adaptive for all vertebrates and is in fact exhibited by all of them prenatally, postnatal facilitative behavior should appear as well. Since it does not do so except among endotherms, it must have some adaptive effect peculiar to birds and mammals.

Byers (1984) has tentatively offered the following evolutionary explanation of play in terms of endothermy. Endothermy makes energy conservation important, and any disposition that contributes to such conservation is likely to be selected, including the atrophy of unused bones and muscles as well as the hypertrophy of heavily used ones. Thus endothermic development was selected to maintain only the biomass that is necessary for performing the four Fs. As endothermy evolved, then, the use dependence of certain muscular systems became more pronounced.

> Juveniles with use-dependent musculoskeletal systems could prepare the systems for motor-tasks (e.g. prey capture, fighting flight) likely to be closely linked to survival and reproductive success before the task was encountered for the first time.... In other words the ancestral function of play was motor-training, and the necessary precondition of this, highly selective use-dependence in musculoskeletal systems, had already emerged as a consequence of the evolution of endothermy (Bekoff & Byers 1985: 250).

For all its value as an account of the evolution of "motor-training," as an account of the evolution of play, this new hypothesis suffers from all the objections lodged against the previous one. Either it's not an account of the evolution of play, or play is being redefined to refer to behavior that includes much nonplay activity, and may exclude some *bona fide* play as well.

We may grant that endothermy places a premium on minimizing energetic costs, that one way to minimize such costs is to atrophy and hypertrophy certain skeletal-muscular systems, and that there has been enough time and selection pressure for mammalian evolution to have this effect. Here finally use and disuse find a non-Lamarkian role in adaptational explanations. For use and disuse build up and reduce muscular systems, and if they work on the right ones, the ones either very important for survival or quite unimportant, they will tend to conserve energy, as endothermy requires.

But here again at most we have an adaptive explanation for why the young of a mammalian or avian species should exhibit certain patterns of movement, running, springing, flying, or crouching. We have no explanation of why these motor-training behaviors should be packaged together into phenomena we would label "play." There certainly are other possible ways in which such use-dependent musculoskeletal systems could be organized, with the same effect on future fitness. That is there will be others unless any combination of such motor-training behaviors will count as play. But in this case, the word will turn out to have little in common with what the ordinary term "play" means.

Doubtless what we call play emerges from "involuntary" motor activity. Bekoff & Byers (1985: 251) note that

> Many of the first interactions of young animals, either with litter-mates, parents, or objects, seem to develop almost reflexively from fidgeting and mouthing. For example, early rooting and mouthing movements used in nursing, when transferred to the leg or face of a litter-mate, are usually called play.

But simply nursing on a paw instead of a teat is not play. What makes such motor-training activities constitute play is the way they are organized, in accordance with one or more of the characteristics Bekoff & Byers enumerate. Were these motor training movements produced in similar quantities but in random and disorderly patterns, they would still have the same effect on use-dependent musculoskeletal systems. So, on the one hand their beneficial consequences for endothermic adaptation does not spill over to explain the adaptiveness of play-behavior by endotherms; and on the other hand, what needs to be given a selectionist explanation is the patterns into which these behaviors are arranged. That is, this is what must be explained if we are to seek an evolutionary biology of play. This is not to gainsay the claim that play is dependent on the presence of these motor-training activities, only that their adaptive explanation is insufficient to explain its persistence.

The evolutionary study of play, if there is to be one, must focus on the selection of those capacities that lead various bits of behavior to be put together in patterns we recognize as play. And this of course requires that we identify the capacities before we turn to the adaptational issues. Bekoff & Byers (1985, p. 255) write:

> Study of the function of play is a study of the process through which natural selection shaped this aspect of behavioral phenotype. Therefore, it is different from the study of proximate causation, which seeks to define the immediate stimuli and physiological mechanisms that control play.

Well, yes, but … what *marks* play off from other behavior is to be found in the combination of its immediate stimuli and the physiological mechanisms that together cause it. So, to identify the phenotype for evolutionary study we must first identify the mechanisms, presumably the cognitive ones, that are distinctive of play. In this case at least a study of proximal causation is prior to and necessary for a study of ultimate causation. What's more, such a study may reveal that there is no distinctive phenotype here to be given an ultimate explanation.

How can we learn more about the mechanisms, physiological, cognitive, or other, that control play? The most obvious starting place for such a study is ecological. If we can discover how play varies with environmental contingencies, we will have at least a first approximation to the informational content of the causes of play. What is interesting about the play-behavior of mammals in particular is its degree of sensitivity to environments. As Bekoff & Byers (1985: 252–53) note, "habitat type, resource availability, and the social environment affect the performance (type and amount) of play activities." When the risks or the energy costs attending play are high, its frequency falls, though it is rarely extinguished. Within species, there are striking differences in play as a function of environmental differences. Thus, Bekoff & Byers report that desert sheep living among cacti play significantly less than conspecifics inhabiting grassy fields and sand bowls. The structure of play also differs between these groups. Desert sheep are not observed to run rapidly, and do not play in large groups, unlike other species. Moreover, reports suggest that animals reduce their play during periods of resource scarcity, that they reduce their periods of play as they grow older, and that in some species, the ibex, for instance, young are encouraged to play by mothers, who "show" their off-spring how to do it, and then stand back and watch. This of course suggests that play is controlled in part by information about its risks and rewards, information animals acquire from the environment which of course requires them to have fairly sophisticated information processing capacities. The more one studies play, the more apparent it becomes that play, its manifestation, character and duration, is very sensitive to environmental factors

This of course does not rule it out as a phenotype. We long ago ceased to view the phenotype along a strict nature-nurture line of demarcation. All phenotypic expression is the result of gene-environment interaction. Manageable, tractable phenotypes will be those in which the genes narrowly constrain phenotypic expression, even across wide environmental variation. In such cases the actual character of the phenotype can be almost wholly explained by the genetic basis. A well-worn example is the sickle-cell trait. By contrast there are phenotypes in which particular environmental factors play a crucial role, so that their presence or absence is essential to the explanation of the phenotype. An equally well-worn example is phenotypic malaria resistance, a phenotype which would not exist but for the interaction of the sickle-cell gene and the anopheles mosquito. Then there are phenotypes not open to powerful evolutionary explanations at all. These will be ones whose genetic constraints are broad, so that exactly where within genetic constraints the actual phenotype lies will be a matter of environmental influence. For instance, our genetically endowed capacity to speak a language does not determine that we will speak any language, still less which language we speak. That is a matter of environment.

Play seems likely to be in this last category of phenotype. It's just not going to be the sort of phenotype for which anything like a single selectionist explanation is available. Too much of the explanation will include reference to environmental contingencies. What is more, even those determinants of play-behavior that can be traced to inherited components will not be specifically selected for their effects on the enhancement of the capacity to play. The reason is that these components will turn out to be the cognitive capacities that control environmentally appropriate behavior generally, and the neural system(s) that respond to operant reinforcement, or whatever leads organisms to what they derive satisfaction from. These capacities, and this system, however have been selected for a large variety of adaptational responses. The contribution, if any, that their effects in encouraging play makes to their selection will, I dare say, be extremely small, compared to the adaptational significance of their other effects in flight, foraging, fighting and reproduction.

As Byers (1984) notes, no one is foolish enough to claim a unitary function for the mammalian hand, so why do so for play. True enough. A unitary function is too much to demand for adaptational explanations. But a small and manageable number of independently identifiable functions is required. At least this is what is required if there is to be an evolutionary explanation for the emergence, persistence and diversity of play as a natural kind of behavior.

Literature Cited

Bekoff, M. & Byers, J. 1985. The development of behavior from evolutionary and ecological perspectives in mammals and birds. In: *Evolutionary Biology*, Volume 19 (ed. by M. Hecht, B. Wallace, & G. France), pp. 215–286. New York: Plenum Publishing Co.

Byers, J. 1984. Play in ungulates. In: *Play in Animals and Humans* (ed. by P. K. Smith), pp. 45–65. Oxford: Blackwell.

Dennett, D. C. 1983. Intentional systems in cognitive ecology. *Behavioral and Brain Sciences*, 6, 343–390.

Fagen, R. 1981. *Animal Play Behavior*. New York: Oxford University Press.

Fisher, J. A. 1990. The myth of anthropomorphism. In: *Interpretation and Explanation in the Study of Animal Behavior* (ed. by M. Bekoff and D. Jamieson), pp. 96–116. Boulder, Colorado: Westview Press.

Wilson, E. O. 1975. *Sociobiology: The New Synthesis*. Cambridge, Massachusetts: Harvard University Press

———. 1977. Animal and human sociobiology. In: *The Changing Scenes in the Natural Sciences* (ed. by C. E. Goulden), pp. 273–281. Philadelphia, Pennsylvania: Academy of Natural Sciences.

Chapter 15

Intentionality, Social Play, and Definition

Colin Allen and Marc Bekoff

Introduction

Many behavioral biologists consider play an important behavioral phenotype. They have a hard time, however, coming up with a consensus definition of play. Most biologists who have observed mammals in the field can give examples of behaviors they consider to be playful, and while there may not be consensus about a definition, there is considerable consensus about cases—biologists agree that many mammals and some birds engage in play, especially during the early years of their lives. Sometimes play is reported in other classes of organisms, such as reptiles, but there is less consensus about these cases.

Putting aside, for the moment, the question of how to define play, and accepting biologists' intuitive classifications of some behaviors as playful, we can illustrate the importance of understanding play by identifying some of the questions that have been asked about it. Such questions include: why has play evolved in some species but not in others, how do ecological variables influence the expression of play, why are there species differences in the structure or form of play and for when play is "scheduled" during the life of the animal, how does the development of play in individuals affect the later behavior of those individuals, and how is play related to learning, socialization, and cognition. Although it is easy to speculate about these questions, they are not easily answered empirically, due to the difficulties of conducting the long-term field observations that would be required to answer them.

Social play—i.e., play involving interaction between two or more individuals—is especially interesting because of the degree of communication and cooperation that is required between the participants. For example, social play in canids (wolves, dogs, coyotes) frequently involves behaviors such as growling, and biting accompanied by shaking the head from side-to-side, actions that would normally preface or accompany aggression. (Other behaviors seen in play include those associated with courtship and mating.) Similar types of social encounters are observed in many primates and other mammals. Participants in such play interactions must have some way of controlling aggressive responses (or sexual responses) to such behaviors. Indeed, in canid species several stereotyped signals, such as the "play bow" have evolved apparently for this purpose. From one perspective, play signals seem to be about other signals. For example, play bows can be glossed as indicating that subsequent signals, such as growls, do not have their normal meaning because "what follows

From *Biology and Philosophy* 9 (1994): 63–74. © 1994 Kluwer Academic Publishers. Reprinted by permission of Kluwer Academic Publishers.

is play." This has led some play researchers to describe play signals as "metacommunicative"—communication about communication.

Researchers are also interested in studying the cognitive dimensions of human social play. For example, Flavell et al. (1987) consider pretend play to be an important step in the cognitive development of human infants. Whether or not participants in such play must possess the concept of pretense is discussed below, but insofar as non-human play is similar to human play, clearly it is tempting to think of non-human play and play signals in both cognitive and intentional terms. Given the present state of research and knowledge about play, we don't think this temptation should be resisted. If we are right, then an evolutionary account of play could provide insights into the evolution of cognition and intentionality. The study of play is potentially important because it offers an opportunity to expand cognitive ethology into an area that includes species other than the usual primates and dolphins (and a lone parrot) that are targeted for comparative research in animal cognition. However, such expansion is not without its critics (Bekoff and Allen 1996). Alexander Rosenberg (chapter 14 of this reader) thinks that if one succumbs to the temptation to characterize play intentionally then one can no longer have an evolutionary account of play. We shall argue that he is mistaken.

Biologists and psychologists alike have found the task of defining behavioral phenotypes vexing, and they have found the task of defining play particularly vexing. Wilson (1975), Fagen (1981), Bekoff and Byers (1981), Martin and Caro (1985), Mitchell (1990), and Bekoff (1995) all explicitly refer to the difficulties of defining social play. As Wilson puts it, "No behavioral concept has proved more ill-defined, elusive, controversial, and even unfashionable" (1975, p. 164). Some of these authors even express skepticism about the merits of providing a definition of play (Bekoff and Byers 1981; Martin and Caro 1985) yet they go ahead and attempt to give one. The emphasis on providing definitions seems to be a hangover from the influence of behaviorist psychology, which saw precise definition of terms as necessary for empirical rigor. Even though behaviorism is no longer the force it was, the common view persists that definitions are needed, else how can we know what we are studying? This common view skirts dangerously close to the paradox of the *Meno*, where Socrates refers to the "trick argument that a man cannot try to discover either what he knows or what he does not know" which he expands by saying "he would not seek what he knows, for since he knows it there is no need of the inquiry, nor what he does not know, for in that case he does not even know what he is to look for" (Plato 23rd C BP: 1961, 80e). The point here is that requiring a rigorous definition prior to empirical research may unreasonably require possession of knowledge that must first be gained by empirical research.

Nonetheless, Rosenberg uses the problem of defining play to motivate his claim that there will not be an evolutionary theory of play, ordinarily understood. He argues that play is a category that is unlikely to have an evolutionary explanation because it must be intentionally and functionally characterized. Rosenberg thinks that, at best, biology can provide a theory of "play-behavior," which must be defined in such a way that the resulting concept will be "only metaphorically connected to our ordinary conception" of play (p. 222 of this reader). In this paper we question the soundness of Rosenberg's arguments.

Although Rosenberg's arguments are directed specifically against play, parallel arguments could be formulated for many other behavioral phenotypes, threatening many projects in ethology. The attack on intentionally characterized phenomena is especially worrisome for cognitive ethology. Our critique of Rosenberg's arguments should be seen as a general defense of certain explanatory projects in ethology, cognitive ethology, and behavioral biology, against a class of attacks exemplified by his concerns.

The Arguments

Rosenberg uses two arguments to support his claim against an evolutionary theory of play. Schematically presented, they are:

A	(1)	Play is a (high)-order intentional activity.
	(2)	There can be no evolutionary biology of intentionality.
Hence	(3)	There can be no evolutionary biology of play.
B	(1)	Our common conception of play is a functional characterization.
	(2)	Because play is functionally characterized, actual cases of play have heterogeneous causes and effects.
Hence	(3)	There can be no evolutionary biology of play.

Argument A has, we shall argue, one dubious and one false premise. In argument B we have no complaints with the premises, but we do not think it is valid. Our reason for doubting its validity is closely related to the reason for disagreeing with premise A(2). Rosenberg presents these arguments in the reverse order that we have them here. For expository reasons we treat A first.

Argument A

Premise A(1): The term "intentional" in this premise (and the next) is used in its philosophical sense, meaning having representational content. Ordinary intentions to act are intentional in the philosophical sense, but so are beliefs, desires, and a whole host of other mental states (see Allen 1995 for an explanation of this terminology).

Rosenberg argues for A(1) first by considering E. O. Wilson's (1975) characterization of our intuitive notion of play as "a set of pleasurable activities ... that imitate the serious activities of life without consummating serious goals" (Wilson 1975. p. 164 as quoted by Rosenberg on p. 220 of this reader). Rosenberg (but not Wilson) calls this characterization of play a definition and draws attention to the notion of imitation that it contains. He states that imitation requires "a representation of the behavior to be imitated, together with the recognition that [one's behavior] will be produced as a pretence" and a little later on the same page he claims that imitation entails an organism "bringing [its behavior] under the description of a pretense" (p. 219 of this reader). Accepting this characterization of play would commit us to the intentionality of play (a degree of intentionality which Rosenberg thinks we should be unwilling to attribute to animals—but see below for a criticism of this). Rosenberg then tries to establish the high-order intentionality of social play. He argues that when one organism plays with another we must be prepared to attribute at least third order intentionality in Grice's (1957) sense. According to this scheme, simple beliefs (or other propositional attitudes) about material states of affairs display first-order intentionality, beliefs about beliefs are second-order, beliefs about beliefs about beliefs are third-order, and so on (see Dennett 1983 for an application of Gricean orders of intentionality to experimental design and interpretation in ethology). On Rosenberg's view, for animal *a* truly to be playing with *b*, it must be that "*a* does *d* [the playful act] with the intention of *b*'s recognizing that *a* is doing *d* not seriously but playfully.... So, *a* wants *b* to believe that *a* wants to do *d* not seriously but with other goals or aims" (p. 220 of this reader). This is third-order because *a desires* that *b believes* something about *a's desires*.

Is the concept of pretense or third-order intentionality required for play? Take the concept of pretense first. Flavell et al. (1987) report that the tendency for human children to engage in pretend play (e.g., manipulating an object as if it is something else) is biologically preprogrammed and first appears at around 12 months. The ability to answer questions accurately about the pretend-real distinction comes much later, but before 3 years old. Of course, verbalization is not the only test of concept possession, but between 1 and 3 years old, parents play a significant role in teaching children to distinguish between play-based imaginings and reality. Initially, pretend play by children may be imitative of adult behaviors without the child being able to reflect on the distinction between pretense and reality.

The Gricean analysis of two-party play seems similarly fanciful when applied to infants. Following Millikan (1984, chapter 3), who questions the applicability of a Gricean account to linguistic meaning in adult humans, we will consider the attribution of intentional states significant only if they correspond to actual changes in the organism's cognitive machinery (i.e., its nervous system) and these changes are causally responsible for the behavior in question. Given this understanding of intentional state attributions, it seems to us unlikely that play with inanimate objects should be analyzed in terms of third-order intentional states since it seems unlikely that anything corresponding to such states is causally responsible for infant play. At *most* play with an inanimate object might involve a second order belief about one's own goals or motives, and there is no reason why play with another organism could not be initiated on the same terms, i.e. without reference to any model of the internal representations of the other organism. However, even second order intentionality (representation of one's own goals or motives) seems implausible in the case of 12 month old children who play. Hence one is faced either with denying that very young children play (in the ordinary sense) or with denying that play really requires high-order intentionality. If Rosenberg accepts the first horn of this dilemma, we suggest he is the one who is not dealing with the ordinary conception of play.

Premise *A*(2) does not specifically mention high order intentionality so perhaps premise *A*(1) does not require high order intentionality to support the conclusion *A*(3). We believe that play does manifest cognitive abilities in organisms, and that these cognitive abilities are intentional in the philosophers' sense (Bekoff and Allen 1992; Jamieson and Bekoff 1993, chapter 5 of this reader). We are more than willing to concede that play is intentional. Even with this admission, however, Rosenberg's argument fails because of the falsity of its second premise.

Premise *A*(2): Our strategy in denying the second premise has two parts. First, we attempt to give a *reductio* (reduction to absurdity) of the premise. Second, we indicate some positive arguments for the view that evolutionary biology needs intentional notions (these arguments appear in greater detail in Allen 1992a, b).

Consider the following argument scheme:

A^* (1) X is an intentional activity.

     (2)   There can be no evolutionary biology of intentionality

Hence   (3)   There can be no evolutionary biology of X.

Suppose that arguments having the form of A^* are valid and consider some possible values for the variable X. In particular, imagine running A^* on kin recognition or language speaking. Both of these seem to be intentional activities, yet it would be surprising if either lacks an evolutionary explanation. Of course, the surprisingness of a conclusion is no guarantee of its falsity, but evolutionary biologists do attempt to explain both kin recognition and language. So, unless the actual practice of behavioral biologists is profoundly misguided there is good reason to think that kin recognition and language are suitable subjects for evoutionary explanation. On the assumption of the validity of A^*, this constitutes a *reductio* of the second premise.

Whether or not A^* is valid we can both challenge the positive arguments often produced in favor of $A(2)$ and provide a positive argument for the view that intentional notions are essential to the practice of cognitive ethology.

Rosenberg does not make clear why he thinks that an evolutionary biology of intentionality is unlikely to be forthcoming, but his reasons appear to be derived from arguments found in Dennett (1969) and Stich (1983). Rosenberg asks whether we could attribute the concept of mouse-catching to a cat, asking "Does it have the concept of mouse, *Mus musculus* in Linnaean terms?" (p. 219 of this reader). Dennett and Stich use similar examples to argue that there can be no science of intentionality (partly) because the difficulty of specifying the contents of animal cognitive states shows that intentional descriptions cannot be made precise enough for scientific purposes. Allen (1992a) argues that these arguments are unsuccessful because they presuppose an improper account of content specification. Applied to Rosenberg's version of the argument, the objection is that if his question is asked of pre-Linnaean humans we should answer "no," but we should not infer from this that those humans had no concept of mouse. (Even if you think they didn't have the same concept as us, it does not follow that they have no concept at all. For a discussion of what kinds of evidence might support concept attribution in non-human animals see Allen and Hauser 1991, chapter 4 of this reader.) Failing to share our conceptual scheme does not rule out the possession of some other conceptual scheme. Nor is it required that these other conceptual schemes be neatly describable in contemporary English. Neither Rosenberg's, nor Dennett's nor Stich's examples establish that attributing concepts (or other intentional states) to animals is inappropriate, so the examples do not support the stronger claim that science cannot make use of such attributions.

A more direct criticism of $A(2)$ can be derived from considerations that seem to require the use of intentional language in evolutionary biology. The selective advantage of cognitive states appears to be that they enable organisms to react appropriately to their environments *in a variety of circumstances* (Griffin 1992). If it were not for the functional capacity for *flexibility* in cognitive systems, there would be no advantage over simpler, hard-wired mechanisms. Allen (1992b) argues that attributing intentional content enables cognitive ethologists to describe the evolutionary significance of cognitive states. Evolutionary accounts explain the presence of certain phenotypes because those phenotypes are produced (in part) by present genotypes which are in turn descended from earlier genotypes which produced phenotypes with a selective advantage. No matter what the actual causal mechanisms linking genotype to phenotype, and phenotype to selective advantage, the selective advantage that results is what is important for explanations in evolutionary biology. We characterize the phenotypes in terms of the *functional* capabilities they provide. For example, light-sensing organs have appeared independently at several different times in the evolution of species on this planet. The evolutionary biologist believes this convergent evolution can be explained in terms of the similar benefits provided to individuals possessing such organs. Notice however, that to describe an organ as light-sensing is to understand its role in a functional analysis (Cummins 1975) of an organism's behavior, and to ignore the specific details of how such a functional capacity is implemented. Of course, under selective pressure, more efficient implementations will be selected over less efficient ones, all other things being equal. But if efficiency is not a significant factor, only functional capacity will be important to the fitness of the organism. (In most real cases there is a complex interplay between functional capacity and implementation-specific properties, such as energetics.) Insofar as an evolutionary account can be given of the convergent development of light-sensing organs, it is in virtue of the common selective advantage of the functional capacity for sensing light in organisms of different species.

Our discussion of the implementation-independent specification of phenotypes (i.e., those traits suitable for evolutionary explanation) may be usefully compared to Sober's (1984, 1993) discussions of the supervenience of fitness on the physical properties of organisms. Sober points out that biologists are concerned with formulating principles, such as Fisher's (1930) *fundamental theorem of natural selection* which relates rate of evolution to variance of fitness within a population. Such principles apply across species that vary widely in their physical characteristics so it is extremely unlikely that there will be a single physical explanation of the empirical applicability of the theorem. Sober extends this argument to the behavioral phenotype of predation. Biologists try to come up with theories to predict changes in the ratio of predators to prey that apply equally to, e.g., lion-antelope predation and plant-insect predation (Sober 1993) or bird-spider predation (Riechert 1993). Clearly the physical basis for predation in lions is much different than in Venus fly traps, but the equations describing the ratio of predators to prey are intended to apply equally to each case. Despite Rosenberg's misgivings about physically diverse, functionally characterized behavioral phenotypes such as play, evolutionary biology is rife with such phenotypes, which biologists theorize about and attempt to study empirically.

Where does this leave intentionally characterized phenotypes? Well, organisms with *cognitive* capacities differ from those that are without them partly in virtue of the plasticity of their behavior in response to different environmental conditions. A reasonable hypothesis is that members of species with limited cognitive capacity are less able to survive in conditions which differ from those in which the species evolved or in which their neural systems were conditioned. If so, the proper functional characterization of cognitive systems is that they allow for an organism to represent and respond to local environmental conditions. All things being equal, it doesn't really matter just how this is done; what is important is *that* it is done. Just as an evolutionary account of light-sensing organs is committed to functional characterization of these organs, so too is an evolutionary account of cognition committed to functional characterization of cognitive abilities. But the functional characterization of cognitive abilities describes them as representational, and hence, in philosophers' jargon, intentional. So, it seems not just that there *can* be an evolutionary account of intentionality, but that there is good reason for thinking that evolutionary accounts of cognition must include intentionality. So, we conclude that Rosenberg's premise $A(2)$ is false. Play can be characterized intentionally without jeopardizing its suitability for evolutionary explanation.

Argument B

It should now be obvious from our account of the premise $A(2)$ why we think that the argument B is fallacious. It is worth, however, examining the reasons behind Rosenberg's view.

Rosenberg thinks that there can be no unified evolutionary account of functional concepts because there are too many different causes and effects which make some piece of behavior an instance of play. He draws an analogy between play and clocks, pointing out that because there are so many different mechanisms that constitute clocks there is no "single general explanatory theory that really explains what clocks do, how and why they do it" (p. 229 of this reader).

The problem with this argument is that the kind of "single general explanatory theory" referred to is not (and should not be) the kind of thing evolutionary biology is necessarily concerned with. Such univocal explanations may rule out other important causal factors or delay progress in coming to terms with a multifactor process (Hilborn and Stearns 1982). While it is the concern of some branches of biology (particularly molecular and cellular) to explain *how* certain organs do what they do, evolutionary theory is generally concerned with *what* they do and *why* they do it. So while it would be foolish to expect a singular molecular or cellular account of light-sensing capabilities across species, it is not foolish to expect unity in some aspects of the evolutionary explanations of the development of such organs (although, of course, there will be differences in the evolutionary histories across different species). Indeed, if the arguments above are correct, evolutionary explanations *typically* deal with functionally characterized phenomena, abstracting away from specific mechanical details, except insofar as these details affect the fitness of organisms or give clues about evolutionary history.

Almost every topic behavioral scientists study is functionally characterized rather than mechanistically characterized. Sober's example of predation, discussed above, is a case in point. One more example should serve to convince. Consider the wide interest (since Darwin) in mate choice and its effect on sexual selection. Darwin himself supposed that a single account of sexual selection could be provided across all species (Darwin 1871), despite the obvious point that the specific causes and effects of sexual behavior vary enormously across species as do the secondary sexual characteristics. Mate choice in birds is influenced by very different physical properties (e.g., tail size and color) than mate choice in frogs ("rivitt ... rivitt"). And the behavioral effects of mate choice are also very different, unless one unifies them under a functional characterization such as "egg fertilization".

If Rosenberg is right that there can be no evolutionary theory of functionally characterized phenomena which are implemented by a wide variety of causal mechanisms, then there can be no evolutionary theory of sexual selection. Indeed, one wonders whether, given Rosenberg's view, there can be evolutionary theory at all, except as an historical account of the development of phenotypes.

Defining Behavioral Phenotypes

The practice of giving explicit definitions in the behavioral sciences has its roots in behaviorist criticisms of 19th century comparative psychology (especially Watson 1930). Comparative psychologists frequently deserved the charges of anthropomorphism leveled against them by behaviorists. (See Burghardt 1985 for an historical account of the rise of behaviorism particularly as it affected comparative psychology and ethology.) As a result of the criticism directed at the earlier excesses of comparative psychologists, the tendency among many students of behavior is to want to specify precisely what they are talking about before presenting empirical results. The lingering influence of behaviorism is beneficial insofar as definitions may facilitate the design and subsequent interpretation of experiments. Definitions may also facilitate communication between scientists. We think it is a mistake to treat definitions as anything more than working definitions—i.e. as rough guides to the phenomena under investigation—and it is therefore a mistake to try to discount whole areas of scientific research on the basis of definitional problems, as Rosenberg attempts to do for play. Although some of the points we make in this section about definition may seem to many philosophers to be too obvious to belabor, the substantial degree of effort that behavioral scientists put into definitional issues indicates the need for such labor.

Scientific rigor does not come via precise *a priori* specification of the concepts used to pick out the examples, but in precise application of experimental techniques to compare and contrast putative examples with respect to observable characteristics. Examples tentatively identified by a working definition (or even just a hunch) should be examined rigorously for similarities and differences. If similarities are found that allow for interesting theoretical generalizations, then confidence in the usefulness of the category increases. On the basis of empirical work one refines the concept and the working definition. Of course, in some cases the refined concept may end up quite different from what one starts with. Also, if one finds that there are no consistent similarities which support theoretical generalizations then one may give up on the idea that the things examined constitute a scientifically interesting natural category.

The question of whether or not it is useful to recognize a category of behavior such as social play is a question of theoretical usefulness: Are there useful generalizations about the behaviors lumped together in this way? The study of a topic like play ought to be approached like the study of any other (candidate) natural kind. To study play, one ought to start with examples of behaviors which superficially appear to form a single category—kittens chasing one another, colts romping in a field, lion cubs wrestling each other, dolphins dunking turtles, human children playing cops and robbers—and look for similarities among these examples. If similarities are found, *then* we can ask whether they provide the basis of useful generalizations, for example in terms of a common evolutionary explanation, or whether a common adaptive function is served (see Bekoff and Byers 1981, p. 315, for a comparative chart for play in eight different species).

In the unlikely event that science is ever complete, then it may be possible to give precise stipulative specifications of the theoretical terms used by science. In the interim, the best that we can hope for is to pick out phenomena by more or less rough criteria and use comparative methods to test hypotheses about which similarities are the theoretically useful ones. The importance of conceptual analytical work should not be underestimated in this process. Working definitions and other means of specifying the conceptual commitments of a given theoretical apparatus serve as important catalysts to the formulation of empirical questions (Bekoff and Allen 1992). However, such working definitions ultimately do not determine the extensions of the concepts they purport to define.

Given this conception of the proper role of definitions, we view Rosenberg's insistence that a piece of behavior is (really) play only if it is intentional to be premature. Whether play, or any other behavioral phenotype, is intentional is an empirical question. It is not something to be decided by definition. So, even if Rosenberg's premise $A(1)$ is true, it is not true *by definition*—it requires empirical support. Empirical investigation might support a common adaptive explanation for all the behaviors biologists lump together as play, or perhaps only for the subset of those behaviors that are intentional. It is also possible that empirical work would support the view that none of these behaviors form an interesting class from the point of view of evolutionary explanation. They might, for example, be evolutionarily insignificant side-effects of a selected feature such as having a nervous system of a certain complexity. In Sober's (1984) terminology, it may be that there was selection *for* other behavioral phenotypes resulting in selection *of* play. It might also turn out that some of the behaviors that we are initially inclined to consider play are not usefully put in the same category as others. The same is true of any behavioral category applied across species, e.g., communication, deceit, learning, or murder.

Likewise, if concerned about the intentionality of a particular type of behavior, one should look at the purported examples and decide whether they provide evidence of intentionality. For example, in two-organism play do specific signals serve to initiate or terminate the play (Bekoff 1975; Bekoff 1977)? If so, then this *may* provide evidence that animals are communicating in their intentions to each other (Bekoff 1975: Bekoff and Allen 1992). Of course, to determine that this is evidence for intentionality requires a theory of what counts as evidence for intentionality. Whether or not the category of intentional behaviors is a useful category is itself an empirical question. In other words, are there useful generalizations that can be formulated by regarding some behaviors as belonging to the class of intentional behaviors? We believe that there are theoretical reasons for recognizing such a category. Whatever the case, we think the task of theory building is ultimately more interesting than that of picking over definitions.

Acknowledgements

Discussions with many of our colleagues have been influential on our ideas here, but none should be blamed for our arguments or views. (MB especially thanks Alex Rosenberg for discussing their differences.) We thank the following people who have all provided written comments on one or more earlier versions: Bonnie Beaver, Gordon Burghardt, John Byers, Heather Gert, Marc Hauser, Dale Jamieson, Jon Kvanvig,

Allen Moore, Alan Nelson, Susan E. Townsend, Gary Varner, and an anonymous reviewer for this journal.

References

Allen, C.: 1992a, "Mental Content," *British Journal for the Philosophy of Science* 43, 537–553.
Allen, C.: 1992b, "Mental Content and Evolutionary Explanation," *Biology and Philosophy* 7, 1–12.
Allen, C.: 1995, "Intentionality: Natural and Artificial," in J.-A. Meyer and H. L. Roitblat (eds.), *Comparative Approaches to Cognitive Science*, MIT Press, Cambridge, Mass.
Allen, C. and Hauser, M. D.: 1991, "Concept Attribution in Non-human Animals: Theoretical and Methodological Difficulties Ascribing Complex Mental Processes," *Philosophy of Science* 58, 221–240.
Bekoff, M.: 1975, "The Communication of Play Intention: Are Play Signals Functional?" Semiotica 15, 231–239.
Bekoff, M.: 1977, "Social Communication in Canids: Evidence for the Evolution of a Stereotyped Mammalian Display," *Science* 197, 1097–1099.
Bekoff, M.: 1995, "Cognitive Ethology, Folk Psychology, and the Explanation of Nonprimate Behavior," in J.-A. Meyer and H. L. Roitblat (eds.), *Comparative Approaches to Cognitive Science*, MIT Press, Cambridge, Mass., pp. 119–149.
Bekoff, M. and Allen, C.: 1992, "Intentional Icons: Towards an Evolutionary Cognitive Ethology," *Ethology* 91, 1–16.
Bekoff, M. and Allen, C.: 1996, "Cognitive Ethology: Slayers, Skeptics, and Proponents," in R. W. Mitchell, N. Thompson, and L. Miles (eds.), *Anthropomorphism, Anecdotes, and Animals: The Emperor's New Clothes?*, SUNY Press, Albany, NY.
Bekoff, M. and Byers, J. A.: 1981, "A Critical Reanalysis of the Ontogeny and Phylogeny of Mammalian Social and Locomotor Play: An Ethological Hornet's Nest," in K. Immelmann, G. W. Barlow, L. Petrinovich and M. Main (eds.), *Behavioral Development: The Bielefeld Interdisciplinary Project*, Cambridge University Press, Cambridge, pp. 296–337.
Burghardt, G. M.: 1985, "Animal Awareness: Current Perceptions and Historical Perspective," *American Psychologist* 40, 905–919.
Cummins, R.: 1975, "Functional Analysis," *Journal of Philosophy* 72, 741–764.
Darwin, C.: 1871, *The Descent of Man*, J. Murray, London.
Dennett, D.: 1969, *Content and Consciousness*, Routledge & Kegan Paul, London.
Dennett, D.: 1983, "Intentional Systems in Cognitive Ethology: The Panglossian Paradigm Defended," *Behavioral and Brain Sciences* 6, 343–390.
Fagen, R.: 1981, *Animal Play Behavior*, Oxford University Press, Oxford.
Fisher, R. A.: 1930, *The Genetical Theory of Natural Selection*, Oxford University Press, Oxford.
Flavell, J., Flavell, E., and Green, F.: 1987, "Young Children's Knowledge about the Apparent-Real and Pretend-Real Distinctions," *Developmental Psychology* 23 (6), 816–822.
Grice, H.: 1957, "Meaning," *Philosophical Review* 66, 377–388.
Griffin, D. R.: 1992, *Animal Minds*, University of Chicago Press, Chicago, Illinois.
Hilborn, R. and Stearns, S. C.: 1982, "On Inference in Ecology and Evolutionary Biology: The Problem of Multiple Causes," *Acta Biotheoretica* 31, 145–164.
Jamieson, D. and Bekoff, M.: 1993, "On Aims and Methods of Cognitive Ethology," *Philosophy of Science Association 1992*, volume 2, 110–124.
Martin, P. and Caro, P. M.: 1985, "On the Functions of Play and its Role in Behavioral Development," *Advances in the Study of Behavior* 15, 59–103.
Millikan, R.: 1984, *Language, Thought, and Other Biological Categories*, MIT Press, Cambridge, Mass.
Mitchell, R.: 1990, "A Theory of Play," in M. Bekoff and D. Jamieson (eds.), *Interpretation and Explanation in the Study of Animal Behavior, Vol. 1, Interpretation, Intentionality, and Communication*, Westview Press, Boulder, CO, pp. 197–227.
Plato: 23rd C BP: 1961, *Meno*, in E. H. Hamilton and H. Cairns (eds.), *Plato: The Collected Dialogues*, Princeton University Press, Princeton, NJ, pp. 353–384.
Riechert, S. E.: 1993, "The Evolution of Behavioral Phenotypes: Lessons Learned from Divergent Spider Populations," *Advances in the Study of Behavior* 22, 103–134.
Rosenberg, A.: 1990, "Is There an Evolutionary Biology of Play?," in M. Bekoff and D. Jamieson (eds.), *Interpretation and Explanation in the Study of Animal Behavior, Vol. 1, Interpretation, Intentionality, and Communication*, Westview Press, Boulder, CO, pp. 180–196.

Sober, E.: 1984, *The Nature of Selection: Evolutionary Theory in Philosophical Focus*, MIT Press, Cambridge, Mass.

Sober, E.: 1988, *Reconstructing the Past: Parsimony, Evolution, and Inference*, MIT Press, Cambridge, Mass.

Sober, E.: 1993, *Philosophy of Biology*, Westview Press, Boulder, CO.

Stich, S.: 1983, *From Folk Psychology to Cognitive Science: The Case Against Belief*, MIT Press, Cambridge, Mass.

Watson, J. B.: 1930, *Behaviorism*, W. B. Norton, New York.

Wilson, E. O.: 1975, *Sociobiology*, Harvard University Press, Cambridge, Mass.

Communication and Language

Chapter 16

Communication and Expectations: A Social Process and the Cognitive Operations It Depends Upon and Influences

W. John Smith

Introduction

Signals performed by one animal often influence the behavior of other individuals. The phenomenon can be studied as communicating, which is a social process, or through the cognitive operations of individual animals as they signal or respond to signals. Each kind of study can contribute to the other.

Because animals are not simply affective machines whose behavior is controlled by their changing emotional states, each individual responds to stimuli through more or less complex assessments of the contextual relationships of information from diverse sources. The individual must continuously predict the course of unfolding events, flexibly developing and tuning its expectations on the basis of both current stimuli and experience. It appears actively to organize and store acquired knowledge to provide an essential foundation of information for its continuous anticipation of circumstances. The mechanics of its operations on information are the focus of cognitive research.

The social environment is the arena for studying social communication. A crucial part of every individual's world is made up of other individuals, many of whose actions must be anticipated and influenced. These tasks are facilitated by signaling behavior, which is specialized to share information. When one animal's signals influence another's behavior, the latter's responses are context dependent. It is the evaluation of information "in context" that is centrally important to studies of both cognition and communication. Communication cannot be understood without taking into account the mental operations that integrate information from many sources. And signaling gives cognitive research a convenient and powerful starting point. If the information made available by signals can be fully interpreted by investigators, attempts to understand the mental operations that underlie either intentional performance of or responses to those signals can be greatly facilitated.

"Communication," as the term is used in this chapter, is a process in which an individual shares some of the information that it has with other individuals. Information is a property of entities and events that renders them, within limits, predictable (in the broad sense of knowable at other times). Although making information available is inevitable, since any individual's body and all of its actions make information available, there are also structures (e.g. crests) and acts (e.g. vocalizing) that have been specialized to be informative. These diverse specializations are simply termed "signals" herein, and the communicating that is discussed always involves them. To restrict the terms "communication" and "signals" in this way is arbitrary, but it is convenient for some purposes. It provides an appropriate focus: devices specialized to be informative ("formalized," Smith 1977: 326–330) are especially salient to animals as they deal with one another (Smith 1977: 207, 459).

Communication affects expectations—an individual's expectations are the predictions it makes as it continuously interprets information. These span different durations, in different detail, with more or less flexibility. They provide guidance as the individual adjusts to its changing circumstances.

Although communication is a social process, formulating and working with expectations is not. The latter is instead a set of cognitive procedures taking place within a single individual's mind. There are rules governing inter-individual behavior that operate at an interactional level of integration and, when known, enable prediction of social events. There are also rules of cognition that govern how individuals handle information. The study of cognitive operations of *communicating* individuals (whether signaling or receiving signals), however, necessarily involves research in both social and individual realms. This combined endeavor cannot be developed properly without adequate and explicit models of both communication and cognition.

Social behavior and cognition can each be studied apart from the other, of course, and often are. In *The Behavior of Communicating*, for example, I focused on communication as a social phenomenon, and for many purposes excluded consideration of cognition (Smith 1977). Despite that perspective's focus on the social properties of communicating, however, a pivotal issue incorporated into it is in fact cognitive: in responding to signals, individuals must evaluate sources of information contextual to the signals and somehow bring information from the different sources together as they select their responses.

Context-dependent responding appears both to enrich communication and to render it flexible. It enriches by enabling the use of each signal in an array of circumstances, thus achieving more than one function per signal. It engenders flexibility by permitting adjustments in responding to different conditions. It permits an individual to calibrate the signals of other individuals. That is, by gaining experience with the inevitable idiosyncrasies of signal use characteristic of each of its associates, an individual can tailor its expectations to fit what can be realistically predicted. Such calibrating provides the individual with a defense against being misinformed by any associate who is frequently unreliable, and can also facilitate dealing with ontogenetic and other changes in behavior (Smith 1985).

Context-dependent responding joins the issues of communication to those of cognition. It provides the common theme, being based on a set of cognitive processes that are essential to communication in all but the most rudimentary forms. And the mental operations by which individuals continuously generate and use "expectations" provide the bases for context-dependent communicating.

The following sections deal with, first, how animals (including humans) continuously develop sets of expectations with which to prepare themselves to cope with their uncertain worlds. Second, I argue that signaling provides a rich array of sources for a significant part of the information from which individuals construct their expectations. The special properties and distinctive informational contributions of each of several different repertoires of signaling behavior are outlined, and the dependence of communication on cognitive procedures that enable animals to respond to signals in context is emphasized. The final section focuses on the central importance of information for study both of cognitive processes of individuals participating in communication, and of the social process of communicating. We must determine the kinds of information that are available from different sources, and then learn how this information is dealt with as individuals formulate sets of expectations.

Expectations

Animals deal with changing circumstances without being continuously surprised and unprepared. They must be able to expect the sorts of changes that usually occur; that is, to anticipate and to be prepared for events.

Expectations can be scaled as needed. For instance, a narrowly focused expectation may be a prediction that current circumstances make some event, "a" likely, or that they make "a" more probable than another event "a" or "b." Alone, such predictions would be insufficient to guide most animals, who must embed narrowly focused predictions within wider ones as they select their behavior. Further, individuals should continuously construct what I have termed "predictive scenarios" (Smith 1991). Briefly, this proposal entails the following:

Any cognitive individual continuously collects and evaluates information from various sources, seeking to anticipate unfolding events. It takes whatever relevant information it can glean and compares this with expectations based both on the current situation and on information that has been stored previously (also see Menzel & Wyers 1981; Wyers 1985). It assesses how closely its current circumstances have aligned with its recent expectations, and adjusts further expectations accordingly. The individual thus continues to generate and test "running predictions" (Gregory 1975), both to guide its behavior moment by moment and to provide perspective for evaluating further information as it becomes available. It is then prepared to cope with change, and even to gain some control over the course of events.

It has been suggested that humans operate in this way. We have been shown to store information about the usual progression of events, using cognitive structures that have been termed "scripts" (Schank & Abelson 1977) or "memory organization packets" (Schank 1982). We construct "generalized event representations" for recurrent patterns of events, and use these to guide our behavior in unfolding episodes (Nelson 1986).

A "predictive scenario" is a specific projection, tailored to a particular episode and derived from generalized expectations about events similar to that episode. As a proposed cognitive construct it is very closely related to those of the aforementioned authors, yet differs in at least three ways. First, it is specifically focused on the process of projecting events from current and stored clues, whereas their constructs are concerned more with the organized storage of information, as a basis for projections. Second, I assume that an individual continues to formulate predictive scenarios even when having no particular goal. This keeps the individual prepared to cope. "Coping" is an unceasing generalized yet essential goal that is served when no more specific goal has been set. Third, whereas the other conceptualizations incorporate the individual's actions into the picture in all cases, predictive scenarios can at times simply project the course of events in the individual's environment.

Nelson suggests that the ability to form memories of generalized sequences of events is "an innate property of the human cognitive system" (1986: 241). She has shown that even very young children construct almost flawless generalized representations for familiar events. Animals of other species, all sharing the same need to anticipate unfolding events every waking moment of their lives, may have some very similar ability. Indeed, this seems more reasonable than the unfortunately common idea that they are merely ruled by "affect." Having human speech or language is not necessary for cognitive processing (Weiskranz 1988; Bekoff & Jamieson 1991). Even as adults, probably the majority of the expectations we form are not verbalized.

The ability to respond with continued flexibility to uncertain events is enhanced if competing predictions are generated simultaneously and chosen among as events develop. An individual should thus entertain multiple working hypotheses. Predictive scenarios are representable by flow diagrams with branching points and alternative courses.

As an event progresses, an individual could assess whether available information supported primarily one prediction, or left important ambiguity and risk; whether significant information was missing; and whether that lack was acceptable in the circumstances, or unexpected and troublesome. When uncertainty is high the individual must elect to seek further information or switch to some other opportunity, or follow a program chosen to fit a class of scenarios. For instance, it might adopt a "typical case" scenario if experience suggested that the situation was favorable. Even with sparse information, responding might then be initiated based on "rules of thumb" consistent with the most frequently encountered trend of this class of events (Smith 1985: 68). Usually such responses would be appropriate, and could be altered as warranted. Conversely, however, an individual might invoke a "worst case" scenario and behave cautiously or pre-emptively to avoid possible dire consequences (Smith in press). Choosing worst case scenarios should be especially likely when events may involve predators or other severe dangers.

To recapitulate: Three main steps are postulated in conceiving of an animal's basic, moment by moment cognitive activity as a continuous cycle of generating and testing expectations that are incorporated into predictive scenarios. First, the individual is viewed as continuously seeking, even actively "extracting" (Owings & Leger 1980) information from various sources in its current circumstances. Second, the individual continuously compares this information with information it has previously stored, much of which is organized into "generalized event representations" that suggest probable developments (Nelson 1986). Third, from the results of this evaluation, the individual makes and updates predictions, selects among them, and generates new ones.

All of these steps are part of the *continuous* mental processing of every individual. Most of the effects are ephemeral, because most of the operations take place within what is called "working memory" and are lost, although some specific information and some effects of problem-solving techniques can be passed into long-term storage. Even for humans, much of the processing seems not to require conscious awareness. (Nonetheless, when consciousness is involved it could have major effects.)

Expectations are based on information. The information is obtained from diverse sources. Signals are a special, often very important source, and this brings us to consider communication.

Communication

Much of the information upon which each individual bases its expectations is "private." That is, although the information is available to that individual, it is not available to other individuals. For instance, an individual may be predisposed to certain actions by a feeling of hunger, or by changes in blood chemistry of which it is not consciously aware. This internal information is available to the individual itself, but, if the individual is acting on more pressing needs, the information does not become public. What the individual can be seen to be doing, however, makes other information publicly available. Finally, some information that is initially private is made public by the special behavior here termed "signaling": for example, information about what the individual may do next.

Sharing information by signaling enables one individual to influence another individual's expectations, and hence its behavior. A signaler can profit if its signals cause other individuals to behave in ways useful to it, for example to defer to it, to be less likely to attack it, to cooperate with it in any of various ways. Such advantages drive the evolution of signaling. (There is a second side to this evolution. Most recipients of signals will behave in these ways only if the behavior is advantageous to them, too. Signaling specializations co-evolve with dispositions to respond to them, a fundamental constraint too often underestimated by modelers of evolution.)

The signaling of nonhuman animals may usually have more effect on a recipient individual's expectations of social than of nonsocial events. Social expectations are derived from many sources, of course. There is each individual's familiarity with different ways of interacting, and the parts its associates customarily play in different interactions. Each individual knows its special relationships with, and bonds to, different associates, and the composition and structure of the groups of which it is a member. Such knowledge is basic, and rooted in experience. In fact, many social phenomena exist only in the minds of individuals who are party to them. A territorial boundary, for example, exists only as a social convention between neighbors, a convention that puts them into a special relationship and governs certain expectancies they form of each other's behavior. However, in any given territorial confrontation more precise expectations pertinent to the immediate event are essential to efficient interacting, and are fostered by signaling. Signaling is crucial to the "negotiations" (Hinde 1985) that lead to establishment of a boundary in the first place (i.e. to the first experience with each other of two individuals who become socially bonded as "neighbors"). Signaling, in fact, is essential to efficient social behavior. A great many species have not only territoriality but also much other interactional behavior that is complex and intricate enough to make considerable demands on communication.

Signaling also influences individuals' expectations of their nonsocial environments. For instance, there are circumstances in which an individual who signals may have a low probability of traveling along with its companions as they leave or pass a site. Its signals may raise expectations that it has discovered a localized food resource there. In other circumstances, an individual who signals that it has a high probability of fleeing may have detected an approaching predator, and its signal may raise expectations among its associates of the imminent possibility of a life-threatening event. The signal may even be performed only when the predator, even a particular kind of predator, has been detected, and in no other kind of event. This could lead those responding to the signal to expect such a predator.

What a human observer sees, of course, is the altered behavior of individuals who perceive signals, and not their mental "expectations." There are fundamental things we need to know about communication if we are to understand how signals affect the behavior of their recipients, and if we are to use observations of these effects to learn

about the nature of expectations. For one thing, we must know the formal characteristics and properties of different kinds of signals. For another, we must know what
kinds of information are contributed by signaling.

Signal Repertoires
The point of "formalization" (specialization to be informative) is that it binds particular acts, adornments and the like to particular information such that all members of
some group or population somehow recognize the linkage. The acts and structures,
called "signals" herein, become special vehicles for sharing information, and thus for
influencing expectations. Formalization, whether by processes of genetic evolution or
through cultural means, results in several repertoires of signal behavior. Each repertoire deals in distinctive kinds of information and makes its own kinds of contributions to social behavior. Signals of more than one repertoire contribute together in
most events, contextually to one another (Smith 1986). The different repertoires can
be broadly characterized as follows:

Displays   The primary units of signal behavior have usually been termed "displays"
by ethologists. These vocalizations and other sounds, ultrasounds, postures and movements, releasings or depositings of pheromones, touches, vibrating of substrates, and
so forth have been the main subjects of ethological study of communicating. They
are, in many respects, the most readily studied behavioral signals—particularly those
that are easily heard or seen by us. Although display forms may intergrade, and in
some species do so extensively, we can usually separate the displays of a species at
least roughly into units of a repertoire, and study the occurrence of each such unit.

Modes of Varying Display Form   The forms of the primary display units are modifiable. Much as a word in English speech can be uttered loudly or softly, shortened
or prolonged, raised or lowered in pitch, and can be harshened, quavered, or made
shrill, so can a laugh, a shriek, or a moan—or a vocal signal of most other species of
mammals or birds. Visible, tactile and other signals are similarly modifiable. Some
modifications produce intermediates between display units.

  Many of the ways of modifying signal form are themselves formalized. Thus each
species has a repertoire of signals that are momentary, reversible ways of altering the
forms of members of the primary display repertoire. Each such signal unit is a distinctive way of altering form within some range of values. The use of any signal in
this repertoire of form variations is, of course, contingent upon performance of a
display, but the informative contributions of form variations need not be at all
secondary (see below).

Modes of Combining Displays   A third set of signaling specializations is seen in patterned combinations of display units. Some are simultaneous compounds, for instance
of a vocalization with a movement (as "mew" calling occurs with the "forward" position of a herring gull, *Larus argentatus*, Tinbergen 1959), and "gakker" combines with
various head sets and movements of laughing gulls, *L. atricilla*, Burger & Beer 1975).
Others are sequential combinations, specialized by various sorts of performance rules.
At the simplest, a special sequence can be formed by repeating a single kind of display while keeping the duration of intervals between successive instances roughly
regular within some standard range, as a black-tailed prairie dog, *Cynomys ludovicia-*

nus, does when it "barks" continuously (Smith et al. 1977). Or performances can be constructed of two or more different "song forms" in rule-bound sequences, as in the singing of such birds as the eastern wood-pewee, *Contopus virens* (Smith 1988) or the yellow-throated vireo, *Vireo flavifrons* (Smith et al. 1978). While the singing patterns of these birds admit various sequential recombinations of song forms, other rule-bound sequences of vocalizations have single, fixed orders in which variation is in the presence, absence and number of successive components (as in "chick-a-dee" calls of black-capped chickadees, *Parus atricapillus*, (Hailman et al. 1985, 1987).

Not just birds, but all vertebrates and many invertebrates, employ displays in patterned combinations. Cases that have been described include the gill cover and fin erections, fin and tail movements, and colorings of fighting fish (*Betta splendens*, see Simpson 1968), the combining of body movements with crest erections, lateral flattening of the body, tongue protrusion, color changes and tail movements by *Anolis* lizards (see, e.g. Hover & Jenssen 1976; Jenssen 1977), and, in primates, song sequences of titi monkeys (*Callicebus moloch*, Moynihan 1966) and the "F + Whistle" combinations of cotton-top tamarins, *Saguinus oedipus* (Cleveland & Snowdon 1982; McConnell & Snowdon 1986).

Formalized Interactions   A "formalized interaction" may involve a single cooperative act or a routine that entails a sequence of acts. In either case, the signaling unit incorporates behavioral contributions of individual participants into a mutually produced, orderly product that is itself specialized as a signal. Common examples include both whole greeting sequences and some of the behavior they incorporate (such as a handshake between two facing humans, or the walking in parallel of two gulls doing "forward" displays).

Individuals who greet, challenge, court, play or converse signal to each other by adopting and maintaining a prescribed interactional routine. Together, they produce the relevant formalized interaction for the kind of event. The formalized interaction *per se* is usually not their whole behavior, but is a signal or extended signaling routine that frames the event. As is also typical of predictive scenarios, there are alternative branchings that give freedom and flexibility to accommodate to, negotiate and exploit different circumstances.

The organizational framework of a formalized interaction allots parts to each participant. Each part entails a specific act or range of acts, delimiting the procedures a participant can employ as it interacts. Formalized order in the interaction derives partly from synchronous and turn-taking actions of the participants and, in extended routines, from patterned sequences of moves. Usually there is also formalized spatial patterning, based on special mutual orientations and relative spacings of the participants. Detailed analyses of the geometry and timing of such moves in jackal (*Canis aureus*) courting (Golani & Mendelssohn 1971) and human conversational interactions (Kendon 1977) show how remarkably choreographed everyday performances can be.

When engaged in a formalized interaction, participants are guided and constrained by its rules. They have to do "what is expected of them." That is, each participant in the event has some expectations that are shared by the others because of the formalized features. These features provide both the framework for the overall interaction and certain moves to be made at particular junctures. In essence, a program for a class of predictive scenarios has been brought into the public domain by formalization.

Of a very large number of possible scenarios for a circumstance, one set that offers something to all participants has been selected, and a formal routine has been devised for keeping behavior within the bounds of this set. The formal routine must be kept evident throughout such an interaction. This is especially apparent at each juncture where change may occur. Participants must then signal their continued adherence to the routine, or to some particular subroutine. They may use many devices, such as specially timed glances or specific facial orientations (Kendon & Ferber 1973) or striking poses such as the canid "play bow" (Bekoff 1977). If they do not, the interaction falters.

Since formalized interactions can be single jointly performed acts, such as a handshake, or multiple acts combined into extended routines, such as the typical sequential format of a human greeting (see Kendon & Ferber 1973), the phenomenon encompasses interactional analogues of two of the repertoires of signals that a single individual can perform. There is also an analogue of the repertoire of variations in signal form. Thus signaling behavior, as a whole, has two parallel elaborations of form: one for single and the other for multiple performers. However, the classes of information involved and thus the functions served by these two lines diverge.

Informative Contributions of Signals
The importance of the several classes or repertoires of signal behavior just outlined is that each repertoire contributes in a distinctive way and can be combined with performance of the other repertoires. Having several classes of signals, all of which may be brought to bear even in a brief event, thus considerably enlarges the scope of communication and of a signaler's capacity to provide sources of information that are contextual to each other. What sorts of information are involved, and how do these differ among repertoires of signals?

Units of the primary repertoire of displays each provide several kinds of information. Typically, each display has distinctive features of form that identify a signaler. The forms of audible signals also provide information that permits a signaler to be located by a binaural recipient. Each display also correlates with, and therefore provides information about, the conditional performance of several kinds of behavior. Most of these kinds of behavior are alternatives to each other, and information is also provided about their relative probabilities of being selected by the signaler. To take an especially simple example: a display may make available information about three kinds of behavior, enabling prediction that the signaling individual may flee or may attack, but is most likely to behave indecisively while evaluating the situation further. Other displays may predict more broadly that the decisive alternative to escape is not necessarily attack, but some activity specified only insofar as it cannot be done while fleeing. (Again, these are very simple examples. For a fuller account of predicted classes of behavior see Smith 1977.) There is other, quasi-adverbial information in addition to that about the relative probabilities of performing various classes of behavior, for instance: how forcefully the behavior may be performed, or the direction it may take. Finally, evidence is accumulating that some displays provide information about stimuli to which signalers are responding: particular classes of predators (e.g. Owings & Leger 1980; Seyfarth et al. 1980) or resources (Dittus 1984). Present indications are that such information may always be combined in a display with information about behavior. It may also be the case that the evolution of signals with such "external" referents occurs primarily in conditions in which signalers or the stimuli (e.g. predators or resources) are usually distant from relevant recipients of the information (Smith 1986: 316). We have much still to learn about referents.

Signals that alter the form of the primary display units can contribute at least two different kinds of information. First, they can add information to that made available by the basic signaling. Quavering a vocalization, for instance, appears to add the behavioral prediction that the signaler is likely to quit, abruptly, the activity to which it has committed itself. Second, varying a display's form can modify information that is already present. The relative probabilities of alternatives shift as a gull in an "upright" display posture alters the angle at which it holds its bill: the more downward the bill, the more probable is attack relative to fleeing (Moynihan 1955).

Units of this repertoire of modifications usually encompass continuous shifts in signal form. This gives them the useful property of scaling information continuously, finely grading the changes they convey.

The third repertoire, made up of procedures for combining signal units, has the advantage of enabling a signaler to combine the information from two or more such units in an organized pattern, in effect establishing contextual relations among display units. Given the importance of context to recipients of signaling, this advantage can be powerful. In sequential combining, long continued sequences of signals can present more than one primary unit, can make evident the relative proportions in which different primary units are presented, and can shift these proportions as a signaler's behavior or its predispositions shift. For example, the daytime singing performances of eastern wood-pewees combine two song forms (the primary display units) into long, nonrandom sequences (Smith 1988). To the extent that the more abundant of the song forms predominates in a performance, the singer is receptive to interactional overtures by other individuals—but it is unlikely to work at fostering interactions. As the relative proportion of the other song form increases beyond a certain level, however, the singer becomes more actively involved and will seek out and approach other individuals. Most of the singing is done when individuals are out of sight from each other, and such information about potential interactional behavior should be valuable to recipients as they evaluate the need to come together in particular events. (Note, though, that it is not *a priori* obvious that singers should provide information scaled along this particular continuum of possibilities. The finding is empirical, based on naturalistic observations and tested experimentally; the potential adaptiveness of such information is obvious after the fact.)

Finally, the cooperative signaling performances of repertoires of formalized interactions provide special information that participants need if they are to interact effectively at crucial junctures, at times of imminent change, when the status quo must be checked, or when disparities between participants must be dealt with. The information signaled by adherence to formalized interactional routines predicts that each participant will conduct itself within the constraints of a cooperative framework. In play fighting, for instance, even though many component actions resemble attack, aspects of the sequence itself appear to confirm to participants that the interaction remains playful (Bekoff 1977, and personal communication 1989). Key parts of a particular scenario for an event become fixed, and knowledge of them is shared by the participants through jointly performing the formal pattern. Events that might otherwise become diffuse, chaotic, or hazardous are made orderly and predictable by these signaling routines.

An essential feature of the formalized interaction as a signaling device is that the joint venture is more than just a source of information. It also enables each participant to *elicit* signaling responses from the other within the security of formal constraints. That is, while a display may or may not elicit a signaling response, and may elicit a more direct and undesirable response, moves within a formalized interaction require response signaling. This feature removes or lessens dangerous unpredictability. Negotiation is made easier as participants formally share control of the event.

Context-Dependent Responding

While signals are specialized vehicles for information, and thus important in communicating, they cannot function alone. Recipients rely on information from diverse sources to evaluate information from signals—and vice versa. The site of a signaling event, the current and changing spatial relations of the participants, their familiarity with each other and with similar events in the past, their evaluations of the contestability of resources, can all be crucial determinants of recipients' responses to a signal. Responding is adjusted. Communication is context-dependent.

Context-dependency implies cognitive operations that are more complex than are single stimulus, key-into-lock depictions of classical "releaser" effects. At the simpler end of the scale, context-dependency can be automatic: a key stimulus may be responded to only if certain other stimuli are present (a feature of more realistic releaser models). Yet context-dependency very often leads a single important stimulus to elicit a considerable array of different responses in different circumstances. Fixed preprogramming must usually fail to provide adequate subtlety and flexibility for such response tendencies. Simple rules for assembling and operating on information from multiple sources may be adequate, yet these must often be elaborated into richer procedures that extend the range of events in which a stimulus can lead to useful responses.

Species whose members show finely tuned responsiveness in highly changeable circumstances must extract subtle and intricate relationships from numerous sources of information. Their cognitive operations must be far advanced over those implied by the releaser formulations that were once the dominant ethological model of communication.

Several abilities are necessary for context-dependent responding. The individual must be able to attend to numerous sources of information, and select among them. It must select some information to rank as focal and some other to array as contextual, pertinent in some way for evaluating the former. It must consider information not only from current sources, but also from historical sources that have been stored in its memory or in the genes of its lineage. The individual must also be able to attain a "mental set" of predispositions (see Miller 1951: 225, and Gleitman 1981: 251–52, A36), deriving this from assessments of current needs and opportunities, interpreted and enriched by the experience it can bring to bear.

The assessments underlying an individual's mental set at any time are predictive scenarios. To project such scenarios, an individual must be able to store both basic perceptual schemata and the "generalized event representations" of Nelson (1986). To respond flexibly to uncertain events, an individual must also develop more than one scenario simultaneously, and compare and select among them as events progress. When so much uncertainty exists that animals cannot be reasonably confident of their expectations, they must have procedures for obtaining more information. They may also need such alternatives as "typical case" or "worst case" scenarios, with which to temporize (Smith 1991). Individuals of many species of animals, and especially of birds and mammals, are so effective in sufficiently complex and changeable environments as to suggest that all of the abilities listed here must be widespread.

The ubiquity of context-dependent responding provides an obvious starting point for research on the cognitive effects of receiving signals, a point that addresses a fundamental feature of both communication and information processing. To start here, we must focus on *information*, and on its diverse sources in any event in which an individual responds to signaling. We must understand what information is made available to the individual both by signaling and by sources contextual to each signal in any relevant way. The task is thus to explain what each signal and the overall complex of signaling contribute to the knowledge on which responses are based, and how other knowledge is brought to bear, so that the informational bases for cognitive operations are exposed.

Conclusions and Goals

Communication can be described as one of the means by which an individual can influence another individual's expectations. In communicating, one individual shares information with another: its signals make available to that second individual information that may affect the latter's predictions of events. But a signaler does not, or not simply, determine a recipient's predictions, because those are based on information from many sources: the effects of signals are always context-dependent.

In formulating models of communication as a fundamentally context-dependent process, the concepts of social ethologists converge with "generalized event representation" and "predictive scenario" formulations of cognition. Research on the *social* phenomenon of communicating here identifies a necessary ability of *individual* animals—a particular cognitive capacity or capacities.

This model for communication sees formalized signals of several distinctive repertoires as making up one set of information sources. The nature of the information provided by these sources suggests that such signaling must operate within a system in which animals evaluate signals (as, indeed, they evaluate any stimuli) as relevant within a framework of information derived from many sources. This perspective includes a major role for experience as a stored source of information.

This model for cognition suggests how experience is brought to bear. Individuals abstract patterns from events, and store these patterns in a generalized form that permits prediction of the course of subsequent events (Nelson 1986). Their predictions may take the form of scenarios: continuously assembled projections that are tailored moment by moment to unfolding events. Scenarios help individuals to evaluate information that is received as they attempt to cope with changing circumstances.

There are even cases in which formalizations for communicating reveal cognitive structures that underlie interactional sequences. These are found among the most elaborate kinds of signals, the mutually produced "formalized interactions." Formalized interactional routines reveal the plots or outlines of special shared scenarios. The formalized interactions of courting gulls or grebes, contesting prairie dogs or wildebeest, playing canids, or greeting or conversing humans fix some moves and sequences of "scenarios"—and are functional precisely because they keep their scenarios predictable.

To recapitulate: social communication is context-dependent, and so requires complex cognitive work that evaluates and integrates information from many sources. Key sources of information are experiential. Each participant's responses to signals may be based on cognitive representations of events in generalized patterns, representations that permit the individual to generate predictive scenarios continuously as a basis for its "expectations." Mutual signaling specializations termed formalized interactions even appear to reveal some aspects of such scenarios, which they constrain as a means of standardizing interactions.

How can further research be designed to aid our understanding of both communication and cognition?

Cognitive ethologists seek to understand the mental operations by which information is processed. It is thus necessary to know what kinds of information are available to a subject, and their sources. Signals can be an important focus for this research because they are sources of information that should be important to animals. Signals evolve because they make public information that significantly often *is* useful to animals in dealing with one another. One goal is to learn how signals affect cognitive responses. By knowing what information a signal provides and that its effects are context-dependent, it may be possible to investigate whether animals, like humans, store generalized event representations—and whether they continuously develop and work with predictive scenarios based on these.

In this endeavor, the initial task of an ethologist studying communication is to investigate carefully the *full* range of information that is made available by signals themselves. This information provides an excellent starting point of undeniable relevance, and experiments can be devised to test when and how recipients of signals respond to part or all of it. Other sources of information can often be harder to study. In particular, while information can be provided for a subject to store, the subject's stored sources cannot be fully assessed or fully controlled. Nonetheless, responses to signals provide clues to the kinds of information that would have to be added to that made available by a known signal in order to facilitate a particular response, and can be used as the basis for designing experiments to uncover and manipulate key contextual effects.

Literature Cited

Bekoff, M. 1977. Social communication in canids: Evidence for the evolution of a stereotyped mammalian display. *Science* 197, 1097–1099.

Bekoff, M. & Jamieson, D. 1991. Reflective ethology, applied philosophy, and the moral status of animals. *Perspectives in Ethology* 9, 1–47.

Burger, J. & Beer, C. G. 1975. Territoriality in the laughing gull (*L. atricilla*). *Behaviour* 55, 301–320.

Cleveland, J. & Snowdon, C. T. 1982. The complex vocal repertoire of the adult cotton-top tamarin (*Saguinus oedipus oedipus*). *Zeitschrift für Tierpsychologie* 58, 231–270.

Dittus, W. P. 1984. Toque macaque food calls: Semantic communication concerning food distribution in the environment. *Animal Behaviour* 32, 470–477.

Gleitman, H. 1981. *Psychology.* New York: W. W. Norton.

Golani, I. & Mendelsohn, H. 1971. Sequences of precopulatory behavior of the jackal (*Canis aurevs* L.). *Behaviour* 38, 169–192.

Gregory, R. D. 1975. Do we need cognitive concepts? In: *Handbook of Psychobiology* (ed. by M. Gazzaniga & C. Blakemore), pp. 607–628. New York: Academic Press.

Hailman, J. P., Ficken, M. S. & Ficken, R. W. 1985. The "chick-a-dee" calls of *Parus atricapillus*: A recombinant system of animal communication compared with written English. *Semiotica* 56, 191–224.

———. 1987. Constraints on the structure of combinatorial "chick-a-dee" calls. *Ethology* 75, 62–80.

Hinde, R. A. 1985. Expression and negotiation. In: *The Development of Expressive Behavior: Biology-Environment Interactions* (ed. by G. Zivin), pp. 103–116. New York: Academic Press.

Hover, E. L. & Jenssen, T. A. 1976. Descriptive analysis and social cor-relates of agonistic displays of *Anolis limifrons* (Sauria: Iguanidae). *Behaviour* 53, 173–191.

Jenssen, T. A. 1977. Evolution of anoline lizard display behavior. *American Zoologist* 17, 203–215.

Kendon, A. 1977. Spatial organization in social encounters: the F-formation system In: *Studies in the Behavior of Face-to-face Interaction* (ed. by A. Kendon), pp. 179–208. Lisse: Peter de Ridder Press.

Kendon, A. & Ferber, A. 1973. A description of some human greetings. In: *Comparative Ecology and Behaviour of Primates* (ed. by R. P. Michael & J. H. Crook). New York: Academic Press.

McConnell, P. B. & Snowdon, C. T. 1986. Vocal interactions between unfamiliar groups of captive cottontop tamarins. *Behaviour* 97, 273–296.

Menzel, E. W., Jr. & Wyers, E. J. 1981. Cognitive aspects of foraging behavior. In: *Foraging Behavior* (ed. by A. C. Kamil & T. D. Sargent), pp. 355–377. New York: Garland STPM Press.

Miller, G. A. 1951. *Language and Communication*. New York: McGraw-Hill.

Moynihan, M. 1955. Some aspects of reproductive behaviour in the black-headed gull (*Larus ridibundus ridibundus* L.) and related species. *Behaviour* Supplement IV, 1–201.

———. 1966. Communication in the titi monkey, *Callicebus*. *Journal of Zoology* 150, 77–127.

Nelson, K. 1986. *Event Knowledge: Structure and Function in Development*. Hillsdale, New Jersey: Lawrence Erlbaum Associates.

Owings, D. H. & Leger, D. W. 1980. Chatter vocalizations of California ground squirrels: predator and social-role specificity. *Zeitschrift für Tierpsychologie* 54, 163–184.

Schank, R. C. 1982. *Dynamic Memory: A Theory of Reminding and Learning in Computers and People*. New York: Cambridge University Press.

Schank, R. C. & Abelson, R. P. 1977. *Scripts, Plans, Goals and Understanding: An Enquiry Into Human Knowledge Structures*. Hillsdale, New Jersey: Lawrence Erlbaum Associates.

Seyfarth, R. M., Cheney, D. L. & Marler, P. 1980. Vervet monkey alarm calls: semantic communication in a free-ranging primate. *Animal Behaviour* 28, 1070–1094.

Simpson, M. J. A. 1968. The display of the Siamese fighting fish, *Betta. splendens*. *Animal Behaviour Monograph* 1, 1–73.

Smith, W. J. 1977. *The Behavior of Communicating. An Ethological Approach*. Cambridge, Massachusetts: Harvard University Press.

———. 1985. Consistency and change in communication. In: *The Development of Expressive Behavior: Biology-Environment Interactions* (ed. by G. Zivin), pp. 51–76. New York: Academic Press.

———. 1986. Signaling behavior: contributions of different repertoires. In: *Dolphin Cognition and Behavior: A Comparative Approach* (ed. by R. J. Schusterman, J. A. Thomas & F. G. Wood), pp. 315–330. Hillsdale, New Jersey: Lawrence Erlbaum Associates.

———. 1988. Patterned daytime singing of the eastern wood-pewee, *Contopus virens*. *Animal Behaviour* 36, 1111–1123.

———. 1991. Animal communication and the study of cognition. In: *Cognitive Ethology: The Minds of Other Animals* (*Essays in Honor of Donald Griffin*) (ed. by C. Ristau), pp. 209–230. Hillsdale, New Jersey: Lawrence Erlbaum Associates.

Smith, W. J., Pawlukiewicz, J. & Smith, S. T. 1978. Kinds of activities correlated with singing patterns of the yellow-throated vireo. *Animal Behaviour* 26, 862–884.

Smith, W. J., Smith, S. L., Oppenheimer, E. C. & deVilla, J. G. 1977. Vocalizations of the black-tailed prairie dog, *Cynomys ludovicianus*. *Animal Behaviour* 25, 152–164.

Tinbergen, N. 1959. Comparative studies of the behaviour of gulls (Laridae): A progress report. *Behaviour* 15, 1–70.

Weiskranz, L. 1988. (ed.) *Thought Without Language*. New York: Oxford University.

Wyers, E. J. 1985. Cognitive behavior and sticklebacks. *Behaviour* 95, 1–10.

Chapter 17

Animal Communication and Social Evolution

Michael Philips and Steven N. Austad

Introduction

Social organization requires—and is perhaps reducible to—relatively stable patterns of coordinated behavior between individuals. However, animals do not coordinate their activities with one another by chance. They do so on the basis of information about each other and about the environment. But how much of this information is acquired by communication with other animals and how much is acquired by other means? Can anything general be said about the role of communication in social evolution, or does it vary from taxon to taxon; and if the latter, what explains the variation? More specifically, is there some general relationship between the transfer of information by communication and the achieved level of social complexity. Or is it possible that levels of complexity achieved by means of communication could be achieved through other methods of acquiring information as well? And what, if anything, do our answers to these questions tell us about the evolution of social organization and the evolution of communication? In this paper we will provide a definition of "communication" that enables us to formulate these questions more precisely, and we will offer some observations that may contribute to answering them.

The Nature of Communication

There is a large literature on the topic of communication, but no definition of "communication" in the scientific literature emphasizes all of what we feel are the important components of the process. Because existing definitions obscure these components, scientists find it difficult to formulate the questions we are interested in pursuing. To illustrate the need for a new account we will begin with a brief review of some of the more important biological definitions of communication that have been offered, and point out how they obscure the distinctions we wish to make.

Wilson (1975: 176) defines "communication" as an "action on the part of one organism (or cell) that alters the probability pattern of behavior in another organism (or cell) in a fashion adaptive to either one or both of the participants." Wilson's definition reduces communication to causal impacts (albeit adaptive ones). To retain some connection with the phenomenon of communication, we must assume these impacts occur by transmitting information. Otherwise the ultimate form of communication may occur when a predator eats its prey, thereby permanently altering the behavior of another organism.

Let us call information "useful" to an animal, if it adaptively alters the probability pattern of that animal's behavior. In that case, Wilson's definition entails animal A communicates with animal B so long as its behavior provides useful information to B (in a fashion adaptive to A or B). But now consider what qualifies as communicative: (1) animal A depletes local resources, thereby increasing the probability animal B moves elsewhere (adaptive to B); (2) animal A conceals itself, making it more likely that its predators move on; (3) animal A unavoidably leaves spoor, altering the movement patterns of its predators and competitors.

In general, animals leave traces of themselves by their every action, even their existence, that other animals will respond to in predictable ways. In some cases these traces will count as communicative, but not in every case. Our suggestion is that this distinction is crucial to understanding the evolution of communication. Distress calls, threat displays, and courtship behavior are clearly different from footprints in the sand. And terming both "communication" (even distinguishing them as separate subcategories of communication) blurs a vital distinction.

Dawkins & Krebs (1978: 283) declare that communication occurs "when an animal, the actor, does something which appears to be the result of selection to influence the sense organs of another animal, the reactor, so that the reactor's behavior changes to the benefit of the actor." From the standpoint of evolutionary biologists, the main difference between this definition and Wilson's is that communicative behavior in this case must be advantageous to the actor. Thus footprints in the sand do not constitute communication. However, a predator's paralyzing sting may still be communication with its prey, as is a dik-dik's "freezing" when spotting a predator.

An oddity of both Wilson's and Dawkins-Krebs' accounts is the reference to "advantage" in the definition of communication. Of course, communicative activities evolved because they at one time enhanced fitness. But not all communicative activity now enhances fitness (even on average). Conditions change. Traits or actions that once enhanced fitness may no longer do so. Poachers may now conceivably benefit more from the trumpeting of African elephants than the elephants do themselves, yet this should not invalidate the claim that trumpeting is communication. Moreover, not all communicative behaviors are straightforwardly results of natural selection. Apes now communicate with humans by use of AMESLAN (American Sign Language for the Deaf). The brain capacity that supports this is, of course, a result of selection. But signing itself is not.

As the preceding suggests, there is no essential connection between a behavior enhancing the fitness of the sender (or receiver) and a behavior being communicative. Clearly, we can decide that an action is communicative before we can determine whether it enhances fitness. Notice that if we eliminate the fitness enhancing proviso from the definitions thus far considered, communication is reduced to any kind of causal impact. Again, these definitions obscure the crucial distinction between information acquired from other animals by communication and information acquired by other means.

Smith's (1977) account of communication is not tied to selection in this way. He defines "communication" as "any sharing of information" (p. 13); and more carefully, as any behavior "that enables the sharing of information between individuals as they respond to one another" (p. 2). His stress is on interaction. "Interaction is the arena for communication ... therefore however else communication is analyzed it must be considered from an interactional perspective ..." (p. 12).

Smith's emphasis on sharing and interaction is, we believe, a substantial advance in thinking about communication. However, he does not provide an account of sharing that helps distinguish between communicative behavior and behavior that success-fully coordinates activity by other means (including other means of providing in-formation). Indeed, he offers no clear account of sharing at all and the conceptual tools he introduces for analyzing communication—though useful—limit the role of sharing in his theory. Smith *does* distinguish "formalized" from unformalized signal-ling, which captures something of the distinction we seek, however, by terming both "signalling" and including both in "communication," a crucial distinction is blurred. For instance, Smith (personal communication) considers that if one animal observes another animal eating or sleeping, communication has occurred.

More specifically, Smith distinguishes between the message and the meaning of a signal. The message is simply information encoded by the sender. The idea of mean-ing is less clear, but is usually thought of as how the receiver understands the mes-sage. Since the only evidence of animal understanding we have is behavior, the meaning is operationally taken to be the response to a signal. But as Smith recog-nizes, animals may respond to a given signal in a variety of ways. And if the meaning is identified with any response, then there is no necessary relation between message and meaning. For instance, if a domestic dog unfamiliar with the forest is frightened by the mating calls of an unknown animal, Smith must say that animal has communi-cated with the dog. What now remains of the idea of sharing? Naturally understood, "A shares information with B" entails that B receives all or part of the same infor-mation that A actively sends. But as we have just seen, Smith's account does not require this. In the final analysis, his account shares an unfortunate feature of the Wil-son and Krebs-Dawkins accounts. Since any response (or any response made more probable by the signal) counts as receiving a communication, Smith leaves us no room to distinguish between responses based on decoding signals and other re-sponses. In sum, although his reference to "sharing" indicates an awareness that com-munication requires some relation between what the sender sends, and the receiver receives, Smith does not fully incorporate this insight into his theory. Note that in any case information shared needn't necessarily be true; only that the message sent must be similarly received. Thus predacious fireflies, *Photuris versicolor*, capture and eat males of several other firefly species by mimicking the flashes of females of those species (Lloyd 1981). The message ("I am a female of your species") is a lie, but the information in it is shared, and our intuitive assumption that communication has oc-curred is confirmed.

Slater (1983: 10) defines "communication" as "the transmission of a signal from one animal to another such that the sender benefits on average from the response of the receiver." The notion of a signal is potentially very useful, however Slater defines it in terms of Smith's nomenclature as "the physical form in which the message is em-bodied for its transmission through the environment." Our previous proviso against including fitness-enhancement as part of the definition still obtains. But once elimi-nated, Slater's remaining definition as "the transmission of a signal from one animal to another" is a useful partial definition of communication. By this account, commu-nication occurs in the event that organism B receives (i.e. hears, smells, sees, etc.) a signal sent by organism A. There is no requirement that organism B properly decode the signal. Indeed, there is no requirement that organism B recognize it as a signal at all. Thus by focusing only on the sensory apprehension of a signal, we neglect the importance of proper decoding of the message. The attraction of human hunters to the roaring of red deer should not be considered communication.

One problem with the definitions we have thus far discussed is that they all assert, or imply, that the content of a communication depends on a receiver's response, where any organism whatever can potentially count as a receiver. This means that any given signal may function in an indefinite number of communicative acts. And it implies that the communicative capacity of an organism is a function of the variety of ways in which other organisms in its environment—including organisms of other species—respond to its signals. Thus, an organism's capacity to communicate is increased dramatically when an ethologist enters the field and begins to record, analyze, and write papers about its signals. If we are interested in the evolution of communicative capacities, this is clearly an unwelcome consequence.

A Definition of "Communication"

We propose the following definition. Communication occurs when: (a) an animal transfers information to an appropriate audience by use of signals; or (b) an animal gains information that another animal intends to convey by means of signs. By signals we mean attention-getting behaviors or features of organisms that have evolved to convey information to other organisms. Signals, then, are distinguished from features or behaviors of animals that provide information about them to other animals but did not evolve to do so. That is, the signals at one time conveyed a fitness advantage, although they need no longer do so. An appropriate audience consists of the animal(s) to which the signal evolved to convey information. The evolution of communication, then, is in part the evolution of signalling and the receptivity to signals.

By "signs" we mean any behaviors or features of the environment that animals have invented in order to convey that information. The most obvious example, of course, is human language. But other primates have been taught to sign. And it is arguable that domestic animals invent signs to communicate their desires to their keepers (e.g. dogs bringing sticks to their keepers to convey their desire to play, cats pawing at a door to communicate their desire to go out, etc.). Note that some behaviors (e.g. bird song) may contain features both of signals and signs (song dialects).

When we say that signs and signals convey information, we use "information" in a nonquantitative sense, although nothing in our definition would prohibit a quantitative usage. Thus, animals use signals to convey information about their identity (species, kin group, sex, age), their condition (hungry, injured, sexually receptive, etc.), their behavioral probabilities (willingness to fight or play), features of their environment (proximity of food, predators), and other matters. However they communicate successfully only if an appropriate audience gains information by receiving and decoding the signal.

It is arguable that the evolution of the capacity to sign increased the potential for complex social interactions by orders of magnitude. Most of the ethological literature on communication, however, is about signalling and we shall restrict ourselves to that topic.

Our definition of signalling captures the range of phenomena generally classified under that heading and connects it to the concept of evolution. As suggested, however, the various noises, odors, etc. that organisms make count as signals if and only if they have evolved to convey information. Whether the signal enhanced the fitness of the sender only, or both sender and responder, as it evolved is logically independent of our definition.

Our account suggests that to understand communication we must distinguish between three elements: (1) the *message*—information the signal has evolved to convey, (2) the *interpretation*—information decoded by an appropriate receiver, (3) the *response*—action taken upon processing the reception. Thus:

> *Message*: Information due to natural selection on signal form and content
> *Interpretation*: Message + metainformation in signal = total information in signal
> *Response*: Overt behavior resulting from interpretation + context

Our "message" is similar to Smith's (1965), but differs in that only information which evolution has favored qualifies, although the signal may contain additional information. To make this distinction clear, consider the soft peeping call made by male toads (*Bufo bufo*) during nocturnal fights in murky ponds for receptive females. Size is often the decisive factor in these fights. The pitch of the calls is inversely correlated with body size, probably as an inevitable consequence of the size of their sound-producing organs. Thus while the structure of these calls might signal willingness to continue fighting, males tend to be less persistent if the pitch of their opponent's call is lower than their own (Davies & Halliday 1978). While it might be advantageous to a male toad to acoustically disguise its size, it is not possible. Information about male size is not part of the message proper according to our definition, but qualifies according to Smith's. We will call this incidental property of the signal its metainformation (of which more below).

Interpreting a signal is decoding the information it conveys. The evolution of communication requires not only that organisms signal but also that other organisms are equipped to understand the signals. Without the capacity to decode, communication could not occur. However the interpreter may decode either more or less information than is included in the original message. Signals degrade through space and time, so information dissipates. More importantly, because signals are transmitted via some physical mode originating with the sender, information about the sender not included in the message may be included in the signal (for example, information about the sender's proximity, identity, or size). This information is not part of the message proper if the signal did not evolve to convey it, and is the signal's metainformation. One of the most important types of metainformation may be the identity of the sender. For instance, both white-throated sparrows (*Zonotrichia albicollis*) and stripe-backed wrens (*Campylorhynchus nuchalis*) react differently to the advertisement vocalizations of territorial neighbors than to those of nonneighbors (Brooks & Falls 1975; Wiley & Wiley 1977). Hence metainformation may have an important impact on overt behavior.

Metainformation, however, is not to be confused with information about the sender *per se*. Many signals have evolved to convey information about the condition of the sender (e.g. sexual receptivity, hunger, injury, etc.). And most of these could not have evolved unless they also contained information about the sender's location and certain dimensions of its identity as well (e.g. its species). So this information is part of the message as well. Some signals evolved, moreover, precisely because they convey information about certain dimensions of the sender's identity (for example, its position in a social hierarchy). In the last decade, the ability of many species to make hitherto unsuspected distinctions between kin and nonkin or between individuals of varying degrees of kinship has been developed (reviewed in Fletcher & Michener 1987; Waldman 1988; Hepper 1989). It is not clear at this point whether this information is carried by signals and, if so, whether the signals have evolved to carry it.

Finally, the response is the overt behavioral action taken as a consequence of the receiver's interpretation combined with its physical state and the environmental and social context. The dependence of the response upon a signal's context was also emphasized by Smith (1965), who pointed out that the "kit-ter" call of the Eastern Kingbird (*Tyrannus tyrannus*) is given by males in a variety of contexts; including when landing during a territorial patrol flight, when turning away from chasing a hawk, and when approaching a mate. Although the information received should be identical in each case, depending upon the context a female hearing the call might approach the male, emerge from cover, or simply stand still and allow the male to approach her (Smith 1977).

Metainformation will often play an important role in a response. To take a common human example, one's response to an insulting message left on a telephone answering machine will depend upon whether one recognizes the caller's voice, and if so, one's previous relationship with the caller.

Note that in our account of communication, some signals (i.e. new information) will call for no response. If a subordinate male knows a dominant male is nearby, he may respond to a female sexual receptivity signal by doing nothing. Similarly, some signals may fail to bring about a response because they contain no new information. If an organism is in the act of responding to an alarm call already, a repetition of that call may have no effect on its behavior. Of course, repetition *may* contain new information ("I *still* see the predator"). Given communication accounts that identify the message with the interpretation and conflate the interpretation with the response, these signals must be said to encode no messages: indeed, to convey no information.

Finally, our account also differs from some others in the general model for understanding animal behavior it presupposes. To understand communication as causal impacts, as Wilson and Dawkins-Krebs do, is to portray animals as if they were elements of a physical system related to one another by causal laws. Implicitly, one is trying to understand animal interaction by appropriating the model of physics. By stressing the fact that signals carry information, our account as is Smith's (1977; see also chapter 16 of this reader) is based on a picture of organisms as information processors. On this account, we understand behavior as a response to information. The evolution of behavior—including social behavior—depends on the evolution of an organism's capacity to process different sorts of information in different ways. It is a significant advantage to an organism to be born with the capacity to identify certain features of the environment (e.g. conspecifics, potential mates, foreign territories, dangers) without considerable learning. It is also a great advantage to be able to access information that is not available on the basis of one's own powers of perception. For these reasons, the capacity to produce and decode signals marks a great evolutionary advance; an advance that, among other things, makes social life possible.

Implications for Social Evolution

Does this account help us to understand the evolution of social organization? Our account of communication stresses information transfer, and is distinguished from accounts stressing causal impacts. Thus signalling conveys specific information by means of devices that have evolved to convey just that information and to convey it to others that have evolved to decode it in just that way. The fact that certain groups of organisms are born with the capacity to signal and decode each other's signals (or are genetically predisposed to learn their species-specific language quickly) enables them to enter into social relations with others of their kind. They are, as it were, born into a linguistic community. Members of this community share a certain set of categories corresponding to the information their signals have evolved to convey (for example, danger, hunger, food, territory, dominant male, etc.). The potential for social complexity depends in part on what kinds of information their signals have evolved to convey.

To explore this relation we need to say more about social complexity. Animal social organization is definable as relatively stable patterns of coordinated behaviors between individuals. We distinguish two qualities of social organization—degree of sociality and social complexity. The degree of sociality in an animal group is a function of the extent to which members depend on coordinated behaviors to pass along their genes to future generations; or, what comes to the same thing, an animal group is social to the extent that members of the group are dependent on their relations to one another for the perpetuation of their genes.

This, however, is not social complexity. A society of relatively few types of interrelated individuals with relatively few types of relations between them is less complex than one with a greater number of types and a greater number of relations, even if members of the former group are more interdependent than members of the latter. For instance, among the siphonophoran coelenterates the genus *Nanomia* consists of colonies composed of individuals specialized as floats, propulsion devices and digestive apparatuses (Wilson 1975). Without essentially total coordination of propellant individuals, directional movement would be impossible, and without similar coordination among digestive individuals nutrients would not be appropriately distributed and some would starve. But such colonies are surely less complex than human societies. As this example suggests, complexity is also independent of the precision with which group activities are coordinated. That is a matter of efficiency. Simpler systems are often more efficient—more elegant—than complex ones.

To understand social complexity it is useful to think of what makes any system complex. In general, complexity is a function of: (1) the number of functionally distinct elements (parts, jobs, roles) there are; (2) the number of ways in which these elements can interact to perpetuate the system or to promote its goals (or, if it is an artifact, the goals of its users); (3) the number of different elements (parts, jobs, roles) any individual within the system can assume at different times or at a given time; and (4) the capacity of the system to transform itself to meet new contingencies (i.e. the capacity of the system to produce new elements or new relations between elements).

Conditions (1) and (2) are self-evident. They apply to all systems from machines to languages. Conditions (3) and (4) may apply to a restricted range of systems, but for our purposes it is sufficient that they apply to social organization. A society in which any individual may assume a variety of roles must be more complex than one in which roles are fixed, for the former must have methods for assessing which individuals occupy which roles on specific occasions and recognizing when individuals have changed roles. The fourth condition is plausible for similar reasons. A group that is capable of transforming its structure to meet new conditions must contain some set of procedures for doing this. But there is no evidence that nonhuman animals are capable of changing their social structures in this way.

Given these measures of social complexity, what can be said about the relation between social complexity and communicative capacity?

It might appear that there is no important relation. After all, relative to variation in social complexity, there exists a surprisingly small range of variation in signal repertoire among animals. For instance, Moynihan (1970) suggests that the number of displays within species varies by only a multiple of three or four throughout the vertebrates! Some fishes exhibit as few as ten displays, some primates approach forty. A similar range may obtain among the invertebrates, where ten to twenty signal categories are generally recognized among social insects (Wilson 1975) and perhaps similar numbers among cephalopod mollusks (Moynihan & Rodaniche 1977). Signal information may be enriched or elaborated by grading and combination (Wilson 1975; Brown 1964; Fox 1971). But there is no reason to suspect that the range of combinations and gradations will vary substantially more across species than do signal repertoires, and there is a considerable far greater variation in social complexity.

Although the social complexity of an organism may not *correlate* with signalling capacity *per se*, it is nonetheless correlated with the capacity of an organism to communicate certain kinds of information, in particular, information concerning various dimensions of its identity. Signalling is not the only way organisms can recognize the status of other organisms, but it is clearly a very efficient way. In fact, if this information could not be signalled at all it might be quite costly to acquire.

In the most highly developed groups there are at least four important dimensions of identity: "job," dominance status, kin relations, and nonkin relations (e.g. ally). A very complex nonhuman society might allow four possibilities in each dimension. But it would take signals with just sixteen independent attributes to convey the relevant identifying information. These signals could support a considerable degree of behavioral complexity. For if there are four categories and four possibilities within each category, there will be 256 identifying combinations. To the extent that a decoder's coordinating options with respect to signals depends on the combinations of "identities" that characterize the sender, the laws governing the decoder's response to a signal will be complex.

To put the point differently, the more social differentiation, the greater the range of "significance" a signal may have to decoders. A signal will have different significance to two decoders if—given their identities and their circumstances—the interpretation of the signal demands different responses (i.e. makes different responses adaptive). Thus, as we have seen, a sexual receptivity signal will carry the same message to a dominant male, a subordinate male and a competing female. But the significance of the signal in each case will depend on the identity and the circumstances of the decoder. As this suggests, an organism's capacity to determine the significance of a signal does not depend entirely on its capacity to decode the message the signal contains. Except in the limiting case where the message has only one appropriate response, an organism must also be able to recognize relevant aspects of its circumstances. Some of this information may be conveyed by metainformation in a signal (for example, the age or size of the signaller). But some of it may simply depend on an organism's capacity to process information about its environment that is not contained in a signal at all. Although the evolution of this kind of information processing is a precondition for social complexity, it does not necessarily give rise to it. There is no reason to believe that social lions are any better at it than solitary jaguars.

One particularly interesting and important kind of metainformation is the identity of the sender as an individual (as opposed to his identity as an occupant of a status). The capacity of organisms to recognize each other as individuals is important for three reasons. First, it saves them the trouble of identifying themselves as occupants of a status whenever that is relevant to an interaction. If they can recognize one another as individuals, they don't need continually to remind one another that they are mates, allies, siblings, etc. They can remember that particular individuals occupy particular statuses. Secondly, and more importantly, it provides them with additional information relevant to determining the significance of a signal (or any other behavior), and, in particular, the reliability of the information it contains (e.g. whether it is a bluff, false alarm. etc.). And finally, it makes possible the formation of adaptive subgroups within larger social wholes (e.g. mating pairs, and alliances).

The ability of animals to discriminate among signals' sources may vary enormously—from virtually no discrimination, as perhaps alarm calls in winter foraging flock of birds, to total discrimination, such as individual voice recognition in groups of humans. Highly refined recognition systems are not limited to higher vertebrates. For instance, although female manx shearwaters (*Puffinus puffinus*) recognize the calls of their mates (Brooke 1978), desert woodlice (*Hemilepistus reamuri*) are just as sophisticated, recognizing other family members via odors (Linsenmair 1987). However in the higher vertebrates, communication may be most nuanced due to complex webs of individual alliances. Clearly, the potential for alliance formation will be enhanced to the extent that individual group members are recognized, whether as a result of signal identification or direct identification, simply because the response to any signal may depend upon the sender's identity.

It is not always clear whether information is conveyed as the message in a signal or as metainformation. If discrimination occurs because of chemical emanations of the source, whether the discrimination is communicatory or not depends upon whether the chemicals involved have been selectively favored for their use in discrimination. In rat colonies, for instance, odor is due to individual secretions plus the accumulation of faeces and urine (Brown 1979). The extent to which colonies differ in these odors is probably not a consequence of natural selection for these differences, but it could be. In either case, the greater number of classes of individuals recognized, the greater number of social contexts recognized.

As an example of this last point, imagine a social group composed of six individuals, two unrelated sets of three full siblings. Consider an individual within that group seeking to join two other individuals for the purposes of cooperative hunting. With recognition only of group members versus nongroup members, there is only one recognizable hunting group—himself plus two other group members. If kinship were also recognized, then this individual could discriminate between three kinds of groups (two fellow sibs, two nonsibs, one sib and one nonsib). If all group members were individually recognizable, our focal individual could potentially join twenty unique groups. Thus the range of social contexts, even within a relatively small group, is enormous.

It is also not clear to what extent individual recognition depends on decoding metainformation in signals (e.g. recognizing voices or odors) and to what extent it depends on other kinds of information processing (e.g. recognition of faces). Ultimately then, it is the recognition of individuals or classes of individuals, whether it be via communicative means or not, that determines the range of social contexts which organisms may discriminate and thus enhances the range of significance a signal may have. Therefore an inquiry into the sources of social complexity must begin with an inquiry into the taxonomic or ecological factors influencing the evolution of specific recognition systems. Nonetheless, for reasons cited earlier, signalling is a very efficient means for conveying this information and we might expect it to play a major role.

An inquiry into the evolution of diverse recognition systems is beyond the scope of this paper. However, we note that a great deal of current research is devoted to describing the degree to which animals recognize their kin and the mechanisms by which such recognition occurs (reviewed in Fletcher & Michener 1987; Waldman 1988; Hepper 1989). We suggest that research effort directed at the ultimate goal of understanding social evolution might be fruitfully applied at present to understanding recognition systems of nonkin as well.

Acknowledgements

We are grateful to W. John Smith for his attentive critique of this manuscript. We are also grateful to Portland State University for providing funds facilitating the collaboration of the authors.

Literature Cited

Brooke, M. de L. 1978. Sexual differences in the voice and individual voice recognition in the Manx shearwater (*Puffinus puffinus*). *Animal Behaviour* 26, 622–629.

Brooks, R. J. & Falls, J. B. 1975. Individual recognition by song in white-throated sparrows. I. Discrimination of songs of neighbors and strangers. *Canadian Journal of Zoology* 53, 879–888.

Brown, J. L. 1964. The integration of agonistic behavior in the Steller's jay, *Cyanocitta stelleri* (Gmelin). *University of California Publications in Zoology* 60, 223–328.

Brown, R. E. 1979. Mammalian social odors: A critical review. *Advances in the Study of Behavior* 10, 103–162.

Davies, N. B. & Halliday, T. R. 1978. Deep croaks and fighting assessment in toads *Bufo bufo*. *Nature* 274, 683–685.

Dawkins, R. & J. R. Krebs 1978. Animal signals: Information or manipulation? In: *Behavioural Ecology*, 1st ed. (ed. by J. R. Krebs & N. B. Davies); pp. 282–309. Oxford: Blackwell Scientific.

Fletcher, D. J. C. & C. D. Michener (eds.) 1987. *Kin Recognition in Animals*. New York: Wiley.

Fox, M. W. 1971. *Behavior of Wolves, Dogs, and Related Canids*. New York: Harper & Row.

Hepper, P. G. (ed.) 1989. *Kin Recognition*. Cambridge: Cambridge University Press.

Linsenmair, K. E. 1987. Kin recognition in subsocial arthropods, in particular in the desert isopod *Hemilepistus reaumuri*. In: *Kin Recognition in Animals* (ed. by D. J. C. Fletcher & C. D. Michener), pp. 121–208 New York: Wiley.

Lloyd, J. E. 1981 . Mimicry in the sexual signals of fireflies. *Scientific American* 245 (July), 111–117.

Moynihan, M. H. 1970. Control, suppression, decay, disappearance and replacement of displays. *Journal of Theoretical Biology* 29, 85–112.

Moynihan, M. H. & Rodaniche, A. R. 1977. Communication, crypsis, and mimicry among cephalopods. In: *How Animals Communicate* (ed. by T. A. Sebeok), pp. 292–302. Bloomington: Indiana University Press.

Slater, P. J. B. 1983. The study of communication. In: *Communication* (ed. by T. R. Halliday & P. J. B. Slater), pp. 9–42. New York: Freeman & Co.

Smith, W. J. 1965. Message, meaning and context in ethology. *American Naturalist* 99, 405–409.

————. 1977. *The Behavior of Communicating.* Cambridge, Massachusetts: Harvard University Press.

Waldman, B. 1988. The ecology of kin recognition. *Annual Review of Ecology and Systematics* 19, 543–571.

Wiley, R. H. & Wiley, M. S. 1977. Recognition of neighbors' duets by stripe-backed wrens *Campylorhynchus nuchalis. Behaviour* 52, 10–34.

Wilson, E. O. 1975. *Sociobiology.* Cambridge, Massachusetts: Harvard University Press.

Chapter 18

Animal Language: Methodological and Interpretive Issues

Sue Savage-Rumbaugh and Karen E. Brakke

Whence the Nature and Origins of Language?

A sea lion takes a frisbee to a hoop after watching a person wave her hands in a certain way. A chimpanzee waves its hands and someone then unlocks a door for it. A parrot looks at a clothespin and says "pegwood." A dolphin touches a paddle after searching its tank when someone makes particular arm movements. Each of the behaviors performed by the animals above is in some way similar to the linguistic skills of the human child. Yet science has been reluctant to conclude that a sea mammal has syntax or that a parrot can name things or answer questions. The chimpanzee shares much of our phylogenetic history, but even its ability to grasp basic linguistic functions has repeatedly come under question (Savage-Rumbaugh et al. 1980; Terrace et al. 1979). Language, as opposed to most human characteristics, is believed by many to set us apart from the rest of the animal kingdom. Scientists and lay persons alike maintain that *Homo sapiens* is the only species capable of true language, in spite of increasingly convincing evidence that the bio-linguistic substratum for language exists in other primates.

There is, nonetheless, continuing interest in the nature and origins of language. The ontogeny of human language acquisition has been studied extensively and its course has been fairly well documented (e.g. Bates 1979; Dale 1976; Greenfield & Smith 1976; Lock 1980; Peters 1983). Still under debate, however, are issues concerning the relationship of language to other cognitive skills and the extent to which language is innate or learned (Moerk 1977; Waldron 1985). One approach to addressing these questions is to challenge the "linguistic uniqueness" perspective by attempting to establish linguistic skills in nonhuman species. This has been done in several research programs over the past few decades, yet the results of such studies have been mixed.

Some of the confusion has arisen because of logistical and technical concerns. Because nonhumans do not normally learn language, they must be taught the skills they acquire. And because they usually do not speak, they must be taught communication systems that do not utilize the primary channel of human language, speech. Methodological differences can make interspecific comparisons more difficult by shifting the focus away from the functional aspects of symbolic communication and toward the structure of the utterances themselves. In so doing, the adaptive and functional significance of language, which was undoubtedly crucial to its evolution, can become lost among concerns that have little to do with communication proper.

It would perhaps be productive at this juncture to return to some of the original issues which prompted the research: namely, the degree of analogy and homology between animal language skills and natural human language acquisition. But before it is possible to make fruitful comparisons between apes and other animals who have been taught language-like skills, it will be necessary to have a clearer understanding of what children do as they become competent language users. Most of the studies of single word utterances and the emergence of intentionality in children appeared after the initial reports of ape language. Consequently the early ape-language researchers worked without the benefit of the large body of data now available on early language processes in children. Needless to say, the paucity of such data at the time led to some confusions and misinterpretations of the relationships between ape and child symbol use.

Language Learning in Children

Language is, essentially, a form of intentional communication. As such, it functions to coordinate activity between individuals and to bring about change in one's environment (Bruner 1983). To use language is to engage in the adaptive behavior of altering one's social environment by talking to others. Consequently many investigators in the field of child language have recently begun to study it from a pragmatic rather than structural perspective (Bruner 1983; McShane 1980). Bates (1979: 366), in fact, defines functional communicative intent, which provides the basis for language acquisition, as "a social motivation to communicate, verbally or nonverbally, through shared reference to external objects." The earliest acts of the infant are not intentional, but by the end of the first year the child is clearly addressing its communications to adults; when it wants something, it will look at its intended audience as well as the desired object and will adjust its communicative actions in line with the caregiver's response. How does this change come about?

The development of intentional communication is an interpersonal process that is initiated by those who interact with the infant. That is, "meaning" is imparted to the infant's actions by a caregiver who is already familiar with the communicative and linguistic conventions of the culture. This caregiver will interpret, for example, a temporarily outstretched arm as meaning that the infant desires to be picked up, and will respond appropriately. Note that not only is the action interpreted by the adult but an intention is attributed to the infant by the adult, regardless of whether or not that intention is initially present in the mind of the infant.

As the infant matures and becomes familiar with common routines, it begins to associate certain acts with certain responses and starts to produce those acts in order to elicit the same responses. When the child recognizes and anticipates not only the desired outcome but also the role of the caregiver in fulfilling that outcome, then intentional communication can occur. For example, at this point the infant ceases to stretch its arm fully toward something it cannot reach. Instead, it partially reaches in the direction of the desired object then looks toward the adult and vocalizes. Clearly, the infant now expects the adult to execute the action for him or her and the reach has become a "signal" instead of an action intended to obtain a goal directly.

Behaviorally, an intention will be evidenced by the child's monitoring of the caregiver's responses and by making adjustments to its communicative acts until the interaction has been successfully negotiated and a satisfactory outcome produced (Bates 1979). At the same time that the child is learning how to communicate intentionally, it is also coming to recognize that other animate beings in the world act intentionally as well. Many of the daily routines of caregiver-infant interaction are repeated several times over the course of a week or even a day. They can be as simple as a peekaboo game or as elaborate as going to the grocery store. Each is characterized by a sequence of events that remains relatively invariant. By recognizing the events, or markers, that others use to announce or indicate each routine, the infant is able to predict and take part in that interaction (Bruner 1983). When an adult starts a simple peekaboo game by putting her hand over her eyes, for example, the infant anticipates the adult's next act of removing her hand and saying "Boo!," demonstrating this anticipation by smiling and vocalizing while the hand is still in place. An older infant may also say "Boo!" or reverse the roles entirely, hiding its own eyes.

Often, the behaviors that adults and older children use to mark their intentions are symbolic. For example, rather than putting her hand over her eyes to start a game, an adult may say "Shall we play peekaboo?" To the extent that the young child can extract information from what is said, it will become able to predict future events in its world and consequently to attempt to control them with its own actions. Eventually, the child will recognize that it too can use the same types of symbolic markers (i.e., words) to initiate routines and direct the attention of others.

At this point it is necessary to introduce the concept of "reference." When one says that someone is referring, one generally means that this person is using an intentional symbolic act to accomplish a specific goal (Gauker 1990; Savage-Rumbaugh 1990a). Reference is an inter-individual process in which a symbol (or group of symbols) is employed for the purpose of causing another party to think or behave in a specific way. Symbols used in such a way have the effect of causing the attention of the listener to become focused upon the topic of interest to the speaker. For example, an infant may point toward a toy outside its crib and look at an adult. Here, the direction of the outstretched arm indicates the toy and the desire is conveyed by facial expression and vocalization. No symbols are needed, because the toy is present. However, when the infant says "ball" and gestures toward the couch, the adult infers that the word "refers" to the ball which, among other toys, has been dropped behind the couch. A word is needed here, since the ball is not visually present and pointing would not convey which toy the infant desires. This view of "reference" is not a Lockean one. Rather, it stresses the inter-individual cause-effect nature of the development of the representational process. "Meaning" or "reference" is not seen as extant in the words themselves or even in the mind of the speaker (though it is partially determined by the expectancies the speaker brings to the outcome of his communications). Meaning exists in the interaction between speaker and listener. Words are used by the speaker, in the same way that a tool is employed to solve a physical task. That is, words are used to bring about an intended effect; however, they do not always accomplish this goal and often have unintended effects as well. Word meanings typically change dramatically with each usage. For example, the word "apple" refers to one thing in the context of conversation about fruit and quite another in the context of a conversation about cities. "Reference" is employed here as a descriptive term for the process of using words to achieve coordinated actions toward objects, locations, other persons, and so on. The type of "reference" that is of specific concern in the studies below is the process that occurs when one party, upon being asked, selects a specific object, or set of words, that "go with" a "label." However, the use of the term "reference" for this process is not intended to indicate a specific word-object relationship that exists apart from the process of using the word in an instrumental fashion (Gauker 1990).

The fact that human beings do associate classes of objects with words arises from interpretations of how these words are used in our presence. Cause-effect hypotheses are generated from analysis of word function and these hypotheses are used to generate an internalized language structure. For a thorough discussion of these complex philosophical issues of "reference," and its use by linguistically competent apes see Gauker (1990), Savage-Rumbaugh & Rumbaugh (1991), and Savage-Rumbaugh (1990a, 1990b, 1991, 1993). The perspective of reference expressed in these articles is very similar to that offered by Wells (1987: 20), which is summarized in this statement: "the problem of the origin of language is not, as has often been supposed, that of how sounds could become the signs of thoughts, but of how men discovered how to guide or influence the behavior of their neighbors by any means whatever, and later came to use arbitrary signs." The work with other species is helping to reveal the conditions under which this process does, and does not, come about.

Is Labeling the Learning of Words?

Consider, for example, the symbol-manipulation project undertaken with the chimpanzee (*Pan troglodytes*) Sarah (Premack 1970; Premack & Premack 1983). In this study, Sarah was trained to associate plastic chips with real objects. Her training began at age five with approximately an hour of drilled exercises per day in which she was required to put plastic chips ("words") on a magnetized board before receiving a piece of food. Eventually, Sarah was able to make same/different judgements and complete analogies using the chips (Premack & Premack 1983). It was apparent that Sarah was, indeed, associating the plastic symbols with specific physical objects and attributes.

Yet what was Sarah communicating here? She did not share any new information; the trainer already knew the correct answer. Nor was she initiating the symbolic interactions in order to fulfill an intention. Symbol selection trials were set up by humans and Sarah merely solved the complex problems presented to her. In a statement that tells more about the limitations of this approach than about the limitations of the chimpanzee, Premack and Premack (1983: 34) express their view that, "Chimpanzees, we now know, are not initiators of language; they will, however, engage in dialogue once drawn into an exchange." Given that a primary use of language is the initiation of coordinated activity, however, there appears to be a critical difference between Sarah's symbol system and that of human children. Sarah had no opportunity nor reason to go beyond what she was trained to do and share new information with her experimenters.

A similar argument can be made about the data from Alex, an African Grey parrot (*Psittacus erithacus*) who has been taught via shaping of phonemic production to "label" objects held in front of it (Pepperberg 1981, 1983). For example, upon being shown a triangular piece of wood Alex will, when asked "What shape?," utter "three-corner." He then receives the item. If Alex makes an incorrect response, the trial is repeated until the correct utterance is emitted. Word acquisition is drilled in strict test situations consisting of problems to be solved before receipt of reward. Although Pepperberg is careful in her work not to make overt claims that language exists in the parrot, she insists that the vocal labels used by the parrot are "referential."

In the training paradigms employed by Premack (1970) and Pepperberg (1981, 1983) there is no opportunity for reference to occur, *even on the part of the experimenter*. That is, the experimenter does not use symbols the purpose of causing the animals to carry out a specific set of behaviors. In these paradigms, the experimenter holds up an object and requires the chimpanzee or parrot to produce the appropriate "label." The experimenter is not engaging in "reference" because the object does not indicate, or "refer to" anything. It is merely a stimulus for which one must produce the appropriate response. The subject, upon producing the appropriate label, also cannot be said to be employing that symbol for the purpose of "referring." Certainly, the only anticipated outcome from the subject's point of view is a reward, and selecting the symbol "hat" when shown a "hat" does not mean that the "hat symbol" refers to the reward. It is only selecting a response to receive a reward. Communication *per se* does not occur during such training, for there is nothing to be communicated.

Is "Learning to Do as You Are Told" Language?

In contrast to the symbol-production training with Sarah and Alex, some projects have undertaken study of animals' responses to utterances directed to them (Herman 1987, 1988; Herman et al. 1984; Schusterman & Krieger 1984, 1988). These studies have been conducted with two species of sea mammal: the dolphins Ake and Phoenix (*Tursiops truncatus*) and the sea lions Rocky and Gertie (*Zalophus californianus*). The receptive-language approach was taken with these subjects because of their apparent intelligence and their inability to make the manual or vocal responses conducive to producing signs or symbols. The focus of both studies has been on sensitivity to symbol relations whether, for example, the subjects will "flipper touch the ball" or "fetch the hoop to the frisbee" when instructed to do so, instead of performing some other action or relating the objects incorrectly.

Note that in this paradigm, the experimenter is the one producing the symbols and the subject responds differentially based on the specific instructions it is given. With this training technique, a message is given. The experimenter's signs communicate the behaviors that the person wants the dolphin or sea lion to perform. This context is somewhat more "language-like" than the productive one discussed above and may, in fact, be likened in some ways to the early interactions between human caregivers and infants who are beginning to respond to sentences within routines but cannot yet produce them. Critical differences remain, however, between this and the language learning of human children. Unlike the child, all of the actions carried out by Ake, Rocky, and the others in the test paradigm achieve a single goal—the receipt of a fish to eat (Herman et al. 1984; Herman 1987, 1988; Schusterman & Krieger 1984, 1988). In the routines of daily life, a child learns to carry out different actions for different ends and becomes a functional partner in the interactions. The correspondence between the communication and its result, that is natural for the child, is not present in the dolphin and sea lion studies. For the sea lions and dolphins, the important aspect of the interaction is the relationship between their actions and whether or not they receive food. For the child, the important relationship is between what is said and what is then done.

For example, a young child, upon hearing his friend say "would you like to play 'tagerm'" and then being shown the game, might find he would like to play again. He could initiate the game by asking to play "tagerm" even if he had never heard the word before. The dolphin, however, has little reason to learn in this way, since it a) cannot make the signs the experimenter makes, and b) probably does not particularly want to "take the frisbee to the hoop" in any case. It is more interested in reinstating the "effect" of receiving a fish than in the actions that were the result of the symbols "take the frisbee to the hoop."

In all of the studies described above, training and testing occur in a single context. The subjects are successful in making the responses that they have learned in order to obtain whatever reward is at hand. No data exist which suggest that their symbol use is intentionally communicative or referential. The study paradigms in which they participate do not foster the "social motivation to communicate intentions" that Bates (1979: 366) described. This is not to say that these animals lack intentionality and do not communicate to each other or to humans. Within the test situation, however, these capacities have no opportunity for expression. The utterances of children, by contrast, exhibit many different messages, even at the one word stage. Children learn many words that permit them to affect their world in many different ways. Dolphins learn many words that affect the world all in the same way (they produce a fish). Until training paradigms are utilized that permit the animal to do more than obtain one type of reward, the subjects cannot be expected to realize their potential for symbolic communication.

Language as Immersion in Social Routines
Recognizing the importance of social interaction and routines for the development of communicative intent, some investigators taught American Sign Language (ASL) signs to apes in "cross-fostering" studies (Gardner & Gardner 1969, 1975, 1984; Patterson 1978; Fouts et al. 1979; Terrace 1979).

These studies had several advantages over the "problem-oriented" paradigms reviewed earlier. Symbol use was integrated into routines involving food preparation, play, travel, and other activities which were relevant to the subjects. Experimenters used different symbols to announce different routines, and communication was not limited to one or two hours per day. As with human children, caretakers reacted to the behavior of the subjects as if it were intentional, even if it was not. Eventually, the subjects of each of these studies started producing symbols in ways that topically and structurally resembled those of young children (Gardner & Gardner 1975).

Despite the appearance of rearing environments that were similar to those of human children, there still existed fundamental differences in the teaching of symbols to these apes and what has been reported for normal children. Physical molding of the apes' hands, shaping of desired behaviors, and forced imitation were used as teaching techniques until they could make the signs without prompting. Once a sign was learned, they were required to produce it afterward within certain routines. For example, things to be opened could not be opened until the ape signed "open." Things to be eaten could not be eaten until the ape signed "food." Tickle games, once stopped by the experimenter, could not be continued until the ape signed "tickle." In such situations, the signs added no communicative information. They were merely used as a means of getting the ape or person to do something that was already understood by other means.

Such routines are analogous to the learning of a few words by human children, such as "please" or "thank you," but in most instances the motivation to use words comes from a desire to communicate novel information or information not otherwise apparent to the listener. The child's utterance may occur within a routine, it is true, but adults generally do not withhold items until the appropriate word is said. Rather, they tend to ask the child to talk only when it is otherwise not clear what the child wants. A further difference between early human communications and those of the ape sign projects is that the words or pseudo-words are selected and uttered by the infant. The infant also chooses the message it desires to convey. By contrast, when an experimenter takes a chimp's hands and molds them, even the act of communicating is originating within the mind of the experimenter, not that of the ape. The ape is a passive observer of its own sign. It does not select which sign is to be learned or which message to be expressed.

Nonetheless, if the ape begins to initiate or respond to communicative utterances in different contexts it can be said to be exhibiting language-like behavior, for at this point a process similar to early communications by humans begins. For example, Washoe first produced the sign "toothbrush" while looking at a group of toothbrushes in the bathroom. She had not been trained to use this sign and it was usually used by caretakers at the end of a meal. She had appeared to acquire the sign observationally (i.e. through delayed imitation) and used it in an appropriate context other than that in which it had been learned (Gardner & Gardner 1969). Her behavior in this instance was quite similar to a child who names objects to himself or herself.

Unfortunately, the value of this behavior was not fully appreciated by Washoe's human companions. As soon as it occurred, the investigators required Washoe to produce the sign at the end of each meal, in effect reducing its value as a communicative event. Instead of letting the sign develop spontaneously, they forced it into a rote behavior to be produced in a specific situation before events could continue. Such procedures resemble those employed in the studies by Premack (1970) and Pepperberg (1981) and involve no referential communicative use of the symbols.

Washoe and other ape subjects in these studies have produced many different signs or symbols appropriately. Within context, they appear to act much like human children. However, most of their utterances have been limited to productive requests. Tests of receptive ability divorced from context (e.g. Fouts et al. 1976; Patterson 1978) are virtually nonexistent and thus it is gratuitous to inpute language understanding or comprehension to these animals. Also, many of the functions for which children use language, such as spontaneous naming or statements of intent, have not emerged in these apes, and thus some have concluded that nonhumans are incapable of moving beyond symbolic behaviors that reap immediate, primary rewards (Terrace 1985). Again, these conclusions may reflect limitations of the training paradigms as much or more than those of the animals involved.

The Language Research Center
Understanding the bio-linguistic substratum of language, particularly as it is manifested by apes, has been the focus of the research program at the Language Research Center since the early 1970s. Currently the center houses eleven apes, including five common chimpanzees, four bonobos or pygmy chimpanzees (*Pan paniscus*) and two orangutans (*Pongo pygmaeus*), all of whom are subjects in ongoing studies of bio-linguistic and higher cognitive processes.

The first ape subject at this laboratory, Lana, demonstrated that apes could readily discriminate among geometric symbols and could put symbols in a sequence to form differentiated but structured symbol strings for the purposes of receiving various rewards (for example, "Please machine give juice" to receive a drink of grape juice)

(Rumbaugh 1977; Rumbaugh et al. 1973). By using geometric symbols located on contact-sensitive keys, Lana illustrated the value of providing an ape with a touch-sensitive communication system. The appearance of a system which made symbol production very simple (just press a key) resulted in a sharpening of the scientific focus upon the conceptual and procedural aspects of symbol use, rather than the productive aspects. Because it was now easy for a chimpanzee to produce symbols, and to combine them in the proper sequence, the fact that the ape could construct something that "looked like sentences" was quickly superseded by the questions of how one could legitimately draw parallels between human and ape communications. When, how, and under what conditions was it appropriate to equate symbol presses with words and sentences?

Clearly, as the earlier discussion reveals, questions of communicative competence could not be answered by determining whether or not chimpanzees could learn to answer questions or associate certain movements with different stimuli. The essence of human language lies in our ability to use symbols to tell others something that they do not already know. The more complex the message, the greater the need for structural rules regarding the units of which the message is composed. Did Lana understand the relationships between the symbols she used? Was she using key presses to convey messages or were these key presses simply conditioned responses performed for the purpose of obtaining food? Even more importantly, upon what basis could a legitimate determination of why and how Lana and other apes used symbols be made?

These questions were addressed with the addition of four more common chimpanzees (Ericka, Kenton, Sherman and Austin) to the Language Center's research program. They too learned to differentiate and use symbols. However, unlike Lana and other language-trained apes, they were not taught to label things upon demand but rather to ask for things of interest to them such as foods and tools. As with children, these skills were acquired through a process which stressed the development of communicative intentionality and joint regard (Savage-Rumbaugh 1986). The communications were negotiated first at the nonverbal level and secondarily at the verbal level. For example, when the chimpanzee needed a particular tool to solve a problem, it first expressed this desire nonverbally, by gesturing to the tool. Only later was a symbol learned as an alternate means of expressing which tool was needed. More importantly, a measure of concordance was employed to determine whether or not they knew which tool they had requested. By either replying inappropriately to their request (i.e. giving them the wrong tool) or by offering them the tool kit and allowing them to choose any tool, it was possible to determine whether what they said corresponded with what they then did.

These studies permitted "reference" to be objectified as a verifiable inter-individual process, rather than a postulate of internal mental structure. They put in place a behaviorally valid means of determining whether or not a chimpanzee knew what it said. This verbal-behavioral concordance also made it possible for the chimpanzee to make statements about intended future actions of its own. For example, the announcement of the intent to "tickle" followed by tickling, or the announcement of the intent to "go outdoors" followed by a trip outside, could occur. Previous symbol-using apes did not have announcement skills at their disposal. They had asked for things they wanted and had named things when told to do so, but they had not used symbols for the purpose of conveying their future actions.

This behavioral "legitimization" of the linguistic capacity of apes established that apes could use symbols in many of the same ways as human beings, and that they were not simply engaging in a series of tricks or conditioned routines lacking cognizance of the significance of their utterances. What this work did not do, however, was address one of the most significant aspects of differences between human and ape— the fact that nearly all children acquire language skills not only spontaneously but effortlessly. Adults do not have to teach them; indeed it is hardly possible to prevent children from learning language if they are reared in anything approaching a normal environment. Why did apes need tutoring, and fairly constant tutoring at that?

The addition of four new subjects of a different species, the bonobo, permitted studies at the Language Research Center to address this question (Savage-Rumbaugh et al. 1986; Savage-Rumbaush 1988; Savage-Rumbaugh et al. 1990). These subjects consisted of a wild caught adult bonobo female (Matata) and her offspring (one male, Kanzi, born in 1980; and two females, Mulika and Panbanisha, born in 1983 and 1985, respectively). A female common chimpanzee, Panzee, was born in 1985 and is being reared with the bonobos in a co-rearing study.

Studies with these subjects began with attempts to replicate the findings described above with common chimpanzees. The adult female, Matata, evidenced significantly greater difficulty discriminating symbols and sequencing them than previous subjects. Matata showed similar deficiencies in other areas such as match-to-sample, sorting, and tool use. More importantly, she did not display a stable concordance between her symbolic utterances and her nonverbal behaviors, suggesting that her lexigram usage could not accurately be characterized as "symbolic" or "referential," at least at the procedural level typified by the *Pan troglodytes* subjects Sherman and Austin (Savage-Rumbaugh et al. 1990).

By contrast, all of Matata's offspring (Kanzi, Mulika, and Panbanisha) acquired large symbol vocabularies. The most important finding with these additional ape subjects was that *it is not necessary to train language.* Simply by observing and listening to the caretakers' input, as a child observes and listens to those around it, they began to use symbols appropriately. Their acquisition of these skills has been described in detail elsewhere (Savage-Rumbaugh et al. 1986; Savage-Rumbaugh 1988); however, a brief summary is relevant here.

All of the young bonobos were exposed to caretakers who pointed to keyboard symbols as they spoke. Caretakers talked to them about daily routines, events, and about comings and goings of the laboratory. These events included trips to the woods to search for food, games of tickle and chase, trips to visit other primates at the laboratory, play with favorite toys such as balloons and balls, visits from friends, watching preferred TV shows, taking baths, helping pick up things, and other simple activities characteristic of daily life. They were not required to use the keyboard to get the caretaker to tickle, play, open doors, or give them food. Instead of requiring symbol production, caretakers talked to the apes about what they were doing and what was to be done next. These conversations were characterized by speaking while simultaneously pointing to symbols and were always contextually relevant. They were rarely, if ever, repetitive in the sense that the same word or sentence was uttered over and over. Nonetheless, across days, routines evidenced basic structures or schemata that tended to repeat themselves, just as do the routines of preschool children.

Table 18.1
First lexigrams acquired by infant bonobos

Kanzi	Mulika	Panbanisha
Orange	Milk	Milk
Peanut	Key	Chase
Banana	T-room	Open
Apple	Surprise	Tickle
Bedroom	Juice	Grape
Chase	Water	Bite
Austin	Grape	Dog
Sweet potato	Banana	Surprise
Raisin	Go	Yogurt
Ball	Staff Office	Soap

Unlike apes whose symbol vocabulary was assigned by the experimenter, the bonobos "selected" the symbols they were ready to acquire from the hundreds used around them each day. Like children, their first words were not all the same, though there was overlap (Table 18.1). Also unlike other apes, the bonobos first learned to associate the spoken word with its real world referent, not the geometric symbol. Only after learning the relationship between a spoken word and its referent did they connect the word and the geometric symbol. Their initial acquisition was receptive, that is, they evidenced comprehension of things that were said to them and around them before they began to employ symbols to communicate their own desires.

Decoding Speech

When the input which the ape receives is spontaneous and context-appropriate natural language, each word is inevitably intermingled with others in many different types of sentences. For example, one might hear "balloon" in the sentences "Can you blow up the balloon?," "Can you find the balloon?," "Please don't swallow the balloon," "Would you put the balloon in the backpack?," and so on. From such complex input the ape must somehow abstract the phonemic combination of sounds that forms the word "balloon" and pair these sounds with the object. The ape's initial attempts to assign reference may differ from the accepted referent either by being too specific or too global. However, the constant attempts to interpret utterances produced by the models will eventually result in the appropriate delimiting of the referent for the word "balloon."

When symbols are acquired in this manner, the process of reference and the particular item of reference are comprehended for some time before the symbol is ever produced. Such comprehension is neither paced nor prodded by a teacher; indeed the caregiver may not be aware that comprehension is even occurring, since for the most part such comprehension is covert and self-reinforcing. The ape's motivation is to understand the message that is being directed toward it so that it can predict what will be happening in the social context, not to produce a motor act that will please the teacher and result in receipt of a banana or fish. When apes do begin to produce a symbol which they have already learned to comprehend, they neither expect nor receive a reward for doing so. Instead, symbol production functions to provide information regarding their internal state.

Syntax

In the view of many linguists, language is defined largely by the existence of syntax (for a current review of this issue see Bates et al. 1990). Upon this perspective neither complex communications nor rational thought can take place as long as syntax is absent. It is assumed that all human communications involving more than a simple desire or alarm call need syntax as do all communications about the past and the future and all communications regarding relationships between agents, actions, objects, locations, and events.

The importance which linguists historically attributed to syntax caused these issues to supersede all others in the ape language debate. It was too quickly assumed that single word utterances produced by animals could be explained by the principles of conditioned discrimination learning, generalization, match-to-sample, and imitation (Brown 1973). For many scientists, the study by Terrace et al. (1979) was the final word on ape language. However, the premise upon which Terrace arrived at his negative conclusions was itself fatally flawed. This premise was that if an ape could use different symbols in different grammatical categories and if it could then sequence or properly arrange these categories, it must be said to posses a rudimentary syntax.

There are two reasons why the production of symbols ordered by category is not a sufficient demonstration of syntax. The first is that many words (for example, proper names) can function equally well in different syntactical categories. Thus the knowledge that "Kelly" goes in the agent position in an agent-action-object frame such as "Kelly throw ball" means little unless it can simultaneously be shown that "Kelly" is placed in a different category and different position in a sentence such as "Give the ball to Kelly."

It is noteworthy that Terrace did not search Nim's data for such differential syntactical categorization of common words. Rather, he attempted to determine which words, if any, tended to fall in a particular position such as first or last when they occurred conjointly. On the basis of this tally he concluded that lexical regularities existed in Nim's utterances. Nim's regularities were not positional and were, in some sense, rule based, though Terrace did not attempt to specify any rules that might account for the observed regularities. Terrace concluded that semantic categorical structure was not present because Nim used only a small number of words in most categories. For example, the only signs that served as "beneficiaries" were the synonymous signs "me" and "Nim." With only these signs as "beneficiaries" it is not reasonable to conclude that Nim had developed a functional semantically-based concept of the role of the "beneficiary" or that he could use a syntactically organized sentence.

It is possible to simultaneously accept Terrace's conclusions regarding Nim and question his premise that syntax can be demonstrated by looking at the order of Nim's signs. Simple action-agent-object ordering is not synonymous with syntactical structure. Syntactical structure can be demonstrated only by showing that the semantic relationship between words, which is encoded by order (or other syntactical devices) is understood.

More important, however, is the fact that the basic function of any sequence of words (with or without syntactical markers) is to convey specific novel meanings that cannot be expressed by the utterance of individual words. The communicative effect produced by a combination of a group of words is distinctively different from the production of individual words. The production of novel combinatorial utterances is an extremely powerful communicative process that characterizes all languages. It antedates the emergence of syntax proper, and because a new meaning is created which is not simply an additive result of the separate units, it cannot be satisfactorily reduced to the principles of conditioning, generalization, match-to-sample, or other similar psychological processes.

Novel and Creative Combinations without Syntax

Terrace observed that "There is no evidence, however, that apes can combine such symbols in order to create new meanings." (Terrace et al. 1979: 900) In making such a statement, he assumed that syntax is a necessary condition for the generation of novel meanings, while overlooking the fact that word combinations themselves can be employed to create new meanings. For example, an utterance such as "Car trailer" or "Grouproom Matata," may well convey a novel meaning that its individual components, if uttered alone, could never generate.

The bonobo Kanzi regularly created combinations that differed from those of Washoe and Nim in substantive ways. For example, when Kanzi produced the combination "Car trailer" he was in the car and employed this utterance as a means of indicating that he wanted the car to be driven to the trailer rather than to walk. (The trailer is near the lab and Kanzi generally walked to the trailer when he wanted to go.) He followed the utterance with a gesture toward the trailer. When asked whether he wanted the car to go to the trailer, Kanzi produced a positive vocal response and again gestured to the trailer.

Had Kanzi said "car" alone, this single symbol utterance would have been interpreted as a comment about being in the car and would have simply been acknowledged. Had he said "trailer" alone, the caretaker would probably have simply gotten out of the car and walked with Kanzi to the trailer, since it was a very short distance to drive. However, by saying "car trailer" Kanzi produced a novel meaning and brought about a set of events that otherwise would not have been likely to occur (i.e., taking the car to the trailer).

Kanzi similarly produced the combination "Grouproom Matata" to convey something different than either symbol could convey alone. Kanzi was in the grouproom when he produced this combination and he had just heard Matata vocalize. Generally when he wanted to visit Matata, he would so indicate by simply saying "Matata" and gesturing "go" toward the colony room (where Matata was housed). However, on this occasion, by producing this combination he indicated that he wanted Matata to come to the group room. In response to his utterance he was asked, "Do you want Matata to come to the group room?" He immediately made loud positive vocal noises first to the experimenter, then to Matata, apparently announcing something about this to her. She responded with excited vocalizations also. Had Kanzi said only "grouproom," his utterance would have been interpreted as a comment on his location, just as "car" would have been in the preceding example. However, since one cannot take a room somewhere, the interpretation was that Kanzi wanted Matata to come into the grouproom. Kanzi's vocalization in response to the question and his ensuing behavior affirmed the correctness of this interpretation.

These utterances, which are characteristic of Kanzi, differ from Washoe's "water bird" in that they are not elicited by factors present in the environment and the experimenter's query. While it is not possible to know at any given moment why Kanzi said "Car trailer," "Matata grouproom," or any other of thousands of similar utterances, it is reasonable to conclude these utterances were provoked by an interaction

Table 18.2
Distribution of two-element semantic relations in Kanzi's corpus

Relation	No.	Example (of dominant order)
Action-Action	92	TICKLE BITE, then positions himself for researcher/caregiver to tickle and bite him.
Action-Agent	119	CARRY person(gesture), gesturing to Phil, who agrees to carry
Agent-Action	13	Kanzi.
Action-Object	39	KEEP AWAY BALLOON, wanting to tease Bill with a balloon and
Object-Action	15	start a fight.
Object-Agent	7	BALLOON person(gesture), Kanzi gestures to Liz; Liz gives Kanzi
Agent-Object	1	balloon.
Entity-Demonstrative	182	PEANUT that(gesture), points to peanuts in cooler.
Demonstrative-Entity	67	
Goal-Action	46	COKE CHASE, then researcher chases Kanzi to place in woods
Action-Goal	10	where coke is kept.
Entity-Entity	25	M & M GRAPE. Caregiver/researcher: "You want both of these foods?" Kanzi vocalizes and holds out his hand.
Location-Location	7	SUE'S-OFFICE CHILDSIDE, wanted to go to those two places.
Location-Entity	19	PLAYYARD AUSTIN, wants to visit Austin in the playyard
Entity-Location	12	
Entity-Attribute	12	FOOD BLACKBERRY, after eating blackberries, to request more.
Attribute-Entity	10	
Miscellaneous relations	37	These include low frequency (less than seven) such as attribute of action, attribute of location, affirmation, negation, and those involving an instrument.
Two-Mode Paraphrase	4	CHASE chase(gesture), trying to get staff member to chase him in the lobby.
No direct relation	6	POTATO OIL. Kanzi commented after researcher had put oil on him as he was eating a potato.
Total	723	

Adapted from Greenfield & Savage-Rumbaugh (1990a).

between Kanzi's memory system and information that he was processing at the current time. Moreover, they reflected an attempt to communicate a specific message about his internal state to another party, rather than a simple naming of something pointed out by the experimenter. As such, these two-word messages were communicative and expressed things that the experimenter would not otherwise have known. The same cannot be said of the "water bird" response. (For additional examples of Kanzi's utterances, see Table 18.2).

It is also possible to determine what Kanzi meant as a result of the utterance. One can simply agree with Kanzi and then look to see if his behavior corresponds to what has been agreed to. For example, does he head toward Matata's cage and unlock her door if given the opportunity? Does he sit down in the car and gesture toward the trailer? Since there are an unlimited number of other things he might do other than exhibit behaviors which correspond to his utterance, if he does do things which proceed along the lines of the utterances, it is reasonable to assume that he knows what he has said. It is not possible to use a similar approach with "water bird." This utterance is elicited by the experimenter's query and does not reflect Washoe's internal state in any sense. Whatever she does after the utterance is not relevant to her signing "water bird."

Multi-word utterances, then, can either represent strings of single signs or they can be attempts at the communication of complex messages that are not possible with signs or symbols used individually. Table 18.3 depicts some critical differences that have been delineated in order to evaluate the semantic appropriateness of Kanzi's multi-word utterances (Savage-Rumbaugh 1990). This table contrasts the presently available data on multi-word utterances for the apes that have served in language studies.

While all conditions do not need to be met for each utterance, it is essential that all of these conditions be satisfied in some sense by the total body of data available for the ape or other animal (see Savage-Rumbaugh 1990 for a more complete description of the need for each of these conditions). If the ape's multi-word utterances do not meet these criteria, then the further search for syntactical structures in the utterances would not appear to be warranted. Using the criteria in Table 18.3, it is possible to evaluate and compare the multi-word utterances of different apes, as is done in the table. For example, an utterance such as Washoe's "water-bird" meets only criteria 7 and 8, and fails all others. In some cases the failure to meet a criterion results from Washoe herself, but in other cases it results from a failure to report the behavior associated with the utterance.

Looking at Nim's combinations, we find that they fall into three classes of utterances, 1) those which contain a "wild card," 2) those which are ritualized and must be signed within a given routine, and 3) those in which a single sign is combined with a pointing gesture. None of these types of signs meet the criteria of Table 18.3. It is even questionable whether two-word utterances such as "Food Nim," "Ice Nim," "Hungry me," etc. should be classified as two-word combinations since both the signs "Nim" and "me" are used as "wild cards" or signs that Nim added freely to any utterance.

These data suggest that it is not a tendency to imitate, nor a lack of syntactical competency, that is at the basis of Nim's failure to learn language, as Terrace's argues. Rather, his difficulty is more basic. It appears that Nim is unable to create truly novel two-word combinations regardless of order. Study of videotapes of Nim with his trainers reveals that they constantly addressed questions to Nim with the goal of producing more signs and sign combinations (Savage-Rumbaugh & Sevcik 1984). For example, if Nim wanted an apple that they held (which he indicated by reaching for the apple) he was asked "What this?" "What Nim want eat?" "Nim want eat apple?" "Who eat apple?" until he finally produced a combination such as "Me Nim apple eat." While Terrace maintains that Nim was not explicitly taught combinations, it is clear from these tapes that Nim was not permitted, most of the time, to use single signs to make his wants known. Moreover, the queries used by the trainers contained signs that they wanted Nim to make in order to expand upon the simple communication that he had already made. Consequently, the adoption of a strategy of imitating the teacher's utterance was the only means available to Nim of obtaining food, play, and other important things.

Are Nim's data indicative of the ultimate capacity of the ape? When Nim's data are contrasted with those of Kanzi, an ape who acquired symbols spontaneously without molding or other training, it is clear that Nim's limitations do not extend to all apes. A 5-month corpus of Kanzi's multi-word utterances (collected between April 1 and

Table 18.3
Conditions needed to establish the capacity for true multiword utterances

Ape	Published corpus	Criteria met by published corpus	Criteria met by isolated examples
Washoe	None		1, 5, 8, 9
Moja Dar Tatu	None		1, 5, 8, 9
Ally Booee Bruno	Small corpus (Miles 1978)	9	9
Sherman Austin	Large corpus (Savage-Rumbaugh 1986)	2, 3, 5, 6, 8, 9	2, 3, 5, 6, 8, 9
Lana	Large corpus	1, 2, 5, 6, 7, 8, 11	1, 2, 5, 6, 7, 8, 9, 11
Nim	Large corpus (Terrace 1979; Terrace 1984)	5, 9, 10	5, 9, 10
Sarah	None	Not applicable, No intentional utterances	Not applicable, No intentional utterances
Koko	None		1, 8, 9, 10
Chantek	None		5
Kanzi	Large corpus (Greenfield & Savage-Rumbaugh 1990a)	1, 2, 3, 4, 5, 6, 7, 8, 9, 10, 11	1, 2, 3, 4, & 5, 6, 7, 8, 9, 10, 11

1. Some referents of the utterance are absent in many combinations.
2. The majority of utterances are not preceded by a "What's this?" or "What do you want?" query.
3. The behavior which follows the utterance is observed and recorded in order to verify the validity of the expressed utterance.
4. The meaning or intent of the majority of utterances are not, and could not, be apparent to the listener from the context alone.
5. The majority of utterances are known not to be imitations of the listener's previous comments.
6. The majority of utterances are known to be appropriate to the context as a result of scoring at the time of the utterance.
7. The words chosen for the utterance are significant in that the same words uttered singly would convey an incorrect message or messages and intent could not be deduced from context.
8. The majority of the combinations are not formed by attaching one or more meaningless "wild-card words" to another word.
9. The majority of the combinations are not routinized.
10. The agent, action, and object classes of a multiword combinations all have multiple members which occur in other combinations.
11. If other words were combined it would change the outcome significantly.

September 1, 1986) has been analyzed using the contextual data gathered on Kanzi's behavior at the time the utterance occurred (Greenfield & Savage-Rumbaugh 1991). In each case, the intent of the utterance was determined by Kanzi's behavior. This analysis indicates that Kanzi's combinations differ significantly from those of Washoe and Nim. None of the combinations used in this analysis were imitations (only 2.67% of Kanzi's combinations were either partial or full imitations of the preceding utterance; these were eliminated from analysis for the purposes of this data set). Both the context and Kanzi's ensuing behavior were recorded for each combination. This made it possible to determine whether or not Kanzi understood the utterance and what he intended that it mean.

The majority of Kanzi's utterances were novel and most of the messages could not have been conveyed by single words. Many of the utterances referred to events or objects which were absent at the time of the utterance. As illustrated in Table 18.2,

Kanzi employed a wide variety of semantic relations. Moreover, in the majority of his combinations, he tended to order symbols according to semantic function (see Greenfield & Savage-Rumbaugh 1990, 1991 for discussion). The variety of lexically distinct combinations was so great as to make it impossible for the combinations to have been formed on the basis of lexical position preference. Also, many items occurred in different positions in different combinations. For example, "Grab Matata" occurred as an action-object combination signalling Kanzi's desire to play a game of "grab" with Matata. However, the utterance "Matata bite" was not used to indicate a desire to playbite with Matata, but the fact that Matata had bitten Kanzi quite hard. Similarly, Kanzi used the combination "Hide peanut" to comment that he had just hidden some peanuts in the grass. However, he then formed the combination "Chase hide" to ask the caretaker to play a game of chase and hide with him.

Cuing: How to Draw Accurate Conclusions
The issue of cuing is one that has been, and must continue to be, of concern in this field, as Wilder (chapter 3 of this reader) observes. However, in the past this issue has also been used unfairly to attack the entire field as a questionable one. The purpose of these one-sided attacks has not been to develop standardized methodologies to eliminate cuing, but rather simply to raise doubts as to whether it is possible ever to eliminate the scent of Clever Hans, and thus to argue that no animal studies can be valid under any circumstances. This is patently false. Indeed, it is possible to determine what animals can do using methodologies that control for cuing (Rumbaugh et al. 1990). There are many different ways of doing this, and the "correct" way at any given time depends upon that which one is trying to demonstrate. However, there are some very simple principles that apply to the majority of situations. The first is that it is important to distinguish between what the animal does in training situations or during daily conversation and what it does in testing formats. During training and/or conversation settings, it is to be expected that the experimenter will provide a model for the animal, much as a parent provides a model for its child and that the adult will try to help the animal to communicate. This is an essential process in language acquisition for the child and there is no reason to deny it to animals attempting to learn language. Similarly, some cuing or prompting may be done by parents during this period. The goal, however, is to understand what it is the child or chimpanzee is attempting to say, by whatever means is at hand. Data from such sessions *are not expected to be free of parental or experimental input.* Such data are however, important for revealing many facts regarding the learning process itself.

During *test settings*, all such input must be removed. Test settings must be designed to determine, in an explicit sense, the capacities that the animal (or child) has developed fully enough to be able to exhibit them out of the communicative context when queried under conditions that prevent contextual and/or experimenter input to the response. Wilder (chapter 3 of this reader) at times seems to confuse these two settings in his critique, taking pains to point out that cuing of different sorts can occur in daily conversations with Kanzi. Indeed, if no rapport were permitted between Kanzi and the experimenter in the daily context of language use, it is difficult to see how a functional symbolic communication system could ever develop.

However, Wilder overlooks some important aspects of the daily conversational setting with Kanzi which mitigate against the kind of cuing that is of concern to him. Certainly the experimenter could devise a means of cuing Kanzi in this setting, but the concern of the experimenter is not that of getting Kanzi to say what is "right" or "correct" or to answer a question. Rather, the experimenter is interested in whatever Kanzi has to say. It does not matter where Kanzi goes, what game he wants to play, what he would like to eat, or what he would like to do. There are no experimental constraints which determine this. It is up to Kanzi. Consequently, *there is no pre-programmed correct answer that the experimenter is waiting for or wanting Kanzi to produce.* If Clever Hans could have stomped his foot as many times as he wished, regardless of the question he was asked, it is not likely that he would have begun to look to the trainer for cues.

Blind tests have been a standard control in the field and fully adequate tests to eliminate cuing have been employed by Gardner and Gardner (1984), Herman (1987), Schusterman & Krieger (1984), Rumbaugh (1977), Savage-Rumbaugh (1986), and Savage-Rumbaugh et al. (1986). Fully adequate controls have not been employed by Patterson (1978), Terrace (1979), Miles (1978), or Pepperberg (1981), or by Boysen & Berntsen (1989) in tests of numerical ability. Fouts (1973) initially used adequate controls, but dropped them in some of his later research (Fouts et al. 1984). (It is this work which Wilder criticizes.) Adequate controls require that all potential means of indicating the correct response to the animal, prior to its occurrence be ruled out. This is most easily accomplished by having the experimenter who judges the animal's response be blind. This means that this experimenter either cannot see the animal (and the animal cannot see him/her) or that the experimenter does not know what response the animal is to make (such as left, right, or middle). Sufficient trials must be administered to rule out chance responding. When conceptual or novel responses are of interest, trial one data must be employed.

An ideal example of such a test is the use of headphones to determine comprehension of the English words (Savage-Rumbaugh, 1988). In this test, Kanzi wears headphones so that only he can hear the target word. The experimenter does not know what Kanzi heard, nor does he/she know what lexigrams are available for Kanzi to choose from until after his selection has already been made. Target words and alternatives are selected randomly from trial to trial. Additionally, Kanzi is given food for participating in the test, but food or other reward is never contingent upon a correct response. It is given as requested. The importance of being able to give tests without reward is often underestimated with regard to the issue of cuing (Wilder, chapter 3 of this reader). If the organism has nothing to gain by being correct and nothing to lose by being incorrect, it has no reason to search for cues, inadvertent or otherwise, and it does not do so.

Terrace (1979) and Miles (1978) report no blind tests. Pepperberg (1981) is the judge of whether or not the parrot answers correctly and she is present in the room and knows which item is shown to Alex. Boysen & Berntsen (1989) report too few blind trials to ascertain whether the novel behavior (adding) was chance or not.

Conclusion

Kanzi's ability to combine symbols without drill or withholding of preferred items implies that many fundamental aspects of language cannot be specific to *Homo*. While his capacity for extremely complex syntactical devices remains limited, it is still expanding. It also must be remembered that Kanzi's brain is one-third the size of our own. Given that he can, without training, decode speech into individual words, determine how those function in different and novel communicative settings (Savage-Rumbaugh 1988), use them spontaneously and appropriately in novel combinations (Greenfield & Savage-Rumbaugh 1990), and comprehend sentential relationships (Savage-Rumbaugh 1989), it is reasonable to conclude that the language gap between man and ape may result from a difference in information processing capacity and memory, rather than innate linguistic structures.

We find, then, that it is possible to tap, not train, abilities in other extant species that give evidence of a bio-linguistic substratum for language. Given an appropriate communicative environment and the opportunity to develop skills without rote, reward-based training or drilling, bonobos have developed symbol use that functions much like that of human children. They not only use the symbols to communicate requests, statements, and comments, but they also understand the utterances of others. Additionally, Kanzi, the oldest symbol-using bonobo, has spontaneously begun to use multisymbol utterances to encode information that cannot be expressed with a single symbol. The evidence from Kanzi and the other bonobos casts doubt on two widely-held beliefs in the scientific community: that language is possible because of unique structures in the human brain and that even complex skills are best taught to nonhumans through simplistic shaping and conditioning techniques.

At the moment, it is not known whether the bonobo alone can demonstrate these homologies to children's language, or whether the freedom from methodological constraints has allowed this capacity to develop naturally. There is evidence that some of the cognitive components of language are present in members of other species. Certainly, a correspondence of some kind between sign or symbol and its referent has been established in dolphins (Herman, et al. 1984), sea lions (Schusterman & Krieger 1984), parrot (Pepperberg 1981, 1983), chimpanzee (Gardner & Gardner 1969, 1984; Savage-Rumbaugh 1986; Savage-Rumbaugh et al. 1986, 1990), and gorilla (Patterson 1978). The nature of this correspondence may not be equivalent to that found in bonobos, but its presence suggests that further studies of these and other species is warranted. Future research should focus upon the animal's ability to comprehend symbolic communicative messages which are directed to it. These messages must be able to convey novel propositional information (such as "There is a snake hiding in the blanket") and the motivation to comprehend such messages must reside in their intrinsic worth and the appropriateness of their context. For it is from the comprehension of the novel messages of others that the capacity to produce novel messages of one's own must rise.

Acknowledgements

The preparation of this chapter and research described herein were supported by National Institutes of Health grant NICHD-06016, which supports the Language Research Center, cooperatively operated by Georgia State University and the Yerkes Regional Primate Research Center of Emory University. In addition the research is supported in part by RR-00165 to the Yerkes Primate Research Center of Emory University. This research was also supported by the College of Arts and Sciences of Georgia State University. The authors wish to thank Kelly McDonald, Jeannine Murphy, Elizabeth Rubert, Rose Sevcik, and Philip Shaw for their work with the bonobos. The authors also appreciate the efforts of Robert Astur toward the preparation of this manuscript.

Literature Cited

Bates, E. 1979. *The Emergence of Symbols.* New York: Academic Press.

Bates, E., Thal, D. & Marchman, V. 1990. Symbols and syntax: A Darwinian approach to language development. In: *The Biological Foundation of Language Development* (ed. by N. Krasnegor, D. Rumbaugh, M. Studdert-Kennedy & R. Schiefelbusch). Oxford: Oxford University Press.

Boysen, S. T. & Berntsen, G. G. 1989. Numerical competence in a chimpanzee (*Pan troglodytes*). *Journal of Comparative Psychology* 103, 23–31.

Brown, R. 1973. *A First Language: The Early Stage.* Cambridge, Massachusetts: Harvard University Press.

Bruner, J. 1983. *Child's Talk.* New York: Norton.

Dale, P. S. 1976. *Language Development: Structure and Function.* (2nd edition). New York: Holt, Reinhart and Winston.

Fouts, R. S. 1973. Acquisition and testing of gestural signs in four young chimpanzees. *Science* 180, 978–980.

Fouts, R. S., Chown, W. M. & Goodin, L. 1976. Transfer of signed responses in American Sign Language from vocal English stimuli to physical object by a chimpanzee (*Pan*). *Learning and Motivation*, 7, 458–475.

Fouts, R. S., Couch, J. B. & O'Neal, C. R. 1979. Strategies for primate language training. In: *Language Intervention from Ape to Child* (ed. by R. L. Schiefelbusch & J. H. Hollis), pp. 295–323. Baltimore, Maryland: University Park Press.

Fouts, R. S., Fouts, D. H. & Schoenfeld, D. 1984. Sign Language conversational interaction between chimpanzees. *Sign Language Studies* 42, 1–12.

Gardner, R. A. & Gardner, B. T. 1969. Teaching sign language to a chimpanzee. *Science* 165, 664–672.

————. 1975. Early signs of language in child and chimpanzee. *Science* 187, 752–753.

————. 1984. A vocabulary test for chimpanzees (*Pan troglodytes*). *Journal of Comparative Psychology* 98, 381–404.

Gauker, C. (1990). How to learn a language like a chimpanzee. *Philosophical Psychology* 3, 31–53.

Gill, T. V. 1977. Conversations with Lana. In: *Language Learning by a Chimpanzee: The LANA Project* (ed. by D. M. Rumbaugh), pp. 225–246. New York: Academic Press.

Greenfield, P. M. & Savage-Rumbaugh, E. S. (1990). Grammatical combination in *Pan paniscus*: Learning and invention in the evolution and development of language. In: *Comparative Developmental Psychology of Language and Intelligence in Primates* (ed. by S. Parker & K. Gibson), New York: Cambridge University Press.

————. (1991). Imitation, grammatical development, and the invention of protogrammar by an ape. In: *Biobehavioral Foundations of Language Development* (ed. by N. Krasnegor, D. Rumbaugh, M. Studdert-Kennedy & R. Schiefelbusch), pp. 235–258. Hillsdale, New Jersey: Lawrence Erlbaum Associates.

Greenfield, P. M., & Smith, H. 1976. *The Structure of Communication in Early Language Development.* New York: Academic Press.

Herman, L. M. 1987. Receptive competencies of language-trained animals. In: *Advances in the Study of Behavior Vol. 17* (ed. by J. S. Rosenblatt, C. Beer, M.-C. Busnel, & P. J. B. Slater), pp. 1–60. Petaluma, California: Academic Press.

————. 1988. The language of animal language research: Reply to Schusterman and Gisiner. *The Psychological Record* 38, 349–362.

Herman, L. M., Richards, D. G. & Wolz, J. P. 1984. Comprehension of sentences by bottlenosed dolphins. *Cognition* 16, 129–219.

Lock, A. 1980. *The Guided Reinvention of Language.* London: Academic Press.

McShane, J. 1980. *Learning to Talk.* Cambridge: Cambridge University Press.

Miles, H. L. 1978. Language acquisition in apes and children. In: *Sign Language Acquisition in Man and Ape: New Dimensions in Comparative Psycholinguistics* (ed. by F. C. C. Peng). Boulder, Colorado: Westview Press.

Moerk, E. L. 1977. *Pragmatic and Semantic Aspects of Early Language Development.* Baltimore, Maryland: University Park Press.

Patterson, F. 1978. Linguistic capabilities of a lowland gorilla. In: *Sign Language Acquisition in Man and Ape: New Dimensions in Comparative Psycholinguistics* (ed. by F. C. C. Peng), pp. 161–201. Boulder, Colorado: Westview Press.

Pepperberg, I. 1981. Functional vocalizations by an African Grey parrot (*Psittacus erithacus*). *Zeitschrift für Tierespsychologie* 55, 139–160.

————. 1983. Cognition in the African Grey parrot: Preliminary evidence for auditory/vocal comprehension of the class concept. *Animal Learning and Behavior* 11(2), 179–185.

Peters, A. M. 1983. *The Units of Language Acquisition*. Cambridge: Cambridge University Press.

Premack, D. 1970. The education of Sarah: A chimp learns the language. *Science* 170, 54–58.

Premack, D. & Premack, A. 1983. *The Mind of an Ape*. New York: Norton.

Rumbaugh, D. M. 1977. *Language Learning by a Chimpanzee: The LANA Project*. New York: Academic Press.

Rumbaugh, D. M., Gill, T. V., & von Glasersfeld, E. C. 1973. Reading and sentence completion by a chimpanzee. *Science* 182, 731–733.

Rumbaugh, D. M., Washburn, D., Hopkins, W. D., & Savage-Rumbaugh, E. S. (1990). Chimpanzee competence for counting in a video-formatted task situation. In: *Proceedings of the Hawaii Conference on Animal Cognition* (ed. by H. Roitblat). Hillsdale, New Jersey: Lawrence Erlbaum Associates.

Savage-Rumbaugh, E. S. 1986. *Ape Language: From Conditioned Response to Symbol*. New York: Columbia University Press.

————. 1988. A new look at ape language: Comprehension of vocal speech and syntax. In: *Nebraska symposium on motivation, 35* (ed. by D. Leger). Lincoln, NE: University of Nebraska Press.

————. 1989. Language: Our erroneous but cherished preconceptions. Invited lecture, Animal Language Workshop, University of Hawaii at Manoa.

————. 1990a. Language as a cause-effect communication system. *Philosophical psychology. 3*, 55–76.

————. 1991. Language learning in the bonobo: How and why they learn. In: *Biobehavioral Foundations of Language Development* (ed. by N. Krasnegor, D. M. Rumbaugh, M. Studdert-Kerinedy & R. Schiefelbusch), pp. 209–233. Hillsdale, New Jersey: Lawrence Erlbaum.

————. 1990b. Language acquisition in a nonhuman primate species: Implications for the innateness debate. *Developmental Psychobiology. 23*, 1–22.

————. 1993. Language learnability in man, ape, and dolphin. In: *Proceedings of the Hawaii Conference on Animal Cognition* (ed. by H. Roitblatt, L. M. Herman, & P. E. Nachtigall), pp. 457–484. Hillsdale, New Jersey: Lawrence Erlbaum.

Savage-Rumbaugh, E. S., McDonald, K., Sevcik, R. A., Hopkins, W. D., & Rubert, E. 1986. Spontaneous symbol acquisition and communicative use by pygmy chimpanzees (*Pan paniscus*). *Journal of Experimental Psychology: General* 115, 211–235.

Savage-Rumbaugh, E. S., & Rumbaugh, D. M. 1988. A theory of language acquisition in apes. Paper presented at NICHD Conference, "Biobehavioral Foundations of Language Development." Leesburg, Virginia.

————. 1991. A theory of language acquisition in apes. In: *Biobehavioral Foundations of Language Development* (ed. by N. Krasnegor, D. M. Rumbaugh, M. Studdert-Kennedy & D. Schiefelbusch). Hillsdale, New Jersey: Lawrence Erlbaum Associates.

Savage-Rumbaugh, E. S., Rumbaugh, D. M. & Boysen, S. 1980. Do apes use language? *American Scientist* 68, 49–61.

Savage-Rumbaugh, E. S. & Sevcik, R. A. 1984. Levels of communicative competency in the chimpanzee: Pre-representational and representational. In: *Behavioral evolution and integrative levels* (ed. by G. Greenberg & E. Tobach), pp. 197–219. Hillsdale, New Jersey: Lawrence Erlbaum.

Savage-Rumbaugh, E. S., Sevcik, R. A., Brakke, K. E., & Rumbaugh, D. M. 1990. Symbols: Their communicative use, combination, and comprehension by bonobos (*Pan paniscus*). In: *Advances in Infancy Research 6* (ed. by C. Rovee-Collier & L. P. Lipsitt), pp. 221–278. Norwood, New Jersey: Ablex.

Schusterman, R. L., & Krieger, K. 1984. California sea lions are capable of semantic comprehension. *The Psychological Record* 34, 3–23.

————. 1988. Artificial language comprehension in dolphins and sea lions: The essential cognitive skills. *The Psychological Record* 38, 311–348.

Terrace, H. S. 1979. *Nim*. New York: Alfred A. Knopf.

————. 1985. In the beginning was the "name." *American Psychologist* 40, 1011–1028.

Terrace, H. S., Pettito, L. A., Sanders, R. J. & Bever, T. G. 1979. Can an ape create a sentence? *Science* 206, 891–900.

Waldron, T. P. 1985. *Principles of Language and Mind*. London: Routledge & Kegan, Paul.

Wells, G. A. 1987. *The Origin of Language: Aspects of the Discussion from Condillac to Wundt*. La Salle, Illinois: Open Court.

Chapter 19

Knowledge Acquisition and Asymmetry between Language Comprehension and Production: Dolphins and Apes as General Models for Animals

Louis M. Herman and Palmer Morrel-Samuels

Introduction

The receptive competencies of animals, in general, appear to be more highly developed than are their productive competencies (Herman 1987a). Consistent with this notion is the hypothesis of a basic asymmetry in the receptive and productive competencies of animals trained in language-like tasks (Herman 1987b). Language comprehension, a receptive skill, is therefore likely to be a more valid indicator of a species potential for acquiring some of the fundamental attributes of a natural or artificial language than is language production. In this paper we examine this thesis in greater detail, giving special attention to language work with dolphins and apes. We also review and discuss some relevant concepts and findings from the study of human language that may help to clarify or put into perspective some of the issues and findings in the animal language work.

Receptive Competencies and Knowledge Requisites: An Illustration with the Dolphin

Receptive competencies support knowledge acquisition, the basic building block of an intelligent system. In turn, knowledge and knowledge-acquiring abilities contribute vitally to the success of the individual in its natural world, especially if that world is socially and ecologically complex, as is the case for the bottlenosed dolphin, *Tursiops truncatus* (Norris & Dohl 1980; Wells et al. 1980). Among the basic knowledge requisites for the adult dolphin are the geographic characteristics and physiographic features of its home range; the relationships among these physical features and seasonal migratory pathways; the biota present in the environment and their relevance as prey, predator, or neutral target; the identification and integration of information received by its various senses, including that between an ensonified target and its visual representation; strategies for foraging and prey capture, both individually and in social units; the affiliative and hierarchical relationships among members of its herd; identification of individual herd members by their unique vocalizations and appearance; and the interpretation of particular behaviors of herd members (Madsen & Herman 1980; Herman 1991). This is undoubtedly an incomplete listing and is in part hypothetical, but is illustrative of the breadth and diversity of the knowledge base necessary to support the daily life of the individual dolphin. Similar analyses could be made of knowledge requirements of apes or of other animal species, but the underlying message is the same: extensive knowledge of the world may be required for effective functioning in that world and much of the requisite knowledge is gained through the exercise of receptive skills.

Knowledge-Acquiring Mechanisms and Processes: The Case for the Dolphin Continued

Plotkin (1988) discussed the influence of genetic, developmental, experiential (individual learning), and cultural (organism to organism information transfer) factors on knowledge acquisition by humans. (The cultural transmission of information does not necessarily imply cultural evolution of the species, a process Plotkin [1988] reserves for the human species.) These factors are broad enough in concept to apply to nonhuman organisms as well, although the importance of each factor may differ substantially across species. Here, we briefly consider how each of these factors may contribute to the acquisition of knowledge by the dolphin.

Genetic factors relevant to knowledge acquisition include endowments in sensory apparatus—the interfaces with the outside world—and in central nervous system development. The senses of the dolphin are well adapted to the underwater world and include many unique specializations. The dolphin's hearing and vision function as broadband receivers of fine resolution (Dawson 1980; Herman & Tavolga 1980; Popper 1980; Nachtigall 1986; Ralston & Herman 1989), enabling the individual to detect and monitor most environmental events of biological importance. The eye is highly light sensitive, and is specialized toward the blue end of the visible spectrum, an adaptation to the photic characteristics of the undersea world (Madsen & Herman 1980). Visual acuity is good and is approximately equivalent in air and water (Herman et al. 1975). Echolocation, an active system requiring the integration of sound production and hearing, allows for the interrogation of the aquatic environment under any condition, but is especially useful when viewing conditions are poor. Hearing and vision are thus both highly efficient receivers of information.

The brain of the bottlenosed dolphin is large in absolute and relative size, and has an extensive cortical surface area (Elias & Schwartz 1969; Ridgway & Brownson 1984; Ridgway 1986). The differentiation among areas of the dolphin cortex is not as clear as that in most terrestrial mammals, and the cortical architecture has apparently expanded the features of the early mammalian brain rather than emphasizing the modular plans characterizing the brains of anthropoid apes and of some carnivores and ungulates (Morgane et al. 1986; Glezer et al. 1988). Nevertheless, it has been argued that the very large surface area of the cortex, even given its relative thinness (Ridgway & Brownson 1984), supports considerable information-processing power (Jerison 1978). This hypothesis is given support by behavioral studies showing the exceptional competency of bottlenosed dolphins for carrying out a variety of challenging and complex cognitive tasks (reviewed in Herman 1980, 1986).

These tasks may be carried out at roughly equal levels of proficiency using either visual or acoustic information (Herman et al. 1989a). In a sense, dolphins and old world primates are "cognitive cousins" (Herman 1980) because of the functional similarities in cognition of these otherwise ecologically and evolutionarily divergent life forms. The shared cognitive characteristics provide another illustration of the generalization that different paths in evolution can nevertheless lead to similar functional outcomes.

Bottlenosed dolphins are long-lived (ca. 30 to 40 years), highly social mammals. There is extensive growth in the size of the brain during the first nine to ten years of the dolphin's life (Ridgway 1986). The development of echolocation skill appears to proceed slowly (M. Caldwell & Caldwell 1967), as does the development of the calf's unique signature whistle (M. Caldwell & Caldwell 1979). During the first two years or so of its life the young bottlenosed dolphin remains closely attached to its mother (Wells et al. 1980). Nursing may continue for 18 months or more (M. Caldwell & Caldwell 1972; Sergeant et al. 1973). In some cases, female adult members of a herd may temporarily share responsibility for the protection or care of the young dolphin when, for example, danger threatens or the natural mother is engaged in feeding dives (M. Caldwell & Caldwell 1966; Tavolga 1966; Tavolga & Essapian 1957; Norris & Dohl 1980). Thus, although the period of development and growth of the young dolphin is protracted, and its dependency on adults is long-term, this allows the youngster the necessary time for acquiring the structures, skills and knowledge required for effective functioning in the adult world.

The individual experiences of the developing dolphin are integrated into its growing fund of knowledge of its ecological and social world. However, not all experience need be gained through personal encounters. The dolphin is an adept mimic of sounds and behaviors (Richards et al. 1984; Tyack 1986; Xitco 1988; Herman et al. 1989b; also see review in Herman 1980). It is likely, therefore, that some knowledge may be acquired "culturally" by observation and imitation of others, rather than through direct experience. Such cultural transmission of information is a highly efficient means for acquiring knowledge and reaches its peak as a knowledge-acquiring factor in the human species (Plotkin 1988) where pedagogy is formalized and ritualized. The cultural transmission of information is not limited to the human species: it has been documented frequently in animals, for example macaque monkeys (Kawamura 1963; Mineka & Cook 1988; but see Galef, chapter 7 of this reader), chimpanzees (Goodall 1986; Menzel et al. 1972), birds (Jenkins 1978; Curio 1988), and humpback whales (Payne et al. 1983).

Again, we might have described the knowledge-acquiring mechanisms for some other species than the dolphin, but the same theme would hold: with so many mechanisms and processes devoted to the acquisition of knowledge, and given its importance in the life of the individual, it seems reasonable to assume that evolution has selected for the development of exceptional knowledge-acquiring skills in animals, or what may be more simply termed "receptive skills." The question considered in the remainder of this paper is the relationship between receptive skill (or comprehension) and generative skill (or production), as expressed in language development or competency of humans, apes, and dolphins. Several concepts central to language in general are also discussed including reference and syntax.

Language Comprehension and Language Production in Humans

Although human language is often discussed as if it were a unitary system, language comprehension and production are in certain respects distinct processes, and their respective skills can differ markedly. Clinical studies of patients suffering language disorders demonstrate that lesions can selectively affect receptive or productive capabilities, producing distinct aphasic syndromes (Luria 1965; Geschwind 1969). Patients with lesions in Wernicke's area, for example, have difficulty comprehending language but can speak fluently and grammatically, albeit not necessarily with much meaning. Patients with lesions in Broca's area generally comprehend language well but have difficulty producing fluent grammatical sentences, although these syndromes seldom leave all other perceptual and nonlinguistic skills intact (Lieberman 1984). The implication is that although language production and comprehension in the normal human adult appear to be mediated by a single, unitary language system, they are better conceived of as separate systems that become functionally integrated during the period of development of language skills, and thereafter.

Studies with young children have generally shown that language comprehension precedes and exceeds language production (Fraser et al. 1963; Ingram 1974; Benedict 1979) and that production may involve more complex processes than does comprehension (Bloom 1974; Schiefelbusch 1974). Findings with adults show that receptive vocabularies typically greatly exceed expressive vocabularies, and that when learning a second language adults generally experience greater speed and success in understanding the new language than in speaking it (e.g. Winitz 1981). Of course, understanding of the spoken word is often aided by social, contextual, and nonlinguistic factors. This does not invalidate the premise that the level of receptive language skill exceeds productive skill because, in a sense, these context cues themselves require comprehension, suggesting that the individual can bring to bear a broad range of receptive skills when analyzing the meaning of an utterance.

One factor implicated in the greater difficulty with language production may be the reliance of language production on memory recall processes, in contrast to the recognition processes characterizing language comprehension. To produce a meaningful utterance the mental representation associated with an appropriate word (or gesture) has to be accessed in the speaker's memory, the symbolic code produced, and conversational conventions accommodated so that the addressee can form some notion of the speaker's intended meaning. Such conventions are varied and place considerable constraints on language production. For example, speakers have to maintain a modicum of relevance, brevity, and the like (Grice 1975, 1978) to be understood. Aside from this, and similar issues in the domain of pragmatics, the distinction between language production and comprehension regarding demands on memory processes remains: In a sense, recall is the speaker's central problem, and recognition the addressee's.

At some level, recognition and recall must rely on identical cognitive features (Gregg 1986): for example, knowledge of the lexicon, the presence of mental representations for the semantic units of the language, and the ability to retrieve those representations (Tulving 1968a, 1974). However, there are instances where recall and recognition do not rely on the same features, and cases where the former can exist without the latter, as well as the converse. It is not surprising that recognition can exist without recall. We have all had the experience of being unable to produce an unusual sought-after word although we may recognize it immediately on hearing it (Brown & McNeill 1966). The same young child who uses "doggie" to refer to several different animals (an overextension of meaning) will nevertheless consistently choose the toy dog when asked to select the doggie from among several stuffed animals (Clark 1983). Overextensions may thus reflect the child's difficulty in recalling the correct name for an animal, rather than an inability to recognize the distinguishing features of different animals.

Recall without recognition can also exist (Tulving 1968b). We may be able to recall a word if given an opportunity, but may fail to distinguish it correctly from among alternatives in a multiple-choice test. This type of recognition error is especially prominent when target items are low in discriminability, when they lack differentiation between each other on numerous dimensions (Olson 1970) or are very similar to distractor items in the recognition test (Santa & Lamwers 1974). (However, see Mandler [1972] and Rabinowitz et al. [1977] regarding the difficulty of recognizing objects in some contexts, and Tulving [1981] regarding the counterintuitive effect of similarity between distractor and target.) The double dissociation of the two cognitive capabilities—the fact that each can exist either with or without the other (Teuber 1955)—suggests that different central mechanisms or processes may be involved (Lezak 1976), as proposed, for example, in Anderson & Bower's (1972) model where recall is a two-stage process and recognition a one-stage process. There is evidence that recognition processes develop before recall process in the infant (Piaget 1968; Piaget & Inhelder 1973; c.f. Mandler 1984), suggesting that comprehension skills are supported at an earlier age than production skills.

There are thus several dimensions in which comprehension and production appear to differ at least in part: cognitive structures, cognitive processes, and developmental progressions. The sum of these differences tends to magnify the theoretical distinction between comprehension and production, and heightens the importance of examining for differences in comprehension and production in tests of language competencies of animals and humans.

The Reference and Meaning of Words

The concept of reference has been of heightened interest in some of the recent literature on animal language (e.g. Premack 1985; Terrace 1985; Savage-Rumbaugh 1986; Herman 1988, 1989; Schusterman & Gisiner 1988, 1989). The questions considered include whether words may come to have a referential function for animals exposed to language training, and what criteria shall be used to test for the presence of that function. Again, a brief review of the concepts of reference and meaning as developed in analyses of human language may provide a helpful perspective for subsequent discussions of findings on animal language.

In human languages, content words function to refer to objects, actions, properties and relationships (Luria 1981). The words direct the attention of the listener to those items of interest to the speaker. Bruner (1983: 68), elaborating on earlier work of Putnam (1975), emphasized that "reference is a form of social interaction having to do with the management of joint attention." The mere utterance of the word may not be sufficient, however, for the listener to perceive the speaker's intended meaning, in part because meaning and reference are not necessarily coextensive (though of course it is possible to collapse that distinction for purposes of analysis). Reference—particularly in a brief discussion such as this—resists simple explanation for a number of reasons. Notable among these is the fact that a speaker can use one word to invoke one referent and yet vary the meaning of the utterance by using tropes such as metaphor. Moreover, because words are polysemous (Glucksberg et al. 1985) one word may have multiple referents: a "table" may be a piece of furniture, a listing of data, or a flat plateau. Nor is it the case that a referent must have only one appropriate symbolic label.

Early notions of word-meaning such as the referential theory of meaning (Alston 1972) equated the object and the symbol's meaning: the meaning of the word was simply the thing to which it referred (Mill 1843/1930; Frege 1892; Meinong 1904/

1960; Russell 1905). This definition usually requires that all words (including logical particles such as "if," "the," "and") have specific referents, and that symmetry exists between names and objects, each invoking the other (though admittedly some writers claim it is reasonable to resolve this inconsistency by classifying logical particles as unique cases). It may sometimes be suitable to expect first-graders to see a picture of a small visored beanie and write the word "CAP" alongside it, but it is certainly not the case that the subtleties of nonliteral language use such as sarcasm (Ackerman 1982), antiphraisis (direct contradiction) (Ackerman 1983), irony (Clark & Gerrig 1984; Jorgensen et al. 1984), meiosis (understatement) (Demorest et al. 1983) and hyperbole (Zillmann et al. 1984) conform to such unidimensional theories. For example, if enough background information is furnished, sarcasm can be discerned in a few lines of text even though paralinguistic cues are absent and the literal meaning of the passage directly contradicts its implied meaning (Kreuz & Glucksberg 1989).

Moreover, it can be argued that words refer to concepts rather than to specific entities—to "tableness" (i.e., the defining features of a table) rather than to "tables" (Lieberman 1984). The word and its referent are thus not equivalent, reversible in their function (c.f. Herman 1989; Schusterman & Gisiner 1989). Words have in part a referential function—object words exist to refer to objects—but objects do not exist to refer to object words.

In Austin's (1962) analysis, utterances function as *bona fide* acts that exert a palpable force capable of getting specific things done in specific conversational contexts. In Searle's (1969, 1975) expansions of Austin's thesis, as well as in later revisions (Bach & Harnish 1979; Clark & Carlson 1982a, 1982b), the utterances that a speaker produces are categorized according to their pragmatic effect. For example, effectives (e.g. "I now pronounce you husband and wife") and commissives (e.g. "I promise to be there"), as well as the other four or five types of speech acts, can change the state of the world simply by being uttered in the proper conversational context. In this sense, speech acts are like any other behavior that produces an effect on others or on the material world.

Speech acts retain their power, their ability to accomplish, by virtue of their role as *signals* (see Grice 1957, 1968; Schiffer 1972; Clark 1985). In contrast, *signs* are produced without any overt intention to communicate. (The term "sign" continues to be used by convention when discussing natural gestural languages although such gestures clearly function as signals.) Signals are intentionally offered for the purpose of conveying information. The grunt of a weight-lifter bench pressing 200 kg is a sign; the sound may have communicative value to bystanders, but no intention to communicate was necessarily involved. An eight-year old groaning as she lifts a pencil to do her homework is more likely to be a signal, an intentionally produced symbol meant to have communicative value. The child's groans, and most speech for that matter, are *m-intended* in Grice's terminology, that is, intended to be meaningful.

Speech-act theory is compatible with work that portrays the meaning of an utterance as if it is constructed by the addressee through a series of hypotheses (Harris & Monaco 1978; Neisser 1976). For example, such hypothesis-generation seems involved when addressees attempt to determine the meaning of the gestures that accompany spontaneous speech (Morrel-Samuels 1989), resolve optical illusions (Hochberg 1978), comprehend artificially-synthesized speech (Remez et al. 1981) and interpret written text (Quine 1960; Davidson 1974; Fish 1980; Bechtel 1988). On this view, words lack immutable meaning, but can convey meaning by virtue of the addressee's hypotheses about the speaker's intended meaning (Krauss 1985; Krauss & Morrel-Samuels 1988). In effect, the addressee attempts to account for the linguistic and nonlinguistic contexts in which the speech occurs. Research on animal language competencies likewise suggests that context can play a role in the interpretation given to signals (Savage-Rumbaugh 1986; see Wilder, chapter 3 of this reader). Context-guided interpretations of signals may also appear in natural communication among animals as, for example, when the alarm call of the young vervet monkey is ignored by adults because of its referential imprecision. For example, the alarm call for the martial eagle may be used by the youngster in the presence of a variety of nonpredatory birds (Seyfarth & Cheney 1986).

The implication of the preceding discussion for the animal language work is that reference is a multi-faceted phenomenon not easily tied down by any criterion in isolation nor established by any single experiment or experimental paradigm (Herman 1987b, 1988). A test of symmetry (interchangeability of symbol and referent— Schusterman & Gisiner 1988) or tests for correct symbol use in both production and comprehension (Savage-Rumbaugh & Rumbaugh 1978) are suggested approaches of varying validity and usefulness for analyzing the referential function of symbols. The degree to which a symbol functions to refer requires the application of multiple tests and multiple criteria of reference (see Herman 1987b). Furthermore, the experimenter should be alert to how environmental and linguistic contexts may alter or constrain the animal's interpretation of the symbol's meaning. Some of the most interesting and useful analyses of linguistic and cognitive skills may derive from careful attention to context effects in symbol use or comprehension.

Language Production Skills of Apes

The pioneering sign-language studies of the Gardners (e.g. R. Gardner & Gardner 1969; B. Gardner & Gardner 1971) and the early keyboard studies of Rumbaugh (1977) placed great emphasis on language production by their chimpanzee subjects. The chimpanzees were encouraged to produce gestures or to press symbols on the keyboard to request desired foods or events, to name objects, or to answer simply-framed questions. In both language projects the researchers looked for the appropriate use of symbols, the growth of vocabulary, and evidence of spontaneous combinations of gestures or symbols to create new or expanded meaning, just as takes place with children moving beyond the one-word stage of language (Brown 1973). The early results appeared to indicate that the language development by the chimpanzees followed the course for young children. In later evaluations, however, two issues became of central concern: linguistic reference and sentence construction abilities. The first issue addressed whether the gestures or symbols generated by the apes functioned as references to real-world objects or events, or as non-referential instrumental acts suitable for obtaining a desired outcome. The second issue considered whether the production of sequences of signs or symbols by the animals obeyed any structural (grammatical) rules, whether there was a growth in the mean length of an utterance with growing experience in the language, and whether sequences of symbols added any significant meaning beyond that already available with single signs or symbols.

Savage-Rumbaugh (Savage-Rumbaugh 1986; Savage-Rumbaugh & Rumbaugh 1978; Savage-Rumbaugh et al. 1980a) demonstrated that requesting desirables by use of their "names" did not necessarily result in the names acquiring a referring function. In fact, linguistic competence need not be involved to any degree, because such naming can be explained as the execution of a simple, learned S-R association. Symbol (word) production in this case has an instrumental, or "pure performative" function (Savage-Rumbaugh 1986: 16). However, the referring function of the symbol may be within the grasp of the ape using procedures that specifically train for the management of joint attention by two apes. Savage-Rumbaugh & Rumbaugh (1978) constructed a situation that emphasized both the production and comprehension of symbols and in which communication between two apes through these symbols led to distinct, pragmatic outcomes determined by both semantic and contextual constraints. In effect, as in the tenets of speech-act theory, signal production by one ape affected the behavior of the other in ways intended by the signal producer.

The Gardners (R. Gardner & Gardner 1984) showed that under controlled testing conditions the chimpanzee Washoe was able to produce the appropriate gestural sign for a wide variety of objects displayed on color slides. Similar results were obtained in other ape language studies (e.g. Patterson 1978). However, the use of a gestural sign in these vocabulary tests differs from the demonstrations of Savage-Rumbaugh & Rumbaugh (1978) in that there was no intention to communicate or to affect another's behavior. Although the results of the Gardners and of Patterson are not inconsistent with the notion that the gesture signs are being used referentially, they are not sufficient to demonstrate that function.

Analyses of the sign sequences produced by apes have not, in general, revealed evidence of sentence construction or of any underlying syntactic structure. Apes appear to use signs in relatively arbitrary orders; ordering does not seem to convey differential meaning, and longer sequences do not seem to add new meaning (Savage-Rumbaugh et al. 1980b; Terrace et al. 1979). Furthermore, Terrace et al. (1979) reported that the bulk of the signs and sign combinations used by his chimpanzee Nim were prompted by cues available from the trainers interacting with the ape. Terrace also claimed to find evidence for similar prompting in the Gardners' videotapes of signing by Washoe. Terrace's analyses, if generally correct, mark the question of syntactic understanding as moot, since signing is seen primarily as an act of copying. Terrace's conclusions have been challenged, however, on the grounds that the training procedures he used with Nim, and the conditions under which Nim was maintained, were very different from those used with other signing apes (see e.g. Fouts 1983; Miles 1983; c.f. Terrace 1983). These other investigators have reported more sign spontaneity by their subjects than was found for Nim.

Lana, the ape studied by Rumbaugh (1977), produced sequences of symbols to obtain a desired food or event, name a person, or use a pronoun. Thompson & Church (1980) showed, however, that these symbol strings could be accounted for by at most six "stock" sentence frames, or obligatory sequences, to which Lana simply added the missing symbol for the particular food, event or name. Thompson and Church saw no basis for concluding that Lana had any awareness of the meaning of the obligatory symbols used, a conclusion reached also by Savage-Rumbaugh et al. (1980a). These and other negative results have apparently driven researchers away from the further study of the syntactic processing abilities of the apes, and have at times led them to subordinate the importance of syntax to reference for an analysis of language competency (e.g. Terrace 1985).

Language Comprehension by Apes

Premack (1971, 1976) was the only early researcher of ape language competencies who devoted substantial consideration to comprehension. He provided evidence for the apes' understanding of a variety of concepts and propositions—same-different, if-then, negation, quantifiers, spatial relationships, and so forth—all expressed within the framework of an imposed artificial language in which plastic shapes of various colors stood for objects, actions, and properties. These concepts and propositions were viewed by Premack as "exemplars" of the semantic attributes of a natural language. Premack suggested that competency with these exemplars of language was, in effect, evidence of competency in language, a conclusion contested strongly by Terrace (1979). Terrace's view was that these competencies are demonstrations of problem-solving skills, and of generalization, but that the set of skills, no matter how impressive, does not constitute language.

In other language experiments Premack (1976) showed that the chimpanzee Sarah could respond appropriately to rearranged sequences of symbols, where meaning was partly determined by the sequence—as in (Put) RED ON GREEN versus (Put) GREEN ON RED. The ability to arrange the real-world conditions according to the dictates of the sequence of symbols appeared to be evidence for syntactic processing. Unfortunately, this experiment, as well as some of the others reported by Premack (1976), was flawed by procedural problems, particularly in the establishment of strong, contextually constraining situations that may have guided the responses of the ape (Terrace 1979). On the whole, methodology aside, many of the results of Premack's studies seem reasonable and we have little doubt that if repeated with additional controls substantial evidence of good comprehension would be obtained.

All of the cited studies with chimpanzees have been of *Pan troglodytes*, the common chimpanzee. Recently, Savage-Rumbaugh has begun language studies with *Pan paniscus*, the pygmy chimpanzee (see Savage-Rumbaugh & Brakke, chapter 18 of this reader). *Pan paniscus* is notably different from *Pan troglodytes* in its ecology, physical appearance, vocal repertoire, social structure and behavioral characteristics (Susman 1984). The language work with the pygmy chimpanzee initially focused on symbol production, using a portable plastic keyboard that could be carried around a large natural enclosure by the experimenter as she accompanied the chimpanzee subject (Savage-Rumbaugh et al. 1985; Savage-Rumbaugh 1986). The subject, Kanzi, was not given explicit symbol training but learned to use the keyboard by observing his mother undergoing formal training in its use. However, he soon became more proficient in its use than his mother, and used the keyboard to refer to foods, objects, and places he wished to visit. Unlike most of the studies with *Pan troglodytes*, spoken language was used with Kanzi; the experimenters commented on Kanzi's responses, asked him questions, and called Kanzi's attention to events occurring or about to occur in the habitat. Savage-Rumbaugh has recently formalized the use of spoken language and has demonstrated Kanzi's facility in understanding spoken English imperative sentences (Savage-Rumbaugh 1989). The level of understanding appears remarkably high, and poses a marked contrast to anything that has been demonstrated previously about chimpanzee language competencies through studies of language production (Savage-Rumbaugh & Sevcik 1984).

Language Comprehension by Dolphins

Savage-Rumbaugh's recent demonstration with Kanzi is similar in principle to the comprehension approach taken in language work with dolphins by Herman and his associates (Herman et al. 1984; Herman 1986). Each of two bottlenosed dolphins was tutored in a specially-constructed artificial language. One dolphin was specialized in a language in which words were represented by computer-generated sounds. For the second dolphin, words were represented by gestures of a signer's arms and hands, as in human sign languages. In each case, the words referred to objects, actions, properties, and relationships. Combinations of words, or "sentences," were constructed according to a set of word-order rules that allowed for the creation of more than 2000 sentences, each having a unique meaning. Imperative sentences, up to five words in length, were instructions to carry out named actions relative to named objects and object modifiers. Some sentences (non-relational sequences) required an action to a single object. For example, the sentence LEFT BALL TOSS asks the dolphin to toss the ball on her left in the air. Other sentences (relational sequences) required the dolphin to construct a spatial relationship between two named objects, by taking one object to another or by putting one object inside or on top of another. For example, PERSON SURFBOARD FETCH, instructs the dolphin to take a surfboard to a person (who is in the water).

Different sequences of the same words created different instructions as in the semantic contrasts requesting the dolphin to take the surfboard to the person (PERSON SURFBOARD FETCH) versus the person to the surfboard (SURFBOARD PERSON FETCH). Comprehension of these sequences required that the dolphin take account not only of the meanings of the individual words but of their sequence. Comprehension of the language was measured by the accuracy of response to the instructions. Comprehension was in general good and understanding of new instructions was in most cases not significantly different from the understanding of familiar instructions (Herman et al. 1984).

The dolphin's ability to understand and answer simple interrogatives was also tested (Herman & Forestell 1985). Binary (Yes/No) responses were required to questions about the status of named objects, that is, questions asking whether a named object was or was not present in the dolphin's tank. The sequence HOOP QUESTION, for example, asks whether a hoop is present. Answers were given by pressing one of two paddles to indicate presence ("Yes") or absence ("No"). Overall, the answers accurately described the real-world situation, and reports of "absence" were as reliably given as reports of "presence."

In further work, responses to the "Yes" and "No" paddles were used by the dolphin to, in effect, report her ability to construct a relationship between two objects (Forestell 1988). As an example, in response to an imperative to take a ball to a basket, but with no basket present in the tank, the dolphin transported the ball to the "No" paddle. In contrast, if both the ball and basket were present, the dolphin typically either constructed the relationship requested or transported the ball to the "Yes" paddle. Finally, if the ball was absent, but the basket present, the dolphin pressed the "No" paddle directly. These different types of responses were performed spontaneously by the dolphin on the first occasion presented, were performed reliably thereafter, and were applied to any objects named.

These comprehension studies give evidence of both semantic and syntactic processing by dolphins. The responses of the dolphins were consistent with the meaning of the words in a sequence and with the constraints imposed by word-order, and also appeared to take account of the state of the world. The "sense of grammaticality" of the dolphin within its artificial language was tested further in a series of studies examining responses to anomalous sentence constructions. These were sequences of words that departed from the word-order rules of the language or that contained grammatically and semantically correct subsets of words within longer anomalous strings (Herman et al. 1984; Herman 1986, 1987b, 1988, 1989; Holder et al. 1989). Among other things, the results of these studies revealed the ability of the dolphin to relate nonadjacent words in an anomalous string and to delete extraneous words from the string in order to construct a semantically and syntactically correct sequence. For example, the sequence WATER SPEAKER HOOP FETCH is an anomaly in that (1) there is no existing syntactic rule in the language that relates three object words and, (2) the sequence Object 1 + Object 2 normally communicates that a relationship is to be constructed between those two objects, with the second named object transported to and then placed in, on, or beside the first object, as specified by the sentence's terminal verb (FETCH or IN). In the example given, the second word, SPEAKER, is not transportable since it is mounted on the wall of the tank. In this and similar cases, the dolphin typically deletes the second word of the string and takes the third-named object (e.g. HOOP) to the first-named object (e.g. WATER—represented by a stream of water entering the tank). Evidence that the dolphin recognizes the embedded semantic anomaly comes from the presentation of the shorter sequence WATER SPEAKER FETCH. In this case no transportable object is specified. The typical response of the dolphin with an anomaly of this type is to reject the entire sequence by not responding at all.

These studies of the receptive competencies of dolphins within artificial languages thus demonstrate sensitivity to syntactic constraints, and suggest an awareness of the boundaries of the language's syntactic rules (Herman 1987b). In contrast, the studies with apes that have emphasized their productive skills have found little or no convincing evidence for the understanding or use of syntactic constraints. This contrast between what may be found with emphasis on comprehension rather than on language production is reminiscent of findings from studies of young children in which tests of receptive skills have revealed language competencies of preverbal or nonverbal children (e.g. Ingram 1974; Curtiss 1977), or have demonstrated grammatical competencies beyond those measured through analyses of spoken language (e.g. Strohner & Nelson 1974; Chapman & Miller 1975). Also, as was noted earlier, studies of young children have found that, in general, comprehension of language precedes and exceeds language production (e.g. Ingram 1974). In an interesting parallel, findings with wild vervet monkeys demonstrate that comprehension of social vocalizations or of alarm calls develops before these sounds are produced reliably in an appropriate context (Seyfarth & Cheney 1986; Hauser 1989).

The syntactic rules of their language were not explicitly taught to the dolphins. Nevertheless, they acquired an implicit knowledge of those rules through experience with exemplars of proper strings of 2- or 3-words. However, 4-word strings, which were logical combinations of nonrelational and relational rules for shorter strings, were understood immediately the first time they were given to the dolphins (Herman et al. 1984). Thus, the dolphins' knowledge of the syntactic rules is implicit and is acquired primarily through exposure to grammatically correct sequences. This knowledge allows for effective responding to novel syntactic structures, including those that are grammatically correct and those that are not. Similarly, human subjects exposed to artificial grammars, and who receive no explicit instruction in the underlying grammar, can nevertheless make correct judgments of the grammaticality of novel strings (Reber 1967). Furthermore, these subjects are not able to describe the grammar explicitly if so asked. In other work of Reber and associates (Reber et al. 1980) it was shown that if the underlying grammar was relatively complex, implicit learning was more effective for learning about that grammatical structure than was explicit instruction in the grammar. Children learning a natural language likewise develop a sense of grammaticality through implicit learning attained by exposure to many examples. The dolphins' knowledge of the syntactic rules of their languages thus appears to be acquired in ways analogous to that described for human children, and for human adults in the situations studied by Reber.

The ability of the dolphin to understand a reference to an absent object, and to respond appropriately to such references (Herman & Forestell 1985; Forestell 1988) suggests that the symbols of the language have acquired a referential function for the dolphin. Yet, the existence of this referring function is not necessarily established (or denied) by any single criterion. For example, the claim that exchangeability (symmetry) of symbol and referent is the *sine qua non* of reference (Schusterman & Gisiner 1988, 1989) in effect denies that the referent can evoke mental representations beyond that elicited by the symbol, and that some of those representations may be substantially different from that elicited by the symbol (Herman 1988, 1989).

As we emphasized earlier, an analysis of what words mean to the subject will benefit from a variety of convergent tests using multiple criteria. As an example, some sentences given the dolphins included novel words, where unknown sounds or gestures were inserted into familiar sentence frames (Herman 1987b). Thus, the simple sentence BALL OVER might be re-stated as X OVER, or as BALL Y, where X and Y are vocabulary items not known to the dolphins. Typically, the dolphins rejected these instructions if the unknown word occurred in the terminal position reserved for an action word (BALL Y), but responded to an arbitrary object if the unknown word appeared in the place of an object word (X OVER). The latter type of response was likely a reflection of the early training of the dolphins during which action words were sometimes given alone, and the dolphin was allowed to respond to any object of its choice. But, by rejecting sentences containing unknown action words the dolphins demonstrated knowledge of the lexical boundaries of their language and an understanding that responses cannot be executed without an action term. At the same time, the dolphins' rejection of semantic anomalies containing familiar words where the instruction was not capable of execution (as in the sentence WATER SPEAKER FETCH), indicates that both lexical and semantic analyses of a sentence were made when organizing a response (or deciding not to respond).

Recent work with dolphins at our laboratory has demonstrated their ability to interpret televised images of signers and of highly degraded gestures (Herman 1987c; Herman et al. 1990). In these studies the dolphin looks at a small television screen placed behind an underwater window, and views the gestures of a trainer being televised at a remote location. During the initial tests, the arms, head and torso of the signer were visible on the screen. In subsequent trials the images were progressively degraded, so that only arms and hands, or only hands appeared. Even when the signer's hands were supplanted by two spots of white light tracing out the path of the gesture (a "point-light" display), the dolphin's comprehension remained high despite the fact that no explicit training was involved. As might be expected, performance in the fully degraded point-light condition was significantly poorer than in the less-degraded conditions. Nevertheless, results from a comparative study show that the dolphin's performance was not significantly different from our intermediate-level trainers tested with the same point-light displays shown the dolphin (Herman et al. 1990). These findings—as well as evidence for cerebral asymmetry in the dolphin (Morrel-Samuels et al. 1989)—suggest that dolphins retain representations of gestures in memory, and process those representations in a manner that is similar to the way humans process referential symbols.

These results, together with those presented earlier on responses to absent objects and to lexical and semantic anomalies, provide converging lines of evidence for the referential function of the signs used in the language. More generally, the examination of the receptive skills of dolphins has revealed capabilities for semantic and syntactic processing, and suggests that the dolphins utilize a rich network of mental representations when responding to language-mediated tasks. That such demonstrations have proved rather elusive in studies emphasizing productive skills reflects the difficulty of obtaining objective, replicable data in such studies and, more importantly, supports the hypothesis of an attenuation of productive skills relative to receptive skills.

Conclusions

The language comprehension work with the dolphins, the recent work by Savage-Rumbaugh with the pygmy chimpanzee Kanzi, and some of the earlier work of Premack, have revealed competencies for language not realized in other work emphasizing language production. The message from these findings is twofold: (1) animals, in general, seem engineered primarily as efficient, broadband monitors of their world and through their genetic, developmental, experiential and social endowments are able to acquire, retain and utilize extensive knowledge of that world; and (2) the potential of animals for displaying language competencies is more closely approximated by examining receptive skills rather than productive abilities, bearing in mind that there are apparent substantial asymmetries in receptive and productive mechanisms, processes and skills.

Acknowledgements

Preparation of this paper was supported by Contract N00014-85-K-0210 from the Office of Naval Research and from a grant from the Center for Field Research (Earthwatch). Release time provided by an appointment of L. H. to the Social Science Research Institute of the University of Hawaii provided the opportunity to prepare this paper. We thank Kathy Eblen for her dedicated help in preparing the manuscript.

Literature Cited

Ackerman, B. P. 1982. Contextual integration and utterance interpretation: The ability of children and adults to interpret sarcastic utterances. *Child Development* 53, 1075–1083.
———. 1983. Form and function in children's understanding of ironic utterances. *Journal of Experimental Child Psychology* 35, 487–508.
Anderson, J. R. & Bower, G. H. 1972. Recognition and retrieval processes in free recall. *Psychological Review* 79, 97–123.

Alston, W. 1972. Meaning. In: *The Encyclopedia of Philosophy*, Volume 5 (ed. by P. Edwards), pp. 233–241. New York: MacMillan & Free Press.

Austin, J. L. 1962. *How to Do Things with Words*. Oxford, England: Oxford University Press.

Bach, K. & Harnish, R. M. 1979. *Linguistic Communication and Speech Acts*. Cambridge, Massachusetts: M.I.T. Press.

Bechtel, W. 1988. *Philosophy of Mind: An Overview for Cognitive Science*. Hillsdale, New Jersey: Lawrence Erlbaum Associates.

Benedict, N. 1979. Early lexical development: Comprehension and production. *Journal of Child Language* 6, 183–200.

Bloom, L. 1974. Talking, understanding, and thinking: Development relationship between receptive and expressive language. In: *Language Perspectives—Acquisition, Retardation, and Intervention* (ed. by R. L. Schiefelbusch & L. L. Lloyd), pp. 285–311. Baltimore, Maryland: University Park Press.

Brown, R. 1973. *A First Language*. Cambridge, Massachusetts: Harvard University Press.

Brown, R. & McNeill, D. 1966. The "tip of the tongue" phenomenon. *Journal of Verbal Learning and Verbal Behavior* 5, 325–337.

Bruner, J. 1983. *Child's Talk: Learning to Use Language*. New York: W. W. Norton.

Caldwell, M. C. & Caldwell, D. K. 1966. Epimeletic (care-giving) behavior in Cetacea. In: *Whales, Dolphins and Porpoises* (ed. by K. S. Norris), pp. 755–789. Berkeley, California: University of California Press.

————. 1967. Intra-specific transfer of information via the pulsed sound in captive odontocete cetaceans. In: *Animal Sonar Systems*, Volume II (ed. by R. G. Busnel), pp. 879–936. Jouy-en-Josas, France: Laboratoire de Physiologie Acoustique.

————. 1972. Behavior of marine mammals. In: *Mammals of the Sea* (ed. by S. H. Ridgway), pp. 409–465. Springfield, Illinois: Thomas.

————. 1979. The whistle of the Atlantic bottlenosed dolphin (*Tursiops truncatus*)—Ontogeny. In: *Behavior of Marine Animals: Current Perspectives in Research*. Volume 3 Cetaceans (ed. by H. E. Winn & B. L. Olla), pp. 369–401. New York: Plenum.

Chapman, R. S. & Miller, J. F. 1975. Word order in early two and three word utterances: Does production precede comprehension? *Journal of Speech and Hearing Research* 18, 355–371.

Clark, E. V. 1983. Meanings and concepts. In: *Handbook of Child Psychology: History, Theory and Methods*, Volume 1 (ed. by W. Kessen). pp. 787–840. New York: Wiley.

Clark, H. H. 1985. Language use and language users. In: *Handbook of Social Psychology*, Volume II (ed. by G. Lindzey), pp, 179–231. New York: Random House.

Clark, H. H. & Gerrig, R. J. 1984. On the pretense theory of irony. *Journal of Experimental Psychology: General* 113, 121–126.

Clark, H. H. & Carlson, T. B. 1982a. Hearers and speech acts. *Language* 58, 332–373.

————. 1982b. Speech acts and hearers' beliefs. In: *Mutual Knowledge* (ed. by N. V. Smith), pp. 1–36. London: Academic Press.

Curio, E. 1988. Cultural transmission of enemy recognition by birds. In: *Social Learning: Psychological and Biological Perspectives* (ed. by T. R. Zentall & B. G. Galef), pp. 75–97. Hillsdale, New Jersey: Lawrence Erlbaum Associates.

Curtiss, S. 1977. *Genie*. New York: Academic Press.

Davidson, D. 1974. On the very idea of a conceptual scheme. *Proceedings and addresses of the American Philosophical Association* 47, 5–20.

Dawson, W. W. 1980. The cetacean eye. In: *Cetacean Behavior: Mechanisms and Functions* (ed. by L. M. Herman); pp. 53–100. New York: Wiley Interscience.

Demorest, A., Silberstein, L., Gardner, H. & Winner, E. 1983. Telling it as it isn't: Children's understanding of figurative language. *British Journal of Developmental Psychology* 1, 121–134.

Elias, H. & Schwartz, D. 1969. Surface areas of the cerebral cortex of mammals determined by stereological methods. *Science* 166, 111–113.

Fish, S. 1980. *Is There a Text in This Class?* Cambridge, Massachusetts: Harvard University Press.

Forestell, P. H. 1988. *Reporting on Relationships Between Symbolically-Named Objects by a Dolphin (Tursiops truncatus)*. Ph.D. thesis, University of Hawaii.

Fouts, R. S. 1983. Chimpanzee language and elephant tails: A theoretical synthesis. In: *Language in Primates: Perspectives and Implications* (ed. by J. de Luce & H. T. Wilder), pp. 63–75. New York: Springer-Verlag.

Fraser, C., Bellugi, U. & Brown, R. W. 1963. Control of grammar in imitation, comprehension and production. *Journal of Verbal Learning and Verbal Behavior* 2, 121–135.

Frege, G. 1892. Über Sinn und Bedeutung [On sense and reference]. *Zeitschrift für Philosophie und Philosophische Kritik* 100, 25–50.

Gardner, B. T. & Gardner, R. A. 1971. Two-way communication with an infant chimpanzee. In: *Behavior of Nonhuman Primates* (ed. by A. M. Schrier & F. Stollnitz), pp. 117–184. New York: Academic Press.

Gardner, R. A. & Gardner, B. T. 1969. Teaching sign language to a chimpanzee. *Science* 165, 664–762.

———. 1984. A vocabulary test for chimpanzees (*Pan troglodytes*). *Journal of Comparative Psychology* 98, 381–404.

Geschwind, N. 1969. Problems in the anatomical understanding of the aphasias. In: *Contributions to Clinical Neuropsychology* (ed. by A. L. Benton), pp. 107–128. Chicago, Illinois: Aldine.

Glezer, I. I., Jacobs, M. S. & Morgane, P. J. 1988. Implications of the "initial brain" concept for brain evolution in Cetacea. *Behavioral and Brain Sciences* 11, 75–116.

Glucksberg, S., Kreuz, R. J. & Rho, S. 1985. Context can constrain lexical access: Implications for models of language comprehension. *Journal of Experimental Psychology: Learning, Memory and Cognition* 12, 323–335.

Goodall, J. 1986. *The Chimpanzees of Gombe: Patterns of Behavior.* Cambridge, Massachusetts: Belknap Press.

Gregg, V. H. 1986. *Introduction to Human Memory.* Boston, Massachusetts: Routledge.

Grice, H. P. 1957. Meaning. *Philosophical Review,* 66, 377–388.

———. 1968. Utterer's meaning, sentence-meaning, and word-meaning. *Foundation of Language* 4, 225–242.

———. 1975. Logic and conversation. In: *Syntax and Semantics 3: Speech Acts* (ed. by P. Cole & J. L. Morgan), pp. 41–58. New York: Academic Press.

———. 1978. Some further notes on logic and conversation. In: *Syntax and Semantics 9: Pragmatics* (ed. by P. Cole), pp. 113–128. New York: Academic Press.

Harris, R. J. & Monaco, G. E. 1978. Psychology of pragmatic implication: Information processing between the lines. *Journal of Experimental Psychology: General* 107, 1–22.

Hauser, M. D. 1989. Ontogenetic changes in the comprehension and production of vervet monkey (*Cercopithecus aethiops*), vocalizations. *Journal of Comparative Psychology* 103, 149–158.

Herman, L. M. 1980. Cognitive characteristics of dolphins. In: *Cetacean Behavior: Mechanisms and Functions* (ed. by L. M. Herman), pp. 363–429. New York: Wiley Interscience.

———. 1986. Cognition and language competencies of bottlenosed dolphins. In: *Dolphin Cognition and Behavior: A Comparative Approach* (ed. by R. J. Schusterman, J. Thomas, & F. G. Wood), pp. 221–252. Hillsdale, New Jersey: Lawrence Erlbaum Associates.

———. 1987a. Do animals understand more than they can generate? Paper presented at the *Third International Conference on Thinking.* Honolulu, Hawaii.

———. 1987b. Receptive competencies of language-trained animals. In: *Advances in the Study of Behavior,* Volume 17 (ed. by J. S. Rosenblatt, C. Beer, C. M-C. Busnel, & P. J. B. Slater), pp. 1–60. Petaluma, California: Academic Press.

———. 1987c. The visual dolphin. Paper presented at the *7th Biennial Conference on the Biology of Marine Mammals.* Miami, Florida.

———. 1988. The language of animal language research: Reply to Schusterman & Gisiner. *The Psychological Record* 38, 349–362.

———. 1989. In which Procrustean bed does the sea lion sleep tonight? *The Psychological Record* 39, 19–50.

———. 1990. What the dolphin knows, or might know, in its natural world. In: *School Structure and Social Behavior of Wild Delphinids* (ed. by K. Pryor & K. S. Norris), Los Angeles, California: University of California Press, pp. 349–364.

Herman, L. M. & Forestell, P. H. 1985. Reporting presence or absence of named objects by a language-trained dolphin. *Neuroscience and Biobehavioral Reviews* 9, 667–681.

Herman, L. M., Hovancik, J. R., Gory, J. D., & Bradshaw, G. L. 1989a. Generalization of visual matching by a bottlenosed dolphin (*Tursiops truncatus*): Evidence for invariance of cognitive performance with visual or auditory materials. *Journal of Experimental Psychology: Animal Behavior Processes* 15, 124–136.

Herman, L. M., Morrel-Samuels, P. & Brown, L. A. 1989b. Dolphins recall and imitate action sequences. Paper presented at the meeting of the *Psychonomic Society,* Atlanta, Georgia.

Herman, L. M., Morrel-Samuels, P. & Pack, A. A. (1990). Bottlenosed dolphin and human recognition of veridical and degraded video displays of an artificial gestural language. *Journal of Experimental Psychology: General* 119, 215–230.

Herman, L. M., Peacock, M. F., Yunker, M. P. & Madsen, C. 1975. Bottlenosed dolphin: Double slit pupil yields equivalent aerial and underwater diurnal acuity. *Science* 139, 650–652.

Herman, L. M., Richards, D. G. & Wolz, J. P. 1984. Comprehension of sentences by bottlenosed dolphins. *Cognition* 16, 129–219.

Herman, L. M. & Tavolga, W. N. 1980. The communication systems of cetaceans. In: *Cetacean Behavior: Mechanisms and Functions* (ed. by L. M. Herman), pp. 149–209. New York: Wiley Interscience.

Hochberg, J. 1978. *Perception*. Englewood Cliffs, New Jersey: Prentice-Hall.

Holder, M. D., Kuczaj, S. A. II & Herman, L. M. 1989. A dolphin's response to nongrammatical sequences. Paper presented at the meeting of the *Psychonomic Society*. Atlanta, Georgia.

Ingram, D. 1974. The relationship between comprehension and production. In: *Language Perspectives— Acquisition, Retardation, and Intervention* (ed. by R. L. Schiefelbusch and L. L. Lloyd), pp. 313–334. Baltimore, Maryland: University Park Press.

Jenkins, P. F. 1978. Cultural transmission of song patterns and dialect development in a free-living bird population. *Animal Behaviour* 25, 50–78.

Jerison, H. J. 1978. Brain and intelligence in whales. In: *Whales and whaling*, Vol. 2, pp. 161–198. Canberra: Australian Government Publishing Office.

Jorgensen, J., Miller, G. A. & Sperber, D. 1984. Test of the mention theory of irony. *Journal of Experimental Psychology: General* 113, 112–120.

Kawamura, S. 1963. The process of subculture propagation among Japanese macaques. In: *Primate Social Behavior* (ed. by C. H. Southwick), Toronto: Van Nostrand.

Krauss, R. M. 1985. Cognition and communication: A social psychological perspective. Paper presented at the meeting of the *American Psychological Association*, Los Angeles, California.

Krauss, R. M. & Morrel-Samuels, P. 1988. Some things we do and don't know about hand gestures. Paper presented at the meeting of the *American Association for the Advancement of Science*, Boston, Massachusetts.

Kreuz, R. J. & Glucksberg, S. 1989. How to be sarcastic: The echoic reminder theory of verbal irony. *Journal of Experimental Psychology: General* 118, 374–386.

Lezak, M. D. 1976. *Neuropsychological Assessment*. New York: Oxford University Press.

Lieberman, P. 1984. *The Biology and Evolution of Language*. Cambridge, Massachusetts: Harvard University Press.

Luria, A. R. 1965. Neuropsychology in the local diagnosis of brain damage. *Cortex* 1, 2–18.

———. 1981. *Language and Cognition*. New York: Wiley (English translation).

Madsen, C. J. & Herman, L. M. 1980. Social and ecological correlates of cetacean vision and visual appearance. In: *Cetacean Behavior: Mechanisms and Functions* (ed. by L. M. Herman), pp. 101–147. New York: Wiley Interscience.

Mandler, G. 1972. Organization and recognition. In: *Organization of Memory* (ed. by E. Tulving, W. Donaldson & G. Bower), pp. 139–166. New York: Academic Press.

Mandler, J. M. 1984. Representation and recall in infancy. In: *Infant Memory* (ed. by M. Moscovitch), pp. 75–102. New York: Plenum.

Meinong, A. 1904/1960. Über Gegenstandstheorie [The theory of objects]. In: *Untersuchungen zur Gegenstandstheorie und Psychologie*. Leipzig. (Reprinted in: *Realism and the Background of Phenomenology*. Glencoe, Illinois: Free Press).

Menzel, E. W. Jr., Davenport, R. K. & Rogers, C. M. 1972. Protocultural aspects of chimpanzee's responsiveness to novel objects. *Folia Primatologica* 17, 161–170.

Miles, H. L. 1983. Apes and language: The search for communicative competence. In: *Language in Primates* (ed. by J. de Luce & H. T. Wilder), pp. 43–61. New York: Springer-Verlag.

Mill, J. S. 1843/1930. *A System of Logic, Ratiocinative and Inductive: Being a Connected View of the Principles of Evidence and the Methods of Scientific Investigation*, 8th Edition. London, England: Longmans & Green.

Mineka, S. & Cook, M. 1988. Social learning and the acquisition of snake fear in monkeys. In: *Social Learning: Psychological and Biological Perspectives* (ed. by T. R. Zentall & B. G. Galef), pp. 51–73, Hillsdale, New Jersey: Lawrence Erlbaum Associates.

Morgane, P. J., Jacobs, M. S. & Galaburda, A. 1986. Evolutionary morphology of the dolphin brain. In: *Dolphin Cognition and Behavior: A Comparative Approach* (ed. by R. J. Schusterman, J. Thomas, & F. G. Wood), pp. 5–29. Hillsdale, New Jersey: Lawrence Erlbaum Associates.

Morrel-Samuels, P. 1989. *Gesture, Word, and Meaning: The Role of Gesture in Speech Production and Comprehension*. Ph.D. thesis, Columbia University, New York.

Morrel-Samuels, P., Herman, L. M. & Bever, T. G. 1989. A left hemisphere advantage for gesture-language signs in the dolphin. Paper presented at the meeting of the *Psychonomic Society*, Atlanta, Georgia.

Nachtigall, P. E. 1986. Vision, audition, and chemoreception in dolphins and other marine mammals. In: *Dolphin Cognition and Behavior: A Comparative Approach* (ed. by R. J. Schusterman, J. A. Thomas and F. G. Wood), pp. 79–113. Hillsdale, New Jersey: Lawrence Erlbaum Associates.

Neisser, U. 1976. *Cognition and Reality.* New York: W. H. Freeman.

Norris, K. S. & Dohl, T. P. 1980. The structure and function of cetacean schools. In: *Cetacean Behavior: Mechanisms and Functions* (ed. by L. M. Herman), pp. 211–261. New York: Wiley Interscience.

Olson, D. R. 1970. Language and thought: Aspects of a cognitive theory of semantics. *Psychological Review* 77, 257–273.

Patterson, F. G. 1978. Linguistic capabilities of a young lowland gorilla. In: *Sign Language and Language Acquisition in Man and Ape: New Dimensions in Comparative Pedolinguistics* (ed. by F. C. Peng), pp. 161–201. Boulder, Colorado: Westview Press.

Payne, K., Tyack, P. & Payne, R. 1983. Progressive changes in the songs of humpback whales (*Megaptera novaeangliae*): A detailed analysis of two seasons in Hawaii. In: *Communication and Behavior of Whales* (ed. by R. Payne), pp. 9–58. Boulder, Colorado: Westview Press.

Piaget, J. 1968. *On the Development of Memory and Identity.* Barre, Massachusetts: Clark University Press.

Piaget, J. & Inhelder, B. 1973. *Memory and Intelligence.* New York: Basic Books.

Plotkin, H. C. 1988. An evolutionary epistemological approach to the evolution of intelligence. In: *Intelligence and Evolutionary Biology* (ed. by H. J. Jerison & I. Jerison), pp. 73–91. New York: Springer-Verlag.

Popper, A. N. 1980. Sound emission and detection by delphinids. In: *Cetacean Behavior: Mechanisms and Functions* (ed. by L. M. Herman), pp. 1–52. New York: Wiley Interscience.

Premack, D. 1971. On the assessment of language competence in the chimpanzee. In: *Behavior of Nonhuman Primates*, Volume 4 (ed. by A. M. Schrier and F. Stollnitz), pp. 186–228. New York: Academic Press.

————. 1976. *Intelligence in Ape and Man.* Hillsdale, New Jersey: Lawrence Erlbaum Associates.

————. 1985. Gavagail or the future history of the animal language controversy. *Cognition* 19, 207–296.

Putnam, H. 1975. *Mind, Language and Reality.* Cambridge, England: Cambridge University Press.

Quine, W. V. O. 1960. *Word and Object.* Cambridge, Massachusetts: M.I.T. Press.

Rabinowitz, J. C., Mandler, G. & Patterson, K. E. 1977. Determinants of recognition and recall: Accessibility and generation. *Journal of Experimental Psychology: General* 106, 302–329.

Ralston, J. V. & Herman, L. M. 1989. Dolphin auditory perception. In: Complex Acoustic Perception: *The Comparative Psychology of Complex Acoustic Perception* (ed. by J. R. Dooling & S. H. Hulse), pp. 295–338. Hillsdale, New Jersey: Lawrence Erlbaum Associates.

Reber, A. S. 1967. Implicit learning of artificial grammars. *Journal of Verbal Learning and Verbal Behavior* 5, 855–865.

Reber, A. S., Kassin, S. M., Lewis, S. & Cantor, G. W. 1980. On the relationship between implicit and explicit modes in the learning of a complex rule structure. *Journal of Experimental Psychology: Human Learning & Memory* 6, 492–502.

Remez, R. E., Rubin, P. E., Pisoni, D. B. & Carrell, T. D. 1981. Speech perception without traditional speech cues. *Science* 212, 947–950.

Richards, D. G., Wolz, J. P. & Herman, L. M. 1984. Mimicry of computer-generated sounds and vocal labeling of objects by a bottlenosed dolphin. *Journal of Comparative Psychology* 98, 10–28.

Ridgway, S. H. 1986. Physiological observations of the dolphin brain. In: *Dolphin Cognition and Behavior: A Comparative Approach* (ed. by R. J. Schusterman, J. Thomas, & F. G. Wood), pp. 31–59. Hillsdale, New Jersey: Lawrence Erlbaum Associates.

Ridgway, S. H. & Brownson, R. H. 1984. Relative brain sizes and cortical surface areas of odontocetes. *Acta Zoologica Fennica* 172, 149–152.

Rumbaugh, D. M. (Ed.) 1977. *Language Learning by a Chimpanzee: The Lana Project.* New York: Academic Press.

Russell, B. 1905. On denoting. *Mind* 14, 479–493.

Santa, J. L. & Lamwers, L. L. 1974. Encoding specificity: fact or artifact? *Journal of Verbal Learning and Verbal Behavior* 13, 412–423.

Savage-Rumbaugh, E. S. 1986. *Ape Language:* From Conditioned Response to Symbol. New York: Columbia University Press.

————. 1989. Our erroneous but cherished preconceptions. Paper presented at the *Animal Language Workshop*, Honolulu, Hawaii.

Savage-Rumbaugh, E. S. & Rumbaugh, D. M. 1978. Symbolization, language, and chimpanzees: A theoretical reevaluation based on initial language acquisition processes in four young Pan troglodytes. *Brain & Language* 6, 265–300.

Savage-Rumbaugh, E. S. & Sevcik, R. 1984. Levels of communicative competency in the chimpanzee: Pre-representational and representational. In: *Behavioral Evolution and Integrative Levels* (ed. by G. Greenberg & E. Tobach), pp. 197–219. Hillsdale, New Jersey: Lawrence Erlbaum Associates.

Savage-Rumbaugh, E. S., Rumbaugh, D. M. & Boysen, S. 1980a. Do apes use language? *American Scientist* 68, 49–61.

Savage-Rumbaugh, E. S., Rumbaugh, D. M., Smith, S. T., & Lawson, J. 1980b. Reference—the linguistic essential. *Science* 210, 922–925.

Savage-Rumbaugh, E. S., Rumbaugh, D. M. & McDonald, K. 1985. Language learning in two species of apes. *Neuroscience and Biobehavioral Reviews* 9, 653–665.

Schiefelbusch, R. L. 1974. Summary. In: *Language Perspectives—Acquisition, Retardation, and Intervention* (ed. by R. L. Schiefelbusch and L. L. Lloyd), pp. 647–660. Baltimore, Maryland: University Park Press.

Schiffer, S. 1972. *Meaning.* Oxford, England: Clarendon Press.

Schusterman, R. J. & Gisiner, R. 1988. Artificial language comprehension in dolphins and sea lions: The essential cognitive skills. *The Psychological Record* 38, 311–348.

———. 1989. Please parse the sentence: Animal cognition in the Procrustean bed of linguistics. *The Psychological Record* 39, 3–18.

Searle, J. R. 1969. *Speech Acts.* Cambridge, England: Cambridge University Press.

———. 1975. A taxonomy of illocutionary acts. In: *Minnesota Studies in the Philosophy of Language* (ed. by K. Gunderson), pp. 344–369. Minneapolis, Minnesota: University of Minnesota Press.

Sergeant, D. E., Caldwell, D. K. & Caldwell, M. C. 1973. Age, growth and maturity of bottlenosed dolphins (*Tursiops truncatus*). *Journal of the Fisheries Board of Canada* 30, 1009–1011.

Seyfarth, R. M. & Cheney, D. L. 1986. Vocal development in vervet monkeys. *Animal Behaviour* 34, 1640–1658.

Strohner, H. & Nelson, K. E. 1974. The young child's development of sentence comprehension: Influence of event probability, nonverbal context, syntactic form, and strategies. *Child Development* 45, 567–576.

Susman, R. L. (ed.) 1984. *The Pygmy Chimpanzee.* New York: Plenum.

Tavolga, M. C. 1966. Behavior of the bottlenosed dolphin, *Tursiops truncatus*: Social interactions in a captive colony. In: *Whales, Dolphins and Porpoises* (ed. by K. S. Norris), pp. 718–730. Berkeley, California: University of California Press.

Tavolga, M. C. & Essapian, F. S. 1957. The behavior of the bottlenosed dolphin *Tursiops truncatus*: Mating, pregnancy, parturition and mother-infant behavior. *Zoologica* 42, 11–31.

Terrace, H. S. 1979. Is problem-solving language? *Journal of the Experimental Analysis of Behavior* 31, 161–175.

———. 1983. Apes who "talk": Language or projection of language by their teachers? In: *Language in Primates* (ed. by J. de Luce and H. T. Wilder), pp. 19–42. New York: Springer-Verlag.

———. 1985. In the beginning was the "Name." *American Psychologist* 40, 1011–1028.

Terrace, H. S., Petitto, L. A., Sanders, R. J., & Bever, T. G. 1979. Can an ape create a sentence? *Science* 200, 891–902.

Teuber, H. L. 1955. Physiological psychology. *Annual Review of Psychology* 6, 267–296.

Thompson, C. R. & Church, R. M. 1980. An explanation of language in a chimpanzee. *Science* 208, 313–314.

Tulving, E. 1968a. Theoretical issues in free recall. In: *Verbal Behavior and General Behavior Theory* (ed. by T. Dixon & D. L. Horton), pp. 2–36. Englewood Cliffs, New Jersey: Prentice-Hall.

———. 1968b. When is recall higher than recognition? *Psychonomic Science* 10, 53–54.

———. 1974. Cue-dependent forgetting. *American Scientist* 62, 74–82.

———. 1981. Similarity relations in recognition. *Journal of Verbal Learning and Verbal Behavior* 20, 479–496.

Tyack, P. 1986. Whistle repertoires of two bottlenosedd dolphins, *Tursiops truncatus*: Mimicry of signature whistles? *Behavioral Ecology and Sociobiology* 18, 251–257.

Wells, R. S., Irvine, A. G. & Scott, M. D. 1980. The social ecology of inshore odontocetes. In: *Cetacean Behavior: Mechanisms and Functions* (ed. by L. M. Herman), pp. 263–317. New York: Wiley Interscience.

Winitz, H. (Ed.) 1981. *The Comprehension Approach to Foreign Language Instruction.* Rowley, Massachusetts: Newbury House.

Xitco, M. J., Jr. 1988. *Mimicry of Modeled Behaviors by Bottlenosed Dolphins.* Masters thesis, University of Hawaii.

Zillmann, D., Masland, J. L., Weaver, J. B., Lacey, L. A., Jacobs, N. E., Dow, J. H., Klein, C. A., & Banker, S. R. 1984. Effects of humorous distortions on children's learning from education television. *Journal of Educational Psychology* 76, 802–812.

Animal Minds

Chapter 20

Evolution and Psychological Unity

Roger Crisp

Psychology will be based on a new foundation, that of the necessary acquirement of each mental power and capacity by gradation
—Darwin (1859/1968: 458)

The Principle of Psychological Continuity

Philosophers often make claims which defy common sense, such as that time does not exist or that infanticide is morally acceptable. I want to do quite the opposite in this paper. I shall argue for the common sense view that certain nonhuman animals (henceforth "animals") have conscious experiences and that often we can talk of these experiences in the same terms that we use of our own experiences.

But why argue for what is anyway common sense? For a reason I have already suggested: that people sometimes deny it. Just because a claim is commonsensical does not make it true. So if people deny such a claim, it requires defense. The claim I shall defend has been denied, for example, by Descartes and modern linguistic philosophers (see for example Descartes 1637/1911a; Davidson 1975). Their theses have been well criticized elsewhere, so I shall not discuss them in this paper (see for example Regan 1983: Chapter 1; Routley 1981). But recently a view has emerged that consciousness is a social phenomenon. This view would greatly restrict the scope of our attributions of mental states to animals, and I shall later subject it to scrutiny.

My claim, then, is that the psychology of human beings and animals forms a unity. Animals are not nonconscious, nor are their minds entirely beyond our understanding. One might express this in the form of what Gareth Matthews calls the *Principle of Psychological Continuity (PPC):*

> *PPC.* For any given psychological state, act or function, *p*, if a given animal belongs to some species other than the lowest one and that animal is capable of *p*, then there is an animal of some lower species such that the lower animal is capable of some psychological state, act or function, *p'*, and *p'* is a model of *p* (Matthews 1978: 437).

Clearly a number of questions are begged by *PPC*. The two most obvious concern the notions of one animal's being higher than another, and of the mental state of one animal's being a model of the mental state of another. I shall attempt to offer answers to these questions later in the paper. But before that I want to consider why we should accept *PPC* in the first place.

Arguments for Psychological Unity

The Other Minds Argument

The first argument for the unity of psychology between human beings and animals is negative. It is that there is no reason to doubt the existence of the minds of animals, or rather that any reason we have to doubt the existence of the minds of animals also gives us a reason to doubt the existence of the minds of other humans. We are faced with a choice between attributing mental states to animals and solipsism or skepticism concerning other minds generally. As most of us are quite ready to accept that other human beings have minds, then we should accept that animals too have minds.

Some of the positive reasons for a person to accept the existence of the minds of others—human or nonhuman—I shall discuss below. Now I shall consider one of the most prevalent objections to the Argument from Other Minds: that animals do not have a language, and therefore we have reason to attribute, say, the experience of pain to other human beings and not to animals. (I am assuming here that pain can be described, in a broad sense, as a state of mind.)

One way to defuse this objection might be to show that animals do in fact use language. One might instance the communication behavior of dancing bees, or of chimpanzees using American Sign Language (see for example von Frisch 1967; Gardner and Gardner 1969). There are two problems with this approach. The first is that there is doubt as to whether such systems of communication do indeed constitute a language. For example, they may be said to lack a necessary characteristic of a linguistic system, such as syntactic productivity (Thorpe 1974: 66–76; Terrace 1979: Chapter 11). The second problem is that even if the reply were successful, we would still be required to restrict mentalistic terms to language-using animals. Most animals would remain nonconscious.

A better reply is to accept that the use of language does indeed give us a reason to attribute pain to another human being in certain circumstances, but to deny that the fact that animals do not use language gives us a reason to doubt that they have minds. We may be able to learn the use of the concept "pain" only within a linguistic community, but there seems no reason to believe that to have a certain type of experience *e* one needs to be able to employ the concept of *e* in linguistic communication. If there is such a thing as an Oedipus Complex, then presumably I may develop one despite not only not understanding what is happening to me, but never having heard of the idea of such a psychological state. Nor does it seem plausible to suggest that to experience *anything* requires that one be able to use language. Could we think that a person born deaf-mute remains nonconscious throughout her life?

The Argument from Behavior

When some things behave in certain ways, the attribution of mental states to the thing often plays no role in an explanation of the behavior. If my car keeps stalling, it is only as a joke that I shall explain its behavior by saying that it is in a bad mood with me for driving it too fast last week. Rather, I am likely to suggest that there is something wrong with the carburetor. Likewise, if I place my tomato plant beneath a shelf, and it begins to grow towards the light, it will only be metaphorically that I say that the plant *wants* light. With human beings, the opposite is true. Very often we explain a person's behavior in mentalistic terms: She pulled her hand from the stove because its heat caused her pain; she visited the library because she wanted the new novel by Thomas Pynchon and believed that she might find it there.

What about animals? It seems to depend on the type of animal whether mentalistic attributions will be part of the best explanation. If we consider in a rigorous manner how a paramecium behaves, we shall almost certainly avoid the attribution of consciousness to it. It lacks the behavioral and neurological sophistication required for such an attribution (see the argument immediately below). But now consider the following example. A cat enters my back yard, passing by Fido's kennel. The cat makes a run for it around the corner. Fido chases her, but she is not in the yard. Fido stands barking under the lime tree. It would be very hard to describe this example other than in the following way (see Hebb 1946): the cat was *frightened* by the *sight* of Fido; Fido was *excited* by *seeing* her; the cat *wanted* to escape Fido and *believed* that she could do this by climbing the tree; Fido could not find her in the yard, and so *concluded* that she must be up the tree. Other terms might be used, but they would have to contain mentalistic attributions at some level if we wanted to make sense of the scenario. In particular, my use of *believed* and *concluded* might be questioned. But I think that they can be thought inapplicable only by a person in the grip of a theory such as those in modern philosophy which restrict propositional thought to language-users, and I have suggested already that these theories can be doubted.

The Argument from Neurology

The brains of all multicellular animals, including human beings, are made of the same matter. The fundamental characteristics of neurons and synapses are roughly the same (Griffin 1981: 127). It is the numbers and structures that differ: the brain of a human being contains billions of neurons, while those in an ant brain run only into the hundreds or thousands (Gould 1980: 180). This in itself says little. But it says more than if animal brains consisted of a material entirely different from that in the human brain. The same goes for size of brain. It is again difficult to decide the importance of this factor, since the brain tends to become absolutely larger, but relatively smaller, as the body increases in size through evolution. But at least animal brains are not all the same size as that of an ant. Indeed the brains of small whales, dolphins and porpoises are close in size to those of human beings, both absolutely and in relation to size of body (Walker 1983: 132, 138).

If we restrict ourselves to vertebrates, as regards the parts of the brain, all have a spinal cord, which is involved to an extent in bodily behavior. For example, it causes an animal to withdraw a limb from a painful stimulus (Groves and Thompson 1970). The hindbrain, consisting primarily in the brainstem, has various sensory and motor functions. This again is found in all classes of vertebrate (Walker 1983: 149). All vertebrate brains can generally be described in terms of three main parts: the hindbrain, midbrain and forebrain. The thalamus receives inputs from the eye in all sighted vertebrates (Walker 1983: 181, 192). It can be argued that the little forebrain that is present in nonmammals is not there just for responding to smells, for example, but for some form of cognition. For the cerebral hemispheres of lower vertebrates have various physiological properties in common with those of mammals (Walker 1983: 193).

I do not have the knowledge or the time to go further into the neurological similarities I have mentioned. My discussion is brief and arbitrary, and there is a great deal more to be said even at present, when the study of comparative neurophysiology is still in its relative infancy. But whatever one's views on the specifics of brain function, the general truth that animal brains are anatomically similar to our own must be accepted. And this gives us a reason for believing that the mental events that take place "within" them are in some degree similar to those which occur in our own brains.

The Argument from Evolution

There is a common picture of evolution which is roughly as follows. Members of a certain species all gradually evolve over time, becoming better suited to their environment, whether or not it remains stable. There is a problem with seeing evolution as a "ladder" like this. It does not seem to fit the case of human evolution. There is no ladder among early African hominids, but rather three roughly coexistent lines: *A. africanus*, the australopithecines, and *H. habilis*. There is no development within each line (Gould 1980: 60–61). This is a good reason for seeing evolution as consisting in a group of the original species separating from the original species and evolving separately. The formation of a new species through evolution is known as *speciation*.

Most biologists accept the form of speciation made popular by Ernst Mayr in the so-called *allopatric theory*. A simplified example of allopatric speciation might be the following (see Crook 1980: 18–19). A certain species x has been doing rather well in a certain environment. It has succeeded in reproduction to the point where the central areas of that environment have become overpopulated. Thus, some members of x are forced into areas peripheral to the central area. Here the environment is less conducive to the well-being of members of x. There are more predators and food is scarcer. The mortality rate among the members of x in the peripheral areas is therefore higher than that in the central areas. Those members of x who become adapted better to the new environment are more successful in reproduction than those less well-adapted. After a certain period, a new species—*super-x*—has developed.

What I must show is that a mental life might have some adaptive value for members of x as they develop into *super-x*. If x were a species of plant, it is not obvious what ecological advantage mental states would offer (Dawkins 1980: 119). Plants being immobile, the conscious awareness of pain caused by a predator might not serve any useful function (though perhaps even they could, say, release an antipredatory chemical). But in the case of animals, the advantage is clear. Consider three areas in which the developing members of x must be successful: movement to avoid predators, locating food, and reproduction. How could a mental life help? A mental life may well involve mental images (Griffin 1981: 144–45). If a member of x has mental images of a known predator which it has seen preying on other members of x and of that predator as present now in the distance, as well as the ability to compare the two, it will be better equipped to survive than an animal without these capacities. Mental images may be of use also as search-images in the location of food and suitable mates. They constitute one part of a mental life. There are other aspects, and I suspect that plausible evolutionary advantages could be found for many of them and that one could incorporate them into the story of the emergence of *super-x*.

Julian Huxley has suggested two useful criteria for assessing whether the members of a certain species have made an evolutionary advance (Huxley 1942: 562). First, they should show increasing control over their environment; second, they should become increasingly independent of that environment. Members of *super-x* may meet both of these criteria with the aid of mental states.

It might be objected that the behavior of members of *x* as *super-x* develops could be explained adequately without recourse to the use of mentalistic terms. As I suggested above, whether this is so depends on the sophistication of the behavior and neurophysiology of the animal in question (and, indeed, the sophistication of the researcher; but I should argue that a researcher who explains behavior in non-mentalistic terms is committed to doing so in the human case to the same extent as she is in the non-human [see the argument above and the Principle of Parsimony below]). Let us assume that in the scenario I have described the peripheral areas are far colder than the central areas. If a member of *x* responds to the change in temperature by shivering, we would be unlikely to explain this by suggesting that the animal is aware of the cold and has decided to do something about it. But if the animal starts to build a nest—something that members of *x* in the central areas have never done—we might well explain this by attributing some conscious states to the animal, probably even some primitive form of reasoning. It has been plausibly suggested that one function of consciousness might be to enable an animal to select a particular action from a number of options, the choice being constrained by the environment in which it finds itself (see Shallice 1972; it is argued in Boden [1984: 155] that the flexibility of potential in higher animals provides a *prima facie* case for mental representation).

Before moving on, I should like to provide further backing for the three positive arguments for *PPC*, in the form of two principles. The first is the well-known Principle of Parsimony, accepted in some form or another by most scientists. According to this principle, the simpler of two explanations is to be preferred, if both explanations are of equal explanatory power. I should argue that, in explaining both human *and* animal behavior, neurology, and evolution, the use of mentalistic terms will provide a stronger set of explanations than an alternative set which eschewed such terms. But it might be argued that a particular set of explanations which employed mentalistic terms in the human case, and nonmentalistic in the animal, is of equal explanatory power to a set relying on mentalistic terms in both cases. But here parsimony provides a reason for preferring the latter set, since it employs a single explanatory conceptual system for both cases.

The second principle is the Principle of Conservation (Jerison 1976: 37–40). This principle can be used also to buttress the positive arguments for *PPC*, and it may in itself gain support from the Principle of Parsimony. The Principle of Conservation states that, other things being equal, essential characteristics of a species will be found in the direct descendants of that species. It might be objected that I cannot use the Principle of Conservation to support *PPC*, since it itself rests on the assumption that something like *PPC* is correct. But the Principle of Conservation can be provided with independent intuitive support. Let us adopt the common analogy of evolution with a watch-maker. (I adapt the following example from Simon [1969: 115].) A watch-maker would be well-advised to follow the Principle of Conservation. Imagine a watch-maker who wants to develop a watch which will tell the time in seconds as well as hours and minutes. She has already built a type of watch which will do the latter perfectly adequately. If she is conservation-minded, she will merely attach a second-hand to one of the original watches. To start from scratch, building an entirely new watch from basics, would not only waste time, but probably be inefficient. For the new watch might not tell the time in hours and minutes as well as the old one. Though it may be a mistake to see purpose in evolutionary selection, it is not a mistake to describe it as efficient.

These four arguments, then, provide reasons for accepting *PPC*. The arguments, however, are silent on whether we are justified in speaking of animals as higher or lower on the phylogenetic scale. Because this question is central to *PPC*, I shall turn to it in the next section.

The Phylogenetic Scale

The "ladder" picture of evolution lies behind a common view of the classification of animals. According to this picture, there is a single scale of evolutionary advancement, on which human beings are at the top, unicellular creatures at the bottom, and other animals in between. Even leaving aside the question of whether unicellular creatures are animals, this view of evolution is of course mistaken. The various types of animal have developed separately, with no common ancestry. Even if the "ladder" view were correct, there would be a multiplicity of ladders.

Since this is so, there is no reason to think that an animal in one group which appears more sophisticated in one aspect—say, vision—is going to be superior to another animal from another group which has poor vision. For the animal with poor vision may have a more advanced muscular system for example. These problems with the common view of evolution have led certain researchers—most notably Hodos and Campbell (1969)—to reject entirely the notion of any phylogenetic scale.

It would be foolish to argue for the common view as it stands. But to claim that it is nonsense to say that a chimpanzee is a "higher" animal than a lamprey does seem counter-intuitive. I think that we can avoid offending our intuitions without running into the sort of problems with the view of evolution exposed by Hodos and Campbell. We should first accept that any scale or hierarchy that we construct will be very rough. We should then accept that a single linear scale will not suffice. Rather, we must compare living animals according to, say, recency of origin, phylogenetic relatedness, and adaptation to the environment (see Walker [1983: 117] for an example of such a scale; I should like to acknowledge my debt, in particular in this section, to this excellent book). Another thing we may do is to place human beings at the top of the scale, while admitting that there is no clear biological reason for doing this (the scale is not one of pure behavioral or neurological sophistication). Our justification must be that the scale is to be constructed from *our* point of view. We are trying to understand the points of view of other animals from our own, and for this purpose an anthropocentric scale will be necessary. Since apes will be just below human beings on the scale, we can assume that, other things being equal, their mental states will be more like ours than those of a reptile.

But it might be objected that I have not taken full account of the fact that many animals—such as birds—are unrelated to human beings in phylogenetlc terms. To answer this objection, account must be taken of nonphylogenetic considerations. Ancestry is not the whole story. Rather, we should note the phenomenon of *convergence*. Animals with different ancestries may evolve similar characteristics in response to similarity of environment. Those characteristics similar among animals which are ancestrally related are called *homologous*, those similar among unrelated animals *analogous*. For example, a streamlined body is a homologous characteristic of sharks and goldfish, but an analogous characteristic of sharks and dolphins. As Huxley suggests, we can classify animals into *clades* of environmental adaptation, as well as *grades* of phylogeny (Gould 1976: 115–22). The Principle of Conservation supports the view that we are likely to find homologous psychological characteristics among related animals, while the Principle of Parsimony supports this view and the view that analogous behavioral or neurological features are likely to result in analogous mental states.

There is one final problem suggested by Hodos and Campbell. This is that since, as I have admitted, each species may evolve ecological specializations, a single species is a separate entity. It cannot be used as a representative example of a group or class, or as a basis for making generalizations about groups or classes. Again this seems highly counterintuitive. Surely—at least in certain cases—a pigeon can be taken as an example of a bird?

Stephen Walker argues that the phenomenon of *adaptive radiation* of members of a species into separate environments suggests that this view of species as constrained by environment is too strict (Walker 1983: 124–25). In fact, any species has a *flexible potential*. The obvious example, of course, is the finches of the Galapagos islands. These have developed in dramatically different ways not only from each other, but also from their ancestors and relations in South America. One species (*Camarhyncus palidus*) has become insectivorous, imitating a woodpecker by using its bill to hold twigs which it uses as a lever to extricate insects from the bark of trees (Lack 1947: 58–59).

In these ways, then, by making our phylogenetic comparisons vague and unashamedly anthropocentric, and taking into account ecological convergence, we can add substance to the notion of comparing animals and describing them as "higher" and "lower."

Mental Models

There remains one final notion in *PPC* which requires elucidation. This is the idea of one mental state's being a model of another. In his original outline of *PPC*, Matthews eschews analysis of the notion of "model" that he has in mind, stating "my use of the term 'model' here is meant to express what I take to be a working conception among psychologists and much of the lay public." (Matthews 1978: 438) As far as I can see, neither of these two groups of people has quite the conception of a model that is required for *PPC*. A psychologist will usually see a model of mind, or a particular facet of mind, in the form of a diagram such as a "Black Box" or a computer model. This kind of model is a schematic presentation, and is not at all the same sort of thing as that which is modelled. This notion, then, will not help in the understanding of *PPC*.

The conception of a model held by the lay public is closer to what we want. It is again a representation, though not a schematic one. An example might be a model of a Spitfire airplane, made in plastic to a scale of 1/100. If animal mental states modelled human mental states in this way, they would have little in common with the latter. For the plastic model of the Spitfire has little in common with an original Spitfire. The pain of an animal would be "pain," as the model Spitfire is a "Spitfire."

We can build on the layperson's conception, however, in order to arrive at a notion of model less inimical to our purpose in postulating *PPC*. Imagine a model Spitfire, made this year, which appears identical to the 1941 original (an ex-pilot could not tell the difference). It is the same size as the original. The only important difference between the original and the model is one of origin. I shall call this type of model *model A*. To return to our rough classification of animals, it would seem quite plausible to suggest that the pain of a chimpanzee which is being severely burned is a *model A* of the pain of a human being in the same circumstances. In a thought-experiment in which you could experience both pains, you would not be able to tell the difference. For the only difference is the "location" of the mental state, not its experiential nature.

The obvious objection to my discussion so far is that I have shown bias in selecting a chimpanzee. Why not a rat? Or a fish? Let me introduce a second type of model, *model B*. A *model B* of a Spitfire might be 3/4 scale, have plastic upholstery and no guns. There is now more than a trivial difference between this model and the original, though there are many similarities. One might say that the pain of a rat being burned is a *model B* of the pain of a human in that position. But most animals are lower than rats. Take a fish. (I am aware of the dispute as to whether fish could in fact feel pain even if other animals can. If it is doubted whether they can, one can select an alternative lower animal.) The brain and behavior of a fish is far less like those of a human being than those of a rat. Consider *model C*. A *model C* of a Spitfire might be 1/75 scale, made in Japan and be controlled by a radio-transmitter. But it will still do many of the things that real Spitfires do: engage in dog-fights with ME 109s, take off and land on a runway, and so on. When I say that my goldfish is in pain, then, I may well mean that it is experiencing a mental state which is a *model C* of human pain.

Many people are bewildered when confronted with the proposition that a fish can feel pain. There seem to be two sources of this bewilderment: (i) a difficulty in understanding what it feels like to be a fish; (ii) a difficulty in analyzing what "pain" means. (i) can be dealt with immediately. To know that another person is in pain you do not have to know how it feels *to be that person*. You have merely to understand pain. This leads us on to the second difficulty. It can be resolved by noting that we all know what "pain" means. If we did not, we could not use the term in the present discussion. It might be said that we do not know what it *is*. But we do, for we have felt it. It hurts, we do not like it, it makes us cry. And when we ascribe an experience of pain to a goldfish, we may be saying that it is being hurt, that it does not like it, and even perhaps that it is "crying." (Various alarm calls have been distinguished in fish, including those of "alarm" and "aggravation;" see Milne & Milne [1963: 54].)

Which type of model is in play in any attribution of a mental state to an animal does not depend only on the classification of the animal. It depends also on the sophistication of the state in question. It might be suggested that, say, an Oedipus Complex is a counter-example to *PPC*. For a chimpanzee is unlikely to experience a state which is a model of a human Oedipus Complex. But this ignores the possibility that a chimpanzee might experience a *model B* of an Oedipus Complex. A young male might find himself sexually attracted to his mother, and so feel envious of his father, but without developing a superego.

One other concept is worth introducing here in the hope of further clarifying the implications of *PPC*. This is the notion of *degrees of consciousness*. Trying to get to grips with the notion of consciousness (or mind) sometimes seems rather like the game of apple-bobbing. The concept is too big and slippery for us to obtain a hold on it. I have seen people tire of bobbing apples, take them from the water and cut them up for eating. In the same way, one might divide a mental life into sections, perhaps in the following way: 1. Perception; 2. Memory; 3. Imagery; 4. Dreams;

5. Sensation; 6. Emotion; 7. Intention; 8. Belief; 9. Desire; 10. Reason; 11. Anticipation; 12. Self-awareness; 13. Awareness of other minds.

This list is not intended to be exhaustive, but rather illustrative of the kind of division into sections I have in mind. One can use one's list to speak of degrees of consciousness. For example, an animal which perceived and remembered what it had perceived for some significant time could be said, other things being equal, to have a higher degree of consciousness than an animal which perceived without remembering its beliefs. We could also classify within sections. For example, an adult human being might be said to show a greater degree of self-awareness than an adult chimpanzee.

I should like to include a brief caveat here. Of course, a *model C* of pain will be hard to imagine. But it is not beyond us. There are, however, some mental states which we are quite unable to imagine. Take the experience of a bat as it flies around a dark cave (see Nagel 1974 and Akins, chapter 23 of this reader). We have no grip on what the experience of the bat might be like, for we have nothing comparable to the bat's sense of echolocation. But this is no reason for us to deny that there is such an experience. The arguments of section 2 still apply. So we can say that there is something it is like to be a bat, though we are unable to say what it is.

I shall end this section with what I consider to be a remarkable passage from Aristotle, which should make clear my debt to him in my discussion of models:

> In the great majority of animals, there are traces of psychological qualities or attitudes, which qualities are more markedly differentiated in the case of human beings. For, just as we pointed out resemblances in the physical organs, so, in a number of animals, we observe gentleness or fierceness, mildness or cross temper, courage or timidity, fear or confidence, high spirit or low cunning, and, with regard to intelligence, something equivalent to sagacity. Some of these qualities in man, as compared with the corresponding qualities in animals, differ only quantitatively: that is to say, a man has more or less of this quality, and an animal has more or less of some other; other qualities in man are represented by analogous and not identical qualities: for instance, just as in man we find knowledge, wisdom and sagacity, so in certain animals there exists some other potentiality akin to these. The truth of this statement will be the more clearly apprehended if we have regard to the phenomena of childhood; for in children may be observed the traces and seeds of what will one day be settled psychological habits, though psychologically a child hardly differs, for the time being, from an animal; so that one is quite justified in saying that, as regards man and animals, certain psychical qualities are identical with one another, whilst others resemble, and others are analogous to, each other. (Aristotle 1910: 588a18–b3)

The Social Theory of Consciousness

In 1966, Alison Jolly argued that higher primates have a more developed intelligence than lemurs because their social life is of greater complexity (Jolly 1966). This theory has been elaborated by Nicholas Humphrey with reference to consciousness itself (Humphrey [1983]; the thesis is repeated in Humphrey [1986]; see also Crook [1980]; Crook acknowledges his debt to Humphrey on p. 28.)

Descartes believed that animals reach only the "first grade of sensation":

> To the first [grade] belongs the immediate affection of the bodily organ by external objects; and this can be nothing else than the motion of the particles of

the sensory organs and the change of figure and position due to that motion. The second [grade] comprises the immediate mental results, due to the mind's union with the corporeal organ affected: such are the perceptions of pain, of pleasurable stimulation, of thirst, of hunger ... and the like. (Descartes 1637/ 1911b: 251)

This is strikingly reminiscent of Humphrey's description of the position of our ancestors, which also applies to present-day non-social animals:

Their brains would receive and process information from their sense-organs without their minds being conscious of any accompanying sensation, their brains would be moved by, say, hunger or fear without their minds being conscious of any accompanying emotion. (Humphrey 1983: 48–49)

Humphrey believes that only man and *perhaps* a few of the higher social animals are conscious, have minds (Humphrey 1983: 55). His view clearly poses a threat to *PPC* and the claims I have been making for it.

There are three main strands to what I shall call the social theory of consciousness. The first is the negative claim that "creative intellect" (the ability to infer that something is likely to happen because it is entailed by a novel conjunction of events) has not arisen in the higher primates through a need for practical invention. Animals do not need a great deal of imaginative reasoning to subsist (Humphrey 1983: 17).

The second strand concerns the evolutionary function of creative intellect. The life of the great apes and man may not require much practical invention, but it does call for the possession of a large amount of knowledge of technique and the nature of the habitat. This knowledge is acquired by tradition, in a community. The life of social animals presents a great number of problems, and the role of creative intellect is to hold society together (Humphrey 1983: 19). As this intellect developed, individual animals began to use it to outwit one another, which put further evolutionary pressure on its selection (Humphrey 1983: 22) .

The final strand is the explication of the workings of consciousness. Humphrey resurrects the Argument from Analogy. An individual animal can develop a model of the behavior of others by reasoning through analogy from its own case. Its own consciousness reveals to it by introspection the nature of the consciousness of others. It can then use this knowledge to interpret and predict their behavior (Humphrey 1983: 33–35).

Humphrey supports his case with empirical evidence from his own research (Humphrey 1986: 57–60). He found himself working with Helen, a monkey from whom the visual cortex had been removed. At first, Helen appeared blind. But after six months of encouragement from Humphrey in the form of play and walks near the laboratory, she started to use her eyes again. Humphrey explains what happened to Helen by referring to the case of D. B., who underwent surgery which excised the entire primary visual cortex on the righthand side. It seemed to D. B. that he could see nothing to the left of his nose. But he and those studying his case were surprised to find that he could make highly accurate guesses concerning objects in his lefthand visual field. Helen and D. B. seemed to be experiencing what Larry Weiskrantz calls "blindsight" (Marshall et al. 1974). They can use their eyes to help them get around and so on, but they are not conscious of any visual sensations.

I shall now take these strands of the social theory, and attempt to unravel them. The first two concern the part played in evolution by creative intellect. Humphrey has underestimated its importance. He bases his claim on field observations of the chimpanzee. But this animal is already well-adapted to its environment. As I suggested in my discussion of the evolution of species x into *super-x*, mental faculties may be of great benefit to animals which find themselves in peripheral areas in times of environmental crisis. Chimpanzees have proved themselves in the laboratory to be capable of remarkable inventiveness, and it is likely that this capacity stems from a time when such a capacity helped their ancestors to survive (by enabling them to use sticks to catch termites, for example).

Humphrey places too much importance on the role of consciousness in education by the group. Undoubtedly it is important. The social theory in itself may well be right. But there are other functions for consciousness to perform. And it must not be forgotten that fairly complex skills can be transferred purely hereditarily. Consider, for example, the behavior of a cuckoo. It is assumed by many psychologists that most of the social signals in mammals do not have to be learned through introspection and analogy, but result from innate capacities. Examples include appeasement gestures, some of the facial expressions of primates, and tail positions in wolves. If the behavior of nonsocial animals is nonconscious, then it seems quite plausible that that of social animals is the same. (It is argued in Leyhausen [1965] that the notion of a "nonsocial" animal does not in fact make sense.) The process of one animal's outwitting another, while it may be relevant in discussing the interaction of members of a group, could also take place between individual nonsocial animals of the same species or, indeed, different species.

Humphrey's thesis begins to look most doubtful when we contrast nonsocial animals with an apparently high degree of consciousness with highly social animals who seem to have less developed mental lives. Bears, which are typically nonsocial, differ little in "intelligence" or cranial morphology from social animals such as wolves, whereas bees, which could certainly use knowledge of techniques and habitats, are highly social and, one would think, at a low level of consciousness if at any. Nor do there appear to be great differences between the relatively non-social patas monkey and the gelada or hamadryas, which lead complex gregarious existences. These monkeys are of the same taxonomic group (Crook 1980: 129).

As for the third strand of the social theory, I do not want to quarrel with Humphrey's use of the Argument from Analogy. This is because I suspect that it must enter at some stage in the explanation of our knowledge of other minds. What I am arguing is that he plays down the evolutionary significance of consciousness in nonsocial behavior, and correspondingly exaggerates it in social behavior. I believe that this leads him to confuse consciousness with selfconsciousness. Humphrey believes that consciousness is the set of subjective feelings available to introspection. Animals who do not need to introspect will not introspect, and hence are unconscious. But if an animal feels pain—and there is surely a good argument for the adaptive value of pain even to a non-social animal—should we not describe this animal as conscious? I myself sometimes think that selfconsciousness is merely an advanced form of consciousness (for does not the animal in pain show that—in a sense—it knows that it is *it* and not some other animal which is in pain?), but I do not have to go that far to refute Humphrey. For even if human beings and the higher primates alone are selfconscious, this does not imply that they alone are conscious.

Finally, what of Helen, the blind monkey? I think it is important here to emphasize the fact that both Helen and D. B. had been accustomed to employing their five senses in the ordinary way to obtain knowledge about the world. Once their vision was impaired, they would naturally feel that their damaged eyes were of no use. But once they began to realize that this was not so, that in fact they could make successful guesses, I believe that their mental life was transformed, and with it their consciousness. Imagine that you become like the boy in D. H. Lawrence's short story *The Rocking-horse Winner* (Lawrence 1955: 790–804). When you are on your rocking-horse, you are able to predict the winners of forthcoming horseraces. At first, your guesses would be shots in the dark. You would be unsure about them. But soon your guesses would become reliable hunches, and after that you would begin to treat them as a source of information about the world. You would have developed something like a sixth sense. It is this that Helen and D. B. have developed. But in their case, presumably, the sense is not a new one, but rather a damaged version of the sense of sight. For we are all, in a sense, conscious of the ability to make correct guesses about what is in our visual field *as well* as being conscious of that visual field itself. When the field disappears, we assume that the ability to guess correctly has gone as well. But the cases of Helen and D. B. show that it has not.

Conclusion

In this paper, I have argued for the continuity of psychology, viz. the common sense view that animals are conscious and have mental lives, and that we can speak of their mental lives in the same terms that we use of our own. I formulated this claim in the Principle of Psychological Continuity (PPC). I set out a number of arguments for PPC. I then elaborated the notions of the phylogenetic scale and mental models on which PPC relies. Finally, I criticized the theory that consciousness has evolved purely for facilitating social interaction.

Acknowledgements

I am grateful to Anthony Crisp, Marianne Fillenz, Andy Foggo, Jonathan Glover and the editors for comments on earlier drafts.

Literature Cited

Aristotle. 1910. *Historia Animalium* (Trans. by D. W. Thompson). Oxford: Clarendon Press.
Boden, M. 1986. Animal perception from an AI standpoint. In: *Minds, Machines and Evolution* (ed. by C. Hookway), pp. 153–174. Cambridge: Cambridge University Press.
Crook, J. 1980. *The Evolution of Human Consciousness.* Oxford: Clarendon Press.
Darwin, C. 1859/1968. *The Origin of Species.* Harmondsworth: Penguin.
Davidson, D. 1975. Thought and talk. In: *Mind and Language* (ed. by S. Guttenplan), pp. 7–23. Oxford: Clarendon Press.
Dawkins, M. 1980. *Animal Suffering.* London: Chapman and Hall.
Descartes, R. 1637/1911a. Discourse on Method Part V. In: *The Philosophical Works of Descartes*, Volume 1 (ed. & transl. by E. Haldane & G. Ross), pp. 19–118. Cambridge: Cambridge University Press.
———. 1637/1911b. Reply to Sixth Objections. In: *The Philosophical Works of Descartes*, Volume II (ed. & transl. by E. Haldane & G. Ross), p. 241–258. Cambridge: Cambridge University Press.
von Frisch, K. 1967. *The Dance Language and Orientation of Bees.* Cambridge, Massachusetts: Harvard University Press.
Gardner, B. & Gardner, R. 1969. Teaching sign-language to a chimpanzee. *Science* 165, 664–672.
Gould, S. 1976. Grades and clades revisited. In: *Evolution, Brain and Behavior* (ed. by W. Hodos, H. Jerison & R. Masterton), pp. 115–122. Hillsdale, New Jersey: Lawrence Erlbaum Associates.

————. 1980. *Ever Since Darwin*. Harmondsworth: Penguin.

Griffin, D. 1981. *The Question of Animal Awareness*. New York: Rockefeller University Press.

Groves, P. & Thompson, R. 1977. Habituation: a dual process theory. *Psychological Review* 77, 419–450.

Guttenplan, S. (ed.) 1975. *Mind and Language*. Oxford: Clarendon Press.

Hebb, D. 1946. Emotion in man and animal. *Psychologica! Review* 53, 88–106.

Hodos, W. & Campbell, C. 1969. Scala naturae: Why there is no theory of comparative psychology. *Psychological Review* 76, 337–350.

Hodos, W., Jerison, H. & Masterton, R. (eds.) 1976. *Evolution, Brain and Behaviour*. Hillsdale, New Jersey: Lawrence Erlbaum Associates.

Hookway, C. 1986. *Minds, Machines and Evolution*. Cambridge: Cambridge University Press.

Humphrey, N. 1983. *Consciousness Regained*. Oxford: Oxford University Press.

————. 1986. *The Inner Eye*. London: Faber.

Huxley, J. 1942. *Evolution: The Model Synthesis*. London: Allen & Unwin.

Jerison, H. 1976. Principles of the evolution of brain and behavior. In: *Evolution, Brain and Behavior* (ed. by W. Hodos, H. Jerison & R. Masterton), pp. 23–35. Hillsdale, New Jersey: Lawrence Erlbaum Associates.

Jolly, A. 1966. Lemur social behavior and primate intelligence. *Science* 153, 501–506.

Lack, D. 1947. *Darwin's Finches*. Cambridge: Cambridge University Press.

Lawrence, D. 1955. *The Complete Short Stories of D. H. Lawrence*, Volume III. London: William Heinemann.

Leyhausen, P. 1965. The communal organization of solitary animals. *Symposia of the Zoological Society of London* 14, 249–264.

Marshall, J., Sanders, M., Warrington, E. & Weiskrantz, L. 1974. Visual capacity in the hemianopic field following a restricted occipital ablation. *Brain* 97, 709–728.

Matthews, G. 1978. Animals and the unity of psychology. *Philosophy* 53, 437–454.

Milne, L. & Milne, M. 1963. *The Senses of Animals and Men*. London: Andre Deutsch.

Nagel, T. 1974. What is it like to be a bat? *Philosophical Review* 83, 435–450.

Regan, T. 1983. *The Case for Animal Rights*. London: Routledge & Kegan Paul.

Routley, R. 1981. Alleged problems in attributing beliefs, and intentionality, to animals. *Inquiry* 24, 385–417.

Shallice, T. 1972. Dual functions of consciousness. *Psychological Review* 79, 383–399.

Simon, H. 1969. *The Science of the Artificial*. Cambridge, Massachusetts: Harvard University Press.

Terrace, H. 1979. *Nim*. New York: Knopf, 1979.

Thorpe, W. 1974. *Animal Nature and Human Nature*. London: Methuen.

Walker, S. 1983. *Animal Thought*. London: Routledge & Kegan Paul.

Chapter 21

The Mental Lives of Nonhuman Animals

John Dupré

Introduction

It is commonly supposed that the question whether animals other than ourselves have minds is perfectly simple to understand, but very difficult to answer. We suppose that we know exactly what is at issue, since we know from our own experience what it is to think, or more generally have mental lives; but we are very uncertain how we might ever discover whether animals do the same. In large part, we may also suppose, this is because, being dumb, they are unable to tell us. I want to argue in this paper that almost everything about this set of views is wrong. Our difficulty with this question is hardly at all to do with lack of evidence, but has everything to do with a lack of clarity about what is really involved in the attribution of mental states. I do not, of course, mean that the question about animal minds could be settled independently of any evidence. But I do want to suggest that the empirical facts in question may, in many cases be quite banal. The trick is to decide what the relevant facts are. To put this claim in an imperialistic mode, I am suggesting that the problem is paradigmatically philosophical.

In the first part of this paper I shall expand on the preceding claims and explain in a general way the kinds of questions I do take to be involved in deciding whether an entity is an appropriate subject for the attribution of mental properties. In the second section I shall make some rough and tentative suggestions about the appropriateness of attributions of more specific kinds of mental phenomena. (One important moral of the opening section is that we should avoid assuming that there is some unitary answer to the question about animal minds.) In the final section I shall try to identify some questions that do remain mysterious, and offer some ideas about how light might be thrown upon them.

The Cartesian Legacy in Our Thinking about the Mental

I would like to develop two related themes about the mental states of animals. First, I want to point out the powerful and pernicious influence that Cartesian assumptions, generally—if perhaps ironically—unconscious, continue to exert on much of our thinking about this topic. and to say something of what are the consequences of rejecting these assumptions. Cartesian perspectives are omnipresent in recent discussions of animal minds, not least among those most vocal in support of the view that nonhumans have a wide range of mental capacities. One conspicuous example is the work of Donald Griffin (1984). It is even commonplace among those active in defending the rights of animals to ethical treatment. Marian Stamp Dawkins (1990), for example, rests the case that animals can suffer explicitly on the argument from analogy (for discussion of this argument, see below; see also Crisp, chapter 20 of this reader). My arguments against these Cartesian assumptions owe a great deal to my understanding of the later Wittgenstein (1958); a specific question I would like to explore is to what extent Wittgenstein's insights into the conceptual status of the mental justify us in espousing a kind of behaviorism.

Second, I want to argue against an idea, again more often implicit than explicit, that there is just one fundamental question as to whether animals *really* think. A close parallel here can be drawn with the question whether there are really animal languages, or whether animals can be taught *real* languages. In either case the question can be seen to presuppose a kind of essentialism, the view, that is, that there is some one crucial feature, an *essence*, that is necessary and sufficient to make a thing or phenomenon what it is. The questions then can be raised, What is the *essence* of thought (or language), and do animals have it? The idea that there is an essence of thinking is of course famously connected with the name of Descartes; its denial—and again the same denial for the case of language—is central to the work of the later Wittgenstein. So it should be clear that the issues I have distinguished have much to do with one another.

Descartes thought that the property that distinguished any genuinely mental phenomenon from anything else was its transparency, or indubitability, to the agent experiencing it. This is also the basis for a classical conception of consciousness. Objects of consciousness, on this view, are not only immediately apparent to their subjects, but their nature is unmistakable. Unlike Descartes, more recent thinkers do not necessarily identify mental phenomena with objects of consciousness. I say "mental phenomena," though Descartes would say "thought," because as suggested above one problem Descartes has bequeathed us is much too homogeneous a view of the mental. (In the *Meditations*, Descartes gives a typical list of kinds of thinking as doubting, understanding, affirming, denying, willing, refusing, imagining, and sensing [Descartes 1642/1967: 153, Med. 2].) Something is a pain, say, for Descartes, if and only if it is experienced as a pain by its subject; the nature of pain is unmistakably evident to the subject; and the meaning of the word "pain" is exhausted by its function of referring to that experience. Although Descartes did not consider the minds of animals, presumably because he explicitly considered them to be nothing but machines, this conception of the mental raised a pressing problem about the existence of other human minds that has been prominent in the subsequent history of Western philosophy. It will be useful to approach the problem about other species by looking first at this problem about other members of our own species.

The relevant difficulty to which Descartes' conception gives rise is that the putative essential property of mental phenomena, transparency or consciousness, is accessible to us only in our own case. We cannot—and this is a logical rather than an empirical impossibility—ever have access to this property in the case of another mind. If, even in principle, we can never verify that the essential property of the mental is present in any case but our own, it is natural to ask whether there is any possible justification for believing in the existence of minds other than our own. The traditional answer to this question has been to appeal to what has become known as the argument from analogy. We observe in our own case, according to this argument, that certain of our mental states are correlated with characteristic modes of behavior.

We observe in other people these same patterns of behavior, and infer inductively that they are accompanied by the same mental states (see also Crisp 1990).

It is worth remarking at this point that *if* this is the right way to think about other humans, there is little difficulty about other animals. The behavior of my cat when it has a pain in its paw is very much like mine when I have a pain in my foot; on the other hand it never produces the behavior which for me would be associated with extracting a square root. I would conclude, using the argument from analogy, that it had some but not all of the mental states I experience myself. The trouble is that if such an argument is needed, it is woefully inadequate. An inductive argument based on observation of one case to a generalization over a population of billions is hardly deserving of the title "argument." The reason that we do not accept inductive arguments based on a single instance is that we cannot, in general, have any reason to suppose that the observed case is typical. One would be in error, for example, in concluding on encountering a radio that all hard rectangular objects emitted complex and cacophonous sounds. In the present case, the very point at issue is whether consciousness, the property at issue in the argument from analogy, is a property peculiar to myself or more widely distributed. If the former, skeptical hypothesis is correct then the inductive argument—the argument from analogy—is worthless; to accept it is thus to beg the skeptical question entirely.

A radically different solution is offered by analytic behaviorism. According to this view, pain, for example, just *is* the characteristic set of its behavioral manifestations (see Skinner 1953; a rather more subtle position, though basically behaviorist, can be found in Ryle 1949). Thus to ask whether someone writhing on the ground with a knife in his leg is in pain is nonsense; nonsense of the same kind as the question, I know she has the same parents as I do, but is she really my sister? But attractive though this solution has sometimes appeared, it is obviously unacceptable in this simple form. It is possible that the person on the floor has his leg anesthetized, and is pretending to be in pain. Given this possibility, it cannot be *nonsense* to ask whether the person really is in pain. It is worth noting again that *if* this were an adequate solution to the problem, it too would present no special difficulties of extension to other animals: if they produce the appropriate behavior they have the mental state in question, if not, not.

Since I cannot treat the ramifications of this problem in adequate depth in the context of this paper, I must now be somewhat dogmatic. My own view is that although, for the reason just stated, analytic behaviorism is untenable, there is a good deal right about behaviorism when it is separated from the claim that mental terms can be analytically reduced to sets of behaviors. What I take to be at the heart of Wittgenstein's attack on the Cartesian tradition is the demonstration that there are deep conceptual connections between mental states and the behavior that constitutes their characteristic display. In differentiating this position from analytic behaviorism we must emphasize that a conceptual connection here must be distinguished from a strictly logical connection. The word "pain" is not logically equivalent to some complex description of behavior.

How, then, should we understand the meaning of a word such as "pain"? Wittgenstein approaches meaning through a consideration of what it is to explain meaning. Meaning is what one grasps when one correctly understands an explanation of meaning. Meanings can be explained in many ways, one, but by no means the only, of which is the use of samples of the referent of a word (socalled ostensive definitions).

So in the present context we need to think of what is involved in explaining the meanings of mental terms; and an essential part of the answer, surely, is behavior expressive of the mental states in question. Moreover, as I shall elaborate in a moment, Wittgenstein shows that, contrary to the Cartesian picture, mental terms could not possibly be explained ostensively, i.e. by pointing to the connection between the word and the alleged mental referent.

The moral to be drawn here is not that mental states can be reduced to behavior, but that, contrary to the Cartesian assumption, it must be possible to explain the meaning of mental terms through appeal to behavior (or perhaps behavior plus characteristic causal antecedents). Any explanation, for Wittgenstein, is fallible; it may be misunderstood. However, it must also be possible, if it is a satisfactory explanation, for it to be understood correctly. If it is, then the explainee has acquired criteria for the application of a term. Thus, for example, by observing myself and others in various painful positions, and producing various forms of behavior expressive of pain, I can be taught the meaning of the word "pain." I can then apply it correctly to other cases. The distinction between Wittgenstein's position and that of analytic behaviorism, as well as further insight into Wittgenstein's positive view, can be found in his remark that the word "pain" does not describe pain behavior, but replaces it (1958: 89). Verbal expressions of pain thus become criteria of pain on a par with groaning; and like other criteria they can, on occasion, be disingenuous.

We can now consider the application of this picture to the worry about other minds, whether human or otherwise. I see a person with a nail stuck in his foot groaning and writhing on the ground. Since I am familiar with the criteria for pain, amply realized in the present case, this strikes me as a clear instance of pain. But there remains a philosophical inclination to ask: but is the person really in pain? Suitably expanded, this makes perfectly good sense. I might be asking, is this only a pretense of pain? Perhaps it is a rehearsal of part of a play, for instance. The legitimacy of such questions point exactly to the impossibility of providing a behaviorist reduction of pain. But of course the skeptic about other minds is not someone who wonders whether other people are only pretending to have the experiences they seem to be having. She is someone who wonders whether, in any case but her own, the situation observed really provides evidence of pain at all. But she is thus raising the question whether the criteria that she (thinks she) has learned for the term "pain" really are such criteria. And this is equivalent to the question whether she really knows what it is that she wonders whether she is observing an instance of. The skeptical question thus appears to be self-defeating. And this, finally, suggests that the Cartesian perspective from which it derives must be confused.

This line of argument, though I believe it to be impeccable, seldom convinces. The reason is, I think, that most of us have retained extremely strong Cartesian intuitions. We think of our use of the term "pain" as fundamentally a device for referring to something we are acquainted with in our own private experience, and thus as only contingently related to its typical causes and behavioral manifestations. To address this worry directly, we must turn to the most notorious and controversial part of Wittgenstein's overall strategy, the socalled private language argument. The Cartesian picture, as I have said, assumes that words for mental states function primarily to refer to private internal states; and if the function of a word is primarily referential, it should be possible to explain its use ostensively, by the use of samples of its referent. Thus, just as we explain color words by using objects of the appropriate color, we should explain sensation words by using samples of the appropriate mental quality. And to cut a long story short, this simple Cartesian picture of the meaning of a term such as "pain" is incoherent. No-one could explain the use of a term which functioned simply to refer to a private internal state; no criterion could be communicated for the application of the term, since only the person attempting to explain the term has any access to the private feature that is supposed to serve as a criterion; and hence no distinction could be imparted between correct and incorrect use of the term. This last point is especially crucial. Imparting a distinction between correct and incorrect application of a term is precisely what, as Wittgenstein emphasizes, an explanation of meaning is intended to achieve. So we have reached, in essence, the same point that was arrived at when the skeptical argument discussed above was argued to be self-refuting. The skeptical worry, which derives from this mistaken assumption about the meanings of mental terms, is raised in a way that undermines the meaningfulness of the very question that it is intended to raise.

This leads me, finally, back to the minds of animals. What I want to claim is that the starting point for an adequate approach to this problem is to reject the idea that there is some one "deep" question involved. There is not, in Gilbert Ryle's (1949) memorable figure, some private internal stage across which the referents of mental terms act out their ghostly roles. Since we have no such stages ourselves, we need not inquire whether other creatures possess or lack them. We cannot even begin to consider a range of questions that continue to figure prominently in discussions of animal minds—Are animals really conscious? Are they self-conscious? Do they really know what they are doing? Do they have experiences? Or are they, on the contrary, merely machines?—unless we reject the Cartesian picture, and then ask what are really the criteria for the application of these various terms. When we do so it is, of course, likely that the questions will have rather various answers. In the next section I shall look at some questions about animal minds which, I think, can be answered fairly confidently.

Some Easy Questions about Animal Minds

In this section I shall touch on a number of different questions about the mental capacities of animals: Do they have experiences, beliefs, intelligence, or language? But I shall start with the most general such question: Are nonhuman animals ever in any kinds of mental states at all? As may well have been guessed from the preceding section, I take the answer to this question to be affirmative. However, I want to look briefly at some criteria that have occasionally been deployed to rule out any attribution of mentality to animals whatsoever.

Perhaps the commonest such criterion remains that of Descartes: Are animals conscious? This can be interpreted variously. Donald Griffin, in his book *Animal Thinking* (Griffin 1984: 9), suggests that the issue separating him from more behaviorally minded scientists is "whether animals are mechanisms and nothing more ... complex mechanisms to be sure but unthinking robots nonetheless." Elsewhere he suggests that the problem may be whether animals are aware of their own mental states (or: do they know what they are doing?), or again whether they are aware of objects not immediately present to their senses. (I shall return to this last idea.) The first question suggests exactly the aspect of Descartes' view that raises the insoluble problem of other minds: Whether an entity is conscious might be totally independent of the totality of its behavior and behavioral dispositions. Although there are powerful intuitions in favor of such a possibility, I shall reject it for the reasons outlined in the preceding section: In the absence of behavioral criteria we cannot even attach a meaning to a mental term; so the attribution of mentality cannot be quite independent of behavior.

Awareness of one's mental states, interpreted in one of Griffin's senses as "knowing what one is doing," may seem closer to a genuine and empirical notion of consciousness. We sometimes distinguish, for example, conscious from unconscious mental processes precisely on the grounds of whether the subject is aware of what she is doing. A person acting on a posthypnotic suggestion may offer an explanation of what she is doing in mentalistic or psychological terms, but the explanation may be quite mistaken. Unfortunately, it is pretty clear that this provides no adequate model for explicating the philosophical question about the mental states of animals. A person under post-hypnotic suggestion typically *is* aware of mental states; it is just that she is deluded about what mental states are in fact relevant to explaining her actions. No one, I suppose, wants to argue that animals are conscious alright, but invariably deluded about the motives of their actions. A more appropriate parallel would be with the case of a somnambulist, who, we may suppose, is apparently acting, but in fact is not conscious of anything. But this supposition, assuming it is correct, is based on clear criteria: The somnambulist is glassy-eyed and mechanical in his movements; he displays extreme shock if woken. Here, however, we have a distinction that seems to apply with equal force to animals. My—not especially bright—cat sometimes chases his tail with a degree of nonchalance that strongly suggests that he is not aware of what he is doing. For example, he makes a pass at it with his mouth and, after the tail has eluded him, stares about him in a comic state of puzzlement. He appears at least to have forgotten what he was doing; perhaps he never even knew. On the other hand one is not tempted to such a supposition when, his body quivering with intensity, he is concentrating on stalking a bird. The point of such rather banal examples is not to claim great insight into feline psychology, but merely to indicate that, provided we insist that there are criteria distinguishing conscious from nonconscious states, there is no difficulty of principle in applying them beyond the human case. It will of course be said that I am quite perversely refusing to address the real issue. When he stalks the bird is he *conscious*, or is he just acting mechanically like an "unthinking robot"? But this is just to return to the Cartesian conception of consciousness as quite independent of any behavioral manifestations; and hence of any possible criteria; and hence, I have tried to argue, of any sense. (A distinction between conscious and nonconscious mental states entirely innocent of behavioral consequences has recently been defended by Carruthers [1989; but see Jamieson & Bekoff 1992]. The specific confusions in this neo-Cartesian account cannot be addressed here.)

A somewhat more substantive concern is that animals might be incapable of awareness of anything not immediately present to them. This is an implausible suggestion about many kinds of animals. I suspect it might be less appealing if we did not suffer from such an impoverished sense of smell. If one considers an animal such as a dog without this disadvantage, it seems clear that awareness of the absent must be a major aspect of its experience. Dogs, I take it, can readily distinguish between fresh and stale scents, and can recognize both as the kinds of scents they are. Recognizing the stale scent of an opossum, say, is surely being aware of a spatio-temporally distant opossum. If, as I assume, dogs respond very differently to fresh and stale opossum scents, it would seem that it is precisely the spatio-temporal, or at least temporal, distance observed by the dog that accounts for the difference.

Of course, "being aware of a spatio-temporally distant opossum" may reasonably be seen as no more than a bizarre circumlocution for "being aware (or knowing) that an opossum has passed by here before." But I take it that the reason that spatio-temporal absence has been considered important in this context derives from ideas about intentionality, that thought can be "about" things that are not immediately present. And this is more obviously implied by the paraphrase than in my original formulation. (The new formulation also raises the question of the attribution of states such as *belief* to animals, which I shall consider further below.) Griffin (1984), in a similar vein, discusses some experiments on birds in which they learned to search in a variety of ways for items of food concealed by experimenters, and hypothesizes that perhaps the birds have mental images of the food they are searching for. But what is important here is the appropriateness of the thoroughly intentionalistic expression "searching for"; not whether some—in my opinion wholly mystifying—neoCartesian explanation of this capacity is correct.

More mundane examples come readily to mind. I make a certain noise to communicate to my cats that I am prepared to feed them. If, as is usually the case, they are hungry, hearing this noise causes them instantly to run to the kitchen just sufficiently slowly to make sure I am following and to attempt to trip me up. It will of course be objected that this does not show that they associate this noise with (spatially distant) food. Perhaps they have just been conditioned to respond to a particular auditory stimulus with movement to the kitchen; certainly this response has been rewarded in the past. It is not altogether easy to justify the intuitions common to almost everyone who has interacted with reasonably intelligent animals other than specially bred rats and pigeons, that this is a thoroughly perverse interpretation. One important ground for it is that such behavior cannot be treated in isolation. These cats, for example, frequently exhibit the same behavior without any stimulus, and also with other food suggesting stimuli, such as the sound of a canopener. Again, if they have just been fed, they may not respond at all. It strikes me that the assumption that they associate certain sounds with (absent) food and hence, if they are hungry, go to the kitchen where food is often provided for them, is vastly more parsimonious than any attempt to reduce the phenomena to conditioned pairs of stimuli and responses. In the final section of the paper I shall offer support of a rather different kind for this sort of interpretation.

Let me turn now to a rather different, but I suspect even less problematic, issue: Are animals intelligent? I take the unproblematic answer to be, roughly: Yes, some animals have quite considerable degrees of intelligence, though no doubt some others have very little. I shall not try to offer a rigorous definition of intelligence, partly because I doubt whether such a thing is available or appropriate. A central aspect, I take it, is the ability to find solutions to problems, and to do so with some flexibility. (This is an important general theme of Griffin 1984.) By the latter, I mean to exclude responses that are invariably elicited by a particular stimulus, regardless of whether they are, in the particular circumstances, appropriate solutions to problems; analysis of invertebrate behavior often, though by no means always, shows highly adaptive behavior not to be intelligent on this criterion. The criterion I have offered is, of course, an empirical one, and it might have turned out that animals were entirely stupid. The ethological literature shows this to be far from the case. The observations surveyed by Donald Griffin in his *Animal Thinking* provide an excellent source of illustrations.

There remains, nonetheless, the familiar illusion of a much deeper problem. Once again, this comes down to the idea that however intelligent behavior may appear to be, there is still the question whether we are dealing with a genuinely intelligent being, or merely a "mindless robot." As I have tried to indicate in previous contexts, I take this concern to be deeply incoherent. This misconception of intelligence has been attacked with great brilliance by Gilbert Ryle (1949). Ryle argues forcefully that intelligence is grounded primarily in intelligent *action*. The Cartesian picture, what Ryle refers to as the myth of the ghost in the machine, leads us to suppose that the intelligence of an action (which, for us, will often be a linguistic action) is not intrinsic to the action but resides in some internal and inaccessible mental antecedent of the action. Thus, for the Cartesian, an intelligent move in chess, a witty and *à propos* remark, or a smart piece of base-running are only symptoms from which we may attempt to infer intelligence. But, as we have seen in considering the so-called problem of other minds, if such an inference were needed, it would be very poorly grounded. Ryle argues, on the contrary, that intelligent performances are constitutive of intelligence. Hence, and plausibly enough, it is not an open question whether a person whose remarks and actions are consistently intelligent is in fact intelligent. To put the matter in a Wittgensteinian mode, intelligent performances are criteria of intelligence. They are defeasible criteria, in the sense that we may show that particular, apparently intelligent, performances should be attributed to luck, habit, or whatever. But it makes no sense to ask whether *all* intelligent performances might in fact fail to be intelligent.

It is in the light of these rather straightforward observations that, I want to claim, the question of animal intelligence is a simple one. There is ample evidence that animals are often capable of appropriate and flexible responses to a variety of problem-posing situations. Striking examples drawn pretty much at random from Griffin (1984) include accounts of remarkably coordinated cooperative hunting among lions (pp. 85–87), or the versatility with which captive great tits learn to solve experimentally constructed foraging problems (pp. 65–67). Such responses are not symptoms from which intelligence can, at some intellectual risk, be inferred. They are constitutive of intelligence. So, I conclude, many animals are fairly intelligent.

Turning finally to a topic about which I shall say very little, let me nevertheless say something about nonhuman language and the importance of its alleged nonexistence. It is certain that many animals communicate to some extent with one another, perhaps almost all do to a very limited extent. It is equally certain that we have not encountered anything remotely like a human language in any other species. By the first point I mean that they convey information about such things as their emotional states (grimaces, growls, etc.) and their environments (alarm-calls and the famous waggle-dances of bees); and the behavior by which they do this has the primary function of so conveying information. On the other hand, it is extremely improbable that any nonhuman terrestrial creature has any use for such things as, for example, pluperfect subjunctives, or even subordinate clauses. Exactly how wide this gulf will prove to be remains a fascinating question now undergoing investigation from various directions. Contemporary studies of social animals in the wild, and of attempts to teach nonhumans fragments of quasihuman language may throw light on the extent to which human language is a wholly novel evolutionary creation, or simply a by-product of generally highly developed mental capacities. But I shall not attempt to review these questions here. Rather, assuming that animals do not possess anything like human language (whether or not they may have the capacities for significant parts of it) I want to consider whether this lack shows that they must also be missing other central features of a mental life.

There are a variety of reasons why what I take to be quite disproportionate importance is often attached to the question of animal language. Perhaps the most important of all such reasons are, broadly speaking, political: For a variety of economic religious, or other ideological reasons, it has been important to many people to insist on an unbridgeable gulf between humans and animals, and language has seemed the most promising instrument for achieving this. (These political aspects of the question have been particularly emphasized to me by Harriet Ritvo.) Closer to my present concerns, it has been thought (e.g. by Descartes) that language was a necessary condition of consciousness or of intelligence. Recent philosophers have suggested that language is necessary for a being to possess beliefs. (States such as beliefs, desires, intentions, hopes, fears, etc., which involve a relation between a subject and an actual or possible state of affairs, are often referred to generically as "propositional attitudes," and treated similarly in this context.) I shall briefly consider each of these claims.

Perhaps the easiest such idea to reject is that intelligence should require language. If, as I have suggested, intelligence should be conceived as appropriate and flexible response to problem-posing situations, then it is impossible to see why this should require linguistic ability. It might be suggested that it would be impossible for an entity to show intelligence without the capacity to conceptualize the situations with which it was confronted. For the appropriateness of a response will depend on the kind of situation involved; and for the range of responses to be flexible, the entity must be able to discriminate different kinds of situations which is, perhaps, to exhibit that it has "concepts" of these kinds of situation. But if this is right, then the possession of concepts is a capacity independent of the ability to express them linguistically. It is true that we, as highly linguistic beings, tend to associate concepts very tightly with words we use to express them; and there are no doubt many concepts that we possess that we could not posses if we were not linguistically talented. But if we require no more of the possession of a concept than the ability to discriminate what falls under it from what does not, the connection with linguistic capacity is surely quite contingent. And the possession of "concepts" thus tolerantly conceived is all that is required for at least a modest degree of intelligence.

Let me finally turn to the so-called propositional attitudes, belief, desire, intention, and the rest. As is conventional in contemporary philosophy, I shall focus especially on belief. The best known recent defense of the thesis that without full-blown language a creature cannot properly be said to possess beliefs is perhaps that of Donald Davidson (1975, 1982), and I shall focus on his treatment of the question. Davidson's central argument for the dependence of belief on language is as follows. Human beliefs, at least, are deeply embedded in a very complex structure of belief. By contrast, Davidson considers the attribution to a dog of the belief that a cat is in a particular tree. (The dog in question has been chasing a cat, and is now barking up a tree, though in fact the wrong tree.) Davidson writes:

> [C]an the dog believe of an object that it is a tree? This would seem impossible unless we suppose the dog has many general beliefs about trees: that they are growing things, that they have leaves or needles, that they burn. There is no fixed list of things that someone with the concept of a tree must believe, but without many general beliefs there would be no reason to identify a belief as about a tree, much less an oak tree. (1982: 3)

It is, indeed, plausible that we would not attribute the belief in question to another human unless we supposed that he or she was in possession of the sort of general truths about trees that Davidson describes. But we should be careful about what this shows. In particular, we should carefully distinguish the question whether the dog has something like the full complement of beliefs that we would expect of another human about whom we asserted "he believes that there is a cat up that tree" from the question whether the dog has some belief which has some significant content in common with that former belief. I think that the answer to the first question is negative, but that that is all Davidson's argument shows; and I see no reason to doubt that the answer to the second question may well be affirmative.

I shall say something more about the attribution of particular beliefs to animals in the final section of the paper, but first I should consider further the question whether we are justified in attributing any belief at all to a dog. I take this to be a question about the appropriateness of a general explanatory strategy for dealing with animal behavior, the strategy Daniel Dennett (1971) refers to as "the intentional stance." Roughly speaking, this is the strategy of trying to decide what an animal is aiming to achieve and what it believes are the avenues open, and obstacles, to achieving that goal. This, of course, is the way we standardly explain the behavior of other humans. Someone who objects to using this approach to the behavior of other animals should, I take it, be prepared to advocate some preferable strategy. As far as I can see, the only systematic alternative would be to adopt what Dennett refers to as the "physical stance." That is to say, we analyze the animal as a physical structure, and determine, by appeal to knowledge of the laws of nature, how that structure will behave in response to a given set of environmental stimuli. One research program that more or less fitted this latter model was behaviorism. The characteristics of the physical structure could be taken to have been determined by a past history of stimuli, behavior and rewards, and this history would determine the response of the structure to new situations. But this program has had almost no success in understanding the behavior of animals in anything like natural conditions, and for reasons that are well understood. Animals are more intelligent than the program allows; they have much more interesting internal structure—I am inclined to say, structure of beliefs and goals—than it suggests.

There is a quite different candidate for a physical stance approach to behavior, one that is now widely held to be very plausible, and that is to give a genuinely physical analysis of the internal structure, presumably a neurobiological account. Two points should be noted about this. First of all, no such account is anywhere near being available. So what we are considering is only a possible strategy, not a real alternative. Possibility should certainly not be discounted from a philosophical perspective, and it is certainly an important question whether this possibility is genuine. However, and this is the second point, this possibility in no apparent way distinguishes the non-human from the human situation. There are, indeed, a number of philosophers who believe that some day we will be in a position to replace our intentional stance explanations of human behavior with physical stance explanations grounded in neurobiology. These philosophers go on to conclude that the concepts in terms of which we give intentional stance explanations—beliefs, desires, etc.—would then have turned out to be fictitious. While I am not persuaded of the coherence of this view (see Dupré 1988), the point of present relevance is simply that no fundamental divide between the human and the nonhuman is implied: perhaps, strictly speaking, no one has ever really believed anything; but if so, beliefs certainly do not depend for their existence on language. And if they are simply a fiction we make do with lacking an adequately developed neurology, there seems to be no reason for taking this fiction to be any less necessary for nonhumans than for humans. I do not, of course, want to deny the obvious fact that the majority of beliefs we attribute to humans could not sensibly be attributed to nonlinguistic animals. This is simply because for very many beliefs, perhaps the majority, the only possible criterion is a verbal expression. But there are nonetheless many beliefs that we attribute to both humans and nonhumans on the grounds of simpler behavioral criteria; so, I want to maintain, the difference is ultimately one only of degree.

I have not attempted to exclude every possible ground for drawing a deep divide between human and animal cognition. Indeed, I have not attempted to consider the range of arguments that Davidson deploys toward the establishment of this division. So perhaps I shall conclude this section by using Davidson quite unfairly against himself. The final conclusion of the paper discussed above is that "rationality is a social trait. Only communicators have it." Since many animals are social, and many animals communicate, we should perhaps enlist Davidson in support of the view that there are many kinds of rational animals.

Some Hard Questions About Animal Minds

The general theme of this paper so far has been to argue that certain kinds of "deep" mystery that appear to arise in connection with the question of animal minds are illusory. The suggestion that no nonhuman animal is conscious, sensate, moderately intelligent, or in possession of even the simplest beliefs can, I have tried to argue, be founded only on serious misunderstandings of what is involved in the application of mental descriptions. Thus I want to conclude that there should be no difficulty in deciding that many other kinds of animals *have* minds. However, even a more defensible interpretation of mental language can present deep and perplexing obstacles to the interpretation or characterization of nonhuman minds. In this final section of the paper I shall indicate a perspective on mental language that suggests that such problems, even though difficult, are at least solidly empirical and, in principle, tractable.

Since the first part of this paper depended heavily on an interpretation of Wittgenstein, it may be appropriate to introduce the present discussion with one of Wittgenstein's better known aphorisms: "If a lion could talk, we would not understand it" (1958: 223). This remark develops the intuition that language is deeply integrated with nonlinguistic practices and behavior. Since lions, and other animals, lead wholly different lives, their hypothetical language could make no sense to us. Does this imply—if it is true—that we are necessarily mistaken in applying terms of our language to a lion? To pursue a standard example, a possible reason for hesitation in applying the term "pain" to a lion, would be that while there is much in common between the natural expressions of pain in humans, and the behavior of lions when they are injured, there are also differences. Lions, do not, I suppose, exactly cry. Moreover, again on a Wittgensteinian picture, for humans these natural expressions are often replaced by verbal ones, statements such as "I am in pain." Some kinds of pain attribution seem to depend almost exclusively on verbal criteria. There are perhaps no criteria for attributing a headache to a lion.

Suppose, then, that our lion found its voice and said something that we were (somehow) inclined to translate as "I am in pain." Why might we not be right in this translation, and thus understand the lion? One might imagine a Wittgensteinian answering that the role that such an utterance could, imaginably, play in the life of lions, and its relation to the natural leonine expressions of pain would be different from the equivalent role of the English utterance in the life of humans. If this seems wholly implausible, it is perhaps because the behavior associated with pain is so primitive that it really does extend to many nonhuman species without serious alteration. But then we should certainly be doubtful about the reference of pains for talking whales (which do not groan, still less grimace) let alone for beetles or butterflies.

There is a powerful pragmatic reason for rejecting this line of argument. Most people think it is a very bad thing to torture, or gratuitously injure, lions, whales, and perhaps even beetles, though the extent of these intuitions is notoriously variable. Presumably part of the reason for this is that we think that these animals feel pain, and pain is a bad thing. It would seem that doubts such as I have been raising about the legitimacy of applying our term "pain" to lions or the translation as pain of some term in the vocabulary of a talking lion, would threaten to undermine all such intuitions, and show that the objections to torturing animals must be incoherent. I am inclined to think that this conclusion is a *reductio ad absurdum* of the line of argument that purports to demonstrate it;

But it is also fairly clear that the threatened conclusion cannot be a legitimate inference from the arguments under consideration. Wittgenstein's argument does not show that humans only come to feel pains at the point when they learn to talk about them; on the contrary, they show that if pain did not pre-exist pain language, there could not be such language. Hence whatever we make of the roars and so on of injured lions, their status as expressions of sensation, at least, cannot be undermined by considerations concerning the linguistic incompetence of lions.

I want to suggest that taking the Wittgensteinian perspective a stage further points to an attractive resolution of this difficulty. It is extremely difficult to get rid of the intuition that what we are really concerned with in attributing pain to the lion is a correct characterization of what is going on in the lion's mind: what, if it could only talk, and if we could only understand it, the lion would refer to by its word "pain." Put in another contemporary idiom, we are trying to speculate about part of "what it is like to be a lion"; and that, as has been discussed by Thomas Nagel (1974), is a hard thing to do. But I have recommended rejecting all these interpretations of the problem, and I suggest that we focus instead on the question, What do *we* mean—if anything—by attributing pain to a lion? We should remember, in other words, that "pain," even when applied to lions, is a word in *our* language. And if *this* is the question, then it can be seen that our difficulty in understanding the dicta of hypothetical talking lions is completely irrelevant.

Of course, serious doubts might be raised about whether our term "pain" *should* be extended to lions, whales, or whatever. The facts alluded to above, that the criteria for such applications will differ in some important respects from those appropriate for humans, show that this is an extension of our concept, not a paradigmatic use. But I think that from this perspective it is clearly a natural and obvious extension, comparable, perhaps, to our extension of the term "conversation" to telephone conversations and even rapid exchanges of computer messages. Lions and other animals avoid things that cause them pain, withdraw rapidly from painful stimuli, and generally respond to pains in ways that are more or less analogous to human responses. But perhaps most important, to pick up an earlier point, the concept of "pain" fits into broader aspects of our conceptual scheme, most especially the ethical. We think that causing pain is a very bad thing, because it is a sensation that sentient beings greatly dislike. Since lions are clearly sentient, and show every sign of disliking the experiences which, I am suggesting, we refer to as "pain," we should avoid causing them these experiences. This is another very powerful reason for including their relevant experiences under our concept of "pain."

I think this perspective, if it is accepted, should also defuse some of our worries about the attribution of cognitive states to animals. When we say, to return to an earlier example, that the dog believes that the cat went up the maple tree, we are, obviously enough, saying something in English. Whether such a statement is appropriate or not must surely depend, then, on whether the dog satisfies criteria that we would usually employ in attributing such a belief to a human. It does not depend, for example, on whether the dog is entertaining some proposition in Caninese that would be correctly translated as: "The cat went up the maple tree." Indeed, it seems pretty obvious that we might well attribute this belief to another human on exactly the kinds of grounds proposed for the dog. (We see a man chasing a cat shouting abuse and swinging at it with a stick; the cat darts up an oak tree, and the man continues yelling up the maple tree and shaking his fist, etc.) Of course the majority of beliefs that we attribute to humans probably do depend essentially on linguistic criteria; but many do not, and such may very well be attributed to nonhumans.

There is a slightly different kind of worry that might still be raised, that suggests a serious and pervasive risk of error in such attributions. Richard Jeffrey (1985), in discussing Davidson's example, suggests that although the dog may not have the concept of a tree that Davidson describes it may have a concept of its own that the maple tree falls under; he suggests "marker that a scratcher can disappear up." Although, as I have been arguing, I do not think the question at issue is illuminatingly construed as one about the phenomenological states of dogs or lions, this suggestion does point to a real difficulty. This is simply that it is easy to be wrong in giving intentional explanations of the behavior of nonhumans. Here I mean to identify the point at which armchair theorizing ends, and the difficult empirical task of cognitive ethology begins. To be successful, as opposed to merely logically intelligible, in attributing beliefs to other animals, we need to know a great deal about the animals we are talking about. If we do not know what their perceptual capacities are, and what features of the environment they are capable of discriminating (see Rosenzweig, chapter 12 of this reader); the goals that such animals often pursue; the level of intelligence they are capable of bringing to bear on the pursuit of these goals; their tendencies to stereotyped or habitual responses to certain kinds of situations; and so on, we are likely simply to be wrong in our suggestions as to what their cognitive states are. Hence it is unsurprising that we can make such attributions much more easily and widely in the case of our conspecifics, and after that we are inclined to feel more comfortable with the beliefs of cats and dogs—about which we feel we know a fair bit—than with whales or bats. But I see no reason why, as we come to know more about other creatures, we should not come to be very successful in giving intentional stance explanations of their behavior—explanations in our own language, which is just as well since they probably have none, and if they did we could not, perhaps, understand them.

Acknowledgements

I have been helped by comments on an ancestral version of this paper by audiences at the University of Colorado at Boulder and the University of California at San Diego. I have also benefited greatly from the responses of various people to a previous draft. I am particularly grateful to Marc Bekoff, Dale Jamieson, Peter Hacker, Thomas Kuhn, and Harriet Ritvo.

Literature Cited

Carruthers, P. 1989. Brute experience. *Journal of Philosophy* 86, 258–269.
Davidson, D. 1975. Thought and talk. In: *Mind and Language* (ed. by S. Gutenplan), pp. 7–23. Oxford: Oxford University Press.
———. 1982. Rational animals. *Dialectica* 36, 318–327.
Dawkins, M. S. 1990. From an animal's point of view: Consumer demand theory and animal welfare. *Behavioral and Brain Sciences*.
Dennett, D. 1971. Intentional systems. *Journal of Philosophy* 68, 87–106.
Descartes, R. 1642/1967. *Meditations on First Philosophy*. In: *The Philosophical Work of Descartes* (ed. & transl. by E. S. Haldane & G. R. T. Ross), pp. 131–199. Cambridge: Cambridge University Press.
Dupré, J. 1988. Materialism, physicalism, and scientism. *Philosophical Topics* 16, 31–56.
Griffin, D. 1984. *Animal Thinking*. Cambridge, Massachusetts: Harvard University Press.
Jamieson, D. & Bekoff, M. 1992. Carruthers on nonconscious experience. *Analysis* 52, 23–28.
Jeffrey, R. 1985. Animal interpretation. In: *Actions and Events. Perspectives on the Philosophy of Donald Davidson* (ed. by E. LePore & B. McLaughlin), pp. 481–487. Oxford: Blackwell.
Nagel, T. 1974. What is it like to be a bat? *Philosophical Review* 83, 435–450.
Ryle, G. 1949. *The Concept of Mind*. London: Hutchinson.
Skinner, B. F. 1953. *Science and Human Behavior*. New York: Macmillan.
Wittgenstein. L. 1958. *Philosophical Investigations*. Second Edition (ed. by G. E. M. Anscombe & R. Rhees; transl. by G. E. M. Anscombe). Oxford: Blackwell.

Chapter 22

Inside the Mind of a Monkey

Robert Seyfarth and Dorothy Cheney

For anyone interested in how humans think, there is something especially fascinating about other primates. The social behaviour of nonhuman primates offers a glimpse of minds that have similarities with our own but fall short in important respects. Examining the workings of these "almost minds" may shed light on the origins of human language, cognition and self-awareness. It may ultimately tell us how, in the course of our own evolution, some minds gained an advantage over others. This evolutionary perspective draws attention to the many apparent similarities between human and nonhuman primate behaviour.

The goal of our own research, however, has been to establish where these similarities between us and nonhuman primates break down. We approach the study of primate intelligence from a practical, functional perspective. What problems do monkeys face in their daily lives? What do they need to know, and how might one method of obtaining and storing knowledge give certain individuals a reproductive advantage over others? Eventually, this approach could reveal not only how human intelligence evolved, but why.

To document what monkeys and apes do in their natural habitats, we observed East African vervet monkeys (*Cercopithecus aethiops*) in the Amboseli National Park in southern Kenya, and compared our own observations with studies of other primate species. Our aim was to consider what sorts of underlying mental operations might possibly account for the monkeys' behaviour. From observing a particular event, do the monkeys make the same deductions that we do? Do they underestand kinship and social rankings? Or are they acting out complex strategies without being in any sense aware of what they are doing? To probe further into the minds of our subjects, we conducted experiments designed to test whether the patterns of social behaviour we humans see might also exist in the minds of the monkeys themselves.

We can think of social groups of monkeys and apes as being composed of many different long-term and short-term alliances among related and unrelated animals. To gain a social and reproductive advantage over others, individuals must be able not only to predict each other's behaviour, but also to assess relationships. It is not enough to know who is dominant or subordinate to oneself; an individual must also know who is allied to whom and who is likely to come to an opponent's aid. For this reason, we might predict that individual monkeys would be sensitive to other animals' relationships in any species in which alliances are common.

From *New Scientist*, 1992, 4 January: 25–29. Reprinted by permission.

Monkeys do seem to recognise the social relationships that exist among other group members, and judgments about these relationships seem to underlie much of their behaviour. Males assess the closeness of bonds between other males and their females before attempting a takeover. Females assess the ranks of others when competing for grooming partners. And females and juveniles apparently recognize the ways in which monkeys related through their mother (matrilineal kin) act together in unison, as they direct reconciliation or retaliation not only to individual opponents, but to their opponents' kin as well. In fact, vervets sometimes trigger fights in apparent efforts to retaliate against a slight received by another family member. If, for example, juvenile female Shelley observes her sister involved in a fight with juvenile male Trollope, it is likely that Shelley will threaten a close relative to Trollope.

Knowledge of other animals' social relationships can only be obtained by observing the behaviour of others and making appropriate deductions. Primates may not be limited to an egocentric view of the world: they may be able to step outside their own immediate experience to make judgments about the experiences of others. Monkeys, in this respect, seem to differ from Anthony Powell's infamous character Widmerpool, who was "one of those persons capable of envisioning others only in relation to himself".

The assessments that monkeys make of one another, moreover, are not simple, but seem to occur along at least two dimensions simultaneously. They classify individuals on the basis of kinship or close association at the same time as they recognize differences in rank. Thus two individuals may sometimes be lumped together as members of the same family, while at other times they may be considered separately, one ranking higher than the other. A female who recognises that sisters B and C are closely associated may threaten B after being involved with a fight with C. Nevertheless, the female is also capable of distinguishing B's and C's relative ranks, and in other contexts may groom the higher ranking B in preference to C.

We can make no precise statements about the machanisms that underlie the monkeys' knowledge of each others' relationships. For example, even if monkeys do have abstract concepts such as "closely bonded," their knowledge of these bonds may derive principally from noticing that certain individuals spend a lot of time with each other. Similarly, we cannot be sure that monkeys constructing a dominance hierarchy engage in "transitive inference"—in other words, that having seen that A is dominant to B and B is dominant to C, they infer that A is dominant to C. There is evidence that they do, but it is also possible that they simply memorise the outcome of every interaction between other individuals.

The ability to classify others into abstract categories such as "closely bonded" would have at least two functional advantages. First, it would allow individuals to identify types of relationships quickly, and to predict the behaviour of others based on partial information. As a result, a monkey who joins a new group, or whose group receives an influx of migrants, could make accurate predictions about behaviour without having to observe the interactions of every individual with every other. Secondly, as group size increases, the ability to form categories and to make judgments based on these categories would provide an increasingly efficient method for recognising the characteristics of relationships and predicting what specific individuals are likely to do next.

If we grant that a monkey has concepts, can we also conclude that the monkey recognises the existence of concepts in others? Does a monkey's knowledge of its

Working out What a Grunt Means

Like the players at Wimbledon, vervet monkeys frequently grunt to each other during normal social interactions. The vervets' grunts are harsh, raspy signals that sound like a human clearing his throat with his mouth open. As Thomas Struhsaker originally noted, grunts are given in at least four distinct social circumstances. A female monkey may grunt as she approaches a more dominant individual or a subordinate, as she watches another animal, or as she herself initiates a group movement across an open plain, or when she has just spotted the members of another group.

Even to an experienced human listener, there are no immediately obvious differences between grunts, either from one context to another or between individuals. Even when grunts are displayed on sound spectrograms, it is not possible to detect any consistent differences in acoustic structure from one context to the next. Although grunts are occasionally answered by other group members, in most cases grunts evoke no behaviourial responses. Changes in the direction of gaze, which are difficult to measure in the wild, seem the only obvious response when one individual grunts to another.

From an observer's perspective, watching monkeys grunt to each other is very much like watching humans engaged in conversation without being able to hear what they are saying. The creatures are saying something but we have no idea what it is. Vervet monkey grunts are strikingly different from their alarm calls: alarm calls given in response to different predators are easily distinguished acoustically.

The most obvious way of understanding what is happening is to adopt the influential view of W. John Smith, professor of biology at the University of Pennsylvania. He suggests that the information contained in an animal's vocalisation can be determined by both its acoustic properties and the context in which it is given. According to Smith, animals have relatively small repertoires of signals, each of which conveys a broad, general message. A small repertoire of general signals can nevertheless elicit a variety of different responses because of variation in the contexts in which calls are given.

Applied to vervet grunts, this hypothesis predicts that vervets are using a single vocalisation in a variety of different circumstances. The grunt itself provides general information about the vocaliser's identity, location or subsequent behaviour. Variation in the responses evoked by different grunts is accounted for by variation that the receiver perceives in the context in which they are given. Alternatively, it may be that within what seems to a human observer to be a single type of grunt there are a number of different grunts, each conveying quite specific information that depends more on a call's acoustic properties than on the context in which it is given.

To test these hypotheses, we designed the following set of experiments. First, grunts from the same individual were tape-recorded in each of the social contexts described above. Then, over a number of months, we played each grunt to subjects from a concealed loudspeaker and filmed their responses. For example, we might play Bokassa's "grunt to a dominant" to Duvalier on one day and then, three or more days later, play Bokassa's "grunt to another group".

Throughout these trials we allowed social context to vary freely. Tests were conducted, for instance, when there were dominant or subordinate animals nearby, when the group was foraging or resting, or when animals were at the centre or the edge of their range. We reasoned that if the grunts were really one vocalisation whose meaning was largely determined by context, subjects should show no consistent differences when responding to different calls; responses should be determined by the contexts in which calls were presented. On the other hand, if each of the grunts was different, and if each carried specific information that was relatively independent of context, we should find consistent differences in responses to each grunt type, regardless of the varying circumstances in which it was played.

Eighteen animals were played the recording of a grunt that had originally been given to a dominant animal; then a few days later, they were played a grunt given to another group. Subjects responded in many different ways, but two responses appeared consistently, and were consistently different across the two grunt types. "Grunts to a dominant" caused subjects to look out, towards the horizon, in the direction the loudspeaker was pointing. So "grunts to another group" directed the listener's attention away from the speaker, and in the direction toward which, under normal conditions, the vocaliser would have been facing.

By their behaviour, then, the monkeys seemed to be saying that although their grunts sound more or less the same to us, they contain information. In many cases, this information can include events external to the signalling individual, such as the approach of another group or the movement of animals into an open area.

social companions include knowledge—or at least a theory—about its companions' mental stages?

On 1 October 1972, the *Sunday Times* printed the obituary of Flo, an adult female chimpanzee who had lived in the Gombe National Park in Tanzania, and who had been studied by Jane Goodall for more than 11 years. An excerpt from this obituary read as follows: "Flo has contributed much to science. She and her large family have provided a wealth of information about chimpanzee bahaviour, infant development, family relationships, aggression, dominance, sex ... But this should not be the final word. It is true that her life was worthwhile because it enriched human understanding. But even if no one had studied the chimpanzees at Gombe, Flo's life, rich and full of vigour and love, would still have had a meaning and a significance in the pattern of things."

This final sentence highlights an important question for biologists. If no human observer had ever interpreted Flo's life, could we still say that she had knowledge, motives, beliefs and desires, and that her life was full of vigour and love? Do such mental stages really exist in the mind of any animal? Or are they artefacts, invented by ethologists as the best means of describing what they have seen? When we watch nonhuman primates in the wild and analyse their social behaviour, do we have their minds or ours under the microscope?

Strategic Observations

Watching monkeys, one is tempted to treat them like tiny humans not only because they look rather like us but also because features of their social organisation, for example close bonds among kin and status-striving, look like simplified versions of our own. More important, anthropomorphising works: attributing motives and strategies to animals is often the best way for an observer to predict what an individual is likely to do next.

Descriptions of social behaviour in anthropomorphic terms do not, however, constitute an explanation. After all, one way to describe and predict the behaviour of a cash dispenser is to assume that it wants to help you to do your banking, even though this motive plays no part in the machine's operation. So a key goal of our research has been to dissect the knowledge and motives that make monkeys do what they do. Can we prove that the mechanisms that govern behaviour and communication in vervet monkeys are similar to our own? If they are not, what are the differences? What can we do that monkeys cannot, and how does this make their lives and their view of the world different from our own?

Vervet monkeys, like many other animals, recognise individuals and take note of the interactions that occur among them. The monkeys may also create in their minds a number of representations that describe different sorts of social relationships: for example, mother-offspring relationships, relationships among kin and friendships between males and females. Experiments with captive monkeys have shown that primates compare relationships according to the types of bond they exemplify and not just according to the individuals involved. They judge mother-offspring pairs as the same even if one involves a mother and her adult daughter and the other involves a mother and her infant son. Monkeys appear to make use of such representations in their daily lives. A vervet monkey is more likely to threaten another female if one of her own close relatives and one of her opponent's close relatives have recently fought. Such behaviour is difficult to explain unless vervets recognise some similarity between their own close bonds and the close bonds of others.

Any mental representations monkeys have of social relationships are probably not as abstract and flexible as our own. Language allows us to label different types of relationships, to specify the criteria by which to include a bond in one class or another, and to discuss types of relationships independently of individuals, in general, abstract terms. There is as yet no evidence that monkeys' knowledge of social relationships is accessible to them in a similar way or that their classification of social bonds is abstract enough to include the identification of unfamiliar individuals or social structures. We suspect that a monkey raised among families A, B, C, D and E could tell us that the bond between Mother A and Infant A1 is the same sort of bond as that between Mother C and Infant C1. We do not know, however, if the same monkey could deduce that bonds just like this occur in other vervet groups, let alone in other species.

Humans not only classify social relationships into types but also examine the motives and strategies of others in an attempt to explain why some relationships are alike and others different. When trying to understand behaviour, humans often use introspection as a guide. Knowing that our own actions are often caused by particular mental states, we look for the same processes in others.

We have as yet no evidence that monkeys are aware of their own knowledge or attribute mental states to others. Monkeys are doubtless excellent at monitoring and predicting each other's actions, and they probably have little difficulty recognising that monkey X's actions can have a particular effect on Y's behaviour. It seems unlikely, however, that monkeys take into account each other's thoughts, motives or beliefs when they assess what other individuals are likely to do next.

For example, although their vocalisations certainly function to alert others to the presence of food, danger or each other, monkeys do not adjust their calls according to whether or not their audience is ignorant or informed, and in this sense cannot be said to communicate with the intention of changing a listener's mental state. Similarly, while monkeys are clearly able to acquire novel skills from others through observation, social enhancement and trial and error learning, there is little evidence that they teach or even imitate each other, perhaps because they cannot distinguish between their own states of mind and the states of mind of others.

Even in the case of deception, monkeys' attempts at manipulation seem aimed more at altering their rivals' behaviour than at affecting their rivals' thoughts. Deception, in the human sense, requires the attribution of mental states to oneself and to others. When we lie to someone we recognise a distinction between our own and another person's thoughts, and we depend on the fact that a person's beliefs can affect subsequent behaviour. If we are correct in arguing that monkeys live in a world without attribution, it would also seem to follow that they live in a world without deception.

The issue, however, is more complicated than this. Many animals do act in ways that serve to deceive others. Great tits, for example, give apparently deceptive alarm calls at feeding perches, and they vary their false alarm calls depending upon who is nearby. If the birds at the feeding perch are lower ranking than the signaller, false alarm calls are rarely given, presumably because the caller can simply supplant the rivals by approaching. But when the birds that are feeding are of higher rank and so cannot be supplanted, the lower-ranking birds do give false alarm calls. We have no evidence, however, that the birds use any other signals to deceive each other, or that they use deceptive signals in any other social context.

Such deception in animals is less flexible than human deception. We suspect that many of the differences between human and nonhuman deception ultimately derive from the failure of most animal species to attribute mental states to others. Human deception rests on the assumption that other individuals have mental states that can be manipulated to one's own benefit. Armed with this general theory, humans can modify deceptive behaviour widely, within a single context or from one context to the next. By contrast, animal deception seems to rest primarily on the recognition of certain behavioural contingencies: if I do this, he will do that. It must be learnt and relearnt from one circumstance to the next.

We do not yet know how flexible deception is in monkeys, nor indeed how flexible the detection of deception is. For example, a subordinate male who wishes to mate with a sexually receptive female will often attempt to "deceive" a more dominant male by leading the female behind a bush or a rock before he mates with her. If a dominant male learnt to be wary of a male who attempted to sneak copulations in this way, would he also begin to distrust the male's alarm calls? We suspect that he would not, because to do so would demand that the dominant male would have some understanding of the other male's motives, something he may be incapable of doing if he cannot recognise mental states in others. The dominant male might continue to be distrustful of his subordinate rival whenever his rival approached a female, but still continue to run into trees whenever his rival uttered an alarm call.

Apes may be considerably better than monkeys at attributing mental states to others. Chimpanzees, for example, do seem to recognise thoughts as agents of actions, and much of their behaviour seems designed to alter or control other individuals' states of mind. They deceive each other in more ways and in more contexts than monkeys, and experiments with captive subjects have suggested that chimpanzees can learn to distinguish between ignorant and knowledgeable trainers. More intriguingly, there is also evidence from the Ivory Coast that chimpanzees may actively teach their infants how to crack open palm nuts, suggesting that mothers recognise and attempt to rectify their infants' ignorance.

Even apes, however, seem to have difficulty attributing specific mental states to others. Consider empathy, for example. When his mother Flo died, the young male chimpanzee Flint exhibited many of the behavioural patterns we associate with grief in humans. He avoided others, stopped eating and spent many hours a day sitting in a hunched posture, rocking back and forth. After some days, he died. It is clear from this and other descriptions of death in chimpanzees that these animals experience grief and a sense of loss when an individual close to them dies. Equally striking, however, is the absence of sympathy among other chimpanzees: no chimpanzee has ever been reported to have consoled a grieving companion. Although chimpanzees have mental states and grieve at the loss of close friends, they do not seem to recognise the same mental states in others. As a result, they are unable to share another's sorrow or show empathy towards it.

When we study the social behaviour of monkeys we are tempted to anthropomorphise and treat them as if they were human. There are, however, many ways in which a vervet's view of the world is very different from our own. Monkeys see the world as composed of things that act, not things that think and feel. Like the primatologists who study them, vervet monkeys observe social interactions and draw generalisations about the types of relationships that exist among individuals. But there is no evidence that the monkeys have a "theory of mind" that allows them to recognise their own knowledge and attribute mental states to others.

While vervet monkeys are acutely sensitive to other animals' behaviour, they know little about what causes them to do what they do. A monkey may make use of abstract concepts and have motives, beliefs and desires, but her mental states are not accessible to her: she does not know what she knows.

Chapter 23

A Bat without Qualities?

Kathleen A. Akins

The Bird's Eye View

The other day in a physiology seminar we were discussing the effect of retinal foveation on visual perception. The fovea is a small portion of the retina densely packed with receptor cells—a density that makes possible those visual tasks that require high spatial resolution, the identification of shape and texture, accurate depth perception and so on. The fovea, however, can "see" only a small part of the entire visual field. So, much like directing a telescope across the night sky, foveated creatures move their eyes—shifting the "interesting" parts of the scene in and out of the foveal area. This is why we, but not rabbits, move our eyes about.

Enter the eagle—or, rather, birds of prey in general. They too have foveated eyes, but eyes with even better spatial resolution than our own. The African vulture, for example, can discern live prey from dead at an elevation of 3,000–4,000 metres, an elevation at which it is difficult for us even to sight the bird (Duke-Elder, 1958). Eagles, too, have high resolution foveae. Because they dive for the ground at speeds greater than 200 mph, their eyes must be capable of extremely accurate depth perception. Indeed, given the broad range of visual information that an eagle makes use of in its behaviour, the evolutionary "solution" was the development of *two* circular foveae connected together by a horizontal band of densely packed receptor cells (think here of the shape of a barbell). The horizontal band serves to scan the horizon. The central fovea, like those of most birds, looks to either side, each one (in the left and right eyes) taking in a different part of the world. Finally, the eagle has an extra pair of (temporal) foveae pointing forward, converging on a shared field—a foveal pair much the same as our own except with three times the density of receptor cells (Duke-Elder, 1958). It is this forward-looking foveal region that provides the high spatial resolution. Attending to the scene below via the temporal fovea, eagles spot their prey and dive at fantastic speeds, pulling up at exactly the right instant.

But therein lies a mystery, I thought, the mystery of the "eagle's eye" view. Given two foveal areas and a horizontal band, how does an eagle "attend to" a scene, look at the world? What does that mean and, more interestingly, what would that be like? Here, in my mind's eye, I imagined myself perched high in the top of a dead tree sporting a pair of very peculiar bifocal spectacles. More precisely, I pictured myself in a pair of quadra-focals, with different lenses corresponding to the horizontal band, foveal and peripheral regions of the eagle's eye. I wonder whether it is just like that, I

From M. Davies and G. W. Humphreys, *Consciousness*, Blackwell Publishers, 1993, 258–273. Reprinted by permission.

thought, like peering successively through each lens, watching the world move in and out of focus depending upon where I look. First I stare through the horizontal section and scan the horizon for other predators; then I switch to my left central lens and make sure no one is approaching from behind; then I use the high-powered temporal lens to scrutinize the water below for the shadows of some dinner. Is that how the world looks to an eagle?, I wondered. Is that what it is like to have two foveae?

The Problem: Nagel's Claim and its Intuitive Basis

In "What is it like to be a bat?" (1974), Thomas Nagel made the claim that science would not, and indeed, could not, give us an answer to these kinds of questions. When all of science is done and said—when a completed neuroscience has told us "everything physical there is to tell" (Jackson, 1982, p. 127)—we will still not understand the experiences of an "essentially alien" organism. It will not matter that we have in hand the finer and grosser details of neuroanatomy, neurophysiology and hence, the functional characterization of the system at various levels of complexity— nor will the "completed" set of psychophysics provide us with the essential interpretative tool. For all of neuroscience, something would be missed—what it is like to be a particular creature, what it is like *for* the bat or the eagle.

There are many reasons, I think, both intuitive and theoretical, why Nagel's claims about the limits of scientific explanation have seemed so plausible. Nagel himself, for example, argued for this conclusion by appeal to a theoretic notion, that of a point of view. Phenomenal experience, he said, is necessarily an experience from a particular point of view, hence the facts of experience are essentially subjective in nature. On the other hand, the kinds of phenomena that science seeks to explain are essentially objective, or viewer independent—"the kind [of facts] that can be observed and understood from many points of view and by individuals with differing perceptual systems" (Nagel, 1974, p. 145). So any attempt to understand the experience of an alien creature by appeal to scientific facts (facts about his behaviour and internal computational/physiological processes) will only serve to distance us from the very property we seek to explain: the subjectivity of phenomenal experience. Or so Nagel argued. Nagel's conclusion was that the only possible access one could have to the phenomenal experience of another organism is by means of a kind of empathetic projection—by extrapolation from one's case, we can ascribe similar experiences to other subjects. Needless to say, this is a process that will work well enough given a suitably "like-minded" organism (such as another person) but which will be entirely inadequate for understanding the point of view of more alien creatures. Hence, given only empathetic means, said Nagel, we cannot know the nature of a bat's phenomenal experience.

Nagel's argument, like those of a number of other philosophers (for example, see McGinn, 1983), makes use of a variety of theoretic tenets—about the objectivity of scientific facts, the subjectivity of experience and about the nature of a point of view. In the usual case, such arguments hinge upon a claim that "you can't get from there to here"—that there is no route from the objective to the subjective, from the nonintentional to the intentional, from the sub-personal to the personal, and so on— even given all of the resources of the natural sciences. These are views that must be addressed, I think, by argument, each in its own right or, better, met by a demonstration that the dichotomy at issue can in fact be bridged by scientific insight. Rather than address here these theoretic concerns, about subjectivity, point of view and so on, I want to look instead at the *intuitive* pull towards Nagel's conclusion—why most of us harbour that nagging suspicion that science must fail, that it cannot tell us what we want to know. This is the intuition that science will necessarily omit the one essential element of phenomenal experience, namely its very "feel."

The unfortunate fact of the matter, I think, is that these negative intuitions are well grounded in our everyday experiences. We have all faced the difficulty of trying to communicate the nature of a particular phenomenal experience, good or bad. "It was awful, absolutely horrible!!" you might recount, speaking of a bad migraine headache—but, apart from a fellow migraine sufferer, no one seems the wiser for your description. Frustratingly, despite the listener's own extensive catalogue of aches and pains, any elaboration on the "horribleness" of a migraine seems to do little good. "Yes, it's a bit like that but ..." one will hedge, when asked how a migraine compares to an ordinary headache, one caused by tension or by sinus inflammation. Or is it like having a nasty hangover, a bad case of the flu, or like the stabbing pain one feels when the lights are suddenly switched on in a darkened room? "It's sort of like that, except, only, um ... well ... much, much, *worse!*" This is what a sufferer will typically reply, unsure, even in his own mind, what to make of such comparisons. (Does a migraine differ from a bad hangover only in intensity or is there in fact a difference in kind? Or does the difference in intensity *constitute* a difference in kind?) Ironically, the best descriptions one can give, the descriptions that elicit the most empathetic sounds and nods, are usually not descriptions of the pain at all, but of the beliefs and desires that go along with the migraine. "If I knew the migraine wasn't going to end, I'd seriously wonder whether life was worth living" or "the pain is so intense, you don't even want to roll over, to find a more comfortable position in which to lie"—it is such thoughts that make clear the severity of the experience. Describing the feelings *per se* just does not seem possible. You simply have to have a migraine.

Extend, then, this epistemic difficulty to the phenomenal experience of an alien creature. Suppose that an organism has sense organs of a completely unfamiliar kind and, further, that it processes the information gathered from these strange sense organs in a manner unique to its species (or at least, in a manner unknown to ours). This is an organism that, undoubtedly, will have experiences that we do not: some of its sensations will be nothing like our sensations. So if we think of an organism's phenomenological experience as constituted by the set of all those alien "qualia," the problem of understanding seems insuperable. Given that we cannot comprehend by description the relatively familiar and circumscribed sensations of the migraine sufferer, what could we possibly know about an alien creature's point of view—about an entirely foreign phenomenological repertoire? If we can comprehend only those sensations that we have experienced, and if our own sensations are very unlike those of the bat, then we will be unable to understand a bat's phenomenology. This is the intuitive conclusion grounded in everyday experience.

The problem about the experience of bats, however, was, as Nagel described it, a problem about scientific description—whether science, not everyday conversation, could buy us any leverage on the bat's point of view. So what does common sense tell us here? The answer, I think, is that our conclusions about the ineffable nature of sensations fit hand in glove with another common feeling about the efficacy of science: to the average person, the suggestion that science might resolve these communicative difficulties seems quite strange, if not downright puzzling. How could science possibly help us in this respect?

Suppose, for example, that I am trying to describe to you a certain kind of feeling, say the pain of my broken toe. I might say something like this:

> Well, at first, when I tripped over the broom handle, there was a sharp, intense pain—a blinding flash of "white" that occurred behind my eyes. Then the pain evened out to a dull throbbing in the toe—and, later, by that night, it had turned into what I think of as "pain somewhere." You know, that's the pain of a deep injury—when the pain is clearly where it should be, in this case, in the *toe*, but it's also nowhere in particular. Your whole body feels, well, dragged out.

If you have actually had a broken toe or another injury of this sort, these sensations might sound quite familiar. You know, for example, exactly what I mean by the phrase "a blinding pain." But if you have been fortunate enough to have avoided such traumas, certain parts of the description will seem quite peculiar. (A "throbbing" pain you can understand, but what is it to have a pain that is "blinding" or felt "nowhere in particular"? Surely this is just a figure of speech?) One can, of course, on the basis of the description, obtain *some* understanding of the phenomenological properties at issue (after all, if asked about the pain of a broken toe, you could simply paraphrase the above description!). But it does little to help you understand how the pain actually *feels*. That is the part you cannot grasp given the description alone. Imagine, now, that you are given a completed model of human nociception, a model of all the neurophysiological/computational processess that underlie the production of pain, including, of course, the pain of a broken toe. That this model could in any way help seems entirely dubious. Why would you understand the *pain* of a broken toe any better if presented with a corpus of facts about C-fibres and A-fibres, conductance times, cortical and sub-cortical pathways, transmitter release, the function of endogenous opiates and so on? How could these statements about brain function possibly tell you about the *feeling* of a broken toe?

It is this intuitive sense of puzzlement, I think, that lies behind the more theoretical philosophical arguments of Nagel (1974), Block (1978), Jackson (1982) and McGinn (1989)—behind philosophical arguments that "you can't get from here to there," that there is an unbridgeable explanatory gap between the facts of science and those of subjective experience. In this sophisticated guise, the puzzlement is not given a naive dualist expression: most philosophers do not hold that science must fail to explain phenomenological events because those events occur in a "realm" beyond the physical world. Rather, the materialistic tenets are upheld: descriptions of neurological processes, it is generally agreed, are descriptions of inner sensations *in some sense of the phrase*. Moreover, given that sensations are brain processes, most Nagelians admit that science could not be entirely irrelevant to our understanding of an alien creature's experience. Neurophysiology, psychology and psychophysics will illuminate (no doubt) some aspects of an alien point of view. Still—and this is where the intuitive puzzlement resurfaces—no matter how much we come to understand about a brain's representational or computational capacities (the nature of its functional states at various levels of description, plus their structural and relational properties), the qualitative properties of that organism's point of view will still be missing. Again, it is the "very feel" of the experience that science is said to leave out. But what exactly does this mean? What is given and what is not by science?

Think here of the difference between, say, a pristine page in a child's colouring book, with only the thick black outlines of the picture drawn in, and that same page alive with colour, the trees and flowers and birds given hue according to the whims and palette of a particular individual. In one we have the "basic outline" of the image, the two-dimensional form; in the other, we have that outline plus the hues of the forms—colours that might have been different had the artist chosen otherwise. Now if we were given only the pristine page, various questions about the scene would remain unanswered. "But is the sky blue or is it really grey?" "Is the flower on the left yellow or is it actually white?" Without the completed picture, it is impossible to tell. It is questions analogous to these, then, that are allegedly left unanswered given only the neurological/computational facts about another organism's brain processes. Even if we knew the basic outline or, in Nagel's terms (1974, p. 179) the "structural properties" of an alien creature's representational scheme, the very "colour" of the experiences, the qualia, would still be missing. Like the missing colours of the outlined page, there are any number of ways, consistent with the structural properties of the representations, that those subjective experiences could be. What science can give us, at best, are boundaries on the space of possible qualia, on the pure "colours" yet to be filled in. In this way, our everyday intuitions cast the problem of consciousness, both in its naive and philosophical forms, as largely a problem about the intrinsic or qualitative nature of sensations, about the "greens, reds and blues" of phenomenal experience.

The Film

Imagine, then, that I, having dropped in from some future time towards the end of neuroscience, claim to have a film of "what it is like." I have, that is, a film of the phenomenology of the bat. While such a suggestion might at first seem unlikely, let me assure you that this film carries the stamp of approval of future science. For what science has found out, in the fullness of time, is that just as some people have suspected (Dawkins, 1986), the bat's sonar echo is used to solve the very same informational problems for which we humans use light. The bat uses the informational properties of sound to construct a representation of objects and their spatial relations. This is why the bat's experience can be presented on film to us, the human observers—why it has, I claim, a strangely "visual" quality. Needless to say, this film was made in the appropriate Disney style: a "cinerama" or "sen-surround" film projected on a curved screen, 180 degrees around the theatre, presented to an audience outfitted in "3-D glasses," for the sake of stereo vision. And, of course, the film is in colour.

What, then, does the bat film look like? First, the plot is simple. It shows, from the bat's auditory viewpoint, a boring sort of chase scene: the bat, flying about, uses sonar signals to catch mealworms that have been thrown into the air by an experimenter. (Bats, of course, are not blind—they see as well as hear. For the purposes of this thought experiment, however, I am considering only their auditory sensations.) This feat is accomplished with a manoeuvre characteristic of the Little Brown bat. First the bat flaps around, emitting his Fm sonar signal (a cry that begins at about 60 khz and sweeps downward, through the intermediate frequencies, to a cry of about 20 khz) and waiting for something edible to appear; then when he sights a mealworm, he flies over and manoeuvres until he can swat the mealworm with his

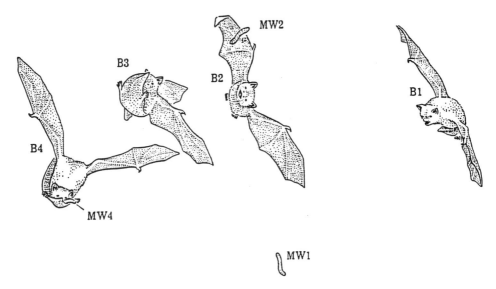

Figure 23.1
A filmed sequence of a bat (*Myotis lucifugus*) capturing, by a somersault maneuver, a mealworm tossed into the air. Shown are the four sequential positions, beginning with the rightmost figure. In the first frame, the bat (B1) spots the mealworm (MWI), which is still rising from the toss. In the second frame the bat uses its wing to deflect the worm downward. Next the bat catches the mealworm in a pouch between his tail and two legs. Finally, the bat ducks down to scoop out his meal. (Adapted from Webster and Griffin 1962.)

wing; performing a somersault, the bat then secures the prey in his tail pouch; finally, he reaches down to grab it, eating the mealworm from his pouch (figure 23.1). (Why bother with the pouch? As someone recently pointed out, "Every good meal deserves to be eaten sitting down."[1]) This is the basic scenario, one that is repeated several times. Now, what the film actually shows to the human observer is a kaleidoscopic display of vibrant colour forms. Swirling and pulsating in three-dimensions, the coloured forms dance across the screen, colliding and dispersing, suddenly appearing or vanishing. That's all. That, I claim, is what it's like. It is not, of course, what we humans would see, if we were acting the part of the bat—if we, with our human visual systems, were trying to catch a mealworm (Nagel, 1974). It is not "visual" in the human sense. On the other hand, this is not a film from our point of view, but from the point of view of a bat.

As you, the reader, will no doubt object, something is clearly wrong with this story. That is, whether or not the film "accurately depicts" some part of the bat's phenomenology—the sensory "colours"—watching the swirling display seems to leave out much of what is surely important to the bat's point of view. First, unlike our experiences during a film of a roller-coaster ride or a hang-glider's flight, we do not feel any of the additional "sympathetic" sensations appropriate to the moment. It does not seem to us that we are making any of the swooping and diving movements that are made by the bat. Nor do we understand the significance of the coloured images. Barring any sub-titles of the form "now the somersault begins" or "now you've got the mealworm in your pouch," you will not know what is happening— what you, as a bat, are doing. When the bright red image swirls across your left "auditory" field, is something (the mealworm? a background object?) moving past you or are you moving relative to it (maybe this is a somersault?)? Then again, is anything even moving at all? Can you infer that the movement of the colours stands for movement in the world? Probably not. And what does the three-dimensional nature of the film buy you? What does it mean when one coloured patch appears behind or in front of another? Is this a spatial relation or ...? All in all, the coloured images hold little insight for the human observer.

As a first pass at explaining what is wrong with this story—why a cineramic film could not tell us what we want to know about the bat—note that, while not particularly helpful in this instance, such "sen-surround" films are extremely useful in understanding the human point of view. When we watch a film of, say, the hang-glider's flight, the pictures go proxy for the real world. The brain interprets the intensity, frequency and spatial cues of the film in much the same way as it would interpret these same properties of light, reflected by real objects in the three-dimensional world. Hence, we really do see (more or less) what is seen during a hang-glider's flight. Indeed, because the visual system informs both the vestibular and the sympathetic nervous systems, we even feel the non-visual sensations—the terror before the leap, the drop in the stomach that follows. Through watching the film, seeing from this novel perspective the world rush by and feeling the sympathetic sensations of movement, a good deal about the experience of hang-gliding is communicated. In other words, we can simulate another person's point of view just because (a) we share a similar visual system, and (b) we can artificially create the hang-glider's visual input.

Similarly, when we watch the film of the "bat experience," we use the spectral cues in ways typical of human vision (what other choice could there be?). But what exactly does that mean? Unfortunately, we do not really know how colour vision works, in what "typical" ways spectral cues are employed. What we do know is that the colours we see depend upon the current ambient light plus the profile of wavelengths that specific materials are disposed to reflect. Further, we suspect that spectral signals are involved in just those visual tasks for which intensity cues prove inadequate. For example, it is often postulated that such cues are used to define equiluminescent borders, highlight the contrast between object and background, and to differentiate objects that are similar in all other respects (e.g. the ripe and unripe pear). (For a short explanation of colour pathways, see De Yoe and Van Essen, 1988; for a more thorough review of colour vision, see Gouras, 1984.) In other words, while we may think of the colour system as whatever neural machinery produces colour sensations, the colour system is more than that: it is that part(s) of the visual system that responds to, discriminates and utilizes spectral cues. It is this system, then, whatever it might be, that is activated when we see the film of the "bat experience."

Needless to say, a bat's colour sensations of acoustic stimuli would be quite another matter. Its sensations would not be tied to the ways in which external objects reflect ambient light nor would its sensations be a part of a system that uses the spectral composition of light for various information processing tasks. The bat's colour sensations would be linked to properties of acoustic stimuli and to its auditory processes involved in spatial processing. As it turns out, although the bat film was presented as consisting of seemingly random coloured patches, I had in mind a specific process for the generation of those images. There was an informational relation between the properties of the visual image and those of the acoustic stimuli about which you, the "viewer," were not told. That relation was as follows. First, the hue of the sensations (red, green, blue, etc.) encoded the frequency of the sound waves; second, the brightness of the colours gave the volume or intensity of the sound; and, third, the configuration of the patches showed, straightforwardly, the spatial properties of the sound waves. Finally, the film encoded the time delay of the echo or the bat's distance from surrounding objects. By making the coloured patches appear at different depths, spatial disparity mimicked a disparity in time—the amount of time it takes for the bat's outgoing cry to bounce off a distant object and return. The longer the delay between the cry and the echo, the further "back" the coloured patches appeared in the "visual" field. In this way, distance was represented by stereoscopic display.[2] Now, such an image of the sound field, in itself, would not buy the bat a sensory system for spatial perception. In order for the bat to perceive spatial relations in the world, something more would be needed: the visual images would have to be hooked up with various other neural processes "further down the line"—with the bat's cortical pattern analysers that decode object shape, texture and identity, with the bat's vestibular and motor systems, and with, well, who knows what else? The fiction of the bat film, however, is that these colour sensations are what the bat experiences, *qualitatively*—a coloured image of the sound field, over time, as the bat pursues a mealworm.

One problem with the bat film now looks relatively clear: as a result of the differences between the human visual system and the bat auditory system, we cannot expect that by inducing colour sensations in ourselves we will understand the role that such sensations play in the bat's phenomenal world.[3] Because a "sen-surround" film produces our visual experience through the usual means, we see the colours as we normally do, as the projection of moving coloured images upon a curved screen. Lacking the auditory/representational capacities of the bat, we do not experience the colours as does the bat, however that might be. All a film can show us are meaningless (albeit coloured!) visual events. Put another way, what the bat film seems to prove is that it is not for lack of the "quality" of the bat's experience that his world eludes us. Even if, *ex hypothesi*, we were able to produce in ourselves the "very feel" of the bat's experience, its 'qualitative' aspect, we would not understand the bat's point of view. Watching the swirl of colours, those sensations lack their proper representational content. We cannot expect to understand the bat's point of view, in other words, without access to both the representational and qualitative parts of its experience. And here we are given but one aspect, the phenomenological "feel" of the bat's world.

Unfortunately, this way of putting things is not quite right, for it does not get to the root of the problem, does not fully explain why a film cannot give us the point of view of the bat. Let me try a different path. Both the description of the bat film as initially given and the conclusions drawn from it above presupposed that there could be a separation of the "qualitative" and "representational" aspects of phenomenal experience. "What the bat hears is just like colour" the reader is told, "except, of course, the colours mean something quite different. Imagine that!" This was how the thought experiment got off the ground. Yet sensible as that request might have seemed, we have no idea how to comply with it, what such a separation could be. As Daniel Dennett has often pointed out (see, for example, Dennett, 1988), what one is asked to imagine, what one can imagine and what one actually imagines are three distinct things. It is not clear that we do know how to separate our conscious experiences into two parts, the representational and qualitative aspects, or whether, indeed, this notion even makes sense. To illustrate this point, suppose that, instead of referring to the bat film, I had requested that you do the following:

> Open your eyes and look around your office (it's the end of term)—at the stacks of books and papers, at the piles of articles, unopened mail and ungraded papers. Note the way the scene looks to you, the inner phenomenology of the event. Now, a bat's consciousness is just like that—the feel of the scene is exactly the same—except, of course, all those visual sensations *mean* something very different to the bat. They represent quite different properties. Imagine that!

The problem is that you cannot imagine that, no matter how sincerely or hard you try. First, it would require that you "strip away" the representational content of the entire office scene (say, by erasing the "black lines" of the image, leaving only the "crayoned" parts?). Then, by some other process, the intentional content of the bat's representations must be "overlaid" upon the remaining bare sensory qualities (by a process akin to drawing in new lines or attaching new labels?). This, I contend, is not something we have any idea how to do: we do not know what the two "parts" would be like, of and by themselves, so we have no inkling how to pull them apart or put them together. Our intuitions do not provide a concrete distinction between the qualitative and representational aspects of perceptions.

Still, you might well ask, why then, if there is no such distinction, did the bat example work at all? That is, in the bat film, we were asked to imagine meaningless coloured patches swirling across the screen—and we did. It also seemed perfectly reasonable to imagine that those colours played a representational role in the bat's experience, one that was different from the role they play in our conceptual scheme. But if there is no distinction between the qualitative and representational parts of experience, how could this be so? Certainly it seemed to us that we could imagine such a distinction.

The answer here is that the description of the film was intentionally misleading: it was designed to play upon a common experience, that of seeing images or pictures we can not identify. Staring at an abstract painting perplexedly, we scan the blobs of colour for form—what could that possibly be a picture of?—when, suddenly, the figure of a man emerges. The apparently meaningless blobs of paint are transformed into a comprehensible image. These are the cases in which we legitimately regard content and "mere colour" as distinct: at first the canvas contains only formless coloured blobs; after the "aha!" experience, the painting has meaning—and this despite the fact that the canvas remains physically unchanged. It was this kind of event that set the stage for the original bat film. Given our familiarity with pictures and drawings, we tried to imagine a similar kind of thing—a film of "meaningless" coloured shapes, non-intentional and non-representational sensory qualities, such that, if only we knew the proper "squint" of the bat, those images would have content for us as well. We imagined, or at least we thought we could imagine, an unchanging substrate of pure sensation—a substrate analogous to the physical paint upon the canvas— onto which the bat's meaning could be affixed. The problem, however, is that our experience of abstract art does not provide a genuine example of what we need, the separation of content from "mere colour." Viewing an abstract painting does not involve an experience of a 'meaningless' image in the proper sense, that is, because the sudden emergence of a form in an abstract artwork is not the experience of having sensory stimuli, devoid of content, instantaneously gain representational properties.

Even if we do not initially see the coloured shapes as the ghostly portrait of a man, we do see the colours as something—as coloured shapes upon a canvas, external to us, 3 ft dead ahead. The same is true for the patches of colour in the bat film. Perceiving (or imagining) moving coloured patches on a screen is an intentional— or at least, quasi-intentional—event, an experience of coloured patches as coloured patches. So when we imagined the bat film, we did not thereby imagine pure sensory qualities, colour qualia devoid of content. Our understanding of abstract art forms was misleading because it fostered the illusion that we could imagine exactly that.

Where does this leave us with respect to Nagel's original question and its intuitive basis? In questioning whether we could ever understand an alien organism's point of view, we intuitively construe this problem as analogous to the everyday task of understanding the phenomenal experiences of each other. Here, because our own difficulties turn around individual sensations, around the "feel" of sensory events— the pain of a migraine headache, the azure blue of the Mediterranean, the "essence" of flamingo pink—we infer that the main stumbling block to understanding an alien creature must be the inaccessibility of those qualia. We treat a conscious experience, in other words, as a mere collection of qualia, as a bunch of individual sense data that have somehow come together to form a phenomenological whole. (Certainly, this is the route that most analytic philosophical debates have also taken. In the "inverted spectrum" problem, for example, the question is asked whether it would be possible for two people to have exactly the same neural structures and functions and yet have their colour experiences be "spectral inversions," one of the other. Could you, my neurological equivalent, see the sky as red even though I see it as blue? In the "absent qualia" problem (Block, 1978), the question is whether an artificial system function- ally identical to one's own brain could be entirely devoid of qualitative experience. If, given a Turing-machine table that described the functional states of my brain, the entire population of China could be talked into instantiating, for one hour, the state types specified by that table, would my aches, tickles and pains be somehow "expe- rienced" (collectively?) by all the citizens of China? These are the kinds of questions —questions phrased in terms of individual sensations—that are currently asked.)

What is overlooked by the intuitive construal of the problem are the following two points. First, because we are able to individuate, identify and catalogue some of our phenomenological experiences and to converse with other people about such percep- tual experiences as "that very colour" (referring, say, to the intense blue-green of the Mediterranean), it does not follow that these sensations come to exist *in vacuo*. This "isolation" of those sensations (whether as a result of some internal process of in- dividuation or merely in virtue of linguistic convention) does not thereby produce sensations that stand apart from our representational/conceptual schemes. What the intuitive view conflates, in other words, is an ability to refer to certain parts of con- scious intentional experience with an ability to pick out its purely qualitative aspects. Isolation does not distil qualia from content. So, whatever the root of our everyday problems in communication, it is not the intrinsic nature of sensations *per se* that makes for trouble—or, rather, there is no reason to think that this is the case given our communicative problems. If our utterances do not refer to pure sensation, one sees that the problems of communicating our phenomenological experience are equally a problem about representational states.

Second, a point of view, as we know from our own—paradigmatic—case, is not a jumble of qualia. In the normal non-pathological subject, consciousness is systematic, representational and intentional (e.g. we represent objects as being a certain way or of a certain type). Moreover, such properties are not "optional" parts of our conscious experience, merely accidental or inconsequential aspects, if they can be considered "parts" at all. Rather, these properties are constitutive of a point of view. That we experience the world in any way at all—that it is like anything to be me—is made possible by exactly these properties. So, given that our own phenomenal experience is the starting point for an explanation of the very notion of a point of view, and that our own experience is not a mere collection of qualia, we must assume that the same holds for the bat. If there is anything it is like to be bat, we have no reason to think—indeed, there is no sense to the suggestion—that that bat's experience is but a collection of pure qualia.

The mistake of the intuitive view, then, was first to think that our problem of communication was one about pure qualitative states, and then, second, to import this interpretation of the problem into the task of understanding an alien point of view. If we construe our communicative failures to hinge upon pure qualitative states of which the speakers do not have a common experience, then what we face in understanding a foreign phenomenology is simply "much more of the same"—for the bat will have more and more purely qualitative states of which we ourselves have had no experience. By misconstruing the nature of an interpersonal problem, the puzzle about another creature's point of view becomes a problem about pure qualia.

The upshot of the bat film, then, is this. Nagel has claimed that we will never understand the point of view of an alien creature. This is a claim that our intuitions support with a nod towards "that something," pure phenomenal experience, which cannot be known merely by description, without personal experience. But if introspection does not yield any clear distinction between the representational and qualitative properties of experience, then we do not know, *a priori*, what insights or even what kinds of insights will result from empirical investigation. Certainly we cannot confidently declare that science must fail to unearth "that something," for we have no clear idea to what this amounts; nor can one say what the scientific approach will necessarily leave out, if it must leave out anything at all. This gives us, I think, good reason to continue on with our empirical investigations of mental representation—to look towards the disciplines of neurophysiology, psychology and artificial intelligence—without undue pessimism about the relevance of their experimental results.

Ourselves as Subject

One consequence of tying together sensation and representational experience is that the nature of our own subjective experience is opened to investigation (Sellars, 1963; Dennett, 1978; Churchland, 1983). It is as legitimate a subject of inquiry as the experience of other creatures. Because the questions about phenomenology are no longer focused on the intrinsic quality of particular sensations but on a phenomenology as a whole—complete with its representational/intentional nature—our ignorance extends to ourselves as well. We, as the "owners" of our point of view, do not thereby understand its representational character. Hence, our study of representational systems is also an investigation into our own point of view.

This consequence is, I suspect, somewhat counter-intuitive. If anyone knows about my subjective experience, it is certainly me, or at least that is what we have always thought about the matter. By way of lending some small amount of plausibility to this result, then, I want to end this chapter by going back to the example at the beginning, that of the eagle. What did learning a simple anatomical fact about the eagle, about the foveation of the eye, tell us about that creature's experience? More importantly, how would a fact about an eagle nudge our sense of self, reflect upon the human experience?

In learning that the eye of the eagle has two separate foveal regions, it suddenly seemed clear that the experience of the eagle must be different from our own. On the other hand, when I tried to imagine *how* the experience of an eagle would differ from my own, I immediately adopted a hypothesis that incorporated my own visual system into the experience. I wondered, that is, whether being an eagle might not be akin to the experience I would have while wearing strange quadra-focals—whether it wouldn't be like shifting my own gaze from lens to lens sequentially. In essence, I incorporated my own foveal field into the experience of being an eagle. (This would give me, in effect, eight different levels of visual acuity: four lenses imposed upon my foveal and non-foveal regions.) Of course, nothing we know about the visual system of the bird of prey constrains its visual "attention" in a similar way. Although my foveae must move from lens to lens sequentially, the bird need not have any analogous "inner" eye that receives, serially, the information from the two foveae and the horizontal band. Because there are parallel lines from all regions of the retina, there is no reason why the brain must process the information sequentially—no reason why, say, the eagle must first attend to the left, then forward, then to the horizon just as I would. The eagle might "attend" simultaneously to all this information at once, no matter how this might conflict with our intuitive notion of visual attention. This is a possibility that the anatomical data reveals.

Note that once we see how a notion of "foveal" processing has been misapplied to the eagle's point of view, it is an interesting question whether or not we have also "moved the eye inward" not merely in thinking about the eagle, but alas in thinking about ourselves. Here, I am referring to the many models of conscious attention that utilize, in one form or another, the "spotlight" metaphor: the "inner eye" of consciousness shifts like a searchlight from one neural event to another, successively attending to different mental events. This, too, is a "foveal" theory of attention, not of another organism's consciousness but of our own. We apply the foveal metaphor to our conscious experience as a whole. Certainly, this is a model with intuitive plausibility. Something about it seems just right. The question that the eagle's eye raises, however, is about the basis of this appeal. Is it appealing because this is, in fact, how our inner experience is, or does it seem right just because the foveated nature of our visual experience colours our understanding of conscious attentive processes as a whole?

First, the former alternative could be true. The spotlight theory might seem plausible because, on looking inwardly at ourselves, we can see by introspection that our consciousness is sequentially focused on single events. That is, the introspective evidence coheres with the metaphor. But is this really so? Recall what it is like to struggle through a recalcitrant screen door weighed down by several bags of groceries. First, you juggle the groceries and grasp the door handle; then you feel a mosquito land on your ankle; then you hear the creaking door hinge and the rip of a paper bag; then the mosquito makes a stab with his proboscis; then you loose your grip on the handle; then the screen slams shut on your shin; then a tin can bounces off your thigh ... Somehow, this strictly sequential narrative does not quite capture the experience, even if it does record the objective order of the external events. The very problem with such experiences is that "everything happens at once." In the midst of the calamity, what happens first—the bag ripping or the mosquito biting or the screen door slamming—is not always clear. On the basis of experience alone, there is no distinct ordering of all of the events, no clear sequence of this event, then this one, then this and finally that.

Perhaps, then, the explanation goes the other way about: perhaps the searchlight metaphor, combined with our story-telling practices and our understanding of the relevant causal chain of events, confer order upon the conscious events only in retrospect. What I am suggesting is that the spotlight metaphor may be adopted just because (a) we are foveated animals and (b) we do not actually perceive any firm order in the events (i.e. such events are not "tagged" for time). Because we are such strongly visual organisms and because eye movements are required for our perception of the world, the metaphor seems plausible. Needing an explanation, we mistake our intuitive grasp of the visual perception of external events for an accurate description of internal attentional processes. We co-opt the visual notions of "searching," "focusing" and "watching" and apply them to all of conscious experience. This, I think, is possible. What the eye of the eagle should make us wonder is whether our conception of ourselves might not be "tainted" with the same foveal metaphors we naturally apply to other creatures.

The above example is not meant as a serious criticism of spotlight theories of conscious attention. Rather, it is given as a suggestive example of how it could come about that we are mistaken about our own inner events—how the way our own attentional mechanisms seem to us could diverge from how in fact they are. It offers a small glimpse of the ways a possible reconception of ourselves, and our point of view, could come about in the light of physiological/computational discoveries.

Still, the central idea of this chapter has been that we do not know what science will explain, just because we lack a firm grasp on the subject matter: the nature of conscious events. If so, we are in a funny position. We will know what science can tell us only after it has done so. Hence, only suggestive examples are now possible. What we can provide, however, are good reasons to wait—to see what science will do. In effect, this is what I have been attempting to show in this chapter.

Acknowledgements

This chapter began as an introduction to paper, "What is it Like to be Boring and Myopic?" (Akins, 1993) where it served, in a much abbreviated form, to motivate the neuroscientific approach to the problem of consciousness used there. An earlier version appeared under the title "Science and Our Inner Lives: Birds of Prey, Bats and the Common (Featherless) Bi-ped" in a collection edited by Marc Bekoff and Dale Jamieson (1990). For their generous comments on and discussion of the manuscript, I would like to thank Marc Bekoff, Daniel C. Dennett, Dale Jamieson, Joseph Malpeli, Wright Neely, Brian C. Smith, Tony Stone, Tom Stoneham and Mary Windham. I would also like to thank Martin Davies for his extensive comments on the final draft.

Notes

1. That someone being Jeremy Butterfield.
2. This way of generating the film was given only for the sake of example, not because I think that this is what a bat's experience is really like. That is, assuming that a bat does have a point of view (and I doubt

that it has), the film represents the properties of the sound field before the sound waves are transduced, processed and filtered by the basilar membrane, midbrain and auditory cortex of the bat. At the level of the auditory cortex (surely the first neural level at which conscious experience would be possible), the informational characteristics of the signal have been significantly changed.

3. It is an interesting question, however, whether, given the addition of dopplershift or velocity information to the visual display, our own visual systems could act as a spatial pattern analyser of some sort—that is, whether if we, given the intellectual knowledge of how the image is produced, were to look at the screen we could learn to use that information to guide our actions, say to walk around a room filled with objects.

References

Akins, K. A. 1993: What is it like to be boring and myopic? In B. Dahlbom (ed.) *Dennett and his Critics*, Oxford: Blackwell Publishers.

Bekoff, M. and Jamieson, D. 1990: *Interpretation and Explanation in the Study of Animal Behavior. Vol. I: Interpretation, Intentionality, and Communication*. Boulder, Co.: Westview Press.

Block, N. 1978: Troubles with functionalism. In C. Wade Savage (ed.), *Perception and Cognition: Issues in the Foundations of Psychology, Minnesota Studies in the Philosophy of Science*, Vol. 9, Minneapolis: University of Minnesota Press, 261–325. Reprinted in Block, 1980a, Vol. 1, 268–306.

Churchland, P. S. 1983. Consciousness: the transmutation of a concept. *Pacific Philosophical Quarterly*, 64, 80–95.

Dawkins, R. 1986: *The Blind Watchmaker*, London: Longman.

Dennett, D. C. 1978: *Brainstorms: Philosophical Essays on Mind and Psychology*. Cambridge, MA.: MIT Press.

Dennett, D. C. 1988: Quining qualia. In Marcel and Bisiach, 1988, 42–7.

De Yoe, E. A. and Van Essen, D. C. 1988: Concurrent processing streams in monkey visual cortex. *Trends in Neuroscience*, 11, 218–26.

Duke-Elder, S. 1958: *System of Ophthalmology: The Eye in Evolution* (Vol. I). St Louis: Mosby.

Gouras, P. 1984: Colour vision. In N. Osborn and J. Chader (eds), *Progress in Retinal Research*, Vol. 3, Oxford: Pergamon Press, 227–61.

Jackson, F. 1982: Epiphenomenal qualia. *Philosophical Quarterly*, 32, 127–36.

McGinn, C. 1983: *The Subjective View*. Oxford: Oxford University Press.

McGinn, C. 1989: Can we solve the mind-body problem? *Mind*, 98, 349–66.

Nagel, T. 1974: What is it like to be a bat?, *Philosophical Review*, 83, 435–50.

Sellars, W. 1963: *Science, Perception and Reality*. London: Routledge and Kegan Paul.

Webster, F. A. and Griffin, D. R. 1962: The role of the flight membranes in insect capture in bats. *Animal Behavior*, 10, 332–40.

Chapter 24

Afterword: Ethics and the Study of Animal Cognition

Dale Jamieson and Marc Bekoff

In the heyday of logical empiricism (circa 1930–1960), science was seen as the purest of human activities. There was a single thing that was "the scientific method"; observations were distinct from and unaffected by theoretical commitments; theories were "sets of sentences" that made no essential reference to knowers; explanation and prediction were regarded as formal relations between sentences that in principle could be made mechanical; and all of this theorizing, explaining, and predicting was thought to be uncontaminated by values.

While many scientists continue to give obeisance to some such picture, it has long since met its demise in the broader intellectual community. Beginning with Quine (1951/1961), influential philosophers argued forcefully against almost every tenet of logical empiricism. Next came historians, abetted by the testimony of important scientific figures. Books such as J. D. Watson's (1968) *The Double Helix* painted a very different picture of scientific discovery than was suggested by the logical empiricist model. Scientists were seen to be sometimes selfish, irrational, motivated by power and prestige rather than The Pursuit of Truth—in other words, all too human. In the wake of these critiques have come moral philosophers, sociologists, and most recently feminists (see for example, Lori Gruen, chapter 2 of this volume). Although many scientists may not be aware of it, there is a swirl of activity addressing almost every feature of the scientific life (Alberts and Shine 1994).

Science, like all human practices and institutions, is a proper subject for moral scrutiny, and there is growing concern about issues that center on human relationships with nonhuman animals (references can be found in Bekoff 1994a, 1995 and Bekoff and Jamieson 1996). Scientists such as Richard Dawkins (1993) have called for legal rights for chimpanzees, gorillas, and orangutans. Top-level administrators in the United States such as President's Clinton's science advisor, John Gibbons, have indicated the need for greater ethical reflection on the use of animals in research.

In this chapter we briefly consider two difficult, overlapping issues about the relationship between ethics and the study of animal cognition. These are (i) the vexing connection between cognition and moral status and (ii) the ethics of various experimental practices in studies of animal cognition and behavior.

Cognition and Moral Status

The philosophical roots of the contemporary animal protection movement can be traced to Peter Singer's (1975, 1990) book, *Animal Liberation*. One important factor influencing the reception of Singer's book is that it appeared against a background of changing attitudes in philosophy, psychology, and linguistics about the appropriateness of appeal to cognitive states in the explanation of human behavior. Chomsky's (1959) review of Skinner's *Verbal Behavior* was widely regarded as devastating to behaviorist attempts to explain human linguistic competence. By the time *Animal Liberation* was published, behaviorism was dead in much of the intellectual world. It was no longer out of the question for scientists to explain human behavior in mentalistic terms. If the social lives of many animals were as complex as some researchers suggested and if there were no good theoretical reasons for eschewing talk of mental states, then it seemed natural to explain animal behavior in mentalistic terms as well.

Viewed in this light, the development of cognitive ethology was inevitable, and perhaps even tardy. The years 1974–1976 saw the publication of Nagel's (1974) provocative paper "What is it like to be a bat?," Wilson's (1975) *Sociobiology: The New Synthesis*, and Griffin's (1976) *The Question of Animal Awareness: Evolutionary Continuity of Mental Experience*. In only two years students of animal behavior were presented with major new ideas in overlapping fields concerned with the comparative and evolutionary study of animal behavior. In *Animal Liberation* Singer discussed research on animals at great length, and although much of the discussion is negative and disapproving, he relied on the ethological work of Jane Goodall, Konrad Lorenz, and Niko Tinbergen to show that many animals have much more complex cognitive and social systems than were previously attributed to them, especially by the behaviorist mainstream, and that they were capable of pleasure and pain. Singer himself noted the irony that scientific research on animals has discovered features of animals such that, in virtue of them, a great deal of behavioral research cannot be justified. Indeed, the very research that resulted in these discoveries may appear immoral in light of their own results.

Questions about the relation between what animals are like and how they should be treated are often in the background of discussions about the complexity of behavior and the "inner" lives of animals (Bekoff and Jamieson 1991; Jamieson and Bekoff 1992; Bekoff 1994a, 1995). These questions should move from the background to the foreground and be openly discussed. While there is no purely logical connection between views about mental continuity and views about moral continuity, there are important psychological connections. A culture that recognizes its behavioral and emotional kinship with nonhuman animals is one that is likely to recognize its moral kinship as well (Rollin 1989; Bekoff et al. 1992; Cavalieri and Singer 1993).

Some have gone as far as to claim that if gaining knowledge of the cognitive skills of wild animals does nothing more than inform the debate about animal welfare, then these efforts are worthwhile (Byrne 1991). Those who study behavior and behavioral ecology in the field are in a good position to make important contributions to animal welfare, although unfortunately they often play only a minor role in informing legislation and regulation. Field workers can help to provide guidelines concerning dietary requirements, space needs, and the type of captive habitat that would be the most conducive to maintaining the natural activity budgets of the animals being held captive, as well as information on social needs in terms of group size, age and sex composition, and about the nature of the bonds that are formed between animals and human researchers. One important result of research in cognitive ethology is that even if animals are physically well-maintained, the individual's state of mind—his or her psychological well-being—must be given serious consideration (Bekoff 1994a, 1995).

Research Ethics for Ethologists

Studies on cognition are performed both under controlled laboratory conditions and in the field. Often research not motivated by an interest in animal cognition but by an interest in behavior suggests that animals are "smarter" than had been previously realized; that they are conscious, have expectations, desires, and beliefs, make assessments and choices based on fine discriminations among various alternatives, and have subjective feelings (Bekoff and Jamieson 1991; Ristau 1991; Griffin 1992; M. Dawkins 1993). Even though apparently clever behavior does not imply cognition, often the attribution of mental predicates is irresistible in these cases. Even those who are officially skeptics about animal cognition often fall into using cognitive language when discussing their work. In some cases they would not know what to say otherwise.

Both laboratory and field research can involve intrusions into the privacy of animals' lives. Because animals living under field conditions are generally more difficult to observe than individuals living under more confined conditions, various manipulations are often used to make them more accessible to study. These include activities such as handling, trapping (often using various sorts of mechanical devices that might include using live animals as bait), and marking individuals, none of which are unique to field studies, but all of which can have important and diverse effects on wild animals who may not be accustomed to being handled by humans or even to their presence. Simply observing and visiting individuals, groups, nests, dens, and ranging areas can also have a significant influence on behavior. Filming animals can have a negative influence on the animals being filmed; reflections from camera bodies, the noise of motor-driven cameras and other sorts of video devices, and the heat and brightness of spotlights (A. Pusey personal communication) can all be disruptive. In a long-term study of coyotes (Bekoff and Wells 1986), it was found that shiny cameras and spotting scopes made the animals uneasy, so this equipment was painted dull black so that it would not reflect much light. In this study, the same clothes were worn when visiting dens so that similar odors and visual images were presented to the coyotes on each visit.

Here are some examples of how what seem to be minor or insignificant intrusions from our point of view can actually disrupt the lives of animals (see also Kirkwood, Sainsbury, and Bennett 1994).

> 1. Kenney and Knight (1992) found that magpies who are not habituated to human presence spend so much time avoiding humans that this takes time away from essential activities such as feeding.
> 2. Major (1990) reported that in white-fronted chats, nests that were visited daily by humans suffered higher nest predation than nests that were visited only once at the end of a typical period of incubation.
> 3. Wilson et al. (1991) found that Adélie penguins who were away from their nests when exposed to aircraft and directly to humans showed profound changes in behavior including deviation from a direct course back to a nest as well as increased nest abandonment. Overall effects due to exposure to aircraft included a decrease of 15% in the number of birds in a colony and an increase

of 8% in active nest mortality when compared to undisturbed conditions, as well as substantial increases in heart rates.

4. Hensen and Grant (1991) found that trumpeter swans do not show such adverse effects to aircraft. However, the noise and visible presence of vehicles did produce changes in incubation behavior by trumpeter females that could result in decreased productivity due to increases in the mortality of eggs and hatchlings.

5. Gales, Williams, and Ritz (1990) found that the foraging efficiency of little penguins (average mass of 1,100 grams) was decreased by their carrying a small device (about 60 grams) that measured the speed and depth of their dives. They referred to the changes in behavior as the "instrument effect." Davis (1991) also found that Adelie penguins fitted with small transmitters showed reduced swimming speed and probably foraging efficiency as well.

6. Pietz et al. (1993) found that free-ranging radio-equipped female mallard ducks, when compared to females who were not radio-equipped, "tended to feed less, rest and preen more, initiate nests later, and lay smaller clutches and eggs" (p. 696).

7. Kinkel (1989) reported that fewer wing-tagged ring-billed gulls returned to their colony site when compared to leg-banded individuals, pair bonds of tagged birds were also broken more frequently than pair bonds of banded birds, and most tagged females who returned to their colony were unable to acquire mates.

8. Burley, Krantzberg, and Radman (1982) showed that mate choice in zebra finches is influenced by the color of the leg band used to mark individuals. Females with black rings and males with red rings had higher reproductive success than birds with other colors. Blue and green rings were especially unattractive on both females and males.

9. Gutzwiller et al. (1994) found that in some species of birds, human intrusion influenced normal singing behavior, the result of which could lower the reproductive fitness of males who are sensitive to this type of disturbance.

10. Bertreaux, Duhamel, and Bergeron (1994) observed that the weight of radio collars influenced dominance relationships in adult female meadow voles. There was a significant loss of dominance when voles wore a collar that was greater than 10% of their live body mass.

11. Laurenson and Caro (1994), in perhaps the most careful and extensive analysis available for a large mammal, analyzed the long-term effects of wearing a radio collar, aerial radio-tracking, and lair examination in wild cheetahs on the central plains of the Serengeti National Park, Tanzania. They concluded that "the behaviour and reproduction of even sensitive mammals need not be affected by field techniques" (p. 547). However, they caution that some of their measures might have been too crude and they note that there might be individual differences in response to stress (for example) that demand close attention. Furthermore, they state (p. 556) that "Recording and reporting such measures should be a routine part of any study using intrusive techniques, as the onus is on fieldworkers to show that their methods have no impact, or at least an acceptable impact, on their study animals" (see also Travaini, Palomares, and Delibes 1993). Needless to say, much more work and discussion is needed to flesh out just what "an acceptable impact" consists in.

While there are many problems that are encountered both in laboratory and field research, the consequences for wild animals may be different from and greater than those experienced by captive animals, whose lives are already changed by the conditions under which they live. This is so for different types of experiments that may or may not entail handling, trapping, and marking individuals. Consider experimental procedures that include (i) visiting the home ranges, territories, or dens of animals, (ii) manipulating food supply and other resources, (iii) changing the size and composition of groups (age, sex ratio, kin relationships) by removing or adding individuals, (iv) playing back vocalizations, (v) depositing scents, (vi) distorting phenotypes, (vii) using dummies, and (viii) manipulating the gene pool. These manipulations can change the behavior of individuals and groups with respect to movement patterns, how space is used, the amount of time that is devoted to various activities including hunting, foraging, anti-predatory behavior, and social encounters including caregiving, play, and dominance interactions. These changes can also influence the behavior of nontarget individuals. Consider, for example, the consequences of reintroducing red wolves into areas in which coyotes already live.

Many specific questions can be asked about the ethics of animal research and we briefly discuss several of these questions in what follows. Although there may be little consensus about the answers to these questions at this time, we believe that better and worse answers can be given.

1. Do wild animals have a different moral status than domestic animals? This is an important question because field studies are performed on both domestic and wild animals, often in the same habitat. Callicott (1980/1989, p. 30) writes that "Domestic animals are creations of man. They are living artifacts, but artifacts nonetheless, and they constitute yet another mode of the extension of the works of man into the ecosystem." Callicott thinks that domestic animals are "stupid" and are not owed the kind of respect due to wild animals. Others, however, argue that there is no distinction in moral status between wild and domestic animals, or that we owe more to domestic animals than we do to wild animals. We may owe more to certain domesticated animals because of the trust these animals invest in humans and the strong reciprocal bonds that develop (Bekoff 1995). Colwell (1989, p. 33) maintains that "Our moral responsibility for the appropriate care of *individual* organisms in agriculture, zoos, or gardens does not depend on whether they are wild or domesticated in origin." He also writes: "I contend, however, that the role of domesticated *species* as coevolved members of our ancestral component community ... places them in a biologically and ethically distinct class from 'wild' species."

2. Is it ever justified, and if so under what conditions, to bring wild animals into captivity? The most frequently cited reason for bringing animals into captivity is to preserve endangered species by allowing individuals to live in a protected environment that facilitates breeding and maintains the species' gene pool. It is sometimes said that the goal of these programs is the eventual return of these animals to the wild. While there are serious philosophical questions involved here (e.g. Do animals have a right to liberty? Do species have interests? Can the welfare of individuals be sacrificed in the interests of species? [Jamieson 1985/ 1994, 1995a]), it should be noted that some of the most severe critics of captive breeding programs are the scientists themselves who have dedicated their lives

to these efforts and who sincerely want them to succeed (e.g. Peterson 1989; Rabinowitz 1986; Schaller 1993). No one should deny the extreme importance of the goals of captive breeding programs. However, half-hearted, haphazard, or incorrect approaches both waste resources and harm the animals involved.

3. How can the number of animals used in research be minimized? In cases in which animals are followed or located repeatedly, it is worth asking whether only one individual has to be marked or fitted with a radio collar if all other animals are individually identifiable using reliable behavioral or other markers. Not only would this entail less handling of individuals, but minimal labeling of the animals might also lead to less disruption of ongoing behavior. If studies produce results whose validity can be legitimately questioned, because, for example, the data come from stressed animals, then attempts to repeat the studies, in one form or another, will result in yet more animals being used.

4. Should individuals be subjected to harmful or painful staged encounters so that we can learn how animals deal with these situations and how their behavior is influenced (Huntingford 1984)? There are many studies of this kind, including those in which researchers intentionally stimulate predatory, agonistic, infanticidal, or other types of encounters. While these sorts of studies can result in useful knowledge, there are many difficult issues involved, and reflecting on them can make people change their minds. As an example, one of us (MB) performed staged encounter studies on the development of predatory behavior in captive coyotes, but on reflection found it impossible to justify them and decided that he would no longer do this sort of research. His decision centered on the psychological pain and suffering to which the prey (mice and young chickens) were subjected by being placed in a small arena in which there were no possibilities for escape, as well as the physical consequences of being stalked, chased, caught, maimed, and killed. One result of his decision is that additional detailed information about the development of predatory behavior could not be obtained because similar data cannot be collected under nonstaged field conditions. Staged-encounter studies are also performed in the field. For example, in a recent study, Small and Keith (1992) released radio-collared Arctic and snowshoe hares to learn how Arctic foxes preyed on them. Infanticide is also often studied using staged encounters. In one study of experimentally induced infanticide in birds, mothers were "collected"—that is, shot to death—to determine how replacement females would treat the young of the females who had been killed (Emlen, Demong, and Emlen 1989). Many motherless chicks were maimed or killed, and the ethics of such a study have been called into question (Bekoff 1993).

Live trapping is also an activity that can be incredibly inhumane, and the experience of being caught in a live trap can be quite painful for an animal. In order to learn about the physiological (endocrinological, hematological) and behavioral responses of captive and free-ranging red foxes to padded and unpadded foothold traps, Kreeger et al. (1990) conducted a 3-year study in which trapped foxes were "euthanized" (killed) by shooting them and nontrapped free-ranging foxes who were used as controls also were shot to death. Kreeger and his colleagues found (p. 147) that "foxes caught in unpadded traps had higher physical injury scores to the trapped limbs than foxes caught in padded traps" and that "heart rate and body temperature increased rapidly after foxes were caught, but returned to mean pretrapped levels after 80 minutes." There were also some important biochemical differences between trapped and control foxes (generally, trapped foxes had "higher levels of adrenocorticotropin, β-endorphin, and cortisol and lower levels of thyroxine and insulin" as well as higher leukocyte counts with a significant neutrophilia and leukopenia, and higher incidences of adrenal and kidney congestion and hemorrhaging in their adrenal glands, lungs, and hearts) and between foxes caught in padded versus nonpadded traps (foxes caught in padded traps generally had higher cortisol levels, but lower β-endorphin levels). There was no significant difference in the mean time spent resisting traps during an 8-hour period between foxes caught in padded (mean of 85.4 minutes) and unpadded traps (mean of 63.8 minutes). Note that animals were allowed to resist traps for cumulative periods of over one hour!

As a result of their efforts, Kreeger et al. concluded that "Red foxes caught in foothold traps developed 'classical' stress responses characterized by increased HR, increased HPA hormones, elevations of serum chemicals, and neutrophilia" (p. 159). Most of the changes in trapped animals were due to resisting traps. The results of their study led the researchers to recommend the use of padded traps in future work. There is no mention at all about the ethics of either the research that they did or that trapping of all kinds is an activity that should be carefully scrutinized and is often ill-advised. That padded traps do, indeed, produce fewer serious injuries had previously been shown by Olsen et al. (1986, 1988) and McKenzie (1989), and one wonders why Kreeger et al.'s research was even necessary. McKenzie modified steel foothold traps and tested them on seven free-ranging black-backed jackals in Botswana. While there were fewer injuries when padded traps were used, six (85.7%) of the jackals trapped still showed lameness of the leg which had been trapped.

Unfortunately, the guidelines of most professional societies are not very explicit about what humaneness consists in nor about schedules of checking traps, nor for that matter, about schedules for checking on animals who are fitted with bands, tags, radio collars, or implanted telemetric devices. For example, the American Society of Mammalogist's guidelines for acceptable field methods (1987, p. 7) state that humane scientific methods, those "that keep the captured mammals alive, uninjured, and in a comfortable microenvironment while contained for subsequent handling," must be used when trapping live animals and that "Live traps must be checked frequently." The (undefined) schedule of checking depends on the type of trap that is used. In the booklet on ethics published by the Association for the Study of Animal Behaviour and the Animal Behavior Society (Stamp Dawkins and Gosling 1992) there is no discussion of recommended trapping procedures. Perhaps developing stringent guidelines for checking trap lines and also for checking marked or instrument-equipped animals should be on the immediate agenda of these and other associations. It seems highly unlikely that anyone who has ever worked with trapped animals could claim that being trapped is not both physically and psychologically harmful or painful for the individuals involved. Alternatives to leghold traps and other devices that restrict an animal's movements should be developed.

5. What responsibility does the research community have to prevent ethical misconduct, and how should this responsibility be exercised? In recent years

various communities of researchers have taken steps to deal with problems of misconduct by adopting codes of professional ethics and refusing to publish papers that violate ethical guidelines. At the same time researchers have too often behaved like physicians in being reluctant to take steps against their own. In cases of conflict there has been a tendency for many scientists to side with more powerful members of the community against the less powerful. Unfortunately, there still is not much agreement about what the collective ethic should be with regard to many of the questions that we ask, nor much sense that the research community has the obligation to encourage high ethical standards within its own community. In many circles there is even a sense of complacency about research misconduct. Yet, in the most exhaustive empirical study to date on the reported incidence of misconduct, Swazey, Anderson, and Louis (1993) found that reports of fraud, falsification, and plagiarism occur at a surprisingly high rate. They conclude that this is a serious problem that needs immediate attention (see also Bulger, Heitman, and Reisler 1993; Silverman 1994).

6. What is the proper relationship between researchers and the animals they study? Because some form of bonding between the animals who are being studied and the researchers is probably inevitable, these bonds should be exploited in such a way as to benefit the animals (Davis and Balfour 1992; Bekoff 1994b). As L. E. Johnson (1991, p. 122) notes: "Certainly it seems like a dirty double-cross to enter into a relationship of trust and affection with any creature that can enter into such a relationship, and then to be a party to its premeditated and premature destruction." Indeed, double-crossing is routinely done as part of many research projects including exploiting the trust of domesticated animals in human beings so that they can be harmed for experimental purposes. Trapping also can compromise the trust that wild animals develop in humans.

7. What principles should we use as ethical guides? Rolston (1988) has suggested that if human-caused pain in animals is less than or equal to what the animal would experience in the wild, then it is permissible to inflict the pain. For many animals it is difficult to know whether this condition is satisfied, for we do not know how most individual animals in nature experience pain (Hettinger 1994). For this reason we must be careful that this principle is not just a rationalization for researchers doing what they really want to do on other grounds (Hettinger 1989). Many other principles have been proposed that perhaps should guide us in our treatment of animals: utilitarian ones, rights-based ones, and so forth (for further discussion see Jamieson 1993). Scientists often operate on the basis of implicit principles and guidelines that are not discussed that should be brought out into the open.

8. Are scientists responsible for how their results are used? This is not a purely "academic" question, since a great deal of research on animals is funded by agencies that want to reduce populations and control behavior. Information about the behavior of tigers or wolves may be useful to those who simply want to make a rug out of them. Those who study marine mammals have been struggling with the question of researchers' responsibilities to the animals they study for more than a decade. Purely scientific information about populations, migration routes, and behavior can be used by those who are involved in the

commercial exploitation of animals. Even when there are hunting bans and restrictions, these may only be temporary.

One idea worth considering is that a scientist who studies particular animals may be morally required to be an advocate for them in the way that physicians are supposed to be advocates for their patients. On this view, the welfare of the animals who a scientist studies should come first, perhaps even before the goal of obtaining peer-reviewed scientific results. Some scientists such as Jane Goodall and Dian Fossey have exemplified this ethic, but they have had many critics from within the scientific community.

9. Perhaps the most fundamental question is why do research on animals at all. Even the least invasive research can be disruptive and costs time and money. In recent years anthropology has been going through a disciplinary soul-searching, and it is time for behavioral biology to go through one as well. Many people study animals for deeply personal reasons—they like being outdoors, they like animals, they don't know what else they would do with their lives—but this hardly amounts to a justification. Several other reasons for doing this research are also frequently given: that animal research benefits humans, that it benefits animals, and that it benefits the environment.

Animal research that benefits humans falls into two categories. One category includes research that contributes to human health; the other category includes research that provides economic benefits. Little field research can be defended on the grounds that it contributes to human health. Animal models for human diseases and disorders are better constructed under laboratory conditions, and even then many of them are quite controversial both on scientific and moral grounds. Animal research that contributes economic benefits often concerns predator control. Much of this research employs morally questionable methods, and also raises questions about where science ends and industry begins. Predator management may be informed by science but in itself it is not science; and if producing direct economic benefits were the only justification for studying animals then very little behavioral research would be justified.

The idea that behavioral research benefits animals and the environment is an appealing one. The thought is that only by studying animals in nature will we know how to preserve them, and only by preserving animals can we protect the natural environment. As noble as these sentiments are, they are rife with dangers. For this attitude can lead very quickly to transforming science into wildlife management; and wildlife management poses important moral challenges (Jamieson 1995c).

Humans face an environmental crisis in part because of their attempts to control, dominate, and manage nature. These attempts have led to the destruction of important aspects of nature, and even to serious threats to human well-being. In attitude and intention, much wildlife management is more of the same. A new generation seems to think that in the past we were incompetent managers but now we know what we are doing. However, as Ziff (1960, p. vii) wrote in a different context, "the induction is depressing." Ludwig, Hilborn and Walters, (1993) call into question the idea that we can manage animal populations in a sustainable way. They argue that science is probably incapable of predicting sustainable levels of exploitation of an animal population, and even if it were possible to make such predictions human shortsightedness and greed would prevent us from acting on them.

The purest motivation for studying animals may be simply the desire to understand them. But even if this is our motivation, we should proceed cautiously and reflectively. For in quenching our thirst for knowledge we impose costs on the animals. In many cases they would be better off if we were willing to accept our ignorance, secure in the knowledge that they are leading their own lives in their own ways (Jamieson and Regan 1985). However, if we do make the decision to study animals we should recognize that we are doing it primarily for ourselves and not for them, and we should proceed respectfully and harm them as little as possible.

Concluding Remarks

There is a continuing need to develop and improve general guidelines for research on free-living and captive animals. These guidelines should be aspirational as well as regulatory. We should not be satisfied that things are better than they were in the bad old days, and we should work for a future in which even these enlightened times will be viewed as the bad old days. Progress has already been made in the development of guidelines, and the challenge is to make them more binding, effective, and specific. If possible, we should also work for consistency among countries that share common attitudes towards animals; research in some countries (e.g. the United States) is less regulated than research in other countries (e.g. the United Kingdom [Gavaghan 1992]). In this evolving process, interdisciplinary dialogue between field workers and philosophers is necessary; no single discipline can do the necessary work alone. Researchers who are exposed to the pertinent issues, and who think about them and engage in open and serious debate, can then carry these lessons into their research projects and import this knowledge to colleagues and students. Not knowing all of the subtleties of philosophical arguments—details over which even professional ethicists disagree—should not be a stumbling block nor an insurmountable barrier to learning.

Perhaps what is most important is to teach well by precept and example. Those who are now students will live and work in a world in which increasingly science will not be seen as a self-justifying activity, but as another human institution whose claims on the public treasury must be defended (Jamieson 1995b). It is more important than ever for students to understand that questioning science is not to be anti-science or anti-intellectual, and that asking how humans should interact with animals is not in itself to demand that humans never use animals. Questioning science will make for better, more responsible science, and questioning the ways in which humans use animals will make for more informed decisions about animal use. By making such decisions in an informed and responsible way, we can help to ensure that in the future we will not repeat the mistakes of the past, and that we will move towards a world in which humans and other animals may be able to share peaceably the resources of a finite planet.

References

Alberts, B., and Shine, K. 1994. Scientists and the integrity of research. *Science* 266, 1660–1661.
American Society of Mammalogists. 1987. Acceptable field methods in mammalogy: Preliminary guidelines approved by the American Society of Mammalogists. *J. Mammal.* 68 (4, Suppl.), 1–18.

Bekoff, M. 1993. Experimentally induced infanticide: The removal of birds and its ramifications. *Auk* 110, 404–406.

Bekoff, M. 1994a. Cognitive ethology and the treatment of nonhuman animals: How matters of mind inform matters of welfare. *Anim. Welfare* 3, 75–96.

Bekoff, M. 1994b. Should scientists bond with the animals whom they use? Why not? *Int. J. Psychol.* 7, 78–86.

Bekoff, M. 1995. Naturalizing and individualizing animal well-being and animal minds: An ethologists naiveté exposed? In: A. Rowan, ed. *Wildlife Conservation, Zoos, and Animal Protection: Examining the Issues.* Medford, Massachusetts, Tufts.

Bekoff, M., Gruen, L., Townsend, S. E., and Rollin, B. E. 1992. Animals in science: Some areas revisited. *Anim. Behav.* 44, 473–484.

Bekoff, M., and Jamieson, D. 1991. Reflective ethology, applied philosophy, and the moral status of animals. *Persp. Ethology* 9, 1–47.

Bekoff, M., and Jamieson, D. 1996. Ethics and the study of carnivores: Doing science while respecting animals. In: J. L. Gittleman, ed. *Carnivore Behavior, Ecology, and Evolution*, Vol. II. Ithaca, New York, Cornell University Press.

Bekoff, M., and Wells, M. C. 1986. Social ecology and behavior of coyotes. *Adv. Study Behav.* 16, 251–338.

Bertreaux, D., Duhamel, R., and Bergeron, J.-M. 1994. Can radio collars affect dominance relationships in *Microtus*? *Can. J. Zool.* 72, 785–789.

Bulger, R. E., Heitman, E., and Reiser, S. J., eds. 1993. *The Ethical Dimensions of the Biological Sciences.* New York, Cambridge University Press.

Burley, N., Krantzberg, G., and Radman, P. 1982. Influence of color-banding on the conspecific preferences of zebra finches. *Anim. Behav.* 30, 444–455.

Byrne, R. 1991. Review of D. Cheney and R. Seyfarth, *How Monkeys See the World. The Sciences* July, 142–147

Callicott, J. B. 1980/1989. Animal liberation: A triangular affair. In: J. B. Callicott, ed. *In Defense of the Land Ethic: Essays in Environmental Philosophy*, pp. 15–38. Albany, New York, SUNY Press.

Cavalieri, P., and Singer, P. eds. 1993. *The Great Ape Project: Equality Beyond Humanity.* London, Fourth Estate.

Chomsky, N. 1959. Review of B. F. Skinner's *Verbal Behavior. Language* 35, 16–58.

Colwell, R. K. 1989. Natural and unnatural history: Biological diversity and genetic engineering. In: W. R. Shea & B. Sitter, eds. *Scientists and Their Responsibilities*, pp. 1–40. Canton, Mass., Watson Pub. International.

Davis, L. S. 1991. Penguin weighting game. *Nat. Hist.* January, 46–54.

Davis, H., and Balfour, D. eds. 1992. *The Inevitable Bond: Examining Scientist-Animal Interactions.* New York, Cambridge University Press.

Dawkins, M. S. 1993. *Through Our Eyes Only? The Search for Animal Consciousness.* San Francisco, W. H. Freeman.

Dawkins, R. 1993. Gaps in the mind. In: P. Cavalieri and P. Singer, eds. *The Great Ape Project: Equality Beyond Humanity*, pp. 80–87. London, Fourth Estate.

Emlen, S. T., Demong, N. J., and Emlen, D. J. 1989. Experimental induction of infanticide in female wattled jacanas. *Auk* 106, 1–7.

Gales, R., Williams, C., and Ritz, D. 1990. Foraging behaviour of the little penguin, *Eudyptula minor*: Initial results and assessments of instrument effect. *J. Zool. Lond.* 220, 61–85.

Gavaghan, H. 1992. Animal experiments the American way. *New Sci.* 16 May, 32–36.

Griffin, D. R. 1976. *The Question of Animal Awareness: Evolutionary Continuity of Mental Experience.* New York, Rockefeller University Press.

Griffin, D. R. 1992. *Animal Minds.* Chicago, University of Chicago Press.

Gutzwiller, K. J., Wiedenmann, R. T., Clements, K. L., and Anderson, S. H. 1994. Effects of human intrusion on song occurrence and singing consistency in subalpine birds. *Auk* 111, 28–37.

Henson, P., and Grant, T. A. 1991. The effects of human disturbance on trumpeter swan breeding behavior. *Wildl. Soc. Bull.* 19, 248–257.

Hettinger, E. C. 1989. The responsible use of animals in research. *Between the Species* 5, 123–131.

Hettinger, N. 1994. Valuing predation in Rolston's environmental ethics: Bambi lovers versus tree huggers. *Env. Ethics* 16, 3–20.

Huntingford, F. A. 1984. Some ethical issues raised by studies of predation and aggression. *Anim. Behav.* 32, 210–215.

Jamieson, D. 1985/1994. Against zoos. Reprinted in L. Gruen and D. Jamieson, eds. *Reflecting on Nature*, pp. 291–299. New York, Oxford University Press.

Jamieson, D. 1993. Ethics and animals, A brief review. *J. Agric. Env. Ethics* 6 (Spec. Suppl. 1), 15–20.

Jamieson, D. 1995a. Zoos revisited. In B. G. Norton, M. Hutchins, E. F. Stevens, and T. L. Maple, eds. *Ethics on the Ark: Zoos, Animal Welfare, and Wildlife Conservation*, pp. 52–66. Washington, D.C., Smithsonian Institution Press.

Jamieson, D. 1995b. What will society expect of the future research community. *Science and Engineering Ethic* 1, 73–80.

Jamieson, D. 1995c. Wildlife conservation and individual animal welfare. In B. G. Norton, M. Hutchins, E. F. Stevens, and T. L. Maple, eds. *Ethics on the Ark: Animal Welfare and Wildlife Conservation*, pp. 69–73. Washington, D.C., Smithsonian Institution Press.

Jamieson, D., and Bekoff, M. 1992. Carruthers on nonconscious experience. *Analysis* 52, 23–28.

Jamieson, D., and Regan, T. 1985. Whales are not cetacean resources. In: M. W. Fox and L. Mackley, eds. *Advances in Animal Welfare Science, 1984*, pp. 101–111. The Hague, Martinus Nijhoff.

Johnson, L. E. 1991. *A Morally Deep World. An Essay on Moral Significance and Environmental Ethics.* New York, Cambridge University Press.

Kenney, S. P., and Knight, R. L. 1992. Flight distances of black-billed magpies in different regimes of human density and persecution. *The Condor* 94, 545–547.

Kinkel, L. K. 1989. Lasting effects of wing tags on ring-billed gulls. *Auk* 106, 619–624.

Kirkwood, J. K., Sainsbury, A. W., and Bennett, P. M. 1994. The welfare of free-living animals: Methods of assessment. *Anim. Welfare* 3, 257–273.

Kreeger, T. J., White, P. J., Seal, U. S., and Tester, J. R. 1990. Pathological responses of red foxes to foothold traps. *J. Wildl. Manag.* 54, 147–160.

Laurenson, M. K., and Caro, T. M. 1994. Monitoring the effects of non-trivial handling in free-living cheetahs. *Anim. Behav.* 47, 547–557.

Ludwig, D., Hilborn, R., and Walters, C. 1993. Uncertainty, resource exploitation, and conservation. Lessons from history. *Science* 260, 17, 36.

Major, R. E. 1990. The effect of human observers on the intensity of nest predation. *Ibis* 132, 608–612.

McKenzie, A. A. 1989. Humane modification of steel foothold traps. *S. Afr. J. Wildl. Res.* 19, 53–56.

Morris, D. 1990. *The Animal Contract.* New York, Warner Books.

Nagel, T. 1974. What is it like to be a bat? *Philos. Rev.* 83, 435–450.

Olsen, G. H., Linhart, S. B., Holmes, R. A., Dash, G. J., and Male, C. B. 1986. Injuries to coyotes caught in padded and unpadded steel foothold traps. *Wildl. Soc. Bull.* 14, 219–223.

Olsen, G. H., Linscombe, R. G., Wright, V. L. and Holmes, R. A. 1988. Reducing injuries to terrestrial furbearers by using padded foothold traps. *Wildl. Soc. Bull.* 16, 303–307.

Peterson, D. 1989. *The Deluge and the Ark. A Journey in Primate Worlds.* Boston, Houghton Mifflin.

Pietz, P. J., Krapu, G. L., Greenwood, R. J., and Lokemoen, J. T. 1993. Effects of harness transmitters on behavior and reproduction of wild mallards. *J. Wildl. Manag.* 57, 696–703.

Quine, W. O. 1951/1961. Two dogmas of empiricism. In: *From a Logical Point of View*, Second edition. Cambridge, Massachusetts, Harvard University Press.

Rabinowitz, A. 1986. *Jaguar, Struggle and Triumph in the Jungles of Belize.* New York, Arbor.

Ristau, C., ed. 1991. *Cognitive Ethology: The Minds of Other Animals, Essays in Honor of Donald R. Griffin.* Hillsdale, New Jersey, Lawrence Erlbaum Associates.

Rollin, B. E. 1989. *The Unheeded Cry, Animal Consciousness, Animal Pain and Science.* New York, Oxford University Press.

Rolston, H. III. 1988. *Environmental Ethics, Duties to and Values in the Natural World.* Philadelphia, Temple University Press.

Schaller, G. B. 1993. *The Last Panda.* Chicago, University of Chicago Press.

Silverman, S. 1994. Process and detection in fraud and deceit. *Ethics Behav.* 4, 219–228.

Singer, P. 1975. *Animal Liberation.* New York, Avon.

Singer, P. 1990. *Animal Liberation.* Second edition. New York, New York Review of Books.

Small, R. J., and Keith, L. B. 1992. An experimental study of red fox predation on Arctic and snowshoe hares. *Can. J. Zool.* 70, 1614–1621.

Stamp Dawkins, M., and Gosling, L. M., eds. 1992. *Ethics in Research on Animal Behaviour. Readings from Animal Behaviour.* London, Academic Press.

Swazey, J. P., Anderson, M. S., and Louis, K. S. 1993. Ethical problems in academic research. *Am. Sci.* 81, 542–553.

Travaini, A., Palomares, F., and Delibes, M. 1993. The effects of capture and recapture on space use in large grey mongooses. *S. Afr. J. Wildl. Res.* 23, 95–97.

Watson, J. D. 1968. *The Double Helix.* New York, Atheneum.

Wilson, E. O. 1975. *Sociobiology: The New Synthesis.* Cambridge, Massachusetts, Harvard University Press.

Wilson, R. P., Culik, B., Danfeld, R., and Adelung, D. 1991. People in Antarctica—how much do Adélie penguins *Pygoscelis adeliae* care? *Polar Biol.* 11, 363–370.

Ziff, P. 1960. *Semantic Analysis.* Ithaca, New York, Cornell University Press.

Contributors

Kathleen A. Akins
Department of Philosophy
Simon Fraser University
Burnaby, British Columbia
Canada V5A 1S6

Colin Allen
Department of Philosophy
Texas A & M University
College Station, Texas 77843-4237

Steven N. Austad
Department of Biological Sciences
University of Idaho
Moscow, Idaho 83843

Marc Bekoff
Department of Environmental,
Population, and Organismic Biology
University of Colorado
Boulder, Colorado 80309-0334

Andrew R. Blaustein
Department of Zoology
Oregon State University
Corvallis, Oregon 97331-2914

Karen E. Brakke
Language Research Center
3401 Panthersville Road
Decatur, Georgia 30034

Dorothy Cheney
Department of Biology
University of Pennsylvania
Philadelphia, Pennsylvania 19104

Roger Crisp
St. Anne's College
Oxford, England OX1 4BH

John Dupré
Department of Philosophy
Stanford University
Stanford, California 94305

John Andrew Fisher
Department of Philosophy
University of Colorado
Boulder, Colorado 80309-0232

Bennett G. Galef, Jr.
Department of Psychology
McMaster University
Hamilton, Ontario, Canada L8S 4K1

Lori Gruen
Department of Philosophy
Lafayette College
Easton, Pennsylvania 18042

Marc Hauser
Departments of Anthropology and
Psychology
Harvard University
Cambridge, Massachusetts 02138

Louis M. Herman
Kawolo Basin Marine Mammal
Laboratory
1129 Ala Moana Boulevard
Honolulu, Hawaii 96814

Dale Jamieson
Department of Philosophy
University of Colorado
Boulder, Colorado 80309-0232

Walter D. Koenig
Hastings Reservation
38601 East Carmel Valley Road
Carmel, California 93924

Steven L. Lima
Department of Life Sciences
Indiana State University
Terre Haute, Indiana 47809

Sandra D. Mitchell
Department of Philosophy
University of California
La Jolla, California 92093-0302

Palmer Morrel-Samuels
Kawolo Basin Marine Mammal
Laboratory
1129 Ala Moana Boulevard
Honolulu, Hawaii 96814

Ronald L. Mumme
Department of Biology
Allegheny College
Meadville, Pennsylvania 16335

Michael Philips
Department of Philosophy
Portland State University
P.O. Box 751
Portland, Oregon 97207

Richard H. Porter
Department of Psychology and Human
Development
George Peabody College
Vanderbilt University
Nashville, Tennessee 37203

Carolyn A. Ristau
Department of Psychology
Barnard College
New York, New York 10027-6598

Alexander Rosenberg
Department of Philosophy
University of Georgia
Athens, Georgia 30602

Michael Rosenzweig
Department of Ecology and Evolutionary
Biology
University of Arizona
Tucson, Arizona 85721

Sue Savage-Rumbaugh
Language Research Center
3401 Panthersville Road
Decatur, Georgia 30034

Robert Seyfarth
Department of Psychology
University of Pennsylvania
Philadelphia, Pennsylvania 19104

W. John Smith
Department of Biology
University of Pennsylvania
Philadelphia, Pennsylvania 19104

Randy Thornhill
Department of Biology
University of New Mexico
Albuquerque, New Mexico 87131

Hugh Wilder
Department of Philosophy
College of Charleston
Charleston, South Carolina 29424

Index